The Civil Se[...]
Britain to[...]

MANCHESTER
UNIVERSITY PRESS

Politics Today

Series editor: Bill Jones

The Civil Service in Britain today

Colin Pilkington

Manchester University Press
Manchester and New York

distributed exclusively in the USA by St. Martin's Press

Published by Manchester University Press
Oxford Road, Manchester M13 9NR, UK
and Room 400, 175 Fifth Avenue, New York, NY 10010, USA
http://www.man.ac.uk/mup

Distributed exclusively in the USA by
St. Martin's Press, Inc., 175 Fifth Avenue, New York,
NY 10010, USA

Distributed exclusively in Canada by
UBC Press, University of British Columbia, 6344 Memorial Road,
Vancouver, BC, Canada V6T 1Z2

British Library Cataloguing-in-Publication Data
A catalogue record for this book is available from the British Library

Library of Congress Cataloging-in-Publication Data applied for

ISBN 0 7190 5223 8 *hardback*
     0 7190 5224 6 *paperback*

First published 1999

06 05 04 03 02 01 00 99   10 9 8 7 6 5 4 3 2 1

Typeset in Photina
by Servis Filmsetting Ltd, Manchester
Printed in Great Britain
by Biddles Ltd, Guildford and King's Lynn

Contents

Preface

Notoriously the Civil Service is secretive, reluctant to let the world know about the matters with which it concerns itself. And ironically enough the public seem to be as reluctant to find out about the activities of the Civil Service as civil servants are reluctant to speak about themselves to the public. Anyone who has been involved in the teaching and examination of government and politics knows very well that there are areas in the syllabus that represent blind spots in the average student's memories of what they have learned. It is well known that there are certain topics which students do not find interesting and indeed some that they find positively boring. And then there are certain matters which, if raised by an examiner, prove to be more like black holes in space rather than the blind spots mentioned above. Not only do the students themselves fight shy of studying these topics but even their teachers are wary of saying anything about them and writers of textbooks seem positively reluctant to write about them.

Local government, and particularly local government finance, represents one such 'black hole'. So also do those underlying pillars of the political system, the judicial system and, of course, the Civil Service. As far as the latter is concerned this is something of a sweeping generalisation in that, encouraged by the success of the television series *Yes Minister* and some highly publicised statements by former Labour ministers like Richard Crossman, Barbara Castle and Tony Benn, there is a certain degree of interest in that single aspect of the Civil Service which is represented by minister–civil servant confrontations, such as were typical of Jim Hacker and Sir Humphrey. Yet, apart from that one very distorted perspective, students steer clear of any deeper examination of the role of civil servants from a mixture of ignorance, indifference and boredom.

This is not to decry *Yes Minister*, a wonderful series which managed to grasp many truths concerning the Civil Service, despite the obvious exaggerations for comic effect, and in so doing managed to throw a revealing light onto some of the more labyrinthine Whitehall machinations. The essential nature of the truth which forms the background to that programme can be judged by the number of times it is quoted as a point of reference in this book. All the same, *Yes Minister* is no more than a television comedy programme, for all its accuracy. There were many aspects of the Civil Service that the programme had of necessity to ignore, either because they were not immediately humorous or because they are developments which only took effect after the programme had ended its run on television.

The fading of public interest in the Civil Service after the series of *Yes Minister* and *Yes Prime Minister* ended conceals the fact that there are still very many things about the Civil Service which cry out for the close scrutiny of students. In recent years political studies have concentrated heavily on constitutional change and in particular on the combined impact that the issues of Europe, devolution and federalism have had on the political structures of the United Kingdom. Yet the same students who concentrate their attentions and interest on constitutional change seem to overlook the equally significant managerial reforms that have revolutionised the whole structure and functioning of the Civil Service since 1986, a form of administrative devolution that has part-fragmented the unified British Civil Service into the kind of federal structure which really does represent a change in administrative practices, every bit as important as any constitutional change to the legislature.

This book is therefore an attempt to clarify the picture as regards the Civil Service at the end of the twentieth century, attempting to outline the position as it has become established in the period of consolidation following the Labour victory of 1997. This is not as easy to do as might be supposed, given that the indifference towards the Civil Service mentioned above as being exhibited by students is true of the degree of interest shown by the media. Whereas the simplest of facts about parliamentary or party politics are discussed and debated endlessly in the media by experts and commentators, major events in the world of the civil servants can pass unreported and unnoticed. For example, when researching this book I discovered that in March 1998, less than a year after the election, the Blair government called a halt to the setting up of any new agencies under the Next Steps programme, thereby ending ending a major, decade-long phase in the modern development of the Civil Service. Yet the important news that the Next Steps programme had ended was not reported in any of the press seen by me, nor did I hear it mentioned on any radio or television news programmes. In other words, since the media do not think the public would be interested in the Civil Service, even the most important of matters affecting the Civil Service go unreported, making it very hard for the student to remain fully informed.

The politics student, however, cannot afford to ignore the Civil Service, if only because the policy process is an increasingly important segment of any government and politics syllabus, at all levels of study. There is also executive accountability, as well as the whole question of standards of behaviour as they relate to the conduct of public life, matters which can only be understood by analysing the ways in which the bureaucrats and administrators have adapted to Thatcherite market forces and to the post-Thatcher political structures and processes.

My thanks and acknowledgments for help in writing this book are due to all the usual candidates. Bill Jones as always was a worthy guide and mentor, as was Nicola Viinikka, Pippa Kenyon and other members of the team from Manchester University Press. Grateful thanks are due to Glynis Sandwith and her associates at the Politics Association and to my friend Dennis Harrigan and other colleagues on the examining team with AQA-NEAB. However, as far as the subject of the Civil Service is concerned, there is one particular debt that I really must acknowledge: in an area about which so little is published such as the Civil Service, the one reference that has proved immensely valuable is the website maintained by the Cabinet Office on the Internet. My sincere thanks therefore to http://www.open.gov.uk/co/ in its many guises, because it is there that information can be found which is just not available elsewhere.

Colin Pilkington

1

Introduction

What is the Civil Service?

In 1952, the late Michael Ventris, an architect but also a keen amateur cryptologist, succeeded in deciphering the Cretan script known as Linear B and work could begin on transcribing the many clay tablets bearing fragments of writing that had mystified archaeologists and others since Sir Arthur Evans first excavated the Palace of Knossos in the 1890s. The excitement felt at the revelations that were expected from these records from the second millennium BC was somewhat dashed by the discovery that they were largely inventories of oil, wheat, wine, servants and so on, or they were records of the amounts of goods paid or owing to someone else. 'To all the gods, one amphora of honey, to the priestess, one amphora of honey'.[1] In other words, these inventories were either some ruler's account books or they were tax returns. For the archaeologist it is exciting to discover records contemporary with the Trojan War, but for the romantically inclined it is disappointing to discover that the few written fragments remaining from that time were not the work of poets but of Mycenaean civil servants.

The decipherment of Linear B is yet more evidence that civil servants can compete with prostitutes and spies for the title of the oldest profession. Officials and administrators in the public service are certainly as old as civilisation; indeed there is an argument which suggests that they are actually the cause of civilisation since what after all does 'civilisation' mean but 'a complex civil organisation of society'? Historians have recognised for some time that the Ancient Egyptian civilisation arose from the need for concerted action to control the River Nile, both to prevent flooding at some times and to provide irrigation at others. Such a major feat of co-ordinated planning and organisation required not only the strong central government represented by the Pharaohs but also the army of scribes, messengers and tax gatherers who actually administered the schemes. If you recall your Bible, Joseph may have been taken into the service of Pharaoh for the sake of his ability to interpret dreams, but he

1

remained in that service because of his organisational ability in the control of food supplies.

Civil servants are most commonly defined in the dictionaries as 'servants of the Crown, other than holders of political or judicial offices, who are employed in a civil capacity and whose remuneration is paid wholly and directly out of moneys voted by Parliament'.[2] That definition, of course, covers many categories of public servant whom we should not normally regard as civil servants, within the terms of this book. What about postmen, or messengers, or the cleaners of government departments? What, indeed, about all the employees of nationalised enterprises? What this book is concerned with is, in fact, that part of the Civil Service which is involved in the bureaucratic implementation of government policy: the area where the government makes a decision and the Civil Service implements that decision. 'The traditional democratic view stipulates that the fundamental decisions must be taken by politicians . . . administrators are regarded as having to conform to the decisions of the political rule-makers'.[3]

The modern Civil Service has four main functions:

- To advise government ministers on policy matters.
- To manage the use of government resources.
- To make decisions in the name of their ministers.
- To carry out the day-to-day administration of government departments.[4]

This is, of course, a very modern interpretation: it is only in the last hundred years or so that the administrative functions of government have become separated from political control. Until quite late in the nineteenth century, the head of a government department was a political nominee who combined in his own person what today are the functions of both minister and permanent secretary. As 'king's servants' there was no real dividing line between minister and bureaucrat – they were usually the same person. Ironically, as we move into the new millennium, there are those who believe that modern trends are leading to a renewed weakening of the dividing line and the re-assertion of a political agenda for the Civil Service. Certainly there is an echo of the dual minister-bureaucrat role in the part played by Commissioners in the administration of the European Union.

The nature of bureaucracy

According to the *Oxford English Dictionary*, the first use of the word 'bureaucracy' in English was by Thomas Carlyle in 1848, when he spoke of 'the continental nuisance called bureaucracy'. The context of that statement shows how bureaucracy was seen from the first as something alien to the British way of life, and hints at the suspicion with which bureaucracy has always been regarded by the British political establishment. In the early nineteenth century the

British ideal was for minimal government and there was general hostility to the idea of a centralised administration with a formally organised structure that was staffed by impersonal functionaries.

Bureaucracy quite simply means government by office and, as an organisational structure, requires individuals to occupy clearly defined offices in a hierarchical pyramid. Authority in a bureaucracy is not granted to any one individual but resides solely in the office to which that individual has been appointed. The early sociologist Max Weber was aware of the problems and dangers of a bureaucratic structure but he also believed that it was the most efficient and rational form of administration for the modern scientific age. As Weber saw it, administrative authority was historically based on tradition or charismatic leadership but this only works in a fairly simple society. On the other hand, 'modern industrial societies have become so complex and so technical that only experts can manage them'.[5]

The distinguishing feature of bureaucracy is the line structure of control and decision-making. The nature of **formal line management** was defined by Henri Fayol, one of the pioneer theorists in the science of efficient public administration. Fayol studied the French PTT (Posts, Telegraphs and Telephones) in 1920 and laid down certain basic principles of efficient administration:

- There should be a clear line of authority from top to bottom of an organisation with clear lines of communication.
- Responsibility and accountability should be linked to a single person in a specific job.
- Each office-holder has the clearly defined duties, powers and responsibilities that are linked with that office.
- Each level in the hierarchy will have its own competence as to which decisions can be taken at that level.
- No subordinate should be subject to the orders of more than one superior and the ranks of office-holders should be so arranged that no one person supervises more than five or six subordinates.

The line is therefore a two-way channel of communication between the top and bottom of the hierarchy for the transmission of orders, information, advice, instructions and questions. The merits of a formal bureaucratic structure are claimed as:

- The rigidity of the rules governing a bureaucracy ensures that there is a consistency in the application of those rules, regardless of special circumstances.
- The impersonal nature of the office means a universally standard of administration without favours being shown to one side rather than another.
- The defined status of each office-holder and the clear channels of communication between them mean that problems can always be tackled at the required level of competence through 'referring up' or 'referring down'.[6]

The traditional British distrust of bureaucracy arises from weaknesses inherent in this formal organisation, largely because of the rigidity of the structure and its inability to adapt to circumstances:

- The need to safeguard the position of office-holders by making and retaining records of actions and decisions means that the bureaucracy becomes immersed in paperwork and red tape. Time-wasting delays can occur because of the constant need for form-filling and consultation of records.
- Office-holders may be afraid that they do not have the level of competence to make a decision demanded of them and that decision may therefore be shelved or referred upwards, leading to somewhat lengthy delays in the decision-making process.
- The inflexibility of the organisation leads to over-reliance on rules and regulations and unwillingness to bend or ignore those rules even when it is recognised that efficiency might suffer from too rigid adherence to those rules.
- Bureaucrats feel most comfortable in a regular routine and therefore are wary of any innovatory development that might upset the status quo. A bureaucracy is conservative, if not reactionary, by nature, and is not particularly good in serving a reforming or radical administration.
- Insistence that only the 'proper' channels of communication should be followed can lead to outsiders only having access to the system at too great a remove from where the decisions are taken, leading to delays as problems are passed up the hierarchy for a decision to be taken, followed by further delays as the nature of that decision is then passed down the hierarchy again to the point of enquiry.

Arguments over the nature of the Civil Service and criticisms of its performance are all influenced by the nature of bureaucracy, and different understandings of that nature have created different models through which the bureaucracy is perceived by politicians and other critics.

The liberal-democratic model of bureaucracy

The traditional British pattern of public administration assumes a neutral, anonymous, permanent and professional Civil Service which advises, serves and supports its political superiors without exercising any independent power or initiating any action for itself. This model of liberal neutrality is that adopted by Sir Robert Armstrong, then Cabinet Secretary, in his guidelines for the service, written after the Westland Affair, in which he states that the Civil Service has 'no constitutional personality or responsibility separate from the duly elected government of the day'.[7]

This model is common to all those countries which are thought of as liberal democracies, although there are obvious variations in characteristics between those countries.

The administrative cadre model

The divorce of administration from political control is probably highest in those Western European states, like France, which have administrative *cadres*, organised on almost military principles, whose loyalties are solely to the state. Many of these states have legislatures that are elected by proportional representation, as a result of which they normally expect to have coalition governments of differing degrees of stability. In any state where governments change frequently, or where periods exist when there is no government while a coalition deal is being negotiated, a strong Civil Service is an obvious necessity in order to ensure the day-to-day functioning of the state in the absence of political direction.

The federal-bureaucratic model

Very few liberal democracies have bureaucracies as centralised as Britain's. In countries like France, and other countries with traditions based on the Napoleonic dispensation, as much as half the administration is devolved from the centre to *départements* or provinces, through a network of prefectures, in what might well be called administrative devolution. Other liberal-democratic administrations are federal, as in the United States. With a federal form of government many Civil Service functions are carried out by the component states, with only a small proportion of those working in the public sector employed at a federal level. This could well prove to be the future model for Britain as the devolution programme becomes established and begins to be extended.

The 'spoils system' model

Nor are all liberal-democratic systems free of patronage. For example, it must be remembered that the American system diverged from its British parent in the late eighteenth century, before reforms in Britain had divided the responsibility for government departments between a minister who was a political appointee on the one hand and a chief administrator who was a permanent career civil servant on the other. In the USA the old British system evolved into that form of patronage known as the 'spoils' system. This refers to the historical practice by which a President, or Governor at state level, would repay political favours once they were elected through appointing friends and supporters to positions within the administration. The President still forms his cabinet and executive by appointing political allies – who are not normally members of Congress – to be heads of the various government departments and bureaux. These appointees are therefore both ministers in the presidential administration and executive heads of their government departments. However, the days when a change of government meant that virtually the entire administration was replaced have long since gone. Nowadays more than 90 per cent of the administration in Washington are career civil servants and only about 2,000 individuals are political appointees who will be replaced with a change of president. This small number does, however, represent the top tier of departmental heads and this hard-core élite does have a damaging effect on career promotion prospects for permanent civil servants. The system also lacks the continuity of a permanent Civil Service, when government departments face a change of senior personnel every time that there is a change of president.[8]

As far as Britain is concerned, the liberal-democratic model is sometimes seen as the ideal goal towards which minister–administrator relationships should aspire but which often falls short of this ideal since power relationships within the model can be moderated by being seen from different perspectives.[9]

The liberal-bureaucratic model

This is an adaptation of the liberal-democratic model in that, while it accepts the traditional view of the politician–official relationship, within which the minister is the senior partner, the truth is more probably that the balance of power is skewed in favour of permanent officials. This is the view of the 'over-mighty servant' which created comedic tensions in the TV series *Yes Minister*, where Sir Humphrey regularly used bureaucratic skills to thwart his minister's intentions.

The Whitehall Village model

This is a belief that all senior civil servants, no matter which department they serve, share a common language and culture and thereby make common cause: not necessarily to thwart the politicians, although that can be the case, but just as often to assist ministers through inter-service contacts. The Higher Civil Service constitutes a parallel communication network which can help or hinder the work of ministers, dependent on the civil servants' own agenda. As one ex-minister has said, 'I do not know where they meet but all civil servants seem to know each other . . . for example, officials from the Welsh Office were closely acquainted with those of the Department of Energy. . . .'[10]

The power-bloc model

This is the nightmare of left-wing politicians like Tony Benn who believe that senior civil servants belong, by education and background, to an Establishment or power élite which imposes its own cultural values on government through its control of the administrative high ground. Tony Benn, and others like Brian Sedgemore, felt that this was why socialist governments have never been able to introduce truly socialist measures – because all radical proposals were vetoed or neutralised by a High Tory and reactionary Civil Service which has long util-ised all its energies to maintain a comfortable status quo.

The bureaucratic over-supply model

This is the equivalent of the left wing's power-bloc model in the demonology of the right wing. According to this model the upper echelons within the Civil Service work in the interests of some civil service ethos, departmental prestige or their own personal standing, rather than in the interests of country or government, and as such have considerably extended the bureaucracy in an empire-building exercise of personal or departmental aggrandisement. It was in reaction to this vision of the spreading tentacles of an over-weaning bureaucratic monster that the Thatcher governments of the 1980s became committed, in some of the lady's own favourite sayings, to 'rolling back the frontiers of the state' or 'cutting the Civil Service down to size'.

Notes

1 J. Chadwick, *The Decipherment of Linear B*, Penguin, Harmondsworth, 1961. It has nothing to do with the subject of the Civil Service but it is a fascinating topic.
2 This commonly accepted definition was first formulated by the Tomlin Commission in 1931 but is quoted by Bill Coxall and Lynton Robins, *Contemporary British Politics* (2nd edition), Macmillan, Basingstoke, 1994, pp. 148–9.
3 Jean Blondel, *Comparative Government*, Philip Allan, Hemel Hempstead, 1990, p. 293.
4 John Alder, *Constitutional and Administrative Law* (2nd edition), Macmillan, Basingstoke, 1994, p. 231–2.
5 Jean Blondel, *Voters, Parties and Leaders*, Penguin, Harmondsworth, 1963, p. 185.
6 Fayol's work is discussed in C. A. Leeds, *Political Studies*, Macdonald and Evans, Plymouth, 1981, pp. 249–52.
7 Sir Robert Armstrong, *Notes and Guidance on the Duties and Responsibilities of Civil Servants in Relation to Ministers*, 1985, quoted by Coxall and Robins, Note 2 above, p. 152.
8 Robert Pyper, *The British Civil Service*, Harvester Wheatsheaf, Hemel Hempstead, 1995, pp. 21–2.
9 The models of power relationships in the Civil Service are those used by Coxall and Robins, Note 2 above, pp. 152–3.
10 Gerald Kaufman, *How to Be a Minister*, Faber, London, 1997, p. 27.

2

The origins of the Civil Service

From the curia regis to Secretary of State

The Civil Service in Britain has its roots in the English *curia regis*, the 'king's court' or royal household, and the first government departments had their origins in the various divisions of servants looking after the needs of that household. The department of Chancery, under the Lord Chancellor, was the king's writing-house where clerks wrote out the various writs, letters, deeds, charters and other documentation required to run the king's affairs. The Exchequer was the king's counting-house, so-called for the checkered cloth spread on the table on which the king's money was counted: the check squares representing an arithmetic convenience for the clerks, like a two-dimensional abacus. Over time these two departments became increasingly involved in the judicial and financial administration of the kingdom, moving as a result out of the domestic into the public domain. Other new domestic departments took their place in the household and these also, over time, assumed a public role and in their turn had to be replaced. The Middle Ages saw a succession of administrative departments created whose names indicate their domestic origins and purpose – the Chamber, the Wardrobe, the Signet and so forth.

The administration and bureaucracy of the medieval state was staffed almost exclusively by churchmen, to the extent that the words 'cleric' for a clergyman and 'clerk' for a minor official are derived from the same word. There was a number of reasons why this should be so:

1)   England in the Middle Ages was an illiterate society – as late as the sixteenth century it has been estimated that only 38 per cent of the population was literate.[1] In medieval society education was strictly according to vocational need and most trades and occupations did not need the ability to read, write or calculate. The nobility placed their young in other noble houses to learn the laws of chivalry and the use of arms; the children of tradesmen were apprenticed to other artisans within the guilds while the majority of children worked

8

alongside their parents in the fields and learned by doing. Only those intended for the Law, Medicine or the Church attended schools or universities and, by so doing, were judged to have entered minor orders.

2)   Churchmen could be rewarded for service by ecclesiastical appointments, benefices or livings within the gift of the king, without any cost to royal revenues. This is what led to the great medieval conflicts between monarch and the Church, such as the dispute between Henry II and Thomas Becket or between John and Stephen Langton. The churchmen had been appointed to their bishoprics or archbishoprics as servants of the king but, once appointed, started to serve the Pope and Church. Memories of those conflicts helped lead to the belief that civil servants should serve just one master, without showing partiality for any personal allegiance they might feel.

3)   Ever since the Civil Service began there has been an element of doubt as to how far civil servants can be trusted to work in the interest of their employer without secretly working more for their own benefit. Particularly suspect are those civil servants who use the profits of their office in the interest of their families, building up an inheritance that can be passed on to their children and succeeding generations. Of course this is an ever-present question which is still surrounded by an aura of distrust. In some ancient empires the question was 'solved' by entrusting public posts to eunuchs who, unable to father children, could be assumed to be disinterested in posterity. In the same way, clerical celibacy in the pre-Reformation Church was supposed to free officials from dynastic ambitions. We know that this supposition was false, that the clergy were not celibate and that the euphemistic employment of the word 'nephew' to describe the illegitimate sons of popes and other churchmen gave us the term 'nepotism' to describe favouritism shown to one's own family. Nevertheless, the hypothetical celibacy of the clergy helps explain why they acquired their dominance in medieval administrations. It also explains why men of quite humble origins – like Thomas Wolsey, the son of an Ipswich butcher – could rise to the highest office in the land on the basis of personal merit rather than on their status at birth: being without issue meant that a churchman's wealth and power would die with him and that therefore the social rise of such an individual represented no threat to the established positions of the nobility.

It must not be assumed that a royal administration staffed by clerics meant a bureaucracy entirely made up of priests and monks. Someone who had completed his elementary education received the tonsure to show his membership of minor orders but he did not necessarily proceed to the major orders as deacon or priest. Instead the educated classes might use their education in a lay capacity as teacher, lawyer, accountant or, indeed, civil servant. Even Thomas Becket achieved the highest post in the civil administration, as Henry II's Chancellor, without being ordained: he was only consecrated as priest one day prior to being made Archbishop of Canterbury. As the Middle Ages proceeded there was an increasing tendency for the majority of clerks in the administration to be clerical only by education rather than vocation and men like Sir Thomas More could study theology at Oxford and enter the service of a bishop without even thinking of becoming priests themselves.

The Civil Service as we understand it today could only really begin with the Reformation because:

1 The disestablishment of so many churchmen required the creation of an entirely new tier of lay bureaucrats and administrators.
2 The dissolution of the monasteries and the break with Rome meant that whole new areas of competence and organisation were put into the hands of the royal administrators as they took over land and property belonging to the Church and appropriated church revenues.

The period immediately prior to the Reformation had seen the reign of Henry VII, a king who had the mind of a cost-conscious accountant. Under his personal guidance the civil administration was totally reformed, the Exchequer in particular becoming noticeably efficient, even if it was slow to function, as are all bureaucracies. It was on the basis of Henry VII's reforms that the Civil Service was restructured under his son, Henry VIII, under the direction of the man who was the first true civil servant, as we should recognise the term – Thomas Cromwell.

Cromwell was a lawyer not a churchman. He made his mark as the protégé of Cardinal Wolsey but, after Wolsey's fall from grace, succeeded where his master had failed in showing how Henry could gain the divorce he was seeking. He consolidated his position by masterminding the dissolution of the monasteries and the sequestration of church property to the benefit of the royal purse. His success and sheer administrative ability gave him the authority to carry out what Elton, the prominent constitutional historian, calls the Tudor Revolution, reorganising the entire royal administration and turning it for the first time into a national rather than a household system of government.

There was a departmental structure to the administration, divided into six offices – the Exchequer, the Duchy of Lancaster, the Court of General Surveyors, the Court of Augmentations, the Court of First Fruits and Tenths and the Court of Wards and Liveries. All six departments were concerned with revenue, some traditionally so, like the Exchequer, others like the Court of Augmentations dealing with revenues that had formerly belonged to the Church. The six departments together with other offices covering judicial, military and foreign affairs combined together under the office, created by Cromwell to replace the Chancellor as the monarch's closest adviser, the Principal Secretary of State. It was his Elizabethan successor in that office, Lord Burghley, who first made the Privy Council the nerve centre of the bureaucracy at the start of the modern age. During the Elizabethan period two Principal Secretaries of State were appointed although the stronger personality of the two, like Burghley, always seemed to dominate: so that to the outsider there might well have appeared to be only one.

Whitehall

Whitehall is, at one and the same time, a geographical location, a generic term and an attitude of mind. It takes its name from York Place, the 'White Hall' that was originally the lodgings of the Archbishop of York in London, and which was rebuilt, embellished and elevated to the status of palace in the late fifteenth and early sixteenth centuries by two powerful archbishops who were also influential public servants. George Neville, who was Chancellor from 1460 to 1472, erected a fine brick-built mansion which served as a lodging convenient for the Chancellor's government business in Westminster. Then, in 1514, Thomas Wolsey was elevated to the see of York and immediately saw York Place as a convenient base for the duties he had in Westminster such as the presidency of the Star Chamber. As at Hampton Court, Wolsey extended and enlarged the buildings and its environs to the extent that he created feelings of envy in the king. When Wolsey fell from grace and power, York Place was among the first of his properties to be seized by King Henry. 'In the year 1529, when Cardinal Wolsey, archbishop of Yorke, was indicted in the Premunire, whereby King Henry VIII was entitled to his goods and possessions: he also seized into his hands the said archbishop's house, commonly called Yorke place, and changed the name thereof into White hall.'[2]

The acquisition of the White Hall came at a propitious moment for Henry VIII. According to the Renaissance theory of kingship, whereby royal prestige was founded on outward show and courtly ceremonial, the king was acquiring a series of evermore magnificent houses and palaces – Hampton Court, Greenwich and Nonsuch – to act as a setting for regal supremacy. It was in line with this policy that, in place of the royal palace at Westminster which had burned down in 1512, York Place was expanded into a Palace of Whitehall in order to become the new seat of administration. Over the years after 1530 Henry acquired extra land in the form of the manor of Westminster and the convent of St James and built a huge and rambling palace covering twenty-three acres and housing more than 600 people, described by the Duc de Saint-Simon at the end of the seventeenth century as 'the largest and ugliest palace in Europe'. More important than its size, however, was the function it was given as it was made to play its part in Henry's administrative policy.

Under Henry VII the seat of government had been the Star Chamber in Westminster Palace where the Council carried out its judicial and executive functions in the same building as parliament exercised its legislative duties. Henry VIII left the judicial duties of the Council with the Star Chamber in the Palace of Westminster but moved the executive powers of the Council – the Privy Council – to the royal quarters in Whitehall. It is from this division that we have inherited the convention that the legislative and judicial powers of parliament are located in Westminster and the executive powers of cabinet government and the Civil Service are based in Whitehall. This division was increased under Charles II when the vast body of servants serving the royal household was reduced and their quarters became available for government officials and officers of state.[3]

Whitehall Palace burned down in January 1698 but important changes had already been made to the site. By 1670 the southern part of the palace had been sold by the royal household and had been bought by George Downing who built houses speculatively along the street which still bears his name. The fire of 1698 completely destroyed the royal apartments and grace-and-favour residences that were situated to the east of the site, between the present-day thoroughfare of Whitehall and the river. But the west of the site, between Whitehall and St James' Park and including the Banqueting Hall and the sports complex known as the Cockpit, was relatively untouched. The Secretaries of State, the Council, the Board of Trade and the Treasury, made homeless by the fire, were rehoused in the remains of the Cockpit building. Even today the Cabinet Office is housed in what is left of Henry VIII's tennis court.

This physical location and the division of function that went with it began the tradition whereby parliament and the legislature were known generically as Westminster, while the Civil Service and government administration gained the generic title of Whitehall. The name of Whitehall is now used for the Senior Civil Service generically in a way totally divorced from any actual geographical location. The principal, policy-making departments, staffed by senior civil servants and directly serving the offices of the Secretary of State, are still said to be situated in Whitehall, even if, like the Department of the Environment, Transport and the Regions, they are to be found in Bressenden Place near Victoria Station.

The growth of government departments after the Restoration

The administrative structure created under the Tudors continued under the early Stuarts and indeed under the republican Commonwealth and Protectorate following the Civil Wars. The restoration of the monarchy in 1660, however, saw a big shake-up in the administration which began to take on a shape that is recognisable as the embryonic pattern for our modern service, structured and operating through departments. The existing two Secretaries of State were differentiated by being put in charge of two departments, known according to their function in foreign relations as the Northern Department, dealing with northern Europe and the protestant countries, and the Southern Department, dealing with southern Europe and the catholic countries.

The Committee for Trade and Plantations, which was instituted in 1621 as the first government department not concerned with revenue, was reinstated after the Restoration as two councils, one for trade and the other for the plantations (which is how the early colonies were known). The two councils were reunited in 1672 and, in 1696 became a committee of the Privy Council known as the Board of Trade and Plantations, although colonial affairs were taken away from the Board's responsibilities in 1768. The Board of Trade was much criticised for waste and indolence and as a result of this criticism Edmund Burke was successful in having the Board abolished in 1782. But chaos ensued and, within two years, the Privy Council Committee on Trade and Plantations was reconvened. It was this committee that was reconstituted as the Board of Trade by an Order in Council in 1786 and it is that order which remains as the authority for the existence of today's Department of Trade and Industry. In a period in which the Civil Service was essentially no more than advisory and regulatory in its duties, the Board of Trade was unique among government departments in being the only interventionist office, albeit in a limited sense. Despite having a largely advisory role, the Board of Trade did play a part, during the late eighteenth and early nineteenth centuries, in regulating working conditions for sailors working in Britain's merchant fleet and in playing a significant supporting role in the movement to abolish the slave trade. It was also the reconstituted Board of Trade which was the first government department to draw a clear line of distinction between ministers and officials, thereby making it the forerunner of a non-political Civil Service.

A product of the Restoration that was just as important as the embryonic Board of Trade was the rise of the Treasury as a major government department. The Treasurer's office had become separated from the Exchequer under Lord Burghley and, in 1660, was recreated as a new government department under five Commissioners. The driving force behind the new powers gained by the Treasury was the Secretary to the Treasury, Sir George Downing, who, as mentioned above, built the street bearing his name, which significantly still houses many Treasury ministers. Downing was a time-serving, duplicitous turncoat, who had spied on royalist exiles in the Low Countries for Cromwell's government but who, seeing the way the wind was blowing, ingratiated himself with the restored monarchy and bought his baronetcy by betraying three fugitive regicides to the hangman. Apart from this career as a double agent in his time abroad, Downing had learned the latest administrative and accountancy techniques for which the Netherlands were noted in the seventeenth century. As Secretary to the Treasury, Downing used the skills he had acquired to double the efficiency of the government's revenue-raising and, through an Order in Council in 1668, established Treasury control over the revenue and expenditure of all other government departments. In other words, the Treasury gained – as it has, at least partially, retained – control over all the rest of Whitehall, a generic term that was already being used for the various government offices housed for convenience in the king's Palace of Whitehall. This pre-eminence of the Treasury has stamped its mark on governments right up to the present day, the prime minister carrying the honorary title of First Lord of the Treasury, while government whips owe their constitutional legitimacy to their descent from Treasury Commissioners.

Apart from the Treasury, the revenue departments and the Councils for Trade and Plantations, the Whitehall administration created under Charles II consisted of various boards and departments under the control of the Privy Council and the two Secretaries of State. For motives which have found an echo in recent years, many government services, like the General Post Office, were operated by private contractors who paid the Crown substantial sums for the grant of a monopoly over the supply of that service.

In March 1782 Rockingham became prime minister in a Whig administration and wished to appoint two prominent Whigs, Shelburne and Fox, as Principal Secretaries of State. The two men, however, hated each other and it was impossible for them to work in harness. It was a suggestion made by George III that resolved the difficulty. The king pointed out that it was ridiculous to make two men responsible for all home and foreign business, and that it would make far more sense to divide the functions and responsibilities of the Secretary of State's office, thereby separating the two incompatible ministers. As a result, the old Northern Department became the Foreign Office, with responsibility for all foreign relations – although without control of the Diplomatic Service at this point. The old Southern Department became the Home Office with the task of dealing with home affairs for the United Kingdom, Ireland, Crown territories like the Isle of Man and the Channel Islands and all the overseas colonies under government control. The Home Office also acted as a dumping ground for all the governmental tasks that had no obvious home elsewhere. The Home Secretary, the Foreign Secretary and the Chancellor of the Exchequer became, as they have remained, the three great Offices of State. They were joined by another Secretary of State in 1801, when the realities of the Napoleonic War demanded the creation of a War Office, under the Secretary of State for War.[4] Responsibility for the Board of Trade rested not with a Secretary but with the President of the Board.

Patronage and purchase

Hennessy has estimated that the number of people employed in the public service by the middle of the eighteenth century must have amounted to around 4 to 5 per cent of the adult male population.[5] Only about 17,000 of these would be civil servants as we understand the term but, importantly, 14,000 of them would be concerned with revenue.

Work in a government office was highly desirable. It was not arduous, it paid reasonably well and it carried a government pension. Except for the very senior men in the departments who were ministers or other political appointees – who could lose their jobs on the whim of a king or prime minister, or with a change of administration – such posts were secure for life. It was also possible, indeed probable, that opportunities for private gain might accrue to the office-holder. Such desirable positions were, of course, not easy to obtain. An aspirant to public employment needed the influence of a powerful patron although even then the position was very often subject to purchase, on payment of a suitable sum of money. The Civil Service was often seen as the obvious place to put a younger son or poor relation of an aristocratic family with no other prospects and no ability to make their own way in the world. According to Charles Trevelyan who was to reform the system, admission to the Civil Service was for the 'unambitious, indolent or incapable'.[6] This was actually seen as desirable because, if the recruits were ambitious, active and able, the chances are that they would use those abilities for their own profit rather than the public good. Throughout the seventeenth and eighteenth centuries, and well into the nineteenth, the service was riddled with inefficiency or corruption or both.

Fascinating glimpses of seventeenth-century Whitehall, which are nevertheless not irrelevant to the study of present-day developments in administration, are revealed in the diaries of Samuel Pepys.[7] Pepys was a distant relative of Edward Montagu (later the Earl of Sandwich) who had been in charge of the navy during the Protectorate. Transferring his allegiance to the monarchy, Montagu was confirmed in his position at the Restoration by being made Master of the Wardrobe and Vice-Admiral of the navy, under the Duke of York as Lord High Admiral. As part of the patronage he could now dispense, Montagu undertook to find a position in the Navy Office for the young relative whom he had already advanced in the dying days of the Protectorate. Formerly working for George Downing at the Exchequer, Pepys was made Secretary to the Fleet in early 1660, receiving his warrant on 18 February. Later, in the early summer, Pepys was told that Montagu had been given the position of Clerk of the Acts to dispose of and that the post was his, with a promised salary of £350 a year and a house owned by the Navy Office. Pepys received his warrant from the Duke of York on 29 June and had the patent guaranteeing his security of tenure sworn on 15 July.

To obtain his office cost Pepys money. Apart from an undisclosed sum disbursed to clear him from his employment with George Downing and the £40 that his patent had cost him, Pepys had to buy off a previous incumbent, paying a Mr Barlow £50 a year if his salary remained at £200, or £100 a year if the salary rose to £350 as expected. Pepys was also, like his patron, expected to make valuable gifts to those who had helped them to their position. 'I took my Lord's £100 in plate to Mr Secretary Nicholas and my own piece of plate being worth above £19.'[8] However, we know that the post was obviously worth more than the salary it paid, if only because of the offers made to buy the office from him. 'Mr Watts, a merchant, offered me £500 if I would desist from the Clerk of the Acts place'[9] and 'a Mr Man offered me £1000 for my office of Clerk of the Acts.'[10]

Samuel Pepys's early career in the Navy Office seems to be typical of all that was later thought of as being wrong in the fabric of the Civil Service. It is also not without relevance to the developments of the present day since the seventeenth-century pattern of small government departments, often with a political or partisan agenda, staffed by nominees appointed by patronage, has an uneasy echo in the quango culture of the late twentieth century. Once again we have a situation where many governmental functions are carried out by agencies outside the formal structure of the Civil Service, their direction being in the hands of political appointees whose appointment, it is sometimes suggested, is in return for political service or favours in the past.

It would seem, ironically enough, that Pepys himself was a good, efficient and energetic secretary to the Admiralty and his role in building what was later to be the supremacy of the Royal Navy has long been recognised. To criticise the system was not to deny that from time to time outstanding administrators did emerge, despite its faults. Nevertheless, a Samuel Pepys was an exception rather than the rule and a system which blended nepotism, inefficiency, bribes and promotion by purchase could not fail to produce significant numbers of personnel who were themselves as inefficient and corrupt as the system.

The situation in the civil administration was mirrored by that in the military where officers received their first commission and subsequent promotions through purchase. And it was one event which spelled the end of patronage and purchase in both the civil and military services: the disastrous errors and blunders, both military and administrative, which characterised the Crimean War in the 1850s, leading to an outcry which demanded change at senior levels in the services and an end to preferment by purchase. 'No less than seven more or less independent authorities shared in the organisation of the army, and helped in reducing it, as Prince Albert aptly said, to a mere "aggregate of battalions". The complication, the muddle, the duplication, the mutual jealousies, the labyrinthine processes of supply and control, were astounding.'[11] The public manifestation of this muddle in the government's mishandling of the war finally gave impetus to the cause of reform in the Civil Service.

Notes

1 Rosemary O'Day, 'An Educated Society', in the *Oxford Illustrated History of Tudor and Stuart Britain*, Oxford University Press, Oxford, 1996.
2 John Stow, *A Survey of London*, 1598.
3 Descriptions of Whitehall Palace are based on S. Turley, 'The Lost Palace of Whitehall', *History Today*, January 1998, pp. 47–52. This article also contains the Duc de Saint-Simon's opinion of Whitehall. Information on Henry VIII's administrative reforms is taken from G. R. Elton, *The Tudor Revolution in Government*, Cambridge University Press, London, 1953.
4 This survey of the history of the Civil Service is necessarily brief and a great deal of interesting information has had to be omitted. Anyone wishing to read about this history in greater detail is recommended to consult the work on which this summary is largely based: Peter Hennessy, *Whitehall*, Secker and Warburg, London, 1989 (Chapter 1, pp. 17–51).
5 *Ibid.*, p. 26.

6 The Northcote–Trevelyan Report is reprinted as Appendix B (pp. 106–31) of the *Fulton Committee Report, Vol. 1*, HMSO, 1968.

7 Samuel Pepys, because he wrote his diary in his own private code, is remarkably frank about his service as Clerk and Secretary to the Navy Office, freely noting down bribes or other payments both paid and received. This information can be found throughout the diaries but the most interesting entries concern the manoeuvring for office at the Restoration and can be found between mid-May and the end of September 1660.

8 Samuel Pepys, *Diary*, 4 July 1660.

9 *Ibid.*, 26 June 1660.

10 *Ibid.*, 6 August 1660.

11 Christopher Hibbert, *The Destruction of Lord Raglan*, Penguin, Harmondsworth, 1963, pp. 27–8. Although this book is about the problems of administering an army in time of war, it is invaluable in its descriptions of bureaucratic muddle, such as the urgent order for hay needed by the cavalry which took eight months to process and was only delivered after all the horses had died.

3

Reform and criticism

The Northcote–Trevelyan Report

The prime mover and main agent of reform for the Civil Service was Sir Charles Trevelyan. Born in 1807, into a family of West Country gentry, Trevelyan joined the administration of the East India Company at the age of nineteen and did his career no harm by marrying the sister of Thomas Macaulay, later Lord Macaulay, whose reform of the Indian Civil Service both preceded and inspired Trevelyan's reforms in Britain.

Having made a significant reputation in India, Trevelyan returned to London and the British Civil Service, and was appointed in 1840 to be Permanent Secretary at the Treasury. It is ironic that the man who was later to claim that the old and unreformed Civil Service was incapable of recognising and rewarding merit, was himself recognised and rewarded by the old system by being promoted to the most senior position in the entire service at the age of only thirty-two: something that would be inconceivable in the Civil Service as it was later established by the Northcote–Trevelyan reforms.

At the head of the Treasury, Trevelyan set about creating an efficient organisation with a quite awesome dedication. By 1848 he was convinced that reform was essential for all government departments, not just the Treasury. Over the next few years Trevelyan, or one of his officials, was represented on each of the economic review teams that looked in turn into the efficiency of the Home Office, Foreign Office, Colonial Office, the Irish Office and the War Office. It was in the course of these reviews that Trevelyan made it clear that he believed that the efficient running of a government department depended on two prerequisites:

1 Work should be divided into mechanical (inferior) and intellectual (superior) labour, and the two kept separate.
2 The recruitment and promotion of personnel should be based solely on merit.

Trevelyan's reform of the Treasury caught the attention of Gladstone when he became Chancellor of the Exchequer in 1852 and the politician shared and encouraged his Permanent Secretary's pursuit of efficiency, particularly since it helped establish the position of the Treasury in guiding and controlling the Civil Service as a whole. Soon after taking office Gladstone asked a former civil servant in the Board of Trade, Sir Stafford Northcote, to conduct an inquiry into the Board of Trade. The resulting report drew conclusions very similar to those drawn by Trevelyan in his own departmental reviews, its principal findings being that what the Board of Trade required was a division of labour between mechanical and intellectual grades of staff and the recruitment of staff by means of competitive examination. In March 1853 Gladstone brought the two men together to undertake an inquiry into the entire Civil Service.

> abolishing or consolidating redundant offices, getting rid of obsolete processes and introducing more simple modes of transacting business, establishing a proper distinction between intellectual and mechanical labour and generally, so revising the public establishments as to place them on the footing best calculated for the efficient discharge of their important functions.[1]

The report took a mere nine months to write and publish. Although very short – only twenty pages – the report covered a great deal of ground and indeed established the framework upon which the service is still in theory supposed to rest. Essentially the proposals can be distilled into four basic premises:

1 Recruitment into the Civil Service should be by open competitive examination, the examinations would be conducted by an independent Civil Service Board who would ensure that entry into the service should be entirely on the basis of merit.
2 Entrants should not be recruited for life into a specific department but would enter a Home Civil Service that would facilitate inter-departmental staff transfers. Civil servants, therefore, would need to have had a general education and to be generalist rather than specialist in their knowledge and experience.
3 Recruits would be segregated at entry into a hierarchical structure of grades, ranging from the lowest (mechanical) level of clerical officers, only capable of simple routine tasks, up to the most elevated (intellectual) administrative level which would provide the ranks of senior civil servants who exist to assist and guide ministers in the formulation and administration of policy.
4 Promotion ought only to be on the basis of merit and should not be on the grounds of preferment, patronage, purchase or simple length of service.

Reaction to the report was almost uniformly hostile, even the Queen expressing herself horrified at the idea of opening up the administration of government and formulation of policy to professional bureaucrats. It has always been a British characteristic to favour the gifted amateur at the expense of the talented professional and the British establishment was determined that the Civil Service should not lose its amateur status. Within months of the report's appearance it was acknowledged that there was no hope whatsoever of passing legislation to put all the report's recommendations into effect. Gladstone did succeed in establishing the Civil Service Commission in 1855 and three commissioners did allocate certificates of fitness to would-be applicants to the service, without which certificate they would not be appointed. But those certificates were not awarded as the result of an examination as the report had intended.

It was not until 1870, under Gladstone's first ministry, with Robert Lowe acting as his Chancellor of the Exchequer, that the government felt able to enact the main recommendations of Northcote–Trevelyan. Even then the two men met with considerable opposition from cabinet and the reforms were only introduced by a pre-emptive strike, when Lowe issued an Order in Council which placed the recruitment of staff for all government departments, except for the Home and Foreign Offices, under the control of the Treasury. The day on which that Order was issued, 4 June 1870, has since been established as the recognised date on which the Northcote–Trevelyan reforms became effective and patronage was largely removed from Whitehall.

The organisation established in 1870 saw a Civil Service divided into two classes, one concerned with routine work and the other a higher tier involved in policy-making. Entry into these tiers of administration would be through an examination administered by the Civil Service Commission, although the actual nature of the examination, including the subjects to be examined, was decided by the Treasury. Even these limited reforms were slow in coming, it being the end of the century before the first civil servants who had entered the service by competitive examination reached the higher administrative levels. One area in which the reforms were not applied for some time was the way in which civil servants remained rooted in their departments, which were in turn hierarchical in esteem, with employees of the Home Office, Foreign Office, Colonial Office and India Office receiving more prestige, bigger salaries and better working conditions than the rest of Whitehall.

It was left to Sir Warren Fisher's reorganisation of 1919 to create something even remotely approximating to the unified Civil Service envisaged by Trevelyan. As Permanent Secretary at the Treasury in the important inter-war years, Fisher did all he could to encourage the unity of the Civil Service. His principal weapon in this was the way in which he 'established the idea that inter-departmental transfers should form a normal part of the middle- and high-ranking civil servant's career. This was secured in the Treasury by Fisher's requirement that all his own officials should previously have worked in other departments.'[2]

There has been a tendency in the past to speak of the Northcote–Trevelyan reforms as though they had created the perfect bureaucratic structure for the governance of Britain. Certainly the actions of those responsible for the Civil Service, right up to the reorganisation produced by the Fulton Report in 1968, seemed to suggest that the service created by Northcote–Trevelyan was the apotheosis of what might be expected and that fine tuning rather than reform was all that was needed in order to retain that perfection. In fact the bureaucratic structure created by the Northcote–Trevelyan Report and Lowe's Order in Council was flawed in its conception and has steadily grown more inappropriate since then. That structure and its faults will be examined at more length later but the flaws might be summarised here as:

• The Civil Service which was established in the middle of the nineteenth century was small and acted in purely a minimal advisory or regulatory capacity: serving what is sometimes known as a 'nighwatchman' state. Yet the service was increasing in size even during the Victorian period. Between the Northcote–Trevelyan Report and the end of the century the service doubled in size, from 40,000 to 80,000.[3] In the twentieth century, both government and bureaucracy became increasingly interventionist through the welfare state, the nationalised industries, *dirigisme* in economic planning and massive defence strategies, and consequently the demands on the Civil Service grew out of all recognition from the service Trevelyan had known. With a huge influx of specialist staff during the two world wars and a constant increase in the tasks laid upon the service through governmental expansion, the number of civil servants had reached 732,000 by the time Mrs Thatcher's first administration took office in May 1979.[4]

• The competitive examination established to regulate entry into the service was rooted firmly in the educational standards of Oxbridge and the curricular preferences of middle-class public schools like Rugby. Degrees in the Classics were highly regarded; it being taken for granted that an ability to be conversant with Latin and Greek is the perfect qualification for a country's senior administrators. This emphasis on a classical public school education, coupled with the grade structure advocated by Trevelyan ensured that, while entry might be based on merit, the same was not true of promotion, because there was always an invisible ceiling on promotion for those who had entered the service at clerical level because of the different social and educational culture to which civil servants of the administrative class belonged.

• Allied to this is the cult of the 'gifted amateur', which permeates the British system, whether we are talking about sport or the professions, and which has ensured that in government circles the emphasis has always been on the generalist rather the specialist civil servant. British values mean that there is an actual aversion to the idea of the professional civil servant who has been trained in public administration, as is normal in continental Europe. A Civil Service College was set up only in 1970 and, even then, had nothing of the power and prestige of France's *Ecole Nationale d'Administration* from which the senior ranks of the administrative *grands corps* are expected to graduate. Even more significant for the British Civil Service in an increasingly technological age is that any scientific or technical qualification is regarded as beyond the pale as far as the culture of the Higher Civil Service is concerned. The high status accorded to engineers in France is mirrored by the fact that the technical *grand corps* of Ponts et Chaussées was founded as long ago as 1714 and the higher ranks of technical civil servants have been educated to degree level at the Ecole Polytechnique since 1794.[5] Not so in Britain! There may be civil engineers in the British Ministry of Transport but they will be directed to the Whitehall equivalent of the tradesman's entrance, and the Permanent Secretary and other senior staff will certainly not be of their number.

Towards Fulton

The history of the developing Civil Service was summarised by the great constitutional historian, G. R. Elton, as a three-stage process:

> The medieval household system was served by men recruited from the church . . . the middle period used clients of Ministers, trained . . . and promoted by and through them; this second method of supply lasted until it was replaced by the modern Civil Service with its examinations.[6]

Elton's definition does not make clear whether the growth of the Civil Service is an evolutionary incremental process or whether it is a revolutionary series of changes in direction. Since his first major book was called *The Tudor Revolution in Government*, it can only be assumed that he believed that change was best achieved through organic revolution, that these revolutions arose from the circumstances of the times and that the Northcote–Trevelyan reforms were the ultimate achievement: the end of an evolutionary ladder.

Revisionist thinking in recent years has shown that there are flaws in Elton's reasoning; largely because he was writing before the Fulton Report and could not see how the service was going to develop in entirely new directions in the aftermath of that report, so that an increasing number of critics would begin to deny that Northcote–Trevelyan represented the apotheosis of bureaucracy: there were even those who began to see Northcote–Trevelyan as little more than a temporary aberration in an entirely different story.

1) Like so many institutions within the British political system, the Civil Service cannot bear to discard old and familiar procedures. Systems devised as expedients to suit the situation obtaining at a particular point in time are retained, even though the situation has changed and moved on. Reform always seems to come too late for the problems of the day and, like generals who are always fighting wars with the strategies and tactics of the war before last, reforms in the civil administration always seem to be better suited to the problems of a previous generation. The important role of government in the twentieth century has been an increased involvement in the management of

the economy and yet, as Will Hutton has said, a Civil Service established in the mid-nineteenth century is just not equipped to deal with this. '[U]nlike France or Germany, Britain had made no systematic attempt to train a class of officials competent in commerce and finance. The accent was still placed on administration rather than intervention; on high policy rather than commercial strategy.'[7]

2)   Present indications seem to suggest that the establishment ordained by the Northcote–Trevelyan reforms is not the perfect outcome of a process of natural selection but more a temporary aberration. Indeed, the period of change ushered in by Margaret Thatcher is less one of revolutionary action than one of counter-revolutionary reaction to the ideas of an earlier time, especially insomuch as the quango culture has reintroduced the spectre of patronage and political appointees. Added to that, the hiving off of government agencies has meant the fragmentation of a once unified service and the lines between specialist and generalist have become increasingly blurred. The Civil Service of the 1990s begins to resemble the Civil Service of the 1790s more than it does that of the 1890s. An academic has recently described the post-Thatcher political establishment, as 'a one-party system marked by 18th-century characteristics'.[8]

Under the conditions of national emergency that existed during the two world wars, many of the formidable barriers and snobberies which existed within the Civil Service were broken down. For the sake of the war effort, academics, businessmen, scientists and other expert specialists were recruited to the various arms of the Home Civil Service. This new blood often vitalised the service and made it remarkably efficient in such operations as the introduction of food rationing in both wars, or the huge process of demobilisation and reconstruction after 1945. Yet any benefit that might have resulted from the new methodologies introduced by these irregular civil servants was lost as their temporary contracts were terminated and the Civil Service was restored as quickly as possible to its generalist traditions by the post-war heads of the Service – Warren Fisher after the First World War, Edward Bridges and Norman Brook after the Second, traditionalists to a man!

In the rapidly changing twentieth-century world involving a mixed economy and an interventionist government, the Civil Service grew steadily in size and responsibilities but otherwise retained those characteristics it had inherited as a legacy of the nineteenth century. Very little had happened, either to the organisational structure or the ethos of the service, that would have required any alteration to the Northcote–Trevelyan consensus by the time the Fulton Report of 1968 found that the Civil Service was 'still fundamentally the product of the nineteenth-century philosophy of the Northcote–Trevelyan Report'.[9] It was the arrival of the Labour government of 1964, with its emphasis on the role of a meritocracy and the importance of technological revolution, that led to the Fulton review of civil service structures and procedures. The new prime minister, Harold Wilson, was known to be concerned about the élitism and amateurism he believed existed in the Senior Civil Service, since he had expressed his concerns to the political scientist Norman Crowther-Hunt in a radio discussion and found widespread sympathy for his viewpoint. When, in February 1966, Wilson instituted a committee of inquiry into the Civil Service under the Vice-Chancellor of Sussex University, Lord Fulton, Crowther-Hunt was a leading member of that committee, and remained the most dedicated advocate of its proposals for twenty years thereafter.

The Fulton Committee was handicapped from the start by having a number of constraints and restrictions placed on what it was supposed to be investigating. It was to be free to examine the recruitment, career structure and management of civil servants but was very firmly warned against any interference in the actual nature of the service or the relationships between ministers and officials. As Wilson informed the House of Commons on 8 February 1966, 'Civil Servants remain the confidential advisers of Ministers . . . and we do not envisage any change in this fundamental feature of our parliamentary system of democracy.'[10] This came about largely because the service which had evolved from Northcote–Trevelyan was generally thought to be closest to that model of the Civil Service sometimes called the 'traditional' or 'liberal-democratic' model: in other words, this essentially nineteenth-century creation was just the type of bureaucracy felt to be suitable for the liberal democracies of the West and thereby the epitome of what the British, steeped in the Whig interpretation of history, expected of their civil administration. According to Norman Crowther-Hunt in later years, this restriction on the committee's terms of reference was contrived by senior civil servants so that they could challenge the committee's findings as inadequate in the aftermath of the report. '[It] enabled Sir William Armstrong, when he subsequently became head of the Civil Service, to argue that the Committee's work was thus unduly circumscribed and, as a consequence, that there were considerable doubts about most, if not all, of its recommendations.'[11]

The Fulton Report

Notoriously, the committee did not work well together and their findings are still regarded as highly contentious. Nevertheless, their report produced one clear-cut conclusion in that it made it very plain that the Civil Service, as it had evolved from the Northcote–Trevelyan reforms, was no longer suited to the needs of the second half of the twentieth century. It was deficient, they said, in four major respects:

1 A dominant Administrative Class, steeped in the ethos of the amateur generalist, preferably with a degree in Classics from an Oxbridge College, was no longer ideally suited to the task of administering the scientific, technological and management-oriented society of the late twentieth century.

2 The division of civil servants into separate clerical, executive and administrative classes, with strict limits on recruitment and barriers to promotion,
denied most civil servants a proper career structure and militated against
efficiency. It was estimated in the preamble to the report that, at the time of
Fulton, there were as many as 1,400 different classes in the Civil Service as
a whole.[12]
3 Too few civil servants were trained managers, suggesting a serious
deficiency in training, personnel management and career evaluation in the
service.
4 Most of these faults were the product of the Treasury's control of the Civil
Service. The Committee made a total of 22 recommendations, the most
important of which can be summarised as:

- Control of the Civil Service should be taken away from the Treasury and
  given to a new Civil Service Department which should be jointly headed
  by the prime minister and another, non-departmental, minister. The
  department would have a Permanent Secretary who would thereby
  effectively be Head of the Home Civil Service.
- The separate classes should be done away with and replaced by a single-
  stem structure for the non-industrial Civil Service with open promotion
  from the lowest to the highest positions according to ability: all civil servants should be able to progress as far and as fast as their ability and training could take them.
- There should be a Civil Service College for training recruits, providing in-
  service training and allowing for the development of specialisms and
  management skills.
- The employing departments should have a greater say in the recruitment and training of staff. With regard to the employment of graduates
  there should be a move away from the dominance of Oxford and
  Cambridge and a greater stress should be placed on the relevance of a
  recruit's degree to the work he or she might have to do. Efforts should be
  made to enhance the career prospects of specialists such as scientists
  and engineers.
- Entry into the Civil Service should be less exclusive, with late entry, lateral
  entry and temporary appointments all being made easier. Movement out
  of the service, whether temporary or permanent, should also be facili-
  tated through a relaxation on rules governing the transfer of pension and
  employment rights.
- All ministers should be able to appoint a small number of personally-
  nominated experts and advisers as temporary civil servants to support
  those ministers in policy formation and decision-taking.
- Departments should be encouraged to improve their efficiency by the
  introduction of modern management practices, including accountable
  management, planning units and management service units.

• The operational responsibilities of departments should be examined to judge whether there might not be certain functions which could operate more efficiently if hived off to non-departmental organisations and agencies.

The Fulton Report was compiled in the face of considerable internal wrangles over a range of issues. There were disagreements between committee members which culminated in a divided view on the proposed reforms and the signing of a minority report. But these arguments over recommendations paled into insignificance compared with the controversy surrounding the question of implementation. The Cabinet was split over the matter because Wilson had circulated a minute proposing the immediate setting up of a Civil Service Department and the removal of responsibility for Civil Service affairs from the Treasury, without having previously informed Roy Jenkins who, as Chancellor of the Exchequer, was in charge of the Treasury and, in theory at least, in charge of the Home Civil Service. At once Jenkins mobilised opposition to the adoption of Fulton's recommendations as they related to the Civil Service Department, the Civil Service College and abolition of classes, all three of which Wilson wanted to put into immediate effect. Jenkins was not necessarily against such reforms but felt that the changes needed to be carefully considered before implementation and not rushed into effect as Wilson was seeking to do. Jenkins's position received the backing of such cabinet heavyweights as Denis Healey, Michael Stewart the Foreign Minister and Richard Crossman.[13]

The Cabinet debated the matter for some time but ultimately gave way to Wilson's wishes. Crossman does report that the politicians took advantage of the dispute to make deals and to take pay-offs for agreement over personal and political differences; however, once these deals were done and the compromises agreed, the critics gave Wilson, 'a very easy time . . . Harold needed a success for himself' and Cabinet consented to his getting it.'[14] If, however, the politicians were finally willing to accept the Fulton Report, the same was not true of the officials. Sir William Armstrong, as head of the Civil Service, was locked in battle with Wilson over fundamental questions raised by the report. Armstrong was ready to accept the proposals for the Civil Service Department and for the Civil Service College: by the time these proposals were accepted they were effectively and substantially emasculated compared with Fulton's intentions. What Armstrong stubbornly fought against was the proposal that internal divisions between the classes should be removed. Over ten years later, Norman Crowther-Hunt collaborated with the political journalist Peter Kellner in writing a book about elitism in the Civil Service, the main message of which was to describe how Armstrong and other senior civil servants had succeeded in destroying the useful and necessary reforms suggested by Crowther-Hunt and his colleagues on the Fulton Committee.[15]

According to what Armstrong said later, Harold Wilson had a very limited view of what was meant by classes in the Civil Service. Rather than the 1,400 classes identified by Fulton, Wilson was concerned solely with the three classes into which the administrative bureaucracy was divided. These classes, which severely restricted the openness of recruitment and promotion, were defined in my youth as meaning that someone who left school at sixteen with a clutch of GCE 'O' levels could hope to enter the clerical grades of the Civil Service; those who stayed on at school to eighteen or nineteen and acquired their 'A' levels could aim to become an Executive Officer; while those hoping to become administrators needed a university degree, preferably in a non-vocational subject and, almost invariably, from either Oxford or Cambridge. Although it was theoretically possible for someone to move on their own merit from bottom to top there were in fact almost insuperable barriers between the clerical, executive and administrative levels.

Sir William Armstrong and Harold Wilson reached a compromise agreement by which Armstrong agreed to give up these divisions between clerical, executive and administrative officers, replacing them with a single-stem Administration Group with open-access recruitment and promotion. What Armstrong was not willing to give up was the division between generalists and specialists and, in effect, the divisions between Oxbridge Classicists and the rest. And here, although Armstrong has always been the one attacked, it has to be said that Wilson is far from being free of blame. It was Wilson himself who brushed aside Fulton's proposal that graduate entrants into the Service should have 'relevant' degrees and who adhered to the notion that a general degree in the liberal humanities was a more suitable qualification for a neutral administrator than a degree with vocational application. By doing so Wilson virtually negated any hope that the Civil Service College and a new commitment to modern management techniques would promote a change in the ethos of senior civil servants. Twenty years later, in 1986, Clive Ponting was able to point out that four of the senior administrators in the Department of Defence, responsible for administering the largest part of a defence budget of several billion pounds, were all Classicists who had read Greek and Latin Literature at Oxford.[16]

These disagreements over the report inevitably led to delays in implementation. The Civil Service Department was set up almost immediately in 1968 and was partially successful in loosening the hold of the Treasury over Civil Service management. However, the impact of the department was always limited and it was one of the first casualties of the Thatcherite new broom – being abolished in 1981. A Civil Service College was opened in 1970 but any hopes that it would be modelled on the French Ecole Nationale d'Administration and would be used to break down the old classical-generalist domination of the Service were soon dashed: initially at least it operated through providing courses of in-service training, often remedial in nature, thereby becoming associated with being only of use to those who had failed in their careers and were thus in need of retraining. The elimination of classes and the introduction of a single, unified administrative structure had to wait until the Conservatives under

Edward Heath had replaced the Wilson government, the change taking effect in 1971. As has been said already, the reforms were only a pale shadow of what Fulton had recommended, removing the horizontal barriers from the career structure but leaving intact the vertical barriers between generalists and specialists.

Other reforms suggested by Fulton were introduced by the Heath government. The suggestion that non-administrative activities might be hived off from departments was realised in the creation of three major agencies: the Property Services Agency, the Defence Procurement Agency and the Manpower Services Commission, harbingers of the Next Steps programme of twenty years later. The government of 1970–74 also saw the first tentative introduction of performance management and business-orientated schemes into Civil Service structures. These also were heralds of the wave of reforms that would sweep over the service in the 1980s.

There is an anomaly over the Fulton Report and its implementation. The need for the Commission and its proposals was prompted by two separate strands of criticism:

1 **The over-mighty servant**: a left-wing critique which was aimed at the elitism inherent in the Higher Civil Service and the ability of Whitehall mandarins to manipulate events so as to preserve the established order and stifle radical reform.
2 **Bureaucratic over-supply**: a right-wing critique which concentrated on the inefficiency of Civil Service personnel based on over-manning, rigidity of procedures and freedom from the discipline of market forces.

The anomaly over Fulton was that the commission was set up by a Labour government, largely for the left-wing reasons mentioned above. Yet those proposals which attempted to meet those left-wing positions were only slowly and partially implemented. It was those proposals which met right-wing critical points which ultimately were most fully implemented; tentatively under Heath and then overwhelmingly under Margaret Thatcher and John Major. It all hangs on the perspective from which the prevailing political establishment views the concept of bureaucracy.

Summary and conclusion

The Fulton Report was supposed to reform the Civil Service according to the preoccupations of the 1960s. In other words the outcome of Fulton was supposed to be, not only a more modern and efficient service, but one that was also more egalitarian in its criteria for recruitment and promotion. Unfortunately, the comparatively few politicians who were willing to implement Fulton were distracted by more serious matters such as the economic crisis which led to the 1967 devaluation of sterling and the intensification of that economic crisis throughout the late 1960s and early 1970s. The politicians left reform of the Civil Service to the civil servants themselves and the result was a series of small cosmetic changes rather than the root-and-branch reform required. 'Until recently, the story of the Senior Civil Service has been one of resistance and self-preservation. Senior civil servants have remained remarkably unaffected by changes that have altered the workings of the rest of the Civil Service.'[17]

The opportunity represented by the Fulton Report was missed, which meant that reform, when it did come under the Thatcher administration, was even more damaging to the traditionalists' view of the Service than might otherwise have been the case.[18]

Notes

1 This is a simplified extract from Gladstone's Treasury Minute of 12 April 1853 setting up the Northcote–Trevelyan Review. A full version of the text is to be found in R. A. Chapman and J. R. Greenaway, *The Dynamics of Administrative Reform*, Croom Helm, London, 1980, pp. 25–6.
2 Robert Pyper, *The British Civil Service*, Harvester Wheatsheaf, Hemel Hempstead, 1995, p. 8.
3 Figures quoted in Peter Hennessy, *Whitehall*, Secker and Warburg, London, 1989, p. 51.
4 Tony Butcher, 'The Civil Service in the 1990s', *Talking Politics*, Autumn 1995, p. 39.
5 A useful survey of the French Civil Service is included in Anne Stevens, *The Government and Politics of France*, Macmillan, Basingstoke, 1992 (Chapter 5, pp. 118–40).
6 G. R. Elton, *The Tudor Revolution in Government*, Cambridge University Press, London, 1953, p. 425.
7 Will Hutton, *The State We're In*, Jonathan Cape, London, 1995, p. 53.
8 Professor John Keane, *New Statesman*, 27 March 1997, p. 51.
9 Lord Fulton, *The Civil Service, Vol. 1, Report of the Committee 1966–8*, Command Paper 3638, HMSO, 1968.
10 Harold Wilson in *Hansard*, 8 February 1966, quoted in Hennessey, Note 3 above, p. 190.
11 Peter Kellner and Lord Crowther-Hunt, *The Civil Servants: An Inquiry into Britain's Ruling Class*, Macdonald, London, 1980, p. 27.
12 The actual wording in the Fulton Report states of the number of classes – 'there are over 1400, each for the most part with its own separate pay and career structure'.
13 The arguments over the Fulton Report were chronicled by Richard Crossman in his diary entries for June 1968 (*Richard Crossman: The Diaries of a Cabinet Minister, Vol. 3*, Jonathan Cape, London, 1977. Also available in a condensed single-volume version, edited by Anthony Howard and published by Methuen, London, 1979).
14 *Ibid.*
15 Kellner and Crowther-Hunt, Note 11 above.
16 Clive Ponting, *Whitehall, Tragedy and Farce*, Hamish Hamilton, London, 1986.
17 Rachel Bayliss and Charlotte Dargie, *The Senior Civil Service in the 1990s*, Chapter 4

in Steve Lancaster (ed.), *Developments in Politics, Vol. 9*, Causeway Press, Ormskirk, 1998.

18 Ian Budge, Ivor Crewe, David McKay and Ken Newton, *The New British Politics*, Addison Wesley Longman, Harlow, 1998.

4

The Civil Service after Fulton

The Civil Service and the delivery of government

There are many public servants who carry out administrative tasks very similar to the work done by civil servants but who are not actually themselves civil servants according to a strict definition of the term. Typical of these public servants are the police, tax inspectors, customs officers and the clerks and officials serving parliament in the Palace of Westminster, plus, of course, the entire bureaucracy of local government. Nowadays, true civil servants can be found in one of four different working environments, although only the first of these represents the traditional Civil Service as we think of it:

1 departments and ministries of state.
2 governmental offices for the regions.
3 non-ministerial departments.
4 executive agencies.

In dealing with the policy-making administrators of the Senior Civil Service we are concerned overwhelmingly with those government departments and ministries that make up Whitehall as we have defined it in a previous chapter. Essentially, the delivery of government in Britain is compartmentalised into specialised administrative areas – agriculture, education or transport being typical examples – known as government departments and it is these which administer the decisions and policies made by government ministers. This administration is largely carried out by civil servants, although direction is political, with each department having a political head in its minister.

No framework of rules or conventions defines the departmental structure of government. Certain major departments, such as the Treasury or the Lord Chancellor's Department, are of medieval origin and over a long period of time have become so fundamentally important to government that they are bound to continue. But, beyond these central departments the Crown is free to create, abolish, merge and divide the other departments as it wishes. Apart from the

Foreign Office, Home Office, Colonial Office, War Office and Board of Trade, the roots of which extend back to before 1800, most modern departments originated with the growth of governmental responsibilities in the nineteenth century. Each new responsibility assumed by government had to have a body created to deal with it in the form of a 'board' or 'committee of the Privy Council' and it was these boards and committees which grew in size and influence to become true government departments. There is no general statutory basis for this structure although some specific statutes do exist, as with the Order setting up the Board of Trade in 1786.[1]

Over the years ministries come into being, grow, diminish, cease to exist or merge with others according to need. Consider a simple history of the Commonwealth Office:

- 1947: India Office and Dominions Office merge to become Commonwealth Office.
- 1966: Commonwealth Office absorbs what is left of the Colonial Office.
- 1968: Commonwealth Office is merged with the Foreign Office to form the Foreign and Commonwealth Office.

During the 1970s there was a fashion for merged 'super-ministries', such as when joint control of the armed services and other elements of national defence passed from the individual concerns of the Air Ministry, War Office and Naval Department to become part of a extra-large Department of Defence. It was around that time that these new 'super-ministries' first became known to the public as Departments of State, and the minister in charge of a Department became more widely known under the title of Secretary of State.

Still later on, some of these extra-large departments proved to be too unwieldy and the process was put into reverse, departments being divided or parts of the department being transferred elsewhere. A typical example was the Department of Health and Social Security which was divided into two under Margaret Thatcher, splitting into the Department of Health and the Department of Social Security.

A Secretary of State has overall responsibility for the functioning of a department. In the second rank are Ministers of State with specific areas of responsibility and, below them, Parliamentary Under Secretaries of State. All ministers, including the Secretary of State, have Parliamentary Private Secretaries as their assistants. An example of how this structure works is that exhibited by the Department for Education and Employment, under the Secretary of State for Education and Employment, where junior ministers divide among themselves the different operational functions of the department:

- Minister for Employment.
- Minister for School Standards.
- Minister for Education and Employment in the Lords.
- Parliamentary Under-Secretary of State for Employment.

- Parliamentary Under-Secretary of State for School Standards.
- Parliamentary Under-Secretary of State for Lifelong Learning.[2]

The Welsh, Scottish and Northern Ireland Offices are different in that they are each responsible for several areas which are dealt with at individual departmental level in England. In the Scottish Office, for example, there is a Secretary of State for Scotland who is in overall general control but there are also Ministers of State with specific responsibilities for education, transport, etc. (See Appendix 1 for a list of departments and ministries, with the number of civil servants employed by them).

Within each department, each minister – junior or senior – has his or her own ministerial team of civil servants, although naturally enough the largest team belongs to the Secretary of State. In the television programme *Yes Minister*, Sir Humphrey Appleby introduced Jim Hacker to the involved structure of the Civil Service in his department: 'I am the Permanent Under-Secretary of State, known as the Permanent Secretary. Woolley here is your Principal Private Secretary. I, too, have a Principal Private Secretary, and he is the Principal Private Secretary to the Permanent Secretary. Directly responsible to me are ten Deputy Secretaries, eighty-seven Under-Secretaries and two hundred and nineteen Assistant Secretaries. Directly responsible to the Principal Private Secretaries are plain Private Secretaries. The prime minister will be appointing two Parliamentary Under-Secretaries and you will be appointing your own Parliamentary Private Secretary.'[3]

Considering the Civil Service as a whole, the largest part is located across the entire United Kingdom. Only 15 per cent of non-industrial civil servants are located in inner London, with a further 8 per cent in the suburbs, obviously meaning that 77 per cent of non-industrial civil servants are based and work outside London. On the other hand, the more senior the civil servant, the more likely it is that he or she will be located in Whitehall itself. 86 per cent of the top three grades of the Higher Civil Service are located in Central London, including all but three of the 36 Permanent Secretaries; whereas nearly 60 per cent of the Principals and Senior Principals who make up grades 7 and 6 are to be found in the provinces.[4]

Distanced from Whitehall and the higher ranks of policy-making civil servants are the national and regional departments of government which have a remit to oversee the application of national policy of several departments within one office in a form of administrative devolution. Examples of this have been the Scottish Office, Welsh Office and Northern Ireland Office, each of which is organised into functional departments dealing with such areas of responsibility as agriculture and fisheries, education, environment, home and health, planning, trade and transport. In England it was always the case that certain ministries such as agriculture or transport administered their policies in the country at large through a series of regional offices.

During the early 1990s, as part of the Tory government's reorganisation of the Civil Service, offices known as integrated regional offices (now known as **government offices for the regions**) were instituted to perform the same service for the English regions as the Northern Ireland, Scottish and Welsh Offices do for the national regions. The Regional Director in each office is responsible for the regional policies of three Departments of State – Environment, Transport and the Regions; Trade and Industry; Education and Employment – reporting to and remaining accountable to the relevant Secretary of State. The ten regional offices and the populations served by each are: London (6.9 million), South East (7.7 million), Eastern (5.2 million), South West (4.8 million), West Midlands (5.3 million), East Midlands (4.1 million), Yorks & Humberside (5.0 million), North East (2.6 million), North West (2.6 million) and Merseyside (1.5 million).[5]

In 1998 the Deputy Prime Minister, John Prescott, announced the setting up in April 1999 of eight Regional Development Agencies (RDAs). These cover much of the same ground as the pre-existing regional offices but the creation of an elected Mayor and strategic authority for London has removed the capital from the list, while Merseyside has been absorbed into the North West region based in Manchester. These RDAs will take a lead in developing regional strategies and will represent the regions to the European Union (EU) but they will also have a say in regional policies on transport, land use and the environment, further and higher education, crime prevention and public health.[6]

The Higher Civil Service and those non-industrial, generalist grades concerned with policy-making and administrative duties are naturally based in ministerial departments. A very substantial part of the Civil Service is, however, employed in non-ministerial departments and agencies which are the executive divisions of government, carrying out and administering the decisions of ministers. Many of these departments and agencies have existed for some time and have a long history as executive offices of ministerial departments but they have only really flourished as semi-autonomous bodies during the process of reform that began in the 1980s with the Next Steps programme and other reforms that will be discussed in later chapters. Nevertheless, and despite the comparatively recent nature of these reforms, the executive agencies and departmental units were responsible by 1998 for employing over 76 per cent of all civil servants. However, a high proportion of these agencies' personnel are specialists rather than generalists, and therefore seldom qualify for the upper ranks of the Higher Civil Service.

Non-ministerial departments are government offices not under the direct control of a government minister but headed by office-holders, board-members or commissioners with specific statutory responsibilities. A great number have responsibilities for government revenue, most notably the Inland Revenue which collects tax in all its forms for the Treasury and the Department of Social Security. Then there is HM Customs & Excise with responsibility for VAT, customs dues on imports and exports and other indirect taxation, including VAT receipts for the EU. The Office of the Paymaster General, founded in 1836, provides banking and financial services for the government, together with its subordinate bodies, the Public Works Loan Board, set up in 1793 to advance loans to local government for capital expenditure, and the National Debt Office, founded even earlier in 1786 and still managing government investment portfolios, including the National Insurance Fund, National Savings and the National Lottery Fund. Land and property belonging to the state is managed by the Crown Estate Commissioners or the Forestry Commission.

Non-ministerial offices supervise and regulate private and privatised concerns that have public responsibilities. For a long time this has included Commissions like the Building Societies Commission, the Friendly Societies Commission and the Charity Commission together with offices such as the Office of Fair Trading. More recently, many regulators have been set up to look after former nationalised concerns, including the Office of Electricity Regulation (OFFER), Office of Gas Supply (OFGAS), Office of the National Lottery (OFLOT), Office of Passenger Rail Franchising (OPRAF), Officer of the Rail Regulator, Office of Telecommunications (OFTEL) and Office of Water Services (OFWAT). The former Inspectorate of Schools in England has become the Office for Standards in Education (OFSTED) or HM Chief Inspector of Schools (Wales) in Wales.[7] (See the second part of Appendix 1 for the main four non-ministerial departments and the number of civil servants they employ.)

There are literally dozens of **executive agencies**, some of long-standing but many others created as a result of the reorganisation to be discussed in subsequent chapters (see Appendix 2). Executive agencies were only introduced in 1988 under the Next Steps programme, with the founding of the Vehicle Inspectorate, and there were still only 12 agencies in existence by 1990. This had grown to 94 agencies by 1994, with a further 11 agencies peculiar to Northern Ireland. When the Blair government issued its first *List of Ministerial Responsibilities* in June 1997 it was able to list 137 agencies in the UK as a whole, ranging in size and importance from the Wilton Park Conference Centre with 37 employees, to the Benefits Agency with 66,300 staff. A year later this figure had increased to 138 agencies and four executive departments. All those working in the agencies are civil servants but their recruitment, pay and promotion structures are autonomous of the old traditional structures, most noticeably in the hierarchical structure which is composed of chief executives and managers rather than the traditional Permanent Secretaries, Deputy Secretaries and Under Secretaries, and with many senior positions being advertised publicly and being open to candidates from outside the Civil Service establishment who are then appointed by the Agency Chief Executive rather than a departmental minister.

Recruitment and promotion: staffing after Fulton

By the mid-1960s, as we saw in Chapter 3, the Civil Service had became set in the pattern established by the Northcote–Trevelyan Report of the 1850s. A Civil Service Commission controlled recruitment to the service through a competitive examination and then granted promotion on merit, although civil servants tended to remain within the class to which they had been recruited. As the first major attempt to reform what by then was a century-old institution, the Fulton Report was very much concerned with eliminating the rigidities created by these class divisions within the Civil Service. A major concern of the report was to isolate four areas where current practices of recruitment and promotion were flawed:

1) *Closed entry* – as a result of which senior positions in the Civil Service were always filled by promotions from within the service. Fulton felt that senior positions should be open to outside applicants who could open up the enclosed, rather claustrophobic, world of the Civil Service to the wider knowledge and experience of the world outside the service.

2) *The cult of the generalist* – whereby senior civil servants were almost exclusively those who had received a general education and were graduates in the Classics or humanities. On the other hand, the attitudes of those responsible for recruiting and promoting meant that those with specialist or professional qualifications, such as scientists, engineers, lawyers or accountants, were effectively prevented from entering the administrative grades. Such an attitude did nothing for the morale of non-administrative civil servants who had to reconcile themselves to being 'second-class citizens' on the promotion ladder, nor did it really serve the interests of people and government in what was an increasingly technological society.

3) *A bias towards Oxbridge graduates.* Despite disclaimers which said that there was no such thing as an 'old boy network' for graduates of Oxford or Cambridge and despite insistent claims that entrance examinations and qualification requirements were open to all and limited by nothing but individual merit, the fact remained that the nature of the entrance examinations and the background of those conducting recruitment interviews was such as to favour Oxbridge candidates at the expense of other institutions of higher education. For example, of the successful candidates sitting the examinations for fast-stream entry to the administrative grades in 1968, 59 per cent were graduates of Oxford or Cambridge.

4) *Lack of mobility.* At the time of the Fulton Report, civil servants were still recruited directly into the clerical, executive and administrative classes and, although it was theoretically possible to move between classes and work one's way through the ranks from clerical to administrative status, this did not happen. There were what were known as 'glass ceilings' – invisible but very much present – between the classes and, no matter what merit and ability might be displayed by the civil servant, he or she tended to remain within the grade to which they had been recruited.[8]

Fulton himself was principally concerned with the division between generalists and specialists, seeing the philosophy of the 'gentleman amateur' and the supremacy of the Oxbridge Classicist as representing the greatest hindrances to the development of a modern government machine suitable for the second half of the twentieth century. He wanted the recruitment and promotion systems changed so as to give more weight to 'relevant' degrees, opening up the ranks of the Higher Civil Service to professional administrators with managerial expertise. Unfortunately for Fulton, it was this area, where he felt that reform was most needed, that was totally overlooked by those reforms that were introduced. This was partly because of resistance to change within the service itself: in 1980 Lord Crowther-Hunt was still complaining that the slowness of reform was due to the dominance of generalists and an Oxbridge elite who were so entrenched within the higher ranks of the service that they could block any changes that might damage their own authority. And it must be admitted that to ask a generalist Higher Civil Service to curtail their own dominance to such an extent as to admit specialists into the higher echelons of the service, would be rather like asking turkeys to vote for Christmas.

Also to blame was the fact that implementation of Fulton was left to the Conservative government of Edward Heath, newly elected in 1970, which was far less sympathetic to the cause of reforming the Civil Service than the outgoing Wilson government. It has to be said, however, that both Wilson and Callaghan, as ex-grammar-school boys, were themselves somewhat suspicious of the narrow interests of the specialist, compared to the wide-ranging talents of the generalist, and were reluctant to upset a system they saw as still working well because of the lifetime of tradition that was backing it. Which is why Crowther-Hunt could still lament the lack of reform in 1980 and why it was left to the Thatcher governments of the 1980s to introduce reforms which went far beyond those dreamt of by Fulton.

Although the reforms were nowhere near as far-reaching as Fulton would have wished, the Civil Service was nevertheless substantially restructured as implementation of the Fulton Report began in 1971. The sprawling and complex structure that had been categorised by class and function was replaced by a wide range of specialist and departmental groups (see Appendix 3) each of which was staffed according to a service-wide unified grading structure. At the same time, in 1972, the former clerical, executive and administrative classes were integrated into a single-stem 'Open Structure' **Administrative Group**, without the intervening class boundaries to act as ceilings to promotion. The top seven grades in the Open Structure of the Administrative Group (see Appendix 4) represent the Senior Civil Service, a grouping of generalist administrators.[9] Within this Open Structure a 'fast stream' of **administration trainees** was established so as to assist the more able applicants to achieve a speedy promotion to the higher echelons of the service. The specialist and professional groups were also given their own fast-stream programmes in the post-Fulton period but the persistence of separate career structures for different groups within the service meant that the generalist fast streamers remained supreme: as late as 1994, more than 60 per cent of the top three grades were generalists, while the only specialist group to make a showing on the promotion ladder was the group including the lawyers, representing about 12 per cent of the Open Structure.[10] We should not, however, overlook the fact that the more able specialist graduates in disciplines such as information technology can command twice the salary from private industry than they could earn as senior civil servants: specialist applicants may pass the fast-stream entrance requirements and start upon a Civil Service career, only to be wooed away by more lucrative offers from the City or elsewhere.

Very much in line with Fulton's recommendations was the **Civil Service Department**, created by the Wilson government in 1968 to take over the running of the Civil Service from the Treasury. In 1970 the Department acquired the Civil Service Commission and began to reform and improve recruitment and training practices, particularly as it related to the 'fast-stream' programmes. Under these programmes, university graduates who had successfully passed the entrance examination were accepted directly into the upper ranks of government departments as administration trainees; with the expectation that they would have the potential to progress to at least the entry level of the Senior Civil Service and to achieve rapid promotion within the top seven grades of the Open Structure.[11] Despite its successes in improving recruitment practices – or perhaps because of those successes – the Civil Service Department was much resented by the Treasury and its powers were slowly eroded over a ten-year period, until it was abolished for not fitting in with the new Thatcher regime in 1981. Recruitment and training were returned with the Commission to Treasury control while actual operational control of the Civil Service passed to the Cabinet Office, with the Cabinet Secretary having the additional official title of Head of the Civil Service.

Also founded as a result of Fulton's recommendations was the **Civil Service College**, set up in 1970 with the implied intention of creating a staff college which would deal with major training courses for graduate entrants, so as to escape the long tradition of 'learning by doing' whereby fast-stream entrants were thrown in at the deep end and expected to carry out their duties on the basis of little more training than an induction course lasting perhaps three or four days. The College, however, never did live up to what was expected of it, mainly because of the way in which the College's courses were perceived by rank-and-file civil servants. Most successful courses in the early years were remedial courses intended to correct faults in management practice. The College was therefore seen as providing courses designed for failing professionals, meaning that to apply for a course at the College was equivalent to confessing a personal failure. This reputation deterred many candidates from the often excellent management courses on offer and the College's importance began to decline; its head being downgraded in 1976 from a College Principal on grade 2 (Deputy Secretary rank) to a Principal on grade 3 (Under Secretary). There has been a recovery in recent years, beginning with a three-week top management programme for aspiring civil servants on grade 3 which has proved both successful and popular.

In 1989 the College became the third executive agency set up under the Next Steps programme and acquired the need to meet market-orientated performance criteria, covering its own costs by charging departments for the provision of courses and ultimately making a small profit. This success has heralded something of a revival in the prestige of the College, especially with business management programmes developed in association with the Cranfield, Manchester, Strathclyde and Open University Business Schools. Over 500 courses are now on offer to a wide range of commercial and public sector organisations as well as all Civil Service departments, with the further advantage that courses can be tailor-made by the College according to the needs of the client organisation, whether it is from the private or the public sector.

Composition of the Civil Service: educational, gender and ethnic origins

The Fulton Report was essentially egalitarian in its intent. We have already discussed concerns about the dominance of the generalist but Fulton was also concerned with the image of the typical senior civil servant as being a public school, Oxbridge-educated white male with a distinctly conservative and reactionary bias. As Kingdom says, 'The mandarins have traditionally come from the same social stratum as those at the heads of industry, commerce, the City, the army, the church, and professions such as law and medicine. They attended the same public schools and universities, belong to the same London clubs and meet at country house parties.'[12] This view of what used to be called 'The Establishment' is rather rooted in the attitudes of the 1960s but it has to be said that, in generalised terms, very little has changed fundamentally in the attitudes and prejudices of the Senior Civil Service. The stereotyped attitude of senior civil servants towards females, for instance, is epitomised in one episode of *Yes Minister*, where Jim Hacker asks Sir Humphrey Appleby:

> HACKER: How many permanent secretaries are there at the moment?
> SIR HUMPHREY: Forty-one, I believe.
> HACKER: Forty-one. And how many are women?
> SIR HUMPHREY: Well, broadly speaking, not having the exact figures to hand, I'm not exactly sure.
> HACKER: Well, approximately?
> SIR HUMPHREY: Well, *approximately* none.[13]

There were periods in the 1980s, ironically during the administration of a woman prime minister, when Sir Humphrey's reply would accurately have been, '*precisely* none'. The relative importance of women in the Civil Service was revealed in *Civil Service Statistics* published by the Government Statistical Service for the Treasury in 1988. According to these figures, there were no female Permanent Secretaries and only 5 per cent of the whole Open Structure were women, most of these being in grades 5 to 7, as Assistant Secretaries or Principals. In the clerical ranks on the other hand, 66 per cent of Clerical Administrative Officers were women, and 75 per cent of Clerical Administrative Assistants. By the 1990s there have been some improvements: in 1993 women represented some 40 per cent of fast-stream applicants and about 33 per cent of those appointed. According to figures released by the Cabinet Office in 1996, women made up 51 per cent of the Civil Service but 90 per cent of those women were at Executive Officer level or below; compared with 58 per cent of men. At that time there were three women with the status of Permanent Secretary (9 per cent of civil servants occupying grade 1). Taking grades 3 to 1 into consideration, 66 were women, representing 11 per cent of those on the three grades. The same Cabinet Office report also stated that a recruitment target had been set which envisages at least 15 per cent of Senior Civil Service positions being held by women by the year 2000. For women this certainly represents a degree of progress but, proportionately, it will still be the case that women are greatly under-represented in the Senior Civil Service, as indeed are ethnic minorities and the products of state schools and redbrick universities.

Three successive annual reports by the Civil Service Commission – 1991, 1992 and 1993 – devoted considerable time and space to examining the reasons for low success rates among fast-stream applicants from the ethnic minorities. The main conclusion of these reports was that there had been a significant increase in the numbers of ethnic minority applicants over recent years but that that increase was not reflected by any noticeable increase in the number of successful applicants. An article in the *Observer* of 12 October 1997 quoted recent statistics to the effect that just 1 per cent of senior civil servants above the status of Assistant Secretary are of Asian origin. When Afro-Caribbeans are considered the figure is 0.34 per cent. It may well be that there are significant numbers of civil servants being recruited from the ethnic minorities but they are overwhelmingly to be found in the lower grades. The greatest hurdle is seen to be the qualifying aptitude test forming part of the fast-stream selection process, which is where most applicants fail. It may well be that the socio-cultural values on which this test is based are the values held by white, upper-middle-class males and this gives an undue advantage to candidates who share those values and satisfy that description. As has been said earlier, the competitive entrance examination introduced in the nineteenth century was rooted in the educational standards of Oxbridge and the curriculum preferences of middle-class public schools like Rugby.

This same underlying educational bias on the part of the selection process may help explain the continued domination of the Senior Civil Service by those educated at public school and Oxbridge. The Cabinet Office figures of 1996 showed that 51 per cent of Permanent Secretaries were educated at public school and 60 per cent were graduates of Oxford or Cambridge. A number of commentators, from Kellner and Crowther-Hunt onwards,[14] have made the point that recruitment procedures in the selection process favour the product of the public school or Oxbridge. In other words, it is senior figures within an organisation who set up the criteria for recruitment and there is therefore an unwitting tendency for these senior figures to recruit those who are cast in their own image.

The Civil Service Commission has introduced a number of positive measures to try to smooth out these recruitment discrepancies, including the specific canvassing of state schools and all universities during careers conferences and the careers fairs known as 'Graduates in Government'. In 1991, Sir Robin Butler, as Head of the Civil Service, introduced a scheme whereby each Whitehall Permanent Secretary or agency Chief Executive adopted a university (including what were then still known as polytechnics) which they then visited on a regular basis, speaking to students in an attempt to recruit them, widening the catchment area for fast-stream applicants.

The Civil Service Management Code contains very firm guidelines on equal opportunities, stating:

> Civil Service equal opportunities policy provides that all eligible people must have equality of opportunity for employment and advancement on the basis of their suitability for the work. There must be no unfair discrimination on the basis of age, disability, gender, marital status, sexual orientation, race, colour, nationality, ethnic or national origin, or (in Northern Ireland) community background.[15]

Summary and conclusion

Following the reforms of the Fulton Report there were still many critics of the Civil Service who believed that civil servants were too powerful in comparison with government ministers, enabling an elite of the Civil Service to manipulate the machinery of government in some way so as to thwart the wishes of an elected government. There were basically two perspectives governing this critique of the Civil Service:

1 **The left-wing perspective** – put forward in a series of memoirs published by former Labour ministers such as Richard Crossman, Barbara Castle and Tony Benn – stating that the Higher Civil Service, as part of the establishment or ruling class, will do everything possible and use all their manipulative powers to maintain the status quo and to prevent the introduction of such radical initiatives as a Labour government might encourage.

2 **The right-wing perspective**, which is more concerned with the size of a proliferating bureaucracy and the inefficiencies inherent in such a structure. The inertia of the Civil Service in favouring consensual, centrist policies was

just as disturbing to the radical right wing, personified by Margaret Thatcher, as it was to Tony Benn and the far left.

The irony is that the Labour prime ministers, Harold Wilson and Jim Callaghan, who might have been expected to reform the elitist nature of the Civil Service after Fulton, never shared the doubts and fears expressed by politicians to the left of them like Tony Benn. The nature of the Civil Service was not seriously challenged until after 1979. Then, the prime minister who did have serious reservations about the Civil Service was Margaret Thatcher, which meant that the far-ranging reforms when they did come were driven by the concerns of the right – concerns primarily about the efficiency of an over-large and over-bureaucratic institution and secondly about the degree to which the introduction of simple market forces could revivify the system.

Notes

1 The definition of a government department is taken from Colin Pilkington, *Politics Today Companion to the British Constitution*, Manchester University Press, Manchester, 1998.

2 The breakdown of the DfEE is based on the *List of Ministerial Responsibilities*, issued by the Cabinet Office, Office of Public Service, June 1997.

3 From *Open Government*, first programme in the BBC-TV series, *Yes Minister*. Jonathan Lynn and Antony Jay, *The Complete Yes Minister*, BBC Books, London, 1984.

4 Bill Coxall and Lynton Robins, *Contemporary British Politics* (2nd edition), Macmillan, Basingstoke, 1994, p. 156.

5 English regionalism was discussed in two articles which appeared at around the same time, Jonathan Bradbury, 'English Regional Government', *Politics Review*, April 1996, p. 16–19, and Gerry Stokes, Brian Hopwood and Udo Bullman, 'Do We Need Regional Government', *Talking Politics*, Spring 1996, pp. 191–5.

6 Peter Hetherington, 'Prescott Gets Half a Cake', *Guardian*, 20 November 1998, p. 23.

7 Pilkington, Note 1 above.

8 The four criticisms made by the Fulton Report are outlined in Robert Pyper, *The British Civil Service*, Prentice Hall/Harvester Wheatsheaf, Hemel Hempstead, 1995, pp. 28–9.

9 George Tyrrell, *Longman Revise Guide – Government and Politics*, Addison Wesley Longman, Harlow, 1996, pp. 86–7.

10 These and subsequent figures on the demographic make-up of the Civil Service are based on statistics released by the Cabinet Office in 1996, based on field work done in 1994, and quoted by Rachel Bayliss and Charlotte Dargie, 'The Senior Civil Service in the 1990s', Chapter 4 in Steve Lancaster (ed.), *Developments in Politics*, Vol. 9, Causeway Press, Ormskirk, 1998.

11 The Fast Stream Development Programme is described in the *Civil Service Management Code*, published by the Machinery of Government and Propriety Division of the Cabinet Office (Office of Public Service and Science), 1996.

12 John Kingdom, *Government and Politics in Britain*, Polity Press, Cambridge, 1994, p. 356.
13 From *Equal Opportunities*, fifteenth programme in the BBC-TV series, *Yes Minister*. Lynn and Jay, Note 3, above.
14 Peter Kellner and Lord Crowther-Hunt, *The Civil Servants: An Inquiry into Britain's Ruling Class*, Macdonald, London, 1980.
15 Cabinet Office, *Civil Service Management Code*, see Note 11.

5

The political culture of the Civil Service

The ideal of a liberal-democratic service

According to the tenets of liberal pluralist democracy, as enshrined in the Northcote–Trevelyan reforms and founded on the ethos of nineteenth-century political society, the British Civil Service was believed to have three particular strengths: it was said to be permanent, impartial and anonymous.

Permanence and continuity

Governments might change their political complexion after a general election, while government ministers regularly come, go and are reshuffled according to the wishes of the prime minister. But the civil servants staffing those ministries continue as though nothing has happened, ensuring a stability and continuity of administration that is in sharp contrast with the fairly short life-span of ministerial appointments and which is very different from the American system of 'spoils' or patronage under which senior officials change every time the elected administration changes.

Ministers in a British government, when they are appointed, know little or nothing about the department they have to run, being more or less ignorant about the work and concerns of that department. Senior civil servants on the other hand have had years of experience as professional administrators, building up a wealth of expertise across a range of departments, ensuring a smooth continuity in the administration of any department's work. This does tend to lead to an unadventurous attitude on the part of officials, since the looked-for continuity is best achieved through a middle-of-the-road approach to policy that avoids unsettling changes of direction by not deviating too much from the status quo and the policies of the previous administration. This in turn has sometimes created problems and tensions between senior civil servants who have become rather set in their ways and those governments that have been elected on a radical manifesto:

Ranged against the politician's claim to be breaking with the past is the belief in the Civil Service that it represents and personifies the seamless integrity of past, present and future government rolled indistinguishably into one. Whitehall is the custodian of the very continuity that the new keepers of Westminster think they have been elected to rupture.[1]

The desire of civil servants for a smooth continuity in any transfer of power means that the not inconsiderable energies and talents of senior policy-making civil servants will be devoted to playing down over-radical demands for change by means of promoting consensual solutions. Many of the changes inflicted on the Civil Service after 1979 were reactionary measures taken in response to the way in which Margaret Thatcher felt that her ideas were being thwarted by an over-powerful Civil Service when she first took power.

The concept of permanence has also given rise to a convention which states that senior civil servants have security of tenure and can only be dismissed from their posts at the specific request of a minister, with the additional approval of both the prime minister and the Head of the Civil Service. In recent years the only instance of a senior civil servant being dismissed in this way was Sir Peter Kemp, the civil servant responsible for the Next Steps programme, whose dismissal was requested by William Waldegrave, as Public Service Minister, in 1992.[2] In fact the appearance of job security for senior civil servants is as illusory as any political convention. Under common law a civil servant is a servant of the Crown and therefore theoretically part of the royal household. As such, a government minister, acting in the name of the Crown, has the right to dismiss a civil servant 'at pleasure', without notice and without giving a reason for that dismissal. Even modern civil servants who have proper contracts of employment have no more claim to security of tenure than any other employee whose employment is only safeguarded by that minimum of legislation which promises redress if unfair dismissal can be proved.[3]

Political neutrality

The continuity of a permanent Civil Service, whereby the same civil servants serve successive governments of different political complexions, presupposes that civil servants should not compromise that ability to serve any master by holding strong political opinions themselves. After all, civil servants do not make policy, they merely carry out decisions made by the politicians, meaning that they themselves should be politically neutral and non-partisan. As one former minister has described their duty to serve the government of the day, regardless of the party that is in power, 'If convinced of the need for action on practical grounds, it [the Civil Service] will assist Labour governments to advance socialism . . . and will equally impartially assist Conservative governments to demolish what the socialists have created. Often the same officials will do both.'[4]

All applicants to join the Civil Service are investigated and carefully screened before appointment and, although this process exists primarily to weed out any candidates with fascist or communist tendencies, the system does tend to throw up those applicants with strongly partisan loyalties. Civil servants are not expected to play any role in party politics at national level, nor to perform any actions which could be interpreted as serving the partisan interests of either government or opposition, nor should they speak in public or publish writings about politically controversial issues. Under the House of Commons Disqualification Act of 1975 which defines those holders of public office who are not allowed to take seats in the House of Commons, civil servants are ruled to be not eligible to stand for election, either to the parliament at Westminster or to the European Parliament. As for political activity in a civil servant's spare time, the position varies according to their place in the service hierarchy. Civil servants in industrial or non-office grades are said to belong to the 'politically-free' category and for these there are no restrictions, except for the normal requirement that a civil servant should not indulge in political activity while on duty. Nor should a politically-active civil servant's connection with the service be made widely known.

Beyond this unrestricted category there is an intermediate group who can indulge in political activity, but only with the approval of their head of department. However, senior civil servants who are directly involved in the policy-making process should play no part in national politics whatsoever: to the extent of not even being expected to express a political opinion in public. As the Civil Service Management Code states:

> Civil servants not in the politically free category must not allow the expression of their personal political views to constitute so strong and so comprehensive a commitment to one political party as to inhibit or appear *to inhibit loyal and effective service to Ministers of another party*. They must take particular care to express comment with moderation, *particularly about matters for which <u>their own Ministers</u> are responsible*; to avoid comment altogether about matters of controversy affecting the responsibility of their own Ministers, and to avoid personal attacks.

However, even the most senior civil servants are permitted to take part in local government politics, with the approval of their heads of department.

Anonymity

Traditionally, civil servants were never named nor was their identity made known to the public. This was the rule for two main reasons:

1 If civil servants with a say in policy formulation or the drafting of legislation are not named they cannot be 'got at' by interested parties, either by means

of bribery or threats. Anonymous and unidentified civil servants find it easier to maintain their necessary neutrality.

2 Civil servants need not fear taking decisive action or giving frank advice to their ministers since, if civil servants are not named, they cannot be blamed if their actions or advice prove to be wrong.

It would be wrong to suppose that the anonymity of civil servants has ever been either absolute or universal. Many lowly officials in the Civil Service, such as counter clerks in social security benefit offices, have daily face-to-face contact with members of the public, and for some time have worn identifying name-badges while doing so. Even in the past, very senior civil servants, like Lord Crowther-Hunt or Lord Normanbrook, had a certain fame and notoriety outside the narrow world of government, certainly among the better-informed members of the public. Nevertheless, there was and is a persistent belief on the part of those civil servants involved in the policy-making process, that the interests of the state and the better functioning of the Civil Service would be best served if their identity could remain hidden from the general public.

These three characteristics of permanence, neutrality and anonymity are inextricably linked to – and form the essential foundation for – the doctrine of ministerial responsibility, which states that a minister is personally responsible for the workings of his or her department and therefore for all the actions of civil servants under his or her control. This convention whereby the minister would take the blame for any wrong actions by unnamed civil servants has been described by Kingdom as 'the very heart of democratic theory . . . Civil servants are not themselves supposed to speak concerning their work; they must remain anonymous; and when praise or blame is apportioned, it must fall on the minister who should, in cases of serious error, resign like an officer and gentleman.'[5]

It has always been a major convention of the unwritten British Constitution that a government minister is responsible for the conduct of his or her department and indeed for the actions or inactions of the civil servants in that department. The minister is accountable for this responsibility to the people through parliament and in the past it was always understood that parliament could require the resignation of a minister for failure to meet that responsibility, even if the fault was that of civil servants rather than that of the minister personally. The classical instance of this was the Crichel Down affair in the 1950s, when a Conservative minister resigned because of mistakes made by his civil servants under the previous Labour incumbent. The most recent example of a traditional resignation on a point of principle was the resignation of Lord Carrington as Foreign Secretary after the Argentine invasion of the Falkland Islands in 1982.

In fact, despite a few honourable exceptions like Carrington, the willingness of ministers to resign has all but disappeared in recent years, even in the face of gross errors and manifest incompetence. Andrew Rawnsley has referred to the current attitude among politicians as 'the spirit of this political age, the guiding principle of which is that nobody resigns'.[6] On the other hand, it has been pointed out that the willingness of ministers to resign can easily be overstated, and has never been particularly noticeable. In 1956, S. E. Finer made the point that he could only find evidence for twenty ministerial resignations in the century since 1855.[7] It has always been the case that erring ministers have attempted to sit tight and brazen it out: what has changed is the increased seriousness of the transgressions which ministers feel can be overlooked.

In 1986, following incidents such as the Ponting prosecution and the Westland affair which we shall discuss shortly, the then Head of the Civil Service, Sir Robert Armstrong, drafted a memorandum which spelled out the responsibilities and duties of civil servants to their ministers, a memorandum that encompassed the service conventions of neutrality and anonymity:

> in general the executive powers of the Crown are exercised by and on the advice of Her Majesty's Ministers, who are in turn answerable to Parliament. The Civil Service as such has no constitutional personality or responsibility separate from the duly elected Government of the day. It is there to provide the Government of the day with advice on the formulation of the policies of the Government, to assist in carrying out the decisions of the Government, and to manage and deliver the services for which the Government is responsible.[8]

Armstrong went on to emphasise that 'the British Civil Service is a non-political and disciplined career Civil Service, and those civil servants who could not accept the consequences of these arrangements should resign'.[9] It is, however, rather ironic that this official definition of Civil Service ethics was only produced in answer to events which had themselves considerably eroded the ethical standards of the service. It is also ironic that the Armstrong memorandum reasserts the non-political nature of the Civil Service at a time when a considerable degree of politicisation had already affected the service and was continuing to do so. Moreover, the slow politicisation of the service was a process in which the author of the memorandum was far from being an innocent bystander!

The politicisation of the Civil Service

Margaret Thatcher's view of the Civil Service was formed by her experiences as Secretary of State for Education between 1970 and 1974 and it is worth looking at that period in some detail because those experiences, and the conclusions Margaret Thatcher drew from them, provided the trigger for what were to become revolutionary changes imposed on the Civil Service during her premiership. Already suspicious of the Civil Service mentality, Mrs Thatcher, as she was then, came into instant conflict with her Permanent Secretary, Sir William Pile, on the day of her appointment. 'Within the first ten minutes of her arrival she uncovered two things to us,' Pile recalls. 'One is what I would call an innate wariness of the Civil Service, quite possibly even a distrust. And secondly a page from an exercise book with eighteen things she wanted done that day.'[10] Unused to demands for instant action, Pile and his officials tried to tone down her demands by offering advice and alternative ideas based on years of experience, only to find that she did not want advice from anyone and totally rejected any facts and arguments put forward. The minister tried to have the official removed. In tears she pleaded with Lord Jellicoe, the Minister for the Civil Service, claiming that Pile and his wife were extreme left-wingers intent on undermining her position prior to bringing down the government as a whole. To another acquaintance she claimed that Pile was a dangerous security risk while he remained in such a senior position within the Civil Service. When the storm over the government's withdrawal of free milk from junior schools broke and the minister became known to press and protesters alike as 'Thatcher the Milk Snatcher', she blamed Pile for not warning her that she was about to make a faulty decision. For her the incident was not a political failure but yet another example of the incompetence of civil servants. All in all, the minister's experiences at Education were highly formative with regard to her perception of the Civil Service. 'We were dealing with someone who basically felt we were not on her side,' said Pile of those years. Her comment on the other hand was, rather more simply, 'Iron entered my soul'.[11]

That iron was tempered and hardened over the next few years, during which time Margaret Thatcher became leader of the Conservative Party. Her brooding over her time at Education engendering a fierce hostility towards the Civil Service that greatly influenced her as soon as the election of 1979 enabled her to do anything about it. 'No government has been elected whose leader was as deeply seized as this one of the need to overturn the power and presumption of the continuing government of the Civil Service: to challenge its orthodoxies, cut down its size, reject its assumptions, which were seen as corrosively infected by social democracy, and teach it a lesson in political control.'[12] As a member of the Heath cabinet which executed its famous U-turn on economic policy, Margaret Thatcher had seen how the machinations of civil servants can divert a government from its radical programme and she was determined not to have her own radical agenda overset by the sort of consensual politics she detested and which she felt permeated civil service attitudes and values. Once she found herself in a position to influence the selection and appointment of senior civil servants she set herself to changing the political complexion of those senior officials. By politicisation we do not, in this instance, mean the direct recruitment of Conservative Party members, but it did mean the appointment as senior officials of candidates who showed the same single-mindedness as the prime minister and the same, almost ideological, commitment to radical change.

Margaret Thatcher was aided in her plan to influence the Civil Service by the fact that, at the time of the 1979 election, three key civil service positions were about to become vacant, enabling her to place her own chosen representatives at the very heart of the administration. The positions were those of Cabinet Secretary, the prime minister's Private Secretary and the prime minister's press secretary. The first of these jobs went to Sir Robert Armstrong, then Permanent Secretary at the Home Office. Armstrong was not an obvious Thatcher choice, being Eton and Oxford educated and formerly Private Secretary to Edward Heath, but the unorthodox duties that he later showed himself willing to perform in the aftermath of the Westland and *Spycatcher* affairs proved how well Mrs Thatcher's choice had been made in political terms. Her choice as Private Secretary, Clive Whitmore, a grammar-school-educated high flyer from the Ministry of Defence, was even more successful, in that, despite being a civil servant, he became totally devoted to promoting the prime minister's political programme, the two of them thinking and acting together as if of one mind. Her choice as press secretary was Bernard Ingham, then at Energy where he had been appointed by Tony Benn. A blunt Yorkshireman, a former journalist and one-time Labour Party member, he was another whose sympathy for Mrs Thatcher was not immediately apparent, but who proved to be the very closest of allies in the years to come. It is one of the ironies of the Thatcher years that those genuine civil servants like Bernard Ingham and Charles Powell, who was later appointed to Margaret Thatcher's private office as her Private Secretary for foreign affairs, were more her political and ideological allies than most of her political advisers. 'He [Ingham] was seen at home and abroad to know her mind, speak for her, even on occasions exceed her in the zeal of his commitment to the cause . . . [Powell] was a man of great ability and great understanding and also, more exceptionally, had developed a close personal rapport with the leader.'[13]

Towards the end of her first term, in 1982, Margaret Thatcher seized on another opportunity to guide the political direction of the Senior Civil Service. Between mid-1982 and the end of 1983 there were no fewer than eight heads of Whitehall departments who were due to retire. These were the older generation, men like Sir Douglas Wass, Permanent Secretary at the Treasury, who retained the old consensual and centrist beliefs that were anathema to the prime minister. The Civil Service Department had been abolished in 1981 and control of the Civil Service had reverted to the Cabinet Office, meaning that Sir Robert Armstrong now became Head of the Civil Service. Even more than ever the prime minister would have an important voice in the appointment of senior civil servants. It is to this period that the expression 'Is he one of us?' belongs, representing the question Margaret Thatcher asked to sound out opinion as to the suitability of candidates for appointment. In asking this, she was not bothered about party membership or affiliation with any particular ideological group. The Thatcherite ideal was someone who:

- was single-minded and determined in their commitment to a policy;
- would not be deterred by a few reverses;
- was a doer not a talker.

The degree of politicisation of civil servants was measured by the precept that you could not have a radical government without radically-minded officials. For Thatcherite policies to succeed it needed officials who had broken with the traditional ethos of the Civil Service. Under the patronage of Thatcher and Armstrong a new breed of Permanent Secretary emerged – like the new head of the Treasury, Peter Middleton, who helped Margaret Thatcher in her bid to get a rebate on British over-payments to the European Community, a particularly sweet victory when the Foreign Office had done its utmost to secure such a rebate but had failed to do so.

Alongside this growing political involvement by permanent civil servants there has also been a very significant increase in the number of political advisers who are appointed to the government team or who become members of the prime minister's private office as temporary civil servants. Increasingly it has been the case that new prime ministers bring with them their own advisers and press officers who are then employed as civil servants and paid by the state, even though they are carrying out a function where the dividing line between government and party interest is very blurred. In certain ways it is a long-standing practice but it was Harold Wilson who was the first to make much of it with his so-called 'kitchen cabinet' of Marcia Williams (now Lady Falkender) and the *Mirror* journalist, Joe Haines. Margaret Thatcher went even further, with all the members of her own policy research unit under Brian Griffiths functioning as civil servants, working alongside her own influential advisers such as Sir Alfred Sherman, Alan Walters and Sir Anthony Parsons. As one Sunday newspaper pointed out, 'Mrs Thatcher had the most extensive retinue of personal advisers of any prime minister in our history.'[14] And what was begun by Margaret Thatcher was continued by John Major so that, by April 1996, the number of special advisers employed by the government had risen to 38, compared with the 13 that had existed in 1979. Just over a year later and the situation had moved on yet again as the advisers imported by the new Labour government increased the number of political appointees to more than 50.

From the very start of his administration Tony Blair has been much criticised for what has been called his 'cronyism'; namely the appointment of personal friends and advisers to high positions. This was especially true of the way in which significant numbers of Labour's election campaign team were moved *en bloc* into Number 10 to form an unofficial private office for the prime minister. Only two days after the election, an Order in Council established that political appointees, including at that stage Tony Blair's chief of staff, Jonathan Powell, his press secretary, Alastair Campbell, and his policy adviser, David Miliband, would have the ability to exercise executive authority over civil servants. Shortly afterwards, Sir Michael Bett of the Civil Service Commission warned that, 'if there was a horde of political appointees being made civil servants, they would not be being made on the principle of fairness and open competition'.[15] A month after the election the team of advisers appointed to Number 10 was as large as 20, some of them paid for by the Labour Party but many of them employed and paid as civil servants. And the situation at Number 10 was mirrored in most government departments, as in the case of Gordon Brown who had five advisers, including the high-profile and controversial appointee, Charlie Whelan, who later paid for his political activities by being required to resign.

Civil Service concern at this increase in creeping politicisation under Labour was first publicly expressed when it was reported that Tony Blair wanted to appoint his chief of staff, Jonathan Powell, to be his Principal Private Secretary, an important position within the Senior Civil Service career structure and a post that has been held by up-and-coming career civil servants since the 1920s. Sir Robin Butler, as Head of the Civil Service, immediately moved to block Powell's appointment as being inappropriate and after some discussion produced the compromise agreement that a career civil servant would be appointed to the position of Private Secretary, while Powell himself would retain the title of Tony Blair's Chief of Staff, with particular responsibility for policy matters. By June 1997 the number of political appointees to Number 10, and to the political offices of other cabinet ministers, was so great that it took on the outward appearance of the American spoils system, where all holders of senior positions in the administration are changed with a new president. The government denied any intentional wrong-doing, claiming that the existence of political special advisers would protect the Civil Service itself from politicisation in that 'the government must be run by political parties rather than by officials'.[16]

Over the first year of the Blair government, criticism of the place of political advisers in the Civil Service became focused upon the activities of Alastair Campbell in his work for the Number 10 Press Office, where he combined his civil servant status with intensive spin-doctoring activity for the Labour government. Concern about Campbell's role was so great that the Commons' Public Administration Select Committee chose to investigate the politicisation of the government's press office, failing, however, to agree in its criticisms of Campbell when it reported in August 1998. Such was the disagreement within the committee on this matter that two separate and quite contradictory reports were produced. The majority report, by mainly Labour MPs, found 'no clear evidence' of the press office having given certain of the media preferential treatment for political reasons. On the other hand, a minority report by Tory members, and the one LibDem member, Mike Hancock, was highly critical, claiming that the press officer was 'not politically neutral but a hatchet man for the Labour Party'. This minority report also went on to claim that press officers who rank as civil servants should either stop working for political interests or they should be paid out of party funds rather than by the tax-payer.

Letting some sunlight into the dark corners

The British governmental system in general, and the Civil Service – as the central executive arm of that system – in particular, is almost pathologically secretive. According to Clive Ponting the British system represents, 'A powerful and persistent culture of secrecy – reflecting the basic assumption that good government is closed government.'[17]

There are over 100 statutes in existence to prevent disclosure of information outside government closed circles. The most important of these statutes is the Official Secrets Act of 1911, as amended and reissued in 1920, 1939 and 1989. Originally drawn up to tighten security in the run up to the First World War, the main purpose of the Act was to combat espionage but it managed to embrace all aspects of government work. Even today, fifty years after the end of the Second World War and a decade after the end of the Cold War, the Act still has to be signed and observed by anyone joining the Civil Service, at whatever rank, no matter how humble.

The part of the Official Secrets Act which causes most concern is Section 2, a catch-all provision stating that public servants must not disclose any information to any unauthorised persons which they may have learned in the course of their work. This might sound reasonable enough in time of war, if it were applied to classified information, but the Act is nowhere near so specific. A strict application of the rule would make a public servant liable to prosecution for divulging anything whatsoever learned at work and, carried to ridiculous extremes, it would be possible to prosecute an official messenger for telling his wife the price of a packet of biscuits in the Ministry of Defence canteen. That is a ludicrous example, and not seriously intended, but it is not too far from some of the decisions that have been made in the past to prosecute under the Official Secrets Act.

Beyond these statutes governing secrecy, a variety of rules and conventions reinforce governmental secrecy. The Thirty Year Rule, for example, forbids the publication of official documents such as cabinet papers within what is seen as the working lifetime of the people involved: 30 years being the normal length of the moratorium, although very sensitive material can be kept concealed for 50, 60 or 100 years, or indeed indefinitely. Another set of rules was drawn up to advise civil servants on the withholding of information and the evasion of awkward questions on such occasions as their appearance before parliamentary select committees. Originally written by Edward Osmotherly of the Civil Service Department in 1980, and therefore known as the Osmotherly memorandum, these guidelines are a little out-of-date but remain valid as what has been described as 'twenty-five pages of how to say "I'm sorry, Chairman. I can't answer that question. May I refer you to my Minister?"' [18]

Something of a problem is created by the fact that so many of the secrecy rules surrounding government are concerned with political matters rather than issues of state security. This is because there are a number of factors in the

British political system that automatically encourage the growth of a culture of secrecy:

- The adversarial nature of the two-party system which encourages the government to keep secret all its workings in case the opposition might find out and use the knowledge for political advantage.
- The doctrine of collective responsibility, and the need for the government to present a united face to the world, means that internal government disagreements, within Cabinet or between ministers, have to be kept from the outside world in case the external appearance of government solidarity is undermined.
- The doctrine of ministerial responsibility and the anonymity of civil servants conspire to make it necessary that the workings of government be kept concealed in order to prevent blame ever being attached to an individual, whether politician or official. The justification for this is because civil servants in particular will be unwilling to embark on the risky innovative measures necessary for progressive government if they feel threatened by the risk of blame becoming attached to them if the measure should go wrong.
- The link in the British system between executive and legislature, with the need of government ministers to be elected, creates a desire on the part of ministers that their errors and misjudgments should never be known to the voters who must re-elect them.

As can be seen from this list of factors, the imposition of secrecy is implemented less in the explicit interest of national security and more in the implicit interest of not embarrassing the government. For many years civil servants accepted this without question and quite cheerfully did what they were told. But one of the factors which affected the neutrality of the Civil Service during the 1980s was the way in which civil servants became increasingly reluctant to carry out instructions unquestioningly if those instructions offended their consciences. After the last war there was severe and widespread criticism of those German public servants who had carried out atrocities ordered by the Nazi Party and then pleaded innocence on the grounds that they were 'only obeying orders'. Civil servants in Britain who were asked to perform tasks which offended their consciences were aware that 'only obeying orders' was no longer regarded as an acceptable excuse and therefore became less willing to participate in strategies designed to keep from the public what might be interpreted as unacceptable government behaviour. And this in turn led to three notorious cases of civil servants breaching the secrecy rules in the period 1983 to 1985.

In October 1983, a clerk in the Foreign and Commonwealth Office (FCO), Sarah Tisdall, sent the *Guardian* newspaper copies of two memorandums written by Michael Heseltine about the disposition of cruise missiles at Greenham Common air base, memorandums which hinted that the Defence Secretary was not being totally open in informing parliament. The *Guardian* printed the information and was immediately the target of an intensive police investigation to find the source of the leak. The newspaper tried to protect its source but, under legal threat, had to give up the leaked photocopies, the source of which was easily identified from internal evidence, making it clear that Sarah Tisdall was the guilty party. She was arrested by the police, charged under Section 2 of the Official Secrets Act, tried at the Old Bailey and, in March 1984, sent to prison for six months.

In the meantime, in November 1983, an administration trainee in the Employment Department, Ian Willmore, sent the magazine *Time Out* a copy of minutes from a meeting between Michael Quinlan, recently appointed Permanent Secretary at Employment, and Lord Donaldson, then still Sir John Donaldson, Master of the Rolls. The minutes contained comments about trade union rights that were inappropriate for a senior civil servant and which should certainly never have been made by a senior judge, particularly one who was about to hear a sensitive industrial relations case on appeal. An internal investigation revealed Ian Willmore's probable guilt in leaking the minutes but there was very little evidence to convict him and he was finally allowed to trade a full confession in return for being allowed to resign without prosecution.

The most famous of the three cases, however, was that of Clive Ponting, a senior civil servant in the Defence Ministry. During the Falklands War of 1982 much concern had been expressed about the circumstances which surrounded the sinking of the Argentinian battleship, the *General Belgrano*, criticisms of government action being led by the Scottish Labour MP, Tam Dalyell. Ponting became convinced that Dalyell and the House of Commons were being misled by ministerial disinformation and, to clarify matters, sent Dalyell two documents relating to the affair, only one of which was marginally confidential. In 1985 Ponting was prosecuted for leaking official information under Section 2 of the Official Secrets Act, on the grounds that his breach of secrecy was against the national interest; the case hinging on two different interpretations of the expression 'national interest'.

1 For Clive Ponting it was in the national interest for the public to know the truth and therefore, by releasing this information, he saw himself as serving the national interest.
2 For the government and prosecution (and this indeed was the position adopted by the judge in his summing-up), the national interest equates with the policy of the government of the day. According to this view, a civil servant has a primary duty to uphold government policy, including the concealment of information, if that is the wish of the government.

Ponting argued – apparently with the agreement of the jury because he was acquitted – that his actions were not against national interests but merely against the party political interests of the Conservative government. In a climate that quite regularly used the argument of national interest and the weapon of the Official Secrets Act to cover up certain government actions, the judicial ruling that a civil servant could not be considered guilty of a misdemeanour, if his or her action had merely been against a political decision that was not within the remit of the Civil Service, was very important.

The jury in the Ponting case had sent a clear message to the government that a civil servant should place his or her duty to the community at large before any loyalty to a partisan administration. This verdict, together with other cases such as the *Spycatcher* affair, led to calls for a reform of the Official Secrets Act. Even senior judges joined in the demand: one judge writing to the press, 'For heaven's sake legislate now before our law, our courts and our reputation as a free country become the laughing stock of the world.'[19] At the time when that plea was written the House of Commons was debating a private member's bill promoted by a Conservative back-bencher, Richard Shepherd, which would have reformed the Official Secrets Act by allowing someone accused under the Act the defence of prior publication or public interest. However, the government killed off Shepherd's bill by imposing a three-line whip against the bill on its second reading and replacing it with its own amended Official Secrets Act.

The Official Secrets Act of 1989 was presented by the government as reforming Section 2 of the 1911 Act and thereby satisfying critics such as Richard Shepherd. It does clarify parts of Section 2 by allowing large quantities of harmless information to be revealed without penalty. But in other respects the Act became even more severe than its predecessor:

- Certain categories of disclosure become criminal without the prosecution having to prove that disclosure is harmful.
- Criminal liability extends not only to those disclosing any secrets but also to those publishing those secrets, such as newspaper editors.
- Neither the fact of the information having been published previously elsewhere, nor the claim that disclosure was in the national interest, would be available as an argument for the defence, thus denying any future Ponting the same defence as had proved successful in his trial.

Ponting's was an exceptional case, however, and comparatively few civil servants before or since have proved willing to thwart the political will of their ministers. As Will Hutton says, 'if ministers are minded ruthlessly to bend the state to serve hegemonic party ambitions the Civil Service must go along with them'.[20] Hutton goes on to list the ways in which civil servants were used to serve political ends during the last few years of the Conservative administrations of Margaret Thatcher and John Major:

- The Treasury paid a substantial contribution towards the legal costs of the then Chancellor of the Exchequer, Norman Lamont, in a rent dispute with a sex therapist who had become a sitting tenant in his house.
- Treasury officials were used to cost the Labour Party's proposed spending plans, so that they could be used disparagingly in Conservative election literature during the 1987, 1992 and 1997 general election campaigns.

- Senior civil servants in the Department of Health were required to campaign publicly for the establishment of hospital trusts despite their official neutrality on the issue.
- Officials of the Department of Employment made more than 30 changes to the definition of unemployment during the 1980s and early 1990s, in a bid to massage the worst of government unemployment statistics.
- The Scott Report into the Arms for Iraq affair found that Senior Civil Service officials and lawyers from Whitehall departments did try to prevent crucial evidence about arms sales from being revealed and, although it could not be called a conspiracy, ministers and officials did collude in concealing government policy from parliament. There were echoes of the Arms for Iraq affair in 1998 with the involvement of FCO officials in concealing the intervention by the arms company Sandline in the internal affairs of Sierra Leone.

All these factors came on top of a period in the 1980s when the doctrine of ministerial responsibility and the convention of neutrality in the Civil Service both seemed to lose their importance and relevance, changing forever the traditional relationship between ministers and their officials. For some time it had ceased to be the practice of ministers to resign because of the mistakes of their civil servants, but the Westland Affair, in 1985, probably represents the very first time that it became almost routine for ministers actually to name particular civil servants as being the ones to blame rather than themselves.

The Westland Affair was the result of an attempt to allow the British-owned Westland helicopter company to be taken over by a European manufacturer rather than the American company which was currently bidding to take control. The European option was the preferred solution of Michael Heseltine, then Secretary of State for Defence, but was opposed by Leon Brittan, the Trade and Industry Secretary, who wanted Westland to be taken over by the American firm. Although never explicitly stated, Brittan had the ear and sympathy of the prime minister, while Heseltine was out of favour for his pro-European stance. The Defence Secretary very publicly walked out of his cabinet position because he felt his arguments were being ignored by Mrs Thatcher and not being put before Cabinet. The takeover battle thereupon became something of a personal duel between the two men, who were consequently rather less than scrupulous in the tactics they used. In an attempt to discredit what Michael Heseltine had to say Leon Brittan actually ordered his Director of Information, Colette Bowe, to leak a confidential letter from the Solicitor-General, Sir Patrick Mayhew, assessing the legal basis of Heseltine's arguments. The act of leaking a letter from one of the government's law officers is regarded by precedent as behaviour verging on the criminal and the convention of ministerial responsibility would normally have required the immediate resignation of Leon Brittan as the minister responsible. Instead of which, Brittan attempted to claim that it was nothing to do with him and actually named Colette Bowe as being the civil servant responsible for the leak. She in turn made it clear that she had only released the letter at the orders of her minister and after having cleared the action with Number 10, and named Bernard Ingham and Charles Powell as the persons in the Downing Street office who gave that consent. The convention regarding the Civil Service was therefore repeatedly broken since not only were civil servants publicly named and blamed, but the politicians who had ordered that action – and, by inference, that included the prime minister herself – avoided resignation by claiming that civil servants had acted on their own initiative.

It had been to avoid incidents like these that Sir Robert Armstrong had written his memorandum on the duties and responsibilities of civil servants. Armstrong made it clear that he was the most senior civil servant as Cabinet Secretary, but according to convention he was merely the servant of the Cabinet and, as such, did the bidding of the prime minister. As Hugo Young said, 'As Cabinet Secretary, Robert Armstrong occupied a post which all its previous incumbents had succeeded in keeping shrouded in mystery. In the persons of Norman Brook, Burke Trend and John Hunt, the Cabinet Secretary was the mandarin of mandarins, a high priest of administration, endowed with power and influence he took care to maximise by the device of being neither seen nor heard outside the most secret places of government.' Yet, on a number of occasions, Mrs Thatcher required Armstrong to breach his own guidelines by making him face the public and reveal his involvement in government policy. As Young went on to say in the same passage, 'He [Armstrong] was soon driven from behind the veil of a cherished privacy to become one of the most highly and damagingly publicised men of his time.'[21]

The first time Armstrong had acquired something of a notoriety with the public had been through his role in the dispute over union rights at, Government Communication Headquarters (GCHQ) but his first exposure to the full glare of the spotlights came after the Westland Affair when he was summoned to give evidence to the Defence Select Committee – representing the first time that a Cabinet Secretary had ever been summoned before parliament to answer the sort of questions on policy which, theoretically, were the responsibility of the prime minister. The evidence given to that committee formed the basis for the famous Armstrong memorandum, which once again exposed Sir Robert to the public. Then, in 1988, Armstrong was made to do something no civil servant had ever been asked to do before.

At that time the prime minister was obsessively trying to prevent the publication of a book, *Spycatcher*, by the former MI5 officer, Peter Wright, insisting that the book could not be sold in Britain, despite its having been published in America, with imported copies of the book being widely available in the UK. Wright lived in Australia and, when the British government attempted to take out an injunction against the book, the case had to be heard in that country, hearings being before a court in New South Wales. The person sent out to Australia to give evidence as to why the government wished the book to be suppressed was not a government minister nor a law officer but the Cabinet

Secretary, representing the Civil Service to which Peter Wright had once belonged. Armstrong was forced to face hostile questioning in a court of law, despite the fact that the policy he was called on to defend was a political decision rather than a matter for the administration of the Civil Service.

What intensified the already brilliant spotlight on his evidence was the admission by the Cabinet Secretary, paraphrasing Edmund Burke, that, while he had not actually lied in his public statements about the workings of government, he had indeed been 'economical with the truth'. In making such a public spectacle of her most senior civil servant and exposing him to the ridicule of the press, Margaret Thatcher had destroyed what was left of even the appearance of 'anonymity' and 'neutrality' in the Civil Service. From that point on the structure and organisation of the Civil Service could be completely reformed because the ethical basis of the Whitehall culture had been changed out of all recognition. We shall return in Chapter 8 to the impact of all this on the accountability of civil servants, as reflected in codes of conduct drawn up for the Civil Service. Aiding the cultural change that affected the service was another factor of politicisation, the unionisation of the Civil Service and a growing militancy which showed itself in an increased readiness on the part of civil servants to look after their own interests.

Unionisation: pay, trade unions and strikes

Until the 1970s the idea of trade unionism was alien to the Civil Service as a whole, except for manual workers among the industrial civil servants who filled the lower strata of the service. The white collar ranks of the service were represented by staff associations rather than unions and these organisations enjoyed a rather cosy relationship with the employers through the medium of the Whitley Councils, which were originally set up in the aftermath of the General Strike in the 1920s and within which pay and conditions were agreed in nonconfrontational negotiation between employers and employed. The pay of civil servants was fixed within fairly rigid pay scale bands, the civil servants being paid according to the position they filled and moving up the pay scale by annual increments, the only barrier to a smooth promotional progression being adverse comments on a civil servant's standard of work being made in an annual report written by the civil servant's immediate superior.

During the 1960s and 1970s, however, there was an upsurge of white collar unionism in society at large. There was a realisation among white collar workers, particularly those working in the public sector, that trade union militancy had led to quite considerable pay increases for the working classes but that the genteel middle classes, with their staff associations and Whitley Councils, were being left far behind. In the ensuing upsurge of support for white collar unionism the Civil Service was well to the fore, the first-ever Civil Service strike taking place in 1973. Six years later there was a major departure in labour relations within the Civil Service when civil servants throughout the country embarked on a nine-week pay dispute that was ultimately settled by the Clegg Commission in the unions' favour.

Although, in theory, civil servants can join any one of a number of white collar unions, there are in fact seven specific unions which come together in the Council of Civil Service Unions. The vast majority of civil servants, including cleaners and messengers as well as clerks and managers, belong to one of two unions, the Civil and Public Services Association (CPSA) or the National Union of Civil and Public Servants (NUCPS). Civil servants in Northern Ireland have their own separate union, as do prison officers and those working in the Inland Revenue Department. Scientists, accountants, lawyers and other specialists tend to belong to the Institute of Professional Civil Servants (IPCS). The high-level executives and administrators of the Senior Civil Service have their own staff association known as the First Division Association.

These were the unions who extracted a highly inflated pay settlement out of the Clegg Commission in 1979. The Clegg Commission was instituted by the Labour government and its pay recommendations were originally made in the climate engendered by that government. Because of the 1979 general election, however, the settlement of the Clegg awards had to be made by the newly elected Conservative government under Mrs Thatcher. The outcome therefore was critical for the Thatcherite reforms to be described in the next chapter. It was not just that Margaret Thatcher resented the over-generous public sector awards made by Clegg and the fact that circumstances had forced her to grant those awards despite her dislike of them. She was also already committed to cutting back on the size, cost and influence of the Civil Service. The role of the unions in the dispute of 1979 made her see that any reform of the Civil Service could only come about when she had smashed the power of the Civil Service unions. This was just part of the hidden agenda that made the Civil Service strike of 1981 so bitter and so important for government policy.

The dispute began in an unremarkable way with a claim by the Civil Service unions for a 15 per cent pay increase, to which the government replied with an offer of 7 per cent, which was 1 per cent more than the government-imposed cash limit on pay offers. Christopher Soames was put in charge of negotiations for the government and instructed to stick to the 7 per cent offer regardless. The unions therefore began to take industrial action in March 1981, concentrating their efforts on the computerised benefits and revenue agencies. The strike had immediate effect on benefits claimants who were not paid but the government also suffered in that income tax revenue was not collected. The dispute lasted 21 weeks before being settled at the end of July with a settlement of 7.5 per cent. At first there were claims that Mrs Thatcher had miscalculated over the strike and somehow lost the argument. Not only had the strike cost between £500 million and £1,000 million in lost revenues and additional interest payments but it transpired that the government could have had exactly the same deal in early June, which would have saved at least half of the projected costs. Many people were suggesting that the prime minister should resign over her miscalculation.

Later it became obvious that there had been no miscalculation. In fact Margaret Thatcher was determined to prolong the confrontation and had threatened to resign in June if the cabinet had accepted the 7.5 per cent deal then. It was not enough that the Civil Service unions should be defeated; they had to be totally discredited and reduced to impotence by a display of actions that were extremely unpopular with the public. It was part not only of her strategy to smash trade union power but of a way in which she could emasculate the Civil Service unions, rendering them impotent in the run-up to the complete overhaul of the nature and structure of the Civil Service.

In the year after the strike there were a number of important developments arising from it. First, Christopher Soames was dismissed as Civil Service Minister for being too lukewarm about government policy and being too friendly with senior civil servants. There is also a suspicion that Mrs Thatcher just did not like him, as he was a Tory grandee of the old school who had also been proved right over the detrimental effects and the costs of the strike. Following the dismissal of Lord Soames, the next stage was the winding-up of the Civil Service Department and the compulsory early retirement of its Permanent Secretary, Ian Bancroft, and the return of the Civil Service to the joint control of the Treasury and Cabinet Office.

Also produced in the aftermath of the 1981 strike was a dispute that would last with all its repercussions for the remainder of the Thatcher years. This was the argument over the GCHQ, an intelligence listening-post based in Cheltenham. On 25 January 1984, the Foreign Secretary announced that no employee of the GCHQ would be allowed to belong to a trade union, since certain selected staff at GCHQ had withdrawn their labour during the strikes of both 1979 and 1981, leading the government, backed by the American CIA, to decide that union membership at GCHQ, with its consequent threat of strike action, was detrimental to the security of the Western alliance. Protests by the Civil Service unions followed and, although 95 per cent of GCHQ employees accepted the decision, legal arguments with the remaining 5 per cent were pursued as far as the Court of Appeal and actions were still being brought in the courts as late as 1988. The final straw came at a meeting between the prime minister and Len Murray, then General Secretary of the TUC, at which the TUC leader was told that union membership was incompatible with a citizen's patriotic duties and, in a phrase that became infamous, that the unions represented 'the enemy within'. The ban on union membership at GCHQ was removed by the new Labour government in 1997 but by that time the Civil Service unions had been rendered powerless and a wholesale reform of the Civil Service had been forced through.[23]

Notes

1 Hugo Young, *One of Us*, Macmillan, London, 1989, p. 153.
2 Robert Pyper, *The British Civil Service*, Harvester Wheatsheaf, Hemel Hempstead, 1995, p. 12.
3 John Alder, *Constitutional and Administrative Law* (2nd edition), Macmillan, Basingstoke, 1994, p. 230.
4 Gerald Kaufman, *How to Be a Minister*, Faber, London, 1997, p. 35.
5 John Kingdom, *Government and Politics in Britain*, Polity Press, Cambridge, 1994, p. 369.
6 Andrew Rawnsley, *Observer*, 8 January 1995.
7 S. E. Finer, '*The Individual Responsibility of Ministers*', *Public Administration*, Vol. 34, No. 4, 1956.
8 The Armstrong memorandum is quoted at length by Geoffrey Fry, *Policy and Management in the British Civil Service*, Prentice Hall/Harvester Wheatsheaf, Hemel Hempstead, 1995, p. 53.
9 Quoted by Fry but taken from Report HC 92. 1985–86, *Seventh Report from the Treasury and Civil Service Committee: Civil Servants and Ministers, Duties and Responsibilities*.
10 Quoted by Young, Note 1 above, p. 71.
11 *Ibid.*, p. 74.
12 *Ibid.*, p. 153.
13 *Ibid.*, p. 445.
14 Robert Harris, *Observer*, 27 November 1988.
15 *Guardian*, 3 June 1997.
16 Ewan MacAskill, 'Civil Service Makes Way for Blair's Elite', *Guardian*, 3 June 1997.
17 Clive Ponting, *Secrecy in Britain*, Basil Blackwell, Oxford, 1990.
18 Originally said by Hennessey and Smith in the *Strathclyde Analysis Paper Number 7*, 1992, but quoted by Pyper, Note 2 above, p. 125.
19 Lord Scarman, letter to *The Times*, 7 January 1988.
20 Will Hutton, *The State We're In*, Jonathan Cape, London, 1995, p. 35.
21 Young, Note 1 above, p. 355.
22 The Civil Service strike of 1981 and its aftermath are described in detail by Young, Note 1 above, pp. 227–9.
23 Colin Pilkington, *Issues in British Politics*, Macmillan, Basingstoke, 1998, p. 52.

6

The managerial revolution

The three Es: economy, efficiency and effectiveness

In the public mind there is a subtle distinction between public organisations – which are administered – and private organisations – which are managed. Both administration and management have goals and objectives; both seek to use resources to best effect; both have persons within the organisation who make decisions and carry out policy; and both types of organisation are involved in planning, organising, co-ordination and control. For the administrative organisation, however, the important factor is the procedural, bureaucratic structure which maximises consistency in practice. The important thing for the managerial organisation is how best to achieve organisational goals while extracting maximum value for money in the expenditure of resources in order to achieve those goals.

Traditional administrative cultures have tended to be heavily bureaucratic, heavily centralised, very much accountable for their use of resources and therefore very cautious and unadventurous in performance. A public organisation like the Civil Service, as established according to the classic Northcote–Trevelyan mould, was heavily biased towards administrative rather than managerial practices. 'In the private sector, the management function precedes the administrative one. In public organisations, because of their primarily political goals and accountabilities, and the priority given to procedures, it is the administrative function which is prior to the management one.'[1] The main trend underlying all the Civil Service reforms of the 1980s and 1990s which strove to modernise organisational structures was primarily to do with reining back bureaucracy and encouraging the Civil Service in its transition from an administrative to a managerial culture.

Applying the techniques and processes of management, particularly financial management, to the structures of the Civil Service has a long history. It is customary, however, to look in the first instance at the *Plowden Report on the Control of Public Expenditure* in 1961 to discover – particularly in the way it

63

applied financial controls – the true beginnings of the managerial revolution and the emergence of a managerial agenda. It was the recommendations of the Plowden Committee which resulted in the establishment of the Public Expenditure Survey Committee (PESC), a body made up of senior departmental civil servants, which had the task of forecasting the trends in economic growth and estimating the need for public expenditure over a period of five years. It was the work of the PESC which promoted the role of the Treasury in developing financial management services. Equally important, however, was the fact that the Plowden Committee, although primarily concerned with financial matters and monetary control, nevertheless did cast an eye over the management of the Civil Service in general, stressing the importance of managerial efficiency for each individual government department. 'It is becoming increasingly necessary,' said the report, 'for the Permanent Secretary to devote . . . personal time and attention to problems of management . . . to ensure that approved policies are carried out economically and that his Department is staffed as efficiently as possible.'[2]

Once Plowden had proposed looking at the Civil Service in managerial terms, the concept was revisited frequently during the early 1960s, until the Wilson government appointed the Fulton Committee in 1966, with the specifically stated aim of examining the efficiency of the service. And it was the report from that committee, in 1968, which first openly expressed the belief and intent that civil servants ought primarily to be efficient managers, but voiced the criticism that, because of the generalist Oxbridge cultural tradition they shared, too few senior civil servants saw their role in those terms or were willing to relinquish their generalist nature and 'amateur status' so as to acquire the necessary skills and techniques to provide efficient management. It was the Fulton Report which first hinted at the possibility that Civil Service activities could be divided into separate functional departments and, even more importantly, that *not all those functions needed to be executed by traditional civil servants*. This would allow for certain tasks to be carried out by autonomous agencies or even contracted out of the service altogether to outside providers in the private sector.

As has already been examined in Chapters 3 and 4, the Fulton programme of reforms addressed two critical assessments of the Civil Service:

1 The left-wing view of an élitist service, staffed by Whitehall mandarins dedicated to thwarting the more radical measures of a reforming government.
2 A right-wing view of a proliferating and inherently inefficient bureaucracy, overmanned, rigid in procedure and undisciplined by the realities of the market place.

Also as has been described earlier, there was a certain degree of action by the Wilson government on recruitment, staffing and training in the light of the Fulton Report, in order to meet some concerns of the left as to the élitism of the service. However, as far as the rest of the Report was concerned, the successive Heath, Wilson and Callaghan governments did very little to challenge the size and inefficiencies of the Civil Service. After his surprise victory of 1970, the Heath government did put some minor reforms into effect that were designed to increase the efficiency of the service, and a team of businessmen, including Derek Rayner of Marks and Spencer (who was to play a more important, if similar, role later), was seconded to Whitehall in order to examine the systems and processes of government. It was this team that was primarily responsible for the White Paper of 1970, *The Reorganisation of Central Government*, which suggested three ways in which the machinery of government could be reformed:

1)   To make the Civil Service more compact by the contraction and merger of the proliferating number of small ministries into a more manageable number of 'super-departments'. This was a process that had been begun by Harold Wilson under the influence of the 1960s belief that 'big is beautiful', and massive government departments like Defence, Environment and Health and Social Security had emerged as a result. The process was described in Chapter 4, as was the subsequent break-up of some of these super-ministries as enthusiasm waned for extra-large departments. But, despite some scepticism about the merits of size for the sake of size, the fact remains that, as from 1970 onwards, there was a significant decrease in the overall number of government departments and the structure of Whitehall became far more streamlined.

2)   As a possible counter-balance to the 'giantism' inherent in the super-department idea, it was proposed that certain departmental functions should be hived off into separate, autonomous agencies, the staff of which may or may not be civil servants. As we shall see, this ultimately became the basis for the most significant changes but, although a pattern of semi-independent agencies was advocated enthusiastically in the 1970 White Paper, no more than three agencies were established during the 1970s, although these three were large and very important agencies. They were the Defence Procurement Executive, the Property Services Agency and the Manpower Services Commission (MSC), delivering services to the armed forces, government departments and the unemployed respectively. Accountable to ministers but independent of departmental control, the three agencies were of some significance, not least because of the huge budgets they were allowed to manage for themselves. The MSC, for example had responsibility for a wide range of government programmes during the soaring unemployment years of the late 1970s and administered as much as £1 billion a year for just one of those programmes – the Youth Training Scheme (YTS).

3)   The creation of super-departments and autonomous agencies were major examples of structural change but an attempt was also made to alter the process of government with the introduction of such concepts as performance management. One example was the process known as Programme Analysis and Review (PAR) which enabled civil servants and ministers to prioritise their

decision-making so that rational choices could be made as to the best policies to pursue. But these new processes and programmes did not go down well with inherently conservative senior civil servants, who began to drag their feet over what seemed to them the undue speed with which innovative changes were introduced. This was partly because of suspicions on the part of the Whitehall mandarins that the new programmes were intended to remove the taint of amateurism from their generalist ranks and therefore struck at the very heart of Civil Service beliefs and its value system.

Yet it must also be admitted that this was an awkward time for taking innovative measures: the 1970s being noted for a succession of crises, from the oil price crisis of 1973 to the collapse of the pound and IMF intervention by the International Monetary Fund in 1976, from runaway inflation throughout the decade to the numbers of unemployed soaring way above the 1 million mark in the run-up to the 1979 election. With so much to occupy their minds in terms of the national and international economy, it is not surprising that senior civil servants felt that this was no time to be bothered with what they saw as feeble tinkering with management procedures, an appearance of fiddling while Rome burned. And the suspicions of senior officials towards the reform programme was mirrored in a political lack of will to do anything about it, since most ministers in the Wilson and Callaghan Labour governments were not convinced that techniques developed for the efficiency of American big business were necessarily best suited to the British Civil Service.[3]

This meant that the structural efficiency of the Civil Service was not likely to be seriously challenged until the culture of the Senior Civil Service had changed and the catalyst for that cultural change would prove to be the new leader of the Conservative Party, Margaret Thatcher. After 1979, when she first took power, her pre-existing distaste for the Civil Service, created by her time at Education, as described in the last chapter, ensured that her government's approach to the service was driven by the concerns of the right rather than those of the centre-left normally associated with the liberal-democratic model of bureaucracy:

- Primarily, the right was concerned about the lack of efficiency implied in an over-large and over-bureaucratic institution.
- Secondly, the right worried about the degree to which the introduction of simple market forces could revivify the system.

The government elected in 1979 had no clear programme of action to deal with the Civil Service. There was just a general hostility on the part of the prime minister which gradually formed itself into four vague aims which she began to pursue without necessarily developing those aims into firm political policies:

- Aim one said that the 'frontiers of the state' must be rolled back.
- Aim two argued that the size of the Civil Service must be reduced.
- Aim three made it a priority that public expenditure must be cut.

- Aim four suggested that the bureaucratic structure must be made more efficient.

These sort of vague intentions were not new. They were not unlike most of the comments that had been made by all sides and from across the political spectrum since Plowden first investigated the economic efficiency and effectiveness of the government machine. But this time the intentions were reinforced by an ideological pattern of beliefs which suggested four ways in which those four intentions could be carried out.

1 The market was the best way of allocating resources and distributing wealth and the Civil Service must now learn to live and work under the discipline of market forces.
2 Private organisations are regarded as being more efficient than public bodies and therefore public bodies should adopt those managerial structures that had been developed by the private sector.
3 The Civil Service must lose its privileged position and the power of Civil Service unions must be curbed.
4 The culture of the Civil Service must be changed to an entrepreneurial respect for giving value for money in carrying out the 'business' of government.

This was the vague but increasingly defined basis upon which the most radical reforms that had ever been made to the Civil Service were initiated: a programme of reforms that began slowly enough in the period 1979–85, but which rapidly acquired a new momentum after 1986, as Margaret Thatcher approached her third term.[4]

According to Peter Hennessey, in a review of the first two terms of the Conservative government between 1979 and 1987, 'Mrs Thatcher has had more impact on the management of the Civil Service than any previous prime minister.'[5] Margaret Thatcher had come to power in 1979 pledged to reduce the role of government, and that primarily meant cutting back on the Civil Service, reducing the service in both numbers and powers, transforming it from an administrative to a managerial culture and bringing it far more directly under political control. Some of the impact of Thatcherism on the Civil Service has already been examined in Chapter 5 but the more obvious changes are summarised below:

- Between 1979 and 1995, under a series of programmes initiated by the Thatcher administration, the number of civil servants was cut, from 732,000 to 524,000.[6]
- The appointment of senior civil servants to the position of Permanent Secretary in the major government departments was closely supervised by Mrs Thatcher and the Cabinet Secretary, Sir Robert Armstrong. Appointees were considered as to whether they were 'one of us'. They did not have to be Conservatives but they did have to share the prime minister's confrontational,

conviction view of policy. There was a large turnover of senior civil servants during the first two Thatcher administrations, 11 Permanent Secretaries being replaced between 1981 and 1983. It was noted that the new appointments were all given to men liked and admired by the prime minister – men such as Peter Middleton, the man who had drawn up Mrs Thatcher's 'money back' campaign in Europe. 'The permanent secretaries of most major departments are now known as Mrs Thatcher's personal appointments, often promoted over the heads of more senior candidates.'[7]

• Any input into policy formulation that had been granted to the Civil Service over the years was now taken away. The Central Review Body (the Think Tank) was abolished in 1983, and the role of giving serious advice to prime minister and Cabinet that had previously been seen as the prerogative of senior civil servants was now given to special policy advisers such as Sir Alan Walters, Mrs Thatcher's economic adviser, or to right-wing groups like the Adam Smith Institute.

• In response to cases such as those of Sarah Tisdall or Clive Ponting, where civil servants had expressed doubts about carrying out policies with which they did not agree, Robert Armstrong issued guidelines which stated that civil servants are responsible to their ministers and senior officials, not to parliament or the people. Under that ruling there was official recognition that civil servants are obliged to follow the instructions of politicians, even when those instructions are in the interest of a political party rather than in the national interest.

• The Civil Service Department that had been founded in the wake of the Fulton Report was disbanded in 1981 and control of the Civil Service passed jointly to the Treasury and the Cabinet Office.

The Efficiency Unit

Almost the first action of Margaret Thatcher after the election, apart from the formation of her government, was the establishment of an Efficiency Unit in Number 10, headed by Derek Rayner of Marks and Spencer. Sir Derek (later Lord) Rayner was a highly respected businessman who had revolutionised the success of Marks and Spencer by the introduction of new managerial systems. Between 1970 and 1972 he had served a two-year term advising the Heath government on the improvement of efficiency and effectiveness at the Ministry of Defence and it was this which enhanced his reputation as the man most likely to reform the managerial practices of the Civil Service. Based in Downing Street, Rayner was very close to the prime minister in all senses and she placed complete trust in him, conceding considerable powers to him to act as her principal lieutenant in achieving one of her imperatives in government. As he wrote of her, 'She was and has stayed determined that there should be a radical change in the quality of management. Without this, my work and that of my successor could not have been effective'.[8]

Over the four years he served as head of the Efficiency Unit in Downing Street, Rayner had two main tasks :

1 He had to institute real economies and improved efficiency in the way that civil servants did their job.
2 He was expected to increase the regard in which managerial skills were held by senior civil servants. If senior civil servants could be encouraged to regard management as a vital part of their duties, then the entire culture of the Civil Service might be transformed from an administrative to a managerialist perspective.

The process by which the Efficiency Unit achieved these changes progressed in three stages:

1 There was a hunt for 'value for money' (VFM) in terms of the three Es of economy, efficiency and effectiveness; mainly through a series of departmental scrutinies – a form of efficiency audit.
2 In 1982 the scrutiny programme was superseded by the Financial Management Initiative (FMI) which was intended to 'improve the allocation, management and control of resources throughout central government'.[9] The FMI was set up and put in motion by Rayner but continued its work long after he had left to return to Marks and Spencer in 1983.
3 It was Rayner's successor, Sir Robin Ibbs, who instituted the third stage of the reform programme to coincide with Mrs Thatcher's third term in government. The Next Steps programme introduced by Ibbs was designed to change the Civil Service for ever through separating the service's policy-making functions from its executive role as a deliverer of services and it has to be said, now that the Next Steps programme has completed its initial stages, the intended change has indeed taken place.

The scrutiny programme

Underlying the idea for carrying out the 'scrutinies' was the realisation of just how much money was being spent on actually running the Civil Service. Even after some years of being subjected to scrutiny the running costs of the Civil Service during the financial year 1985–86 represented a total of £12.3 billion, or 3.4 per cent of GDP; out of which some £5.8 billion was spent on wages and salaries.[10] Every extra £1 billion spent on the Civil Service accounts for one extra penny on the basic rate of tax; a significant figure for a government dedicated to cutting taxes.

The way in which a 'scrutiny' worked was that a specific area of a department's activity would be chosen for close examination. This would not and could not be done by the Efficiency Unit itself, which had a very small permanent staff anyway; instead the task was given to teams of civil servants recruited as 'scrutineers', usually under the guidance of a civil servant of Principal rank. These civil servant scrutineers would investigate an area chosen by themselves and conclusions would be drawn that again were entirely their own. On the other hand, their methods of working and the nature of the questions they were required to ask were very clearly defined for them by Rayner and his team. 'None of the scrutineers could have doubted what they were expected to do. They were to ask radical questions.'[11]

There is no clear picture as to how successful the scrutiny programme may have been. Certainly it uncovered some startling examples of waste and inefficiency, such as the fact that government research laboratories were breeding their own experimental rats at a cost of £30 each, when they could be bought commercially for £2 each; or that administration of grants to farmers cost the Exchequer £40 for every £100 received as grant. By 1985 the Efficiency Unit was claiming to have identified potential savings of £600 million a year and by 1992 this figure had climbed to between £1.5 and £2 billion. Not that all these potential savings were necessarily realised. A National Audit Office review in 1985 showed that:

- Savings of £112 million a year had been rejected by ministers as unattainable or contrary to government policy.
- Savings of £38 million had been recommended but were left awaiting decisions from ministers.
- Recommendations valued at £171 million a year had been implemented.
- Recommendations valued at £100 million a year had been approved and were awaiting implementation.[12]

The Civil Service itself was very sceptical about the effectiveness of the scrutinies. Clive Ponting, a high-flying young civil servant, who later became even better known for something quite different as we have already seen, initially made his reputation by carrying out a scrutiny of the supply of food to the armed forces by the Defence Ministry. In this he uncovered such massive instances of waste and inefficiency that he was asked to make his report directly to the prime minister, who in turn was so impressed by his findings that Ponting was awarded an OBE for his efforts. However, rivalry between the army, navy and air force meant that all the reforms and savings recommended by Ponting were blocked long before they could ever be implemented. This induced a cynicism in Ponting which led him to say, at the time of Rayner's quitting the Efficiency Unit in 1983, 'some small victories had been won, but Whitehall had absorbed Raynerism, as it had all the other schemes for reform and improving efficiency'. Concerning the success or otherwise of the economies made, he said, 'the Civil Service could certainly be said to have emerged leaner, but not necessarily fitter; it has been not so much slimmed down as hacked around the edges'.[13]

Alongside the scrutiny programme, an individual initiative came from the Department of the Environment (DoE) where the Secretary of State, Michael

Heseltine, instituted his own efficiency and economy project, slimming down the number of civil servants in the DoE by 15,000, or 29 per cent, over four years. Heseltine was also interested in the extent to which the management techniques of the private sector could be applied to the administration of the public sector. From his own experience in industry, Heseltine introduced a system designed to provide ministers and senior civil servants within the DoE with detailed information about the cost and effectiveness of departmental programmes.

> The head of each of the DoE's 57 directorates . . . was told the costs of the people working under his direct authority and he analysed the time and cost devoted to each task. The result was a book which set out his management structure, his objectives and the costs of the work in hand, and set targets for six months ahead.[14]

This was the Management Information System for Ministers (MINIS), the general adoption of which by all government departments was advocated without success by Heseltine in 1982, although Margaret Thatcher was very enthusiastic and did everything she could to promote his ideas to other departments. Another initiative within the DoE was the Joubert Report of 1981 which created an entirely new accounting system for the department. MINIS, the Joubert Report and a variety of Rayner scrutinies came together in 1982 as the joint basis of the Financial Management Initiative (FMI).

The FMI

The FMI was launched by Rayner's Efficiency Unit in May 1982, with three main aims which were intended to streamline the bureaucracy and apply business efficiency methods to Civil Service practice, along the lines advocated by Michael Heseltine at a Cabinet meeting in February where he had been enthusiastically received by Margaret Thatcher, but less enthusiastically by Cabinet colleagues. According to the White Paper setting up the FMI, the aims were that managers at all levels within each department should be able to:

- clearly define the objectives of the department and the means of measuring the performance of the department in meeting those objectives;
- define responsibility for the best use of resources, including a value for money scrutiny of performance;
- identify the training needed by staff, and the availability of expert advice to enable the department to maximise its performance.

There was no uniform FMI across the whole Civil Service but each department developed its own response to the general brief, often giving them individual names as if to emphasise their different approaches. The Department of

Trade and Industry (DTI) developed a programme known as ARM (activity and resource management), the Home Office had APR, and there was even LOCIS (the Lord Chancellor's information system).

There is no clear picture as to the extent to which the FMI was or was not successful. In 1985 the Treasury certainly seemed to think that it was working well. Sir Peter Middleton, Permanent Secretary at the Treasury, said that, 'productivity improvements in the public sector have been at least as good as those achieved in the private service sector'. This estimate appeared to be borne out by a report by the National Institute for Economic and Social Research, which claimed to find a growth in productivity for the Civil Service of between 2 and 3 per cent over the five-year period, 1979–84: every bit as good as growth in the private sector.[15] Another survey showed that the measures introduced by the FMI had resulted in the saving of £1 billion in spending by the Civil Service over FMI's first five years of operation between 1982 and 1987.

In 1985 a Cabinet Office report on the FMI recommended that all policy proposals made by government departments should be accompanied by plans for measuring the effectiveness of that policy. From 1985 Performance Review Reports were part of every department's implementation of the FMI. In 1986 the Treasury added to these performance indicators by introducing running cost controls and cash limits for government departments. As a result, government departments which exceeded their estimated day-to-day running costs would be unable to cover the shortfall by transferring funds from capital expenditure, except with the explicit approval of the Chief Secretary to the Treasury and parliament. The financial stringency involved gained the hearty approval of the National Audit Office and the Comptroller and Auditor General.

However, there were others who were not so impressed with the application of the FMI. Rayner himself believed that the Civil Service would not be able to proceed much beyond a simple level of saving because administrators steeped in Civil Service values would fail to feel any urgency in doing so since, as public servants, they were not subject to the profit and loss constraints suffered by those working in the the private sector. Clive Ponting saw that much of the FMI initiative was irrelevant to the problem of introducing managerialism to the Civil Service: the main thrust in the application of FMI procedures was simply a means of cutting costs and reducing bureaucracy, rather then forcing a root-and-branch modernisation of public administration through managerialist measures. In a report published in 1989 by the London PA Consulting Group, a group of management consultants very much in the Michael Heseltine mould, it was said of the FMI that it was of 'little continuing value' and 'should be radically rethought'.

As Margaret Thatcher moved towards her third term in 1987 so the government felt that it now sufficiently firmly based that it could afford to apply in full measure its thoughts on reforming the Civil Service. Opinion therefore moved from a process that left intact the administration's traditional ways of working, however much reformed, and turned to investigate the means by which the

Civil Service might be radically restructured through introducing market forces into the process of administration. The task of looking into this was given to Sir Robin Ibbs, another seconded businessman, in this case from ICI, who had succeeded Derek Rayner as head of the Efficiency Unit in 1983. In the autumn of 1986 Sir Robin had made a preliminary report on the progress of Civil Service reform since 1979 and Mrs Thatcher had confessed that she felt bitterly disappointed that so little had been done in the previous seven years and that so much still remained and needed to be done. It was in order to see just what it was that needed doing that, in November 1986, Kate Jenkins, Karen Caines and Andrew Jackson of the Efficiency Unit were commissioned to look into what the next steps of the reform programme should be. These three are named as the authors of the report but, as a result of Sir Robin's position as Head of the Efficiency Unit, it is more generally known as the Ibbs Report.

That report into the structure and workings of the Civil Service, entitled *Improving Management in Government: The Next Steps*, was finished in early 1987 but was judged to be so sensitive that its findings were kept secret until after the 1987 general election and it was only published in February 1988. The principal aim was to split up the monolithic structure of the national Civil Service into a number of discrete operational areas of activity, each of which would have its own management structure free of the Civil Service hierarchy and within which there would be a clear divorce between the policy and operational areas of competence. It marked a very clear change in the nature of the Civil Service.

Notes

1 David Farnham and Sylvia Horton (eds), *Managing the New Public Services*, Macmillan, Basingstoke, 1993, pp. 40–5.
2 Lord Plowden, *The Control of Public Expenditure* (Command Paper 1432), HMSO, London, 1961.
3 The discussion on post-Fulton attitudes is based on Robert Pyper, *The British Civil Service*, Harvester Wheatsheaf, Hemel Hempstead, 1995, pp. 52–5.
4 Sylvia Horton in Farnham and Horton, Note 1 above, pp. 132–3.
5 Peter Hennessey, 'Mrs Thatcher's Poodle', *Contemporary Record*, Vol. 2, No. 2, 1988, p. 4.
6 Figures taken from Tony Butcher, 'The Civil Service in the 1990s: The Revolution Rolls On', *Talking Politics*, Autumn 1995, p. 39.
7 *The Economist*, 10 March 1984.
8 Lord Rayner, *The Unfinished Agenda*, University of London, 1984, pp. 4–5.
9 Quoted by Sylvia Horton in Farnham and Horton, Note 1 above, p. 135.
10 The figures are taken from *Civil Service Statistics 1986*, quoted by Geoffrey Fry, *Policy and Management in the British Civil Service*, Prentice Hall/Harvester Wheatsheaf, Hemel Hempstead, 1995, p. 61.
11 Alan Bray, *The Clandestine Reformer: A Study of the Rayner Scrutinies*, University of Strathclyde Papers on Government and Politics No. 55, Glasgow, 1987.

12 National Audit Office figures quoted by Fry, Note 10 above, p. 63.
13 Clive Ponting, *Whitehall: Tragedy and Farce*, Sphere Books, London, 1986.
14 Michael Heseltine, *Where There's a Will*, Hutchinson, London, 1987, quoted by Fry, Note 10 above, p. 64.
15 Peter Middleton and others quoted by Fry, Note 10 above, p. 67.

7

The Next Steps programme

The Ibbs Report

Improving Management in Government: The Next Steps – otherwise known as the Ibbs Report into the structure and workings of the Civil Service – was finally published in February 1988, although it had been completed in early 1987, its findings being thought to be so sensitive that it was kept secret for the best part of a year so as not to imperil the Conservative Party's chances in the forthcoming 1987 general election. That sensitivity arose because, very early in the report, it became clear that at the very heart of the policy being advocated by Ibbs was the idea that the structure of the Civil Service should be split up into a number of discrete operational areas of activity. To quote paragraph 10 of the report:

> The Civil Service is too big and too diverse to manage as a single entity. With 600,000 employees it is an enormous organisation compared with any private sector company . . . A single organisation of this size which attempts to . . . carry out functions as diverse as driver licensing, fisheries protection, the catching of drug smugglers and the processing of Parliamentary Questions is bound to develop in a way which fits no single operation effectively.[1]

The new structure for the Civil Service would consist of a small central core of government departments with their ministers and senior civil servants, the entire core comprising no more than 20,000 staff. Since the team compiling the Ibbs Report had estimated that almost as much as 95 per cent of the Civil Service is primarily concerned with the provision and management of services, it was felt that the more than 5 per cent represented by that central core of 20,000 or so staff should be all that would be required to maintain the policy and decision-making departmental functions of the Civil Service. As a consequence, most of the staff and much of the work which had formerly belonged within the Whitehall departments could and should be transferred to executive agencies over which ministers would have no operational control. Departments would decide on policy, fix the size of an agency's budget and monitor the agency's work but beyond that the agencies would have almost complete autonomy. Where it appeared to be required, some agencies could go beyond even this level of autonomy to become completely independent of government, or alternatively their functions or activities could be contracted out to a private supplier. Little wonder therefore that many civil servants were dismayed by the Ibbs Report and fearful for their jobs.

For many critics the Ibbs Report was seen as little more than preparation for the wholesale privatisation of the Civil Service and many horrified adherents of the old school – to whom such widespread change appeared to be the end of civilisation as they knew it – were prepared to defend the existing system to the death. On the other hand, for many critics on the right the report was seen not to have gone anywhere near far enough and the more radical members of the Thatcher government were seriously advocating full-scale privatisation, taking entire government departments out of Treasury control and imposing compulsory competitive tendering on the remainder for the provision of any public services whatsoever. Even Margaret Thatcher herself was heard to say that those government agencies whose tasks were largely commercial would probably do better if they were removed entirely from within the ambience of the Civil Service. Unlike the prime minister however, Nigel Lawson, then Chancellor of the Exchequer, was very much opposed to the Ibbs Report, probably because he was in sympathy with his Treasury officials who feared that their traditional domination of the Civil Service would be lost through this increased autonomy.

It was this controversy and internal disagreement over the implementation of the Ibbs Report, among politicians and officials alike, which led to the delay in the report's publication until 1988 and there is evidence that the report as it was finally issued is somewhat watered down in its conclusions from the original positions adopted by its authors. When Mrs Thatcher announced the main provisions of the Ibbs Report to the House of Commons on 18 February 1988 and confirmed the government's determination to implement the report, she made it clear that two of the main scenarios anticipated by the critics were unlikely to happen, since:

- The Treasury would continue to retain control over all matters relating to pay and personnel management in the Civil Service – at least for the time being and for as long as the Civil Service remained a unitary service.
- The autonomy of government agencies did not mean that those services which had always been held to be accountable to parliament would now cease to be so. It was just the nature of accountability that would change.

In order to implement the reforms, the prime minister appointed Peter Kemp to be Second Permanent Secretary in the Cabinet Office, acting in that capacity as Project Manager for the Next Steps programme. Kemp was an unusual figure who had been an accountant in the private sector and who had joined the Civil Service as a state-educated, specialist professional recruit, without the benefits of the traditional Oxbridge generalist background favoured by Whitehall mandarins. Yet he had, despite these disadvantages, risen to the position of Assistant Secretary in the Treasury with special responsibility for Civil Service pay. In that position he had worked alongside Nigel Lawson and Lawson looked on Kemp with an approval that he was unwilling to extend to Sir Robin Ibbs. Lawson was to say of Kemp that he did 'a remarkable job' in developing the Next Steps programme.[2]

Initially, a form of market evaluation was devised by which the best way forward for Civil Service activities was formulated so as to facilitate the formation of government agencies. Under this system, in a pattern that would be almost exactly replicated in the 'Prior Options' programme of 1993, each single activity within the service was measured against three possible criteria to decide between three possible outcomes:

1 *The activity needs to stay with the government department* – there should be no change in the organisational structure.
2 *The activity can be best managed outside the control of either government or civil service* – the activity should be either contracted out to a private supplier (privatised) or passed to a non-governmental organisation (quango).
3 *The activity should be controlled by government but managed outside the Civil Service* – the activity should be passed to a government agency.

Ibbs had recommended that the chief executives of agencies should have significant management freedoms over pay and personnel matters and should be directly accountable to parliament as well as to their departmental ministers. However, Mrs Thatcher overruled this. Although agency staff could be questioned and required to give evidence to departmental select committees, in the same way as departmental civil servants were required to do, such appearances would not make agency staff accountable themselves: their function rather being to assist the minister who is the actual person accountable to the committee. As regards an agency dependent on a government department, ministers would be responsible for policy but would no longer be accountable for operational matters. Chief executives of the agencies are therefore answerable to the government, through the agencies themselves, but are accountable to parliament only in the most indirect fashion. According to a leader in the *Guardian*, the aim was to create a state where 'a simple majority in the House of Commons will run a federation of executive agencies and semi-autonomous departments . . . complete with an increasingly casualised workforce, as the old Civil Service disappears'.

Next Steps

Although the decision to reform the Civil Service had been made by the Thatcher government, the Next Steps process got off to a very slow start under her leadership and it was only under John Major that any real progress was made.[3] In the first year a mere eight agencies were in existence, and these were mostly agencies of peripheral importance, like the Stationery Office (HMSO) which had been in existence for some time, although not with the degree of autonomy it would enjoy from now on. But, in spite of the slow start and despite criticism from Opposition parties and the unions, those agencies which did exist or that were created during the early period were showing every sign of being successful. In 1991, Sir Robin Ibbs's successor in the Efficiency Unit, Sir Angus Fraser, published a report, *Making the Most of the Next Steps,* which increased the tempo considerably.[4]

Back in 1988 when the Ibbs Report was first published and the Next Steps programme was initiated, there were only 12 possible candidates for agency status, employing a total of only 70,000 people. And, of these 12, it was only the Employment Service Agency, whose 35,000 employees staffed the nation's Job Centres, which seemed to be of any real importance.[5] The actual first agency to be set up under the programme was the Vehicle Inspectorate, which dates from August 1988, but as late as March 1990 only 12 agencies had been established and there was talk that this was yet another initiative that would fizzle out and be killed off by the intransigence and passive resistance of the Treasury and the Whitehall Old Guard.

As early as May 1988, Peter Kemp rejected these criticisms in advance and claimed that, despite what might possibly be a very slow start, the Next Steps agencies would prove to be the most effective way forward for a Civil Service trying to come to terms with a post-Thatcherite world. Tackled as to the extent of growth in the number of agencies which would be created and asked to guess how many civil servants would be employed within those agencies by 1998, in ten years time, Kemp answered that he anticipated that three-quarters of all civil servants would be located in government agencies before the end of the century. His estimate proved to be extremely accurate, the actual proportion in 1998 being 76 per cent.

In 1992, in the light of the Fraser Report and John Major's election victory, major changes were made to the Next Steps programme which resulted in a serious shake-up for the Civil Service. During the formation of his new government, John Major announced that there was to be a new office, the Office of Public Service and Science (OPS), that would not only take responsibility for the overview of science from the old Department of Education and Science, but would take charge of the Next Steps programme and such spin-offs as the Citizen's Charter, Prior Options and Market-Testing. This office was to be the prime responsibility of a Cabinet Minister, the Chancellor of the Duchy of Lancaster, thereby making reform of the Civil Service part of the government's central planning. Control of the Next Steps programme passed to the Next Steps and Management Development Group, situated within the OPS. Peter Kemp, who had been Project leader since 1988 came into conflict with the new Permanent Secretary of the OPS and with William Waldegrave as Chancellor of the Duchy of Lancaster, ostensibly over the matter of the market-testing programme, although there were many who believed that Kemp's non-traditional origins jarred on Waldegrave and his Whitehall associates with the result that 'Kemp's face did not really fit'. In 1992 Kemp was virtually forced to resign from the Civil Service and surrender his control of the Next Steps project.

Despite Kemp's departure, the reform programme initiated under Next Steps increased in pace and became linked with a number of other devices intended to improve the efficiency of the Civil Service through the introduction of market forces. Typical was the relaunch of the *Citizen's Charter* initiative. The concept of a citizen's charter that would ensure the public's satisfaction with public services had been the brainchild of John Major in 1990, although it was rethought and relaunched both before and after the 1992 election. Public services were encouraged to set targets of consumer satisfaction, with penalties being imposed for failure and successful performances being rewarded. The scheme was intended for all public services, especially the privatised utilities, but it was particularly well suited to the Next Steps agencies, nine of which took immediate steps to issue their own charters.

The practice of *market-testing*, which was the particular development over which Kemp fell out with Waldegrave, was developed as the result of *Competing for Quality*, a White Paper issued in 1991. Government thinking followed the competitive tendering initiatives introduced into local government and the NHS during the 1980s and required government departments and agencies to market-test their activities to see whether those activities could be more efficiently provided by outside organisations instead of continuing rather expensively in-house. There was a two-fold purpose in this exercise in that, if the service could be provided more efficiently and economically by an outside contractor, then there was a gain. But even if it were decided to keep the activity in-house, the act of considering it for tender would have involved the staff in a re-evaluation of the activity which in itself might lead to more effective execution of that activity.

The market-testing programme was opposed by the unions from the start. In 1992 and 1993 the Council of Civil Service Unions (CCSU) published papers attacking the project. According to the message delivered by the Citizen's Charter, the aim of the government in introducing market-testing was increased efficiency and improved services. Nonsense, retorted the CCSU, the sole aim of the government was to cut costs. 'The hype of "value for money" is a smokescreen for cuts. The Government concentrates on efficiency at the expense of effectiveness.'[6] What obviously raised concerns in the unions were certain statements issued by the government, such as one in 1992 which stated that the government's aim was the transfer of 25 per cent of departmental work to outside bodies. But the government pressed on regardless, with some obvious success by its own criteria: by the end of 1993, 389 market tests had been carried out, with average savings of 'over 22 per cent'. By October 1994 some £2.1 billion worth of activities had been considered, many of those activities being contracted out as a result, at the cost of the jobs of 27,000 civil servants. Only about 68 per cent of market-tested activities remained in-house with the Civil Service and, according to the second annual report of the Citizen's Charter, '113 activities were contracted out as a result of a strategic decision to employ an outside employer'.[7] Critics of the market-testing programme, particularly those in the unions, have mostly concentrated on the dramatic contraction in the Civil Service and the loss of jobs. Nevertheless, other fears have been expressed, including doubt about the implications for accountability. 'It is clear that so long as any firm carries out the requirements of a contract no minister will be able to interfere with the work of that firm either . . . in operating methods, or in terms of policy.'[8]

Market-testing was only one way among several in which the Civil Service was being asked to contemplate contracting-out or privatisation as part of the government's search for greater efficiency. Now that the Civil Service had finally embarked on a serious programme of reform, the government and its supporters saw no reason to relax the momentum: the reform programme was intended to be permanent and continuous and the government intended to ensure that such was the case. In 1992 the government launched the **Private Finance Initiative (PFI)** as a means of using private money to finance public facilities: private firms or consortia of firms would raise the capital, build the facility and then recover their investment through an income from the facility. The initiative was not popular with the Opposition parties and projects were slow to appear. However, the road bridge over the Thames at Dartford and the bridge linking Skye with the mainland were both built with private money, although in the latter case the excessive bridge tolls charged by the contractor, who had a monopoly on crossings to the island, led to charges of the government selling out the public interest in the name of privatisation.

Even after Labour became the government in 1997 and it might have been expected that the Labour Party's known hostility to the initiative would mean that the PFI would be kicked into touch, the Labour government nevertheless pressed ahead with the most controversial of all the measures, a toll road running parallel with the M6 to be known as the Birmingham Northern Relief Road, which got the full go-ahead from John Prescott in the autumn of 1998. That statement from a minister who had been one of the leading critics of the PFI really was indicative of the extent to which the private sector has penetrated and become involved with wide areas of public administration.

In 1993 it was announced that Next Steps agencies would review their activities every five years under a process known as **Prior Options**. This process demanded that an agency should look carefully at each activity in which it was involved, and make a choice from the following options:

- the activity is no longer required and should be abolished;
- there is a continuing need for the activity to be provided by the government agency;

- there is a continuing need for the activity, but it should be market-tested for possible contracting-out; or
- there is a need for the activity, but it would be more effectively delivered if it were privatised and removed completely from government control.

The government made it clear that reviews of Next Steps agencies would be announced to the public in advance, thereby obviously inviting the private sector to become involved, perhaps by putting in their own bids to acquire agencies from the government, either in part or in total under some such measure as the PFI.

By April 1996, after the Next Steps programme had been in operation for little more than seven years, a total of 125 government agencies had been set up, including 11 within Northern Ireland, which seemed to show that the programme was successfully on target to meet the aims and objectives set out by Peter Kemp in 1988. Even parts of the Civil Service that had not been hived off into agencies, like the Inland Revenue, were reorganised internally on the agency model and functioned as what are known as non-ministerial departments. By March 1998, as the Blair government considered the first year of its life, 76 per cent of all civil servants, 383,000 in all, were known to be working in 138 Next Steps agencies, or were working under Next Steps conditions in four government departments.[9] Although 1998 marked the end of the agency creation phase of the Next Steps programme, the government announced that they might well create a further 50 agencies, employing a total of 84,000 civil servants, which would bring the numbers of civil servants employed within the agency structure by the year 2000 to over 450,000, more than 80 per cent of the whole.

Organisation and structure of the Next Steps agencies

There is no uniform standard pattern for the government agencies created as a result of the Next Steps programme. They come in all sizes, from the very large – such as the Benefits Agency, with no fewer than 66,296 on its staff – to the very smallest, which is the Wilton Park Conference Centre, with a mere 37 employees (for a full list of government agencies, see Appendix 2). These very different agencies cover an enormous range of central government services and the Fraser Report of 1991 identified various different categories. Generally, however, they can be said to fall into two main groupings, albeit with several sub-groups. The two general groupings are:

1) **Mainstream agencies**, which exist either to carry out the specialised functions of their respective government departments or to execute the regulatory or statutory functions of those departments. This group includes some of the largest and most important agencies such as the Benefits Agency (for the Department of Social Security), the Employment Service Agency (for the

Department of Education and Employment), and the Prison Service (for the Home Office). These three agencies are the three largest in the Next Steps programme and, as such, have not only assumed massive operational functions that were once the direct responsibility of Whitehall departments, but, in the drive for efficiency and savings, have made quite considerable changes in the way staff employed in the ranks of the Civil Service are distributed, since the three agencies between them are responsible for a staff of nearly 140,000.

2) **Specialist service agencies,** which supply support services either to other departments or to the public. Such agencies include bodies like the Central Office of Information, which acts as the advertising agency or press office for all government services, or the Meteorological Office which provides invaluable weather information to the armed forces, merchant shipping, farmers and fishermen as well as initiating the weather forecasts on radio and television.

A number of these agencies are operated as what are called *trading funds*. They can either operate as commercial concerns and introduce market-orientated profitable enterprises as a subsidiary to their main purpose – as in the case of the Royal Mint which not only produces the nation's notes and coins for general circulation as it has always done but also produces special commemorative mint coins and medals in presentation sets for sale to numismatists and other collectors. Alternatively, a trading fund can be an agency which is funded from income, freeing the agency from government control over the management of its funds and capital investment, and allowing it to increase its income through the marketing of the agency's services.

Those men and women at the head of the agencies, the chief executives, were originally all career civil servants, internally appointed. However, under pressure from the Treasury and the Civil Service Select Committee of the House of Commons, and as part of the changes to be discussed in the next chapter, the procedure was changed and since the mid-1990s nearly all chief executive positions have been openly advertised, both inside and outside the Civil Service. Over half the appointments of chief executives under open recruitment have gone to applicants from outside the Civil Service – quite frequently from the private sector. For example, one prominent chief executive, Derek Lewis, the controversial head of the Prison Service, who was dismissed by Michael Howard, had previously held a senior position with Granada, the leisure group.

One reason for resentment on the part of those who have spent their working lives as career civil servants is that, without exception, the chief executives of the leading agencies have been paid much higher salaries than have been available to their civil servant counterparts and predecessors. An example of this again is Derek Lewis, who was paid a salary of £133,280 for running the Prison Service, whereas the comparable grade in the departmental Civil Service at the time was worth a maximum salary of £73,000. It used to be the case that senior civil servants were criticised for being 'generalist' administrators without the skilled expertise that might be needed to run their departments and it might be thought that in this respect this recruitment from outside could not help but be beneficial, with an influx of former businessmen introducing the disciplines of commerce and the market place into public administration. Yet critics have pointed out that it need not necessarily be thought progressive to replace non-specialist administrators with industrialists or businessmen who are no more specialists in that particular service than were the bureaucrats: for example, why should a man skilled in the running of TV rental shops and motorway service areas, as Derek Lewis had done at Granada, be thought particularly capable of running Her Majesty's Prison Service?

Accountability in the 'new' Civil Service

Politically and constitutionally, the most significant aspect of the Next Steps programme is the key factor that the agencies and their chief executives are not themselves accountable to parliament or the electorate, as government ministers and their departments used to be. In the new situation created by the Next Steps agencies, with chief executives at their head, a new convention had to be created which divided the onus of responsibility as it lay between ministers and chief executives. In a Treasury paper of 1989 on the accountability of agencies, it was made clear that the various 'Chief Executives' authority is delegated to them by Ministers who are and will remain accountable to Parliament and its Select Committees'.[10] The paper continued, 'The Chief Executive will be able to inform the Committee how his agency has performed its responsibilities. Ministers themselves will remain fully accountable for all Government policies.' This was an early attempt to frame the convention that in terms of accountability, chief executives will answer as to operational decisions, while ministers will answer as to policy matters. Which is all very well, as long as senior personnel, whether politicians or officials, answer for their own responsibilities and do not use potential ambiguities in their position to duck or evade responsibility.

These ambiguities are of no particular importance when an agency is peripheral to public concerns, as with something like the Weights and Measures Laboratory. It is, however, of major importance when public welfare is in question, as with the agencies supporting the Department of Social Security. When the Child Support Agency was proved to be so ineffective and maladroit that it was in a virtual state of collapse, questions in the House of Commons produced the response from the then Secretary of State, Peter Lilley, that 'it has nothing to do with me'.

Much the same response was made by Michael Howard, Home Secretary in the Major government, over errors and inefficiencies in the Prison Service which led to a series of actions which showed very clearly what the implications of the Next Steps agencies might be for the traditional Civil Service virtues of neutrality and anonymity as they apply to the questions of accountability and ministerial responsibility.

The story behind that incident is that, in October 1995, Michael Howard sacked Derek Lewis as Director General of the Prison Service over a series of blunders, internal disturbances and escapes affecting the Prison Service, the cumulative effect of which had been to embarrass the government. In response to his dismissal Lewis counter-attacked by accusing Howard of improper interference in the day-to-day running of the prison service. Some indication of the extent to which Howard had become involved in the minutiae of prison administration was given in the Learmont Report into lapses of security in the Prison Service. According to Learmont, Howard had demanded at one point that Lewis provide him with 1,000 documents, including 137 'full submissions' in just four months. Lewis also offered to provide evidence that the Home Secretary had intervened in internal prison disciplinary matters; even attempting to influence the choice of which prison it should be to which certain offenders should be sent. All of which seemed to run counter to claims that the Home Secretary was accountable only for policy matters and had no interest in operational issues.

The most important charge against the Home Secretary was the accusation that Howard had overruled Lewis in dealing with the aftermath of a breakout at Parkhurst Prison. Lewis had wanted to transfer the governor, John Marriott, to non-operational duties, pending a disciplinary hearing, but Howard had overruled Lewis, saying that Marriott was to be dismissed immediately. There was evidence that a large part of the blame for problems at Parkhurst lay at the door of the Home Office but that Howard avoided any suggestion of blame by reiterating his claim that he, as minister, was responsible only for policy decisions while the Prison Service was responsible for operational matters. Lewis continued to claim that his dismissal was wrong and this seemed to be upheld by Judge Tumim, the Chief Inspector of Prisons, who said that the Home Secretary's distinction between policy and operations was 'bogus'.

Christmas Eve 1995 saw the retirement of John Marriott, the former governor of Parkhurst Prison, who had been removed from his post by Michael Howard. Free to speak now that he was retired, Mr Marriott used BBC Radio 4's *World at One* to launch a bitter attack on the then Home Secretary, accusing him of incessant meddling in prison affairs, indecisiveness and incompetent leadership. Papers were also leaked by Lewis which proved conclusively that while a disciplinary hearing into Marriott's conduct was proceeding at Parkhurst a telephone intervention by Howard had insisted on Marriott's immediate suspension: a clear case of an operational rather than a policy decision being imposed by a minister on an agency chief executive.[11]

There is a clear constitutional implication in these problems. Members of the public who have a complaint against the administration always used to be able to challenge the government minister concerned through their MP and hold him or her to account for the mistakes of his or her department. This is no longer the case because there is no one clearly accountable for the actions of these agencies, particularly when the relevant government minister refuses to accept responsibility for the operational actions of those agencies that come within the organisational structure of the ministerial department: even if the minister concerned constantly chooses to interfere in the day-to-day operations of the agency.

A recent article which compares the accountability of Next Steps agencies in Britain with similar executive agencies in Germany and Sweden,[12] concludes that any British reforms in the management of public services have so far proved to be far less radical than their equivalents in Northern Europe, particularly in Sweden where the agencies have far more autonomy *vis-à-vis* government ministries than they do in the UK. Comparing it with the now infamous row over Parkhurst Prison described above, a dispute which showed the Home Office to be far more extensively involved in operational prison matters than was supposed to be the case, the authors examine what happened as a result of a prison riot at Tidaholm in Sweden during July 1994. The Ministry of Justice was not involved in any effective way; simply being informed as to the fact of the riot having taken place. On the other hand, the Swedish National Prisons Administration (*kriminalvårdsstyrelsen*) handled the whole thing, investigating cause and effect as well as dealing with the mass media and setting up the necessary reforms to prevent a recurrence. In Sweden separation between ministries and agencies at the operational level is a fundamental constitutional principle.

Nevertheless, there is one lesson to be learned from Sweden and Germany that is worth bearing in mind and it is that the institution of executive agencies does not necessarily create a clear division between operational areas and involvement in policy decisions. Indeed the evidence from Europe is that any operational experience gained by the agencies leads directly in their hands to the formulation of policy decisions. In their article Elder and Page go on to suggest that, for all the protests that there were over Michael Howard and the Prisons agency, some Next Steps agencies in Britain such as the Social Security Benefits Agency are themselves becoming increasingly involved with a direct input into the policy process.

Conclusion

For all of Margaret Thatcher's rhetoric about 'rolling back the frontiers of the state', it was only after her departure that the Civil Service was really transformed from the deadweight bureaucracy that she so much distrusted. The Next Steps programme and the delegation of Civil Service activity to a network of agencies really did change the nature, structure and even the function of the service.

There were those who believed that the advent of a Labour government in 1997 would reverse these changes because of four major concerns about the impact of the Next Steps programme, as expressed by critics of the Conservative government:

1 **Confusion over accountability.** This involves not only the operational/policy dichotomy of ministers and chief executives, but also the problem of whether it is the agency or the department that has financial accountability.
2 **Loss of the national, unified Civil Service.** The many different agencies, each with its own market imperatives, staffed by civil servants with differing pay scales and career prospects, has led to a 'balkanisation' of the old Civil Service, breaking it up into its component and competing parts: the implication being that the various divisions of the service no longer freely co-operate for the common good.
3 **Looming privatisation.** In 1992 the then head of the Efficiency Unit, Sir Peter Levene, claimed that the growing proliferation of agencies was still not enough and nothing less would do than the full privatisation of all government activities.
4 **Loss of the public service ethic.** It was often said that a key element of Thatcherism was the doctrine of 'look after number one' and there is little doubt that the traditional and altruistic Civil Service ethic of doing things for the public good has been considerably eroded by a regime of managerialism which includes market-testing, performance-related pay and competitive tendering.

For all four of these reasons there were many Labour supporters who expected the Blair government to throw the reform programme into reverse, restoring some of the old virtues and reversing some of the measures disapproved of by the Left. But such a reversal or U-turn in policy did not happen. Partly it was the case that the changes had gone too far to be reversed and, in any case, it was not as if New Labour was out of sympathy with many of the changes made: the Next Steps programme seeming to gel remarkably well with the concept of the stakeholder society. There may have been doubts about such constitutional questions as accountability but, as regards straightforward operational questions, there is little doubt that the Next Steps agencies have been generally successful; despite the Child Support Agency. In simple terms, performance targets have been met in 75 per cent of cases and the numbers of staff employed in the Civil Service have been quite significantly reduced without sacrificing the quality of service.[13]

Shortly after the election, as had been promised in successive Labour manifestos, trade union rights were restored to those few workers at the Government Communication Headquarters (GCHQ) who were still interested. However, that was the only aspect of the Civil Service where Conservative policy was actually reversed after May 1997. Indeed, the greatest change imposed by Labour was the vastly increased presence of political advisers in Downing Street and Whitehall already discussed in Chapter 5 and that, as has been said, was merely continuing a trend, begun by Harold Wilson but increasingly practised by Margaret Thatcher.

David Clark, Tony Blair's first Chancellor of the Duchy of Lancaster, with responsibility for the administration and funding of the Civil Service through the OPS, gave evidence to a Commons committee not long after the election. In this he very significantly managed to describe the role of the Senior Civil Service without ever actually mentioning their having a policy role. A Freedom of Information Act was promised by the new government, which would free the Civil Service from the tyranny of the Official Secrets Act, but which would also play its part in the further erosion of the traditional anonymity of the service. Clark also stressed the change of Civil Service function from bureaucratic administration to corporate management, describing the Civil Service as the 'corporate oil within which the wheels of government will actually work'.[14]

The immediate impression of the Blair government during its first couple of years in office would seem to be that they are consolidating and extending the reforms introduced under the Conservatives. But it would be easy to overestimate the extent of change:

> It [the Civil Service] . . . is now focused on corporate management rather than policy advice . . . The effects of change are reflected in the debates about politicisation, accountability and culture. The new government is committed to continuing many of the reforms of the previous government . . . However, there remains a smaller, more diverse Senior Civil Service at the heart of all these changes . . . and they are likely to remain for the foreseeable future.[15]

The extent to which the traditional Civil Service has managed to resist reform can best be seen by examining the structure of the new Senior Civil Service as the Major government of 1992 attempted to create it, appreciating the massive inertia which is always present to combat change in the Civil Service.

Notes

1 Efficiency Unit, *Improving Management in Government: The Next Steps. Report to the Prime Minister* (the Ibbs Report), HMSO, London, 1988.
2 Geoffrey Fry, *Policy and Management in the British Civil Service*, Prentice Hall/Harvester Wheatsheaf, Hemel Hempstead, 1995, p. 106.
3 The Next Steps programme prior to 1994 was reviewed in two articles by Tony Butcher: 'The Changing Civil Service', *Politics Review*, September 1995, pp. 18–21; and 'The Civil Service in the 1990s: The Revolution Rolls On', *Talking Politics*, Autumn 1995, pp. 39–43.
4 See Andrew Gray and Bill Jenkins, 'The Management of Central Government Services', in Bill Jones (ed.), *Politics UK* (2nd edition), Harvester Wheatsheaf, Hemel Hempstead, 1994, p. 434.
5 Robert Pyper, *The British Civil Service*, Harvester Wheatsheaf, Hemel Hempstead, 1995, p. 73.
6 Council of Civil Service Unions (CCSU), *Competing for Quality: Jobs for Sale*, CCSU,

London 1992. The CCSU also published a follow-up document in 1993: *CCSU Comments on the Government's Guide to Market Testing*.

7 Fry, Note 2 above, p. 122.

8 B. O'Toole, 'The British Civil Service in the 1990s: Are Business Practices Really Best?', *Teaching Public Administration*, Vol. XIV, No. 1, 1994, p. 29.

9 Statement made to the House of Commons by Dr David Clark as Chancellor of the Duchy of Lancaster, 12 March 1998. The four non-ministerial departments that operate on Next Steps lines are the Inland Revenue, Customs and Excise, the Crown Prosecution Service and the Serious Fraud Office.

10 Quoted by Fry, Note 2 above, p. 115.

11 Colin Pilkington, *Representative Democracy in Britain Today*, Manchester University Press, 1997, pp. 179–80.

12 Neil Elder and Edward Page, 'Accountability and Control in Next Steps Agencies', *Talking Politics*, Winter 1999, pp. 123–5.

13 Ian Budge, Ivor Crewe, David McKay, Ken Newton, *The New British Politics*, Addison Wesley Longman, Harlow, 1998, p. 255.

14 Quoted by Rachel Bayliss and Charlotte Dargie, 'The Senior Civil Service in the 1990s', in Steve Lancaster (ed.), *Developments in Politics*, Vol. 9, Causeway Press, Ormskirk, 1998, p. 95.

15 Bayliss and Dargie, Note 14 above, p. 96.

8

Towards a 'new' Civil Service

After Next Steps

The Next Steps programme, alongside the Financial Management Initiative, market-testing, Prior Options and all the other reforms to which the Civil Service has been subjected, have helped move the service from its traditional administrative roots to a more managerial model, changing the emphasis of its existence from being a centralised, unitary service to its being a loose federation of discrete component parts.

Prior to 1993, the power and authority to control and direct the Civil Service was centralised in the joint hands of, on one side, the Treasury and, on the other, the Office of Public Service and Science within the Cabinet Office. Change from a unitary to a federal model by loosening this centralised control was given form and approval by the Civil Service (Management Functions) Act of 1992. This Act allowed the Treasury and the OPS either to delegate their powers to another specific agency or department, or alternatively they could delegate a whole range of powers to all government agencies and departments in general. Departments and agencies were thus given responsibility for their own management structures as well as being able to determine their own pay and conditions of service without reference to the centre. The new arrangements were confirmed by a Civil Service Order in Council in 1995 and the new structure was set out in a management code of practice which clearly makes the point that 'the Cabinet Office (OPS) retains the right to inspect and monitor observance of this Code in departments and agencies, but the aim is to keep such inspection and monitoring to the minimum.'[1]

Whereas the Civil Service used to have a single hierarchical structure for all departments, with uniform national pay scales and central recruitment, the Civil Service Act of 1992 was yet another step along the way whereby the various agencies of government have acquired considerable autonomy in these areas of staff management. Further moves in this direction were made when, as from April 1994, any government agency with more than 2,000 staff (at that time this meant as many as 21 different agencies) was permitted to fix its own pay scales and conditions of service, and to negotiate independently with the unions; special emphasis being laid upon performance-related pay. From the start of the Next Steps programme in 1988, the agencies had possessed the ability to recruit their own staff below the administrative level of Principal, without reference to the Civil Service Establishment or Civil Service Commissioners. They were also able, even at that early date, to alter the terms and conditions of service for their members of staff, without reference to the centre. The new measures merely increased the extent and scope of the agencies' autonomy and pointed the way to an extension of these reforms first to the chief executives of Next Steps agencies themselves and then, in a bold move at a later date, to the Senior Civil Service as a whole.

With the start of the Next Steps programme the arrangements which had to be arrived at for the recruitment and appointment of agency chief executives meant that the Civil Service became aware of the criteria used in recruiting senior staff by large private organisations. It was recognised that there was a need, not only to recruit executives of ability, but also to reward them in a manner commensurate with that ability, and also sufficiently generously as to retain their services against the attractions and lures thrown out by alternative employers. Agency chief executives had to be offered service contracts the terms of which would compare favourably with any contracts offered by the private business sector.

Chief executives' posts were therefore:

- advertised for recruitment through open competition;
- offered on a fixed contract with performance targets set; and
- partly rewarded through performance bonuses.

A number of high-profile chief executive positions went to recruits from outside the Civil Service. A typical example was Derek Lewis who was recruited from the Granada Leisure Group to become chief executive of the Prison Service at a salary more like that paid by Granada than the sort of money which had hitherto been associated with Home Office agencies; Lewis receiving a salary of £133,280 at a time when the maximum salary for a grade one civil servant was supposedly £73,000. As the establishment worked out just what was involved in remuneration on the open labour market, it became not uncommon for the chief executives of agencies subordinate to government departments to earn considerably more than the departmental Permanent Secretaries who were their nominal superiors.

As far as the autonomy of government agencies in recruiting staff was concerned, originally the agencies were only given control of staff below the rank of Principal and therefore the rulings that were made on matters of autonomy, such as the Civil Service Act of 1992, affected normal rank-and-file civil servants of the old clerical and executive grades far more than it ever affected senior levels of the administration. But, in the early 1990s, fears began to be expressed that the federalisation and politicisation of recruitment methods and personnel matters were threatening the size, coherence and nature of the Senior Civil Service itself and that there might be a collapse in the structure of the service unless fairly urgent measures were taken to deal with factors affecting the more senior of civil servants. In July 1992, the Cabinet Secretary, Sir Robin Butler, as Head of the Civil Service, and Sir Peter Levene, as the prime minister's adviser on efficiency matters, commissioned the formation of a committee to carry out a special study into recruitment and personnel management at senior civil servant level. The Committee carrying out the study was led by John Oughton, Head of the Efficiency Unit, whose brief was:

> to consider the policies and practices for ensuring the adequate supply of suitably qualified people to fill senior posts in departmental headquarters, agencies and executives, whether from internal sources or after open competition . . . [and to examine] . . . current arrangements in departments for identifying and developing those with potential for appointing to top posts.[2]

The Committee, whose report appeared in November 1993, lavished attention on the traditional Civil Service virtues of integrity, objectivity, impartiality and non-political stance but nevertheless pointed out the manifest weaknesses in the attitude of senior civil servants, as shown in their reluctance to adapt their ways of working to meet managerial imperatives. One senior civil servant giving evidence to the committee said that they should be looking for people with the merit to provide value for money rather than merely the ability to 'ask clever questions'. Another official noted that 'even for high policy, you need to know the trade'. A civil servant on grade 3 level said of those officials more senior to him on grades 1 and 2 that they needed to get out from behind their desks and 'leave their rooms. They see themselves as top policy advisers to Ministers, not managers.'[3] Therefore the underlying suggestion implied in the report was that senior civil servants were intellectual dinosaurs, unaware of the 'real world' and disguising their general ignorance through the use of pedantic and academic language.

The recommendations of the Oughton Report were:

- There was a need for leaner and 'flatter' management structures through the removal of unnecessary management layers in Civil Service departments.
- There should be rapid upward progression through the service for outstanding individuals.
- There was a need for explicit written contracts for senior civil servants (although the Committee refused to recommend the fixed-term contracts held by certain agency chief executives).
- There should be flexible pay arrangements to reward and retain high-flying staff, in the form of performance-related pay.[4]

These recommendations were addressed in *Continuity and Change*, the White Paper of July 1994 which set out to increase further the efficiency of the Civil Service through a form of managerial revolution applied to the higher ranks of the service. This was the work of William Waldegrave as the minister in charge of the OPS, who stated that the aim of the new reforms was to 'map a way forward for the Civil Service to the end of the century and beyond'.[5] The White Paper declared that the most important task was the completion of the Next Steps programme but added that much else needed to be done to realise the 'considerable potential for further improvement' in both the efficiency of the Civil Service and the quality of the services provided by government departments and agencies.

The Civil Service White Paper of 1994[6]

Much criticised by Sir Peter Kemp and right-wing commentators such as those writing for *The Economist*, for 'allowing the mandarins to get away with it',[7] the White Paper known as *Continuity and Change* nevertheless contained much that was of considerable consequence for the future of the Civil Service. The contrary view, taken by Kemp, was that yet again the Senior Civil Service had escaped the logical consequences of those reforms in the service which so drastically affected the lower and middle ranks. As he said, ironically, 'For the great bulk of the Civil Service the changes now in hand will continue, while for mandarins the *status quo* will not change. That is presumably why the document is called *Continuity and Change*.'[8]

There were seven major proposals included in the White Paper:

1 Departments and agencies must be given full autonomy in the development of efficiency programmes – including forward planning through annual performance reviews.
2 Departments should take far more responsibility for pay and staffing matters for all rank-and-file officials below senior administrative levels.
3 There should be the development of a 'leaner and fitter' service by removing unnecessary layers from the hierarchical management structures.
4 The creation of new senior management dispensations under which the old 'Senior Open Structure', which included the top three grades of the Civil Service, will disappear and be replaced with the broader structure of a new 'Senior Civil Service', taking in the top five grades of the Civil Service and including the chief executives of government agencies.
5 Members of the Senior Civil Service should be given individual service contracts, with their pay fixed according to the criteria of responsibility and performance.
6 All senior posts must be openly advertised, with the aim of attracting the most talented people available, the intention also being to encourage high

flyers from the world of industry and commerce to apply for entry into the Civil Service.
7 Trimming of Civil Service numbers to continue, with what remains of the Civil Service to be cut to a total of less than 500,000 by 1998.

At the heart of these proposals was the desire to seek ever-greater efficiency as a continuation of the Next Steps programme. In order to allow departments and agencies to do so they were permitted to choose their own plans and measures for improving efficiency. As of 1995, departments were presented with a budget which placed a ceiling on spending over a three-year period and individual departments were then expected to draw up annual efficiency plans that would keep department spending strictly within the limits imposed by the three-year budget. The ability to choose the means by which these budget targets were observed was delegated to the departments and agencies, leaving them free to *market-test, contract out* or *privatise* as they wished but also offering new management techniques such as linking costs to objectives through **priority-based cost management**; comparing performance with the best practice of other organisations in the process known as **benchmarking**; or rethinking current procedures in **process re-engineering**. New budgeting procedures known as **resource accounting** were to be introduced as of April 1997 so as to provide more accurate information about the costs borne by a department in providing its services, encouraging departments to seek alternative and cheaper ways of working.

By 1994 some 60 per cent of civil servants had their pay and position in the grading structure fixed within their own departments as a result of agreements which delegated pay bargaining from the centre to the place of work. The 1994 White Paper extended this process to all civil servants below senior administrative levels, as of April 1996. As a result, the centrally-negotiated national Civil Service pay agreements, that in some ways had not been altered since the days of the Whitley Councils set up in the 1920s, were now replaced by a more federal model which encompassed many diverse and autonomous arrangements. And a major factor in these arrangements, as stated in the Management Code, was the recognition that there should be a 'close and effective link between pay and performance'.

One factor which was heavily stressed in the White Paper was the excessive number of management levels in the bureaucratic hierarchy of any average government department. The central grading system of the time allowed for anything up to a total of 14 levels between the top and bottom of a departmental hierarchy. Bearing in mind the way in which bureaucratic practice demands that communications are passed up and down the chain of command until the need for a decision reaches the required level of competence, there was a feeling that departments and agencies were over-large and too stratified for efficient running, with lines of communication becoming over-stretched. There was talk of 'delayering' by which the intention was to strip out the unnecessary layers or levels from the department. The intention of this creation of a 'flatter' service was:

- to remove 'unnecessary layers' in the management chain;
- to enable management decisions to be carried out at the most appropriate level;
- to remove 'unwarranted supervision and duplication of effort'; and
- to empower officials to make decisions without the need to refer the question up or down the hierarchical chain.

It was repeatedly stressed that these reforms were all to do with efficiency, with the smooth running of government services and nothing more, but suspicions were aroused by the emphasis that was placed on 'delayering', together with the declaration in the White Paper that Civil Service numbers should be reduced to a figure 'significantly below' 500,000. Critics, especially those in Labour, the other opposition parties and in the unions, found it easier to believe that 'delayering' was simply a more acceptable way of saying 'staff cuts', and represented a politically correct euphemism for redundancy. Because of the way in which trade union activities had been sidelined by successive Tory administrations there was very little that the Civil Service unions could do except protest at these new cuts, protests that could be dismissed as an old-fashioned hankering for the past which would resist any progressive move for change.

The new Senior Civil Service

These moves towards greater efficiency in the service were mere sideshows, however, compared with the main proposal of the 1994 White Paper, which was the intention to restructure completely the higher grades of the Civil Service. Until 1996, when *Continuity and Change* was put into operation, the most senior officials within the policy-making structure of the service, the administrators known familiarly as 'Whitehall mandarins', were represented by the 'Open Structure', made up of about 650 officials on the top three grades. The White Paper replaced these with a much larger senior management group called the Senior Civil Service, made up of all civil servants of grade 5 and above, including the chief executives of Next Steps agencies, and numbering about 3,500 officials.

Remuneration for this Senior Civil Service was also due to change, so as to produce a 'smaller but better paid Civil Service'. There were two main reasons for increasing the salaries paid to these senior positions:

1)   Posts in the Civil Service no longer had the security of tenure they once had. Civil servants in the past had quite cheerfully accepted less pay than senior personnel elsewhere as a price worth paying for a 'safe' job. The loss of that

security meant that civil servants could well demand equality of pay with the private sector, since senior officials accepted risks equal to those faced by senior management in industry and commerce.

2) The government wanted to see senior management from industry and commerce applying for positions in government agencies. They particularly wanted the chief executives of large private concerns to transfer and become the chief executives of Next Steps agencies. And, if the agencies were to have any hope of attracting the desired talent from the private sector, this would obviously involve paying a package of salary and performance-related bonuses which together more nearly approached the current market rate for the job. And, since the chief executives of the larger agencies were equivalent of the grade 2 level of departmental civil servants, the sort of remuneration thought suitable for agency executives was applied by inference to all senior civil servants.

The new pay structure involved a single pay range for all Permanent Secretaries, the position of an individual Permanent Secretary within that range being determined by the Senior Salaries Review Body (SSRB) and the Permanent Secretaries Remuneration Committee. Below the level of Permanent Secretary the old system of grades, based on a centrally agreed spine, was replaced by a framework of 9 overlapping pay bands linked to responsibility and ability and according to what is known as 'job weight'. Each Permanent Secretary would place members of their staff on a point within a salary range commensurate with the marketability of the individual's skills, experience and ability to handle responsibility: in other words, a form of performance-related pay.

As regards recruitment, the Civil Service Commission only become involved where recruitment from outside the service is concerned. Internal appointments and promotions within the Senior Civil Service are all at the dispensation of the departments themselves; except for appointments to grades 1, 1A and 2, these top three pay bands being known as the 'SASC Group' of posts because these appointments are made by the prime minister on the advice of the Cabinet Secretary as Head of the Civil Service, who is advised in turn by the Senior Appointments Selection Committee (SASC).

There were those who expected this latest batch of reforms to get rid of the Fast Stream as a means of recruitment for generalist graduates into the administrative structure of the service. However, a *Review of Fast Stream Recruitment*, carried out by the OPS and published alongside the 1994 White Paper, recommended that the practice should continue, simply because the graduate labour market remained highly competitive. 'Whatever the fluctuations from year to year, it makes no sense for the Civil Service to withdraw from the top end of the graduate market.'[9]

It should be very clear that the White Paper of 1994 did not produce a 'new Civil Service' but what it did make clear is the fact that, while what we tend to think and speak of as the Civil Service is in fact just this small elite group of senior civil servants, the Whitehall mandarins, there is another larger and possibly more significant Civil Service that tends to be ignored. As Sir Peter Kemp said:

> What the White Paper finally recognises is that there are two (or perhaps many more) Civil Services. Essentially, on the one hand, there are top people we all think we know about, now about 3,500, to be entitled the Senior Civil Service . . . on the other hand about 500,000 invisible people, who do the work. The White Paper at last addresses the existence of an enormously diversified set of services, delivering what needs to be done in the best way it can be done, whether publicly or privately. It finally buries the idea of the old monolithic Civil Service, which has hampered thinking for so long.[10]

Report of the Treasury and Civil Service Committee

At the same time as the government had been preparing its White Paper, an important Commons' select committee was also looking critically at the role of the Civil Service. The report of the Treasury and Civil Service Committee (TCSC) was published not long after the appearance of the White Paper and largely endorsed the government's reforms; particularly the Next Steps programme and the Citizen's Charter initiative. On one issue, however, the TCSC was hesitant and doubtful. This issue was the issue of accountability.

Members of the Committee admitted to being confused over the dividing line between government ministers and agency chief executives and particularly as it affected the difference between control of policy and operational control. The constitutional convention of ministerial responsibility, by which a minister is responsible for the actions of all the officials under his or her control, remained theoretically in force. Yet the question remained as to how far ministers could be held responsible for the actions of government agencies that have been given a considerable degree of autonomy and that are often expected to respond to the demands of market forces. The new convention grew that ministers are responsible for policy matters while chief executives are responsible for operational matters. The question then becomes one of concern as to how parliament can hold an agency accountable for its actions when the new cop-out for a minister is to claim that all questions raised by parliament are to do with operational matters over which he or she has no responsibility. One of the recommendations made by the Committee to resolve this dilemma was that officials in charge of government agencies should be made accountable to parliamentary select committees rather than to a departmental minister. At the same time the Committee warned about declining standards in the Civil Service as the reforms introduced under the Next Steps programme for the sake of cost efficiency came into conflict with the traditional values of impartiality and integrity on the part of civil servants. The issue of accountability will be considered in more detail in the next chapter.

Taking both the 1994 White Paper and the TCSC report into consideration, the government proposed in January 1995 that there should be a new Code of Conduct for the Civil Service which would spell out in concrete terms just what was to be expected of the service. It was also proposed that there should be a new appeals procedure whereby breaches of the new code could be reported to the Civil Service Commissioners. There was surprise on the part of many observers at the acceptance by the government of the Code of Conduct because the traditional Civil Service values enshrined within the code were seen as often incompatible with the managerial revolution within the service (for full details of the Civil Service Code, see Appendix 5). However, although the government accepted the idea of a Code of Conduct as put forward by the TCSC, they were unwilling to accept any moves which were intended to make agency chief executives directly accountable to parliament. The government were determined that ministerial responsibility would remain as the sole conventional expression of accountability to parliament.

Civil Service morale

Government and parliament had shown in the White Papers and Committee reports of 1994 that they were happy with the scope and direction of those reforms that had been imposed on the Civil Service. Very little attention, however, was paid to what the civil servants themselves thought of these changes. However, in 1996, the *Observer* newspaper commissioned the research organisation ICM to examine much more closely the attitudes assumed by civil servants in respect of the various changes that had been carried out to reform the service and, by inference, what the attitude of civil servants was towards those Conservative governments which had initiated the reforms. In 1996 this was obviously relevant given the imminent prospect of a change to a Labour administration after the 1997 election. The research findings[11] showed that changes in the Civil Service have indeed led to a significant decline in the standards and morale of the service:

- 92 per cent of civil servants believed that morale was much lower in 1996 than it had been in 1992.
- 91 per cent believed the government had gone too far in its privatisation of Civil Service functions.
- 77 per cent said they would welcome a change of government.
- 73 per cent claimed that they would not recommend the Civil Service as a career to young people today.
- Only 28 per cent of respondents believed that their jobs were secure.

It was this general feeling of unease in the Civil Service, coupled with the suspicion on the part of many civil servants that the worst aspects of Civil Service reform were the product of an ideological stance by the Conservative administration rather than being intended to improve the general quality of the service, which led many members of the Civil Service to come round to an attitude of mind which actually welcomed the thought of an incoming Labour government. Senior civil servants and shadow ministers were involved in serious discussions on the policy implications of the Labour manifesto for quite some time before the election of May 1997 and the smooth handover of power after that election was a tribute to the way in which civil servants fell in behind the new government's strategies with a degree of commitment towards making them work.

As for the new government's attitude towards the Civil Service there seemed to be very little change at first. The one positive move towards reversing policies introduced by the Tories was the restoration of trade union rights at Government Communication Headquarters (GCHQ) but it was so long after the original ban and there were so few workers left at GCHQ who were still affected by it, that the lifting of it was little more than symbolic, carrying out a commitment written into Labour policy as long ago as the 1980s but which could only now be fulfilled. In another respect, however, as has already been discussed at length in Chapter 5, comments that had been made by Labour politicians in the past about feeling uneasy over the replacement of Civil Service advisers by political appointees, proved to be rather hollow when the Blair administration managed to employ almost twice as many advisers as any previous government and Tony Blair even attempted to have his political chief of staff, Jonathan Powell, appointed as his Private Secretary in place of a career civil servant.

A month after the election, on 17 June 1997, the then Chancellor of the Duchy of Lancaster, Dr David Clark, who had special responsibilities for the Civil Service through the Office of Public Service, delivered a speech after which he answered questions about the new government's attitude towards the Civil Service. The main point seemed to be that there was little change of direction foreseen in the immediate future, the emphasis seeming to be upon the continuation of the managerial revolution, consolidating and extending the reforms introduced over the last two decades. Points made by Clark included:[12]

- There would be a Freedom of Information Act, which would mean a further erosion of Civil Service anonymity. Ironically, as will be discussed in the next chapter, this measure has proved very slow to emerge amid the other constitutional reforms introduced by the Blair government; a delay which seems to bear out the old adage that governments and bureaucracies thrive on secrecy.
- There is a commitment to retaining, improving and expanding management structures for the Civil Service. Clark described the Civil Service as 'the corporate oil within which the wheels of government work'.
- Reform of pay structures will continue, including devolved pay, performance-related pay and conditions of employment that are in line with the commercial world.

- There ought to be a greater interchange of personnel between departments, agencies and outside organisations. As Clark said, 'Most of the top Civil Service posts will continue to be filled by people with substantial experience in departments and agencies. They will be working alongside others who have been successful in the open competitions and can bring outside experience to bear on the problems we face.'
- The public service ethos, 'that has slipped in recent years . . . because of restraints imposed by politicians', should be restored.

Nine months later Dr Clark announced a change of direction for the Next Steps programme which rather consolidated the programme reviews and committee reports of the last few years. According to Clark, the target of extending the Next Steps programme to cover 75 per cent of all civil servants, a target which had seemed virtually impossible back in 1988, had finally been achieved in 1997, with no less than 76 per cent of all civil servants (a total of 383,000) working in the 138 agencies and four departments which now operate on Next Steps lines. Speaking of the many improvements in efficiency produced by the Next Steps policy, Clark went on to say that he felt that

> the full potential benefits from this change to Civil Service organisation remain to be achieved. We have analysed agency performance data and have found that we need to look more closely at performance, which has been overshadowed by the emphasis on agency creation. Although some new agencies will continue to be created, we have decided to close off the agency creation phase of the Next Steps policy, and launch a new phase with the focus on performance.[13]

On the same day as Clark made this statement, the *Next Steps Report 1997* was published, outlining four areas of action for the future:

1 Ministers must take a close interest in the targets they set for their agencies, not only in monitoring their performance but also in the way that performance is reported, so that everyone can receive all the information they require so as to make an objective assessment of that performance.
2 Agencies must assess themselves for best practice in being able to improve the quality and efficiency of services, through comparing the standard of service they offer with a whole range of similar organisations, in both the public and private sectors, both in this country and abroad.
3 Agencies must be encouraged to co-operate not only with other government agencies but with other bodies in both the public and private sectors, so that through this co-operation the public might have access to the very best of services.
4 Ministers must work to remove all confusion as to where accountability of agencies should lie. For the sake of efficiency there has to be some delegation of responsibility from Ministers to the executive staff of the agencies but sight must not be lost of the fact that the creation of agencies does not itself affect ministerial accountability to parliament.[14]

Recruitment and appointment in the 'new' Senior Civil Service

As has been discussed previously, the reforms of recent years mean that virtually all civil servants are appointed and promoted by the departments in which
they work, often with pay and working conditions being dictated by autonomous departmental agreements. The case of senior civil servants from the old
'Open Structure' is rather different, however. Permanent Secretaries and
Deputy Secretaries are appointed at the centre by the prime minister. The prime
minister is assisted in this by the Cabinet Secretary as Head of the Home Civil
Service and both of them are helped and guided by the Senior Appointments
Selection Committee (SASC), which sifts through names put forward by the
departments in order to draw up a short list.

The SASC has changed somewhat in recent years, its composition now
being determined by guidelines laid down in the 1994 White Paper,
Continuity and Change. The most important member of the committee is the
First Civil Service Commissioner who has the final say on certain key decisions but the committee is also required to have at least one woman member
and one member from outside the world of government or public administration, such as a senior business executive (in 1998 the representative outsider was Sir Michael Angus, Chairman of the Whitbread group of
companies). Also as a result of *Continuity and Change*, the position of First
Civil Service Commissioner is advertised when vacant and appointed by open
competition.

The key in these senior appointments, however, lies with the relationship
between prime minister and cabinet secretary and with the role that the prime
minister chooses to play. The prime minister may be a totally passive observer
who cheerfully rubber-stamps suggestions made by the Secretary to the Cabinet
and the SASC. On the other hand, the prime minister can be very active indeed,
scrapping short lists and insisting on names not being otherwise considered.
Margaret Thatcher was notorious for her involvement in the appointment of
Permanent Secretaries; witness the notoriety achieved by her query, 'Is he one
of us?' When Sir Douglas Wass retired as Permanent Secretary at the Treasury,
he wrote a carefully reasoned memo to the prime minister recommending a
senior civil servant as his successor. It was a convention that a senior civil
servant's nomination of a successor was almost always a formality as it would
inevitably be accepted. On this occasion, the suggestion was rejected outright
by Mrs Thatcher who wanted her own preferred candidate, Peter Middleton, for
the job. A politician who saw Sir Douglas's memo said that it was 'a consummate piece of mandarin analysis. But it pointed towards a man whom the prime
minister, in her determination to have the right machine in place, did not want
to have.'[15]

Traditionally, all senior civil servants were appointed centrally in this
way, usually from a list of internal candidates. Reforms such as those
ushered in by the Oughton Report and others have led to a much greater

proportion of senior posts being openly advertised, with appointment being subject to open competition and candidates from outside the service being welcomed. As was said in the White Paper, *Continuity and Change* (on page 3). 'Departments and agencies will always consider advertising openly posts at these levels when a vacancy occurs, and then will use open competition wherever it is justifiable in the interest of providing a strong field or of introducing new blood.'

When senior positions become available for appointment, the First Civil Service Commissioner will advise as to whether open competition or internal appointment would be more appropriate. The sort of question to be asked when making that decision was outlined in *Continuity and Change* (on page 41): 'Is there a sufficient field of candidates already within the department, or in order to get a strong field is it necessary to extend the search to the wider Civil Service or to full open competition?' Yet, despite these pressures for posts to be openly advertised and competitive so as to encourage outsiders to apply, all the evidence is that while an increasing number of vacancies are open to external candidates, the actual proportion of external candidates who are actually appointed is going down. According to government figures issued in 1996, the situation in 1992 was that 16.3 per cent of vacancies were openly advertised and 10 per cent of those appointed were external candidates. By 1995 the percentage of vacancies advertised had risen to 29.6 per cent but the proportion of external appointments had barely risen to 13 per cent. Even the Next Steps agencies, which deliberately set out to attract chief executives from the private sector, fared no better. Research by Horton and Jones for the *Public Policy and Administration* journal in 1996 showed that 69 per cent of the 131 chief executives then in place were recruited by open competition but that only 37 per cent of those openly recruited were outsiders. Even the terms 'insider' and 'outsider' are deceptive here: the term 'outsiders' does not necessarily imply the private sector but only that the candidate is external as far as the Civil Service is concerned: more often than not it refers to candidates from elsewhere in the public sector or from the armed services. Of 175 chief executives considered by Horton and Jones between 1988 and 1996, only 13 per cent actually came from the private sector.[16]

Generally speaking, the terms of employment for the service as a whole, including the new Senior Civil Service, has moved from a centrally recruited service, with rigidly fixed grades of pay and security of tenure, to a service where officials have individually determined pay scales and employment according to a written contract of service. Many senior civil servants are now appraised for their managerial skills and part of their pay is performance-related but, nevertheless, there is still a distinction between the terms of employment offered to a departmental civil servant and to a civil servant employed in a government agency.

Conclusion

The question remains as to how far the changes in the Civil Service can be described as revolutionary. And the answer has to be that the changes fall drastically short of anything that might be called even mildly revolutionary. There has been:

- decentralisation and a growing autonomy of departments and agencies;
- changes to a managerial rather than a bureaucratic organisational structure;
- open competition for appointments and the encouragement of external candidates;
- performance related-pay, individually rather than centrally negotiated; and
- contracts of employment and service.

Yet the Civil Service remains recognisably the territory of generalist and graduate career civil servants, recruited and promoted from within. Sir Peter Kemp called his monograph on the 1994 White Paper *The Mandarins Escape Unscathed* and this epitomises the position as it exists in that, no matter how much or how often the service may be reformed, restructured, revitalised, revolutionised or even stood on its head, the Sir Humphrey Applebys of the service will continue to flourish, virtually indistinguishable from their predecessors.

Notes

1 Cabinet Office, *Civil Service Management Code*, Machinery of Government and Propriety Division of the Cabinet Office (Office of Public Service and Science), 1996.

2 Efficiency Unit, *Career Management and Succession Planning Study* (the Oughton Report), HMSO, London, 1993, p. 1.

3 These comments, made to and reported by the Oughton Committee, are quoted in Geoffrey Fry, *Policy and Management in the British Civil Service*, Prentice Hall/Harvester Wheatsheaf, Hemel Hempstead, 1995, pp. 127–8.

4 Rachel Bayliss and Charlotte Dargie, 'The Senior Civil Service in the 1990s', in Steve Lancaster (ed.), *Developments in Politics*, Vol. 9, Causeway Press, Ormskirk, 1998, p. 82.

5 Reported in the *Financial Times*, 14 July 1994 and quoted in Tony Butcher, 'The Civil Service in the 1990s: The Revolution Rolls On', *Talking Politics*, Vol. 8, No. 1, Autumn 1995 – source of much of the information given here as to the reform programme after Next Steps.

6 White Paper Cm. 2627, *The Civil Service: Continuity and Change*, HMSO, London, 1994.

7 *The Economist*, 16 July 1994, quoted in Fry, Note 3 above, p. 130.

8 Sir Peter Kemp, *The Mandarins Emerge Unscathed*, Parliamentary Brief 2, No 10, 1994, p. 49.

9 Report by the OPS, 1994, quoted by Fry, Note 3 above, p. 133.

10 Kemp, Note 8 above, p. 50.

11   Research conducted by ICM/*Observer* during March 1996. 10,000 questionnaires were given to members of two civil service unions. 1,911 completed questionnaires were returned, despite warnings from Sir Robin Butler, Head of the Civil Service, that the survey should be ignored.
12   Reported by Bayliss and Dargie, Note 4 above, p. 95.
13   Dr Clark made his statement on the Next Steps programme, in the Commons, on 12 March 1998, in answer to a parliamentary question from Alan Williams, MP for Carmarthen East and Dinefwr.
14   Command Paper No. 3889, *Next Steps Report 1997*, HMSO, London, 1998.
15   The story is told in Hugo Young, *One of Us*, Macmillan, London, 1989, p. 337.
16   Figures given by Bayliss and Dargie, Note 4 above, p. 83.

9

Secrecy and accountability

The civil servant as secret servant

Open government is a contradiction in terms. You can be open – or you can have government.   Lynn and Jay, *Yes Minister*, 1981

The Civil Service has always been notorious for being rather less than open with the general public – the people whom it is supposed to serve – and has instead developed a reputation for being a closed system, hidden from the wide world which lies outside government circles. Between civil servants and the public a barrier of sorts has been erected which is constructed from a mixture of part secrecy and part manipulation of the truth. It was Sir Robert Armstrong, as Cabinet Secretary, who recast a saying of Burke's to imply that while civil servants may not actually lie for their political masters they were certainly capable of being 'economical with the truth', concealing what truth there may be in over-complex arguments and over-verbose documentation.

The image presented by the Civil Service is therefore all too often one of obsessive secrecy and the prevention of facts being made available, as if the mere fact of revealing the truth might in itself cause the Civil Service irreparable harm. In the past, this air of secrecy and arcane mystery which has pervaded the Civil Service, along with the draconian discipline of the Official Secrets Act, has managed to keep many salient facts about the country's administration away from the eyes and ears of the public at large. Obviously, this has also had considerable implications concerning the nature of accountability in the Civil Service, since the question which must naturally be asked is how can civil servants be held accountable for their actions when the actions themselves, and the persons carrying out those actions, are shrouded in self-generated mists of secrecy? In other words, how can you obtain answers and an explanation, if you do not know what the question should be in the first place? This inclination towards secrecy is further obscured by the doctrine of ministerial responsibility and the conventional anonymity of civil servants, which means that any member of the public wanting to call the administration to account for some action or another is unable to point the finger at the actual persons responsible, and instead has to submit a vague and non-specific accusation.

In the past, any assumptions on the part of a trusting general public as to the nature of Civil Service accountability took the form of passive acceptance that a strong sense of public duty felt by civil servants would ensure that they only worked for the general good: the use of the word 'service' in the term 'Civil Service' being taken literally as meaning an altruistic need to be of service to the community. Moreover, it was felt that any failure of this public-spirited altruism would be rectified by the ability of ministers and senior officials to keep civil servants in line, in the name of good and smooth government, using the carrot-and-stick approach in which the carrot is the chance of promotion and an OBE on retirement while the stick is the Official Secrets Act.

In recent years, however, a public opinion that had grown increasingly sceptical about the good intentions of government was rendered ever more cynical by abuses such as the 'Arms for Iraq' scandal and the general air of sleaze which filled the last years of the Major government. Disillusioned about the probity of the Civil Service, public opinion has swung its support behind the idea of demanding openness in government, with a growing certainty that we should not place too much reliance on civil servants having such a highly-developed sense of duty. The general view of the accountability of civil servants has therefore moved away from reliance on some loose form of regulation by senior officials and ministers to a belief that public servants should be accountable first and foremost to the actual general public which both employs them and represent their customers and clients. Furthermore, public opinion has also realised that there should be a recognisable framework for this accountability.

While recognising the considerable range of duties and activities that are encompassed within the Civil Service as a whole, it is nevertheless possible as a generalisation to divide the work of civil servants into three broad categories:

1 There is the central core of the Whitehall departments, mostly represented by senior civil servants, in which the duty of officials is to provide policy advice for ministers, giving verbal and written submissions and briefings, drafting legislation and helping ministers to uphold their policies in the light of scrutiny.
2 The management function of the Civil Service is to ensure that departments of state and executive agencies are efficient and well-run. This includes, first and foremost, the effective financial management of budgets, staffing and resources to provide both the *correct* and the *efficient* use of those budgets, staff and resources.
3 Finally, there is service delivery, which is the main working activity of the majority of civil servants. This can be as simple as manning a desk in the local Job Centre or dealing with social security claimants; at a higher level,

if the civil servant belongs to a minister's private office, it could mean accompanying their minister on an official visit to a Midlands factory, maintaining their minister's appointments diary or carrying out routine duties in the minister's name.[1]

These three types of tasks and functions carried out by the Civil Service are mirrored in the three ways by which civil servants might be regarded as being accountable.

1 Internal accountability: by which civil servants are accountable to their own line managers and ministers within the department or agency for the effectiveness of their actions.
2 External accountability: which largely means accountability to the people through parliament, either in the normal indirect way through the department minister, or directly inasmuch as civil servants may be accountable to a parliamentary select committee or to the Parliamentary Commissioner for Administration (Ombudsman).
3 Public accountability is a more recent development in that it makes officials answerable to the general public, often through what was originally called the Citizen's Charter but which is now part of Labour's 'Better Government' programme under the title 'Service First'.

According to the constitutional convention of ministerial responsibility, which makes a government minister personally responsible to the people, as represented in parliament, for the actions of all civil servants in the departments and agencies under his or her control, the constitutional position is clearly that 'the accountability of civil servants begins and ends with internal accountability'.[2] And, as was said in the previous chapter, when discussing the 1997 Next Steps report, we should not lose sight of the fact that the mere act of creating semi-autonomous agencies does not in itself affect ministerial accountability to parliament. And this in turn makes the nature and extent of a civil servant's internal accountability all the more important.

The Civil Service Management Code

The terms and conditions of employment in the Civil Service, including the place of civil servants on the hierarchical ladder of the service, together with the nature of their duties and responsibilities within the line management structures of their departments or agencies, are all set out in the Civil Service Management Code, much of which is now included in a civil servant's contract of employment. The Management Code is a defining document that was issued as the result of a Civil Service Order in Council of 1995 and which incorporates rules drawn up at that time by the Minister for the Civil Service in answer to the demands of the Civil Service (Management Functions) Act of 1992.[3] The 1992

Act was itself the product of reforms in the 1980s and early 1990s which had delegated a degree of autonomy to departments and agencies, granting them a certain discretion to determine for themselves the terms and conditions under which the staff of each individual department might be expected to work.

The purpose of the 1992 Act, and the Management Code that was issued to reinforce it in 1996, was to replace the former constitutional position whereby all responsibility for the Civil Service was in the hands of the Treasury and the Cabinet Office – the latter being represented by the Office of Public Service and Science (OPS). It was to these two departments that all civil servants were accountable prior to the 1990s but there was an anomalous situation in that this concentrated centralisation was directly contrary to a belief in the necessity to 'roll back the frontiers of the state', the anti-statist ethos common to those Conservative governments which held office between 1979 and 1997. As the then Chancellor of the Duchy of Lancaster and Minister for the OPS, William Waldegrave, said of this centralised regime during the course of the House of Commons debate introducing the 1992 Act, 'Whether it is sensible or not – I do not think that it can be – decisions affecting the working conditions of all 560,000 or so civil servants must conform to rules laid down by the two central departments, and those rules, like the laws of the Medes and Persians, must then be obeyed.'[4] The purpose of the 1992 Act, according to Waldegrave, was to move away from this centralisation so that personnel management functions previously operated solely at the centre were to be progressively devolved to departments and agencies for their individual development.

The ultimate responsibility for holding civil servants accountable within government departments is quite clearly shared between the Secretary of State and the Permanent Secretary but the matter is less clearcut in those government agencies where there is already doubt as to the dividing line between the minister responsible for policy and the chief executive responsible for operational matters. The actual code states that 'the presumption is that functions delegated to ministers and office holders will, in respect of agencies, be exercised by agency chief executives but the precise extent to which ministers and office holders may wish to allow the exercise of their powers by chief executives is a matter for them to determine'. The problems that can arise from a vagueness and imprecision in assigning accountability in this area, as for example the problems experienced by Derek Lewis at the Prison Service, have already been fully discussed.

The general principles of the code of behaviour to which the Civil Service works, according to the Management Code, are very much in line with the old Civil Service ethos, in particular that:

- Civil servants must be, and must be seen to be, honest and impartial in the exercise of their duties and must serve without fear or favour whichever political grouping happens to form the government of the day.

- Civil servants must not allow their judgment or integrity to be compromised by any suspicion of self-interested behaviour, or by the acceptance of gifts or favours which might compromise their independence of judgment.
- Civil servants must not misuse information for their own ends, particularly for their own financial benefit, nor should they offer themselves for employment in a situation where knowledge or experience gained in the Civil Service might be of particular use to their new employer.
- Civil servants must not take part in political activities nor exhibit partisanship over contentious matters, in such a way as either to undermine or to influence unduly the position of their own minister.

These and other prohibitions are listed in the Civil Service Code of Conduct (see Appendix 5) which was issued on 1 January 1996 at the request of the Treasury and Civil Service Select Committee of the House of Commons and which is directly modelled on the Code of Conduct for Members of Parliament demanded by the Nolan Committee. The Civil Service Code is published as a separate document but it is also included as an integral part of the Management Code and can be said to list those sorts of activities for which civil servants might be held accountable, with particular regard to internal assessment, scrutiny and discipline.

The two-way process within the Civil Service by which the administration of discipline in handed down and the accountability for an individual's actions is referred up, follows the rigid channels of line management within a bureaucratic hierarchy. The senior civil servants within a government department are, in ascending order:

- Assistant Secretary;
- Under-Secretary;
- Deputy Secretary;
- Permanent Secretary.

Each of these is accountable to the rank immediately above their own within the department, except for the Permanent Secretary who fills the department's most senior position in the department, other than the minister himself or herself, and who therefore is answerable to only one superior in the person of the Cabinet Secretary as Head of the Civil Service. Below the senior officials of the department, the hierarchy extends downwards, with everyone down to the level of clerical officer having an immediate superior to whom they are answerable for their efficiency and effectiveness at work. Much the same pattern exists in the government agencies, although there is a dilemma over accountability at the top, as we have already discussed at some length, because it is not too clear as to whether it is the minister or the chief executive who is accountable for decisions on operational matters.

One aspect of accountability that has always had an importance for public administration is the field of financial management and control; the very word 'accountability' carrying overtones of auditing the accounts. Ever since the days of Gladstone there has been an awareness that the Civil Service is responsible for spending public money which has been contributed by the nation's taxpayers and it is therefore inevitable that there have to be procedures by means of which any such expenditure is justified to the satisfaction of those same taxpayers. To this accountability for the *correct* use of public money, the reforms of the 1980s, such as the Financial Management Initiative (FMI), added accountability for the *efficient* use of public money.

In 1985 a Cabinet Office report on the FMI recommended that all policy proposals made by government departments should be accompanied by plans for measuring the effectiveness of that policy. As of 1985, Performance Review Reports therefore formed part of every department's implementation of the FMI. In 1986 the Treasury added to these performance indicators by introducing running cost controls and cash limits for government departments, as a result of which those government departments that exceeded their estimated day-to-day running costs would be unable to cover the shortfall by transferring funds from capital expenditure, except with the explicit approval of the Chief Secretary to the Treasury and parliament. The financial stringency involved as a result of these measures gained the hearty approval of the National Audit Office and the Comptroller and Auditor General.

These measures gained even more importance with the introduction of the Next Steps programme since each executive agency was given performance targets, standards of service and performance indicators, these in turn being linked with the agency's strategic objectives. In terms of internal discipline the line management within both departments and agencies has become as much concerned with the efficiency and cost-effectiveness of civil servants as with their conduct within the traditional Civil Service ethos.

External accountability

As is well known, there are channels in parliament through which MPs can question ministers but, as a means of controlling the executive, it is flawed by the principle of ministerial responsibility, under the conventions of which civil servants are anonymous and their actions shrouded in secrecy. Hence the impotence and inability of an individual MP to get at the truth when faced with the silence of an intransigent minister or the blank wall of Civil Service secrecy. If the minister is reluctant to accept responsibility and the identity of the responsible officials remains unknown there is very little an individual MP can do, either to extract an explanation or to force the executive to make amends.

However, events such as the prosecutions of Sarah Tisdall and Clive Ponting in the 1980s or the revelation of Colette Bowe's complicity in the government's dirty tricks operation during the Westland Affair, events which resulted in the publication of Sir Robert Armstrong's Memorandum on Civil Service behaviour (all matters discussed at length in Chapter 5), have combined with a growing reluctance on the part of ministers to accept responsibility for the actions of their departments, to give rise to new calls for more open government, including new demands for administrators to be held accountable for maladministration.

Since the Fulton Report in the late 1960 the opportunities which exist for challenging the conduct of the administration through parliament have considerably increased and there are now two main parliamentary avenues open:

1 An individual MP, acting on behalf of an individual member of the public, or a group, can challenge the government through the constitutional device of the Ombudsman.
2 If those challenging the government have more influence – if they have the support of the Opposition, a major pressure group or the media, for example – then they may be able to force an examination of the issue by a parliamentary select committee.

The term **Ombudsman** is Swedish and literally means *a grievance man*. Originating in Scandinavia, the Ombudsman was created as a sort of 'tribune of the people' to whom individuals could take their complaints about bureaucratic mistakes or the errors of government. These complaints the Ombudsman would then investigate in a judicial sense, seeking redress if the administration was found to be at fault.

Demands for the creation of such a post in Britain came with a report published in 1961 by the legal group *Justice*.[5] This called for the introduction of an independent judicial figure who could deal with errors and faults in government bureaucracy. The suggestion was much resented by senior civil servants and constitutional lawyers who saw the creation of such a post as subverting two mainstays of the constitution – the supremacy of parliament and ministerial responsibility – as well as discarding Civil Service anonymity and neutrality. In the face of this opposition and hostility the report was shelved for a time.

However, under Wilson's Labour government in 1967, the post of Parliamentary Commissioner for Administration (PCA) was created as the result of a bill introduced by Richard Crossman. The Ombudsman himself was to be assisted by a staff of between 60 and 90 civil servants, supervised by a nine-member select committee. According to Crossman, the remit of the Ombudsman was to check on such bureaucratic abuses as 'bias, neglect, inattention, delay, incompetence, ineptitude, perversity, turpitude, arbitrariness, and so on'.[6] This sounded like a satisfactory remit but the position, when finally defined, was considerably more restricted than had originally been envisaged, in terms of both access and jurisdiction. This was made clear in 1977 when *Justice* published the Widdicombe Report, an examination of the first ten years' operation of the PCA's office,[7] and found that the office of Ombudsman operated rather less effectively than had originally been envisaged, because of a large number of restrictions that had been imposed during the framing of rules governing the institution:

- *There is limited access.* Members of the public are not allowed to approach the PCA directly themselves but must go through the medium of their constituency MP. This is not the case for the Ombudsmen for either National Health or Local Government, who can be approached directly: which presumably explains why the NHS ombudsman deals with almost double the number of complaints as the PCA, while the Local Government ombudsman receives something like fifteen times as many. Many people since the Widdicombe investigation have pleaded for there to be the right of direct access to the PCA, including requests for this from the PCA himself, but so far without success.

- *There is no adequate definition of maladministration.* Despite Crossman's claims as to the wide range of complaints the PCA could deal with, there is a limited number of cases where the PCA has jurisdiction. The Ombudsman is not allowed to question the *nature* of decisions but only faults in *procedure*. Which means that even decisions that are shown to be grossly unfair cannot be challenged if correct procedures have been followed. This in turn has meant that only about 10 per cent of complaints have been upheld, because so many complaints fall at the first fence when they are judged not to come within the PCA's remit.

- *The ombudsman has limited jurisdiction.*
    - (i) The PCA must not deal with any matter which might more easily and effectively be dealt with by a law court or tribunal.
    - (ii) The PCA is barred from any consideration of the government's commercial or contractual undertakings.
    - (iii) Only 14 per cent of quangos and other extra-governmental bodies are open to scrutiny by the Ombudsman.

- *There is only limited autonomy.* Many of the early PCAs were former civil servants, the majority of PCA staff are currently civil servants, the department is funded by the Treasury and legal advice comes from government lawyers. This means that investigations into Civil Service maladministration are largely carried out by representatives of the Civil Service, turning the work of the Ombudsman into what is very much a form of self-regulation. When a former Ombudsman, Sir Edmond Compton, gave evidence to the PCA Select Committee he paid tribute to former Civil Service colleagues by suggesting that the fact that he made so few adverse judgments was indicative of the general excellent standard of British administrative procedures – a cynic may have another explanation.

- *Decisions are hard to enforce.* When the PCA has concluded an investigation their reports go to the MP who originally referred the matter to them, with a copy of the report to the department concerned, and there the matter may well rest. There is no mechanism by which the Ombudsman can ensure that any of his recommendations are carried out. This is not true of the Northern Ireland Ombudsman because there the complainant can apply to a county court for redress, if the finding is in their favour. Other than in that one, specifically regional instance, government departments can feel free to ignore any decisions made by the Ombudsman.

Most successful complaints taken before the PCA are in respect of very minor procedural details, the resolution of which does very little for the image of Civil Service accountability. One significant judgment that has been made by the Ombudsman was the Barlow-Clowes case in 1989 where the Department of Trade and Industry was judged to have mishandled their rules and advice on investment and the government was forced to pay out large sums in compensation to aggrieved investors. On the whole, however, it is very seldom that complaints against a government department result in much more than a verbal rebuke.

Select committees

One significant change to the general accountability of civil servants suggested by the Ibbs Report on the Next Steps initiative, was the recommendation that the chief executives of agencies should be directly accountable to parliament as well as to their departmental ministers. However, this was overruled by Mrs Thatcher's government. Although agency staff could be questioned and required to give evidence to departmental select committees, in the same way as departmental civil servants were required to do, such appearances would not make agency staff accountable themselves: their function rather being to assist, support and clarify the position of the minister who is the actual person accountable to the committee.

The modern departmental select committee system with its investigative powers really only dates from the 1960s. There was a feeling then that those faults of the British parliamentary system which can be ascribed to the secrecy with which government surrounds itself could be dispersed if only Britain possessed investigative bodies along the lines of the Congressional committees which exist as important checks and balances in the governmental system of the United States. It was particularly felt that opposition and back-bench MPs were at a distinct disadvantage in countering the government, because they lacked that vital information which government ministers and their civil servants kept concealed from them. The need was felt for a system of committees which could examine government actions with the force and authority of a court of law and with the all-important ability to demand the production of evidence and witnesses from a reluctant administration.

As Leader of the House in Wilson's government of 1966, Richard Crossman used the establishment of departmental select committees to act as a weapon in his proposed reforms of parliamentary procedure, as he had done with the introduction of an Ombudsman. Under his guidance, committees were set up to examine such subjects as agriculture, education and Scottish affairs and were given powers such as the right to 'send for persons, papers and records' but the idea did not progress very much further for the next ten years. It was a Procedure Select Committee of 1976 which recommended the establishment of a series of investigative select committees, each of which would examine the work of an individual government department, 'with wide terms of reference, and with power to appoint specialist advisers as the committees deemed appropriate',[8] and the introduction of departmental select committees was one of the major reforms undertaken during the early days of the Thatcher government of 1979.

> For a government self-consciously bent on radical change, the Stevas reforms of the House of Commons should have been a badge of seriousness . . . Commons select committees shadowed the Whitehall departments from the start of the Thatcher years: a major innovation which ensured that a government which showed great resistance to all forms of openness and accountability was sometimes invigilated quite uncomfortably. The leader had not really wanted this. Stevas pushed it through cabinet when her mind was on larger matters in 1979.[9]

In the course of the Stevas reforms there was a complete shake-up of the select committee system, with some existing committees being abolished while others, such as the Public Accounts Committee, were strengthened. The important innovation, however, was the establishment of departmental committees which had the specific aim of closely scrutinising the departments which they shadowed. From the very first, 12 of these **investigative departmental select committees** were formed. These were: Agriculture, Defence, Education, Employment, Energy, Environment, Foreign Affairs, Home Affairs, Social Services, Trade & Industry, Transport, and Treasury & Civil Service. Very shortly afterwards committees for Scotland and Wales were formed, while the Energy Committee was disbanded when that department was merged with the Department of Trade and Industry in the mid-1980s. As of the 1992 election the number of select committees was 16, due to the formation of committees dealing with Health, National Heritage, and Science & Technology. In 1994, as part of negotiations over the peace process and as a gesture towards the Unionist lobby, a Northern Ireland Committee was formed, although with a different composition and a slightly different remit compared with the others.

The politician members of the committees are helped by officials, who are civil servants from the Clerk's Department of the House of Commons; between three and six being assigned to each committee. Most committees also have one or two full-time research assistants to help with their specialisation; the assistants often being young graduates on short-term contract. Because the committees are dealing with specialised issues and politicians cannot be guaranteed to have, or be in a position to acquire, the expertise required, all the committees also have specialist advisers, usually academic experts from the universities or research establishments, either called in as necessary on a specific inquiry or sometimes holding a watching brief for the whole life of the parliament and committee.

Powers and effectiveness of select committees

• Committees are appointed for the full life of a parliament so that they cannot be dismissed if a government is angered by their findings.

• The choice of topics for investigation is entirely in the hands of the committee members and will be examined even if the government would like to keep the matter concealed. In this way the existence of the committees acts as a deterrent to over-hasty action on the part of ministers or officials, since a minister knows that he or she may be called before a committee to justify and defend publicly his or her actions, while it has long been established that *civil servants have no right to anonymity if censured and called before one of these committees!*

• Committees are free to call anyone to give evidence before them, whether from within or outside parliament, and to call for documentation from any source, having legal powers to compel attendance or submission. They are thus an important agency for open government since they have access to people and information that cannot be reached by MPs' questions on the floor of the House.

• The committees also represent an important way to get information from civil servants and others onto the public record since, not only are committee meetings regarded as public hearings and thus open to press, radio and television, but all the data contained in the written and oral evidence submitted and heard is published for distribution to interested parties.

• Being members of the same specialised committee for several years, and having the services of specialist advisers, the committee members can acquire a substantial and specialised expertise in the area of interest that will prevent ministers and civil servants being able to pull the wool over their eyes. The work of the select committees ensure that MPs of all parties are better informed about the workings of government and are thus better able to challenge government departments and agencies over their conduct of affairs.

There is little doubt that the system of investigative select committees is an important weapon in enforcing the accountability of government ministers and civil servants. Since their introduction in 1979 the committees have produced hundreds of reports and have had a moderate success, perhaps not so much in influencing government policy but certainly in amending or forcing reconsideration of a whole range of legislative or administrative issues such as defence, energy conservation, health service provision and various privatisations. The greatest impact in the long term, however, is probably the deterrent effect represented by the mere existence of the committees. As two political commentators have stated, there is 'much evidence that ministers and civil servants are influenced in policy-making by the knowledge that what they propose may well come under the scrutiny of these committees and by the very process of committee inquiries'.[10]

Shortcomings of the select committees

Having entered on an investigation the committees can still meet with difficulties. It is not so much the difficulty of getting some people, like senior civil servants and ministers, to appear before them, as the difficulty of getting them to answer questions once they are there. This situation was made very clear during attempts by the Defence Committee to investigate the behaviour of civil servants during the Westland Affair in 1985. When the Permanent Secretary of the Department of Trade and Industry, Sir Brian Hayes, was reminded by the committee that they could demand the attendance of the civil servants in question, Hayes replied that they could get the civil servants to attend the committee but their ministers could still forbid them to say a word. Later, Sir Robert Armstrong, Cabinet Secretary and Head of the Civil Service, went before the committee himself to tell them in even stronger terms that the civil servants in question would not appear before them at any time.

As long ago as 1980, an official in the then Civil Service Department, Edward Osmotherly, drew up a Memorandum of Guidance for Officials Appearing Before Select Committees. The Osmotherly memorandum, as it is known, rules out the possibility of any comments being made by civil servants on the subjects of cabinet committees, government legal departments, inter-departmental links, matters of policy or anything that might be regarded as politically controversial. As has already been mentioned in an earlier chapter, the Osmotherly memorandum has been described as 'twenty-five pages of how to say "I'm sorry, Chairman. I can't answer that question. May I refer you to my Minister?"' [11] In 1993, the BBC-TV programme *Scrutiny* unearthed a video-tape made by the Central Office of Information in 1987 which had the express purpose of training officials to become skilled in the evasive techniques which could be used when giving evidence to a select committee. The same programme also unearthed links between civil servants in the departments and those civil servants seconded to help the select committees; links which meant that departmental civil servants very often had advance warning of the questions they were likely to be asked by the select committee.

Because of these flaws it would be easy to dismiss the actions of select committees as being futile but investigation by a select committee does in fact draw the public's attention to an issue and it is a useful weapon to be used against excessive government secrecy. It therefore seems to be the general view that, for all the faults inherent in the system, of which the shortage of resources is the most serious, the departmental select committees have proved the most effective means of democratic scrutiny to have emerged in recent years although, as two prominent commentators have said, 'scrutiny . . . has improved considerably in the last decade; what remains inadequate is parliament's own ability to deploy to maximum effect the information they provide.' [12]

Serving the citizen

The two forms of external accountability mentioned above, the Ombudsman and departmental select committees, have one thing in common: neither exist to make the Civil Service directly accountable to the people, any more than do extra-parliamentary institutions such as the courts, tribunals and public inquiries which are said to be available for the redress of grievances. A member of the public with a grievance against a public service, whether it takes the form of a complaint against a single civil servant or whether it is aimed at an entire government department, is unable to approach the relevant body in person but must take action through a third party, who may well be a lawyer but who is more often than not the complainant's MP.

The idea that the various managerial reforms of the Civil Service, involving as they did a mixture of performance indicators, value for money and the quality of service delivery, should be extended so as to include the direct public accountability of departments and agencies, came rather late in the day. At the end of 1987, just as the Next Steps programme was about to get under way, a Civil Service seminar on management techniques in public administration was addressed by a manager of British Airways on the subject of the newly privatised airline's 'customer first' policy for serving the consumer – a policy which measured the extent of effectiveness of performance purely in terms of customer satisfaction. One participant was overheard to wonder aloud why it was that customer satisfaction was such an alien concept in public life that a public enterprise had to be privatised before account was taken of the customers' needs. Out of such comments made at this seminar was born the idea that was later to be developed into the Citizen's Charter.[13]

The charter came about as a personal initiative by John Major after he was elected to the leadership in 1990 and was announced to the public by him in 1991.[14] The aim of the charter was to provide 'a revolution in public service' which would, to use a new buzz-word of the period, *empower the people*, who were to be regarded as customers by civil servants. At first the scheme was restricted to civil servants working in those bodies, largely agencies, which have direct contact with the public, like staff behind the counter in benefit offices or job centres. Later the remit was extended to any part of the administration where the public might feel that they had received faulty or deficient service and included in that were, not only all government departments and agencies, but also the privatised utilities, local government services and universities. The scheme as a whole was run by a special Citizen's Charter unit within the Cabinet Office, headed by an advisory panel composed of a mixture of business people, academics and special government advisers.

Part of the remit of the Citizen's Charter lies in making it very clear to the public just how well or badly civil servants and others are performing in the delivery of quality public services and, above and beyond that, making civil servants and others answerable for the standards of service they are providing. To this end, service targets are published, together with performance figures to show the success or otherwise of agencies to meet those targets. This open publication of targets and achievements is controversial and not always popular, as with the examination league tables published for every secondary school in the country which met with a critical outcry as many teachers and teachers' unions claimed that the league tables grossly misrepresented their efforts. Many public servants would claim that this aspect of public accountability is flawed in that the lay observer might misunderstand raw statistical information which very often requires interpretation in order to be understood by the non-specialist. Nevertheless, despite all these reservations, in the view of one commentator, the Citizen's Charter initiative 'stands as a positive step in the direction of enhanced external accountability of the Civil Service'.[15]

There are six principal criteria or service standards against which the performance of public services is measured:

1 **Standards:** meaning the setting, monitoring and publishing of the standard of service expected, together with the publication of performance figures to show the extent to which standards are successfully met.
2 **Accessibility of information:** meaning the provision of full, accurate information framed in the sort of simple, plain language that can be easily understood by the public.
3 **Choice:** meaning that the public services should always contain some element of choice that can be offered to the consumer.
4 **Courteous service:** of particular relevance to those who have daily contact with the public – on a Department of Social Security counter for example – and meaning that these public servants, many of whom might well be required to wear a name-badge so as to be identifiable, should always be polite, helpful and ready to extend their services to all those people who are entitled to them.
5 **Redress:** meaning that if things go wrong the fault will be acknowledged, an apology offered, an explanation given and the situation remedied. This presupposes an established complaints and redress procedure being set up.
6 **Value for money:** meaning that efficient and economic services should be provided, the provision of which should be capable of being realised while keeping within the limitations imposed by the extent of those means and resources available to society.[16]

The first few years of the Citizen's Charter can be regarded as being rather less than successful, despite the prime minister's personal enthusiasm for the initiative. In 1992 John Major had to revamp and relaunch the initiative twice, both before and after the election of that year, because of faults and omissions that had emerged. Many aspects of the charter programme were regarded with cynical amusement by the public who regarded the programme as a somewhat futile public relations exercise rather than having any sense of the initiative being in the public interest. A typical case was the 'Traffic Cones Hot Line', a telephone number that was prominently displayed near every major road works on motorways and main roads and which was supposed to keep the public informed about the work of the Highways Agency. Most motorists were too annoyed and frustrated at the delays caused by coned-off sections of the motorway to be much pacified by the chance of engaging in a telephone conversation about them. Yet, at least the public knew about the cones hot line; other services had a much lower public profile and were not so lucky. Charterline, a telephone help line to assist members of the public in finding the right person or office to whom they should complain, was launched as an experimental pilot scheme in the East Midlands during 1993 but was abandoned inside the year, well before it was due to be launched nationally. The problem was that the public knew nothing whatsoever about it, were ignorant of its function and even of its existence. Therefore, virtually nobody used it: during its very short period of existence it was receiving no more than 25 calls a day, at an average cost to the government of £68 a call.

Yet, despite these early setbacks, the whole charter programme took its place as just one of a whole series of moves leading towards a more open system of government, although it is doubtful whether the idea was quite such a cure for all known ills as John Major would have had the electorate believe. Certainly the idea went hand in hand with the growing number of Next Steps agencies and, as the charter programme became institutionalised in the mid-1990s, there was a proliferation of charters floated by a variety of governmental and non-governmental bodies. There was some doubt as to whether the Labour government elected in 1997 would carry on with the Citizen's Charter, about which the party had been somewhat critical in opposition but, as it happens, the Blair government accepted the initiative with a degree of enthusiasm.

Soon after the government took power in 1997, David Clark, in his capacity as Chancellor of the Duchy of Lancaster and head of the Office of Public Services, announced the start of a new '**Service First**' initiative, also subtitled, 'the New Charter Programme'. Labour had always supported the charter programme, said Clark, claiming indeed that the original idea behind the initiative was pioneered by Labour-controlled local authorities in the 1980s. 'But while that programme has some significant achievements to its credit, it now needs to be renewed . . . in the next phase of the programme, as an integral part of our broader Better Government initiative. It builds on what has been achieved so far but gives a new emphasis to promoting quality, ensuring effectiveness, and working together. Our aim is to help public services deliver a better society for our citizens.'[17]

Under the banner of the Service First programme a new series of major national charters have been instituted, the areas covered including charters for tax-payers, recipients of benefit, employers, jobseekers, road users, the courts, NHS patients, parents and students. Some of these charters – particularly those dealing with taxation – are applicable throughout the United Kingdom. Others, such as those dealing with employment and welfare benefits, are common to all of Great Britain, while charters for further and higher education, patients and parents are different for the national entities of England, Scotland and Wales, the last of these duplicating all charters issued in both English and Welsh language versions. Northern Ireland has a whole range of charters that are unique to the province, including a Citizen's Charter governing the RUC.

Accountability under the Service First programme is further assured by the publication of performance records. Most of the services thus examined are local services which are assessed by the Audit Commission in England and Wales, the Accounts Commission in Scotland and the Local Government Auditor for Northern Ireland. Being largely concerned with the performance of local authorities and the work of local government officials, they do not really represent the accountability of civil servants. Nevertheless, performance records at a national level are produced which show how the central government departments and agencies perform in providing the six service standards laid out in the Citizen's Charter. There are also reports on Health and Education for each of the four national divisions of the United Kingdom.

In the name of accountability and open government there is now a Machinery of Government and Standards Group within the Cabinet Office secretariat. It is their responsibility to make the nature of the various charters public and to publish the performance indicators. All this information is freely available in leaflet form, or it can be accessed through special telephone help lines or, in line with modern technology, all Service First information is made available to the public through the government's own websites on the Internet.[18]

Access to information

Before the 1997 general election the New Labour manifesto made much of the party's promise to open up government to public scrutiny as part of the proposed programme of constitutional reform. 'Unnecessary secrecy in government leads to arrogance in government and defective policy decisions,' it said. 'We are pledged to a Freedom of Information Act, leading to more open government.'[19] The same manifesto promised a reform of the Official Secrets Act, particularly the notorious Section 2, in the light of what has been considered the failure of the 1989 Official Secrets Act to put right the shortcomings of earlier versions. Yet, as the director of the Campaign for Freedom of Information has pointed out, 'Freedom of information has been a constant Labour policy for 25 years. It has featured in every general election manifesto since 1974.'[20] There was every reason to hope that on this occasion these piously uttered manifesto promises would finally be fulfilled, simply because so many of the present generation of prominent Labour politicians have suffered some form of surveillance in the course of their lives, through being regarded as security risks in their more radical youth – significant among them being the new Home

Secretary, Jack Straw. There was a feeling that this was a government that understood the negative aspects of government secrecy and that, as a consequence, something would be done this time.

This was just one of the areas where Labour seemed to fail its supporters by not fulfilling its promises. When David Shayler, a former MI5 employee, broke the story about the security services' surveillance of Jack Straw, Peter Mandelson and others, he was prosecuted in just the same way as those other whistleblowers, Clive Ponting and Peter Wright, had been. The government spent much of 1998 attempting to extradite Shayler from France. This appeared to show that New Labour is no different from any other governing party in wanting to cloud its activities in secrecy. Suspicions about the government's motivation appeared to be confirmed when the promised Freedom of Information Bill was removed from the legislative programme for Labour's first year in office. It was stated repeatedly that this was purely a temporary measure because of the pressure of other constitutional legislation like devolution or reform of the Lords but for a long time there was no immediate indication as to when the promised bill would be reintroduced. Nor was the cause of open government advanced by the fact that David Clark, the minister entrusted with guiding the Freedom of Information Act through parliament, was one of the casualties of Tony Blair's first cabinet reshuffle.

What appeared in place of the Freedom of Information Act, amending parts of the Official Secrets Act, is the government's Code of Practice on Access to Government Information,[21] issued under the Citizen's Charter programme and binding on all departments, agencies and public bodies under the jurisdiction of the Ombudsman. This avowedly had the aim of trying:

- to improve policy-making and the democratic process by extending access to facts and analyses;
- to protect the interests of individuals and companies by ensuring that reasons are given for administrative decisions;
- to support and extend the principles of public service established under the Citizen's Charter.

The undertakings on disclosure made by the Code of Practice can be summarised under five basic headings which represent obligations on the part of those departments and public bodies under the jurisdiction of the Ombudsman:

1 To publish the facts and factual analysis which the government has considered important for the framing of major policy decisions.
2 To publish, or make available, explanations for departments' dealing with the public, so as to assist understanding of departmental actions.
3 To give a full explanation of administrative decisions to the people most affected by those decisions.
4 To publish full information, under the terms of the Citizen's Charter, as to the

services provided by government departments or agencies and also make fully available the performance indicators of those services, again according to the Citizen's Charter.

5 To answer, in full, any reasonable request for information about the departmental remit or an agency's area of responsibility.

There are a number of other clauses which lay down such things as a reasonable time scale for response to requests for information and the amounts of money which departments should be allowed to charge for processing a request for information. Other clauses seek to differentiate between the public's rights of access under the code and any pre-existing statutory rights of access to such things as medical or educational records. All these elements of government openness are, however, in Part I of the Code of Practice. There is also a Part II which is rather like the infamous second section of the old Official Secrets Act in that it gives reasons for the imposition of secrecy over government procedures and which helps to maintain the inherent secrecy of the Civil Service.

Part II begins with the statement: 'The following categories of information are exempt from the commitments to provide information in this Code.' It then goes on to list no fewer than 15 categories which together are so comprehensive as to make any concept of *open* government seem ludicrous:

1 **Defence and foreign affairs:** representing any information which could harm national security; harm international relations; or represent a breach of confidence over information received from a foreign source.
2 **Internal confidentiality:** representing those factors responsible for the conventions of Civil Service anonymity and collective responsibility. In other words it covers those areas of discussion such as meetings of the Cabinet or internal communications between ministers, civil servants, advisers etc.; or indeed any area where discussion would be inhibited or less than frank if participants knew that their words would be widely disseminated.
3 **Communications with the Royal Household:** meaning that exchanges between members of the Royal Household and ministers or officials are meant to be kept confidential. In particular this refers to the confidentiality of meetings of the Privy Council.
4 **Law enforcement and legal proceedings:** meaning that information should not be made public if the result of that information becoming known might prejudice the detection, investigation or prosecution of a crime, or might in any way prejudice the administration of justice through the courts.
5 **Immigration and nationality:** means the confidentiality of all information concerning the administration of immigration controls.
6 **The economy:** which restricts all information that might harm the government's ability to manage the economy; which might enable an individual to profit from market operations; or which might affect the government's ability to collect taxes.

7   **Effective management of the public service:** meaning a bar on information whose 'disclosure would harm the proper and efficient conduct of a department or other public body, including NHS organisations'.

8   **Public appointments and honours:** meaning that advance publicity should not be given to appointments, promotions or recommendations for honours made by Ministers of the Crown.

9   **Vexatious requests:** meaning requests for information that are unreasonable in number or nature; or which would require too great a share of resources to answer; or which are too vague and general in nature.

10 **Premature release of information:** meaning the release of information before the official publication day, the premature release of which could well lead to political or economic damage.

11 **Research and statistics:** which primarily refers to the release of information that can be harmful because it is based on incomplete or unfinished research or data.

12 **Individual privacy:** meaning the unwarranted disclosure of personal information about an individual, including the situation where that individual is dead, to the extent of which the disclosure represents an invasion of that person's privacy.

13 **Commercial confidences:** meaning that trade secrets must not be disclosed.

14 **Confidential information:** which covers a variety of circumstances such as: (a) revealing information only given on assurances of confidentiality, (b) a source of information that would dry up if the supplier were not assured of confidentiality, and (c) highly personal information such as medical records disclosed by a doctor.

15 **Statutory secrecy:** including any disclosure that would breach Parliamentary Privilege or would offend European Community law.

Conclusion

There has been a great deal of talk in recent times about open government and the necessity to make officials answerable for their actions. Yet a close examination of the various procedures and initiatives that have been introduced only goes to show that civil servants are really only accountable to self-regulation within the service. The true extent of the openness of government can best be seen in the Code of Practice on Access to Government Information. On the surface, Part I of the code seems to preach total freedom of access: a freedom backed up by the twin authorities of the Citizen's Charter and the Ombudsman, and supervised overall by the Open Government unit within the Cabinet Office. A closer look, however, takes one into Part II and the realisation that, with an admitted 15 exemptions from full disclosure, any civil servant worth his or her salt could find any number of reasons for preserving the secrecy of Civil Service actions.

Notes

1 This categorisation of Civil Services tasks can be found in Robert Pyper, *The British Civil Service*, Harvester Wheatsheaf, Hemel Hempstead, 1995, p. 65.

2 *Ibid.*, p. 119.

3 Cabinet Office, *Civil Service Management Code*, Machinery of Government and Propriety Division of the Cabinet Office (OPS), 1996.

4 Waldegrave is quoted in Geoffrey Fry, *Policy and Management in the British Civil Service*, Prentice Hall/Harvester Wheatsheaf, Hemel Hempstead, 1995, p. 125.

5 J. Whyatt, *The Citizen and the Administration*, Justice, London, 1961.

6 Richard Crossman, quoted by John Kingdom, *Government and Politics in Britain*, Polity Press, Cambridge, 1994, p. 534.

7 D. Widdicombe, *Our Fettered Ombudsman*, Justice, London, 1977.

8 Philip Norton, Chapter 17 of *Politics UK* (2nd edition), Harvester Wheatsheaf, Hemel Hempstead, 1994, p. 337.

9 Hugo Young, *One of Us*, Macmillan, London, 1989, p. 209.

10 J. A. G. Griffith and M. Ryle, *Parliament*, Sweet and Maxwell, London, 1989, p. 520.

11 Pyper, Note 1 above, p. 125.

12 Bill Coxall and Lynton Robins, *Contemporary British Politics* (2nd edition), Macmillan, Basingstoke, 1995, p. 219.

13 An account of the 1987 meeting was given by Andrew Gray and Bill Jenkins, *The Management of Central Government Services*, in Bill Jones (ed.), *Politics UK* (2nd edition), Harvester Wheatsheaf, Hemel Hempstead, 1994, p. 436.

14 Cm. 1599, *The Citizen's Charter: Raising the Standard*, HMSO, London, 1991.

15 Pyper, Note 1 above, p. 135.

16 Cm. 2101, *The Citizen's Charter: First Report*, HMSO, London, 1992.

17 David Clark MP, Foreword to *Service First: The New Charter Programme*, Machinery of Government and Propriety Division of the Cabinet Office (OPS), 1997.

18 Anyone interested in open government information provided on the Internet can try one of two websites: – http://www.servicefirst.gov.uk/ or http://www.open.gov.uk/

19 New Labour, *Because Britain Deserves Better*, Party Manifesto, 1997, p. 33.

20 Maurice Frankel, *The Long Wait*, Citizen (journal of Charter 88), Winter 1998/99, p. 6.

21 Cabinet Office, *Open Government: Code of Practice on Access to Government Information. Second Edition 1997*, Machinery of Government and Propriety Division of the Cabinet Office (OPS), 11 December 1997.

10

Formulating policy and making decisions

Formulation or implementation?

The role of the Civil Service in the policy-making process is crucial, of growing importance and has been much studied in recent years. For some time now one of the principal areas of political theory to occupy the minds of serious political scientists has been the area which deals with the dynamics of the policy process, with the result that an increasing multiplicity of theoretical models has been created to analyse the policy-making cycle. There is, however, one important factor that is often overlooked by the theorists and that is the fact that the Civil Service has comparatively little to do with the polemics of policy creation, unlike the partisan positions adopted by politicians and all those many policy units and think tanks that are nowadays to be found within the fold of most modern political parties. Unlike politicians, civil servants are not much concerned with the rights and wrongs of policies that are formulated purely on a party political or ideological basis.

The Civil Service has many critics and is therefore constantly at the mercy of politicians who wish to change or reform the service in the light of what they see as its shortcomings. For example, the reforms of the 1980s and 1990s were largely produced by critics on the right who were eager to follow Margaret Thatcher's avowed intention of pushing back the frontiers of the state, because of a belief that the Civil Service was the over-bureaucratic servant of an over-powerful government, seeking to impose a monolithic and statist regime on the nation. On the other hand, before the 1980s the fiercest political critics of the Civil Service were almost always to be found on the left. Politicians of the left such as Richard Crossman, Barbara Castle and Tony Benn were very much to the fore in complaining about the ways in which the reactionary conservatism of the Civil Service had thwarted the socialist thrust of successive Labour governments: through the ability of senior civil servants to impose their own agenda on the government, to negate the implementation of socialist policies and to replace them with policy suggestions more sympathetic to the ideas of the right wing of the Conservative Party.

Such criticisms have been repeated so often that this view of senior civil servants as being inherently right wing has been accepted as fact, especially by those who have always regarded the social and educational background of senior civil servants as having the effect of leaving them irrevocably tainted by élitism. Yet one point which is often overlooked by the prejudiced observer is that this bias on the part of officials has very little to do with the party preferences of civil servants and everything to do with the fact that civil servants dislike over-much change, preferring to have continuity, stability and the maintenance of the status quo wherever that is possible.

The advice and assistance given to politicians by their civil servants during the processes of policy formulation and implementation has therefore very little to do with the left or right wings of politics but everything to do with the cosiness of adopting a nice, easy, centrist solution; firmly eschewing anything that might be regarded as radical or innovative, whether that comes from the radical right or from the radical left. The Senior Civil Service may indeed be conservative by nature but it is conservative with a small 'c' rather than the large 'c' of the party label, and it is a well-known historical fact that the mandarins of Whitehall were every bit as alarmed by Margaret Thatcher's policy initiatives as they would have been had they had to put the socialist ideas of the Bennite left into practice.

One of the main functions of the Civil Service is to implement government policy and it is therefore easy to understand why it should be that civil servants always look at government policy from the perspective of how easy or difficult it would be to put that policy into practice. A conservative policy which seeks to maintain the status quo is regarded as the ideal by civil servants because the conservative nature of the policy ensures that it has been tried before, perhaps many times before, and is probably a variant of the policy currently in force. Most importantly, previous experience of policies of this kind and the repetition of such experiences has shown that a policy works. Radical policies on the other hand are, *per se*, untried and untested and are therefore a leap in the dark as far as a government's officials are concerned. To them an untried policy is a policy that might just possibly work but which is rather more likely not to do so. It therefore logically follows, not only that civil servants will always work extremely hard to implement a policy in which they can believe, but that they will work every bit as hard and every bit as long in order to thwart a policy in which they do not believe. As a former minister has said:

> The question that civil servants ask themselves when required to advise on implementing polemical proposals is not, 'Do I agree with it?' but, 'Can it be made to work?' If they think it can, they will help you to make it work. If they think it cannot, they will do their best to stop it. This is not a very heroic posture, and it can be very irritating, even maddening. Politicians who want to excite the country with imaginative proposals find them watered down in the interests of practicality.[1]

The role taken by the Civil Service in policy formulation is therefore critical in that civil servants will attempt to shape the nature and purpose of a policy decision from start to finish, but, in order to understand the bureaucratic approach, it is necessary to know that the Civil Service sees its own role entirely from the perspective of a policy's practical application, based on pragmatism rather than principle.

Theoretical models of the policy process

The policy-making process requires an input of political ideas from a very wide variety of sources, which ultimately come together through a number of for-malised procedural mechanisms, and which result in turn in an output of many different and differing government decisions. Within that process, the considerable differences which exist in the relative importance of resources, inputs, structures and decisions result in a wide variety of alternative theoret-ical models being formulated to explain how the policy makers arrive at their decisions. There are very many different models, some of which are extremely theoretical, while others are more practically inclined. Whether theoretical or practical, however, these models are sufficiently vague as to range over the whole field of decision-making, within which policy formulation is just one small part. It is, however, possible to simplify matters by ignoring minor differences and having thus simplified the matter, being able to distinguish four clear descriptive models:[2]

The pluralist model

Groups which can be described as pluralist are not dissimilar to what are defined later in this chapter as 'policy networks', or which are described else-where as 'policy communities',[3] in that the pluralist model envisages a network of interest and pressure groups; a network which is interdependent because of the need to negotiate between the various interests of its component groups. It recognises that government departments and agencies, as well as pressure and interest groups, sometimes work together very well while at other times they may compete hard among themselves. The political environment in which these departments, agencies and groups can operate and make decisions is formed as a result of interaction between these various groups, whether that interaction is consensual or based on conflict.

The corporate model

Corporatism was most notably the hallmark of Italian fascism under Mussolini but it has since been applied, often pejoratively, to any system in which certain favoured interest and pressure groups play a central role in the policy-making process, these groups often having a status equivalent to that of a quasi-governmental body. The label 'corporatist' was disparagingly applied to the Wilson and Callaghan Labour governments of the 1960s and 1970s by critics from across the entire political spectrum, ranging from Margaret Thatcher on the right to Tony Benn on the left. Typical of what were categorised as corporatist bodies at that time was the National Economic Development Council (affectionately known as 'Neddy'), formed in the early 1960s and making up a forum in which new policies for forward economic planning could be evolved, and a body on which the trade unions and employers' organisations had equal status with representatives of the government. Industrial relations were given a human face during those years of Labour government by cultivating the image in the media of strikes and industrial unrest being settled during a friendly afternoon's discussion by trade union leaders who just happened to have called in for 'beer and sandwiches with Harold at Number Ten'.

The parliamentary model

This is the traditional model which envisages policy as principally being developed by the main political parties and their members in party policy units or focus groups, perhaps with the support and intervention of the annual party conference. The policy as developed by the party is then presented to the public in the party's election manifesto. The grass-roots origins of policies under this model can be said to mandate the implementation of those policies by the party's MPs, working through parliament on behalf of their constituents, either to support or oppose government policy. From this viewpoint, policy formulation is yet another extension of the concept of parliamentary sovereignty.

The Whitehall model

This argues that, since the implementation of policy is very much in the hands of civil servants, then the Civil Service is the key to understanding policy decisions. An American political scientist, Graham Allison, studied the policy and decision-making processes of the Kennedy administration during the Cuban Missile Crisis of 1962 and came to the conclusion that a true fully-rounded policy decision can only emerge from bargains and compromises made between themselves by government ministers and civil servants – from a whole range of competing departmental interests and priorities.[4] In other words, the persons who have most influence on the direction taken by policy-making are senior civil servants. Within the British experience this factor can be glimpsed in the measures and negotiations concerned with government decisions on cuts in public spending, during which long process the decisions concerning which services to cut and how much money to reduce are subject to keen debate by the rival bureaucracies of spending ministries and the Treasury. This means that the parameters of negotiation are laid down by civil servants long before ministers and politicians become involved. It is as a product of this model that the system of beliefs and practices constraining the role adopted by the Civil Service can also be known as the 'Treasury ethos'.

As with any series of theoretical models, there is probably no single model that can be stated to be true in the strictest sense of the term, although there is very probably at least a small element of truth in each and every one of them. And there is probably rather more truth if they are regarded collectively.

Policy formulation: issues

The starting point in the policy-making process, the key to initiating the process, is very often rooted in discussions surrounding the resolution of a political issue. However, there are many different kinds of issue and they have a varying impact on the political process depending on the length of time any specific issue spends at the forefront of the public's mind. Some issues, particularly those with an ideological basis, are in a sense always with us, although they may fluctuate in importance, changing in form and seriousness but, nevertheless, maintaining a continual presence from which the political parties cannot escape without developing policies and strategies to deal with them.

Ideological issues are therefore part of the fabric of political parties as, for example, support for a free market economy is part of Tory party policy or a stance supportive of the working classes is typical at least of Old Labour. Other issues have no history in party politics but suddenly appear out of nowhere, very often spawned by unexpected events which become very important for a time, and then fade away again. On the whole, however, political issues can be divided into two main types:[5]

1)   **Position issues** comprise all those issues to which political parties offer different and often ideological solutions. The voters' choice of party is determined by their own preferred solution and their perception of which party will best meet that preference. If, for example, voters feel that the most efficient way forward for industry is the removal of state control and regulation, then they would vote for the Conservatives since they are seen as the party of private enterprise.

2)   **Valence issues** comprise all those issues which all parties agree are important, although they do not have to agree on how to deal with them. The choice for voters here concerns which party do they feel will be most competent to deal with that issue? For example, all voters and all parties might well agree on the importance of the National Health Service. However, historically, many voters have felt that, since the Labour Party is the party which feels most strongly about the NHS, it is therefore the party best able to manage the efficient functioning of the service.

The matter is rather more complex in that, in attempting to understand the making of policies and decisions, we should first look beyond this basic typology of issues and attempt to understand what makes an issue, how is it defined, how is it sustained and what effect does it have on the policy-making process?

• **Ideological issues** are defined by the political parties themselves and then refined by the mass media of communication. Parties stress the effectiveness of their own policies for dealing with the problems of the country and denigrate the policies of the opposing party or parties, their message being reinforced by coverage in Britain's highly partisan media, something like 70 per cent of it traditionally biased in favour of the Conservatives. Such a highly partisan press pushes wherever possible those news stories which show their favoured party's policies in a favourable light or sensationalises stories that undermine the opposing party's viewpoint. There is also the daily experiences of the electorate, who realise that their way of life or standard of living is determined by political actions. Most people support a particular political party and that support, together with the depth and extent of the support, is partly determined by the party's attitude to certain issues and the policies they put forward to deal with those issues.

• **Issues of public concern** begin with a feeling that something is wrong or that something needs doing. Sometimes that concern is merely part of a general unease at injustice, unfairness or the way things are going, but in other areas concern may be sparked off by the warnings of experts. Environmental issues are typical of concerns which have increasingly affected people in recent years and which have caused people who hitherto had nothing to do with politics to become involved in political activity. In early 1995 there was so much protest-group activity, especially over environmental issues like the export of veal calves or the extension of motorways, that there was talk of a new militancy appearing in the normally-moderate middle classes and among middle-aged men and women. But a similar phenomenon had been identified by Mike Moran ten years previously when he saw growing middle-class involvement in pressure-group activity as being merely part of a growing disillusionment with the class-based partisanship of the two-party system.[6]

Event-led issues are something else again. Harold Macmillan, when he was prime minister, was once famously asked what he found was the most difficult issue to deal with in government. 'Events, dear boy,' he said, 'Events!' And events retain the ability to upset all politicians because, quite unexpectedly, as a result of an event overseas perhaps, or it may be the irrational behaviour of a disturbed individual, something will suddenly cause even the most apathetic members of the public to become politically involved and motivated. In recent years that event has, with disturbing frequency, been the result of a serious policy mistake or misjudgment on the part of government. Patrick Dunleavy has said, 'Britain now stands out amongst comparable European countries . . . as a state unusually prone to make large scale, avoidable policy mistakes.'[7] The Civil Service is very often concerned with this type of issue since it is frequently a mistake or misjudgment by civil servants that has precipitated the event and, very often, the very fact of government or Civil Service involvement in an event helps to amplify the importance of an issue, particularly if it is badly handled and even more particularly if it has to do with public health. As Rob Baggott has said, 'one can identify a range of issues – food additives, pesticide pollution, salmonella poisoning, lead in petrol, smoking and alcohol abuse. In all these cases governments have been reluctant to take action to protect health, even where the consequences are potentially disastrous.' [8]

Policy formulation – the consultation process

Once an issue has been raised, whether that issue has its roots in the media, in parliament or within the political parties, the obligation to formulate a policy to meet that issue will pass to the Civil Service who will also begin to devise strategies not only as to how government policies can be realised but, if a general election is looming, how the alternative policies advocated by the opposition can be made to work equally as well. In his book of advice to a would-be government minister, Gerald Kaufman described the situation exactly:

> When you enter your department after your election victory, your officials will know at least as much about your policies as you do. They will have studied all your party's policy pronouncements, read all its pamphlets. More than that, they will have spent the months leading up to the election preparing actively for your arrival, just in case you win . . . That is why Whitehall was ready for Labour in 1974 and equally ready for the Conservatives in 1979. [9]

Much the same message was included in the first programme of the TV series *Yes Minister*:

> HACKER: Humphrey then produced draft proposals, to implement my policy in a White Paper. I was flabbergasted. The efficiency of the Civil Service is quite astounding. All of these draft proposals are available to me within thirty-six hours of the new government being elected and within minutes of my arrival at my office. And on a weekend! Remarkable chaps. [10]

There is therefore a very strong working relationship between ministers and senior civil servants in the field of policy formulation and this relationship can be affected by many different factors. Pyper was able to identify eight variables in the relationship: [11]

1) Ministers have parliamentary and/or constituency duties that keep them out of their departments for a great deal of the time. In this respect the Civil Service is left to get on with policy formulation on their own and independently of ministerial influence.

2) The average life of a minister within a department is fairly short: promotion, demotion, the musical chairs of a cabinet reshuffle, resignation or electoral defeat can remove or move on a minister at any moment and, although there have been ministers with very long tenure of their offices, the average length of time spent in a department is usually rather less than two years. In connection with long-term policy development spread over a number of years this can mean that two, or even three, ministers may be involved at one time or another. With a ministerial presence in the policy process being a variable factor the only constant to give continuity to the process is the part played by civil servants.

3) The relationship between ministers and their senior civil servants is very strictly circumscribed by procedural rules as set out in the Ministerial Code of Conduct.[12] One example is that a Permanent Secretary in a department will work very closely with the Secretary of State but will not be bound by decisions of junior ministers. Similarly the Code of Conduct also makes it clear that, while ministers are advised to heed the advice of civil servants, they are not bound to do so. Indeed, over the years there have been many instances, not all of them widely known, where there have been serious differences between a ministry's ministers and the civil servants attached to that ministry.

4) The relationship between the minister and his or her senior officials, particularly with the Permanent Secretary, can be crucial for the efficient running of a department. Most often such relationships can be smooth and business-like, occasionally they can be warm and friendly, but every now and then they can turn stormy and confrontational. Pyper mentions as an example the relationship of Richard Crossman with Dame Evelyn Sharp, his Permanent Secretary at the Ministry of Housing between 1964 and 1966, a case of cat and-dog skirmishing that produced two years of constant conflict and disagreement. Earlier, in Chapter 5 of this book, full consideration was given to the air of unease and mistrust which characterised the relationship of Margaret Thatcher and Sir William Pile, her Permanent Secretary at Education in the 1970 Heath government.

5) The knowledge and expertise possessed by a minister can be important. Sometimes the minister may have personal knowledge of the department's work as, for example, when a doctor becomes Secretary of State for Health. More often, however, ministers will have no specialist knowledge at all and, until such time as they have mastered their brief they will be dependent on the expertise of civil servants who may have worked in that department for ten or more years and who are therefore totally familiar with the subject.

6) The personal importance and prestige of a minister can affect relationships with civil servants. Officials are far more likely to respect and obey ministers who are well-known in both political and public circles and who have many years of experience behind them. Civil servants will listen with respect to the thoughts of experienced ministers concerning policy matters where they would ignore the views of a minister who still needs to prove his or her credentials. The experienced minister is also likely to be less adventurous and

innovative and therefore more ready to accept the conservative and pragmatic approach of senior civil servants. As well as all this, when it is a highly experienced minister who sets his or her face against accepting the advice of officials, those officials are far more likely to back down in the face of ministerial determination, knowing that such determination has a solid foundation based on experience and is not an immature whim of an inexperienced newcomer. On the other hand, there are always those unimportant, insignificant or inexperienced ministers who do not have the respect of their officials and who therefore have very little to contribute to discussions about the more contentious policy issues.

7)   All departments do not have equal status and therefore their ministers and officials do not have equal clout over policy matters. The three great offices of state – the Treasury, the Foreign and Commonwealth Office and the Home Office – are always important, but the relative importance of other ministries shifts with time, with obvious consequences for the comparative weight of ministers appointed to those departments, not to mention the effect on the effectiveness and self-esteem of officials working in those departments. Consider the Ministry of Agriculture, Fisheries and Food which, for much of the time, deals with routine administration but which, just occasionally, as the result of media hype or public concern, becomes the centre of attention, either because of a food scare like the BSE crisis or perhaps because of an argument with the European Union over fish stocks or farming subsidies.

8)   Similarly, certain departments or specific policies can become the focus of attention for the electorate, as a result of statements or decisions made by government or opposition parties. Such statements can transform a mundane policy initiative into what is seen as a keynote issue which then becomes part of the party's flagship policy. As a result, the need for policy formulation becomes an imperative conducted in the full glare of public attention. For example, in the run up to the 1997 election, Tony Blair very famously stated that Labour's three priorities were to be seen as being 'Education, Education, Education'. That declaration coloured the election campaign from that moment on, ensuring that education policies evolved by the Department of Education after the Labour administration took power were subjected to close and continuous review by the media, political commentators and opposition parties alike, with a certain measure of disillusionment when the issue did not seem to receive the promised priority treatment.

Interest and pressure groups

In order to keep ahead of the politicians in policy formulation, civil servants need to call on the services of various interest and pressure groups, many of which have regular and continuing links with civil servants at both a formal and an informal level and which perform the same service for the Civil Service as think tanks, focus groups and policy units do for the political parties. In this respect it is also useful to consider the concept of *insider* and *outsider* interest groups, terms which relate to the acceptability of various groups in the eyes of government and the Civil Service. Baggott defined the difference between them as: '**insider groups** are viewed as legitimate by government and are consulted on a regular basis, while **outsider groups** either do not wish to become involved in a consultative relationship or cannot secure recognition'.[13]

It is of course possible for groups to be classed as either insider or outsider at different times, or indeed to count as being both insider and outsider, depending very much on the perspective of the observer or on such relative factors as political context. Consider, for example, the trade unions in the period 1974 to 1979, when they were welcomed as very close insiders or allies by the Labour government, and compare that situation with the position adopted by the Thatcher governments after 1979, which very firmly locked the unions out from any sort of contact with government circles, labelling them at one point as the 'enemy within'.

At various stages in the policy-making process, from framing the government's response to an issue born out of scare stories in the media, right up to the consultation prior to framing draft legislation, the Civil Service will seek information, guidance and advice from a variety of interest groups that might be called insider groups but which could more properly be called 'legitimate' groups. These groups acquire legitimacy because the government knows and believes that, through consulting these groups and getting their consent for its policies, it can attract even wider support for those policies because of the influence and standing of the groups' membership.

Any consultation between civil servants and interest groups can take place in a variety of ways and through a variety of channels and links.

Formal consultation

There are very many ways by which officials can seek advice in the consultation process through some kind of formalised structure. The most impressive of such structures is a **Royal Commission** which, usually under the guidance of a senior judge, has wide-ranging powers for calling evidence, summoning witnesses, initiating research and making recommendations. There was once much more enthusiasm for creating Royal Commissions than there is now, but a waning of interest began under Margaret Thatcher, who believed that, as many people suspected was the case under Harold Wilson, the call for a Royal Commission to be set up was often little more than a strategic device operated by the government and the Civil Service in cahoots as a way to buy time for the politicians, through diverting attention and postponing controversial decisions. Nevertheless there have been a number of important Royal Commissions in recent years; most notably, two important inquiries into the fight against crime in the Royal Commission on Criminal Procedure of 1981 and the Royal Commission on Criminal Justice of 1993.

Most such commissions are temporary and disband as soon as they have made their report but a few are more or less permanent, such as the Royal Commission on Environmental Pollution which has been a major advisory body on pollution control since 1973 and has been responsible for such major policy initiatives as the promotion of unleaded petrol. All recent changes in the structure and nature of local government have been produced as the result of Local Government Commissions, most recently the Banham Commission which was appointed by John Major to examine local government in England; a commission whose results were reported in 1995.

Another formal structure used in the consultative process is a **departmental committee of inquiry** which, like the Royal Commission, has the ability to seek advice from a wide spectrum of opinion. Like a Royal Commission, the departmental committee seeks to create policy by building a cross-party consensus in answer to a problem. As such, just as with the idea of a Royal Commission, the use of departmental inquiries fell out of favour during the Conservative administrations of the 1980s, since Margaret Thatcher did not favour any instrument which hinted, as these committees did, at the desirability of consensus or compromise.

At a lower prestige level than either the Royal Commission or the departmental committee of inquiry is the **advisory group** or working party which is often set up at the request of government to give expert advice in those areas where neither ministers nor officials are likely to have the necessary expertise. Most departments will have at the very least one advisory committee assigned to them and the subjects covered represent a wide spectrum. Examples might be a Home Office committee advising the police on recruitment from ethnic minorities; or a committee advising on the relationship between industry and pollution; or a committee giving advice concerning the misuse of drugs. Interest groups, professionals, academics and politicians are all represented on these committees but their distinguishing feature remains an expertise in the relevant field that cannot be matched by civil servants who are invariably generalist in education and training.

Possibly the most formal type of consultation is the consultative document that is widely and popularly known as a **Green Paper**. There are in fact a very great number of consultative documents circulated by government departments: according to Baggott it could be anything between 200 and 300 a year.[14] Many of these documents are of minor importance, have a restricted circulation and are little known. Indeed, sometimes there is no real substantive purpose in distributing these items, they are just sent to interested parties out of courtesy or for information only. However, during the 1960s, the then Labour government, intending to introduce legislation on regional employment, decided to seek out informed opinion about its intentions by circulating a sample draft of the proposed legislation. It had been long-established government practice to publish advance notice of legislation proposed by the government, but any such publications, known now as White Papers, more or less represented the final draft of the bill as it would be presented to parliament. The document issued for the first time in 1967, however, was not the final version and it was specifically issued so that interested parties could read it, comment upon it and, hopefully, put forward their own opinions which might thereby have the opportunity of influencing government thinking. Unlike the previous publications of final drafts that had been printed on ordinary white paper these consultative documents were printed on green-coloured paper, hence the names White Papers and Green Papers.

A Green Paper might be issued if the government was seeking general views on a controversial but non-partisan issue such as hanging, abortion or divorce. Alternatively, for a newly-elected government, a Green Paper might be issued to seek public endorsement for party policies developed while the party had been in opposition but which had become particularly relevant now that the party was the government party. There is always a possibility that a Green Paper, like a Royal Commission, is merely a time-wasting exercise to fob off critics. Gerald Kaufman for example, from the ministerial point of view, says that Green Papers, 'have the great merit of fending Parliament off for a time while you try to think of what you actually want to do about some particularly intractable problem'.[15] Having issued the Green Paper, the department concerned will wait for about ten weeks, sometimes receiving written submissions from interested parties and sometimes – particularly when there are existing informal links – receiving visits from interest groups which will come to put their case direct to politicians and civil servants.

Informal links

For all that there are formal arrangements which enable pressure or interest groups, trade or professional associations or, indeed, interested individuals to become involved in the consultation process when certain issues are being discussed or policies developed, these contacts are intermittent and concern specific issues or just one policy at a time. In most cases these contacts are part of an ongoing process in the form of informal contacts between interested groups and officials that are made regularly and constantly. Some groups, which would clearly like to be designated as 'insider' groups, cultivate their contacts with certain civil servants on an almost daily basis, with most of these contacts being made by telephone, although from time to time the two sides will meet face to face. It is even known for groups that have really close and friendly relations with civil servants to invite those civil servants to attend meetings or seminars run by the group, just as group members may themselves be invited to attend meetings with civil servants in Whitehall.

Civil servants involved in these informal links tend to be from the lower ranks of the Senior Civil Service, that is to say from grades 4 to 7. Top senior civil servants above the rank of Under-Secretary tend only to become involved when a formal meeting or contact has been arranged and senior personnel are involved on all sides. Any close or continuous relationship with the groups is more likely to be maintained by civil servants who are still senior but who are located at the Principal or Assistant Secretary level. These civil servants are more likely than their seniors to deal with the day-to-day management of issues or development of policy and therefore find it easy to build up a friendly working relationship with officers of the interest or pressure group involved since such group officers are probably working on the self-same issue at the same time and at about the same level. Senior civil servants, like senior officers of the relevant group, are only likely to be called on in a formal capacity to give approval to an agenda that has already been drawn up and agreed by their more junior colleagues in informal session.

As has been said, most contacts are by telephone but face-to-face encounters do take place and can be as informal as meeting for drinks, lunch or dinner. The most fruitful ground, however, is as a by-product of such things as conferences, exhibitions or trade fairs which junior ministers might well be invited to attend, often with a support team of civil servants in attendance. Consider, for example, a major exhibition of Commercial Vehicles which might well be attended by one or more trade or transport ministers with their attendant civil servants. That setting would be the ideal opportunity for minister and civil servants to be approached informally by officers and members of such groups as the Road Haulage Association, the Road Users' Association, bus companies and so on.

These informal contacts represent a facet of personal friendship networking that works best when those taking part share a common social or educational background. Those groups that are most successful in maintaining informal contacts, to the extent of being recognised as insider groups, are those whose membership shares the same male, middle-class, university-educated profile as that of the Civil Service. The more extreme interest groups tend not to be seen as acceptable, not so much because of the radical nature of their beliefs but because the personalities involved on both sides are incompatible.

Civil servants and the world outside

One of the ways in which links are built between the Civil Service and the more competitive world of the private sector is by a civil servant's opting to move out of the Civil Service into the world of industry and commerce; either through a retired civil servant taking a job in the private sector after retirement or by secondment to industry while still remaining on the establishment strength of the Home Civil Service. It is no secret that it is very useful for a company's future planning if they have knowledge of the way the government has been thinking recently, together with some indication of the thrust likely to be taken by the government's future policy direction, both for trade and industry in general and for that specific company in particular. This has made senior civil servants very useful targets for the headhunters of industry and commerce. One political commentator has noted that the team of civil servants which handled the privatisation of British Telecom had been totally dispersed in a very short space of time after the privatisation was complete; they had all been 'lured by private sector employers impressed with the relevant knowhow of the privatisation process'.[16]

Fearful of the possibilities of malpractice that might arise from self-interested civil servants making decisions that might thereby influence their own careers and line their own pockets, a Code of Conduct was introduced for senior civil servants by which there has to be a waiting period between the civil servant's actual retirement and his or her taking up employment within the private sector. A committee appointed by the prime minister – the Advisory Committee on Business Appointments – can scrutinise all applications for employment made by former civil servants to employers in the private sector, for a period of up to two years after the civil servant has left the Service (see Appendix 6).

As well as the strong possibility that former civil servants may be recruited by the private sector after retirement, another major link between the private and public sectors is the policy of secondment between the Civil Service and outside organisations. As the Civil Service Management Code[17] says, 'The policy of the Civil Service is to encourage inward secondment to promote the exchange of ideas and experience . . . recruitment principles may be relaxed to facilitate transfers of people into the Civil Service for this purpose.' Most such secondments are purely temporary – the majority being for less than three years – and the permanent employer must keep the secondee's position open so that he or she can return when they wish to do so. In most instances the firms and organisations concerned are approached by establishment officers of the Civil Service who invite them to nominate those of their employees who might benefit from secondment, bearing in mind that anyone nominated by industry should be capable of working as a civil servant. The secondment programme was promoted strongly during the Thatcher governments and, according to Baggott, the number of secondments rose rapidly, to reach a total of 1,502 by the year 1990.

The underlying purpose of such secondments is to expose the Civil Service to those new ideas and practices that have proved effective in the outside world. In return, of course, the outside organisations are looking to improve their own informal policy network links with the Civil Service. There is also, of course, the point that outsiders seconded to the Civil Service may return to their permanent employers with a grasp of government thinking and practice that could be very useful to those employers, given that there are not the same safeguards in place to prevent returning secondees from revealing what they have learned as there are safeguards in place to constrain those retired civil servants who may be recruited by the private sector.

The reverse of outsiders being seconded into the Civil Service is the secondment of present-day civil servants to positions in the private sector. The Bridge Programme, 'to build more bridges between government and industry', was instituted by the Thatcher government in 1989 and was considered a great success. The seconded civil servants were regarded as very useful by private employers while they themselves received benefit of two kinds; not only did they gain experience that would be useful when they returned to their duties as civil servants, but they also gained personal experience that might serve them in good stead if they were seeking employment after leaving the Civil Service.[18]

Policy networks

The concept of policy networks is not dissimilar to the idea we have already mentioned which classifies some groups or interested parties as 'insiders' and some as 'outsiders'. Sometimes known as policy communities, these policy networks are made up of government departments or agencies, advisory bodies and interest or pressure groups involved in an area of policy or decision-making, as well as those bodies or individuals likely to be affected by the policies in question. In other words, a policy network is made up of everyone liable to be involved with or affected by decisions taken in a specific policy area, every member of the network having, or expecting to have, an input into the policy consultation period.

The authors of *The New British Politics*[19] include, in their chapter on environmental policy, a list of the component parts of what could be called a British environmental policy network. To take this as a typical example of what a policy network might comprise, those component parts are:

On the government side, represented by both politicians and civil servants:

- *The Minister of the Environment* within the Department of the Environment, Transport and the Regions. Other government departments with specific interests in the environment include the *Ministry of Agriculture, Fisheries and Food*, together with the *Scottish, Welsh* and *Northern Ireland Offices*.
- *The Environment Agency*, established in 1995 but formerly the National Rivers Authority and responsible for pollution control.
- *The Environment Select Committee* of the House of Commons and a number of similar environmental committees in the House of Lords, some of which represent the European Union interest.
- *Royal Commission on Environmental Pollution*. A major standing investigative, regulatory and advisory body. The commission is backed up by a number of other advisory bodies, both official and unofficial.

Who regularly meet with the non-governmental interested parties in this policy network:

- *Local authorities*. Who are involved in the implementation of environmental policy but outside the remit and authority of national government and the Civil Service.

- *Environmental Pressure and Interest Groups* such as Green Peace, Friends of the Earth, RSPB, World Wide Fund for Nature etc.
- *Interested bodies* such as the water companies, road transport firms, farmers etc.

Client group status

This represents the ultimate in close relationships between interest groups and civil servants. Rob Baggott has defined the relationship as being where 'the group has been seen as the principal representative of interests whose co-operation is essential to the achievement of the government's policy objectives'.[20] In other words, it is the relationship that exists between the Civil Service and an interest group which is so much an insider group that there is an identity of interest.

Lynn and Jay, while exaggerating as always for the sake of laughter, gave a very clear picture of this situation in the *Yes Minister* episode 'The Bed of Nails':

> All government departments – which in theory collectively represented the government to the outside world – in fact lobbied the government on behalf of their own client pressure group. Every Department acted for the powerful sectional interest with whom it had a permanent relationship. The Department of Employment lobbied for the TUC whereas the Department of Industry lobbied for the employers, Energy lobbied for the oil companies, Defence lobbied for the armed forces, the Home Office for the police, and so on.[21]

One point does need to be made. The implication in the *Yes Minister* television programme and in the comments of other critics is that the Civil Service is being manipulated by the interest groups concerned. In fact the real danger of these so-called client group relationships is more likely to be the direct opposite in that the interest groups become so enamoured of their close relationship with government that they will not say or do anything critical which might jeopardise that relationship and therefore, far from the group manipulating government, it is more the case that civil servants can manipulate the interest groups for the sake of the government.

The policy process: decision-making

So far we have looked extensively at the consultative aspects of policy formulation and the way in which officials will gather together information from their own experience, from inquiries and from consultation with interested parties in order to draw up policies that will satisfy manifesto pledges or cope with important political issues. What we have to consider now is the way in which this extensive consultation can be turned into reality through legislation and transferred from the field of policy to that of operational matters as a result of decisions taken by government and officials. It is worth remembering at this point that it is the exclusive responsibility of the politicians in government to make policy decisions: hence the dispute between a minister, like Michael Howard as Home Secretary, and the chief executive of an agency, like Derek Lewis as head of the Prison Service, as to who has operational responsibility for running the prisons: a dispute that was settled by a blunt statement that in general terms a minister was purely concerned with policy decisions while it was the chief executive who had complete operational control.

The traditional public administration, liberal-bureaucratic, text-book model of the policy process underlines this clear split of responsibilities. 'This model assumes a clear dividing-line between political decision-making, which is what ministers do, and administration, which is the job of civil servants in tendering advice and carrying out decisions'.[22] However, as Coxall and Robins go on to say, this division of labour is a counsel of perfection towards which ministers and officials aspire but which is often not attained because of the practical reality of the situation, 'a variety of factors often tilt the balance of power in a Department away from the minister and towards the permanent officials'.

Therefore, despite the role of the civil servant being theoretically restricted to the giving of advice, the Civil Service has a significant part to play in the framing of policy decisions and their execution. It also naturally follows that there are a number of devices in existence by which senior civil servants can contribute to the formulation of a policy decision:

Submissions

The submission, is very important in being the draft document by which senior officials put forward various issues to their respective minister. The submission may take a variety of forms, some of which are purely bureaucratic in nature. Nevertheless, if a minister has asked his or her civil servants for a proposed solution to an issue or problem; if a senior civil servant wishes to suggest a way in which electoral promises made by the minister's party might be made good; if officials should wish to convey to their minister any suggestions and proposals made by advisory and interest groups within the department's policy network: for all these purposes the initial action to be taken is for a senior civil servant to write an outline of the proposal or proposals. Such a document is called a *submission* when written from a civil servant to a minister; the corresponding note from a minister to a civil servant is known as a *minute*.

Some senior civil servants are very prolific and seem to spend most of their time in the writing of submissions, as was explained by Gerald Kaufman who, in commenting on the writing of submissions by civil servants, said 'the most prolific there ever has been or possibly ever will be – was a superb Deputy Secretary at the Department of Industry – brilliant, inventive, humourous, loyal – called Ron Dearing'.[23] Dearing's reputation as an efficient and effective civil servant led him later to be given the key positions of head of the Post Office, chairman of Camelot, running the National Lottery, and the last Conservative-appointed watchdog over Education, but that reputation was built on his supreme expertise in a skill unique to the Civil Service, the ability to write a neat, persuasive submission.

The key point to remember about submissions is that they represent a form of briefing from civil servants to their ministers. As such they can be a straight-forward exposition recommending a single course of action or they can be more subtle, offering ministers an apparent choice in what it might be possible to do while simultaneously gently steering them in the desired direction and the looked-for decision.

Meetings

Meetings form the life-blood of the Civil Service. Gerald Kaufman remembers Harold Wilson being asked by his secretary what ministers actually do all day long. To which the firm and comprehensive reply was, 'They hold meetings'. All too often meetings are ineffective and non-productive because civil servants are prone to become bogged down in ineffectual and time-wasting discussion and argument, unless the meetings are chaired by a firm and effective minister or senior official whom the civil servants respect. From his experience as a minister Kaufman makes certain suggestions to ease the problems over meetings:

- meetings should not go on too long because, after a certain length of time (an hour and a half has been suggested) discussion ceases to achieve anything and, in fact, begins to undo what has been achieved already
- discussion about anything other than the supposed subject of the meeting should be halted immediately before the meeting is distracted
- if any decisions are made, a deadline should be set as to a time within which those decisions should be carried out. A follow-up meeting should be scheduled to allow for feedback on the progress of carrying out those decisions
- membership of meetings should be limited to the civil servants of one department or they will play one side against the other, with each department's officials recognising the authority of their own ministers but refusing to acknowledge the other
- wherever possible, action should take the form of administrative action, such as the use of statutory instruments etc., which does not have to be referred to parliament, does not have to receive collective ministerial approval in Cabinet and, above all, does not require Treasury approval.

Treasury involvement

Treasury involvement is a major problem in the policy and decision-making process because no department can carry out its policy decisions without spending money; the Treasury controls the money; and the Treasury will do anything possible to avoid spending any money. Many of the problems encountered in meetings are produced because the Treasury has set department against department over the allocation of resources and the approval of spending plans. It is this sense of competing for a share of rare resources that makes so many inter-departmental relationships adversarial in nature and why there has to be some formalised structure that will co-ordinate departmental views and aspirations.

Ministerial committees

Ministerial committees is the name given to the network of committees – each with 100 per cent civil servant membership – which shadows the organisational structure of cabinet committees, the latter of course having a mixed membership of politicians and civil servants. These 'shadow' committees exist to co-ordinate policy between departments and to resolve inter-departmental disputes before the ministers of those departments meet in Cabinet or in Cabinet committees. It should incidentally be remembered about Civil Service participation in Cabinet committees, or if civil servants take part in any policy-making committee of ministers, that civil servants fall into two quite separate categories at these meetings. Some will be there in their own right with information or advice to contribute, while others are there in the capacity of secretariat – to keep minutes, draw up the agenda etc.

Drafting legislation

Possibly the most important part of the policy process comes when ministers and officials combine to turn the theory of policy into practice, usually through the introduction of legislation. There is a regular procedure governing the way this is handled which may differ in details between different issues but which generally follows much the same lines.

• The first step, as has been suggested, lies in the submissions made by officials of the department to the department's ministerial team. These submissions may be submitted at the initiative of the officials, either in response to government policy statements or to some issue that has become regarded as important in the press or in the minds of the public. Or, alternatively, the submissions may be made in answer to a request made by the minister, stating that it was time that the departmental position on a particular issue was more widely known.

- The submission is discussed in a series of meetings with both the department's senior officers and the departmental ministerial team. Both sides will have their say on the rights, wrongs, shortcomings and inaccuracies of the proposals but, in most cases, any advantage lies with the ministerial team rather than the civil servants since the politicians can cite the democratic mandate of the elected.

- When agreement has been reached within a government department, the matter passes to the appropriate Cabinet committee which will vet the proposal in their turn, giving the proposal its policy approval which, at the same time, smooths its way through Cabinet proper. The Civil Service aspect of this will have been settled in the string of 'shadow' committees set up to co-ordinate government policy before it goes forward through committees. As a result of meetings of Cabinet committees, which in turn will be endorsed by the full Cabinet, proposed legislation will find its way onto the government programme.

- There is one hurdle that any emerging legislation has to face and that is to receive the blessing of the Treasury. Any act of legislation costs money and the financial consequences of what is proposed have to be mapped out and costed by a Treasury minister, whose name will then be appended to the Bill as a sort of guarantor of financial rectitude.

- Alongside and parallel with the political and financial arguments, the civil servants within the relevant department will begin the consultation process, seeking advice and opinions from those sources mentioned earlier in this chapter, such as interest and power groups, technical and professional experts, think tanks and advisory groups and even members of the public who have a serious contribution to make, the various contributions being gathered together to help make up the raw material out of which the legislation will be framed.

- As the consultation process and policy meetings draw to a close, the Leader of the House will make an order that the drafting of the bill should begin. The actual legislation is drafted by a number of specialist lawyers known as 'parliamentary counsel' who go about their work fully briefed and supervised by departmental civil servants and only after long briefing meetings in the relevant department. It is the task of parliamentary counsel, obviously with assistance from civil servants, to draw up an outline bill that is as short and as uncomplicated as possible, while allowing that there will always be flaws which opponents will try to exploit. Despite all the efforts of professional drafters, there have been many flawed pieces of legislation and civil servants responsible for drafting legislation have had to face sustained criticism because of government bills that are still being corrected and amended even at such a late stage as the House of Lords. In an analysis of work done by the House of Lords it emerged that during the 1992/93 session of parliament the Lords passed 1,674 amendments to 28 government bills![24]

- The draft legislation is checked by a committee largely composed of officials, located in the Cabinet Office and known as the Legislation Committee of the Cabinet. It is this committee which gives the go-ahead for a bill to enter the legislative process. The bill as drafted is carefully checked at this stage, particularly by law officers such as the Attorney-General, who will mostly be looking for legal loopholes and other flaws overlooked by the parliamentary counsel or the departmental civil servants.

• As an alternative to the immediate issue of a parliamentary bill, ministers and their officials are often willing to extend the consultative process with the issue of a White Paper. This is prepared in a sequence of actions almost exactly similar to the actions involved in drawing up a bill.One particularly important form of White Paper that the Civil Service has to draw up is when a paper is issued in order to reply to a report made by a select committee and the civil servants in question must respond in detail to any select committee proposals.

• Once the proposed bill has begun its progress through parliament the team of civil servants from the relevant department will continue to service the legislative process, briefing their minister and the managerial team as the bill progresses and writing operational papers on how to absorb amendments made during the committee stages and how to manage the final draft form of the bill as it goes through the process of becoming an Act of Parliament.

Civil servants and parliament

Assistance given to ministers during the consultative and drafting phases of the legislative process is merely a fraction of the total amount of involvement by civil servants in the workings of parliament. The total amount of work connected with legislation undertaken by civil servants is not negligible and will include such things as supporting the departmental minister with necessary information during debates and committee stages of the bill, as well as drawing up answers to spoken and written parliamentary questions (PQs). The devices and conventions that have emerged by which means civil servants help ministers to deal with parliamentary procedures, 'illustrate the important role played by civil servants as policy advisers, departmental managers and policy administrators'.[25]

One important type of **written question** takes the form of a letter written by an MP to the minister, normally in response to the concerns of a constituent, although it could be on behalf of other interested bodies. Such letters are regarded as being extremely important and for an answer will be passed on upon receipt to a senior civil servant whose seniority represents at least grade 5 in the open structure, such as an Assistant Secretary in the relevant department. This senior official will immediately get an investigation under way into the nature and problems of the letter's subject while the actual answer will take the form of a lengthy and detailed reply to the MP who originated the question: an answer researched, checked and written by a team of civil servants whose expertise consists in the drafting of such responses.

Parliamentary questions represent a formalised channel for questioning the actions and policy decisions of government departments and represent the most obvious form of parliamentary scrutiny of ministerial accountability. Such PQs can take two forms, depending on whether they demand a written or a spoken reply.

- **Written questions** are by far the easiest to deal with, even though they might ask for and expect extremely complex and detailed answers, very often statistical in nature. A written question will be exhaustively researched and answered at length by a cross-section of the department's civil servants, the process being led and co-ordinated by a senior civil servant of at least grade 7 of the open structure, namely an official at Senior Principal or Principal level. The answer arrived at goes initially to the MP who asked the question but copies are made available to parliament and to the public through parliament. It is the publication and distribution of these answers which distinguishes them from the simple written questions mentioned above.

- **Oral questions** to be answered in Question Time in the Commons chamber, are shorter than written questions and do not need such a detailed response. However, while the minister has to have advance notice of what is contained in the initial oral question, the MP who has asked that initial question then has the right to ask a supplementary question, the thrust of which does not have to be made known beforehand and which can be about something else entirely. The unexpected question can therefore form a device by which back-bench and opposition MPs can attempt to wrong-foot and catch out the minister. This means that the team of civil servants carrying out research in the department, again under the direction of a Principal, will not only have to frame answers to known questions but also attempt to anticipate the areas about which the minister might be subject to questions and thereby to guess at precisely what supplementaries are likely to arise, drawing up tentative answers to questions that may or may not be asked.

Standing committees and **debates** on the second and third readings of a bill are also occasions when a small team of senior civil servants will accompany the minister to parliament in order to prepare spoken and written briefings in advance of the debates or committee meetings. During the course of those debates and meetings the officials will continually pass notes of guidance to their ministers as new points and arguments arise.

Devices such as PQs are intended to test the accountability of ministers but there is also a sense in which they can also be concerned with the accountability of civil servants. In the previous chapter we dealt at some length with the external accountability of officials, particularly over financial matters, through the twin means of departmental select committees or the Ombudsman. But there is also a sense in which, indirectly, that external accountability of officials to parliament, particularly in the areas of the formation and implementation of policy decisions, is made possible through devices such as PQs which 'cast light into the dark reaches of officialdom, thereby obliging civil servants to enlighten their ministers and official superiors about the actions they have or have not been taking'.[26]

Conclusion

The theory of a neutral Civil Service suggests that, in the course of the policy process, civil servants should assist ministers by providing information and advice and by helping to implement policy decisions. But the theory also suggests that they should leave it there and that their involvement should fall short of participating in policy formulation. Experience tells us, however, that civil servants are not only involved in policy formulation but indeed play a major and crucial part in that process.

Notes

1 Gerald Kaufman, *How to Be a Minister*, Faber and Faber, London, 1997, p. 35.
2 Bill Jones, 'The Policy Making Process', Chapter 25 in Bill Jones (ed.), *Politics UK*, Harvester Wheatsheaf, Hemel Hempstead, 1994, p. 536.
3 Rob Baggott, *Pressure Groups Today*, Manchester University Press, Manchester, 1995, p. 25.
4 The work of Graham Allison is discussed by Bill Coxall and Lynton Robins, *Contemporary British Politics* (2nd edition), Macmillan, Basingstoke, 1995.
5 The discussion of issues is based on Colin Pilkington, *Issues in British Politics*, Macmillan, Basingstoke, 1998, pp. 1–6.
6 Mike Moran, 'The Changing World of British Pressure Groups', *Teaching Politics*, September 1985.
7 Patrick Dunleavy, A. Gamble, I. Halliday and G. Peele (eds), *Developments in British Politics*, Vol. 5, Macmillan, Basingstoke, 1997, p. 335.
8 Rob Baggott, 'Where is the Beef? The BSE Crisis and the British Policy Process', *Talking Politics*, Autumn 1996, pp. 2–8.
9 Kaufman, Note 1 above, p. 37.
10 Jonathan Lynn and Antony Jay, *The Complete Yes Minister*, BBC Books, London, 1984, p. 16.
11 Robert Pyper, *The British Civil Service*, Harvester Wheatsheaf, Hemel Hempstead, 1995, pp. 80–2.
12 Cabinet Office, *Ministerial Code – A Code of Conduct and Guidance on Procedures for Ministers*, Cabinet Office, July 1997.
13 Baggott, Note 3 above, p. 18.
14 *Ibid.*, p. 90.
15 Kaufman, Note 1 above, p. 46.
16 Jones, Note 2 above, p. 549.
17 Cabinet Office, *Civil Service Management Code*, published by the Machinery of Government and Propriety Division of the Cabinet Office (Office of Public Service and Science), 1996.

18 Geoffrey Fry, *Policy and Management in the British Civil Service*, Prentice Hall/Harvester Wheatsheaf, Hemel Hempstead, 1995, p. 95.

19 Ian Budge, Ivor Crewe, David McKay, Ken Newton, *The New British Politics*, Addison Wesley Longman, Harlow, 1998, p. 572.

20 Baggott, Note 3 above, p. 101.

21 Lynn and Jay, p. 435, Note 10 above. The passage quoted comes from a note purported to be Bernard Woolley explaining the role of the Civil Service in making policy.

22 Bill Coxall and Lynton Robins, *Contemporary British Politics* (2nd edition), Macmillan, Basingstoke, 1995, p. 152.

23 The quotation about Ron Dearing, along with other information about the formulation of policy decisions, comes from Kaufman, Note 1 above. The quotes in question come from Chapters 4 and 5, pp. 27–45.

24 Colin Pilkington, *The Politics Today Companion to the British Constitution*, Manchester University Press, Manchester, 1999. Included in the glossary entry for the House of Lords, p. 77.

25 Pyper, Note 11 above, pp. 120–2.

26 *Ibid.*, p. 121.

11

The Civil Service beyond Whitehall

Relocation

The days have long since gone when all civil servants and all government offices clustered together in Central London. Larger government departments and offices have always had regional branches, particularly those which have to carry out the executive functions of government; take, as an example, the very many locations that have always been needed to house the Inland Revenue Service. In recent years, however, it has become increasingly the case that the head office or principal location of a branch of government is also located outside the London area, largely since the government itself is attempting to set a good example to private sector business and industry in those campaigns that are aimed at persuading large organisations to ease pressures on transport and accommodation by relocating their staff away from London and the over-crowded Home Counties. This is not so much true of government departments and the ministries themselves, those principal administrative offices and policy units which contain the senior civil servants of the department, senior personnel who must remain in Whitehall and close to government ministers. But relocation has certainly applied to such government services as the Royal Mint, which has transferred to Llantrisant in South Wales, or the Ordnance Survey's headquarters, which is located in Southampton. And it is even more true of the various government departments' many executive agencies, even those that are long-established, as well as those set up under the Next Steps programme. Consider the largest agencies of them all, those associated with Social Security: the National Insurance Contributions Agency has been located in Newcastle for many years and has long since been joined by the main Benefits Agency office in Leeds and the Child Benefits Agency at Dudley in the West Midlands.

Now, however, the relocation of civil servants away from London is having to be considered, not only for the social or economic imperatives of decentralisation but because the monolithic structure of the Home Civil Service itself is becoming somewhat fragmented and taking on the aspect of a federal structure. A key factor in this is the way in which the Civil Service is having to serve a number of masters other than simply the central UK government in Westminster. What we are talking about in fact is, on the one hand the need to provide a bureaucracy for the new devolved administrations of Scotland, Wales and Northern Ireland, and on the other hand playing a part in staffing the secretariat of the European Union (EU).

The Civil Service and devolution

Over the next few years the area which will demand the most fundamental changes to the Civil Service concerns the bureaucratic dispositions needed to cater for a growing number of newly-devolved administrations. Currently the Scottish, Welsh and Northern Ireland Offices cover all aspects of administrative devolution by implementing the decisions, actions and policies of the UK parliament at Westminster insofar as the respective countries or provinces are concerned. However, devolution will mean that, with the exception of certain reserved powers, the direction of policy and legislation will be passed down from Westminster to the Scottish parliament or to the Welsh and Northern Irish Assemblies and they in their turn will require the help of bureaucrats in order to implement their decisions.

It must, however, be borne in mind that there is no uniform answer since there is no one single form of devolution that is common to all three provinces. Circumstances dictate that a different form of administration has been envisaged and devised for each of the three, with quite different powers available to them and with each of them having differing degrees of legislative autonomy from Westminster. And, if there are three different forms of assembly for the three provinces, there also have to be three different solutions as to how the Civil Service will be arranged in the three administrations. And this can be seen by the terms which the various Devolution Acts have imposed on the nature of the administration available to the devolved assemblies. One word of warning, however. With the exception of the dispositions for Northern Ireland, the practicalities of the Civil Service structures that have been set up are largely unknown as yet and the guidelines laid down in the Devolution Acts might change considerably in the light of experience, once the devolved assemblies are up and running.

Northern Ireland

The arrangements for Northern Ireland are unusual in that there is a pre-existing bureaucratic mechanism already in place as a functional body which has not gone away since a devolved parliament last existed at Stormont prior to 1972. Until the direct-rule legislation of 1974 the province had its own

Northern Ireland Civil Service (NICS) based on Stormont Castle, which ran all those executive functions over which the Stormont Parliament had legislative power. After the introduction of direct rule from Westminster in 1972 the Northern Ireland Office was established along the lines of the Scottish Office, and it was the Northern Ireland Office which officially took over the running of the province under legislation passed in 1974. The NICS was not abolished, however, but remained in being after direct rule, continuing to provide staff for the six government departments which had previously been headed by Stormont ministers, ministerial responsibilities for the province being assumed under direct rule by two Ministers of State and two Under-Secretaries of State within the Northern Ireland Office.

The six Northern Ireland departments were and are:

- the Department of Agriculture;
- the Department of Economic Development;
- the Department of Education;
- the Department of the Environment;
- the Department of Finance and Personnel;
- the Department of Health and Social Services.

The specific concerns of these six departments were known as 'transferred powers' because responsibility for their administration had been transferred to Stormont but there were also 'reserved powers' that remained the concern of the UK parliament in Westminster. These reserved powers obviously included law and order but also took in taxation, any other Treasury concerns, foreign affairs, defence and constitutional matters. With the 1998 Act restoring devolved government to Northern Ireland there was yet again a reassignment of the reserved and transferred powers as they had been disposed since 1974.

> The Constitution Act provides for executive power to be devolved. Heads of departments will take charge of the administration. The Secretary of State will cease on devolution to be responsible for the *transferred* matters with which departments were concerned, though s/he or other United Kingdom ministerial colleagues will remain responsible for *reserved* and *excepted* ones.

It should be noted that, by the 1974 Act, there were under direct rule no heads of departments; departments being subject to the direction and control of the Secretary of State.[1]

Some idea of the impact the existence of a Northern Ireland Civil Service has had upon the UK Home Civil Service can be gained from examining Appendix 1, which lists the staff employed by various Whitehall departments. It is interesting to note that, while the Welsh Office employs 2,050 civil servants and the Scottish Office 4,936, the Northern Ireland Office appears to require a mere 205. Since it would seem unlikely that Northern Ireland requires only one tenth of the administrative work demanded by Wales, there has to be another explanation. And that, of course, is that the 205 civil servants from the UK Home Civil Service are employed purely on the business of the Northern Ireland Office, while the six departments administered by the NI Office are staffed by the NICS. Further evidence of this can be found in Appendix 2 where a list of government executive agencies shows a total of 24 agencies that are exclusively located in the province, often duplicating exactly the pattern of agencies existing in Great Britain, as with the Northern Ireland Prison Service, or the Northern Ireland Ordnance Survey. These agencies are staffed by the NICS rather than the Home Civil Service and there is no doubt that this situation will continue to exist after devolution.

Wales

Of the three devolved assemblies to be established, that for Wales is the one likely to have least effect on the Civil Service. The Welsh Office already represents administrative devolution in the fields of agriculture, education, culture, economic development, environment, health and local government as well as controlling a rather large number of quangos within the Principality. In a very simple move the control of these departmental functions will be transferred directly to the members and officers of the Welsh Assembly but since, unlike the situation in Northern Ireland, there is no separate Civil Service in Wales, the implementation of departmental policy will remain very firmly in the hands of the Home Civil Service. As is very clearly stated in the Act setting up the Assembly, 'the Assembly has the power to appoint staff and *such staff are to be members of Her Majesty's Home Civil Service'* (author's italics).

For those drawing up the devolution legislation one very important consideration is that the Home Civil Service is common to all parts of the United Kingdom and therefore its continuance is a guarantee of the continuing union between England, Wales and all other UK component parts. The key factor is that, where civil servants in Whitehall have the ministers in charge of government departments as their political chiefs, that function in Wales will be assumed by the Assembly along the lines suggested in the Civil Service Management Code. As the Welsh Office's commentary on the bill setting up the Welsh Assembly puts it:

> the Assembly has functions related to staff management in the same way as they are currently delegated to Ministers in charge of Government departments under the Civil Service (Management Functions) Act 1992. The Assembly or any of its committees, the Assembly First Secretary or any of the Assembly Secretaries can delegate any of their functions to the staff of the Assembly. In such cases, the Permanent Secretary to the Assembly (the Assembly's senior civil servant) will determine responsibility within the Assembly staff for such functions.

As far as Wales is concerned the Secretary of State will fund the Assembly out of money provided by funds voted for annually by the Westminster parliament. The expectation is that the Secretary of State for Wales will pass virtually all of these funds to the Assembly; the Secretary of State retaining only a small amount from the funds to cover the costs of his own office. The amount and timing of payments to the Assembly remain a matter for the Secretary of State's discretion, although in practice payments to the Assembly will continue to be determined by the so-called 'Barnett formula', under which funds are allocated to Wales according to its population relative to England. The value of this funding is currently around £7 billion per year.

Secondary offices connected with the Welsh Assembly include an office of the Welsh Administration Ombudsman (*Ombwdsmon Gweinyddiaeth Cymru*) and the Welsh Development Agency (WDA), which is to take over the functions of the Development Board for Rural Wales (DBRW) and the Land Authority for Wales (LAW).[2]

Scotland

In control of the governance of Scotland after devolution will be a body known as the Scottish Parliamentary Corporate Body (SPCB) which will oversee the administration of the devolved parliament, and which will have the powers to appoint staff, hold property, and enter into contracts. Among the most immediate duties of the SPCB will be to organise the staffing of the parliament itself, first estimates for which show that approximately 200 staff covering a wide variety of duties will be required.

As far as Civil Service requirements for Scotland are concerned:

- Scottish ministers may appoint whomsoever they wish onto the staff of the Scottish Administration;
- staff so appointed and any holders of other non-ministerial office in the Scottish Administration will be members of the Home Civil Service; and
- responsibility for the management of such staff will ultimately remain with the Minister for the Civil Service (i.e. the Prime Minister). However, provision is also made enabling responsibility for the day-to-day management of such staff to be delegated to the Scottish ministers and those office-holders in the same way as happens at present for government departments.

The Devolution White Paper states that it is the government's wish that staffing arrangements for Scotland should reflect the traditional values of the Civil Service, making it clear that all such staff will be managed as members of the Home Civil Service. The staff of the Scottish Administration will be extended to cover such personnel as the staff of the Lord Advocate in the Crown Office or in the Procurators Fiscal service. The holder of any office in the Scottish Administration which is neither a ministerial office nor a member of the staff of the Scottish Administration is judged to be in service with the Home Civil Service. Offices in the Scottish Administration which are not ministerial offices are defined by statute and include such posts as the Registrar General of Births, Deaths and Marriages for Scotland, the Keeper of the Registers of Scotland and the Keeper of the Records of Scotland. The intention of these regulations is that all staff of the Scottish Administration should be regarded as civil servants in the UK Home Civil Service since, as was the case in Wales, maintaining a unified Home Civil Service is considered to be essential for preserving the unity of the United Kingdom.

All conditions of service in Scotland are according to provisions regarding the management of the Civil Service contained in the Civil Service Management Code. This reflects the constitutional arrangement under which ultimate responsibility for the Civil Service will remain with the Minister for the Civil Service. Under the terms of the Civil Service (Management Functions) Act 1992 the Minister for the Civil Service has the power to delegate, to ministers and others, those functions vested in him for the management of the Civil Service. This also enables the responsibility for day-to-day management of the Civil Service of the Scottish Administration to be delegated to the Scottish Executive by the Minister for the Civil Service in exactly the same way as responsibility for the day-to-day management of the civil servants in government departments is at present delegated to the ministers of those departments. Staff will be subject to the provisions of the Civil Service Management Code which contains within itself the Civil Service's Code of Conduct setting out the standards of behaviour expected of civil servants, such as political impartiality or integrity.

The duty has been imposed on the Scottish Parliament to provide for the investigation of certain complaints of maladministration in connection with action taken by or on behalf of members of the Scottish Administration. In making such provision, the parliament is required to take account of the Parliamentary Commissioner Act of 1967. It also provides that the Scottish Parliament may make provision for the investigation of complaints in respect of office holders in the Scottish Administration, Scottish public authorities, and action taken by cross-border public authorities in connection with devolved matters. In the UK context, the Parliamentary Commissioner for Administration (often known as the Parliamentary Ombudsman) is independently appointed to investigate complaints about the government's handling of matters. He will continue to deal with complaints from Scotland about the UK's handling of matters where responsibility has not been devolved. For complaints about the handling of devolved matters, there will be similar arrangements for Scotland, based as closely as possible on the UK Ombudsman legislation.[3]

The European dimension

There was a time not so long ago when the part played by the Civil Service in relation to Europe would not have been worth much more than a brief footnote to the main text. However, the principal institutions of the EU – the Commission, the Parliament and the Court of Justice – have very small bureaucracies of their own, and what secretariat as there is is mostly taken up with the translation of EU documents into the 11 languages of the Community. Indeed, one institution, the Council of Ministers, which is the guiding hand and legislative body for the Community, has virtually no secretariat of its own, recruiting temporarily at need from the secretariat of the Commission or using officials from the various member states. And what is true for the Council of Ministers is equally as true for the Community as a whole: the bureaucracy of the EU is very largely provided, directly or indirectly, by secondment from the bureaucracies of the member states.

As the impact of EU membership on the United Kingdom has grown ever greater over the years, so has the number and complexity of the bureaucratic links which exist between Brussels and Whitehall. Civil Service involvement with Europe is on several different levels and for very different purposes but the result is that every civil servant, in every department and on every grade, has to treat work done for the institutions of the Community as being just as much a part of their natural environment as their own Whitehall ministry. Increasingly an important slice of Civil Service duties is taken up in liaison with the bureaucracies of other member states or in dealings with the European Commission. It must also be borne in mind that there is a very considerable amount of work on European matters which is carried out by civil servants who, despite all the amount of work they do on European matters, remain themselves securely part of the British Home Civil Service:[4]

First and foremost in the European involvement of British civil servants is their role in implementing EU secondary legislation as it applies to the UK. Secondary legislation means all those legal instruments devised and issued by the Commission of the EU to administer the policies laid down by the Council of Ministers, legislation which is then passed to national governments for acceptance and implementation. The types of legal instrument issued to national governments for implementation include:

• *Regulations*, which become immediately effective as law within the member states without the need for any national legislation to endorse them nor indeed any need to change the form of the regulation as it was determined in Brussels. However, although regulations become law in the form that was agreed in Brussels the Civil Service of a member state is free to suggest that additional legislation may be required for greater effectiveness, and it is then the task of the domestic civil servants of the member state to suggest and make the necessary modifications.

- *Directives*, which are not as complete and detailed as regulations. In essence they consist of policy objectives that are binding on member governments but which do not have a specific form dictated by the Commission. The method by which the objectives are to be achieved is left to the discretion of national governments and the formulation of that method is left open to the bureaucracies of those national governments.
- *Decisions*, which are not directed to all member states but are specifically directed at one country, firm, organisation or individual. Because these decisions are very specific they are often administrative rather than legislative acts and as a result have very little to do with officials in the member states.

In any one year more than 12,000 legal instruments are issued by the Commission and have to be dealt with by the Home Civil Service. Two-thirds of these are purely routine administration, dealing with matters such as price levels in the Common Agricultural Policy. Of those instruments that can be considered legislative, 4,000 are regulations, 500 are decisions and 100 are directives. The majority of these represent delegated legislation enacted by the European Commission under powers delegated by the Council of Ministers and is largely administrative detail arising from legislation already agreed by the Council. For civil servants in the UK and other member states most of this work is pure routine that does not need much extra activity or effort but it does take up an increasing amount of time for an increasing number of officials.

At first the implementation of European regulations and directives was officially entrusted to the Foreign and Commonwealth Office (FCO), which has always claimed the leading role in anything to do with Europe. The FCO has within it two executive departments specifically designated to deal with European matters, although it was not until the Blair government of 1997 that there was an actual Minister of State at the FCO charged with looking after EU affairs. The two departments are:

1 the European Community Department (Internal), dealing with European matters in the UK.
2 the European Community Department (External) dealing with British interests in Europe.

The above dispensations are based on the FCO's official viewpoint that relations with the EU are to be regarded first and foremost as facets of the UK's overall foreign policy, which should therefore be dealt with exclusively by the Foreign Office. Nevertheless, even as early as the time of Britain's accession to the European Community under Edward Heath there was an alternative perspective in existence, which was to ignore any connection with foreign affairs, seeing any business associated with the European Communities as merely representing a European dimension to what are basically domestic British government and politics. Over the years the FCO has been forced to cede work on European issues to the Cabinet Office and other government departments until, according to Cabinet Office statistics issued in early 1999, there were no fewer than 16 separate UK government departments dealing with policy issues that have a specific European dimension.

A belief that the EU is an important aspect of British domestic policy rather than a concern of British foreign policy led government departments apart from the Foreign Office to cast around for an alternative and better conduit for co-ordinating the concerns of Whitehall and Brussels than the two European Community Departments of the FCO. This they did by establishing an important European Secretariat in the Cabinet Office.[5] Through a weekly meeting with the UK's Permanent Representative in Brussels this small secretariat, numbering no more than about 20 civil servants seconded from other departments, plays a major part in coordinating European matters:

- handling all those European matters likely to be included on Cabinet or Cabinet Committee agendas;
- helping to frame agreements on common responsibilities between departments where European issues are involved;
- briefing departmental civil servants on the present and future implications of British policy in Europe;
- overseeing the scrutiny of European legislation by the European Select Committees of both Houses of Parliament, work which includes the briefing of committee members on EU matters;
- checking that the UK complies to the full with any requirements demanded by the European Commission in the implementation of EU legislation.

Within their own Whitehall departments there is a great deal of work for civil servants to do in support of those ministers who are carrying out their European role as members of the Council of Ministers; something which becomes a particularly onerous task during the UK's presidency of the EU. When a minister attends a Council meeting, he or she will be accompanied by a team of civil servants from the relevant department who will act as advisers during meetings of the Council, as well as providing a secretariat to record the findings of the meeting and note the actions to be taken. This Council work for the Civil Service reaches far beyond the actual Council meetings and includes regular contacts within and between national delegations over a period of several weeks in order to prepare the ground for the actual Council meetings. Council meetings are themselves so short that they rely on the national delegations having reached a provisional conclusion as to the final form any agreement will take before the actual meeting takes place. The importance of the officials is that they leave their ministers comparatively little to do at Council meetings, politicians concentrating on the hammering out of the final details while passing the main issues by the prior agreement established by the officials.

The member states of the EU take turns to hold the Presidency of the EU, the term for which the presidency is held being six months. During that time, ministers from the presiding member state chair the various Council meetings so that, for example, during the British Presidency in 1997 all meetings of the Council of Finance Ministers, ECOFIN, were chaired by Gordon Brown as Chancellor of the Exchequer, while the General Council was chaired by Robin Cook as Foreign Secretary. Ministers chairing these meetings rely very heavily on national officials to provide them with support, there being something of a dual servicing of the presidency so that, at Council meetings, the minister in the chair sits with officials from the Brussels secretariat on one side, and his or her own national officials on the other. The smooth running of European Council meetings becomes a matter of pride for national officials and the relevant Permanent Representatives.

British civil servants in Brussels

British civil servants can therefore do a considerable amount of work for the EU without losing their place in the domestic structure of the Home Civil Service. Yet possibly even more work can be done by civil servants seconded to work in Europe while themselves remaining part of the British Home Civil Service. Typical of this are those civil servants appointed or seconded for service with the **UK Permanent Representation (UKREP)** on the **Committee of Permanent Representatives**, or **Coreper** as it is popularly known.

As a group of permanent representatives to the EU from each member state, and an institution which plays an important and decisive role in the functioning of the EU, Coreper often exerts tremendous influence on EU policy. Comprising the 15 EU states' ambassadors to Brussels and serviced by the small Council of Ministers' secretariat-general, Coreper is the last line of official-level decision-making before proposals reach EU ministers. Although its members are ultimately accountable to their member states' governments, with the status of diplomats or civil servants, with clear guidelines from their national capitals on how to approach any issue, Coreper has wide-ranging abilities to negotiate deals within the EU legislative process and therefore plays a much wider role in the policy-making and decision-taking processes than would be normal for officials if they were working according to the practices of their own countries of origin.

At first a preparatory body set up to hammer out the details written into the 1957 Treaty of Rome, Coreper has gradually developed, for the reasons given above, into one of the most powerful groups of officials in the world. Over the years the committee has begun to devolve its more mundane duties to specialists and, as a result the national representations comprise literally hundreds of officials, splitting for convenience into two bodies, Coreper I and II, in 1962. Coreper II was designated the senior, its core membership comprising the 15 permanent representatives, while Coreper I became a forum for their deputies. Coreper II generally meets on Friday, while Coreper I meets on Wednesday.

The two committees into which Coreper is divided are responsible for:

- keeping the EU's institutions and the governments and bureaucracies of the member states informed of each others' work;
- ensuring that national and European policy are not at loggerheads;
- finding compromises so as not to undermine core national positions.

In practice these different functions are difficult to separate and merge into the more general aim of keeping the EU working smoothly.[6]

The permanent representatives who make up Coreper are, of course, the equivalent of ambassadors to the Community and the British representatives are for the most part regarded as being senior diplomats from the FCO, UKREP having a regular staff of about 40 officials plus ancillaries. The Permanent Representative in person is a career diplomat from the FCO, with the same status as a senior ambassador, ranking in seniority alongside the ambassadors to Washington or Paris. The UKREP staff in its entirety, however, is only partially provided by either the FCO or the Diplomatic Service, as much as two-thirds of the staff in fact being from other Whitehall departments, including the Deputy Permanent Representative who is traditionally a member of the Department of Trade and Industry.

UKREP has three main functions:

1)   UKREP officials provide advice, information and secretarial support in traditional Civil Service fashion for ministers and senior civil servants who are temporarily in Brussels or elsewhere in the Community on EU business.

2)   The Permanent Representative and UKREP officials act to co-ordinate actions and liaise between the British government and EU institutions. UKREP will lobby the Commission and European Parliament on behalf of British interests, while the British government will be kept in touch by means of the Permanent Representative attending meetings with the Cabinet Secretariat in London at least once a week.

3)   As part of the EU legislative process, Coreper provides **working parties** which do developmental work on proposals put by the Commission to the Council of Ministers. These working parties are made up of officials and experts provided by national governments, either seconded directly or via the Permanent Representation. A member state such as Britain might have up to four of its nationals as members of a working party. It is worth noting that, as there may be anything up to 10 such working parties operating at any one time, the contribution made by the national delegations can be quite substantial and significant.

Civil servants working within UKREP are the only British representatives permanently based in Brussels, although there are a variety of other reasons for the temporary long- or short-term secondment of national officials to Community institutions. One major European duty that can best be filled by a senior civil servant is by secondment to the support team of one of the two British Commissioners. All Commissioners have a small group of aides or advisers known as their *cabinet* to assist them in their work; the word 'cabinet' being used here in its French sense which would be better translated into English as 'private office'. The members of a commissioner's *cabinet* are usually civil servants who have been seconded, either from the commissioner's own national civil service, or from another part of the EU bureaucracy. It is only natural that the convenience of familiarity means that it is not unusual for members of the *cabinet* to be fellow-nationals of the commissioner, even though convention expects at least one to be from another member state. British Commissioners, for example, on their appointment to Brussels and being asked to nominate suitable candidates for their *cabinet* may well find it more comfortable and probably more productive to ask for specific officials they had known in their days of political service in the UK, thus fulfilling a need to have at least some people they know and like as members of their *cabinet*, familiar faces whom they know they can work with and who will help them to cope better with their new tasks.

Joining the Eurocrats

Around two-thirds of the administrative staff of the EU are employed by the Commission. Despite a public perception of a massive bureaucracy, fuelled by a tabloid press which seeks to portray Brussels as so over-burdened with red tape that it suffers from the condition known as Euro-sclerosis, the actual size of the Commission's staff (approximately 15,000)[7] is remarkably small, being no larger than the average government ministry in one of the member states and, with an annual budget of £58 billion, spending less than half the budget of the British Department of Social Security. One factor that swells the numbers which are required to service the workings of the EU is the question of translation and interpretation: about 3,000 staff – almost 20 per cent of the total – being involved in translation work alone.

Staff of the Commission are permanently employed and, for the most part, are appointed on merit. In the case of senior or specialised staff, that merit is judged by means of highly competitive open examination. There is a career structure and most promotions are internal but the ever-present question of national jealousies prevents the organisation being truly meritocratic. Something in the nature of a national quota system does exist, at least for those senior administrators who can initiate legislation and it is still not unknown for outsiders to be seconded from their national Civil Services into the service of the Commission as and when they are needed in order to preserve something like a balance of nationalities.

The Commission administration is divided into 23 policy responsibilities, similar to government ministries, each headed by a Director-General. These Directorates-General are not known by their area of responsibility but by a Roman numeral preceded by DG for Directorate-General: hence DGVI for agriculture, DGXVI for regional policy, and so on. The normal hierarchical structure divides the Directorates-General into directorates and the directorates into divisions. The pattern is not uniform, however, because the size of the Directorates-General varies so much: DGIX for example, which deals with important budgetary matters, has a staff of more than 2,500 while DGXXII, dealing with structural policy, has a staff of less than 60. Some of the smaller Directorates-General have directorates but no divisions, while others have divisions but no directorate. Each Director-General is answerable to a Commissioner but there is not a precise match between the areas of responsibility given to the Directorates-General and the portfolios given to Commissioners.

The internal career structure of the Commission's secretariat is not very different from that of the British Civil Service. Members of the staff are divided into four categories:

- **Category A**: reserved for university graduates and represents the senior administrative staff; this is the nearest equivalent in the EU structure to a senior civil servant in the open structure of the UK Home Civil Service. There is also a parallel **category LA** for those administrative grade officials working as translators or interpreters in the *Joint Interpretation and Conference Service*.
- **Category B**: executive grades.
- **Category C**: secretarial and clerical officers.
- **Category D**: manual and support service staff.

How to be a Eurocrat

The Civil Service Management Code[8] states quite clearly, under the heading 'Service with the European Institutions':

> Departments and agencies should encourage staff with potential to consider service with the European institutions as part of their developmental training. Work in the institutions should normally be regarded as experience which will be valuable to the department or agency on the officer's return.

Recruitment for service with the EU bureaucracy is therefore encouraged by the Civil Service Establishment and entry to service in Europe is by way of the normal recruitment channels of the Home Civil Service, even though successful candidates who are offered permanent service with the EU are required to retire from the UK Civil Service immediately upon appointment and it might be thought that the Home Civil Service which had had the expense of training these civil servants might resent losing their services once they were trained. However, there is a source of national pride for member countries in getting as large a number of their citizens as possible into service with the Community's institutions, competition for permanent places with the European institutions being very keen among would-be Eurocrats from all 15 member nations.

However, permanent service is not necessarily the main aim of either the applicants in question nor the Civil Service Establishment which has encouraged their application. It is equally as likely that, rather than seeking a permanent position, British applicants are looking for long- or short-term secondments to work in Europe, either for a specific purpose or simply to gain experience with European institutions as a career-building move, experience that can be useful both to the civil servants themselves and to the departments or agencies which employ them and to which they return after their time in Brussels or elsewhere in Europe.

There are basically three types of secondment available to British civil servants:

1)   The *Stagiaire* schemes offered by the European Commission's **Bureau des Stages** in Brussels provide two 5-month periods of in-service training, known in English as '**the Stage**', which involve work experience in the Commission together with lectures and visits to other institutions. The two courses are open to university graduates and public service employees below the age of thirty and run from 1 March and 1 October each year. *Stagiaires* receive a cost of living allowance from the Commission.

2)   The **Detached National Expert** schemes represent a specific form of secondment to the European Commission since here civil servants are recruited for their own particular expertise which is placed at the disposal of the European institution for periods of one, two or up to three years. The greatest number of such secondments lies in the field of science and scientific research, recruitment being through the Directorate-General for Science, Research and Development (DGXII). The seconded specialists will continue to be paid by their own departments but will also receive a living allowance from the European Commission.

3)   There are a number of schemes, such as the *Agent Temporaire* and *Auxiliaire* schemes, which offer temporary contracts for anything up to three years. These contracts are for specific employment within EU institutions such as the European Parliament, the European Court of Justice but most probably the Commission. The three factors that distinguish these people from permanent employees of the EU are:

• employment is for a fixed term, after which time the official returns to his or her own original employment in their home country.
• those seconded to Europe need not resign from their own department. Indeed their own departments are required to grant unpaid leave for the term of the secondment and to be prepared to re-employ them after their return from Europe.
• staff on secondment will continue to be paid by their home department or agency, who will also be responsible for superannuation payments. There is also a responsibility for ensuring that their living conditions do not suffer and many of those on secondment will be paid a cost of living allowance

under the particular rules that the department or agency has for those of its employees posted overseas.

A **permanent transfer** to work for the Commission is a career move open to any British civil servant, who can apply for transfer through the European Staffing Unit within the Cabinet Office or indeed by direct application to the Directorate-General for Personnel and Administration (DGIX). However, since 1990 when the scheme was introduced, the normal method by which UK nationals qualify for employment as senior civil servants at category A of the EU bureaucracy is through an application for and acceptance onto the European Fast Stream Programme. The Fast Stream recruitment programmes were mentioned in Chapter 4 as a system of fast-track training and promotion for university graduates entering the Civil Service. These programmes have a part to play across the entire Civil Service but the European Fast Stream is of particular importance because it addresses two quite separate objectives in one single measure: the programme is primarily intended to increase the number of UK nationals working within the EU, but it simultaneously creates a substantial and influential section of the Home Civil Service which has considerable experience in dealing with European issues within a UK context.

Applicants for the Fast Stream programme do not have to be civil servants at the time of making their application; they need merely to be UK nationals, with a first or second class honours degree and aged no more than 41 at the time of entering the programme. The age limit is fixed at 41 because they aim to move on to work in Europe after a couple of years' training and there is an upper age limit of 45 for anyone applying to work for the Commission or other EU institutions. There is no particular preference for one kind of degree rather than another, the European Fast Stream is as generalist as any other, but a degree in a suitable discipline such as law, economics, European or political studies or a modern language is considered helpful, while reasonable fluency in a second EU language is also desirable, although candidates who are accepted will attend regular intensive language classes as part of their training programme. If accepted as a European Fast Streamer the applicant becomes a full time UK civil servant, working in a UK government department or agency but, as the European Staffing Division puts it, 'the big difference is that their work has an emphasis on European policy issues, so they learn how the EU machinery works and how Brussels and Whitehall interact'.[9]

Once recruited by the Cabinet Office, the Fast Streamers are allocated to whichever department can offer sufficient EU policy work, although developments in the EU mean that there are very few departments that do not show an increasing involvement in European issues. By late 1998 there were European Fast Streamers employed in no fewer than 16 different UK departments. Within these department the Fast Streamer will tackle a normal Civil Service work load but obviously there is a specialised concentration on European matters. They also spend a fair amount of time on special European training courses laid on by the Civil Service College and will naturally apply for and undertake at least one short-term secondment in Europe. Again according to the 1998 statistics issued by the Cabinet Office, thirty out of the eighty current European Fast Streamers were working on secondment in Brussels at any one time, most of the secondments being with the Commission.

At regular intervals applicants will be invited through the *Official Journal of the Commission* to put their names forward and sit the highly competitive written and oral examinations that are the only possible way of entry into the EU recruitment schemes. If a candidate is successful they will take up their allocated post in Brussels or Luxembourg and will need to resign from the UK Civil Service since they will undertake upon taking up their new positions to place loyalty to the EU above any national loyalties. There is a high level of success for UK Fast Streamer applicants: the same 1998 report mentioned earlier had noted the names of eleven European Fast Streamers who had recently passed competitions for permanent posts with both the Council of Ministers Secretariat and the European Commission. Even those who fail the competitive examinations are not particularly penalised since the training received on the Fast Stream Programme will be invaluable in a career with the UK Civil Service, particularly in the handling of relations and interaction between Whitehall and Europe. As the Cabinet Office report says of unsuccessful candidates, '[they] could stay in the UK Civil Service and put [their] experience and training to good use there'.

Conclusion: towards a federal service?

Examples in this chapter of the extent to which large sections of the Home Civil Service are deployed outside Whitehall, and indeed outside Britain, seem to confirm a thesis put forward, by Robert Pyper among others, which claims that the old monolithic and highly integrated Civil Service is dying if not already dead. It is noteworthy that the Devolution Act setting up a Scottish Parliament is insistent that the need for civil servants to service the devolved administration should in no way weaken the integrity of the UK Civil Service as a whole. As is quoted earlier in this chapter: 'this ensures that all the staff of the Scottish Administration should be civil servants in the Home Civil Service . . . [since] . . . maintaining a unified Home Civil Service is considered to be essential for preserving the unity of the United Kingdom'. Perhaps that unified service may be maintained but there are those critics who may equally argue the case that the damage has already been done and the Civil Service is irrevocably fragmented and balkanised beyond repair.

Pyper's arguments are chiefly based on the reforms carried out in the 1980s and 1990s such as the Next Steps programme or the Financial Management Initiative but the more recent moves to set up extensions of the Civil Service in Edinburgh, Cardiff or Brussels can be seen as being equally as important, if not more so. The result according to Pyper is that, 'A much looser federation of reasonably discrete organisational entities, each with its own ethos and subculture, seems to be taking the place of the old monolith. Government employees will be more likely to identify with their particular agency or department than with a huge organisation.'[10]

Other commentators agree on the changes that have taken place but would not necessarily agree that the changes were indicative of disintegration but more the product of the changes in public service provision that took place in the 1980s and which have redefined the public sector as an 'enabler' or 'facilitator' rather than a provider. According to Peter Hennessy, the Civil Service has changed through a process of decentralisation, the delegation of responsibilities and a recognition that the nature of state provision has changed completely since the idealised model of a service was established by the Northcote–Trevelyan Report in the nineteenth century.[11] Another knowledgeable commentator, Sir Robin Butler, presided over the more significant changes as Cabinet Secretary and, while he recognises both the merits of the reforms and how unlikely it is that any future government might seek to change or reverse them, nevertheless he feels that a quiet period of consolidation is necessary if the Civil Service is not to disintegrate beyond repair.[12] He describes three necessary precautions:

1 A halt should be put on the creation of new agencies before the service becomes so fragmented that there is no proper co-ordination on policy or staffing matters between branches of the same department.
2 Greater efforts should be made to prevent the politicisation of civil servants, with a consequent loss of the ethos of neutrality and anonymity.
3 The growth of open recruitment and appointment should not deprive the Civil Service of its ability to recruit and train its own personnel to the highest ethical standards.

We can be certain that the Civil Service has not yet disintegrated and that there is still a remarkable persistence of beliefs and structures that have their roots way back in the service's history. Yet there have been very significant changes over the past two decades involving decentralisation, delegation and devolution. The structure of today's Civil Service is less centralised and unitary and far more federal.

Notes

1 The information on Northern Ireland devolution is based on a series of explanatory booklets about the peace and constitutional settlement, prepared by the Northern Ireland Office and available from them or HMSO. All the information is also freely available on the Internet at the Northern Ireland Office website at http://www.nio.gov.uk

2 Information and quotations relating to Welsh devolution is based on a booklet written and published bilingually by the Welsh Office, *The Government of Wales Act 1998 – An Explanatory Guide*, which is available from the HMSO but which can also be read by those with access to the Internet on the Welsh Office website at www.assembly.wales.gov.uk/govact/

3 A considerable amount of information about Scottish devolution and its effects, as published by the Scottish Office in July 1998, is available from the Constitution Group at the Scottish Office, Victoria Quay, Edinburgh EH6 6QQ. Or on the Internet at http://www.scottish-devolution.org.uk

4 An outline of Civil Service involvement in Europe is given in Colin Pilkington, *Britain in the European Union Today*, Manchester University Press, 1995, pp. 142–5.

5 Robert Pyper, *The British Civil Service*, Harvester Wheatsheaf, Hemel Hempstead, 1995, p. 176–7.

6 Details of Coreper are taken from an article by Alistair Keene in *Europa*, a discussion journal published by the European Commission, 1997.

7 No one source seems able to agree on the exact size of the Commission staff – figures quoted range from 13,000 to 16,000, the figure chosen depending on variable factors. The figure I give is only approximate and relates to the situation in 1995, but that does not invalidate the point that, for a busy bureaucracy with wide-ranging responsibilities, the Brussels establishment is very small.

8 Cabinet Office, *Civil Service Management Code*, Machinery of Government and Propriety Division of the Cabinet Office (Office of Public Survey and Science), 1996.

9 Cabinet Office, *Guide to Working in EU Institutions*, European Staffing Unit of the Cabinet Office (OPS), 1998 edition.

10 Pyper, Note 5 above, p. 181.

11 Peter Hennessy, 'Questions of ethics for government', *FDA News*, January 1993, p. 3.

12 Sir Robin Butler, 'The Future of the Civil Service', *Public Policy and Administration*, Vol. 7, No. 2, pp. 1–10.

Appendix 1

Part I: Ministerial departments and ministries, as of the structure constructed by the Labour government, May 1997

Listed are the main government Departments of State, often with their subsidiary ministries where those ministries have a title and clear function. This is the structure of government according to Tony Blair in 1997 and is listed here purely as an example: any other prime minister – and indeed Blair himself at a later date – is quite free to change the structure completely. The figure right represents the **total** number of **permanent, non-industrial** civil servants employed in that department, according to the quarterly figures released in April 1998. The figure is a total figure and includes civil servants employed in agencies subordinate to that department. Not included in the statistics is the Northern Ireland Civil Service with its agencies.

Ministry of Agriculture, Fisheries and Food	9,657

Ministry of Defence
  Armed forces
  Defence procurement
	104,637

Department for Education and Employment
  Employment and equal opportunities
  School standards
  Lifelong learning
	33,117

Department of the Environment, Transport and the Regions
  Transport
  Environment
  Local government and housing
  Regions and planning
	15,215

Foreign and Commonwealth Affairs Office	5,449
Department of Health Public Health	4,596

Home Office	10,840
Police and criminal policy	
Prisons, probation and immigration	
Department for International Development	1,055
Law Officers' Departments	10,048
Attorney General and Solicitor General	
Lord Advocate and Solicitor General for Scotland	
Lord Chancellor's Department	
Department of National Heritage	612
Film and tourism	
Arts	
Sport	
Northern Ireland Office	205
Privy Council Office	31
President of the Council and Leader of the House of Commons	
Office of Public Service (and Cabinet Office)	1,823
Chancellor of the Duchy of Lancaster	
Scottish Office	4,936
Home affairs and devolution	
Education and industry	
Local government and transport	
Health and Arts	
Agriculture, environment and fisheries	
Department of Social Security	87,218
Minister for Women	
Welfare reform	
Department of Trade and Industry	8,493
Trade	
Science and energy	
Competition in Europe (shared with Treasury)	
Consumer Affairs	
Small businesses	
Export Credits (agency)	
HM Treasury	893
Chancellor of the Exchequer	
Chief Secretary	
Paymaster General	
Financial Secretary	
Economic Secretary	
Welsh Office	2,050

Sources: Cabinet Office (Office of Public Service and Science), 1997; Government Statistical Service, August 1998.

Part II: Non-ministerial departments operating fully on Next Steps lines

The number of permanent, full-time civil servants employed within them, as of mid-1998

Inland Revenue	49,383
Customs & Excise	23,400
Crown Prosecution Service	5,489
Serious Fraud Office	149

Sources: See Appendix 1, Part I above.

Appendix 2

Executive agencies, as of June 1997

The agencies are listed alphabetically without regard for size or importance. The department or ministry responsible for the agency is given in parentheses. A substantial proportion of all agencies are concerned with serving and supplying the armed services and a disproportionate number are therefore responsible to the Defence Secretary. The total number of agencies is also somewhat swollen by the need to provide agencies for Northern Ireland which correspond to existing agencies in Great Britain. The figures to the right show the number of permanent, non-industrial civil servants employed by that particular agency, as of August 1998, although these figures are not available for Northern Ireland agencies. There are also some bodies not included in this list as regular agencies since their work extends across two or more departments, and for which figures are also not available. This includes such bodies as the Forestry Commission and National Heritage.

Armed Forces Personnel Administration Agency (Defence)	110
Army Base Repair Organisation (Defence)	2,725
Army Base Storage and Distribution Agency (Defence)	3,371
Army Individual Training Organisation (Defence)	4,488
Army Personnel Centre (Defence)	1,058
Army Technical Support Agency (Defence)	809
Business Development Service (Northern Ireland Office)	n/a
Cadw: Welsh historic monuments (Welsh Office)	170
CCTA *information technology*] (Duchy of Lancaster)	170
Central Office of Information (Duchy of Lancaster)	314
Central Science Laboratory (MAFF)	547
Centre for Environment, Fisheries and Aquaculture Science (MAFF)	412

Civil Service College (Duchy of Lancaster)	220
Coastguard (Environment, Transport & Regions)	941
Companies House (DTI)	839
Compensation Agency (Northern Ireland)	n/a
Construction Service (Northern Ireland)	n/a
Court Service (Lord Chancellor)	8,670
Defence Analytical Services Agency (Defence)	117
Defence Animal Centre (Defence)	62
Defence Bills Agency (Defence)	677
Defence Clothing and Textiles Agency (Defence)	511
Defence Codification Agency (Defence)	119
Defence Dental Agency (Defence)	135
Defence Estates Organisation (Defence)	1,112
Defence Evaluation and Research Agency (Defence)	10,666
Defence Intelligence and Security Centre (Defence)	139
Defence Medical Training Organisation (Defence)	102
Defence Postal and Courier Services Agency (Defence)	330
Defence Secondary Care Agency (Defence)	690
Defence Transport and Movements Executive (Defence)	146
Defence Vetting Agency (Defence)	341
Disposal Sales Agency (Defence)	62
Driver and Vehicle Licensing Agency (Environment, Transport & Regions)	3,931
Driver and Vehicle Licensing [Northern Ireland]	n/a
Driver and Vehicle Testing Agency (Northern Ireland)	n/a
Driving Standards Agency (Environment, Transport & Regions)	1,756
Duke of York's Royal Military School (Defence)	99
Employment Service (DfEE)	28,612
Employment Tribunals Service (DTI)	568
Environment and Heritage Service (Northern Ireland)	n/a
Farming and Rural Conservation Agency (MAFF)	530
Fire Service College (Home Office)	253
Fisheries Research Services (Scottish Office)	227

Forensic Science Agency of Northern Ireland	n/a
Forensic Science Service (Home Office)	1,238
Forestry Commission Research Agency (Forestry Commission = Scottish Office, MAFF and Welsh Office)	n/a
Forestry Enterprise (Forestry Commission)	n/a
Government Car and Despatch Agency (Duchy of Lancaster)	225
Government Property Lawyers (Attorney General)	95
Government Purchasing Agency (Northern Ireland)	n/a
Health Estates (Northern Ireland)	n/a
Highways Agency (Environment, Transport & Regions)	1,545
Historic Scotland (Scottish Office)	627
HM Land Registry (Lord Chancellor)	7,810
HM Prison Service (Home Office)	39,363
Industrial Research and Technology Unit (Northern Ireland)	n/a
Insolvency Service (DTI)	1,345
Intervention Board [*implementing EU's CAP*] (MAFF, Scottish, Welsh and NI Offices)	1,102
Joint Air Reconnaisance Intelligence Centre (Defence)	155
Land Registers of Northern Ireland	n/a
Logistic Information Systems Agency (Defence)	188
Marine Safety Agency (Environment, Transport & Regions)	n/a
Meat Hygiene Service (MAFF)	1,030
Medical Devices Agency (Health)	133
Medical Supplies Agency (Defence)	231
Meteorological Office (Defence)	2,144
Military Survey (Defence)	690
Ministry of Defence Police (Defence)	3,589
National Savings (Chancellor of the Exchequer)	4,083
National Weights and Measures Laboratory (DTI)	48
Naval Aircraft Repair Organisation (Defence)	1,516
Naval Bases and Supply Agency (Defence)	7,823
Naval Manning Agency (Defence)	97
Naval Recruiting and Training Agency (Defence)	1,497

NHS Estates (Health) 133

NHS Pensions Agency (Health) 403

Northern Ireland Child Support Agency n/a

Northern Ireland Prison Service n/a

Northern Ireland Statistics and Research Agency n/a

Office for National Statistics (Chancellor of the Exchequer) 2,968

Ordnance Survey (Environment, Transport & Regions) 1,856

Ordnance Survey of Northern Ireland n/a

Patent Office (DTI) 746

Pay and Personnel Agency (Defence) 850

Pesticides Safety Directorate (MAFF) 193

Planning Inspectorate (Environment, Transport & Regions) 642

Planning Service (Northern Ireland) n/a

Property Advisers to the Civil Estate (Duchy of Lancaster) 190

Public Record Office (Lord Chancellor) 416

Public Record Office of Northern Ireland n/a

Public Trust Office (Lord Chancellor) 543

Queen Elizabeth II Conference Centre (Environment, Transport & Regions) 55

Queen Victoria School (Defence) 68

Radiocommunications Agency (DTI) 512

RAF Logistics Support Services (Defence) 374

RAF Maintenance Group Defence Agency (Defence) 4,377

RAF Personnel Centre (Defence) 224

RAF Signals Engineering Establishment (Defence) 576

RAF Training Group Defence Agency (Defence) 2,161

Rate Collection Agency (Northern Ireland) n/a

Registers of Scotland (Scottish Office) 1,057

Rivers Agency (Northern Ireland) n/a

Roads Service (Northern Ireland) n/a

Royal Mint (Chancellor of the Exchequer) 964

Royal Parks Agency (National Heritage) 231

Scottish Agricultural Science Agency (Scottish Office) 121

Scottish Court Service (Scottish Office)	828
Scottish Fisheries Protection Agency (Scottish Office)	256
Scottish Office Pensions Agency (Scottish Office)	144
Scottish Prison Service (Scottish Office)	4,702
Scottish Record Office (Scottish Office)	113
Security Facilities Executive (Duchy of Lancaster)	475
Service Children's Education (Defence)	712
Ships Support Agency (Defence)	2,294
Social Security Agency (Northern Ireland)	n/a
Social Security Benefits Agency (DSS)	66,296
Social Security Child Support Agency (DSS)	7,909
Social Security Contributions Agency (DSS)	7,382
Social Security Information Technology Services Agency (DSS)	1,913
Social Security War Pensions Agency (DSS)	947
Student Awards Agency for Scotland (Scottish Office)	126
The Buying Agency (Duchy of Lancaster)	134
Training and Employment Agency (Northern Ireland)	n/a
Treasury Solicitor's Department (Attorney General)	374
UK Hydrographic Office (Defence)	754
UK Passport Agency (Home Office)	1,276
Valuation and Lands Agency (Northern Ireland)	n/a
Valuation Office [*Inland Revenue*] (Chancellor of the Exchequer)	4,029
Vehicle Certification Agency (Environment, Transport & Regions)	81
Vehicle Inspectorate (Environment, Transport & Regions)	1,507
Veterinary Laboratories Agency (MAFF)	1,029
Veterinary Medicines Directorate (MAFF)	103
Water Service (Northern Ireland)	n/a
Wilton Park (FCO)	37

Sources: Cabinet Office (Office of Public Service and Science), June 1997; Government Statistical Service, August 1998.

Appendix 3

Occupational groups into which the Civil Service is divided

Administration Group

Curatorial Group

Economist Group

Graphics Officer Group

Information Officer Group

Legal Group

Librarian Group

Marine Services Group

Police Group

Professional and Technology Group

Research Officer Group

Science Group

Secretarial Group

Social Security Group

Statistician Group

Training Group

Appendix 4

Senior Civil Service – Open Structure

Grade	Rank	Position or comparable status
Grade 1	Permanent Secretary	Head of a major government department
Grade 1A	Second Permanent Secretary	Head of department or policy division
Grade 2	Deputy Secretary	Director of policy area, head of professional group or large executive agency
Grade 3	Under Secretary	Head of policy programme, most senior line manager
Grade 4	Executive director band	Senior professional
Grade 5	Assistant Secretary	Head of policy section
Grade 6	Senior Principal	Head of regional office
Grade 7	Principal	Head of local office

Appendix 5

A Code of Conduct for the Civil Service

The Civil Service Code sets out the constitutional framework within which all civil servants work, together with the values they are expected to uphold. Based on a draft drawn up by the House of Commons Treasury and Civil Service Select Committee, the code came into force on 1 January 1996 and forms part of the terms and conditions of employment of every civil servant.

The Civil Service Code

1 The constitutional role of the Civil Service is, with integrity, honesty, impartiality and objectivity, to assist the duly constituted Government, of whatever political complexion, in formulating policies of the Government, carrying out the decisions of the Government and in administering public services for which the Government is responsible ...

2 Civil servants are servants of the Crown. Constitutionally, the Crown acts on the advice of Ministers and ... civil servants owe their loyalty to the duly constituted Government.

3 This Code should be read in the context of The Ministerial Code of July 1997 which set out the duties and responsibilities of Ministers, including:

- accountability to Parliament;
- the duty to give Parliament and the public as full information as possible;
- not to deceive or knowingly mislead Parliament and the public;
- not to use public resources for party political purposes;
- to uphold the political impartiality of the Civil Service;
- the duty to give fair consideration ... to informed ... advice from civil servants;
- the duty to comply with the law ... and to uphold the administration of justice.

4 Civil servants should serve the duly constituted Government in accordance with the principles set out in this Code and recognising:

- the accountability of civil servants to the Minister or ... office holder in charge of their department;

- the duty of all public officers to discharge public functions reasonably;
- the duty to comply with the law.

5 Civil servants should conduct themselves with integrity, impartiality and honesty. They should give honest and impartial advice to Ministers, without fear or favour, and make all information relevant to a decision available to Ministers. They should not deceive or knowingly mislead Ministers, Parliament or the public.

6 Civil servants should endeavour to deal with . . . the public sympathetically, efficiently, promptly and without bias or maladministration.

7 Civil servants should endeavour to ensure the proper, effective and efficient use of public money.

8 Civil servants should not misuse their official position . . . to further their private interests or those of others . . .

9 Civil servants should conduct themselves in such as way as to deserve and retain the confidence of Ministers and . . . those whom they may be required to serve in some future Administration. They should comply with restrictions on their political activities . . .

10 Civil servants should not without authority disclose official information which has been communicated in confidence . . . They should not seek to frustrate or influence the policies, decisions or actions of Government by the unauthorised, improper or premature disclosure outside the Government of any information to which they have had access as civil servants.

11 Where a civil servant believes he or she is being required to act in a way which:

- is illegal, improper or unethical;
- is in breach of constitutional convention or a professional code;
- may involve possible maladministration; or is otherwise inconsistent with the Code;

he or she should report the matter in accordance with procedures laid down in departmental . . . rule of conduct. A civil servant should also report . . . if he or she . . . is required to act in a way which . . . raises a fundamental issue of conscience.

12 Where a civil servant has reported a matter covered in paragraph 11 . . . and believes that the response does not represent a reasonable response . . . he or she may report the matter in writing to the Civil Service Commissioners.

13 Civil servants should not seek to frustrate the policies, decisions or actions of Government by declining to take . . . action which flows from ministerial decisions. Where a matter cannot be resolved by the procedures set out in paragraphs 11 and 12 . . . he or she should either carry out his or her instructions, or resign from the Civil Service. Civil servants should continue to observe their duties of confidentiality after they have left Crown employment.

Footnote

The above is an edited and abridged form of the Code. If anyone wishes to read the text in full a printed version is available from:

Machinery of Government and Propriety Division,
Room 132E/1,

Cabinet Office (Office of Public Service),
Horse Guards Road,
London SW1P 3AL.

Alternatively the complete text can be read on the Internet at the Open Government website <http://www.open.gov.uk/co/cscode.htm>

Appendix 6

Civil Service Management Code – rules on the acceptance of outside appointments by Crown servants

It is in the public interest that people with experience of public administration should be able to move into business or other bodies . . . It is equally important that when a former Crown servant takes up an outside appointment there should be no cause for any suspicion of impropriety . . .

. . . Rules provide for the scrutiny of appointments which former Crown servants propose to take up in the first two years after they leave the service. To provide an independent element in the process of scrutiny, the Advisory Committee on Business Appointments is appointed by the Prime Minister . . .

. . . The aim of the rules is . . .

a. to avoid any suspicion that the advice and decisions of a serving officer might be influenced by the hope or expectation of future employment . . .

b. to avoid the risk that a particular firm might gain an improper advantage over its competitors by employing someone who, in the course of their official duties, has had access to technical or other information . . .

Index

Note that throughout this index the initials C.S. are taken to mean 'Civil Service'.

OEDIPUS
UBIQUITOUS

The

Family

Complex

in

World

Folk

Literature

ALLEN JOHNSON AND
DOUGLASS PRICE-WILLIAMS

Stanford University Press
Stanford, California

© 1996 by the Board of Trustees of the
Leland Stanford Junior University

Printed in the United States of America

CIP data are at the end of the book

Stanford University Press publications are distributed exclusively
by Stanford University Press in the United States, Canada, Mexico,
and Central America; they are distributed exclusively by Cambridge University Press throughout the rest of the world.

PREFACE

We first began this project nearly a decade ago. At the time, our knowledge of world folklore and of techniques for its study was limited. Over the years, many valued colleagues have given generously of their knowledge and advice to help us find our way through a maze of unfamiliar sources and contending approaches. Robert Desjarlais, Kunae Kim, Bonnie Taub, and James Wilce served at various times as research assistants, and each went beyond the call of duty to make fully professional contributions to the collection and analysis of the folktales presented here. Their work was supported by many small grants from the UCLA Academic Senate. Early advice from Roy D'Andrade, Gerardo Reichel-Dolmatoff, Christine Goldberg, Larry Peters, and Johannes Wilbert helped us find firm footing in new territory.

Harry Brickman, Bradley Daigle, Samuel Eisenstein, Leslie Horton, Albert Hutter, David Markel, Joseph Natterson, Marvin Osman, and Albert Schrut read an earlier draft and commented helpfully. Douglas Hollan, John Ingham, and Melford Spiro commented extensively on a later draft. The friendly and enthusiastic support of these readers encouraged us to proceed, and their thoughtful commentaries helped us avoid many errors and find balance among perspectives.

Ariane de Pree helped us sort out the inevitable difficulties in tracking down the permission holders for many of the tales in Part II, and in acquiring the necessary rights to reproduce the tales in our collection. Complete permissions information is included in a section entitled "Permissions to

Reproduce the Folktales" following the References Cited in the back matter. Permissions information included with the source notes at the start of each tale is not complete.

Since our manuscript went to press, colleagues who have learned of our work have sent us further examples of family complex folktales that we could not include in this book. Our own field studies conducted while we were compiling folktales showed that when you ask people about family complex tales, they usually know of some. We hope that our work will encourage fieldworkers to ask for such tales in the future, to help enlarge the corpus of tales that, in this work, should be considered only a beginning.

A.J.   D.P.-W.

CONTENTS

South and East Asia

Oceania

A NOTE TO THE READER

In preparing this collection of folktales for what we hope will be a wide and varied audience, we have made several editorial decisions.

First, we decided to adopt a policy of generally ignoring foreign language accents. The tales in their original sources varied widely in this regard, depending on who published them and for what purpose. Rather than reproduce a confusing welter of accents and special characters of interest chiefly to linguists, we opted to simplify matters by omitting most accents. Readers interested in the original orthography of the tales can follow the trail to the original versions.

Second, we decided to reproduce the tales as they appeared in the sources with no attempt to provide a unifying editorial "voice." Most tales occurred as self-contained stories, but a few bear the marks of the collector or are even retold or summarized by the compiler of the source where we found them. We have limited ourselves to occasionally noting this fact with a bracketed comment where it might be confusing to the present reader.

Third, the reader will note that there are often two sources given at the base of the opening page of a tale. The primary source is often older and available only to readers with access to very complete libraries. We usually found the tale in the secondary source, we always reproduce the tale from the secondary source, and we have listed the primary source data mainly for readers interested in checking the context in which the tale originally appeared.

PART I

ANALYSIS

CHAPTER 1

INTRODUCTION

Freud regarded the Oedipus complex as the centerpiece of psycho-analytic theory, "the shibboleth that distinguishes the adherents of psycho-analysis from its opponents" (quoted in Simon 1991: 641). Based upon analysis of his own dreams, and his study of Sophocles' *Oedipus Rex* and Shakespeare's *Hamlet*, he concluded that every boy passes through a phase in which he wishes to kill his father in order to marry his mother.

In learning to control and reject these unacceptable wishes, Freud argued, the growing boy acquires morality and discipline, enabling him to achieve maturity and to find satisfaction in socially approved forms of work and love. The old wishes, however, are not abolished but repressed; they live on in the unconscious. Oedipal stories are evidence that residues of the Oedipus complex, resolved though it may be, continue to inform human activity throughout life.

An oedipal story, in the strict sense, is about a youth who kills his father and marries his mother. More loosely, it is about some sort of struggle between an older, father-like man and a younger man who stands in a son-like relationship to him, and an inappropriate closeness, often erotic, between the younger man and a motherly woman.

Strictly speaking, oedipal stories are not very common. Loosely speaking, they are everywhere. As may be imagined, this gap between strict and loose interpretations leaves plenty of room for argument over exactly what an oedipal story is. We may illustrate this with the story of Aladdin (or Ala al-Din; see Mardrus 1972). Although not a folktale but a story from great litera-

3

ture (*The Book of the Thousand Nights and One Night*), its familiarity to contemporary audiences as a children's story and as the subject of more than a dozen movies serves as a useful starting place. To our knowledge it has never been identified as an oedipal story.

Aladdin is an idle and disobedient youth whose father grieves for him and then one day dies. Aladdin and his mother are left in poverty until a powerful Moorish magician, posing as Aladdin's father's brother, lures Aladdin to a secret location "at the end of a deserted valley filled only with the presence of God" (Mardrus 1972: 377). There he tricks Aladdin into obtaining the treasure and the magical lamp that "had been written, by the powers of earth, in the name of Ala al-Din" (Mardrus 1972: 382). The magician fails in his effort to steal Aladdin's treasure, and Aladdin prospers, eventually marrying the Sultan's beautiful daughter. But the magician, ravaged by envy and rage, steals both the wonderful lamp and Aladdin's young wife, whom he tries unsuccessfully to seduce. Aladdin survives an attempt by the Sultan to behead him and rescues his wife, killing the magician. Before the story ends, the magician's brother makes another attempt on Aladdin, but Aladdin beheads him. Thereafter, Aladdin, his wife and mother, and the Sultan live happily until, when the Sultan dies of old age, Aladdin assumes the sultanate.

Strictly speaking, this is not a oedipal story. Father is a good man, a concerned parent, troubled by his son's lack of enterprise. The villains of the piece are the Moorish magicians who try to steal the youth's rightful treasure, and, for a while, the Sultan who wants to behead him. And, far from marrying his mother, who is described in the story as "old and ugly," he marries the Sultan's beautiful fifteen-year-old daughter.

Loosely speaking, however, the story has a strong oedipal flavor. The villainous Moor pretends to be the father's brother, a very close stand-in for father; although he is not involved with Aladdin in a jealous struggle for Aladdin's mother, he is involved in a jealous struggle for his wife. Senior males of various sorts, including the two Moors, the Sultan, and the Sultan's powerful Wazir (vizier), are all enviously hostile to Aladdin at various points in the story and seek to destroy him; he responds by killing the two Moors and completely dominating the Sultan and Wazir. And, while it is true that Aladdin marries a young maiden, when the story ends he is united with mother in a forever-after happiness, seated on the Sultan's throne, with father (and all father figures) scoured out of the picture. It is not too far-fetched to describe this ending as an "oedipal triumph."

In popular versions of this story, not all the elements are retained. In the recent animated Disney film, *Aladdin*, for example, Aladdin's mother has been left out altogether. To a concerned Arab-American, this reflected the film's tendency to stereotype Arabs as sword-bearing mutilators and killers, which would have been softened by including "a humane character,

Aladdin's lovable mother, an Arab woman willing to sacrifice everything for her son's happiness" (Shaheen 1992). From our perspective, however, this omission has another significance: removing the mother diminishes the oedipal impact of the story. This is also achieved in the film by eliminating the father's two brothers altogether, concentrating all evil intent into the vizier, and simplifying the Sultan into a chubby, kindly, endearing little fellow without a trace of danger in him. With mother gone and the connection to father safely attenuated, the oedipal story has been, as we shall argue later, "detoxified" for popular consumption.

In this book we will be concerned with the occurrence of what we call "family-complex folktales"—stories of incest and family violence—around the world. "Folktales" are to be distinguished from more literate products like the *Thousand Nights and One Night* (although those literary achievements may depend heavily for inspiration on folk literature), and from more serious stories, sometimes distinguished as "myths." We will look into these terminological questions further in the next chapter.

Considering the impact of Freud's concept of the Oedipus complex on twentieth-century thought—whether to stimulate agreement and extension of Freud's ideas or disagreement and rejection of them—the existence of oedipal stories and their distribution around the world are of decided interest. It has been widely assumed that the presence of an oedipal tale is a sign that the Oedipus complex must be present as well. We will need to examine this assumption later, but it is an appropriate starting point for our inquiry: if oedipal stories are universally found in human societies, then perhaps the Oedipus complex is universal too.

This is a controversial point. Just as much as Freud assumed the Oedipus complex was a human universal, so have Freud's critics argued that it is far from being so. Some have seen the Oedipus complex as either limited to the Viennese society of Freud's late-nineteenth-century upbringing, or worse yet, merely the daydream of Freud alone, a well-to-do, self-satisfied patriarch. Even if it did apply to Freud's circle in Vienna, it did not necessarily apply to Viennese women and probably not to the lower economic strata of that class-structured society. Family conflict may well be a human universal, but the strength of the conflicts, and the particular forms they take, is open to wide variation, just as the family and its community context varies widely from one society to the next.

From the beginning psychoanalysts have raised doubts about the universality of the Oedipus complex. In recent decades the emergence of a powerful new paradigm focusing on the "self" (Kohut 1977) has continued this long-standing controversy: here, the "oedipal situation" is regarded as a developmental stage that can be successfully, even "joyfully," negotiated if the child is treated from birth with appropriate empathy and acknowledgment by its caregivers. An Oedipus complex is not necessary and when troubles are associated with this developmental stage, the oedipal conflicts are secondary, epiphenomenal compared to the underlying defects in early childrearing. Thus, the universality of the Oedipus complex is far from accepted even within psychoanalysis.

We became interested in this topic when, in the course of a seminar in Psychocultural Studies, we came to examine a folktale from the Matsigenka Indians of the Peruvian Amazon. These nonliterate hunter-horticulturalists of the upper Amazon rainforest tell of Shakanari (106 in our collection), a boy who married his mother. This story is oedipal in the strict sense: although Shakanari does not kill his father, the two fight and later his father dies.

We wondered how widespread such stories were and realized we simply did not know. We wrote a small grant proposal to search for "Oedipus-type stories." Many years and several small grants later, we have reached the startling conclusion that oedipal tales are universal. We were startled because, when we set out on this project, although we assumed that stories of conflict and even sexual feeling within the family would be common around the world, as anthropologists we assumed that the form of these stories would vary widely, and that different societies of different scale and with distinct patterns of family organization would generate systematically different kinds of family-complex stories.

It is not so much that we were dead wrong as that we had the wrong emphasis. As we will demonstrate, there is indeed a wide diversity of family-complex tales in our collection. What we did not anticipate was how many of them would fall into a narrow range of variation, which we have come to call the "common form" of family-complex tales. The part of this common form that pertains to the son, father, and mother is quite similar to the Oedipus complex as described by Freud, although some modifications suggested by his critics are needed to account for the majority of our tales. Tales about daughters, however, tend to be quite different from what Freud described, and in fact lend support to the feminist critique of Freud that has gone on within psychoanalysis as well as without.

Our main emphasis will be on the value of folktales as evidence concerning the theoretically crucial issue of the universality of the Oedipus complex. We proceed first by briefly reviewing the debates in which folk literature has been cited as evidence for or against that universality. This allows us to establish the context within which our sample of folktales, which is larger and more global than in preceding studies, can be examined. We then examine our collection and describe our findings.

Two findings are especially impressive. The first is the existence of the common form of the family complex just alluded to. The second is that the strongest dimension on which family-complex folktales vary cross-culturally is from small-scale, nonstratified societies to complex, stratified ones: we find clear evidence that tales told in smaller societies are more blatant in presenting sexual and aggressive actions in the family than tales like *Aladdin*, told in complex societies where delicacy and deception mask the passions at the core of the tales. We will argue that this is unique evidence of a higher degree of repression of intrapsychic conflict in members of more complex societies, a finding that may not be surprising but for which hitherto we have had little concrete evidence.

The question remains whether the existence of oedipal tales is evidence of the importance of the Oedipus complex in the lives of the audience for such tales. Following our examination of the tales, therefore, we turn to the theory connecting the content of folktales to unconscious mental life. Finding existing theory on this point vague and inadequate, we revise it into a form that can account for the unconscious meaning of family-complex folktales. As it happens, this brings us full circle to a reexamination of Freud's ideas on the Oedipus complex in light of our folktales and improvements in our understanding of cultural and social evolution since his day. Although there is much to disagree with in Freud's formulations, there is perhaps more to agree with than might have been thought. The debate over the strict versus loose interpretation of oedipal tales will remain, but the sense that there is "something there" in Freud's assertion of the universality of the Oedipus complex is not easily dismissed.

CHAPTER 2

A BRIEF HISTORY OF RESEARCH ON FAMILY-COMPLEX TALES

F reud's use of the Greek story of Oedipus as evidence of the universality of the Oedipus complex in the general population has always been controversial. A group of Freud's close followers embraced his views completely, while a larger group of scholars were sympathetic but skeptical and sought to revise aspects of his theory. Many others, of course, found his ideas clearly in error, or simply unhelpful.

PSYCHOANALYTIC AND ANTHROPOLOGICAL APPROACHES

The common response within anthropology as well as psychoanalysis was a guarded approval from scholars who accepted some of the framework of Freud's original ideas about the Oedipus complex but disagreed with Freud in significant ways concerning the meaning of oedipal stories. The ultimate importance of these differing viewpoints is that, one way or another, each calls into question the universality of the Oedipus complex.

Freud on Oedipus

Although most readers will be familiar with Freud's views on the universality of the Oedipus complex, a brief review here will help set the stage for the critiques that follow. For Freud it was clear that the story of Oedipus appealed to audiences because it reflected every boy's own unconscious wish to kill his father and marry his mother: "His destiny moves us only because it might have been ours" (1900: 262).

According to the Greek folktale (3), King Laius and Queen Jocasta of Thebes, frightened by the prophecy that their newborn son will grow up to kill his father and marry his mother, pierce his feet and expose him to die. He is saved, however, and eventually is raised by the king and queen of a neighboring kingdom. Called Oedipus (swollen-foot) because of the mutilation inflicted upon him by his parents, he leaves his adoptive home as a young man on a hero's journey. On route, during an argument at a crossroads, he kills a man later discovered to be his father, King Laius. He saves Thebes from the Sphinx and assumes the throne, unwittingly marrying his mother. These crimes against the gods eventuate in Jocasta hanging herself and in Oedipus blinding himself with his mother's garment pin.

Freud saw such folktales as part of a larger category of symbolic constructions, including dreams, jokes, and sayings, where unconscious mental life is given expression. People find folktales and jokes interesting because they express unconscious wishes. He found oedipal content in many other stories, including *Hamlet* (1900: 264–66). But he said in his autobiographical essay (1925: 69) that he left serious treatment of folklore to others.

The reasons why Freud believed the Oedipus complex to be universal, and the profound part it played in his conception of what it is to be human, are best approached by way of his argument in *Totem and Taboo* (1913). Its importance lies in Freud's effort to imagine the nature of the change in emotional life that had to take place before our animal antecedents could be transformed into our human ancestors.

In his view, our animal antecedents were impulsive in seeking sexual pleasure and venting aggression. In particular, they were promiscuous sexually, and males used violence to monopolize females. Humans, by contrast, carefully control sex and aggression, providing only a few proper outlets for the expression of either. Working backwards from his knowledge of primitive human society, Freud noted that at the heart of tribal society was the clan, with two key prohibitions: first, a clan totem animal which no member of the clan could kill or eat; and second, marriage rules (exogamy) prohibiting marriage within the clan. These ancient prohibitions must control powerful and basic human desires (1913: 31–32).

Freud inferred that the marriage rules were instituted to prevent incest. In his view, primitives were imbued with a "horror of incest" so great that they not only prohibited marriage between immediate family members, but extended those prohibitions to certain aunts, uncles, and cousins who were regarded as like parents and siblings. He also inferred that the totem animal of the clan, which is not to be killed or eaten, is in fact a symbolic father of the group. He then asked, why would these two prohibitions, on marriage within the clan and on eating the totem animal, be so fundamental? And this led him to his famous conclusion that the clan originated in a crucial moment in prehistory when a group of brothers, who had conspired to kill their violent father and seize his women for themselves, experienced guilt and agreed forevermore to prohibit incest (via marriage rules) and parricide (via totemism).

Hence, marriage rules that prevent fathers and sons from fighting over the women of their family group represent the first step from Nature to Culture, from animal to human. And the first cultural rules were just those that create the Oedipus complex: the boy must relinquish his early, primitive wishes to kill his father and marry his mother, in exchange for a stable nurturing family in which to grow, with the promise that one day he might have his own wife and be in turn protected from his sons' wrath.

It is worth emphasizing that Freud viewed these developments as inevitable in an evolutionary sense: the stable human family and social group was an adaptive advance that began the human dominance of nature we observe today. The sacrifice of wanton sexual and aggressive behavior in favor of impulse control, mediated symbolically, was the price paid for the evolutionary advantage of the human family, with the father present not only as a defender but also as a collaborator in acquiring and sharing food.

But the price paid was in fact a sacrifice of freedom. The impulses remain, and can be detected in the ample evidence of ambivalence between family members, such as the mixture of admiration, dependence, envy, and disappointment a child feels toward a parent, or our complex feelings at the death of a loved one. Contradictory feelings toward family members often cannot be expressed openly, and folktales are a common arena in which they find indirect voice.

Why are ambivalent feelings unsafe to experience directly? According to Freud, owing to the principle of the "omnipotence of thoughts": Children, "primitives," and neurotic persons, he believed, fear that their own wishes can come magically true. Some of these wishes are dangerous, including sexual and aggressive wishes toward family members. Normal adults repress their wishes, which would be threatening if allowed into consciousness. Neurotic persons construct elaborate obsessive-compulsive rituals to prevent their dangerous wishes from becoming realized, and primitive men construct public rituals, such as those of totemism, for the same purpose.

Since the emergence of culture and the Oedipus complex were, in this view, simultaneous—indeed were the same event—we should expect that all human cultures would show evidence of the Oedipus complex. Freud (1913: 158) believed that these primordial events had been permanently seared into the collective mind of humanity. Hence, the universality of the Oedipus complex, and by implication such evidences of it as oedipal-type folktales, was fundamental to Freud's notion of the human condition.

As we can see, the core of the Oedipus complex concerns the son's competition with the father for an exclusive, "marital" relation with the mother. But Freud's concept of the Oedipus complex was broader in theory, for he saw the "complete Oedipus complex" as involving virtually all possibilities for erotic and aggressive feelings within the nuclear family. He opposed, for example, Jung's introduction of the term "Electra complex" to label the girl's attraction to her father and consequent competition with her mother, preferring instead to label this the "feminine Oedipus complex" (Freud 1920: 155; cf. Freud 1940: 194, n.1). Add to this two further ideas, first that bisexuality underlies a "negative Oedipus complex" where erotic attachment to the same-sex parent leads to jealousy toward the opposite-sex parent (1923: 33–34), and second, that brothers and sisters can displace their erotic attachments from parents onto each other (1916: 205, 210; 1917: 333–34), and "the Oedipus complex is enlarged into a family complex."

Freud did not address brother-sister relations in much detail. In addition to seeing their erotic attachment as a later development out of earlier attachments of son to mother and of daughter to father, he thought the most significant early feelings between siblings would be the older child's anger and disappointment upon being displaced as the youngest and neediest child.

In his early formulations, he saw the feminine Oedipus complex as a mirror image of the masculine one. But later he discovered asymmetry between the two, in that the girl's erotic object shifts from mother in the preoedipal phase to father in the oedipal, whereas the boy's primary attachment remains with mother. As a consequence, the boy is free to split off his ambivalence toward his mother and direct all hostility toward his father during the oedipal phase, whereas the girl is unable to do so. Terror of castration impels the boy then to reverse field, incorporate father into superego and reject mother as a sex object, initiating growth to full masculine maturity. The girl, not fearing castration (according to Freud, because she believes it has already happened to her), is less driven by terror and less certain to form the full sexual attachment to father that brings about "definitive femininity" (1931: 232). She is likely to follow two other pathways, either the cessation of her whole sexual life or a defiant overemphasis on her masculinity (1931: 225–35).

Freud did not speculate on how differences in the various forms of the Oedipus complex might be reflected in folktales. The feminine Oedipus complex seems more ambiguous, with ambivalence toward mother and a good chance of never being clearly resolved, but it is difficult to predict how such a difference might make its way into a folktale. We also have no basis on which to speculate whether the brother-sister tie, seen here as an early sibling rivalry overlaid later with erotic feelings displaced from parents, might stimulate the creation of a unique style of brother-sister folktale.

We may reorder the above points to summarize Freud's argument:

1. The powerful adaptive advantages of human social organization and cultural transmission depend upon family stability, which in turn depends upon control of two deeply rooted impulses: to mate with available females (including mother [and sister and daughter]) and to kill competing males (including father and son).

2. The last enactment of parricide and incest was a crucial moment in human history, when our ancestors renounced fulfillment of these destructive impulses and accepted prohibitions. This dramatic moment is seared forever in the collective mind of humanity.

3. Owing to the fear caused by the omnipotence of thoughts, the knowledge of oedipal desires, though collectively shared, is repressed.

4. Repressed thoughts do not disappear, but seek indirect expression in many different ways, including folktales.

5. Oedipal feelings and their repression being universal human attributes, their expression in folktales and other outlets will also be universal.

6. The Oedipus complex can be generalized to a "family complex" by introducing the negative Oedipus complex (bisexuality) and the feminine Oedipus complex, and recognizing that older children may displace erotic and aggressive feelings from parents onto siblings. In Freud's own work, however, we have no clues as to how this generalization of the Oedipus complex to the whole family might reveal itself in folktales about erotic and aggressive relations between diverse family members.

The Focus on Oedipus

Although Freud expanded his concept of the Oedipus complex to include the whole nuclear family (the "family complex"), his interest remained primarily with the father-son-mother triangle, and virtually all subsequent theoretical and empirical work on psychoanalytic theory in a cross-cultural frame of reference retained this focus, whether it sought to support Freud or criticize him.

Rank did most to apply the emerging psychoanalytic approach to world folk literature. In *The Incest Theme in Literature and Legend*, first published in German in 1912, Rank (1992) finds oedipal story lines in dramas not only about Oedipus, but also Hamlet and Julius Caesar. He also extended his analysis to medieval fables, to Christian legends, and finally to contemporary literature. In each of the stories he found evidence not only of oedipal wishes, but also of "defenses," features of the story that were meant to make it more palatable to audiences, such as the severe punishment of the oedipal protagonists (for example, Rank 1992: 100–101).

Rank also moved beyond the father-son-mother triangle to find stories of father-daughter and brother-sister incest. He argued that, although folktales often present father-daughter incest as originating in the father's wish, it is a mutual attraction that is being depicted: "The mother's death when her daughter reaches marriageable age not only is an expression of the father's wish to exchange his spouse for his daughter but, as Riklin points out (1908), also corresponds to the jealous wish of the daughter, who wishes to take her mother's place with the father (identification)" (Rank 1992: 309; cf. Dundes 1980: 51).

Rank follows Freud in seeing sibling incest as displacement of the boy's desire for mother onto sister, and of the girl's desire for father onto brother. Although by and large limiting his scope to ancient and modern European stories, he also referred to folktales in other parts of the world, especially in his discussion of brother-sister incest.

Money-Kyrle (1929) turned his attention not to folklore but to ritual, specifically rituals of sacrifice. He believed that the universal Oedipus complex included parricidal wishes and that sacrificial rites from around the world evidence such wishes. But, since parricidal wishes may be disguised and expressed in many ways, he viewed the Oedipus complex as a generator from which diverse types of sacrificial rites have emerged. We shall return to this notion of a core complex as a generator of many distinctive forms of expression in our discussion of family-complex tales in the next chapter.

THE EARLY REVISIONISTS. We may examine the way in which folktales were used to bolster or undermine Freud's views by starting with those authors who accepted the basic ideas of ambivalence within the family, repression of frightening wishes, and expression of such wishes indirectly in folktales. Later we will consider separately those folklorists and structural anthropologists who either reject or are simply not interested in the possibility that folktales reflect repressed mental contents.

Despite the controversial nature of *Totem and Taboo*, especially its highly speculative imagining of the Primal Crime, it received a warm response from many in anthropology. The famous exception was Alfred Kroeber's (1920) review of the English edition. He rigorously exposed Freud's lack of data on key points (how do we know the sons killed and devoured the father?) and challenged his interpretations (the twin taboos on incest and killing the totem animal are not necessarily the oldest of all taboos). Kroeber was especially upset at what he saw as the "insidiousness" of Freud's argument, how it builds compellingly from one chapter to the next toward an "unsubstantiated convincingness" (Kroeber 1920: 52–53). He ended his review with a plea for psychoanalysts to become more familiar with the wealth of available anthropological knowledge rather than rely on outmoded scholarship: "ethnology, like every other branch of science, is work and not a game in which lucky guesses score" (Kroeber 1920: 55).

Other anthropologists seemed more content with Freud's lucky guesses. Margaret Mead (1930) made constructive use of his discussion of ambivalence between close family members, and a good deal of attention was given to the widespread occurrence of the Oedipus complex (for example, Kluckhohn 1959: 273–75). Stephens (1962) examined correlates of the oedipal situation in a quantitative cross-cultural study. For example, he hypothesized that the existence of a post-partum sex taboo would intensify mother-child closeness (at the expense of husband-wife) and hence the sex attraction between mother and son: cross-cultural data showed that the post-partum sex taboo correlated with initiation rites for adolescent males, severe mother-in-law avoidance, and severe sex training, all of which Stephens saw as evidence that the Oedipus complex exists, at least in certain societies.

In light of such support, La Barre (1957: 451) concluded that "the essential insights in *Totem and Taboo* have ended in virtually unanimous acceptance among professional anthropologists." This seems to us a considerable exaggeration, however. Many anthropologists remain indifferent or skeptical. Freeman (1967) is nearer the anthropological center in expressing enthusiasm for Freud's basic ideas while insisting we reject many of his specific points on the basis of modern research.

In fact the momentous response to *Totem and Taboo* by an anthropologist remains that of Bronislaw Malinowski. Virtually all future debate on the cross-cultural validity of the Oedipus complex would be played out on the field identified in early papers (Malinowski 1923; 1924) and later elaborated in *Sex and Repression in Savage Society* (1927). Malinowski accepted the basic Freudian ideas of repression and unconscious conflict, but disagreed that these conflicts always take the form of an Oedipus complex. He insisted that family life varies widely from one society to the next, and that typical "nuclear complexes" would also vary:

> The problem therefore emerges: do the conflicts, passions and attachments within the family vary with its constitution, or do they remain the same throughout humanity? If they vary, as in fact they do, then the nuclear complex of the family cannot remain constant in all human races and peoples; it must vary with the constitution of the family. The main task of psycho-analytic theory is, therefore, to study the limits of the variation; to frame the appropriate formula; and finally, to discuss the outstanding types of family constitution and to state the corresponding forms of the nuclear complex. (Malinowski 1927: 19)

He argued that the family structure of the Trobriand Islanders among whom he had done long-term ethnographic fieldwork was so distinct from that of Freud's Viennese community that the nuclear complex of the Islanders was quite unlike the Oedipus complex.

Because we are concerned here mainly with the use of folk literature as evidence in arguments concerning family complexes, we turn to Malinowski's use of the Trobriand folktale of Dokonikan and Tudava (67). It is evident that there is a partial oedipal feel to this tale: a boy is very close to his mother, who teaches him to make a strong spear and gives him fighting magic with which he kills a fearsome ogre. The mutilation of beheading suggests castration, and there is even a wounded foot here, albeit the mother's. But several discrepancies from the Sophoclean tale stand out: there is no incest or marriage between mother and son; Tudava's father is never even mentioned in the tale; Tudava himself is never harmed and ends the story as a hero, rewarded for his bravery; and the mother's brother plays a central role in the story (actually he does also in the Sophoclean play: Creon was Jocasta's brother; but this is rarely mentioned in the psychoanalytic literature on the subject).

For Malinowski, these discrepancies were highly significant. He considered the Tudava tale to be just as representative of matrilineal Trobriand society as the oedipal tale was of Western patrilineal society. In the West patrilineal succession ensures powerful ambivalence in the father-son relationship, whereas in the Trobriand Islands the father is a friendly helpmate of the growing boy. Succession to power and property pass through the mother's side of the family, from mother's brother to sister's son.

> The mother's brother is the appointed guardian of her and her family. Yet this is a duty which both weighs heavily upon him, and is not always gratefully and pleasantly received by his wards.
>
> When Dokonikan is killed his head is presented in a dish of wood to the maternal uncle. If it were only to frighten him by the sight of the monster, there would be no point in disguising the head in the taro pudding. Moreover, since Dokonikan was the general enemy of humanity, the sight of his head should have filled the uncle with joy. The whole setting of this incident and the emotion which underlies it receive meaning only if we assume that there is some sort of association or connivance between the ogre and the uncle. In that case, to give one cannibal's head to be eaten by another is just the right sort of punishment, and the story contains then in reality one villain and one conflict distributed over two stages and duplicated into two persons. (Malinowski 1927: 104–5)

As we see, Malinowski suggests that the tale of Dokonikan and Tudava contains a split of the mother's brother into two images, the ineffective but ultimately good mother's brother who at first abandons Tudava (and his mother) but later gives him a bride, and the utterly evil enemy of humanity, Dokonikan. The tale of Tudava is the story of the Trobriand equivalent of Western civilization's Oedipus.

Malinowski also argued that the sexual passion within the Trobriand family did not flow from son to mother, but between brother and sister, who remain close throughout life. In support of this he offered the tale of the Origin of Love and Magic (66), about a girl who accidentally falls under the spell of her brother's love magic and pursues him into the shallows of the seashore, where they copulate repeatedly until they both die of shame.

Because Malinowski believed that matrilineal society preceded patrilineal society in social evolution, his argument is actually profoundly antagonistic to Freud's. He regarded the Oedipus complex as a recent, localized phenomenon at best. Jones (1925: 128) recognized the danger of this attack immediately: "On Malinowski's hypothesis the Oedipus complex would be a late product; for the psycho-analyst it was the *fons et origo*."

Malinowski was not alone in regarding Freud's Oedipus complex as limited to patriarchal society. Others argued that the link was to class-structured patriarchal society, and most especially commercial, competitive societies such as our own. Karen Horney (1937; 1939) strongly objected to Freud's assumption that every human child is constitutionally impelled to harbor incestuous and homicidal wishes. Modern parents, she held, stimulate hostility in children through insensitive, unreliable, critical, domineering, and narcissistic behavior.

Erich Fromm, in part through an exchange of views with Horney (1939: 13, 78), elaborated the theme that the core of the oedipal situation is a boy's legitimate rebellion against an oppressive father: "Inasmuch as social and parental authority tend to break [a child's] will, spontaneity, and independence, the child, not being born to be broken, fights against the authority represented by his parents; he fights for his freedom not only *from* pressure, but also for his freedom to be himself, a full-fledged human being, not an automaton" (Fromm 1947: 157).

Fromm reexamined not only *Oedipus Rex* but also Sophocles' *Oedipus at Colonus* and *Antigone*. He concluded that these plays were essentially about powerful, irreconcilable hatred between fathers and sons. Fromm saw the Oedipus tale as referring to a time when Greece was in transition from matriarchal to patriarchal society. The Oedipus complex has little to do with the mother at all: "We arrive at the result that the complex centered around the boy's incestuous strivings toward his mother and his resulting hostility against the father is wrongly called an Oedipus complex. There is a complex, however, which fully deserves to be called an Oedipus complex, the rebellion of the son against the pressure of the father's authority—an authority rooted in the patriarchal, authoritarian structure of society" (Fromm 1948: 445–46).

Along these lines, it has been noted that many examples in folk literature depict the conflict between father and son without including mother. Viewed from the son's standpoint, though he may love and identify with his father, this implies the contradictory wish to replace him, to fill his shoes. From the father's standpoint, he does not wish to lose position to his son, yet he simultaneously wishes to become immortal by living on in his son (Steinmetz 1985). In Girard's (1979) view, these contradictions have only led to father-son conflict in recent Western society, where the breakdown of paternal authority makes the father and son more equal, hence more likely to compete.

Many other books and articles have explored this basic theme of the social causes of the Oedipus complex and the variability of nuclear complexes from society to society. These arguments question the biological origins of the Oedipus complex, and, not incidentally, have the effect of exonerating the child of blame for whatever hostility or "thwarted sexuality" he may harbor. A few of these arguments are significant enough to merit brief discussion here.

Kardiner (1939) developed perhaps the most explicit model of how it is that folktales and other expressive systems come to reflect emotional conflicts in the individual. Like Freud, he saw the individual bound to life in society and culture by the adaptive advantages of technology and social organization. But, creation and maintenance of technology and a social order require continuous impulse control of individuals, creating institutionalized frustrations: "When these frustrations are general, and apply to every member of the community, then we can expect some manifestation of this pressure in folklore, religion, and perhaps in other institutions" (Kardiner 1939: 445).

Kardiner gives us the impression of pressures, stresses, and frustrations building up in socially controlled individuals that must find an outlet, along the lines of the energy discharge model psychoanalysts were working with at that time (Gill 1983). Contemporary psychoanalysis has developed a far richer conception of the mind in recent decades, and later we will return to consider the implications of this development for our theory of the relationship between folktales and mental life.

Kardiner also shared Fromm's view that the Oedipus complex was not universal. Assuming that folktales reflect current realities in society, Kardiner held that as societies change, their typical or favorite tales would change too. He used the example of society and folklore in the Marquesas Islands to argue that no Oedipus complex was found there, evidence that tales of the oedipal type are not embedded in a "racial unconscious" (1939: 99–100; see also Langness 1990).

An important tangent off this main line of argument focuses on the damaging hostility and seductiveness of parents to their children. Devereaux (1953) used a number of Greek stories to show that Laius's homosexual aggression had brought about the curse that Oedipus would kill him and marry Jocasta: "the Oedipus complex appears to be a consequence of the child's sensitiveness to its parents' sexual and aggressive impulses" (Devereaux 1953: 139). This general theme of parental hostility and sexuality toward children has also been explored fruitfully in a set of papers compiled by Pollock and Ross (1988).

Another development of the Malinowskian critique has been the further elaboration of alternative nuclear complexes. Malinowski called his the "matrilineal complex," to distinguish it from the Oedipus complex.

Harris (1977) finds the origin of the Oedipus complex not in human nature but in tribal warfare, where the emphasis on fierce, competitive males creates a "male supremacy complex" in which women are subordinated and used by men for sex, reproduction, and exchange (alliance formation):

> All of the conditions for creating castration fears and penis envy are present in the male supremacy complex—in the male monopoly over weaponry and the training of males for bravery and combat roles, in female infanticide and the training of females to be the passive rewards for "masculine" performance, in the patrilineal bias, in the prevalence of polygyny, competitive male sports, intense male puberty rituals, ritual uncleanliness of menstruating women, in the bride-price, and in the many other male-centered institutions. Obviously, wherever the objective of childrearing is to produce aggressive, "masculine," dominant males and passive, "feminine," subordinate females, there will be something like castration fear between males in adjacent generations—they will feel insecure about their manliness—and something like penis envy among their sisters, who will be taught to exaggerate the power and significance of the male genitalia. (Harris 1977: 65)

In Harris's view, since warfare is not universal but arises under specific conditions, the male supremacy complex (and hence the Oedipus complex) is not universal either.

Parsons (1964) examined the family structure in Naples, Italy, and concluded that she had found still another complex, called the "Madonna complex." There men fantasize a sexually pure Madonna-like wife, turning against their actually sexual wives, pursuing prostitutes in the street while vigorously defending their sisters' and daughters' chastity. Mothers attend church and are deeply attached to their "beautiful doe-eyed sons," while grown men avoid church and, in the streets and taverns, curse the Madonna and make sexual jokes (compare Dundes 1985: 26). The father is not perceived as close to the son, nor as powerful or especially frightening. Cross-sex parent-child eroticism is basic in the Madonna complex.

In a similar vein, Kosawa (1950) and Okonogi (1979) have identified a distinctive nuclear complex among the Japanese, called the "Ajase complex," after the tale of Ajase (49). In this story, some hostility of the son toward the father is present, but the center of the story concerns a mother's selfishness. The resolution of the mother-son tension comes as a result of the mother's patience and forgiveness. There is no sexual relationship in the tale, and one cannot help but wonder if the focus here is on a preoedipal mother.

Ramanujan (1983) has also argued for a distinctive nuclear complex in

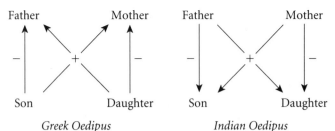

Fig. 1. Greek and Indian oedipal tales compared.
Derived from Ramanujan 1983:252.

India. Examining newly discovered oedipal narratives—a previous scholar had failed to find any and concluded that India lacked the Oedipus complex—Ramanujan found a pattern generally similar to the Greek one. However, he found the emphases shifted: in Indian tales (see 46) it is fathers who tend to kill their sons, and it is mothers who are fated to marry them. Ramanujan conceived the helpful idea of diagramming the tales to illustrate this difference of emphasis (Figure 1).

In a subtle way blame sneaks into the analysis here. These diagrams tend to originate incestuous and homicidal wishes in the child in the Greek case and in the parents in the Indian case. In fact a somewhat covert part of the Freud versus the Revisionists debate concerns who is to blame for unacceptable impulses: oversimplifying, we could say Freud blames the child and the Revisionists blame the parents. Any time theorists originate the unacceptable impulses in a particular individual, they are explicitly or implicitly taking a position on the question "Who is to blame?" As we shall see, folktales usually also take a stand on where the blame for oedipal wishes lies. We will return later to consider the need to distance our theory of family-complex folktales from such implicit blaming.

In sum, the critiques we have examined, which directly or indirectly derive from anthropological theory and data, pose a number of difficulties for Freud's position:

1. The Primal Crime, in which Freud believed firmly, is pure speculation for which no evidence can be adduced.

2. Exogamy and totemism are not the original human taboos Freud supposed them to be.

3. Different socioeconomic conditions produce different family constellations, affecting the specific frustrations children experience growing up.

4. Accepting the validity of Freud's connection between forbidden impulses, repression, and folktales (and other forms of expression of unconscious mental life), different childhood frustrations should produce different folktales; the obverse of this is that differences in folktales, like those found in the stories of Tudava and Oedipus, signal different nuclear complexes.

5. It follows from this that the Oedipus complex is not universal, built into the collective mind, but is found only under specific historical circumstances:

a) societies with authoritarian patriarchal structure and competition for wealth that stimulate rivalry and hostility; and

b) parents, as agents of the social order, who harbor hostile and erotic feelings for their children, bringing into being the Oedipus complex where otherwise it would not exist.

We will consider the first two criticisms later, when we explore our fuller understanding of sociocultural evolution since Freud's time. Now we turn to the remaining points, which are all part of a single argument.

THE FREUDIAN RESPONSE. Within a year of the publication of Malinowski's first two papers, Jones (1925) had prepared a response. He argued that the social importance of mother's brother in matrilineal society, and the erotic brother-sister tie, were social-structural defense mechanisms against oedipal conflicts: a boy's erotic attachment to his mother is deflected onto the less dangerous person of his sister, and his hatred and envy of his father is deflected onto the less threatening person of his mother's brother. Jones thus agrees with Malinowski that a split has taken place in the senior male in Trobriand society (he calls it a "decomposition"), but it is not the mother's brother who has been split into good and bad versions. It is the father figure who has been split into a friendly father and an authoritarian mother's brother.

Jones's belief that matrilineal social structure is a primitive defensive structure against oedipal strife is unacceptable, however (Ingham 1963: 10). Evolutionarily speaking, matrilineal systems like the Trobriands are quite advanced, very possibly having occurred only after the invention of agriculture in the last ten thousand years. Prior to that most societies were probably roughly bilateral in kin reckoning, lacking the property relations and lineage systems of the Trobriands. They would have had to deal with oedipal issues without matrilineal social structure. And, extrapolating from our knowledge of contemporary small-scale societies, close, warm ties between fathers and sons were prevalent.

Stimulated in part by Malinowski's critique of the Freudian Oedipus complex, Roheim (1932) set out to study several distinct cultures, including that of Normanby Island, near the Trobriand Islands. His detailed analysis of folktales, dreams, and songs convinced him that, while brother-sister incest was indeed a preoccupation of the Normanby Islanders, this was secondary to a boy's strong sexual feelings toward his mother and a corresponding fear of being killed and eaten by his father (Roheim 1932: 147, 158; 1941).

In particular, Roheim analyzed a folktale about a boy whose mother is abandoned by her husband and brothers as they flee a man-eating giant who is killing all the people. After many adventures, the boy kills the giant and then joins his mother at the bottom of the sea. This tale is undoubtedly cognate to the Trobriand tale of Dokonikan and Tudava (67): "Whichever way we look at it, it is clear that the Man-eater is the father; the hero is the victorious son who ends in an everlasting life-death at the bottom of the sea in close union with his mother" (Roheim 1950: 226).

Roheim's critique was aimed not just against Malinowski's proposal of a matrilineal complex, but against the general assumption of anthropologists that "all interpretations can only be meaningful in their cultural context" (Roheim 1950: 2). He, by contrast, believed that the "psychic unity of humankind" included intrinsic tendencies to create common expressions everywhere, despite cultural differences. A belief in witches, for example, is the outcome of the child's tendency to project its own oral aggression onto its mother; "a *flying bird* is always and everywhere a symbol of an erection in dream"; and so on (Roheim 1950: 3–4, 262).

Dundes (1985: 18) comments, "One finds no reference to Roheim in mainstream folklore scholarship." This may be in part due to "his chaotic and undisciplined writing style (almost like free association!), coupled with a rather dogmatic way of asserting what a given item's symbolic meaning is" (Dundes 1985: 17). It would be a mistake, however, for any serious student of comparative folklore to let Roheim's style act as a deterrent from awareness of his often deep and provocative insights.

Ingham (1963) applauded Roheim's critique of Malinowski and used further evidence from Trobriand folklore to argue for the presence of oedipal content in Trobriand mental life. He concluded

> that Malinowski did not like psychoanalytic theory for the same reason he disliked theory in general. On the one hand, it would have implied that human behavior is systematically determined and on the other, he could not accept notions about the unconscious, the libido, and so forth because they had no obvious behavioral counterparts; his pragmatic empiricism did not allow him to see patterned relationships and generalizations beyond those immediately given by his intuition and senses. (Ingham 1963: 11)

Spiro's (1982) reexamination of Malinowski's Trobriand material also reaffirms the Freudian position. Using folk literature, among other kinds of evidence, Spiro counters Malinowski's main arguments. He argues that the *absence* of mention of the father in the tale of Dokonikan and Tudava (67) actually points to him as a highly salient figure:

> The matrilineal family comprises four important statuses—child, mother, mother's brother, and father—the absence of a representative of one of these statuses, that of father, must surely be accounted as the most conspicuous *structural* feature

of the myth. That the status of father is replaced by that of cannibalistic ogre—in addition to mother, son, and mother's brother, Dokonikan is the only other character in the myth—must be accounted, therefore, as the most conspicuous *sociological* feature of the myth. (Spiro 1982: 51)

In short, where Malinowski saw Ogre ≅ Mother's Brother, Spiro sees Ogre ≅ Father.

In an earlier work, Malinowski (1922) had provided evidence of ambivalence in the father-son tie, in a Trobriand story of a man who conceals from his son a valuable item he has obtained in inter-island trade. Angered by his father's treachery, the son abandons him on a sandbank and sails away. But the father survives and later, in revenge, attempts to drown his son. This story makes the inference Ogre ≅ Father plausible (Spiro 1982: 54–55).

Using folktales and other evidence, Spiro establishes the existence in the Trobriands of six "correlates" of the Oedipus complex:

1. Strong incestuous desires for sister and adolescent daughter, displaced from mother. Evidence found in the brother-sister incest tale (66) and in a father-daughter incest tale (68).

2. Strong male sibling rivalry, deriving from brothers competing for mother's love. Evidence found in two tales of fratricide.

3. Men's strong jealousy of their own wives and desire for the mates of other men. Evidence found in a folktale about adultery.

4. Avoidance of parents, especially in relation to sexual matters. Evidence found in the custom of extrusion of adolescent sons from the household.

5. Unconscious castration anxiety. Evidence found in two tales (including 68) of self-castration by phallic-aggressive males.

6. Splitting of the maternal image into a "good mother" and a "bad mother." Evidence found in several folktales, worth describing in some detail here.

We consider first a narrative collected in the Trobriands in 1975 by Edwin Hutchins after Spiro had sent him a manuscript copy of *Oedipus in the Trobriands*. In it, an ogress, aggressively greedy and sexual, compels a chief to abandon his pregnant wife and come live with her. The wife is rescued by a sea eagle and carried to his nest on top of a tree, where her son is born. When he is grown, the son returns to his father and denounces the ogress, who has grown so fat that when she comes out of her house she breaks the stair, crashes to the ground, bursts open, and dies.

Other tales represent women as sexual aggressors and men as passive (also true of the brother-sister incest tale, 66). For example, Trobrianders speak of islands to the south where women gang-rape, sexually exhaust, and humiliate any man who passes by. There is also the legend of Kaytalugi, the island of "sexually rabid women." Here, there are no men, and the women sexually use up any hapless man who travels there, until he sickens and dies. These women's own sons do not survive to maturity due to their mothers' relentless sexual abuse. Trobriand men are greatly amused by these tales and eagerly relate them (Spiro 1982: 120–28).

Trobrianders also know several tales in which female genitalia are criticized and mutilated, often with the woman dying as a result. They tell of flying witches whose poisonous emanations from vulva and anus can kill. These witches are considered to be more dangerous than male witches, for they kill and eat men on land or sea. Yet Trobriand men are sexually aroused by women who are reputed to be witches.

Here Spiro makes a provocative linkage between preoedipal and oedipal mother images in folktales. He sees the split into good and bad mother as originating in the preoedipal period. Like other such peoples, the Trobrianders practice a post-partum sex taboo and lengthy nursing period during which a boy is isolated with his mother in a deeply erotic intimacy, not lessened by the mother's enforced sexual frustration and the son's developing genitality (boys nurse for three years or more). Such a sensually charged dependence fills the young boy with fears of being overwhelmed and damaged by his mother (compare Gedo 1979: 137).

Roheim (1948) also noted the simultaneous occurrence of oedipal and preoedipal concerns in witchcraft beliefs on neighboring Normanby Island. There, a witch is a representation of mother and sister that emphasizes their stinginess with food and their cannibalistic urges. Yet witches also have sexual desires for young men, and regularly have sexual intercourse with the ruler of the underground (the Normanby Island equivalent of Satan), whom Roheim regarded as a representation of the father as ogre (Roheim 1950: 218).

As the child's preoedipal relation to its mother is transformed during the oedipal stage, the child's early fantasies of possessing the mother confront the fear of punishment ("incest also contains the exclusion and destruction of the third in the triangle" [that is, father; Loewald 1979: 765]). Spiro (1982: 139) further argues that, in repressing the powerful incestuous attachment to the mother, the Trobrianders have projected their own destructive wishes onto ogresses and witches, and into mythical situations where women are raped, mutilated, and murdered.

Spiro concludes that the Oedipus complex is not absent from the Trobriands, but rather is stronger there than many other places. The expected ambivalence in family emotional life is fully present, including love-hate between the son and both his parents. Spiro draws from his detailed analysis of this famous "negative case" a conviction that the Oedipus complex is indeed universal, varying only in intensity and outcome from one society to another.

Spiro's evidence of the Oedipus complex in the Trobriands, a matrilineal society, not only casts doubt on Malinowski's argument, but indicates that other suggested complexes (Madonna, Indian Oedipus, Ajase) need to be examined in an equally careful manner before they can be accepted as truly nonoedipal family complexes.

Recently, Kurtz (1991) has argued that Spiro's analysis implies that Trobrianders' child development is pathological. He offers evidence to suggest that, through sexual experiences in play groups, young Trobrianders follow a culturally appropriate development of erotic interest away from family members and toward playmates, leading eventually to marriage. He argues that oedipal feelings, or an "oedipal situation," need not imply the neurotic or pathological outcomes sometimes associated with the "Oedipus complex."

Other Kinds of Family Complex

In contrast to the rich literature on the father-son-mother triangle in folktales, other dyads and triads in the family have received little attention. (The "negative family complex," with its focus on homosexual incestuous desires, has been even less discussed: we did not search for such folktales and omit this potentially important topic from detailed examination in this book.)

FATHER-DAUGHTER INCEST. In the Freudian tradition it is possible to view the father-daughter relationship in folk literature as a variant of the oedipal triangle. Bettelheim (1976) pointed out that, in the case of Cinderella, there are many versions of the story from Europe, Africa, and Asia in which Cinderella escapes from a father who wants to marry her, or who wants more love than she can give. "There are many examples of the 'Cinderella' theme in which her degradation—often without any (step)mother and (step)sisters being part of the story—is the consequence of oedipal entanglement of father and daughter" (Bettelheim 1976: 245).

Dundes (1980: 217), examining the story of *King Lear*, concludes that in

> daughter-centered fairy tales, the girl would like to eliminate her mother and marry her father. Many folktales begin with the queen or original mother already dead—perfect wish fulfillment! So in *King Lear*, there is no Queen Lear—leaving the father available as a sexual object for his daughters. But just as the son's wish to marry his mother is taboo, so the daughter's wish to marry her father is equally so. Consequently, in the fairy tale projection, it is always the father who insists upon marrying his own daughter.

Dundes makes an important point here. He describes what he sees happening in *King Lear* as "inverse projection." Just as the folktale father-king's effort to kill his son may be seen as an inversion of the living son's wish to kill his father (Rank 1992), Dundes sees Lear's desire for his daughter as an inverse projection of a daughter's actual desire to marry her father (Dundes 1985: 29–30).

This interpretation of such tales, which, as we shall see, tends to locate the incestuous desire most frequently in the daughter and not the father, has not gone unchallenged. In fact, the aspect of the feminine Oedipus complex that has received the most attention has been what many consider Freud's male-centered view of feminine development, in particular his view that girls and boys develop identically until the oedipal period, when girls discover their lack of a penis (their "castration") and develop lifelong penis envy.

The idea that women's femininity is a secondary development overlaying a primary masculinity appears to have been completely rejected. By 1968, Stoller (1973: 272) had asserted that a "core of femininity" develops in very little girls as a "simple acceptance of the body ego," well before "penis envy, identification with males, and other signs of femininity in disrepair" appear. A decade later, Blanck and Blanck (1979: 85) could say with confidence, "We agree with those who have questioned the postulate that there is a phallic phase in girls. That view of female psychosexuality was based on the assumption that the psychosexual maturation of boy and girl proceeds for both through a phallic phase (Freud 1905). But it is no longer tenable in the light of the present view that there exists a primary femininity in girls (Galenson 1978)." Dundes (1985: 22) has observed that penis envy is rarely represented in folklore anywhere, grounds for doubting its assumed universality.

In a similar way, the difference in the girl's emotional relationship to both father and mother has come to be seen in a positive rather than a negative light. Chodorow (1974), for example, argues that a girl's gender identity is actually stronger than a boy's through identification with mother: she does not turn as sharply away from mother as a boy must, and hence remains more complex interpersonally, more connected with others. In *The Reproduction of Mothering* (1978: 131–32) Chodorow writes:

> There are reasons other than the presence or absence of a penis which can account for the clinical finding that boys repress and resolve their Oedipus complex in a way that girls do not. I read the clinical account as showing that the difference between a boy's oedipal relation to his mother and that of a girl toward her father produce this gender difference in processes of oedipal resolution. Compared to a girl's love for her father, a boy's oedipal love for his mother, because it is an extension of the intense mother-infant unity, is more overwhelming and threatening for his ego and sense of (masculine) independence. Reciprocally, as we have seen, a mother is invested in her baby boy (and probably baby girl) in a way that it is unlikely that a father will be invested in his young daughter, since his relationship to her does not have the same preoedipal roots. This mother-son love threatens her husband and causes him to resent his son. The intensity of the oedipal

mother-son bond (and of the father-son rivalry) thus causes its repression in the son.

By contrast, as we have seen, a girl's attachment to her father does not become exclusive, nor is it as intense as that of a boy's to his mother. It is mitigated by her attachment to and dependence on her mother and is not reciprocated by her father with such intensity.

The greater part of the literature on father-daughter incest is clinically oriented: what are the characteristics of fathers, mothers, and daughters in incestuous households, what are the damaging consequences of the incest, and how effective are the available interventions (Matisse 1990: 31–60; Willner 1984: 144)? An older literature tended to focus on the low intelligence of such families, and on the collusion of mother and daughter in the incest, but this has come under criticism: "because psychiatric literature and studies of family dysfunction apportion responsibility to the mother and daughter, and because psychological literature traditionally dissociates the father's actions from any social context, the legacy of patriarchy remains unimpaired" (Matisse 1990: 34). Matisse's anthropological study of father-daughter incest in middle-class white American families led him to conclude that "it is the father, not the mother or the daughter, who seems responsible for initiating and continuing the incestuous relationship" (Matisse 1990: 382).

It seems that here, again, we find a central concern with identifying who initiates or is responsible for the incest, that is to say, who is to blame. If Freud emphasized the daughter's seductiveness at the expense of the father's, modern scholars are more likely to focus on the daughter as victim of the father's distorted development (Herman 1981; Willner 1984: 145). Fields (1983: 17), however, draws attention back to the mutual seductiveness that can occur between father and daughter and that, if properly managed, helps prepare the girl for mature love relationships outside the home (compare Dundes 1985: 21–22). As Kestenbaum (1983: 126–27) writes, "The girl who is fortunate enough to have experienced in childhood a mature father's frank expression of his pleasure in all aspects of his daughter's femininity is usually comfortable with her body and accepting of her femaleness in adolescence. Such a girl has the advantage of bringing a quality of pleasure in her womanliness to subsequent relationships in adult life." It is the father's responsibility to love his daughter in the appropriately "desexualized" way that allows her to find a suitable husband in her own generation, a resolution artfully represented in the story "Beauty and the Beast" (Kestenbaum 1983: 125).

Carroll (1986) has examined father-daughter incest as a theme in a number of North American Indian Trickster tales. In these tales, which are historically related to each other but have diffused to many quite distinctive societies, Trickster feigns death in order to reappear in disguise and have intercourse with his daughter (see, for example, 87, 89, and 99; compare also 63, 107, and 121). In the first such effort we are aware of, Carroll uses differences in the contents of tales from different societies to test hypotheses about the unconscious meaning of the incest.

Not surprisingly given our above review, he comes up with alternative hypotheses: either the incest wish originates in the daughter or in the father. Following some rather lengthy reasoning and relying on indirect data, Carroll finds support for the wish originating in the father, not the daughter.

In sum, the clear tendency since Freud has been to shift the locus of the incestuous wish from daughter to father, just as in the masculine Oedipus complex it was to shift the origin of hostility from son to father and, to a lesser degree, of erotic love from son to mother. There is also much less sense of a *triangular* complex in the father-daughter situation: daughter is seen as maintaining emotional closeness with mother and the alliance between mother and daughter against Trickster-father in the folktales seems to reflect this.

BROTHER-SISTER INCEST. Evidence suggests that in Western societies father-daughter incest is far more common than mother-son incest, and that brother-sister incest is still more common than either (Willner 1984: 139). In a curious reversal, it appears that published theoretical discussion of incest is most concerned with mother-son incest, and least with brother-sister incest (although father-daughter incest is probably in the forefront in clinical literature).

Moore (1964) notes that many tales of brother-sister incest are actually tales accounting for the origin of the human race or of a particular people, a brother and sister playing the Adam-and-Eve role of First Couple. Although this may be seen as nothing more than a convenient way of solving the problem of where humans came from, Moore argues that, owing to age and generation, brother and sister are actually more likely mating partners than are parents and children (Moore 1964: 1313).

Furthermore, in many kinship systems, brother and sister remain linked throughout life by way of their responsibilities, both ritual and practical, for each other's children. The brother and sister, in fact, often become symbolic parents of their respective children, as for example when a father's sister is called "female father" (Moore 1964: 1317). Even if actual brother-sister incest were absent, in the realm of symbolism (including myth), "relationships which are not sexual or filial in reality may be expressed in symbols having a sexual or filial content. Just as fictive kinship may be resorted to, to bind unrelated persons socially, so fictive incest and fictive parenthood can be part of the idiom of descent" (Moore 1964: 1317). This in itself may account for the appearance of brother-sister incest in folk literature.

A dominant theme concerning brother-sister incest has been the disputed occurrence of brother-sister marriage in certain historical settings. Allowed marriage between full siblings has long been used as evidence that incest prohibitions are cultural, not biological, in origin, and many have assumed that brother-sister marriages were common in ancient royal families. Bixler (1982), however, has examined the evidence for brother-sister marriage among the royal families of Egypt, the Inca, and Hawaii, and concluded that the evidence for marriage between full siblings is very scant indeed.

Part of the problem with these famous cases is that much of our knowledge of the royal families comes from legends rather than historical documents. A further problem arises from the kinship terminologies of these peoples: using classificatory principles, father's brother was usually called "father" and mother's sister called "mother." Thus, father's brother's daughter and mother's sister's daughter were both called "sister." Marriage between such parallel cousins would have been described as between brother and sister. Verifiable cases of marriage between full siblings are very rare and some of these were clearly political contrivances, such as the marriage between Cleopatra, in her twenties, and her twelve-year-old brother, Ptolemy XIII (who died two years later, probably murdered by Cleopatra).

Scholars, however, seem to agree that during the first two centuries A.D. in Roman Egypt full sibling marriage occurred with some frequency among commoners. "Both Egyptians and Romans announced weddings that appear to have been between full-siblings" (Bixler 1982: 273; see also Hopkins 1980). This is the only evidence for brother-sister marriage among commoners in any society.

Brother-sister incest has been a key element in the controversy over the Westermarck (1922) hypothesis that brothers and sisters reared together will have no sexual interest in each other. According to this line of argument, the evolutionary dangers in sibling in-breeding have led to a biologically based propensity to avoid sexual intercourse with close relatives or others who, like close relatives, have been reared together from childhood (Wolf 1966). A disinclination to mate between conspecifics that have been reared together has been noted in many animal species, including several primates (Bixler 1982: 266).

Two difficulties with the Westermarck hypothesis arise. One is that brother-sister incest appears to be rather common, far more common than father-daughter incest or the very rare cases of mother-son incest (Willner 1984: 139–40). These cases are usually among siblings raised together.

The other difficulty with the Westermarck hypothesis has always been that if siblings have no interest in marrying each other, then why prohibit it? Or, apropos the present book, why tell folktales about brothers and sisters who fell passionately in love and suffered harsh consequences as a result? In terms of the theory of folktales we will develop later, we would not expect tales of brother-sister incest to be told at all if Westermarck's hypothesis were true.

NON-PSYCHOANALYTIC PERSPECTIVES FROM FOLKLORE AND ANTHROPOLOGY

Folkloric interest in the Oedipus tale long predates Freud, and it would seem many were not impressed by his interpretation. Robert Graves (1955: 13), for example, writes:

> Was Oedipus a thirteenth-century invader of Thebes, who suppressed the old Minoan cult of the goddess and reformed the calendar? Under the old system, the new king, though a foreigner, had theoretically been a son of the old king whom he killed and whose widow he married; a custom that the patriarchal invaders misrepresented as parricide and incest. The Freudian theory that the "Oedipus complex" is an instinct common to all men was suggested by this perverted anecdote; and while Plutarch records (*On Isis and Osiris* 32) that the hippopotamus "murdered his sire and forced his dam," he would never have suggested that every man has a hippopotamus complex.

It is undeniable that Freud's influence would have been severely restricted had he tried to convince people that they had hippopotamus complexes.

Myth and Folktale

Unlike most anthropologists, folklorists often make a distinction between myth and folktale, understanding folktale as a traditional narrative and myth as a sacred tale. Voegelin (1950: 778) bases the distinction on the appearance in the story of a deity or deities as principal actor(s), or at least that the tale is related to a corpus in which a deity is involved. Failing that, the tale is classified as a folktale. Given this distinction, the Oedipal story—specifically tale type 931 in the Aarne and Thompson (1961) standardized collection—is counted as a folktale and not a myth.

Nevertheless, for many scholars this reasoning does not sit well. Stith Thompson (1949: 409) himself considered that myth is a branch of the folktale. The classicist Kirk (1970: 9) pointed out that what had formerly been accepted as classic myths, such as the stories of Perseus, Medusa, Andromeda, Gilgamesh, and those relating to the Oedipus tale, were not about gods. He (Kirk 1970: 37–41) saw the distinction between myth and folktale this way: "Myths often have some serious underlying purpose behind that of telling a story. Folktales, on the other hand, tend to reflect simple social situations; they play on ordinary fears and desires as well as on men's appreciation of neat and ingenious solutions."

Anthropologists and psychologists have treated the terms differently. Indeed, some anthropologists have leaned more towards equating myth and folktale. Kluckhohn (1959), for example, referred to the "Oedipus-type myth." Benedict (1933) considered that myth could not be divorced from folklore, but did allow that myths are tales of the supernatural world. Bettelheim (1976: 41), a psychoanalyst, made a distinction based on postulated structures of the mind: he thought of myths as being a product of superego demands, while fairy tales are more linked to satisfaction of id impulses.

There would thus appear to be debate and lack of consensus as to the distinction between myth and folktale. We could as easily follow the folklore convention of labeling the story of Oedipus a folktale as call it a myth. For clarity, we have avoided use of the term "myth" in this book, as a way of avoiding an issue that is secondary to our present purpose.

There is an issue, however, on which we need not equivocate. Many so-called "oedipal" tales are in fact cognates of the story of Oedipus and belong to the Aarne and Thompson tale type 931. Many others, however, have no demonstrable link to Oedipus and do not belong to tale type 931. It is these latter we will refer to here as "oedipal" tales, reserving the term "Oedipus-cognates" to refer to those belonging to tale type 931 (see Edmunds 1985).

Classical Approaches

Early folklorists developed a diversity of perspectives on the Oedipus tale. One was that it was a legend based on historical fact, as in the Graves quote above. The German folklorist Carl Robert (1915) tried to trace the historical roots of the story of Oedipus by inspecting the cult places associated with it. He identified the area of Boiotia, and more specifically the village of Eteonos, as the place in which the saga of Oedipus was native. Robert claimed that Oedipus was exiled by Creon to die within the borders of Boiotia, as his death was prophesied to bring the place good luck and crop fertility, and that he was buried in the grave of Demeter, the earth goddess. Earlier, Comparetti (1867) had also taken the position that Oedipus was an ordinary human being whose history was inflated into legend.

Robert also developed the idea that Oedipus was actually a mythical version of the god of vegetation, who is born in spring and dies in winter: "The earth goddess Demeter, in whose sanctuary the bones of Oedipus rest, was originally his mother. . . . The child born of the earth mother in the early year (Spring) had to endure torture or death in Winter. . . . Later saga and poem have embroidered and variated this suffering of Oedipus in the most diverse way; blindness, imprisonment, wandering in misery and drifting on the sea" (Robert 1915: 46). On the matter of the parricide of Laius, Robert argued: "A child of mother earth doesn't need to have a father. If one maintains this, in the context of nature religion it (the father) can only be one which is identical to him (Oedipus) in form, the old year-god, that he must kill, so that he himself can become the god of the year. . . . Yearly Oedipus kills Laius, yearly he marries his mother" (Robert 1915: 58).

A popular argument links Oedipus to the sun. Following Max Müller's (1983) idea that all Aryan mythologies really were attempts to explain solar phenomena such as dawn and the seasons, Breal (1877) saw Oedipus as a personification of Light. When Oedipus blinds himself, "this is the name of the sun at the moment when it touches the horizon" (Breal 1877: 184). The contest with the Sphinx is the struggle with the Storm Cloud, which obscures the Light and is classified with other mythological monsters like the Gorgon. Oedipus therefore is a hero who is the vanquisher of the Sphinx and restorer of the Light.

George Cox (1870) similarly linked Oedipus with Perseus and Herakles as versions of the solar myth. Cox sees the Sphinx as like other monsters (Python, Typhon, Vritra, Zohak, Fafnir, and Cacus) that pertain to darkness: for example, Fafnir is the "dragon of winter, who guards the treasures of the earth within his pitiless folds." Oedipus needed to vanquish the Sphinx, "a dark and lowering cloud," in order to restore the power of the sun. His marriage to Jocasta also restores the sun. The incest, in this view, is incidental to the story, whereas the Sphinx is central.

Another common approach has been to isolate a feature or thread from a tale and track its similarity to features in other tales. Sir George Frazer took up the theme of Oedipus's exposure as an infant and related it to similar features of biblical stories. He wrote of Moses' exposure on the waters among the bullrushes:

> While this story of the birth and upbringing of Moses is free from all supernatural elements, it nevertheless presents features which may reasonably be suspected of belonging to the realm of folk-lore rather than of history. In order, apparently, to enhance the wonder of his hero's career, the story-teller loves to relate how the great man or woman was exposed at birth, and was only rescued from imminent death by what might seem to vulgar eyes an accident, but what really proved to be the finger of Fate interposed to preserve the helpless babe for the high destiny that awaited him or her. (Frazer 1919: 439)

Frazer sees Oedipus as another example of the same story line, but does not offer any special interpretation for it.

In his book *The Hero*, however, Lord Raglan (1936) did identify a set of features as comprising the Myth of the Hero, a distinctive tale type. Inspired by the folktale of Oedipus, he studied many heroes of tradition, like Robin Hood, Cuchulainn, and King Arthur, and found that they shared a number of similar elements: the hero's mother is a royal virgin, his father is a king, an attempt is made at birth to kill him, on reaching manhood he returns to his future kingdom, he marries a princess, he becomes king, he meets with a mysterious death, and so on.

Specifically, there were 22 elements in the pattern that he discovered. Some of the heroes had all of the 22, some had less. The Greek hero Theseus had 20 elements, the Roman Romulus had 18, Dionysos had 19, Moses had 20. Oedipus, according to Raglan, scored the full limit. For Raglan, therefore, Oedipus is not the exemplar of the incest-parricide tale that Freud held it to be, but simply one among many examples of the Myth of the Hero, another tale type altogether.

Dundes (1980: 223–24) finds that the life of Jesus also conforms to Raglan's hero pattern. He notes Raglan's willingness to take as examples three figures from the Old Testament—Joseph, Moses, and Elijah—but not Christ: "Raglan . . . was anxious to show that the lives of traditional heroes were 'folklore' rather than history. Thus it was perfectly all right to argue that Old Testament or Jewish heroes were folkloristic rather than historical. But heaven forbid that a proper member of the British House of Lords should apply this line of reasoning to the life of Jesus!" Folklore, Dundes concludes, while frequently a source of pride and fascination, can also be a source of embarrassment.

The Oedipus Tale in Historical Context

Several writers have attempted to place the tale of Oedipus in historical context. Vernant (1972) faults psychoanalytic writers for overlooking the social context of Oedipus's time. He saw no basis for assuming that the marriage of Oedipus and Jocasta had a sexual component. For the Greeks of his time, familial affection was based on *philia*, a kind of identity between all members of the immediate family. *Philia* was clearly opposed to *eros*, the erotic love between non-family persons. In Vernant's view, identifying familial attachment with incestuous desire was confounding two types of sentiments that the Greeks had carefully distinguished and even opposed.

Vernant also pointed out that Sophocles' play *Oedipus Rex* must be understood in light of the development of the tragic theme in Greek theater. Many writers have noted that the Oedipus tale had two endings (Graves 1955: 14). An earlier one, reported by Homer, has Oedipus living on as king long after his crimes of incest and parricide are revealed, and dying heroically in battle. It was only in the time of Aeschylus (Stritmatter 1987) and Sophocles (Vernant 1972) that the self-punishment of blinding was added. This suggests at least that the attitudes toward such crimes had hardened in the meantime, and that the shift in society toward patriarchy and stratification was the main variable behind the change in attitudes.

A version of this approach has been that the story of Oedipus represents a historical transition of power from matrilineal to patrilineal succession. Propp (1983) argued that the earlier form of succession in ancient Greece was from king to his son-in-law (his sister's son in a matrilineal system), married to his daughter. When the change came to patrilineal succession, the prophecy of parricide arose. Under the matrilineal system the man who would be king simply married the princess; under the new system, however, the hero did not marry the daughter, since the throne no longer passed through her line. Now the hero had to marry the king's widow, and hence kill the king first: "When the king's daughter disappears, her role passes to the king's widow. Oedipus marries his mother. The old role has been transferred to new characters created by changes in the social order" (Propp 1983: 112).

Stritmatter (1987) has similarly viewed the Oedipus tale as a reflection of the break-up of the power of local kin groups dissolving in the formation of the state. In the time of Homer there was a relative lack of concern about incest, "which is treated as an anomaly and not a crime" (Stritmatter 1987: 55), whereas by Aeschylus's time Oedipus is made to blind himself as a sign of guilt over his act.

A Marxian analysis is also possible: Thomson (1977: 287) has argued that the historical change in Greece around the time the Oedipus plays were written centrally concerned the growth of commodity production and the division of labor: Oedipus was "the new man, the individual owner of commodity-producing society, cut off from his kin, independent, free."

Slater (1968) and Lefkowitz (1986) both find that women in ancient Greece held more power (in the domestic sphere) and were treated with more respect in folk literature than previously thought. Slater sees women's frustration with philandering husbands as leading them to be vindictive with their children, who were under their power: this might help account for Jocasta's complicity in the abandonment and exposure of the infant Oedipus. For her part, Lefkowitz doubts whether the incestuous events in Greek myths really indicated sexual passion. In her view Oedipus was not sexually attracted to Jocasta, nor was Thyestes to his daughter: the latter pair, for example, had intercourse because the oracle had said that their son would avenge the murder of his (Thyestes') other children by his brother, Atreus.

Thompson (1952) puts this last position perhaps most forcefully:

> Certainly the Oedipus story of Sophocles involves only quite accidental events and, so far as I can see, has no bearing whatsoever upon the so-called "Oedipus complex." The only enmity Oedipus has is toward an unknown man who tries to drive him off the road. From the Greek point of view, the fact that this man happened to be Oedipus' father came entirely from the workings of fate and not from any psychological law. The same is exactly true of the unwitting marriage with his mother.

Structural Approaches

The structuralist interpretation of Oedipus is quite distinct from both the Freudian and the folkloric. Levi-Strauss (1967), following the emphasis of the linguist Jakobson upon basic oppositions, looks in folktales for such opposites as black-white, up-down, and raw-cooked. Applying his method to the Oedipus tale, he discovers two basic oppositions at work. One is the "overvaluation of kinship" versus the "undervaluation of kinship." The overvaluation of kinship is represented by the mother-son incest, whereas the parricide represents its undervaluation.

The second opposition is a bit more complicated: it refers to the clash between the ancient Greek belief in the origin of humankind by emerging from underground (the "autochthonous origin of man") and the knowledge that human beings are born from the union of man and woman. The tale of Oedipus stresses the killing or overcoming of a half-human/half-beast like the Sphinx that, in Levi-Strauss's words, represents "a denial of the autochthonous origin of Mankind." Levi-Strauss believes that the names of not only Oedipus ("swollen-footed") but also his father, Laius ("left-sided"), and grandfather, Labdakos ("lame"), all refer to the difficulty of Man emerging from the earth, unable to stand upright or walk straight.

Other structural analyses also follow the approach of looking for basic oppositions in the Oedipus myth, but identify different specific oppositions. Turner (1969) identifies the key oppositions as kinsmen versus non-kinsmen and as between consecutive generations. Carroll (1979) focuses on the opposition of affirmation versus denial of patrilineal kin ties. Paul (1982), in a more successful blend of psychoanalysis and structuralism, explains oedipal themes in Tibetan symbolism also in terms of the succession of generations, but focuses on the broader social organization rather than the individual life course. We will review his interesting notion of a "precultural atom" of junior and senior males in conflict over the females of the group later, when we look at Freud's ideas about the "Primal Crime" in light of modern evolutionary theory.

Structural analysis of folklore, while tangential to psychoanalytic analysis, should be regarded as complementary rather than contradictory to it. At various points, psychoanalytic theorists have made use of structuralist insights and methods to enhance their analyses (Carroll 1992: 295; Paul 1982; Spiro 1982). Nor do structural analyses, such as Mosko's (1991) of "sweet" (edible) versus "dirty" (inedible) substances in North Mekeo, preclude the possibility of psychoanalytic interpretations of the same ethnographic materials.

Discussion

Views such as these reflect the wide range of interests that may be brought to bear on any folktale, not just that of Oedipus. Many of them are tangential to psychoanalytic interests and do not preclude psychoanalytic interpretations. Whether Oedipus was a historic figure or symbolically connected with the sun may illuminate the meaning of the story without denying a psycho-analytic perspective.

Alan Dundes, who describes himself as "a Freudian folklorist," is notable for exploring the unconscious meaning of folklore. He finds a middle ground between the universalism of psychoanalysis and the relativism of folklorists, taking a position similar to that of Kardiner (Dundes 1985: 19–22; 1987: 24–25) in the Freud versus the Revisionists debate. Unlike most other folklorists, he regards folklore (including "fairy tales, myths, jokes, manners, customs, sayings, colloquial language" [1987: 16]) as largely unconscious, primary-process material, reflecting early modes of thinking: "Fairy tales, after all, are always told from the child's point of view, not the parents'" (1987: 37).

He and Edmunds (Edmunds and Dundes 1983) have compiled a collection of oedipal folktales. Many of them belong to tale type 931 and are assumed to be cognate to the Greek version. It would make sense that these tales diffused from a common origin sometime in the past. Others, however, do not appear to be cognate, but still have an "oedipal theme." Although Dundes does not stress the point, it is implicit in his approach that some of the universalistic ideas of psychoanalysis can be employed here to explain how similar but historically unrelated stories can co-occur around the world. This, of course, is the main focus of our present book.

Dundes has been especially innovative in extending psychoanalytic interpretations of folklore to contemporary popular culture. He finds strong parallels to oedipal themes in the television series *Star Trek* and the movie *Star Wars* (Dundes 1987: 42–46). In the latter, for example, he notes the incestuous tease in the relationship between Luke Skywalker and Princess Leia (they turn out to be brother and sister after a long, tantalizing semi-romance), and the phallic light-sword battle between Luke and Darth Vader (son and father [Vader]). He even examines the unconscious symbolism of the Apollo moon landing, where Apollo, brother of Artemis the moon, must build up enough rocket thrust to free himself from Mother Earth and land on the moon, where a fellow named Armstrong plants a flag in virgin soil!

Dundes aside, however, it is striking how often theorists pose their interpretations of the Oedipus myth as a denial of the Freudian view. This difficulty in recognizing that the psychoanalytic perspective can coexist with complementary ones is interesting in itself, as examined in Spiro's (1979) "Whatever Happened to the Id?" After a review of the literature in structural and symbolic anthropology, Spiro came to the following conclusion:

> The received opinion in many quarters of cultural anthropology holds that the body, or its drives, or the affects and motives to which they give rise—but most especially those related to sex and aggression—are seldom the concern of cultural symbol systems. If the latter appear to be concerned with sex or aggression, it is

the job of the anthropologist to uncover the reality behind the appearance. (Spiro 1979: 5)

As one example, Spiro reviews Levi-Strauss's (1969) analysis of a Bororo folktale (closely related to our 114), in which a son has sex with his mother (or stepmother), survives many efforts by his father to have him killed, then revenges himself by killing his father and his father's wives. By lengthy and involved structural analysis Levi-Strauss concludes that the incest in the tale really stands for a "close attitude" between mother and son, and that the father-son aggression stands for a "distant attitude" between them (reminiscent of the "overvaluation and undervaluation of kinship" in his analysis of the Oedipus tale). By further comparative analysis of related folktales from other cultures, Levi-Strauss concludes that the meaning they share concerns the origin of cooking fire and, ultimately, of culture.

Spiro comments, with some irony, that a story about sex and aggression in the family is really about sex and aggression in the family. It is not necessary to seek some utterly hidden and counterintuitive meaning for it.

SUMMARY

According to Freud, the transition from nature to culture, from animal to human, depended upon our ability to control impulsive behavior within the family, especially aggressive competition between males over sexual access to females. This control was achieved, but at a cost: the prohibited wishes remain alive in an unconscious region of the mind, continually haunting our dreams and artistic expressions.

Many who agreed with his general approach, however, disagreed with his specific model of the Oedipus complex, and especially with his implication that every child brings oedipal wishes into the world at birth. For many scholars, the degree of father-son hostility varies from one society to the next, reaching its peak in competitive, patriarchal, class-structured societies. The origin of the complex has been shifted from the shared biological makeup of the human species to distinct social and historical circumstances, and the responsibility for it shifted from the children to the parents and their culturally conditioned seductive and destructive wishes toward their own children.

Meanwhile, the larger "complete family complex" of Freud has failed to draw much attention. Father-daughter incest has become the focus of political concerns over the abuse of power by fathers in patriarchal society, and brother-sister incest the focus of debate over the Westermarck hypothesis. Comparatively little has been written about the occurrence of these forms of incest in folk literature, nor about the forms of aggression that may or may not accompany such incest in the tales.

Folklorists appear not to have been influenced by Freud or the subsequent debate. They generally find that both the incest and the aggression in such tales is either incidental and trivial or actually about something else entirely. Our analysis leads to the opposite conclusion. As we turn now to examine the worldwide occurrence of oedipal tales, we will discover that there is a common core out of which the great diversity of specific tales is arising, and that this core indeed expresses passionate erotic and hostile feelings within the human nuclear family.

CHAPTER 3

THE EVIDENCE FROM WORLD FOLK LITERATURE

As we have seen, a good many writers have been working on the assumption that folk literature contains valuable evidence of the content of unconscious mental life. If oedipal folktales are universal, we would certainly want to consider the possibility that oedipal mental concerns are also universal. We will need to examine this assumption of a link between folktale and unconscious mental life in more detail. But first, let us examine some of the evidence for the universality of oedipal folktales.

IS OEDIPUS UBIQUITOUS?

The Greek story of Oedipus was unique and had a particular social and cultural context. Yet, close historical relatives of the story can be found widely in both the old and new worlds, presumably all sharing a common origin in some ancient past, perhaps in southern Asia or the Middle East (see, for example, 8, 48). Beyond this, oedipal tales, which may or may not be historically related to the Greek one (Lessa 1956), are found far from the Eurasian cultural sphere. Beginning with the ancient Greek version, we trace the oedipal tale through this widening circle of geographical and cultural regions.

The Greek Tale and Its Relatives

The tale of Oedipus has been at the center of the storm ever since Freud named his core complex after it. Freud relied on the play by Sophocles for his version of the story. Here we use the folktale on which the play was apparently based (3). Very similar tales, clearly historically related to this one, are told elsewhere. Edmunds' (1985) review of such tales uncovered many common features. The element of prophecy is rarely absent completely, the parricide nearly always precedes the incest, and mutilation is a common theme (although it is rarely the foot that is injured). Usually, also, these tales combine the element of the Hero's Journey: the boy leaves home as a youth, has many adventures, and overcomes obstacles to achieve greatness as a villain or hero. Edmunds also observes that in these tales "the action does not flow from the protagonist's inner self, nor does it culminate in any sort of self-consciousness" (Edmunds 1985: 39). The protagonists are swept along by fate and have no real responsibility for their actions.

In his analysis of "oedipus-type" tales in Oceania, Lessa (1956) identified three major criteria that such tales should have: prophecy, parricide, and mother-son incest. Minor criteria to be looked for included being exposed and then saved as an infant, being reared by another king, and tragic consequences to the oedipal crimes. In his review of such tales in Oceania, he found that no stories had all the criteria, and that most of them were lacking at least one of the three major criteria, while half of them were lacking all the minor criteria. This is not surprising, since many of these tales (if not all) may have no historical connection to the ancient Greek one. But it should prepare us to expect that even close historical relatives of the Oedipus story may differ from it in significant ways.

The Oedipal Tale in Time and Space

We can get a good sense of the kind of similarity that exists across different versions of the oedipal tale from several examples in our collection. In a relatively modern Yugoslavian tale (8), we find a story quite different in its details from the story of Oedipus yet obviously similar in its main features: prophecy, exposure of the infant, safe upbringing in another place, a journey in search of true parentage, parricide, incest, disaster. This version concerns the villainous Judas. More commonly, the oedipal figure is saved by penance or some great act and becomes a hero like Pope Gregory (Propp 1983: 81) or the Buddha (54).

What has changed in the Yugoslavian story are details of local color; the core is unchanged. Yet two millennia separate the Greek and Yugoslavian versions. To be sure, the Greek version was preserved in literature and could be passed on with little change among literate people. But the Yugoslavian tale is part of an oral tradition that was being passed from narrator to narrator, translated into a completely different language, and undergoing modification in dozens of specifics. The core of the tale shows a remarkable persistence.

It is not so far to travel from Greece to Yugoslavia, but equally similar tales are found separated by great distances. The story of Eugene the Found (13), for example, was collected from a seventeen-year-old Creole storyteller on the island of Guadeloupe in the West Indies. This version is not only over two thousand years removed from Oedipus, but thousands of miles as well. It too has undergone local transformation, but the core of the story remains. Prophecy is only suggested in the warning of Eugene the Bohemian that Eugene the Great must kill his first son, who could be dangerous to him. The other key elements are in place. There is even the familiar variation that the servant designated to kill the boy kills an animal instead and brings back the bloody knife (see also 29).

Edmunds (1985) and Edmunds and Dundes (1983) have documented the widespread occurrence of Oedipus-cognate folktales. There is no doubt that the core elements of the story identified by Lessa and Edmunds constitute a highly stable tale type that has withstood a great deal of local creative reworking without losing its fundamental integrity. Versions of the tale have been found throughout Europe, the Middle East, as far east as India (46), Burma (Krappe 1983), and perhaps even medieval Japan (48). It is also found in Africa (19) and in Euro-America (13).

We will not discuss such tales further here, but "The Boy Who Married his Mother" (10), from Finland, is worth notice as perhaps the least elaborate version known. The departures here from the Greek tale—absence of prophecy, the death of the father before the son returns, the mother's merely fainting—are well within the range of variation found in the large number of Oedipus-cognate tales now known to us. Either this minimalist version is a descendant of the Greek tale, or both share a common ancestry.

How Do We Know a Tale Is Oedipal?

The variation from tale to tale raises the issue of how many differences there may be before we must refuse to call a tale "oedipal." This can be a controversial issue, as we already saw in the conflicting opinions about whether the Trobriand tale of Dokonikan and Tudava (67) is oedipal. Often we are confronted with a tale that "feels" oedipal but lacks most or all of the major criteria listed earlier.

During his fieldwork in Burma, for example, Melford Spiro attempted to collect oedipal folktales. A woman, after offering to tell him the story of Maung Ba Cein (53), became confused, wondering why she had thought it was an oedipal tale. The tale she told of a boy who slays the queen's husband, a dragon, in order to marry the queen, has an oedipal feel to it, but it lacks a prophecy, as well as the crucial elements of parricide and incest. Spiro suggests that the tale must have had a latent oedipal meaning to the woman. We can accept this if we are willing to assume the symbolic similarity of Dragon and Father and of Queen and Mother.

We will argue later that such equations can be justified in light of the evidence from a large number of oedipal tales. For now, however, we have a much better reason to call "Maung Ba Cein" an oedipal tale, as may be seen in another version of the same story, called "Pauk Tyaing" (52), reported in 1917 by Brown. In this version of the story, the queen *is* identified as the boy's mother, from whom he was separated when lost in the forest as a child. The dragon is not directly his father, but rather the beast that killed his father and married his mother. In order to marry his mother and become king, the youth must slay the dragon, who becomes a spirit being worshipped under the name of "the Great Father." Perhaps the Burmese woman who told Spiro about "Maung Ba Cein" had heard this other version of the tale and retained a dim or repressed memory of the explicitly oedipal details. But whether she did or not, we can see that her intuition that "Maung Ba Cein" is an oedipal tale is true to the fundamental structure of the story.

Furthermore, Krappe (1983: 129) has argued that this tale is a relative of the Oedipus story:

> Regardless of what one thinks of this legend, it is certainly not of Burmese origin. It is, first of all, a famous tale of Persian or Sanskrit origin, incorporated into the *Book of Tobit*. Another tale, that of the incestuous marriage from which twin sons are born, came along and attached itself to it. Therefore, there cannot remain the slightest doubt about the fact that it is a variant of the classic Oedipus myth which emigrated to India.

The use of variants of a tale to provide evidence of its oedipal nature has been described by Dundes (1987: 167–77). For example, if the king threatens to kill the hero by chopping off his head in one variant, and by castrating him in another, this is evidence that decapitation is the symbolic equivalent of castration. The castration and decapitation are "allomotifs": one may be substituted for another without changing the basic meaning of the story.

One advantage of the analysis of allomotifs is that it can give us some clues to the meaning of elements in a tale for their intended audience. In most cases, folktales are not presented to us in their cultural context, with their local meanings spelled out. For example, among the Tukano of Colombia, women are often equated with fish (Reichel-Dolmatoff 1975: 105–6). So, if in a tale two brothers are said to have "gone fishing," a Tukano audience would know exactly what this meant. But this type of information is rarely provided with folktales, making a comprehensive symbolic context impossible to discover. Discovery of allomotifs provides at least some of that symbolic context. Carroll (1992) has also made use of allomotifs to support his psychoanalytic interpretation of native North American folktales.

In many cases, especially in areas where relatively little work has been done by folklorists, we will have only one version of a tale. We will not be able to test our intuition that a tale is oedipal by finding allomotifs in more explicit versions, if indeed they exist. We need rules of thumb to guide us in identifying more subtle expressions of oedipal content.

Before we suggest what these rules should be, we will give a further example of a tale where the oedipal content is fairly well hidden, yet can be exposed with the evidence of allomotifs from related stories. We collected this tale (14) in 1988 from a nonliterate storyteller in rural northeastern Brazil. It concerns a folk hero, Camoes, who always tricks the king without ever actually getting into trouble. In this tale, in order to prove to the king that all women are evil, he tricks the king into believing that he, Camoes, has seduced his own mother.

After translating this tale upon returning from Brazil in 1988, we had a similar experience to that of Spiro's informant. The tale had seemed oedipal on first hearing, but careful inspection turned up neither parricide nor incest. This was just a joke by Camoes at the king's expense. The storyteller, however, had told this story only after he was asked directly if he knew any stories of mother-son incest. His first response had been, "No," but after a longish silence he continued, "I know one about Camoes."

Actually, there are several related stories in which the incest is made much more explicit. In a medieval European story (6), the Greek philosopher Secundus is said to have become mute by his own choice after testing his mother's virtue: having heard there was very little good in women, he tried to seduce his mother, disguising himself. He succeeded and, rather than have sex with her, uncovered his disguise, causing her to die instantly of shock.

In the story of Solomon the Wise (12) from Chihuahua, Mexico, Solomon proves that women are "selfish, untruthful, and bad" by having a servant seduce his mother, then showing up in place of the servant for the assignation; his mother gasps upon seeing him, then breaks into tears. A very similar tale (34) was told of the Bodhisattva and his 120-year-old mother in ancient India.

In the general form of this story, therefore, son (in disguise, to be sure) seduces mother, proving her base and passionate nature, then removes his disguise himself, humiliating her. Knowing this, we can take the Brazilian tale and say that it is not the king who is being fooled, but the audience. The message that mother could feel passionate desire for son has been softened not by disguising or substituting for son, but by playing a joke where it only appears mother has been seduced. Here the equation is "appearance of seduction = seduction." We may also want to infer the equivalence of king and father in the Brazilian tale, but this is generally a type of oedipal tale in which father's role has been minimized.

On the basis of our examination of the stories in our collection, we conclude that tales that have an "oedipal feel" are usually oedipal at core, even when they lack specific oedipal content. Several kinds of transformations tend to mask or dilute the oedipal content of a story. These variously affect the three protagonists: son, father, and mother. Father can be substituted for by any senior male, but especially by a powerful individual such as a king (46, 139, 24), guru (34), ogre (67), dangerous animal (for example, a lion [54] or dragon [52]), or priest (48, 25). Father is often split into two characters, a dangerous evil one who must be killed and a kindly protective one who should be rewarded. In the latter case, a humble man such as a fisherman (64) often plays the Good Father role. Mother's new husband can also stand for father (90).

In a similar way, mother is frequently substituted for by a queen (139), animal (109), or devil woman (85). Mother-in-law (99, 111), mother's brother's wife/father's sister (72), father's new wife (15, 16, 41, 94, 114, 22, 30), and grandmother (98, 101, 135) can also substitute for mother. Mother, too, can be split into an evil woman who must be avoided or destroyed, and a kindly protective one (94).

It is less common in these tales to disguise son, since he is more often than not the main protagonist from whose point of view the story is told. But any handsome youth, a student (34), or a grandson (98), or a son-in-law (99), can stand for son.

The key relationships between these protagonists are sexual love and violent aggression. In the tales we have collected the sexual love between mother and son is generally explicit for at least one of the partners. That is, either son desires mother (16, 79) or she desires him (7, 15). As we shall see, in Oceania and native America, it is common for their desire to be mutual (64, 122, 123, 127, 129). In other parts of the world, it is common for the two to marry without knowing who they are (3, 8, 45), so that their incest is not deliberate; or, one partner will violently object to the incestuous wish on the other's part (18). In still other stories, son overcomes father while remaining close to mother, protecting and enriching her but never marrying her (19, 27, 33). These representations of innocence, violent opposition to incest, or filial loyalty in the tales will be viewed here as correlates of repression, protecting audiences from too direct an experience of the anxiety-provoking incestuous wishes.

Similarly, the typical relationship between father and son is violent aggression. This may take the form of an affectionate relationship gone sour over the incest. Often, it is represented as one-sided, with Good Father being attacked by Jealous Son (41, 48), or vice versa (2). In such cases, the good partner generally suffers various attacks but defends himself and ultimately vanquishes the bad one. Sometimes, father's role is limited: He dies early (106), dies while traveling (10), weakly fails to confront incestuous mother and son (90), or is never mentioned (67). These too may be devices for softening the impact on sensitive audiences of the unacceptable desires and acts of the participants in the full oedipal drama.

Perhaps not surprisingly, the relationship between mother and father is often ignored in these tales. They are just a married couple, without evident resentments or histories of trouble. Nor are they described as particularly in love or passionate with each other. The focus is centrally on how son feels toward each of them and how they feel toward him.

Oedipus in the Rest of the World

So far we have examined tales that are widespread throughout Europe and Asia. Most of them, except the Camoes-Secundus-Solomon tale, are historically related to the story of Oedipus. Presumably, this is a type of tale that has been told and retold since ancient times, refashioned according to local culture, but remaining essentially unchanged in its core. When we think of the countless storytellers and languages it has passed through, across millennia and continents, the stability of this core is remarkable. Parts must have been forgotten over and over again, new dramatic twists added by creative storytellers, parts of other tales imported to embellish this one, and yet the enduring core seems unaffected.

One folkloric explanation for such a wide dissemination of a tale is diffusion. And it cannot be denied that many oedipal tales have a common ancestry, what Dundes (1985: 2) calls "monogenesis." But to say that a tale came from somewhere else does not explain why it is widespread. We want to know why this tale is so widespread, while most others are of local distribution only.

We turn now to examine instances of oedipal tales that are outside the range of the historical relatives of Oedipus, where diffusion is unlikely. That is, the tale must have been invented independently (polygenesis). We will identify a core which is the oedipal tale, and a range of variation around that core. At that point we will be able to return to the question of why such a tale should be of such wide distribution.

OEDIPUS IN FAMILY-LEVEL SOCIETIES. In the previous section all our examples were drawn from complex societies. Are comparable tales told in simple, small-scale societies? The smallest-scale human societies we know of are "family-level societies" (Johnson and Earle 1987). They are much smaller in scale and simpler in social organization than many frequently cited examples of "primitive" societies from Africa or Melanesia. Often, they lack systematic or intensive warfare and do not have the complex systems of lineage, clan, and totemism commonly attributed to primitive society. They tend to live in small extended family groups, ranging in size from perhaps 7 to 25 members, to live mainly off the land as mobile foragers, and to have comparatively egalitarian relations between spouses and between households. Ethnographers consistently describe warm, intimate relationships between parents and children, with great respect for individual integrity, even toward small children. If oedipal conflicts arise from patriarchal, competitive social forms, as we have already seen some theorists suggest, we would predict that people in family-level societies would not experience an Oedipus complex. They do, however, tell oedipal tales.

The story of Kauha (21), told by the !Kung hunter-gatherers of the Kalahari desert, is quite different from the ones we have been looking at so far, yet it is undoubtedly an oedipal tale in the psychoanalytic sense. Son kills father and does his best to marry mother. Some elements considered central to the Oedipus tale—prophecy, abandonment and rescue of the boy, the hero's journey, the horror upon discovery of the crimes of parricide and incest, and the tragic consequences—are missing. The identities of the protagonists are not hidden from themselves or from the audience. The passive tragic figures doomed by fate to sin and suffer are replaced by self-centered actors of undisguised motivation. Mother seems to take some pleasure from son's growth and replacement of father and appears willing to go along with it. There is no evidence of guilt or remorse. On the other hand, not only are there parricide and incest, there is mutilation, twice: father is cut in half, and son's penis is bitten and swollen. Abandonment and rescue occur, although it is mother who is abandoned by father and rescued by son. And parricidal son can be said to have been punished by the mutilation of his penis and his inability to consummate the incest.

The frankness of this tale is striking after the roundabout way in which the oedipal drama is played out in the cognates of the Greek tale. We must be careful, however, not to assume that a single tale from a small-scale society stands for all such tales and societies. The Eskimo story "The Woman and her Husband" (90) has a distinctive character of its own. Here, wife and mother are the same person. In effect, following his rebirth, son is his own father, a common oedipal theme (Dundes 1985: 29). Wife's second husband, the father-competitor in this oedipal triangle, is shown to be a pretender and acts like it, slinking away as soon as envious son grows instantly to full manhood. Benevolent son, having displaced father without bloodshed, thereafter magnanimously gives him gifts of meat from his successful hunts.

This version of an oedipal tale is less raw, more constrained than the !Kung example. The incest is masked by emphasizing that the woman is the hero's wife. Her mother role is given a spiritual quality and lasts a very short time. There is no mutilation and a violent confrontation is avoided when the second husband immediately takes his things and moves out. His silence suggests he is holding in some powerful emotion that is better left unexpressed.

We could speculate that the constraint evident in the Eskimo tale is culturally appropriate. In *Never in Anger*, Briggs (1970), who spent a long winter in an igloo with a small Eskimo family, is vivid in describing the suppression of antagonistic feelings in this tiny, isolated human group. A similarly rich account of !Kung emotional life, *Nisa* (Shostak 1981), reveals a more exuberant expression of anger in open verbal battles and even physical fights between family members. One wonders whether an Eskimo audience might have been uncomfortable with the more explosive !Kung version of the oedipal tale.

Another tale, collected among the Matsigenka Indians of the Peruvian Amazon in 1973, also comes from a remote people with an intact culture and could not have diffused any time recently from the West. It is the story of a young man, Shakanari (106), whose marriage to his cross-cousin founders when he fails to leave home and reside with her family in the traditional pattern known as "bride service."

Although the story does not explicitly describe incest, when the storyteller was asked if Shakanari made love to his mother, she replied, "He treated her in all ways as his wife." And, although parricide does not occur, it is father's death that allows Shakanari to move back in with mother. There is also a fair amount of violence in this story: Shakanari strikes mother, father strikes him, his wife's father and brothers beat him badly, then he is clubbed to death by the neighbor from whom he has stolen plantains.

The oedipal triangle may be seen in the fight with father and his subsequent death, and the marriage to mother; we note also the triangle between Shakanari, his wife, and her father and brothers. The worms that grew in Shakanari's ear after he was beaten by his in-laws could be seen as a form of mutilation. Shakanari's punishment, of course, also includes death.

Yet this may also be seen as a story of a boy who refused to leave his mother and start his own family. It may be a morality tale about why it is necessary for Matsigenka youths to move in with their wives and provide bride service for their fathers-in-law. The theme of food, found in Shakanari's outrageous giving of meat to mother instead of his wife, and of his stealing plantains, ties in with this "preoedipal" aspect of the story. Preoedipal themes occur frequently in oedipal tales, and we will return later to consider in more detail their presence as a variable in the cross-cultural occurrence of oedipal tales.

These last three tales occur in societies at the opposite end of the developmental spectrum from the civilizations in which Oedipus and its cognates are found. We can see that much of what has been considered central to the Oedipus tale is lacking in these versions. Prophecy, the hero's journey, the "family romance" that one's true parents are royal or wealthy, the protagonist as an innocent leaf in the unaccountable winds of fate—all are lacking. Of particular interest is that in two of the tales the identity of the protagonists is explicit, and even in the Eskimo tale, mother and her husband know that this man who is her original husband was moments earlier her young son. The motivation of these protagonists, and in particular the son, is not in doubt: he wants to marry mother, and he is envious of the husband who stands in his way.

The problem of father is handled in various ways. In the !Kung tale father is chopped in half; the Matsigenka father beats son, but then dies conveniently; the Eskimo father simply loses legitimacy and ignominiously flees the household. Such differences may reflect differences in the cultural appropriateness of open expressions of passionate feelings in general and of aggression in particular. But the most we can say with assurance is that we should expect differences at least as great as these in the oedipal tales we find in different cultures, especially considering that there is no evidence for the kind of historical connection between these tales that accounts for the often striking similarities in the Oedipus-cognate tales of Europe and Asia.

This last point deserves emphasis. In considering the stability of the Oedipus tale across two millennia and thousands of miles, we could not entirely rule out diffusion, especially considering the presence of written traditions in those societies. It is at least theoretically possible that all the colorfully distinct folk versions of Oedipus still derive from ancient written versions in Sanskrit, Persian, or Greek. In the current three cases, however, such an argument is untenable. The only way these tales could have diffused from a common source is if that source were extremely ancient, at least older than the migrations 10,000 or more years ago that carried what La Barre (1984) calls the Paleolithic *Urkultur* into the New World.

To retain diffusion as the main explanation of a pan-human distribution of oedipal tales, we must come to terms with what that implies: namely, that oedipal tales were passed on across hundreds of generations in the absence of writing, transported through every conceivable form of environment and across innumerable linguistic barriers, and are still being told in nonliterate societies today. Other cultural universals, such as fire, are explained not by diffusion alone but by their great usefulness (Brown 1991: 95). Should oedipal folktales prove to be universal, some similar explanation beyond diffusion must also be sought in their case.

THE OEDIPAL TALE AS PAN-HUMAN. Now we may extend our evidence for the universality of the oedipal tale from family-level societies to a larger pan-human frame of reference. Beyond the smallest family-level societies there used to be a huge diversity of egalitarian or mildly ranked societies where the economic base is subsistence from hunting, collecting, fishing, or horticulture, and the main basis of social organization lies in such institutions as extended kinship reckoning and ceremonial feasts and exchanges of valuables, generally linked to pervasive warfare.

As we saw, Freud and Jones raised the question of whether such peoples have less emotional control than people in complex societies, and hence have a greater horror of incest. On the basis of fieldwork and familiarity with ethnographic reports from many small-scale societies, we find that there is some truth to the first part of this idea but none to the second. Such peoples are generally calm and emotionally controlled. Their control takes the form of courtesies that include polite sharing of resources and a quiet, pleasant manner of speaking. But one discovers that they are also very self-assertive and emotionally impulsive. They will share food reluctantly, even stingily, if they feel they have only enough for themselves, and it is extremely difficult to shame or embarrass them into changing their minds. They also express emotions freely when aroused, whether to joyful play with children or to furious tirades and agonistic displays when angered. When the emotion is spent, however, it tends to disappear without lingering guilt or desires for revenge, unless something truly damaging, like theft or homicide, has occurred.

Contrary to Freud and Jones, however, this emotional spontaneity does not lead to a greater horror of incest, or other transgressions, but rather a lesser one. That is not to say that incest or other prohibited behaviors are tolerated or encouraged. Rather, there is a general perception among such peoples that each individual has a substantial integrity that must not be violated. People should be generous, for example, and children are taught generosity. But if one grows up to be stingy, there is little others can do about it except to regulate their relations with the stingy one to protect their own self-interest.

A case of culturally defined incest observed during fieldwork among the Matsigenka Indians of the Peruvian Amazon is instructive (O. Johnson 1978: 98–99):

> A man seeking to establish new affinal ties . . . can manipulate and redefine existing relationships in such a way that incestuous relationships are made marriageable. . . .
>
> An example . . . is Acensio's marriage to his stepdaughter Elva. Although it is common for a man to marry a widow and her daughter from a previous marriage, this case is unique, because Acensio had taken Elva's mother, Rosa, as a second wife when Elva was six years old, and had been treating Elva as his daughter for seven years. When Elva reached puberty, Acensio took her as his third wife, proclaiming that she was not Rosa's daughter but the daughter of Rosa's classificatory sister, who had died many years before. In effect, Rosa was no longer Elva's real mother, Acensio no longer Elva's father, and incest was averted.

People like the Matsigenka are basically moral according to their codes, which prohibit incest and frown on extramarital sex, among other prohibitions on violence, theft, laziness, and so forth. But they are not obsessed with enforcing rules. Although they find many culturally appropriate channels for enthusiastic self-expression in dance, humor, singing, and playing, and in the creative aspects of such work as hunting, fishing, weaving, and arrow making, they seem to understand that people have unacceptable impulses and will sometimes act on them even in the face of community disapproval.

In the tales we are about to encounter, we will see two related trends. The first of these is less repression in the tales, as compared with the Oedipus-cognate tales. The incest and hostile feelings are apparent to the protagonists and the audience as they occur. Protagonists are presented as willful actors, often ruled primarily by the pleasure principle. Whenever identities of protagonists are disguised, or their motivations are obscured, we will argue that this is done to protect the audience from anxiety. In principle, by noticing where such repressions occur, we can gain insight into the level and type of anxiety the oedipal tale stirs in an audience.

The second trend is the relative absence of expressions of guilt and remorse on the part of the protagonists. They may be punished (so that the audience is told that their behavior was wrong), but they do not express guilt for their transgressions. This is in contrast to the great remorse, hand-wringing, penance, and other suffering to which oedipal protagonists subject themselves or are subjected to by the fates in the Oedipus-cognate tales.

"The Little Woodpecker" (123), from the Yamana Indians of Tierra del Fuego, is a good example. It is not an absence of horror that makes this a less "repressed" tale than its civilized counterparts. Incest prohibitions are universal in human societies, and the group of women in the story is the chorus expressing this prohibition. Their horror is at the violation of a taboo. Father also is horrified, but at the size of son's penis and the knowledge that he could, indeed, successfully have intercourse with mother. His horror is less the horror of incest in the abstract than of being deceived by his own wife and son.

Less repression is seen, however, in the emphasis on the pleasure mother and son derive from their incest. Guilt and remorse have no place in their actions. Father's rage and his castration of son likewise occasion no remorse or penance. Incestuous son is transformed into an animal, a common fate of protagonists in native American folktales. Typically, the animal thus created is the founder of a species, its powerful and immortal spirit ruler. People sometimes make offerings to such spirit rulers to assure the abundance of the species for human food. The son's metamorphosis could be seen as a punishment, therefore, but it is not certain that it is regarded by the audience in such societies as a fate worse than death.

"The Jealous Father" (94), told by the Cree Indians of North America, offers further evidence of the role of repression in folktales. Although no guilt is expressed, there are examples of repression. First, father has two wives—a form of splitting—and son has incest with stepmother. Apart from this crucial act, she plays no role in the tale. Son's effort to get back to mother, and her efforts to protect and equip him for that task, dominate the tale. On the other hand, father's envy of son is not repressed, nor is their mutual antagonism. When father attempts to placate son near the end of the story, by offering him mats to walk on, it is clear he is afraid of retribution from his now-powerful son, not hiding his rage from himself or the audience.

There appears to be further use of splitting in this tale, however. As distinct from the jealous Bad Father, the Walrus in this story is a powerful male figure who swims son back to land. He could be the Good Father; or, being sent by mother's magic, he might also represent what Bly (1990a) terms a "male mother," an older man other than father who nourishes and guides son's growth to full manhood. In any case, it seems that hostility and affection for a father figure have been split and directed at two different males in the story. Incidentally, willful son does not care for Walrus's safety, since it threatens his own, and he opportunistically lies to Walrus, causing his death from father's lightning. He shows no remorse for this, of course.

The old woman who helps a child overcome the jealous father in this story occurs in many family-complex stories. She is a motherly old woman, like a grandmother. She is not necessarily a split-off mother, however, because many in the audience for such a tale will have their own helpful grandmothers.

The two blind hags with the bony spikes back of their elbows are another matter. They are witches, the dangerous representatives of father, enemies of son's growth and vengeful upholders of the incest taboo (like the chorus of women in "The Little Woodpecker"). On some level, they must represent at least as much mother's punitive side as father's. The comical image of them tricked into gleefully killing each other with their elbow spikes addresses the resentment in the audience toward frustrating social rules (and toward "old biddies" who watchfully monitor enforcement).

Also of interest in "The Jealous Father" is the reappearance of the hero's journey, which seemed to be lost when we left the Oedipus-cognate tales. Here again son is abandoned by father and must make his way home. In the process, he is helped by benevolent others and he grows into a powerful man capable of displacing father and earning his rightful place at mother's side. This story fulfills the oedipal wish completely: son kills father and spends the rest of his life with mother. That they then both become birds is perhaps a sign of repression, that is, done to reduce the audience's anxiety: the dangerous oedipal triumph is removed completely from the world of contemporary men.

"Sikhalol and his Mother" (64), from the Pacific atoll of Ulithi, is the least compromised representation of oedipal triumph we have yet found in any folktale: son kills father and marries mother without punishment. Despite the complete acceptance of the oedipal triumph, this tale has some elements of repression in it. Mother's denial of the existence of the baby she abandons in the surf, and the ignorance of both mother and son at the onset of their incest, can be said to tone down their responsibility for their crimes.

These elements, as well as the rearing of the boy by a benevolent foster father and the marking of mother's face (a mild mutilation) for identification purposes, are similar enough to warrant speculation that this may somehow be an Oedipus-cognate tale. Lessa (1961), in fact, believes this is so. His reasoning, however, is based heavily on his belief that oedipal tales occur only in Europe, Asia, and Oceania, having diffused from an ancient point of origin in "a 'patriarchal' type of society somewhere in a broad belt from Europe to south Asia." Our present evidence indicates oedipal tales are of worldwide distribution, placing much greater strain on monogenesis and diffusion as explanations.

Furthermore, on internal evidence it is doubtful whether the tale of Sikhalol is an Oedipus-cognate folktale. Not only are other elements of the Oedipus tale missing, including prophecy and the hero's journey, but the entire tone of the latter part of the tale is different. When mother and son discover their incest, rather than react in guilt and remorse, they decide they like it and continue. Son knows who father is when he kills him (although father does not know son). Then son and mother go off to live—a presumably happy married couple.

The conjoining of mother and son "happily ever after," whether as married couple or as birds that fly off together, is a common element in tales from small-scale societies, though hardly universal.

"Uken" (18), from Uganda, is striking for the way it represents mother's role in the incest. Oedipal tales face the difficulty of managing the age difference between mother and son. Many Oedipus cognates mention that when son arrives at mother's, she is "still beautiful," and he falls in love with her. In primitive societies one device is to have son grow quickly or instantaneously into manhood, while mother is still young, as we saw in the Eskimo tale (90) and in "The Little Woodpecker" (123). In "Uken," mother sheds her old skin for the beautiful one underneath, a device also used in the Chinook story, "Wren and his Father's Mother" (101), a tale of grandmother-grandson incest. In "Uken," mother's regret at her own aging and her wish to be son's lover are more dramatically represented than usual.

Uken's sense of disgrace is evidence of repression, to isolate mother's passion as a one-sided deviation. But it is also part of the next phase of the story, when Uken is reborn. This almost has the quality of a hero's journey to it, and may provide a clue to the intrapsychic meaning of the hero's journey in other oedipal tales. The story of Uken seems to be saying this: Sensuous mother wants to possess son like a husband, jealously preventing him from forming his own family. To escape her, son must die and be reborn in the care of Old Woman, who helps nurture him into full manhood, when he is admired by the community. Before he can take his rightful place in that community, however, with supportive Old Woman at his side, sensuous mother must be slain.

This tale contrasts with previous ones in describing the separation of mother and son, rather than their union. It may metaphorically represent the meaning of the male initiation rites common in primitive societies, especially those with endemic warfare where sons must grow up to be warriors. In the civilized Oedipus tale, the abandoned son is usually raised by Kind Man. Here it is Old Woman, reminiscent of the story of the Jealous Father (94). Once again, it is tempting to equate Kind Man and Old Woman with Bly's "male mother," a caring figure other than mother and father, who guides son's development into powerful manhood where he can challenge father and find a bride "just like the girl who married dear old Dad."

DISCUSSION. This examination of a few examples of oedipal tales from nonstratified societies, where a historical derivation of the tale from the civilized Oedipus tale is unlikely or impossible, suggests that we need to revise our conception of what the basic oedipal tale is. In the broad, cross-cultural view, the core oedipal tale is one of jealousy and aggression between father and son and of romantic desire between mother and son. It can be diagrammed simply (Figure 2). We note that the arrows go both ways and the "−" stands for jealousy and aggression while the "+" stands for romantic desire. Few tales actually present even this simple structure fully, however. Often in any given tale, an arrow goes only one way, and the meanings of the "+" and "−" are often softened, distorted, or denied outright. When am-

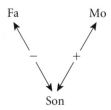

Fig. 2. The core oedipal tale.

bivalence ("$+/-$") is present in a tale, it is common to do so through a split, such as the Jealous Father and the protective Walrus, or Woodpecker's erotic mother and the horrified chorus of women. It is rare for the relationship of either mother-son or father-son in the tales to be a fully complex one with an ambivalent "$+/-$."

For example, the jealousy and aggression between father and son usually begins with one or the other. The Jealous Father abandons his vulnerable son on islands far from shore; only later does son respond with rage. Kauha initiates the aggression against mother, justifying son's rage. Similarly, either son or mother unilaterally instigates the romantic involvement. Shakanari refuses to leave home and join his wife's family. Uken's mother tricks him into sleeping with her.

A corollary of this simplification of the core oedipal structure is that most folktales are told from a particular perspective. There is an underlying moral point of view, a judgment of good and bad implied. Thus, the audience understands that Shakanari should have willingly left home, that Uken's mother should have let her son go, that Kauha should have respected his wife.

The versions of the oedipal tale found in complex societies, however, often further distort the motivation of the protagonists. Son accidentally kills father while innocently pursuing his own course. Mother and son, separated from birth, set eyes on one another and immediately fall in love. The horror of the innocent lovers suddenly made aware of the extent of their sin is poignant. Still, they are identified as guilty and punished.

The core structure of the tale is often attenuated by imbalance. In many tales, father is not mentioned altogether, dies offstage, or passively witnesses the love affair between mother and son. Likewise, in other tales the focus is on the struggle between father and son, with mother present as a focus of their competition, or as a sustaining presence, but not as son's romantic partner. We will return shortly to consider the importance of these imbalances in the oedipal tale.

In this regard, we can see that much of the theoretical debate over the meaning of oedipal folktales has amounted to the same kind of reduction of the core structure as may be found in the tales themselves (Figure 3). Freud insisted on the triadic structure, but tended to have the erotic and aggressive wishes going in one direction. Fromm reduced the structure to a dyad, also with a one-way wish. Ramanujan kept the triadic structure but simply reversed the direction of the wishes. And so on. It seems that in theorizing about the Oedipus complex we have as much trouble as the rest of the world in encompassing its fullness, even though it is a simple and elegant structure.

The core oedipal tale can be incorporated into a variety of larger stories. The Oedipus version, with its emphasis on prophecy, abandonment and res-

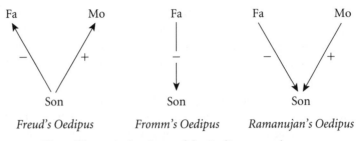

Fa Mo   Fa   Fa Mo

− +   −   − +

Son   Son   Son

Freud's Oedipus *Fromm's Oedipus* *Ramanujan's Oedipus*

Fig. 3. Theoretical variants of the Oedipus complex.

cue, revelation of sin and subsequent punishment, incorporates the core tale into a larger story characteristic of the culture area in which it originated. Many of these themes are inappropriate in other cultural settings where, for example, the idea of "relentless fate" is absent (Lessa 1956: 65).

In other cultural settings, the core tale is made part of stories that explain the origins of the sun, agriculture, or even of people themselves. Naturally, scholars mainly interested in matters like fate or origin theories will regard those aspects of the tales as primary and the oedipal core as incidental. This is probably why Graves considered the parricide and incest in the Oedipus myth to reflect the incorporation of a "perverted anecdote" which was incidental to the tale's real significance as a history of Oedipus, the thirteenth-century invader of Thebes who suppressed the old Minoan cult of the goddess and reformed the calendar.

Variations on a Theme

The oedipal tales we compiled for this project represent every continent and societies at every level of social complexity. They occur in matrilineal as well as patrilineal societies, and in societies where lineality is not reckoned. And they are found in egalitarian societies with warm father-son relations no less than in hierarchical societies with authoritarian father-son relations.

This statement depends, however, on accepting that the core structure of the oedipal tale is not itself a tale but a generator out of which tales emerge in great variety. The Trobrianders' "Dokonikan and Tudava" (67) is an oedipal tale despite the attenuation of the mother-son love affair into a close alliance by means of which older males are mastered. The Eskimo tale "The Woman and her Husband" (90) is oedipal despite the attenuation of the father-son struggle into the hasty retreat of a father figure from his son's claims of priority.

This assumption is bound to be controversial. Why insist that all tales of dyadic father-son hostility are generated out of the triadic core structure identified here? Or that all tales of dyadic mother-son unity are similarly generated? Why not different structures lying at the bases of different tale types? We argue that these dyadic tales are imbalanced versions of the core oedipal tale.

THE FATHER-SON DYAD. Stories of battles between fathers and sons for control of a kingdom are common in stratified societies. The ancient Greek story, "The First Gods" (1), where son conspires with mother to castrate father, is frequently mentioned. This tale and others like it in ancient Greek mythology support the position of Fromm that the core concern of the society that generated the Oedipus tale was the struggle of son against cruel authoritarian father. As we saw, so convinced was Fromm of this that he finally decided that Oedipus's marriage to Jocasta was a meaningless incident in the story. We saw in the previous chapter how others have joined Fromm in regarding the mother-son incest as insignificant.

Despite these arguments, we do better to see such tales as variants on the triadic oedipal core than as a completely distinct tale type. In "The First Gods" it is untenable to argue that the relationship between mother and son is incidental to the story. It is mother and children who suffer, and it is mother who plans and instigates the castration of father; she even created the new material, grey flint, used to fashion the cutting blade. It is also typical of many oedipal tales from around the world that the focal son of the story is the youngest of her children. True, son and mother do not commit incest, but they do conspire to eliminate father's sexual access to mother.

Similarly, there is no basis for assuming that the relationship between Oedipus and Jocasta was "pure" maternal and filial love. Oedipus arrived in Thebes a hero and married the queen. They had two children together, and this was not accomplished by *philia* alone. Jocasta, as she began to suspect the truth (in Sophocles' version, at least), tried in vain to pretend Oedipus was not her son and then hung herself when the truth came out. The guilt and remorse of incestuous mother and son are absolutely central to the tragedy. If there was no *eros*, why the guilt, remorse, and self-punishment?

In the story of Arjuna and Babhruvahana from the *Mahabharata* (40) Babhruvahana's father, Arjuna, arrives in his son's territory threatening battle. Son goes forth to greet father lovingly, but father is furious: "Damn you! You fool. You know the rules for warriors yet you greet me peacefully when I have come to fight!" Son is confused and stands with head bowed until father's wife (son's mother's co-wife) assures him that this is what father wants. Then, "an unequaled battle begins between the father and his son, both of whom are described as being delighted." Son finally kills father with an arrow through the heart. Mother comes forward to castigate co-wife for allowing this fight, and mother and son begin a fast to death in mourning. But co-wife reveals that this battle and father's death were a part of a cosmic bargain by which Arjuna may do penance for a previous immoral killing. Co-wife proceeds to resuscitate father (Arjuna) and the story ends happily.

Again, the focus here is upon the battle between father and son. But mother is centrally present, split into two parts: the first (father's co-wife) encourages son to battle and, thus, kill father, while the second (mother) regrets the violence and mourns father's death. Then son and mother prepare to fast to death, an image of eternal mother-son union. Is incestuous love simply absent here, or has repression touched this story to soften its impact on a civilized audience?

Fromm is right that this type of tale is common in patriarchal society. It reflects the intergenerational male conflicts so significant in stratified warrior societies. The Zulu story "Usikulumi Kahlokohloko" (19), for example, focuses on a son whose father tries repeatedly from birth to kill him until son finally vanquishes father, kills off his whole army, seizes all his cattle, and leaves, taking mother and sister with him.

Heroic son is subjected to evil father's destructiveness. Mother (and sister) and son are united at the end of the tale, and it is mother who saves son from infanticide at the beginning of the story, "for it was a son she loved exceedingly." In the quasi-historical story of Shaka (33), the great Zulu military leader, these same elements of son's undissolved attachment to mother and father's fierce hostility toward son are vividly present, as though life imitated art.

In this light, the story of Oedipus, with the actual marriage of Oedipus and Jocasta, must be seen as much more a core oedipal tale than some other father-son tales. But even in the latter, where the mother-son tie remains apparently innocent, there is a direct or indirect conspiracy between them to bring about father's death and enable a "forever after" closeness between them. As we see next, one could argue that this mother-son tie is a preoedipal, and hence nonerotic, attachment, but it cannot be held that the sole focus of the story is on murderous father-son relations.

THE MOTHER-SON DYAD. Is the mother-son tie in oedipal tales really a preoedipal attachment in which father is essentially trivial or dispensable? Since the mother-son tie is preoedipal before it is oedipal, it makes sense that mother would appear in both forms in world folk literature. Aside from a few discussions reviewed in Chapter 2, however, little attention appears to have been paid to preoedipal mother images in oedipal folktales.

We may assume that in many of the tales we have already reviewed, the fantasy of mother-son closeness or union holds an appeal for audiences that goes beyond sexual gratification. It must originate in the actual experienced early union and the safe, nurturing, and acknowledging environment that mothering ideally creates. In that light, many of the oedipal tales we have already reviewed are actually tales of sons and mothers who do not want son's full growth to manhood, with its inevitable separation, to take place. Indeed, once when we presented the Matsigenka tale of Shakanari (106) to an audience of psychoanalysts, one rose to say, "Shakanari sounds to me like a boy who doesn't want to grow up!"

Whether we think of the difficulties in the early mother-child relationship primarily in terms of instinctual conflicts or of deficits and empathic failures, it seems likely that the resulting disturbances would be repressed and might well make their way into folktales. "Origin of the Stars and of Certain Animals" (112), told by the Bororo Indians of South America, might convince some that we need a category of preoedipal, essentially dyadic, mother-son tales to broaden our frame of reference and make room for theoretical advances in contemporary psychoanalysis.

The central issue in this mother-son relationship is mother's stinginess with food, withholding it even though it is abundant. There is no easily discernible father in the tale, yet this *is* a story of a boy who refuses to stay small and dependent: "Since he [is] not at all interested in spending his time with the women," he refuses to go back with mother to the corn field, and she beats him mercilessly. The missing father may be vaguely present in the birds, especially the little hummingbird who ties the rope in the sky by which the boys escape, or perhaps in the male group that escapes together. But this is a family-complex tale with significant differences from the oedipal tales we have been looking at (Figure 4). Here mother's desire for son is for a small, compliant boy, and son's hostility toward her for this desire completely replaces the union portrayed in the predominantly oedipal tales.

Whereas the oedipal-type tale depicted son and mother as being opposed to their ultimate separation, often at the expense of son's fullest growth and development, this tale shows son prepared to fight for growth against infantilizing mother. The two types of tales represent different facets of the same dilemma: how is son to grow up and separate from mother while they remain attached to each other?

Some tales vividly portray the dangers involved in this movement. In the

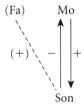

Fig. 4. A preoedipal tale? (112).

"Myth of Nata" (78) from Aboriginal Australia, son crawls back inside mother's vagina and finds the ultimate union with her. This story has a curious mix of the wish to return to the womb with phallic elements like the stick and the *tjurunga* (bull-roarer). The inappropriateness of a growing child returning to the womb is clear in both mother and son becoming *tjurunga*. Is mother welcoming son as an infant back into her womb or as a phallic, sexual son? Perhaps the tale condenses a dilemma between dependent child and separate sexual man.

The story of Tapir Woman (109) of the Mehinaku Indians of South America also seems to mix oedipal and preoedipal images of the mother-son relationship. With little effort this could be described as an oedipal tale: Tapir Woman ≅ Mother, Anus ≅ Vagina, Arm ≅ Penis; the punishment for incest is castration. Only father is missing.

But it might equally be viewed in preoedipal terms: the child is alone at home, crying for his mother; Tapir Woman ends up in a grove of fruit trees, gorging herself until her massive defecation finally releases the poor boy's arm. The child's dependence, together with oral and anal images, suggests that this son gets in trouble by having sex with a greedy, retentive, bad mother (compare 85). Again, a range of conflictual material concerning a boy's growth and development is condensed into a small but graphic story.

One more story will help fill out this picture. It is "The Mother's Boy" (23), told by the Muntshi of Africa. This tale is unusual in presenting the hoped-for resolution of the Oedipus complex. The tale says that son needs father's guidance in order to separate from mother and start his own family. The images are all positive: mother is nurturing, father promotes masculine growth, son is obedient and loyal. The tale emphasizes that son follows his proper path of growth when it is pointed out to him by father, and that mother cannot be counted on to do this by herself (compare Bly 1990b). We are brought back to the triadic model of the oedipal tale. Even when the central issue is mother-son union versus son's growth and separation, father is implicated: in his absence, or when he is attacked and destroyed by son, mother, or both, then the forever-after mother-son union is possible, usually with disastrous results.

DISCUSSION. Each folktale configures a portion of the possible relationships among family members and presents it as a story with a moral viewpoint. Particular tales, then, may support one or another version of oedipal theory. Such stories are simpler than the complex whole from which they are drawn, and hence are easier to understand.

The whole from which these folktales have been derived is the family complex. At the core of the family complex lie conflicts over impulse control in relationships with family members. Each member of the family impulsively

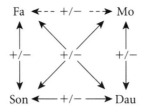

Fig. 5. The family complex.

experiences wishes toward the others: that they would stay or go, give what they appear to be withholding, or accept what they appear unwilling to receive. Yet, Freud argued, the functioning of the human family depends on some degree of control of such wishes, many of which threaten the integrity of the family over time. In Figure 5 ambivalence between each family member is taken for granted (compare Freud 1923: 33–34). The relationship between husband and wife (Fa-Mo) is rendered with dashed lines because few tales in our collection ever comment on the relationship between father and mother. One is left with the impression that they are an ordinary married couple. The action in the stories generally involves a focal child in relation to each parent separately. (The hatred of mother for Ouranos in "The First Gods" [1] is an example of the kind of information about the mother-father tie sometimes given in folktales.)

The family complex modeled in Figure 5 includes daughter's oedipal relationship, which is generally assumed to include the wish to marry father and to kill mother, and the possibility of brother-sister incest and violence. We turn now to consider these neglected versions of the family complex.

FATHER-DAUGHTER INCEST TALES

As we saw in Chapter 2, the implication of Freud's view of the feminine Oedipus complex was that we would find a triangle in which a daughter develops an erotic attachment toward father and a corresponding antagonism toward mother; father may have reciprocal feelings, but will normally have mastered them, as will mother have mastered her jealousy over daughter. But new understanding of the development of gender identity led to a substantially different view, in which father originates the sexual desire that daughter either rejects or is ambivalent about; for her part, mother is seen as remaining close to daughter, who need not reject her identification with mother in order to fulfill her proper gender role. Figure 6 models these two views.

Of the 23 tales of father-daughter incest originally included in our collection, only one represents anything like the "classical view." That one is the story of Myrrha and Cinyras (Ovid 1955: 238), where Myrrha madly desires

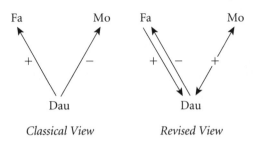

Fa   Mo   Fa   Mo

+   −   +   −   +

Dau   Dau

Classical View   *Revised View*

Fig. 6. Father-daughter incest models.

her father, Cinyras, and finally manages to sleep with him through the intervention of an old nurse. When Cinyras discovers his daughter's identity, after many nights of lovemaking under cover of darkness, he is outraged and tries to kill her. There is no mother-daughter antagonism in the story; if the old nurse is a maternal figure, she plays the role of facilitator enabling the incest.

Virtually all of our other tales depict father as the lustful one who rapes daughter or tricks her into incest against her will. Typical of these are Trickster-type tales discussed in Chapter 2, in which a selfish, impulsive father feigns death (87, 89, 107, 121) in order to return in disguise and marry his daughter. Impulsive fathers also play other tricks to fulfill their incestuous desires, as when Tiki tricks his daughter into thinking his erect penis is a stick she must pull from the sand (63), or tells his daughter that it is not he, but her brother, who is surreptitiously sleeping with her at night (57). Similarly, Raven (96) tricks his daughter into placing his penis in her burned vagina, having told her it is the stalk of a healing plant, and Yakoviri (134) has intercourse with his daughter while pretending to be possessed by a benevolent spirit.

In other similar tales, father does not even bother to hide his identity through trickery. He strongly desires daughter and simply rapes her or attempts to do so (68, 77, 95, 108, 131). Whether he tries trickery or sheer force, however, there is no suggestion in these tales that daughter has acted seductively toward father or that she is sexually attracted to him. In some cases she escapes, like the She-Bear (Basile 1932: 170; also 47), or commits suicide after the fact (56, 68, 118). Most often, when she discovers father's true identity, she turns to mother and together they drive father away: Tiki's (57) wife and daughter plot to kill and cook him, Sunawavi's (87) wife and daughter turn him into a wolf who must continually run around biting his tail, and Woodpecker's (107) wife and daughter beat him until he flies up in the air and becomes a bird. In a few cases incestuous father is killed (68, 95, 113).

There are a smaller number of tales, however, in which either mother or daughter comply in the incest. We have said that Myrrha's old nurse might be a maternal figure conspiring in the incest; in the Greek tale of the birth of Dionysos (4), Persephone's mother, Demeter, actually encourages and abets her daughter's incest with Zeus. Tiki (57) only commits incest when his wife leaves after telling him, "You have your daughter." The beast Ngarara (62) is about to kill his wife's young daughter when she points out to him that if he spares the girl's life he can marry her when she grows up.

And there are a few cases where daughter simply goes along with the incest, as Persephone apparently did: when Prajapati (39) divides himself in two, his female half is shocked at his incest with her but she goes along with it and bears him many children; Tiki (63) and his daughter become lovers; Woodpecker (107) marries his daughter, as does Guanaco man (121). Only in the case of Sun and his daughter (131), however, is it spelled out that daughter enjoys the sexual relationship: here, she likes it so much she sickens and nearly dies and is restored to health only when Sun blows smoke over her.

In sum, our collection of father-daughter incest tales presents a dominant theme of father as initiator and daughter as resister of sexual relations, with a minor theme of daughter more or less passively going along with father. Mother never appears as a jealous antagonist to daughter, and most often appears as her close ally and supporter in her struggle to free herself from father's importuning. Not even where mother conspires to bring about the incest is there any suggestion that she does so out of antagonism toward daughter.

To this point in our argument, therefore, we may say that the tales in our collection conform more to the revised model than to the classical one. We must still consider, however, the possibility that our tales have disguised the true intrapsychic situation. That is, as Dundes (1980: 217–18) argues, tales locating incestuous wishes in father are deflecting the listener's attention from their actual location in daughter. We will defer discussion of this basic issue until the next chapter, in our exploration of the meaning of family-complex folktales.

TALES OF BROTHER-SISTER INCEST

As we saw in the previous chapter, we have even less theory available to us about how brother-sister incest themes might appear in folk literature than we had in the case of father-daughter incest. The idea that incest prohibitions are so culturally variable that some societies actually permit brother-sister marriage has proven to be a great exaggeration, with only one even moderately well-documented case in the world. On the other hand, the Westermarck theory that siblings have no erotic feelings for each other—owing to the innate sexual disinterest that is supposed to arise between children who are reared together—would suggest that, in terms of our theory of folktales as expressions of forbidden desires, there should be no tales of brother-sister incest at all.

Our collection provides evidence to show that tales of brother-sister incest are of worldwide distribution. In about half of them (17 out of 32) brother desires sister but she does not return his desire. Rather than give in to him she may run away (28, 31), cut off her hands (Basile 1932: 170–77) or breasts (91) and give them to him, castrate him (17), and even kill him and cook and distribute his meat to the village (92). If he overpowers and rapes her, she becomes angry, causing him to be transformed into an animal (128, 129), or she may escape (132) and even kill herself (43).

Although in these tales brother is initiator and sister resists, ambivalence on sister's part does make its way into some tales. If brother tricks her, she may go along with him, though without evident desire (55, 59, 73). Although brother remains the initiator, her compliance is occasionally more than passive agreement (58, 119, 125).

In a fourth of the tales (eight) it is sister who is the initiator if not the aggressor. Usually in these cases, brother is horrified and rejects her strongly (104) or kills her (93) and perhaps himself as well (88). Less commonly, brother appears reluctant but goes along with her (133, 20).

In the remaining brother-sister incest narratives the two are compliant lovers. In a few cases, this is a device for explaining the peopling of the earth by an original sibling couple (60, 20); here, sexual desire, morality, and punishment are minimal or lacking altogether. But in several cases we find a passionate mutual love that gets the pair into deep trouble with their parents: either brother (110) or both of them (115, 124, 137) escape their parents' wrath by fleeing into the forest, where they become animals. In one case they die of shame after copulating (66), and in another their enraged parents take them and their newborn child to the swamp and drown all three (26).

It is mainly in the tales where brother and sister are mutually in love, then, that the parents enter the tale as forceful, and profoundly hostile, actors. Hence, if only one sibling has sexual desire, the tale is a struggle between the evil sexual one and the good nonsexual one, whereas if the sexual desire is mutual, the siblings together embody evil in a struggle with the good parents.

We may say that these tales take for granted that erotic desire may arise between brother and sister. Although the greater number of tales assume that this desire occurs exclusively in brother, many assume either that it occurs exclusively in sister or that the feelings are mutual. A fraction of the tales present the incest as an essentially passionless mating needed to originate a human population.

VERSIONS OF THE FAMILY COMPLEX

Our generalized model of the family complex in Figure 5 showed a nuclear family of mother, father, daughter, and son, each directing erotic and hostile feelings toward all of the others. We suggested that by taking only some of the possible dyads and triads out of this matrix, and simplifying their relationships to single valences (using splitting to handle the problem of ambivalence), an ample supply of new stories could be generated. Although this is undoubtedly true, our exploration of many specific folktales suggests that the situation is not nearly so fluid.

On the contrary, family-complex folktales more likely than not will depict just a few of the possibilities inherent in the general model of Figure 5. The basic oedipal tale is the triangular one of mother-son erotic closeness and father-son hostility. Although specific tales often simplify the relationships to have the erotic or hostile feelings originating in only a single partner of the dyad, cross-culturally we do not find patterns suggesting that one partner, whether parent or child, is more likely than the other to be represented as the "perpetrator" (Figure 2).

The situation in father-daughter tales, however, is quite different. The predominant scene portrayed there has father sexually attracted to daughter, who does not return the feeling. When he pursues his attraction through trickery or force, daughter turns against him, usually joining an alliance with mother to oppose him. This is not at all a mirror image of the basic oedipal model, but is quite close to the position to which the revisionist critique of Freud has brought us (Figure 7).

Turning to the brother-sister tales, we find again that a few possibilities dominate the field. Most common is the tale of the passionate brother rejected by sister. One variant reverses the dominant tale, brother rejecting passionate sister, whereas another presents parents united against incestuous brother and sister (Figure 8).

These patterns lead us to revise our model of the family complex. Instead of broadly representing all the erotic and hostile feelings possible within the family (Figure 5), we should represent only those that appear to dominate our tales (Figure 9). The resulting model is notable for two reasons. First, it is based upon a relatively large sample of folktales rather than on a preexisting theory. And, second, the unique picture it provides has a kind of intuitive plausibility with sexual action tending to originate in the males of the family,

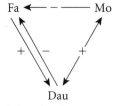

Fig. 7. The basic father-daughter incest tale.

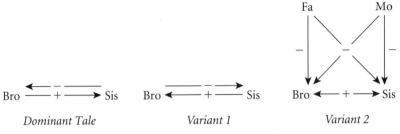

Fig. 8. Brother-sister incest tales. Theme and variations.

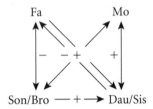

Fig. 9. A common form of the family complex as seen in folktales.

with the primary bonds of affection running between mother and both children: in this model, father is an outsider to the family, a potential aggressor and liable to rejection by the other family members. In the next chapter we will return to this theme, when we examine the arguments concerning the evolution of the human family in light of recent research on primate social organization.

RESULTS OF QUANTITATIVE ANALYSIS

Our original collection contained 164 separate entries. We have removed 33 of these from the present collection, either because they are already included in the collections of Edmunds and Dundes (1983) and Edmunds (1985), or because upon later reflection they were not appropriate to this collection: for example, we have removed a song, a drama, and several stories from literature, such as incest tales by Ovid. The items included in our original sample but excluded from this book are listed in Table 1.

Using the original sample of 164 tales, we coded the tales on a number of variables, including sociocultural variables about the societies from which they came (politically stratified or not, patrilineal or matrilineal, and so on) and internal features of the tales themselves, such as whether the partners knew in advance that they were committing incest, or whether aggressive acts like mutilation and abandonment were done at the birth of an infant.

TABLE 1
Changes from the Original Collection (Quantitative Analysis) to the Present Collection

1A. Tales included in the original collection but omitted in the present work. Although these tales do not appear here, they have been included in the analysis that follows.

Title of Tale	Provenance	Source
Myrrha and Cinyras	Rome	Ovid 1955:233–38
Byblis and Caunus	Rome	Ovid 1955:215–21
Hippolytus	Rome	Ovid 1955:347–48
The She-Bear	Italy	Basile 1932:170–77
The Girl with the Maimed Hands	Italy	Basile 1932:232–40
South Slavic Oedipus I	Yugoslavia	Edmunds and Dundes 1983:11–13
Janos	Hungary	Edmunds and Dundes 1983:23–24
Potametes	Modern Greece	Edmunds and Dundes 1983:134–36
The Abandoned Son	Puerto Rico	Edmunds 1985:223
The Fairy's Curse	Albania	Edmunds and Dundes 1983:6–9
Salamon Premunde	Romania	Edmunds 1985:96–97
Edward	England	Brooks, Purser, and Warren 1938:435
The Sultan's Son	Turkey	Edmunds 1985:198–99
The Rabbi and His Son	Israel	Edmunds 1985:199–202
The Man Who Killed His Father and Married His Mother	Israel	Edmunds 1985:202–3
The Farmer's Son	Israel	Edmunds 1985:203–5
The Boy Who Killed His Mother	Israel	Edmunds 1985:205–6
Nimrud	Medieval Egypt	Edmunds 1985:69–73
The Boy Thrown in the Nile	Sudan	Edmunds 1985:212–14
Jean	Medieval Egypt	Edmunds 1985:73–79
Izanaga and Izanami	Ancient Japan	Eliade 1967:94–96
Prankster Tricks Own Father	China	Ting 1978:208–9
A Gurung Shaman's Chant	Nepal	Mumford 1989:143
Sherpa Dance Drama	Nepal	Paul 1979:286
Mayo Myth	Philippines	Cole 1913:173–74
The Origins of the Kalangs	Java	Edmunds and Dundes 1983:23–34
Sagome and His Mother	New Guinea	Roheim 1952:484–85
The Boy and the Chief	Ponape	Edmunds 1985:209–12
Gufa	New Guinea	Edmunds and Dundes 1983:43–46
Ratananomby	Madagascar	Edmunds 1985:216–20
Asare	Ge	Wilbert and Simoneau 1978 (II):40–41
Podwo and His Unfaithful Wife	Ge	Wilbert and Simoneau 1978 (I):368–71
The Troublemaker	Ayoreo	Wilbert and Simoneau 1989:35–36

1B. Tales added to the present collection after quantitative analysis was completed. These tales were not included in the analysis that follows.

Title of Tale	Provenance	No. in Collection
Camoes and his Mother	Brazil	14
Purusa	Ancient India	38
Prajapati	Ancient India	39
The Flood	Hmong (Laos)	55
Loro Sama Lilaka	Tetum (Timor)	86
The Story of Aishish	Klamath	104
Bachue	Muisca	138
La Cacica	Muisca	139

THE EVIDENCE FROM FOLK LITERATURE

The results of this preliminary data processing must be taken with caution. Despite the relatively large numbers and worldwide distribution of tales in our sample, it still remains an "opportunity" sample about which we cannot say very much. It is necessarily biased: for example, we have far more oedipal tales from Eurasia and Oceania than father-daughter or brother-sister tales; the distributions are more equal for the Americas and Africa. There are undoubtedly other biases that we cannot know about because no one knows how to obtain a random sample of family-complex folktales, and hence we will work with what we have, keeping in mind that these findings are not made definitive simply by attaching a statistical estimate of significance.

In fact, one very strong pattern emerged from the quantitative approach we employed: that tales from societies coded as "stratified" showed much greater evidence of repression than tales from "nonstratified" societies. Although this result was not predicted by any of the theories we reviewed for this project, we were not surprised because this was intuitively obvious to us from handling so many folktales as we prepared our collection. And, such a conclusion is probably implicit in Freud's contention that "civilization is built up upon a renunciation of instinct" (Freud 1930: 97).

The most interesting results regarding repression in stratified societies are three very strong associations in the data. First, we asked whether sexual activity is present in each tale. We found that tales from nonstratified societies were much more likely to include sexual activity than those from stratified societies ($\chi^2 = 7.84$, $p < .005$). We also found that aggression at birth (mutilation, abandonment) was much more common in tales from stratified societies ($\chi^2 = 8.56$, $p < .005$). These two findings suggest to us that audiences in stratified societies are more anxious about incest than those in nonstratified societies: in their stories they are more likely to avoid explicit mention of sexual activity and to portray severe punitive actions of parents against helpless, but potentially dangerous, infants.

We also found a weaker but intriguing link between stratification and the appearance of expressions of shame or guilt in the tales. As would probably be predicted by those familiar with the literature on shame and guilt societies (Piers and Singer 1953), guilt is more likely to appear in stories from stratified societies ($\chi^2 = 3.61$, $p < .06$), emphasizing the importance there of remorse following family-complex crimes.

A possibly related finding emerged when we asked whether the actors in the tale know of their kinship relation before they commit incest, or discover it only after they have innocently sinned. We expected this to be significantly related to stratification, but the relationship is weak at best ($\chi^2 = 2.08$, $p < .15$). There is, however, a very strong relationship between a lack of foreknowledge of incest and aggression at birth: tales in which the actors do not know who they are (do not know in advance that their sexual relationship constitutes incest) are much *more* likely to include aggression at birth than are tales where the partners are aware of their true kinship ($\chi^2 = 16.98$, p < .001). If we assume that folktales tell us something about attitudes or conflicts in the audience that hears them, we could speculate that aggression at birth in a folktale indicates hostility toward the impulsive child self. In their folktales, societies where such hostility is great mask the will and intention of the actors to commit incest (by saying they didn't know better) and introduce cruelties inflicted on infants.

Another set of findings distinguish stories involving mother-son incest from father-daughter or brother-sister incest tales. We sought variables that might distinguish the latter two types of tales from each other, but to no avail. Yet several findings indicate that these two are quite similar to each other and together are distinct from mother-son tales. The strongest finding is that mother-son tales are far more likely to include aggression at birth than father-daughter or brother-sister tales ($\chi^2 = 13.97$, p < .001). Because our sample is biased toward oedipal tales from Eurasia, however, this may mainly reflect our disproportionate number of Oedipus-cognate tales (aggression at birth is a key part of tale type 931). The finding is so strong, however, that we do not rule out the possibility that greater aggression at birth in mother-son tales reflects a deeper anxiety and outrage over this kind of incest in comparison with that between father-daughter and brother-sister.

We also asked to what degree the partners to the incest in a tale were willing participants, and we found that the partners in mother-son tales are far more likely to be "both willing" than in father-daughter or brother-sister tales ($\chi^2 = 7.30$, p < .01). As we have seen, in many of the tales from Eurasia (many of which are Oedipus cognates), both partners are willing but have no knowledge of their close kinship. This finding supports our conclusion, based on inspection of individual tales, that the erotic attitude of mother and son in family-complex stories is bilateral, whereas the attitude is unilateral— usually from father to daughter and from brother to sister—in the other tale types.

Since the literature on Oedipus has stressed so much the transition from matrilineal to patriarchal society in the genesis of that tale, we coded societies according to lineality. We found few significant associations, but three are noteworthy. First, in tales from matrilineal societies, the partners to incest are more likely to know of their kin relation than in patrilineal societies ($\chi^2 = 4.75$, p < .05). Second, sexual activity is more likely to appear in matrilineal tales ($\chi^2 = 3.93$, p < .05). There is also a weak tendency for aggression at birth to be more common in tales from patrilineal societies ($\chi^2 = 3.04$, p = .081). From this we infer that matrilineal tales show less evidence of repression than patrilineal tales. In our sample, there is no relationship between stratification and lineality, so this result is not merely the artifact of greater stratification in patrilineal societies, as implied by the arguments of Fromm and others.

In any case, the variables describing aggression at birth and incest partners' knowledge of their kinship relationship are strongly related to social stratification and, somewhat less strongly, to lineality. We take innocence of the kinship tie to be a device for protecting the audience from the anxiety that would be provoked by "primitive" incestuous actors who openly desire each other. We further take aggression at birth to be an expression in the tale of the harsh attitudes of the audience toward Trickster-child impulsiveness. These differences in tales between nonstratified and stratified societies suggest that stratification is accompanied by higher degrees of repression of unacceptable impulses in the family: these differences in the tales do not change the core situations being depicted, but increasingly mask their fundamental nature from the audience.

One intriguing finding deserves mention. We coded tales according to whether the protagonists in the tale were human, animal, or supernatural. With a χ^2 of 7.2 (p < .05), when the protagonists are animals, they are most likely to know in advance that their sex partner is an incestuous relation, whereas, when they are supernaturals, they are *least* likely to know that their sexual relationship will be incestuous. When the actors are human, their likelihood of knowing in advance is intermediate. We cannot help but note that this pattern has the most "id-like" actors (animals) openly incestuous and the most "superego-like" actors (supernaturals) ignorant of the incest; the "ego-like" humans fall somewhere in between. Our results are summarized in Table 2.

TABLE 2
Statistical Associations of Features of Family-Complex Folktales

Association of Features in Tale			χ^2	$p<$
1. sexual activity	↔	society unstratified	7.84	.005
2. aggression at birth	↔	society stratified	8.56	.005
3. guilt expressed	↔	society stratified	3.61	.06
4. incest foreknowledge	↔	society unstratified	2.08	.15
5. no incest foreknowledge	↔	aggression at birth	16.98	.001
6. aggression at birth	↔	mother-son tales	13.97	.001
7. lovers both willing	↔	mother-son tales	7.30	.01
8. incest foreknowledge	↔	society matrilineal	4.75	.05
9. sexual activity	↔	society matrilineal	3.93	.05
10. aggression at birth	↔	society patrilineal	3.04	.08
11. animal protagonists	↔	incest foreknowledge ⎫	7.20	.05
supernatural protagonists	↔	no foreknowledge ⎭		

NOTE: n = 164.

SUMMARY

We have examined the tales in our collection for evidence concerning the variation and distribution of family-complex folktales. Review of narratives historically related to the Greek tale of Oedipus showed remarkable similarities persisting across vast distances of time and space. Although the availability of a written record of the tale may have contributed to this stability, it is still impressive how much the local color of the story can vary while its essential structure is hardly disturbed.

Some of that structure falls away, however, when we view oedipal folktales worldwide. The Myth of the Hero is usually absent from such tales, as is the depiction of helpless protagonists propelled by relentless fate. What emerges is a core oedipal tale of mother-son intimacy, usually eroticized, and of father-son hostility. We argue that tales where the focus is on a single dyad (a fight between father and son, or a union of mother and son) usually involve the attenuated presence of the other party to the triangle: the father-son fight still implicates mother, and the mother-son union still implicates the problem of son's growth and ultimate separation from mother and movement into the masculine world.

In father-daughter and brother-sister tales the incestuous wish tends to originate in father or brother, to be resisted by daughter (often with mother's solidarity and aid) or sister. Quantitative analysis showed these kinds of tales to be different from father-son-mother tales, with less aggression at birth, perhaps indicating less anxiety (and need to represent punishment for infantile wishes).

We concluded that the general model of the family complex (Figure 5), with its emphasis on erotic and aggressive feelings among all family members—describing the family as a nest of ambivalence—is useful for thinking about the great diversity of folktales of incest and aggression. We also concluded, however, that we can be more specific about what the most common types of tales appear to be (limitations on our sample making all such conclusions provisional). Our model of the common form of the family complex (Figure 9) shows the oedipal core with mutual intimacy between mother and son (erotic) and mother and daughter (not erotic), mutual hostility between father and son, one-way desire from father to daughter and brother to sister, and a one-way hostility from daughter to father. The positive mother-child bond is emphasized, and mature males are viewed with suspicion.

The strongest quantitative pattern in our tales had to do not with types of tales but with the degree of repression evident in the manner in which the tales are told. Tales from nonstratified, smaller-scale societies are bold and direct in depicting sexual and aggressive actions between family members. Tales from stratified societies, on the other hand, mince words, mask actors' identities and intentions, lay stress on remorse and punishment, and generally tone down the sexual and aggressive actions. We view this as evidence that audiences in stratified societies are more anxious about family-complex situations than in nonstratified societies, and that tales have evolved to strike the delicate balance between the boringly tame and the shockingly explicit. Tales like "Kauha" (21) or "The Little Woodpecker" (123), if rendered literally on stage, might well be "banned in Boston" and everywhere else, even in our current "liberated" era, whereas *Oedipus Rex* is free to represent the same fundamental story without complaint.

CHAPTER 4

THE THEORY OF THE FAMILY COMPLEX IN FOLK LITERATURE

In Chapter 2 we examined the background of theoretical debates against which we viewed our collection of folktales in Chapter 3. Although there remain grounds to defend both the psychoanalytic revisionists and the folkloric and structuralist interpretations discussed there, we have found a degree of support for Freud's views that, to us at least, was initially surprising. This has led us to reexamine his theory of the genesis of the family complex and of how it becomes represented in folktales. After revising and updating the old theory of how folktales reflect unconscious mental life, we return to *Totem and Taboo* to evaluate its vision of the universality of the Oedipus complex.

PREVIOUS THEORY IN LIGHT OF OUR COLLECTION OF FOLKTALES

The key debate with which we began our exploration of family-complex folktales concerned whether the tale of Oedipus marked the existence of an invariant Oedipus complex. The arguments over whether the Trobriand tale of Dokonikan and Tudava (67) was oedipal were really, as we saw, over whether the Oedipus complex is universal. The role of folklore in this debate was to show either that oedipal tales are universal (indicating a universal complex) or that they are only one among a number of diverse tale types (indicating a range of distinct family complexes).

Our research tends to support the universalist approach, although it does not describe the same Oedipus complex Freud believed in. That is to say, our folktales tend to support Freud's triangular view of the male Oedipus complex, but not to support his view of the female Oedipus complex, tending instead to support the revisionist critique.

These tendencies were summarized in Figure 9 as the "common form" of the family complex. However, there is a great diversity among our folktales, reminding us that our original model of the family complex (Figure 5) is still useful in showing how "exceptions" to the common form can be generated by selectively emphasizing particular relationships and reducing mutual ambivalence to dramatic one-sidedness.

The usual family-complex folktale is quite simple. There are two or three central protagonists who stand in primary kinship relations to each other, and the direction and content of their emotions toward each other are clear and univalent. But some tales explore the possibilities of the family complex more fully. In the Ozarks joke about Jack and his family (11), for example, by the time the punch line has been reached, all the possibilities for heterosexual incest within the nuclear family have been realized. One of the present authors heard this joke from a boyhood friend in northern California in the early 1950s and remembers it as a joke that made one want to laugh and groan at the same time. The folklorist Randolph (1976: 56) comments: "There are endless variations on this story, with the dialogue assigned to different combinations of family members. [It has been reported from Indiana several times since the 1890s.] Legman says he also heard it in London in 1954, and further points out that it is often related as the dirtiest story the teller knows."

We suggest that what makes this such a dirty story is the delight with which all the members of this family practice incest, without ambivalence or danger (Figure 10).

Even the enlarged scope of this tale, however, is still limited to positive erotic feelings. If there is any hostility expressed here it is in the subtle competition where Jack (and Paw) prefer Jenny to Maw. As Randolph points out, the joke can be modified slightly to refocus the competition: for example, a joke where Jenny tells Jack he's better than Paw (and Maw agrees). Hence, the model for Jack's family might itself be seen as a kind of mini-generator for a series of closely related family-complex stories.

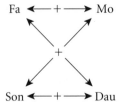

Fig. 10. Jack's family (11).

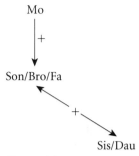

Fig. 11. A tale of incest (7).

"A Tale of Incest" (7), from France, manages to cover all the possibilities for incest that Jack's family does, but by exploiting the kin confusion that incestuous childbearing produces. Here, mother, jealous of teenage son's efforts to seduce a servant girl, takes her place in son's bed and yields to "an abominable pleasure." She becomes pregnant, and then compounds her sin by sending son away so that he, and their daughter (simultaneously son's sister and daughter), do not know each other and are free to fall in love when fate brings them together. When they marry, they ignorantly and blissfully commit simultaneous father-daughter/brother-sister incest. With his father removed early from the tale, son is free to enjoy incest with mother, sister, and daughter, all without knowing and hence without guilt or retribution (Figure 11).

Though these tales are richer in relationships than is usual in family-complex tales, both remain much simpler than the full family complex. We may find still larger expressions of the family complex if we look to elaborate and sophisticated productions of literate society—*The Marriage of Figaro*, for example (Mozart 1959 [1786]).

We find, therefore, that there is a tendency for family-complex tales to follow a common form, yet there is also ample room for other possibilities suggested by the general model of the family complex. In light of this finding, how do the theoretical arguments we reviewed earlier fare? We may examine them now under two headings: the "cultural relativist" critique that accepts the idea of family complexes but rejects the universality of the Oedipus complex, and the "folkloric/structuralist" critiques that argue that family-complex tales are not about sex and aggression in the family at all, but about other cognitive-intellectual (non-emotional) concerns.

The Cultural Relativist Critique

On the whole, the cultural relativist critique does not fare well in the face of the evidence available to us. The Fromm-Horney-Kardiner axis, arguing that the Oedipus complex is only found in patriarchal and capitalist societies, is not supported. While it remains likely that oedipal conflicts are more intense in patriarchal societies, and particularly in those with the male supremacy complex (Harris 1977), tales like "Kauha" (21) and "The Little Woodpecker" (123) contain the fullest possible expression of both eroticism and violence (including actual or implied intercourse and castration), yet they occur in societies that lack tribal warfare and are as distant as possible, socially as well as geographically, from patriarchal Western society. Adherents of the relativistic viewpoint might want to argue that the existence of oedipal tales has nothing to do with the Oedipus complex, and we will turn shortly to the problem of the relationship between the two. Given the importance that Fromm and Kardiner attached to folktales as windows on unconscious mental life, however, it seems unlikely that either would have endorsed such a position.

Another alternative might be to give some ground, admitting that early family life contains oedipal "situations" that inevitably stimulate childhood fantasies like the oedipal core tale we have identified, but in most societies a wholesome style of childrearing resolves the conflicts before they turn into an Oedipus complex. This would lead to an interesting but probably unresolvable debate over the definition of the Oedipus complex: how much unconscious conflict must be present before a "resolved" childhood fantasy becomes an unresolved adult complex? Our opinion is that the Oedipus complex may be more or less resolved in terms of the behavior of well-adjusted adults, but does not lose unconscious vitality and thus makes for stories interesting even to well-adjusted audiences.

The Malinowski axis, which holds more generally that the core conflicts in the family change with the social context, is not supported by our evidence. The arguments of Roheim, Ingham, and Spiro against Malinowski gain support from our evidence that oedipal tales are found in matrilineal as well as patrilineal (and nonlineal) social systems. We did uncover some evidence that folktales told in matrilineal societies show less evidence of repression than those from patrilineal societies. This implies that the oedipal situation is more harshly experienced in patrilineal societies, perhaps because fathers there are more powerful and authoritarian and capable of instilling a stronger fear of punishment. But we note that the difference is not in the Oedipus complex per se, but rather in the implication that patrilineal societies (like stratified societies) are more "repressed" than matrilineal ones (and nonstratified ones).

Therefore, our finding of patterned differences between tales from nonstratified and stratified societies does not cast doubt on the universality of the Oedipus complex. Oedipal tales are clearly widespread and probably universal and cannot be used as evidence that the Oedipus complex is *not*. What our evidence shows rather is that the same oedipal content that is acceptable to an audience in nonstratified societies must be attenuated and symbolically masked before audiences in stratified societies can hear it without undue anxiety.

At this late date, for example, we can hardly remember the surprise with which we first read "The Little Woodpecker" (123). We imagine that ordinary Western audiences would find that story shocking, disgusting, or "savage." It might confirm their prejudices about "the sexual life of savages." Most tales, from all kinds of societies, do some defensive maneuvering—if nothing more, social disapproval is indicated—but those from stratified societies do their best to disguise the intentions and identities of the actors.

In sum, our collection of folktales does not support the freedom to vary implied by the cultural relativist critique. Rather, it suggests that the three dominant themes of family-complex tales are a triangular mother-son love affair threatened by a father-son struggle, a sexually aggressive father opposed by a resistant daughter and mother, and a sexually aggressive bad brother opposed by a non-incestuous good sister.

Although it is true that we need the full model of the family complex to include all the possibilities for sexual and aggressive feelings between family members in order to account for the many exceptions to the basic themes, none of this suggests that different sociocultural groups focus on locally specific basic themes. The "theme with variations" we encounter here does appear to be one shared by humankind at large.

The Folkloric and Structuralist Critiques

The general critique from folklorists and the Levi-Straussian-style structuralists—that family-complex tales are really about something quite different and unrelated to sex and aggression within the family—must be evaluated differently. Since its adherents disagree with us about what such tales really mean, we cannot use the evidence of the tales in our collection to contradict them: they are entitled to say the Oedipus tale (3) is really about historical transformations of government, or that the Bororo tale (114) is really about conceptions of the kinship system.

No doubt there are good reasons historically for pointing out the link between Oedipus and the sun, or agriculture, or the transition from matrilineal to patriarchal society. But these connections lose much of their significance in a pan-human frame of reference. The sun does appear in a few other tales in our collection (91, 105) but can hardly be said to be a recurrent figure; the same may be said for agriculture (8, 106, 112).

Analyses of oedipal tales that insist on local, historically specific cultural meanings, therefore, cannot account for the underlying common pattern we have identified cross-culturally. This pattern depicts forbidden erotic and hostile actions within the nuclear family. As Spiro (1979: 11) pointed out, the most direct assumption would be that these tales really are about sexual and aggressive feelings toward family members—feelings that remain powerful in psychic life despite the abundant cultural controls arrayed against them.

Still, Graves was right in a way when he said that a "perverted anecdote" had occupied what was actually the story of Oedipus the invading conqueror: the oedipal tale seems almost to have moved around the world, occupying one sort of tale here, another there, like a hermit crab occupying the abandoned shells of other species. Where Graves was mistaken was in taking the oedipal tale as a freak without significance, rather than as the universal story that it is, one that can occupy a tale about the family of a heroic king as easily as one about humble hippopotamuses.

OEDIPAL TALES AND OEDIPUS COMPLEX

To this point we have deferred discussion of the relationship between oedipal tales and the Oedipus complex. We did briefly indicate that one stumbling block would be over the definition of the Oedipus complex: Are we referring primarily to unconscious fantasies dating to a developmental phase that has been resolved and outgrown, or to an essentially pathological developmental arrest? In the latter case, we would be referring to a minority of members of any community, men whose functioning is greatly impaired by fear and hostility toward senior males and repeated seductive relationships with motherly women.

Here, it is the former possibility to which we refer: what might be called "oedipal concerns," which should be broadened to include incestuous and hostile feelings surrounding the father-daughter and brother-sister relationships. In theory, these occupy a place in the unconscious mental life of individuals whether or not their effects are discernible as disruptions in work, marriage, or other spheres of life. To this point in our argument, we have been assuming that the incestuous and violent events portrayed in the folktales in our collection indicate the existence of matching "concerns" in mental life.

Furthermore, it does seem that oedipal tales commonly present situations that would be considered abnormal and unacceptable to their audiences everywhere. One is reminded of the comment of the !Kung storyteller at the end of "Kauha" (21): "The things that went on long ago!" and of the Brazilian storyteller's admiration for the legendary Camoes (14): "Camoes was so sly, a real trickster!" One has the impression of extraordinary events in the past, viewed with surprise, and perhaps some admiration, from the distance of a controlled, well-ordered (and ordinary) present.

Folktales, therefore, may present images of feeling and acting that are unacceptable in the storytelling present; arguably, they reflect repressed, unconscious mental contents. Certainly, folktales do more than that, and not all tales exist only to depict the scenery of the unconscious mind. But an understanding of why and how folktales do portray repressed mental life will provide a key link in the reasoning that leads us to conclude that the Oedipus complex, indeed the "common form" of the family complex as identified here, is a human universal.

We will find that the existing theory linking folktales to unconscious mental life can do with some modernizing. Taking advantage of recent theoretical developments in our understanding of repression and the nature of the unconscious, we attempt to come closer to an appreciation of the kind of satisfaction an audience derives from hearing about anxiety-provoking family complexes in folktales. This in turn leads us to a reevaluation of Freud's effort in *Totem and Taboo* to account for the evolution from primate social organization to the human family embedded in cultural process.

Folktales and Intrapsychic Conflict

The question to which we turn now is: Even if we accept that oedipal folktales are more or less universal in human societies, are we entitled to conclude that matching images universally populate unconscious mental life? Cannot a listener be interested in a story about a boy who kills his father and marries his mother without secretly harboring repressed wishes for the same? In order to develop a reasonable answer to that question, it is necessary briefly to address two subsidiary questions:

1. How does the audience listen to folktales?
2. To what degree do folktales contain repressed content?

THE AUDIENCE IS LISTENING. Folktales are often called "fireside tales" or "twilight tales." In our experience in nonliterate cultures, tales can be told any time there is the leisure to do so, as in a break during work, but are most likely to be told in the evening. In societies without extensive night lighting, which is very fuel-expensive, it is usual for there to be a period of dim light, from a burning taper or the kitchen hearth, around which the family gathers during the period between the evening meal and bedtime. These are generally periods of intense family interaction, with children crawling into one lap or another while the day's events are being discussed.

It is common during this time to recount events that are believed to have occurred in the past, but for which no eye-witnesses now exist. No matter how outrageous the events may seem to us, including metamorphoses into animals, prodigious feats of strength, exercise of spiritual power, and such, the audience accepts these stories as essentially true of the past, when people and the world around them were different. Quite often there is a kind of regret for this lost past, or at least a grudging respect for a time when people were more powerful and courageous than in our present tame era.

The atmosphere surrounding the storytelling is often rapt. A respectful silence, although interrupted by a good deal of coming and going and spontaneous interaction, allows the storyteller to get the story out, even though the audience may respond to the humor, violence, and pathos in the story with outbursts of laughter or expressions of surprise or sympathy. Often, someone will ask the storyteller a question such as, "Isn't he supposed to have met Cedar Spirit before he came to the cave?" The storyteller may say, "Yes, that's true," or "No, I haven't heard that." A discussion may ensue before the storyteller is allowed to continue.

The members of the household are often occupied with tasks while the story is going on. Heavy or noisy tasks will be avoided, but spinning cotton with hand spindles, making artifacts like combs or net bags, repairing harnesses, and so on, can go on without much light or noise. Children will play quietly, groom and be groomed, or doze off in a comfortable lap. They will hear these same tales over and over again throughout their lives, told by different storytellers, and they will tell some of them themselves as they master them.

We have already mentioned that this environment of storytelling offers ample opportunity for revisions of tales as they pass through different storytellers with different life histories. Each performance of a folktale (or ritual, drama, and so forth) is a unique event, in which the meanings of the tale vary subtly or radically from other performances. In addition to differences among storytellers, the variations in the performance are responsive to the particular audience and occasion (Bauman 1975). Yet this is all the more reason to be impressed by the stability at the core of many of the tales in our collection. This stability across time and space is a testimony to the deep and constant meaning a tale-type like the oedipal tale must have if it is to survive the buffeting it takes in such diverse hands.

It is equally noteworthy that the audience is fully engaged, in a relaxed way, with the story. The storytelling is entertaining, filled with vivid details like the sounds animals make in the forest or the cries of men in battle. It is safe to say that a world of the imagination is brought to life just as in the better plays or movies we attend. The experience is emotional as much as it is intellectual, although the story line is important and the audience is concerned to get the "facts" straight.

Given all of this, it must be clear that "boring" stories have little chance of catching on in a community. In our experience, people in nonliterate societies are far from impoverished in their repertoire of stories. It is certainly not the case that any story is better than no story. There is as competitive a marketplace for good stories there as here. The stories we collect when we study the folk literature of other societies have gone through a sort of cultural selection: poor stories will not survive. This process must have been most rigorous in the case of stories that are found again and again around the world, like the basic oedipal tale. What accounts for the extraordinary "success" of such a tale?

REPRESSION AND EXPRESSION IN FOLKTALES. The general approach to folktales by psychoanalysts and psychoanalytically oriented anthropologists is that of Freud, by way of Kardiner. Freud, whose focus was on dreams, assumed that folktales and other artistic productions, like dreams, expressed unconscious wishes. In an essay written with a folklorist (Freud and Oppenheim 1911: 181), he argued that dreams that appear in folktales are more explicit—have less hidden content—than actual dreams: "It is very much more convenient to study dream-symbolism in folklore than in actual dreams. Dreams are obliged to conceal things and only surrender their interpretation; these comic anecdotes [in folktales], however, which are disguised as dreams, are intended as communications, meant to give pleasure to the person who tells them as well as to the listener, and therefore the interpretation is added quite unashamedly to the symbol." Apart from this difference in communicative purpose, however, the authors conclude "that folklore interprets dream-symbols in the same way as psycho-analysis, and that . . . it derives a group of dreams from needs and wishes which have become immediate" (Freud and Oppenheim 1911: 203).

As we saw earlier, Kardiner put this graphically in terms of an energy system, where the charges building from repressed wishes find discharge in the folktale. A common approach to this in anthropology is found in the Whiting Model, in which tensions and frustrations built up in the business of making a living in controlled social settings find their way into "expressive systems" like art, drama, folklore, and, incidentally, religion (Whiting and Whiting 1975: 1).

The energetic view has been succinctly expressed with reference to dreams: "It seems that as need pressure accumulates in the early dreams of a sequence, it is discharged in a pitch of excitement either directly or by a highly dramatic visual representation, and is followed by a period of regression or quiescence" (Trosman et al. 1960: 606). This viewpoint has a kind of intuitive plausibility that cannot be ignored. We know what it is to feel an interior pressure and to experience the sense of release that comes with emotional expression, and we have had some experience of release from drama, literature, art, music, or religion. It is reasonable to suppose that the engagement of the listeners at a traditional storytelling also permits some basic forms of release in laughter, amazement, and sorrow.

In terms of contemporary theory, however, the energetic viewpoint is incomplete, at best. It tends to assume that an image from a folktale somehow gets to the locus of the energy build-up and releases it. This raises a great many theoretical problems that cannot be solved within the mechanistic model of drive discharge (Friedman 1988: 197–221). We would now insist that whatever happens to both the repressed wish and the image from the folktale happens to a person or self for whom both wish and image have meaning (Klein 1976; Gedo 1979; Gill 1983). The image must be *understood*, and if there is any release or pleasure in it, it belongs to the self and not to a physiological process of drive discharge. We must describe, therefore, how the external event of the storytelling reaches the inner lives of the listeners. Only then may we attempt to understand the relationship between oedipal tales and the postulated oedipal conflicts or complexes of individuals.

The question of how the anxiety-provoking contents of oedipal tales are heard, or as we prefer to phrase it, "who" is listening to the unconscious content, is not an easy one to answer in this new theoretical framework. We have become familiar with the notion of a cohesive self as the outcome of normal development, but generally this self is treated as the self-identity we construct as we grow up in family and society. The question arises, what if this cohesive self has rejected oedipal strivings as alien to itself, which we have reason to believe is true for the great majority of humankind? Are we to suppose that this same cohesive self is the listener to the tale? And, if so, just what is it hearing?

CONCEPTS OF SELF. The problem is that there is a basic paradox in our current views of the cohesive self with respect to repression: How can a self hide important information about itself from itself? Who is the deceiver and who is the deceived? As Fingarette observes, the self-deceiver *deliberately* hides a truth from himself yet does not know he is doing so. If it were not deliberate, it would be simply an error, not a deception. Yet, "if one *knows*, why bother refusing to say so at least to oneself?" (Fingarette 1969: 65).

Freud (1915: 146) wrote, "It is not easy in theory to deduce the possibility of such a thing as repression." We saw earlier that Freud understood the motive behind repression to result from the "omnipotence of thoughts" that led the child to fear that its dangerous thoughts would automatically become actions and place it in extreme danger. The way the notion of repression has been employed in a traditional Freudian framework sometimes seems to assume that it takes place bit by bit, as each wish is identified as dangerous and consigned to the unconscious. The wish does not disappear, of course, but remains in a kind of cage or repository whence it continually seeks escape. Jung (1964: 102), critical of this approach to the unconscious, writes, "The ideas of Sigmund Freud confirmed for most people the existing contempt for the [unconscious] psyche. Before him it had been merely overlooked and neglected; it has now become a dump for moral refuse." The possibility that this unconscious realm had a structure or organization or self-like attributes appears to have been given little attention, although Freud did entertain the idea of an unconscious part of the ego in his formulation of the structural model (Freud 1923: 12–66).

Although leading us to the brink of a new understanding of the unconscious, the advances of self-psychology have not resolved this difficulty. Kohut (1977: 177), for example, sees repression as occurring during the emergence of the "nuclear self," where "some archaic mental contents that had been experienced as belonging to the self become obliterated or are assigned to the area of the nonself while others are retained within the self or are added to it."

The key words here are "obliterated" and "nonself." Although Kohut sees the "restoration of the self" as in part a process of the self learning to embrace aspects that were formerly repressed, in his writing he has in effect taken the unconscious to be not only a dump, but a dump beyond the city limits, outside the purview of the self. It is of course difficult not to do so, since our tendency is to see "self" and "identity" as closely related. Gedo (1979: 221, 226), too, speaks of a "split in the self," in such a way as to suggest that what is repressed is in the id, outside the "self-organization" of the healthy individual.

THE SELF AS LISTENER. In Kohut's notion of the nonself and in Gedo's notion of the id, we find zones that somehow belong to the person but are defined as outside the self. The healthy self incorporates as many zones and as much content as possible; indeed, growth includes accepting responsibility for formerly repressed needs and impulses (Loewald 1979: 758–63). But, in this perspective, the self inevitably "consigns" or "relegates" some totally unacceptable content to an external, alien zone. It is such contents, however, that oedipal tales evoke.

Let us recall for a moment the content of oedipal tales. We have seen many examples of contents that even flexible "nuclear selves" or "self-organizations" cannot possibly contemplate with equanimity, such as mother-son foreplay with mushrooms (123), mutilations of eyes (3, 105), feet (3, 67), arms (109), breasts (91), and penises (123, 21), attempted or completed parricides and filicides, anguished self-punishment, and suicides. Even heavily psychoanalyzed selves must admit to anxiety in the face of such images: indeed, we may assume that selves that experience no anxiety about such topics are "out of touch with themselves." Yet this content is not there in the folktales for nothing. It is meant to be heard. But if the self has relegated such content to the nonself, then how can it "hear" it? And, if it is not the self that hears it, who then?

This brings us back to the paradox of self-deception and the perplexing notion of a split *within* the self. It will be helpful if, limiting ourselves to the matter of unconscious content in folktales, we try to answer the following questions.

1. Why is it that, for a human being, having an unacceptable wish so often seems to entail not merely *control* over the impulse to realize the wish, but also *denial* and *repression* of the wish itself? After all, all animals experience the frustration of their wishes at some point, and the more complex animals certainly exercise control, as when a hungry hyena keeps its distance from a kill guarded by lions. Why must human beings take the large additional step from saying, "If I grab that meat, as I wish to do, I will suffer," to saying, "I certainly have no wish to grab that meat (what kind of person do you take me for?)"

2. Given that we do accomplish the unlikely act of repression, how do we do it? How does a self hide knowledge about itself from itself? Deception of others is common in nature and is well documented for our closest primate relatives. But self-deception is another matter and may be limited in other animals to a sort of bravado by means of which individuals underestimate obstacles in order to undertake risky ventures (Trivers 1985: 416).

3. Finally, even if we know why we repress knowledge of our unacceptable impulses and how we do it, that still does not explain why we find expression of those impulses interesting or pleasurable when disguised in symbols of many-layered meaning. In the vernacular, why hasn't *Oedipus Rex* been "banned in Boston?"

THE ORIGINS OF SELF-DECEPTION. In order to answer the last question, which is key, we need answers to the first two questions that provide a clearer sense of who is listening to the "unconscious" content of a folktale. In *Self-Deception* Fingarette (1969) has provided a theory of the unconscious that leads naturally to an understanding of the enjoyment people derive from the anxiety-provoking unconscious content in their folktales.

Fingarette's approach is to focus on the *self* as the agent of the deception. We may think of the child's emerging self as starting out something like folklore's Trickster, who "wills nothing consciously. At all times he is constrained to behave as he does from impulses over which he has no control. He knows neither good nor evil. . . . He possesses no values, moral or social, is at the mercy of his passions and appetites" (Radin 1956: xxiii). This Trickster-child rather quickly learns, however, that aspects of his being, arising from his very essence, are unacceptable to those who care for him. This is the origin of intrapsychic conflict, "tragic" in the classical sense that it is an inevitable consequence of being human.

In self-psychological terms, the reaction of the disapproving caregivers may be described as an absence of acknowledgment and mirroring. We recognize that this lack of acknowledgment is experienced by the child as a loss attended by sorrow. But these phrases may not convey the full danger the emerging human feels exposed to.

In every human society, including those small-scale societies where parents' love, joy, and tolerance for their children is well documented, disobedient children are faced with truly frightening prospects. The remarkably patient and generous Matsigenka parents of the Peruvian Amazon (O. Johnson 1978), for example, discipline their children with threats. In addition to constant verbal instruction and correction, parents with a young child keep in the house a fresh-cut stalk of the nettle, *tanko*, with sharp poisonous spines. Although rarely used, it is often brandished at a recalcitrant child, and it is used enough that the threatened child recoils and placates his angered parent.

A favorite technique of parents in such societies is to jokingly threaten to abandon the child. A constant game of Matsigenka mothers is to tease their ill-behaved children that they will give them away to someone. Children respond to the teasing with a specific kind of grin, as if to say, "You're joking, aren't you?" When a particularly exasperated mother would threaten to give her child to the visiting anthropologist, however, the child's half-grin would give way to sheer wailing terror. Very rarely, an "impossible" child will, in fact, be given away (O. Johnson 1978: 166–75).

Adults observing these disciplinary maneuvers tend to see them as mild and amusing. Children in such societies are rarely beaten and receive so much love that they cannot doubt their safety in the household. In Erikson's (1963) terms, their "basic trust" is solid. Yet the looks on their faces reveal a human truth: young children, with their limited experience and cognitive abilities, tend to understand such threats and the actual painful punishments they receive in harsh and vivid terms. The !Kung woman Nisa, for example, has clear and evocative memories of such parental "cruelties" from her own childhood (Shostak 1981: 52). Therefore, the wishes or impulses that bring children to the brink of such punishments are terrifying. In no community is the transformation of a Trickster child into a responsible member of society an easy matter.

Fingarette points out that what the child is actually terrified of are not raw unprocessed "id impulses" but fantasies arising from those impulses. These fantasies—which are likely to include domination, retaliation, and indulgence—are of the same sort as other, acceptable fantasies arising in the child: as much of the child's self goes into constructing the unacceptable fantasies as the acceptable ones. Being unacceptable to the caretakers and hence to the child's emerging sense of itself, however, the growing child disavows his unacceptable fantasies: "It happens . . . that an individual will be provoked into a kind of engagement which, in part or in whole, the person cannot *avow* as *his* engagement, for to avow it would apparently lead to such intensely disruptive, distressing consequences as to be unmanageably destructive to the person" (Fingarette 1969: 87). The "engagement" in question could be an attitude or desire that the individual believes could bring harm to himself or a beloved other: an example would be a child's feeling toward a parent of "I hate you" or "I wish you were dead." The disavowal amounts to saying "Not I: I have no such attitudes or desires."

This contrasts somewhat with Freud's ideas on the omnipotence of thoughts: it is not the fear that a fantasy will magically become reality that leads to repression, but the much more realistic fear that a self that has such wishes will be painfully punished or abandoned: these dangers are learned in the home and actualized in real punishments and threats of abandonment.

How is this repression accomplished? The capacity for disavowal makes use of the most fundamental of defense mechanisms, the "Ur-defense" of denial, whose primitive oral counterpart is spitting out. Fingarette insists that repression is the person's responsibility, his *intention*: he does the spitting out. In his view, consciousness is intentional: avowal and disavowal "are always, inherently, purposeful self-expression rather than mere happenings suffered by the person" (p. 70). (Of course, there is the mental content Freud called "preconscious," which is neither avowed nor disavowed: it can be acknowledged by a person whose attention has been drawn to it.)

But, what of the disavowed content? Is it consigned willy-nilly to a nonself dumping ground? Fingarette's idea is that it goes into a "counter-ego nucleus." Inspired by a brief effort by Freud (1940: 275–78) at the end of his life to reexamine the notion of a split occurring in the ego during the process of repression, Fingarette appears to be moving toward the notion of a complementary self-organization, a disavowed self, that coexists with the avowed self. Such an organized unconscious is much more like a shadow-being than a toxic waste dump or even a zoo of caged impulses.

Jung has carried this idea to its logical endpoint: "It is on such evidence [as dreams] that psychologists assume the existence of an unconscious psyche—though many scientists and philosophers deny its existence. They argue naively that such an assumption implies the existence of two 'subjects,' or (to put it in a common phrase) two personalities within the same individual. But this is exactly what it does imply—quite correctly" (Jung 1964: 23). This allows Jung to view the unconscious in personal terms, as when he says that "unconscious contents of the mind behave as if they were conscious" (p. 33), able to "pass information on" from "the other side": "In fact, the unconscious seems to be able to examine and to draw conclusions from facts, much as consciousness does" (p. 78). He describes it in part as "our shadow (the dark side of our nature)" (p. 85), although he sees the unconscious as a deep source of goodness and insight to which our conscious selves should learn to listen more carefully.

We note in passing that the unconscious mind to which Jung is referring is not necessarily the product of individual repression as Freud would see it. Indeed, there are mental contents of which individuals remain unaware for reasons other than repression. This is a thorny, though important, issue which we do not directly address here, our focus being on the part played by folktales in the expression of repressed contents of the mind.

Jung, however, appears to see repression as a disease of modern life, causing a disastrous loss of contact with an essentially benevolent, energizing unconscious. He contrasts moderns with primitives and ancients who retained their health-giving link to Nature through the unconscious, and sees a pathway to health for us through learning to live in complementary relationship with our unconscious selves.

For our current purposes, Jung's compelling vision has the limitation of denying the inevitability of repression in human life, of taking the sting out of Freud's irreducibly tragic view that all humans, not just moderns, experience internal conflict and repression. Nonetheless, it is useful metaphorically to think in terms of an unconscious, shadowy self capable of processing information and having attitudes.

It does seem that many psychoanalytic theorists have assumed the existence of a self-like unconscious, without really spelling it out. Here, for example, is Money-Kyrle (1951: 61–62) describing the formation of superego by introjection of the same-sex parent:

> In the normal outcome of the Oedipus complex the child introjects, and identifies himself with the parent of the same sex; and, as he has formed his concept of this parent, as humanity has formed its concept of the gods, in the image of himself, that is, by projection, the outcome includes a reintrojection of something of himself. But the fact that this very parent, in the role of rival, has become the depository of sadistic impulses which the child has disowned—in short, the fact that this figure has become to a great extent a "bad" object must seriously interfere with its assimilation. So only part of what is introjected can be assimilated. *The rest remains as an internal, but foreign element within the self.* [Emphasis added]

Winnicott (1965: 140–52) has a provocative discussion of this problem in his paper on the True and False Self. He sees the "good enough mother" as responding to the infant's needs and sustaining the development of its True Self. By contrast, the "not good enough mother"

> is not able to implement the infant's omnipotence, and so she repeatedly fails to meet the infant gesture; instead she substitutes her own gesture which is to be given sense by the compliance of the infant. This compliance on the part of the infant is the earliest stage of the False Self, and belongs to the mother's inability to sense her infant's needs (p. 145). . . .
>
> The True Self comes from the aliveness of the body tissues and the working of body-functions, including the heart's action and breathing. It is closely linked with

the idea of the Primary Process, and is, at the beginning, essentially not reactive to external stimuli, but primary. (p. 148)

Hence, "the False Self . . . lacks something, and that something is the essential central element of creative originality" (p. 152). Yet, even in healthy development a False Self necessarily appears: "The equivalent of the False Self in normal development is that which can develop in the child into a social manner, something which is adaptable. In health this social manner represents a compromise. At the same time, in health, the compromise ceases to become allowable when the issues become crucial. When this happens the True Self is able to override the compliant self" (p. 150).

It is clear that Winnicott's True and False Selves are related to notions of a disorganized or uncohesive self: health lies in bringing more of the True Self into the self-organization, until the point is reached where, "when the issues become crucial," the True Self can override the False Self. But Winnicott also makes it clear that the outcome remains a compromise, the False Self a requirement of social life.

Winnicott's description evokes a self that is an organization of goals and values under the domination of a hierarchy of aims (Gedo 1979). "Archaic" goals, such as oedipal ones, as well as convenient goals dictated by "social manners," may coexist within the larger organization, available to but somehow under the control of the overarching self-organization, which ideally has a large component of True Self available to it.

As we saw, even Gedo leaves some mental content out of this hierarchical organization, though perhaps more by implication than by design. In fact, it seems generally the case that contemporary theorists are reluctant to specify how the unconscious comes into being and what its relation to the self is (compare Lichtenberg 1989: 273–83).

Yet this need not be so. Saperstein and Gaines (1973) propose the concept of a "supraordinate self" that contains all these aspects we are trying to differentiate and label. This self "has a sense of its own uniqueness, and . . . is actively engaged in intention and planning" (p. 419). It "can exercise options, be aware of and create meaning, operate in terms of aims, motives and intentionality, be aware of its uniqueness, stand for the person, and be capable of being restricted or enhanced in its freedom (in its relation to its parts)" (p. 421).

Such a self would be capable of deceiving itself, and its unconscious or disavowed aspect would still be contained within the supraordinate self. Hence, the unconscious remains "self-like," capable of hearing folktales and assigning meanings to them different from those assigned by the conscious aspect: both meanings would belong to the supraordinate self, yet only some would be available to consciousness (see also Jung 1956: 186–87).

A caution is in order at this point, however. We have not removed the paradox, simply restated it. From a mental health standpoint, one wants to reduce or heal the split in the self, hence the emphasis among clinical theorists on enlarging the scope of the nuclear self, bringing the archaic goals into the hierarchy of the self, minimizing the power of the False Self, and so on.

Friedman (1988) argues, however, that such theorists run the risk of emphasizing the synthesizing function of the mind at the expense of the persistence of qualities that cannot be synthesized, that is, at the expense of *conflict*. In any attempted synthesis of the self, there must be aspects of the self that cannot be synthesized, that are not merely "unbound" but "unbindable" (p. 209).

> There is a sense in which wishes are fulfilled by their synthesis with reality and the rest of the mind. And there is a sense in which wishes are betrayed by that synthesis. (It is a typically Freudian tragic paradox.) . . . Many theoreticians attempt to find a simple description within or outside of Freud's theory to sew the mind back together. Such a simple description always leaves conflict unaccounted for. (Friedman 1988: 215)

We cannot "sew the mind together" by assigning repressed matter to the "nonself," and we must assume that the supraordinate self is never without the pain of a deep division within. We should also be alert to the prejudice conveyed by such adjectives as "primitive," "irrational," "archaic," and "maladaptive," when assigned to the unconscious. The agency that has applied these labels to the unconscious is, of course, the conscious, cognitively dominated, acceptable self-organization with which we do our carefully framed public theorizing. Psychoanalysts have reason to appreciate that this conscious cognitive organization of the self is outraged and horrified by the contents of the unconscious and cannot be trusted to give it a fair appraisal.

SO, WHO *IS* LISTENING? We are now in a position to consider what help the concept of a disavowed or unconscious self is in explaining the audience appeal of folktales. Based on the previous discussion, we might say that the disavowed self is created when the supraordinate self does not allow the avowed self to be aware of aspects of itself that are unacceptable in society. This disavowal has the quality of an attempted, or "phantom," amputation. The exact opposite of a phantom limb, this is a part of the self which remains, though it is imagined to be gone. Even if one reaches for it, one cannot feel it.

Previous formulations which treated the disavowed content as bits and pieces that were discarded or, "healthily," given up, could not adequately account for the amount of pain that disavowal costs the *self* (disavowed and avowed; that is, supraordinate). It required the advances of self-psychology to give us a language in which to understand at what cost aspects of the self are refused acknowledgment and integration in the course of development, which in extreme cases can lead to "the unameable dread experienced when a person feels that his self is becoming seriously enfeebled or is disintegrating, . . . the fragmentation of and the estrangement from his body and mind in space, the breakup of the sense of his continuity in time" (Kohut 1977: 105). We must assume that the supraordinate self knows of its repressions and continuously experiences the losses they entail: of acceptance, acknowledgment, integration, and spontaneous expression.

Our view is that folktales speak to the self, both the avowed and the disavowed. The disavowed self in particular experiences the unacceptable events represented in the folktale as an acknowledgment, in public, of its existence. The telling of the tale is a performance that says to the disavowed self, in effect, "There are people such as you; they must be kept in their place, but they do exist." Each hearing of the tale is in this sense a kind of momentary "restoration of the self" (Kohut 1977). The acknowledgment in the folktale momentarily unmasks the phantom amputation and illuminates a portion of the hidden side of the self. The experience of this is probably more one of relief than of release, in that it is not so much energy bound up in repression that is discharged as the pain of disavowal—perhaps a mix of loneliness and agonized self-reproach—that is relieved.

It is this sense of the folktale as a community of awareness that Hagglund and Hagglund (1981: 53) may have had in mind when they contrasted myth and folklore. Whereas myth is often tied to religion and punishment, "folklore, having its roots in the deepest past of a people, is more descriptive of the human need to create forms of mutually shared understanding of the unconscious impulses flooding the mind in the form of dreams and fantasies, and has never been needed as an instrument of obedience and submissiveness."

This is not to say that hearing the repressed contents expressed in a folktale is analogous to a therapy session. The disavowed content is not acknowledged by the avowed self. There is only the communal experience of the shared tale to provide a sort of half-acknowledgment. Such a half-measure is all that appears to have been available throughout most of human history to soothe the pain of disavowal. In an appropriately balanced drama, one that will not be banned, the listener's avowed self maintains ignorance of the disavowed self, even while the disavowed self enjoys public acknowledgment. Like Andy Warhol's *Everyman*, the disavowed self has its fifteen minutes of fame, but id is not made ego, no permanent change in the structure of the self takes place, and hence the same tale will be told over and over again, generation upon generation. To the degree that the tale does change over time, this signals developments in society and culture that alter the way the tale can be presented to an audience without either boring it or driving it away with anxiety.

If this seems paradoxical, it is. The whole idea of a split within the self, of secrets kept by the self from the self, is paradoxical. How can the avowed selves of the audience, for example, sit idly by while the group turns a light on the disavowed selves they are all individually so concerned to hide? Clearly, there is some sort of conspiracy going on, perhaps not unlike the conspiracies that people enter into in scapegoating members of their own families without completely expelling them from the family.

Another dimension of the paradox is, who reacts emotionally to the tale? Often it seems as though the disavowed self does, as when we say, "I don't know why I cried at that play . . . I felt so silly!" Or, "I know it is just a movie but I can't bear to watch the screen!" These are not id impulses or even archaic fantasies reacting. Someone inside is seeing and evaluating the events on the screen, and is bereft or terrified.

We can gain a better understanding of who is listening to the unconscious content of folktales, therefore, if we conceive of the self as a complex whole (some authors use the term "person" to label this larger self) split into conscious (avowed) and unconscious (disavowed) aspects. But this leaves us with a most difficult problem of conceiving of a mind unified and divided at the same time, what Friedman (1988: 396) calls "the dialectical tension between the synthetic function on the one hand, and conflicting structural interests, on the other." Somehow, in theory we need to accept the contradictory image of a supraordinate self with a tear in it that can be soothed but cannot ever be sewn back together completely.

Totem and Taboo Reexamined

By now we have reached two conclusions:

1. That family-complex folktales are universal and tend strongly to depict Freud's masculine Oedipus complex, but not the feminine one; rather, father-daughter and brother-sister incest tend to be portrayed as initiated by males and resisted by females.

2. That the core content of most of these tales reflects aspects of mental life that have been repressed, or left in the possession of a disavowed self, causing anguish to the supraordinate self that originally effected the disavowal in order to prevent its own abandonment or destruction at the hands of angry parents.

If folktales are capable of expressing disavowed mental contents, and if some of these contents appear to be practically universal, what does that imply? In *Totem and Taboo* Freud assumed that the momentous events following the Primal Crime, when the group of brothers regretted their murder of their father and agreed henceforward to ban parricide and incest, were seared forever into human consciousness, an invariant property of the collective mind. Are we now to agree?

Three general kinds of theories can account for a cultural universal like a kind of folktale. Diffusion is one. We find it possible, perhaps even likely, that family-complex tales, probably similar to the common pattern found in our folktales, were told tens of thousands of years ago and spread with the global migrations of *Homo sapiens*. As an explanation, however, this leaves something to be desired. We do not know how many tales have as wide a distribution as family-complex tales have, but they appear to be few in number. Stories like the Flood or the Hero may be among them (but see Dundes 1985: 22). Why only a few stories diffused around the world, if indeed diffusion is the reason for their widespread occurrence, still requires explanation. After all, practically everything about culture, from language to technology to social organization and religious belief, has undergone diversification in the course of human migration and local adaptation.

Two other kinds of theories offer explanations for the universality of the oedipal tale: one that starts from the universality of the nuclear family in human experience and derives the Oedipus complex and oedipal tale from common childhood experiences, and another that assumes that the course of early human evolution laid down patterns in the human genotype that determine how humans process their world of experience cognitively and emotionally, making oedipal imagery in folktales and other forms of expression a kind of biological imperative.

THE "FAMILY ENVIRONMENT" THEORY. Most contemporary observers would find the first of these approaches more acceptable. Cultural anthropologists are profoundly suspicious of biologically based explanations of human behavior, primarily because they so easily tend toward racism. It is possible to retain a major part of Freud's argument in *Totem and Taboo* without invoking the assumption that the Oedipus complex is hard-wired in the human psyche or requiring that a particular group of sons killed and ate father and then in remorse instituted the first social controls (Dundes 1985: 10).

If we compare humans with our nearest genetic relatives, the chimpanzees and gorillas, we must be impressed both with similarities and differences. The similarities suggest (but do not prove) that our common ancestors had a number of family attributes relevant to the Oedipus complex. A strong bond exists between mother and offspring, who recognize one another and may stay near one another for many years as a stable family group. Because males take turns copulating with females in estrus, it is not easy to assign paternity, and there is no evidence that offspring attach to a father the way they attach to their mother. Separation from the mother may be traumatic, as seen in Goodall's (1986) poignant story of Flint, the young chimp who bullied his old mother, Flo, into nursing him far beyond the normal age, and then, following his mother's sudden death, stopped eating and sat disconsolately at the spot of her death until, after a few weeks, he too sickened and died.

Males provide protection for the group of females and children. The males are hierarchically organized, and the leading, or "alpha," male does not tolerate competition in access to females. He has what Waal (1982) calls the "droit du seigneur," the right to first mating that ensures that his sperm will have the best chance of impregnating a female. He will frequently attempt to keep other males away from a fertile female, although he may enter into an alliance with another male, in which he permits his ally access to fertile females in exchange for support in dominating other males.

Waal describes one case where an alpha male so monopolized access to the females of the group that he was responsible for about three-fourths of the matings before he was deposed by a coalition of two other males. Nondominant males must wait for their turn at a fertile female, although eventually they do gain intercourse, probably at a point when she has already been impregnated. Waal commented, "I sometimes feel I am studying Freud's primal horde; as if a time machine has taken me back to prehistoric times, so that I can observe the village life of our ancestors" (1982: 167).

An interesting aspect of the chimpanzee mating pattern is that females are attracted to junior males and will conspire to deceive the alpha male in order to mate with them. The following field observation of Waal describes such an event:

> On one occasion Nikkie [an alpha male] was so engrossed in grooming Yeroen [an ally] that he did not notice Luit [a competitor]'s silent departure. When, some time later, he glanced at the spot where Luit had been sitting, he screeched and looked round in all directions: the oestrus female had also disappeared. Shocked, Nikkie and Yeroen embraced each other. They had obviously reached the same conclusion, because they both rushed wildly, their hair on end, across the enclosure and only calmed down when they found Luit quietly drinking from the moat. Had their fears been unfounded? They will never know, but I know that they had simply arrived too late. (Waal 1982: 179)

Waal writes, "chimpanzees seem to me to be very jealous creatures" (p. 164), and he argues that males are especially jealous in guarding their sexual access to estrus females in order to enhance their reproductive success:

> A female can only be fertilized by one male. By keeping other males away from her a male increases the certainty that he will be the father of her child. Consequently children will more often be sired by jealous than by tolerant males. If jealousy is hereditary—and that is what this theory assumes—more and more

children will be born with this characteristic, and later they in turn will attempt to exclude other members of the same sex from the reproductive act. (p. 170)

From these vivid descriptions it is not hard to imagine a phase of proto-human evolution in which jealous domineering males guarded their sexual privileges over family units of mothers and young offspring. As offspring matured, adolescent males were forced to accept inferior status which included harshly restricted access to receptive females, whereas adolescent females were incorporated into the pool of fertile females. These ancestors were capable of forming alliances to overthrow alpha males, and thus of remembering past interactions and forming antagonisms as well as friendships. Offspring were capable of recognizing their mothers, but their biological fathers were unknown.

Human family life presents a number of key contrasts to this picture, despite certain similarities (such as an intense mother-child bond, creation of ties of loyalty through grooming and nurturing, and jealousy and deceit). The human family is fundamentally nuclear and monogamous (despite much variation). The majority of households in virtually all human societies are composed of a monogamous couple and their children. While polygyny is frequently an acceptable form of marriage, it rarely accounts for more than twenty percent of marriages in a given community. Polyandry is extremely rare.

Normatively, marriage generally identifies a single male as father, instituting protections on mating that guarantee (to the extent feasible) his reproductive rights, and binding him to that family unit more or less permanently. This to a degree equalizes or democratizes the reproductive rights of males, reducing the ability of alpha males to hoard the reproductive opportunities. It also adds a breadwinner to the household in addition to the female: chimpanzee and gorilla males rarely provide food to others, in contrast to mothers, who provide food for their youngest offspring. The ability of humans to bring their children to maturity for such a long childhood in comparison with other apes probably depends fundamentally on binding the father as a protective breadwinner responsible for the safe maturation of his own biological offspring.

But, as Freud rightly surmised, this achievement is at some cost. Humans may have some "instinctual" biologically based inclination to form monogamous unions, but the picture of the great apes, with their dominant, sexually imperialist males, jealous of the females they have and covetous of others, and their females, accepting dominance but open to mating opportunities with younger males, does not seem utterly foreign to humans. We regulate these apelike impulses, however, through symbolic processes that include the kind of identity formation and disavowal that Fingarette writes about. We regard animals as inferior beings and in folklore identify them as degraded humans who could not control their impulses.

It is possible, therefore, to explain the universality of the oedipal tale without assuming that it exists as a specific image in a collective mind. All human beings share the capacity to control impulses through symbolic processes familiar to psychoanalysts: identity formation, defense mechanisms, sublimation, and so forth. Everywhere, humans grow up in families that pose the same basic problems: how to love and be intimate with family members without erotic action, and how to compete with and hate family members without violent action. These dangerous erotic and aggressive impulses, already transformed symbolically into fantasies, are disavowed and find expression only in certain controlled and safe settings, including the telling of folktales. Given the basic similarity of the family cauldrons in which these feelings simmer, it would be surprising if oedipal tales were *not* universal.

We note also that the content of what we called the common form of our folktales is consistent with the derivation of the human species from the ancestors of our closest relatives, chimpanzees and gorillas. The closest bond reflected in the folktales remains that of mother and children, expressed through fantasies of lifelong closeness, eroticized in the case of mother and son and often consummated in eternal union as the founding spirit ancestors of animal species. By contrast, grown males are seen as less firmly bound to the family, their sexual predation taken for granted; in the tales, they are more likely than not to be banished or killed before the tale is over. We find in these tales, therefore, evidence that the binding of the human adult male to the monogamous family remains incomplete, or in competition with a formerly less exclusive, more generalized role.

THE "COLLECTIVE MIND" THEORY. Why, then, not stop here? The second explanation, assuming some sort of hard-wired mental form for the Oedipus complex (and tale), is not likely to be taken seriously by anthropologists in the present climate, and it does not appear to be needed. Nonetheless, we do want to outline briefly why this second, controversial explanation should not be summarily dismissed. When Freud decided the Oedipus complex resided in the collective mind of humanity, he was making a reasonable assumption: if it is universal, it must be part of human nature. That his genetics were out of step with the newer theories of Mendelian genetics does not mean that his basic idea was wrong.

Paul (1976) has defended Freud's argument with the idea of a "precultural atom" of primordial competition between males of different generations for access to females: out of this atom the Oedipus complex developed as the human capacity for culture emerged in prehistory (Figure 12).

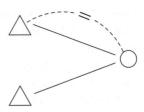

Fig. 12. The "precultural atom."
Derived from Paul 1976:345.

> What I believe that Freud has stumbled upon is the remains of a system of social organization which is typical not only of most primates but of many other mammals whose life is social in nature. This involves a division of the adult males into junior and senior ranks, the distinction being defined not simply by age but also by status within the group: senior males have sexual access to females for the purpose of breeding, and they exercise leadership in the decision-making process of the group; while junior males are excluded from these. (Paul 1982: 11)

This vision of the circumstances surrounding the Primal Crime is consistent with contemporary knowledge about our probable primate ancestors, and is a good starting point for thinking about the evolutionary significance of such a structure as the family complex. Paul, however, does not specifically embrace a biostructural explanation for the existence of that structure (Paul 1982: 12).

Although the pendulum on innate human mental structures is on the swing back after a period of near universal doubt (D. Brown 1991: 98–99, 113–17), we still do not have a language for talking about the possibility that the Oedipus complex and the oedipal tale have some kind of structural analogue or complement in the human genome. Jung, like Freud, assumed that such a thing could exist: his notion of archetypal structure in particular, as distinct from archetypal image, assumes a "built-in" mental structure.

In his work on primitive mythology, Joseph Campbell (1959: 31), influenced by both Freud and Jung, likened Jung's idea of the archetype to a biologically known phenomenon:

> Chicks with their eggshells still adhering to their tails dart for cover when a hawk flies overhead, but not when the bird is a gull or duck, heron or pigeon. Furthermore, if the wooden model of a hawk is drawn over their coop on a wire, they react as though it were alive—unless it be drawn backward, when there is no response.
>
> Here we have an extremely precise image—never seen before, yet recognized with reference not merely to its form but to its form in motion, and linked, furthermore, to an immediate, unplanned, unlearned, and even unintended system of appropriate action: flight, to cover. The image of the inherited enemy is already sleeping in the nervous system, and along with it the well-proven reaction.

Campbell wonders if the chick's image of the hawk is similar to the archetype of the witch as experienced by young children. He concludes that in humans there is at least a susceptibility or receptivity to "imprints" from the environment within a preexisting, innate structure, but that human beings must be distinguished from other animals:

> After the work of Sigmund Freud and his school on the stages of the maturation of the human infant and the force of the imprints acquired in those stages on the responses of the individual throughout life, it will hardly be necessary to argue the relevance of the concepts of "inner readiness" and "imprint" to the sphere of human learning. . . . There is, however, in the human sphere a factor that makes all study of instinct and innate structures extremely difficult; for, whereas even the animals most helpless at birth mature very quickly, the human infant is utterly helpless during the first dozen years of its existence and, during this period of the maturation of its character, is completely subject to the pressures and imprints of its local society. . . . We cannot think of one without the other. (Campbell 1959: 36–37)

The impression one has is of a human potentiality, like a glove, into which the hand of culture and environment must fit in order for the completed person to emerge. The hand and glove need not be of identical size, but their general shape must coincide or the result will be misshapened or crippled. This reverses the usual analogy of the person as the clay that must fit the mold of environment: it asserts that individual and cultural adaptation happens on a two-way street, that culture must do some of the adapting.

Modern theories of language generally assume such a hand-and-glove relationship between the capacity for language with which we are born and the specific language we actually learn. For example, we are innately capable of acquiring rules for distinguishing past and present tense without knowing in advance what the rule will be, or even whether there will be such a rule in any given language. In English we learn talk-talked, hunt-hunted, and so forth, but also several other different rules, such as swing-swung, fling-flung, and so forth; in fact, most adults when given the nonsense verb *spling* will offer the past-tense verb *splung*. It is not the English past-tense rules that are hard-wired, but the capacity to learn and apply such rules quickly and efficiently (Pinker 1991).

Language structure is not the only model upon which we can draw to think about the possible relationship between an innate structuring framework for the Oedipus complex (or, the larger matter of the family complex) and the concrete experience of growth in a family that breathes individual life into the waiting structure. Animal psychologists who have studied chimpanzees have inferred that they must have complex and specific mental structures, or "algorithms" (Tooby and Cosmides 1989; Cosmides and Tooby 1989). For example, the bargaining implied in conspiring to deceive an alpha male or to form a coalition between males requires certain cognitive capabilities, including face recognition, memory of earlier transactions, and ability to recognize and interpret the "values" of one's partner. The algorithms by which information is gathered and processed to permit these specific behaviors are assumed to be part of the innate chimpanzee mental structure.

It may be that, in rejecting Freud's energetics, with its clear sense of instincts clamoring for fulfillment, contemporary psychoanalysts have neglected the problem of how to describe human potentialities, the expectations and inclinations (if those words are not too definite) that we bring into the world with us, however much they may become modified by adaptation to any given environment. The concept of adaptation naturally implies a plasticity in the animal doing the adapting, but as Hartmann (1958) argued, humans are preadapted to an "average expectable environment." And this notion refers not to the environment per se but to the structure of the mind:

> The term, "average expectable environment," has only general roots in biology, anthropology, or evolution. In Hartmann's writings it is most elaborated in his definition of normalcy. Where is the average expectable environment to be found? Not on this or that continent, in this or that village. It is the shape of the soul. It is another name for the nature of Man. It specifies the set of meanings into which life's adventures will inevitably be placed. The average expectable environment is the broad, a priori gestalt of experience. (Friedman 1988: 391–92)

The human infant no doubt "expects" to be fed, held, kept warm and free of rashes, and so forth. When these expectations fail, the child signals its displeasure with squirming and crying. For the older child, there may also be loosely defined expectations about being allowed willful self-expression or, as implied by Jung's concept of the Father imago, about interacting with a masculine figure separate from, and sometimes opposed to, mother. Not all the child's expectations will be realized; childhood (human or not) always entails frustrations. In the case of the human child, a good share of these frustrations will fall within the scope of the family complex.

The similarities in oedipal tales around the world (Figure 9), in contrast to the freedom to vary implied by the general model of the family complex (Figure 5), indicate a significant cross-cultural preoccupation with the particular form of the family complex involving the erotic mother-son union antagonistic to father, and sexually aggressive father and brother. The examination of chimpanzee sexual behavior suggests that the competition between males for control of reproductive access to females is deeply rooted in human phylogeny, and that repression of this competition within the family brings into being an intrapsychic conflict of distinctive importance.

We have some sympathy for Abend (1988: 503), therefore, in his recent defense of the fundamental developmental importance of the oedipal phase, when cognitive development has reached the point where central unconscious fantasies

and progressive biological and social development have made that period of life into the arena for the initial unfolding of *the enduring dramas of human psychology*. Love, jealousy, possession, envy, rivalry, rejection, ecstasy, disappointment, betrayal, power, helplessness, self-esteem, procreation, sexual roles, identity, and function, triumph, defeat, guilt, revenge, restitution, and so on are the familiar themes that so preoccupy us for all the rest of our lives, as our art and literature, not to mention our clinical experience, bear witness. [Emphasis added]

CHAPTER 5

CONCLUSION

Several years ago, when we first confronted the tale of Shakanari (106) in the context of a discussion of anthropology and the Oedipus complex, we were impressed by its Oedipus-like content, yet skeptical that oedipal tales would be a human universal. It is of course startling to come upon such a famous plot in a tiny hamlet of native Amazonians. It could have been one of those odd occurrences familiar enough to anthropologists, like the fact that traditional Eskimos and modern Americans have the same system of kinship terminology. But we were shaken out of this skepticism rather soon thereafter when we examined the existing collections of Oedipus-type tales (Lessa 1961; Edmunds and Dundes 1983; and Edmunds 1985). The newly published collections of native South American folk literature of Johannes Wilbert were also becoming available to us one after another, and our continuing search for family-complex tales uncovered them in still less accessible regions of scholarship. We found little evidence that the motif of the men of the family fighting over the women of the family was a property only of tales told in stratified patriarchal societies. On the contrary, once stripped of phenomena like the inevitability of fate (prophecy) and the fantasy that the hero's parents were really royalty—aspects of the tale limited to complex, stratified societies—the core tale of a boy who struggles to replace father as husband to his mother is remarkably widespread.

Far from being diminished in strength the greater the distance from Freud's Vienna, the tale can actually be bolder in remote societies like those of the !Kung of the Kalahari (21), the Yamana Indians of Tierra del Fuego

(123), or the Pacific islanders of Ulithi Atoll (64). In these tales, and many like them, the actors do not accidentally commit murder and incest, but act willfully and without apparent guilt or remorse. Nonetheless, in most cases they are punished in some way, by mutilation, death, or transformation into animals and/or spirits. In no human society are "oedipal crimes" taken lightly.

Freud's critics within anthropology and psychoanalysis alike have favored the idea that the Oedipus complex is a culture-specific and essentially pathological outcome of male-dominated class-structured society. They tend to argue that, although an oedipal situation is part of the human heritage—son must detach himself from the close early bond to mother in order to join father in the world of grown-up men—it does not need to result in the pathological consequences of the Oedipus complex: namely, the destructive competition that prevents close, cooperative, constructive relations with other men, and erotic compulsions that prevent stable, intimate, sexually satisfying marriages alongside intimate, nonsexualized relationships with other women.

The crux of this debate lies in the distinction between an oedipal situation that can be resolved for growth into healthy maturity, and the Oedipus complex that is not so resolved. There is wide variation in individuals in our own society in the degree to which the Oedipus complex is a source of difficulties in adult life, and our field research in a number of non-Western societies has intuitively convinced us that the "strength and outcome" of the Oedipus complex do indeed vary from one society to another (Spiro 1982: 164).

For the most part, however, we do not detect this variation in the tales in our collection. We did briefly examine the softer Eskimo tale (90) and the harsher !Kung tale (21), associating the difference between them to the wide differences in the way anger is expressed in the two cultures; but that remains speculative. The one large cross-cultural pattern was greater repression in the tales from stratified societies in contrast to the tales of nonstratified societies, which are more explicit. And that difference is not a presence or absence of oedipal content, but rather one of expression.

The apparent universality of the oedipal tale demands an explanation. We could evade this demand by two means. One would be to argue that there really is no "oedipal tale." The tales we have collected are so diverse in details and belong to such distinctive literary traditions that lumping them together is arbitrary.

There are alternative ways of grouping folktales that would sort our collection into dozens of smaller separate piles. An oedipal folktale, like any folktale that has withstood the test of time in a community, is a piece of art with many-layered meanings. Which meaning we emphasize depends on our theory, and focusing on Freud's theory might be thought to imply neglect of other ways of viewing the tales.

Still, we are convinced by working with so many similar tales that the oedipal storyline is neither accidental nor incidental: in most cases, it *is* the storyline of the whole tale. To adopt the personalizing manner of speaking so common in nonstratified societies, we might say that the oedipal tale "likes to be told." Whether as an elemental story like the Finnish tale (10), or decked out in local costume, or embedded in a narrative of more sweeping scope, it is without doubt a popular tale.

The other way to evade the demand to explain the universality of the oedipal tale is to regard it as an unimportant story, without implications or consequences in the lives of people who share in its telling. It appears likely, for example, that oedipal tales comprise only a fraction of folktales from any given community. We have no evidence that they are told very often or given any special emphasis. If we were to equate the oedipal tale's importance to the amount of time people spend hearing it, its importance might be almost infinitesimal.

We can only counter this argument indirectly, on two grounds. First, we have argued that folktales go through a process of cultural selection such that uninteresting (that is, unimportant) tales are discarded over time. Any folktale of any stability and time-depth in a community must be highly interesting, meaningful, and important, even if it is the case that it is heard only occasionally. Infrequent, but dramatic, reinforcement of deeply meaningful cultural meaning systems is common, if not the rule, in human experience. A story with as much depth in time and across cultural space as the oedipal folktale shows a remarkable persistence and is likely therefore to be deeply meaningful.

Second, we embrace a theory of the relationship between folktales and unconscious mental life that gives the oedipal tale importance alongside other repressed, or disavowed, mental contents. Folktales that portray disavowed fears and desires act like mirrors in which the unconscious part of the self can find its own reflection. This partial avowal, we argue, gives satisfaction to the self even while it does not threaten the group conspiracy to keep the offending material repressed. It says something like this: "There were people once, in a more heroic and untamed past, who acted on these unacceptable impulses; they were punished for their crimes, and we today know better than to do what they did. *But, there were such people once.*"

We hold that there is an essential form of the oedipal tale, and of family-complex tales more generally, that is widespread and probably universal in human culture, and that it has deep significance. We have identified the basic form as similar to Freud's Oedipus complex as far as the figure of son is concerned, but similar to the revisionist critique of Freud as far as daughter is concerned. If we were to modify Freud's view of the boy's Oedipus complex, we would follow most modern writers in drawing attention to the active role parents play in shaping the boy's oedipal situation: the portrayal of seductive or compliant mothers and dangerous, hostile fathers in folktales parallels the efforts of contemporary psychoanalysts to balance Freud's emphasis upon the biogenetic, hard-wired origins of the Oedipus complex in the child.

On the other hand, our analysis has led us back to Freud in the affirmative as well. The universality of oedipal tales points to the fundamental importance of the oedipal situation (with or without complex!) in the human condition. Whether we follow those who see oedipal feelings as the outcome of experience (nurture), or those who regard them as a biostructural given (nature) whose genetic basis was laid in the millions of years it took for a divergent ape to evolve into a human being, it would seem that the feelings reflected in oedipal tales are bound to arise in most, if not all, children and to color their emotional lives as adults when they raise their own families. The effort to place blame for oedipal conflicts upon either parents or children is wasted, for the conflicts are inevitable and are replayed throughout life, the players taking on different roles as age and circumstances change them.

The girl's oedipal situation, as viewed through world folk literature, is significantly different from that imagined by Freud. Whereas in the boy's oedipal situation we follow the later Freud in emphasizing the mutual mother-son eroticism and the mutual father-son hostility, in the girl's case we found father most often initiated incestuous actions toward daughter: daughter as a rule did not reciprocate father's interest and did not see mother as a competitor for father's affections. On the contrary, mother was viewed as daughter's ally in fending off father's unwanted advances.

A smaller number of tales that do portray daughter as sexual aggressor toward father, however, again support the idea that a degree of mutuality characterizes the unconscious relations between family members, and that erotic or hostile feelings are rarely unilateral. We need to keep in mind the role of projection in reversing the direction of feelings represented in a family-complex story (Dundes 1980: 217–21). Still, taken along with the preponderance of brother-sister tales in which brother is the sexual aggressor, there is a strong tendency in our father-daughter and brother-sister tales for men to be the sexually interested partners, while women are opposed, indifferent, or passively acquiescent.

We have been tempted by this portrait of the human family, as distilled from our collection of folktales, to explore links to family and social life among our genetically closest relatives, chimpanzees and gorillas. Among them, males are generally the sexually aggressive partners, although estrus females are occasionally active in soliciting matings from inactive males.

Sparse evidence indicates that, when incestuous matings are attempted, it is by brothers toward sisters or sons toward mothers, and in these cases the females protest. The objections of females, therefore, appear to be mainly responsible for the low rate of incestuous sexual intercourse observed among primates.

Male aggressiveness in mating competition is, of course, a major feature of chimpanzee and gorilla social life. Adolescent males are frustrated in their mating efforts by the dominance of the alpha males in their vicinity. It is also true, as Freud anticipated in his story of the Primal Crime, that subordinate males, excluded from mating opportunities, will form coalitions and, by strength in unity, depose and replace an alpha male. Thereafter, they may share the sexual access that was formerly denied them, although eventually one of the coalition partners will emerge as dominant.

The problems of male sexual aggression toward females and domination of other males were no doubt dealt with by early humans by establishing cultural rules concerning sexual access (marriage rules and incest taboos) and aggression (kinship and alliances). These rules brought a crucial male contribution to the family food supply in support of a long maturation period for the human child, democratized reproductive opportunities for males, and helped extend social relations beyond the loose primate "horde" to structured kin-based networks for pooling resources in food supply and territorial defense.

Cultural rules depend on the capacity for symbolizing, but not just in the sense of being able to communicate and share understandings: very specifically, symbolization is needed to bring about repression and new forms of impulse control. It is likely that the evolutionary achievements of symbolization and impulse control were intimately linked. We have such a long time frame available to us now that we need not imagine, as Freud did, that a single momentous event, a dramatic parricide followed by remorse, suddenly brought impulse control (symbolically mediated via totemism) into being. The powerful symbolic means of impulse control available today in even the smallest-scale human societies—including shame, taboo, and threat of supernatural punishment—must have emerged gradually over countless millennia.

Our view of the role of folktales in this process is less that they are morality tales that exist in order to enforce taboos on sex and aggression in the family—although they may play that role, among others—than that they are in some sense the voice of the unconscious: they speak both for and to the unconscious self that exists in everyone. For the human self is created out of the struggle between innate impulses and cultural rules, and seems inevitably to contain a fundamental split. Humans have the ability, and this must be an important part of their capacity for impulse control, to create a self-awareness (a conscious self) that does not acknowledge or avow all attributes of the person it inhabits.

These disavowed attributes of the person are not bits and pieces relegated to a dump or snake pit called the unconscious, but are still properties of a larger, whole, supraordinate self. That self, or the unconscious aspect of it, or an unconscious self—words for this are difficult to find because the whole situation is intrinsically paradoxical—is a listener whenever folktales are told. Modern audiences can be moved to laughter, horror, or tears even while their avowed selves remain apparently neutral, surprised, and even embarrassed at reacting to a story that may seem silly, maudlin, corny, childish, or utterly fantastic. In smaller-scale societies the distance between avowed and disavowed self may be less, for our impression is that audiences there are engaged in the stories without embarrassment or surprise: they find them interesting and do not worry about whether they are entitled to do so.

Yet few of us acknowledge openly to ourselves or others that we share a common heritage of ambivalent feelings toward our most intimate relatives. The family-complex tales we have collected tell stories of aberrant behavior that healthy, normal people consider incomprehensible, if not downright evil. Even exceptionally introspective people have difficulty detecting any such feelings in themselves, even if intellectually they can accept the universality of the family complex we have described here. To us, this suggests the enormous importance to humankind of control over impulsive behavior that could shatter the nuclear family, the extended family, and still larger social units upon which our basic existence depends. Evidently, so dangerous are the erotic and aggressive impulses that even to admit that they exist is prohibited.

In this sense we may say that family-complex folktales are windows on the soul. They open a view into mysterious regions of the self that are otherwise obscure. They allow us to look in upon the one who is listening most intently to the tale as it is told. And as we do so again and again from one folktale to the next, we begin to detect a certain resemblance, evidence of a multilayered, improbable, and yet definite configuration of the human condition.

PART II

THE FOLKTALES

EUROPE AND EURO-AMERICA

1. **THE FIRST GODS.** ANCIENT GREECE

In the beginning there was only Chaos, the Abyss,
But then Gaia, the Earth, came into being,
Her broad bosom the ever-firm foundation of all,
And Tartaros, dim in the underground depths,
and Eros, loveliest of all the Immortals, who
Makes their bodies (and men's bodies) go limp,
Mastering their minds and subduing their wills.

From the Abyss were born Erebos and dark Night.
And Night, pregnant after sweet intercourse
With Erebos, gave birth to Aether and Day.
Earth's first child was Ouranos, starry Heaven,
Just her size, a perfect fit on all sides.
And a firm foundation for the blessed gods.
And she bore the Mountains in long ranges, haunted
By the Nymphs who live in the deep mountain dells.
Then she gave birth to the barren, raging Sea
Without any sexual love. But later she slept with
Ouranos and bore Ocean with its deep currents,

---

1. SOURCE: Hesiod 1993:64–67. Reproduced by permission of Hackett Publishing
Company.

And also: Koios, Krios, Hyperion, Iapetos,
         Theia, Rheia, Themis, Mnemosyne, Gold-crowned Phoibe
         and lovely Tethys.

THE CASTRATION OF OURANOS

After them she bore a most terrible child,
Kronos, her youngest and arch-deceiver,
And this boy hated his lecherous father.

She bore the Cyclopes too, with hearts of stone,
Brontes, Steropes and ponderous Arges,
Who gave Zeus thunder and made the thunderbolt.
In every other respect they were just like gods,
But a lone eye lay in their foreheads' middle.
They were nicknamed Cyclopes because they had
A single goggle eye in their foreheads' middle.
Strong as the dickens, and they knew their craft.

And three other sons were born to Gaia and Ouranos,
Strong, hulking creatures that beggar description,
Kottos, Briareos, and Gyges, outrageous children.
A hundred hands stuck out of their shoulders,
Grotesque, and fifty heads grew on each stumpy neck.
These monsters exuded irresistible strength.
They were Gaia's most dreaded offspring,
And from the start their father feared and loathed them.
Ouranos used to stuff all of his children
Back into a hollow of Earth soon as they were born
Keeping them from the light, an awful thing to do,
But Heaven did it, and was very pleased with himself.
Vast Earth groaned under the pressure inside,
And then she came up with a plan, a really wicked trick.
She created a new mineral, grey flint, and formed
A huge sickle from it and showed it to her dear boys.
And she rallied them with this bitter speech:

"Listen to me, children, and we might yet get even
With your criminal father for what he has done to us.
After all, he started this whole ugly business."

They were tongue-tied with fear when they heard this.
But Kronos, whose mind worked in strange ways,
Got his pluck up and found the words to answer her:

"I think I might be able to bring it off, Mother.
I can't stand Father; he doesn't even deserve the name.
And after all, he started this whole ugly business."

This response warmed the heart of vast Earth.
She hid young Kronos in an ambush and placed in his hands
The jagged sickle. Then she went over the whole plan with him.
And now on came great Ouranos, bringing Night with him.
And, longing for love, he settled himself all over Earth.
From his dark hiding-place, the son reached out
With his left hand, while with his right he swung
The fiendishly long and jagged sickle, pruning the genitals
Of his own father with one swoop and tossing them
Behind him, where they fell to no small effect.
Earth soaked up all the bloody drops that spurted out,
And as the seasons went by she gave birth to the Furies
And to great Giants gleaming in full armor, spears in hand,
And to the Meliai, as ash-tree nymphs are generally called.

THE BIRTH OF APHRODITE

The genitalia themselves, freshly cut with flint, were thrown
Clear of the mainland into the restless, white-capped sea,
Where they floated a long time. A white foam from the god-flesh
Collected around them, and in that foam a maiden developed
And grew. Her first approach to land was near holy Kythera,
And from there she floated on to the island of Kypros.
There she came ashore, an awesome, beautiful divinity.
Tender grass sprouted up under her slender feet.
                                                         Aphrodite
Is her name in speech human and divine, since it was in foam
She was nourished. But she is also called Kythereia since
She reached Kythera, and Kyprogenes because she was born
On the surf-line of Kypros, and Philommedes because she loves
The organs of sex, from which she made her epiphany.
Eros became her companion, and ravishing Desire waited on her
At her birth and when she made her debut among the Immortals.
From that moment on, among both gods and humans,
She has fulfilled the honored function that includes
Virginal sweet-talk, lover's smiles and deceits
And all of the gentle pleasures of sex.

But great Ouranos used to call the sons he begot
Titans, a reproachful nickname, because he thought

They had over-reached themselves and done a monstrous deed
For which vengeance later would surely be exacted.

2. THE BIRTH OF THE OLYMPIANS. ANCIENT GREECE

Later, Kronos forced himself upon Rheia,
And she gave birth to a splendid brood:

> Hestia and Demeter and gold-sandalled Hera,
> Strong, pitiless Hades, the underworld lord,
> The booming Earth-shaker, Poseidon, and finally
> Zeus, a wise god, our Father in heaven
> Under whose thunder the wide world trembles.

And Kronos swallowed them all down as soon as each
Issued from Rheia's holy womb onto her knees,
With the intent that only he among the proud Ouranians
Should hold the title of King among the Immortals.
For he had learned from Earth and starry Heaven
That it was fated for him, powerful though he was,
To be overthrown by his child, through the scheming of Zeus.
Well, Kronos wasn't blind. He kept a sharp watch
And swallowed his children.
                     Rheia's grief was unbearable.
When she was about to give birth to Zeus our Father
She petitioned her parents, Earth and starry Heaven,
To put together some plan so that the birth of her child
Might go unnoticed, and she would make devious Kronos
Pay the Avengers of her father and children.
They listened to their daughter and were moved by her words,
And the two of them told her all that was fated
For Kronos the King and his stout-hearted son.
They sent her to Lyktos, to the rich land of Crete,
When she was ready to bear the youngest of her sons,
Mighty Zeus. Vast Earth received him when he was born
To be nursed and brought up in the wide land of Crete.
She came first to Lyktos, travelling quickly by night,
And took the baby in her hands and hid him in a cave,
An eerie hollow in the woods of dark Mount Aigaion.
Then she wrapped up a great stone in swaddling clothes

2. SOURCE: Hesiod 1993:74–75. Reproduced by permission of Hackett Publishing
Company.

And gave it to Kronos, Ouranos' son, the great lord and king
Of the earlier gods. He took it in his hands and rammed it
Down into his belly, the poor fool! He had no idea
That a stone had been substituted for his son, who,
Unscathed and content as a babe, would soon wrest
His honors from him by main force and rule the Immortals.
It wasn't long before the young lord was flexing
His glorious muscles. The seasons followed each other,
And great devious Kronos, gulled by Earth's
Clever suggestions, vomited up his offspring,
[Overcome by the wiles and power of his son]
The stone first, which he'd swallowed last.
Zeus took the stone and set it in the ground at Pytho
Under Parnassos' hollows, a sign and wonder for men to come.
And he freed his uncles, other sons of Ouranos
Whom their father in a fit of idiocy had bound.
They remembered his charity and in gratitude
Gave him thunder and the flashing thunderbolt
And lightning, which enormous Earth had hidden before.
Trusting in these he rules mortals and Immortals.

3. **OEDIPUS.** ANCIENT GREECE

Laius, son of Labadacus, married Iocaste, and ruled over Thebes. Grieved by his prolonged childlessness, he secretly consulted the Delphic Oracle, which informed him that this seeming misfortune was a blessing, because any child born to Iocaste would become his murderer. He therefore put Iocaste away, though without offering any reason for his decision, which caused her such vexation that, having made him drunk, she inveigled him into her arms again as soon as night fell. When, nine months later, Iocaste was brought to bed of a son, Laius snatched him from the nurse's arms, pierced his feet with a nail and, binding them together, exposed him on Mount Cithaeron. Yet the Fates had ruled that this boy should reach a green old age. A Corinthian shepherd found him, named him Oedipus because his feet were deformed by the nail-wound, and brought him to Corinth, where King Polybus was reigning at the time.

According to another version of the story, Laius did not expose Oedipus on the mountain, but locked him in a chest, which was lowered into the sea from a ship. This chest drifted ashore at Sicyon, where Periboea, Polybus's queen, happened to be on the beach, supervising her royal laundry-women.

---

3. SOURCE: Graves 1955, vol. 2:9–15.

She picked up Oedipus, retired to a thicket and pretended to have been overcome by the pangs of labour. Since the laundry women were too busy to notice what she was about, she deceived them all into thinking that he had only just been born. But Periboea told the truth to Polybus who, also being childless, was pleased to rear Oedipus as his own son.

One day, taunted by a Corinthian youth with not in the least resembling his supposed parents, Oedipus went to ask the Delphic Oracle what future lay in store for him. "Away from the shrine, wretch!" the Pythoness cried in disgust. "You will kill your father and marry your mother."

Since Oedipus loved Polybus and Periboea, and shrank from bringing disaster upon them, he at once decided against returning to Corinth. But in the narrow defile between Delphic and Daulis he happened to meet Laius, who ordered him roughly to step off the road and make way for his betters; Laius, it should be explained, was in a chariot and Oedipus on foot. Oedipus retorted that he acknowledged no betters except the gods and his own parents.

"So much the worse for you!" cried Laius, and ordered his charioteer Polyphontes to drive on.

One of the wheels bruised Oedipus's foot and, transported by rage, he killed Polyphontes with his spear. Then, flinging Laius on the road entangled in the reins, and whipping up the team, he made them drag him to death. It was left to the king of Plataeae to bury both corpses.

Laius had been on his way to ask the Oracle how he might rid Thebes of the Sphinx. This monster was a daughter of Typhon and Echidne or, some say, of the dog Orthrus and the Chimaera, and had flown to Thebes from the uttermost part of Ethiopia. She was easily recognized by her woman's head, lion's body, serpent's tail, and eagle's wings. Hera had recently sent the Sphinx to punish Thebes for Laius's abduction of the boy Chrysippus from Pisa and, settling in Mount Phicium, close to the city, she now asked every Theban wayfarer a riddle taught her by the Three Muses: "What being, with only one voice, has sometimes two feet, sometimes three, sometimes four, and is weakest when it has the most?" Those who could not solve the riddle she throttled and devoured on the spot, among which unfortunates was Iocaste's nephew Haemon, whom the Sphinx made *haimon,* or "bloody," indeed. Oedipus, approaching Thebes fresh from the murder of Laius, guessed the answer. "Man," he replied, "because he crawls on all fours as an infant, stands firmly on his two feet in his youth, and leans upon a staff in his old age." The mortified Sphinx leaped from Mount Phicium and dashed herself to pieces in the valley below. At this the grateful Thebans acclaimed Oedipus king, and he married Iocaste, unaware that she was his mother. Plague then descended upon Thebes, and the Delphic Oracle, when consulted once more, replied: "Expel the murderer of Laius!" Oedipus, not knowing whom he had met in the defile, pronounced a curse on Laius's murderer and sentenced him to exile.

Blind Teiresias, the most renowned seer in Greece at this time, now demanded an audience with Oedipus. [. . .] [He] appeared at Oedipus's court, leaning on the cornelwood staff given him by Athene, and revealed to Oedipus the will of the gods: that the plague would cease only if a Sown Man died for the sake of the city. Iocaste's father Menoeceus, one of those who had risen out of the earth when Cadmus sowed the serpent's teeth, at once leaped from the walls, and all Thebes praised his civic devotion.

Teiresias then announced further: "Menoeceus did well, and the plague will now cease. Yet the gods had another of the Sown Men in mind, one of the third generation: for he has killed his father and married his mother. Know, Queen Iocaste, that it is your husband Oedipus!"

At first, none would believe Teiresias, but his words were soon confirmed by a letter from Periboea at Corinth. She wrote that the sudden death of King Polybus now allowed her to reveal the circumstances of Oedipus's adoption; and this she did in damning detail. Iocaste then hanged herself for shame and grief, while Oedipus blinded himself with a pin taken from her garments.

Some say that, although tormented by the Erinnyes, who accused him of having brought about his mother's death, Oedipus continued to reign over Thebes for a while, until he fell gloriously in battle. According to others, however, Iocaste's brother Creon expelled him, but not before he had cursed Eteocles and Polyneices—who were at once his sons and his brothers—when they insolently sent him the inferior portion of the sacrificial beast, namely haunch instead of royal shoulder. They therefore watched dry-eyed as he left the city which he had delivered from the Sphinx's power. After wandering for many years through country after country, guided by his faithful daughter Antigone, Oedipus finally came to Colonus in Attica, where the Erinnyes, who have a grove there, hounded him to death, and Theseus buried his body in the precinct of the Solemn Ones at Athens, lamenting by Antigone's side.

4. THE DEATH AND REBIRTH OF DIONYSOS.

ANCIENT GREECE

When the great goddess Demeter—we are told—arrived in Sicily from Crete with her daughter Persephone, whom she had conceived of Zeus, she discovered a cave near the spring of Kyane, where she hid the maiden,

---

4. SOURCES: Primary source: Kern 1963:34, 35, 54; Secondary source: Campbell 1959:101.

setting to guard her the two serpents that were normally harnessed to the maiden's chariot. And Persephone there began weaving a web of wool, a great robe on which there was to be a beautiful picture of the universe; while her mother, Demeter, contrived that the girl's father, Zeus, should learn of her presence. The god approached his daughter in the form of a serpent, and she conceived of him a son, Dionysos, who was born and nurtured in the cave. The infant's toys were a ball, a top, dice, some golden apples, a bit of wool, and a bull-roarer. But he was also given a mirror, and while he was gazing into this, delighted, there approached him stealthily, from behind, two Titans, who had been sent to slay him by the goddess Hera, the jealous wife and queen of his father, Zeus. And they were painted with a white clay or chalk. Pouncing upon the playing child, they tore him into seven parts, boiled the portions in a caldron supported by a tripod, and then roasted them on seven spits. However, when they had consumed their divine sacrifice—all except the heart, which had been rescued by the goddess Athene—Zeus, attracted by the odor of the roasting meat, entered the cave and, when he beheld the scene, slew the white-painted cannibal Titans with a bolt of lightning. The goddess Athene thereupon presented the rescued heart in a covered basket to the father, who accomplished the resurrection—according to one version of the miracle—by swallowing the precious relic and himself then giving birth to his son.

5. CONCHOBOR. IRELAND

Conchobor and some of his men chased a flock of birds from Emain Macha. Now these birds were avatars of Deichtire, the sister [or half-sister or daughter] of Conchobor, and of fifty young girls with whom she had lived for three years. When Conchobor and his men chased the birds to the house at Brug, Deichtire and her companions assumed human form again, and Deichtire appeared as the mistress of the house. Conchobor, not knowing that it was Deichtire, demanded to use on his hostess the *droit du seigneur* that was his well-known prerogative. Deichtire begged for a postponement, for she was pregnant, and that night she brought forth a boy who looked just like Conchobor, though Conchobor did not learn until the next day that the woman who had received him was his sister. The child, the future Cuchulainn, was named Setanta; he was brought to Emain Macha to be nursed by Finnchoem, the mother of Conall.

5. SOURCES: Primary source: Gricourt 1954:75–79; Secondary source: O'Flaherty 1980: 168. From O'Flaherty, *Women, Androgynes, and Other Mystical Beasts*, published by the University of Chicago Press, 1980. Reproduced by permission of the publisher.

6. **SECUNDUS.** MEDIEVAL EUROPE

The Greek philosopher Secundus observes a permanent silence. The reason for this strange conduct is the following. Sent away by his parents to famous schools, he soon became a learned man of great renown and after a number of years returned home, where he learned that his father had died in his absence. Wishing to test his mother (he had often heard that there is very little good in women), he went to see her without making himself known to her. Worse, he proposed to her, and she readily granted what he wanted. Yet instead of staining himself with such a sin, he made himself known to her. The woman's shock was such that it cost her her life. Stricken with remorse, Secundus made a vow never again to utter a word. Then he left his home a second time, accompanied only by a servant. The Emperor Hadrian heard about his wisdom and summoned him into his presence, asking him several questions. Not receiving any answer, he ordered his head cut off, not however without giving secret instruction to carry out the sentence only should he be moved, through fear of death, to speak at the last minute. Remaining steadfast in his silence, Secundus was again led before the emperor, who now requested him to put down his answers in writing, which he promptly did. The result was the well-known collection of "maxims," found in many versions of the biography.

7. **A TALE OF INCEST.** FRANCE

When Louis XII was king, the legate at Avignon being then a lord of the house of Amboise, nephew to the legate of France, whose name was George, there was a lady in Languedoc who had an income of more than four thousand ducats. Her name I will not mention, for sake of her relations. She was still very young when her husband died, leaving her but one son; and whether from regret for her husband, or love of her son, she resolved never to marry again.

To avoid all occasion for doing so, she frequented only the society of the devout, thinking that opportunity makes sin, and not knowing that sin forges opportunity. She gave herself up wholly to the divine service, shunning all parties of pleasure, and everything worldly, insomuch that she made it a matter of conscience to be present at a wedding, or to hear the organ played in church. When her son was seven years old, she chose a man of holy life as his preceptor, to bring him up in piety and sanctity.

---

6. SOURCE: Krappe 1927:181–82.

7. SOURCE: De Navarre 1960:273–77.

But when he was between fourteen and fifteen, nature, who is a very mysterious schoolmaster, finding him well grown and idle, taught him a very different lesson from any he had learned from his preceptor; for under that new instruction he began to look upon and desire such things as seemed to him fair and among others a demoiselle who slept in his mother's room. No one had the least suspicion of this, for he was regarded as a child, and nothing was ever heard in the house but godly discourse.

The young gallant having begun secretly to solicit this girl, she went and told her mistress. The mother loved her son so much, that she believed this to be a story told to get him into disgrace; but the girl repeated her complaints so often that her mistress at last said she would find out the truth of the matter: if it was as the girl stated, she would punish her son severely, but if not, the accuser should pay the penalty. In order, then, to come at the truth, she ordered that he should come to her at midnight, to the bed in which she lay alone near the door in his mother's chamber.

The demoiselle obeyed her orders, and that night the mother lay down in the demoiselle's bed, resolving that if her son came thither she would chastise him in such a manner that he should never lie with a woman without remembering it. Such were her angry thoughts when her son actually entered the bed in which she lay; but unable still to bring herself to believe that he had any unchaste intention, she waited for some plainer evidence of his bad purpose before she would speak to him.

But she waited so long, and nature is so frail, that her anger ended in an abominable pleasure, and she forgot that she was a mother. As water retained by force is more impetuous when let loose, so was it with this unfortunate woman, who made her whole pride consist in the violence she did her body. When she began to descend the first step from her chastity she found herself at once at the bottom, and became pregnant that night by him who she wished to hinder from getting another with child.

No sooner was the sin committed than she was seized with the most poignant remorse, and her repentance lasted as long as her life. So keen was her anguish on rising from beside her son, who never discovered his mistake, that entering a closet, and calling to mind the firm resolution she had formed and which she had so badly executed, she passed the whole night alone in an agony of tears. But instead of humbling herself and owning that of ourselves alone, and without the aid of God, we can do nothing but sin, she thought by her own efforts and by her tears to repair the past and prevent future mischief, always imputing her sin to the occasion, and not to wickedness, for which there is no remedy but the grace of God. As if there was but one sort of sin which could bring damnation, she applied her whole mind to avoid that one; but pride, which the sense of extreme sinfulness should destroy, was too strongly rooted in her heart, and grew in such a manner, that, to avoid one evil, she committed several others.

Early next morning she sent for her son's governor, and said to him, "My son is coming to maturity, and it is time that he should be removed from the house. One of my relations, who is beyond the mountains with the Grand Master of Chaumont, will be glad to have him. Take him away, then, forthwith; and to spare me the pain of parting, do not let him come to bid me farewell." Without more ado she gave him money for the journey, and he set out the next day with his pupil, who was very glad of it, and having had what he wanted of his mistress, desired nothing better than to go to the wars.

The lady was long plunged in extreme grief, and but for the fear of God she could have wished that the unhappy fruit of her womb should perish. To conceal her fault she pretended to be ill; and having a bastard brother in whom she confided above all men, and for whom she had done many favors, she sent for him, informed him of the misfortune that had happened to her, but not of her son's share in it, and begged him to save her honor by his help, which he did.

Some days before she expected to be confined, he advised her to try change of air and to move to his house, where she would be more likely to recover than at home. She went thither with hardly any attendants, and found there a midwife, who had been sent for as if to attend her brother's wife, and who, without knowing the lying-in woman, delivered her by night of a fine little girl. The gentleman put the infant out to nurse as his own; and the lady, after a month's stay, returned home, where she lived more austerely than ever.

Her son being grown up, and Italy being at peace, he sent to beg his mother's permission to return to her. But as she was afraid of relapsing into the same crime, she put him off from time to time as well as she could; but he pressed her so much, that at last she gave him leave to come home, having no plausible reason to allege for persisting longer in her refusal. She sent him word, however, not to appear before her until he was married; to choose a wife whom he loved passionately; and not to let his choice be determined by wealth, for if he chose a comely wife that was enough.

During this time the daughter, who had been left with the bastard brother, having grown up into a very handsome girl, her guardian thought of removing her to some place where she should not be known. He consulted the mother on the subject, and it was her wish that she should be given to the Queen of Navarre, named Catherine. The girl was so handsome and well-bred at twelve or thirteen, that the Queen of Navarre had a great regard for her, and wished much to marry her well; but the girl being poor, many lovers presented themselves, but no husband.

The unknown father, returning from Italy, visited the court of the Queen of Navarre, and no sooner saw his daughter than he fell in love with her. As he had his mother's permission to marry any woman he liked, he only asked was she of noble lineage, and being told that she was, he demanded her in marriage of the Queen of Navarre, who very gladly bestowed her upon him, knowing well that the cavalier was as wealthy as he was well-bred and handsome.

The marriage having been consummated, the gentleman wrote to his mother, saying she could no longer close her doors against him, since he brought with him a wife as handsome and as perfect as she could wish for. His mother made inquiries as to the wife he had taken, and found that it was their own daughter, which caused her such excessive affliction, that she was near dying suddenly, seeing that the means she employed to put a stop to the course of her misfortune only served to make it greater.

Finding no remedy for what had occurred, she went to the Legate of Avignon, confessed the enormity of her crime, and asked his advice. The legate, to satisfy her conscience, summoned several theologians, to whom he submitted the affair without naming the person concerned. The decision of this council of conscience was, that the lady was never to reveal the secret to her children, who had not sinned, inasmuch as they had known nothing; but that, as for herself, she was to do penance all her life.

So the poor lady returned home, where soon after arrived her son and her daughter-in-law, who loved each other so much, that never was there a fonder couple, or one more like each other, for she was his daughter, sister, and wife; and he her father, brother, and husband. Their love continued unabated to the last, while their profoundly penitent mother never saw them caress but she withdrew to weep.

8. SOUTH SLAVIC OEDIPUS (JUDAS). YUGOSLAVIA

The curse is ordained by fate.

A man and his wife were wandering through a desolate place in a high mountain range. His wife was far advanced in pregnancy. There in the dark mountain forest, the tired woman sat down under a tree. Her husband asked her: "Why are you sitting down?" She remained silent. "Why are you sitting there?" It weighed heavily on her to admit to him the truth. After a long time she moved a bit. "Don't you realize why I am sitting here. I'm going to have the child. Fate [Bog] has ordained this." "Of course, we have also strived for this," replied the man.

---

8. SOURCES: Primary source: Krauss 1935:358–67; Secondary source: Edmunds and Dundes 1983:19–22. Reproduced by permission of Garland Publishing Co.

All at once a voice spoke up from the forest: "Has the child appeared?" "No, by God, not yet," the reply came. Again the voice sounded: "Is the child already here?" "No, it still isn't." For the third time the voice sounded: "Is the child finally here?" "By God, yes." The first voice spoke: "In the name of Allah, it has appeared at an unlucky hour." "In God's name, why is this so?" "If it had appeared when I asked you the first time, it would have become the ruler of half the world. If it had been born by the time of my second query, truly, a ruler of many peoples would have come from the new-born child. But now he has been born at an unlucky time. He will call himself the executioner of his own father, he will be the lover of his own mother, he will put forth his own hand against God, and worst of all, he will place a noose around his own neck."

The young mother picked up her child, took it in her arms, and went on with her husband. They reached a river, spanned by a large bridge. When they were at the middle of the bridge span, she suddenly tossed the child in a long arc into the water and exclaimed: "By Allah, I don't wish that he be my lover and the executioner of his father."

Exactly at the same time, near some bushes in a meadow on the bank of the river, a pious monk was fishing with his students. The fisherman noticed the child, and the current carried it to them. The monk pulled him ashore. He wrapped him up in the lap of his dolman, carried him to church, baptized him immediately, found a wet nurse for him, and raised him so that the child passed as his own son.

The child was extraordinarily beautiful, like a vila, and he developed splendidly. By his first birthday he was already larger and stronger than almost any three-year-old. He was an unruly, wild child, and had no peer in this respect. He tore up church books in sanctuaries, destroyed holy paintings, broke crosses that were set up, laid waste to gardens around the church. They thrashed him, but he was not in the least bit afraid, because he was and remained a rowdy child.

By his fifteenth year, the monk was already unable to exercise any authority over him. He was too much for him to handle. There remained nothing else to do but to dress and equip him anew from head to toe. In addition, the monk provided him with some money and said to him: "Go out into the world, I no longer can keep you here. You give me more trouble than I can handle."

The youngster now wandered around the world. He went from place to place, from here to there, until he ended up at his father's and mother's home. They were extremely rich people and lived in great abundance. He asked them: "Could you furnish me lodging?" "Surely, why not? You can spend the night here." And in the evening they talked. "Where are you going, young man?" inquired the father. He answered: "I think I want to go into service somewhere."

"Why do you wish to go into service, you who are so young and fine a gentleman?" "By God, I want to do this, if only someone will take me on." "I am ready, if you are inclined to do the job." And so they agreed that he should become their vine-grower.

And thus he went up the steep-sloped vineyard in order to inspect it. The grapes suffered much destruction from the sweet-toothed birds, who were accustomed to frequent the vineyard and who could not be driven away by any means. The young wine-grower prepared a sling, placed a rock in it, ran with it between the vines, and chased away the pests.

One day, the father said: "I must once and for all go and check out what the young man is doing, whether he truly watches over my vineyard. Thank God that we have an overseer!" He crept up to spy out how he performed his duties. At the same moment, the young man picked up a stone and flung it in that direction. The devil directed the throw to the forehead of the father. The rock penetrated the forehead. Struck, his father yelled out in great pain: "Why are you killing me?" The young man took the injured one on his shoulders and rushed home with him. Many gathered around the injured one in order to see what had happened. The father related to them the entire incident and enjoined them: "That was an act of God. Do not place nay blood-guilt on him. He inadvertently hit me, he has not in the least committed any crime against me." After saying these words, he died.

In the meantime, the young man managed the household and farm with the wife of the dead man, his mother. People urged her repeatedly and emphatically: "Look, woman, take this young man as a husband. Do not waste so much effort and your possessions, since this lad, God witness, is an excellent bridegroom."

And so she took him as her husband and they sinned. One night the wife asked before going to bed: "Unfortunate one, who are you really and what is your parentage? You came drifting out of nowhere, you killed my husband, I married you, and to this present day I do not know who you are or where you come from." He confessed to her that a monk had fished him out of the water, had taken him in, and raised him as his son—"And therefore I set out into the wide world to seek my fortune." Horrified, she remembered the whole story. "O, you unhappy man, how did Satan bring you here? May Satan lead you away from here. May no one find out that you set foot in this place." With that she chased him from the house, and he wandered again out into the world.

And so he reached Jerusalem, where he met Christ and the Apostles. He entered into their service, prepared meals for them, served them, washed their dishes, and cleaned house. No one could have done it better than he.

And the Jews tried to bribe him: "Hand Christ over to us." Thus they spoke to him.

"Allah, I'll do it, if you would fill this box of mine with ducats." They gilded twelve of the cheapest coins, added a real gold ducat and presented to him the filled box. He said to them: "Follow me." In the living quarters there were nine doors. He opened one after the other and they followed him step by step. When he came to the room where the holy ones dwelled, he put before them salt and bread on the table, to each the same portion. But he spoke to those accompanying him: "The one to whom I stretch out my hand, that one is the Christ." He put salt and bread on the table for them and pointed with an outstretched hand towards him. A one-eyed man stood with a lance at the door, saw the sign and hurled the spear into the left breast of the Lord. A drop of blood squirted up and struck the guard in his blinded eye. At the very same moment his eye could see again and he yelled out: "Forgive me Lord, I am yours, by God." You know, my dear listener, how they tormented him, how he was dragged before the court and how horribly they finally dealt with him. When Judas realized what he had set in motion, he yelled out bewildered: "By Allah and by God, what have I not done to myself? I became my father's executioner, am called lover of my mother and now I have raised my hand against my God!"

And he bought himself a rope with his ducats and ran with it into a desolate mountain range. He wrote a short note from which people could discern who and what he was, climbed a tall fir tree, fastened around its tip the end of the rope, the other he cast around his neck and thus hanged himself on the tree.

And hanging there he decomposed. The people were greatly astonished because for three years they could not find out what had happened to his carcass, nor where he had hidden himself and what path he had taken. Some hunters got lost in that area and noticed the rope hanging from the tree. At the foot of the tree, directly under the rope, there lay scattered the bones of the hanged one. Tobacco leaves had spouted from these bones. Because of this men should smoke tobacco. The sinner had done repentance, and this leaf should till the end of time in all the world perpetuate the memory of his offense.

9. **ALBAN TYPE.** ITALY

The story of Alban begins with an incestuous union between a king and his daughter. Their child is carried off to a foreign country and thrown on the highway. Some beggars find him and take him to the king of that

---

9. SOURCE: Propp 1983:81. Reproduced by permission of Garland Publishing Co.
NOTE: The text reproduced here is Propp's synopsis of a tale, and the reader will notice that the last two sentences are Propp's commentary.

country. There he is raised. The king claims him as his own son, marries him to the daughter of a neighboring king, and dies. The second king's daughter is none other than the boy's mother. But since he was born of father-daughter incest, his wife is at the same time his mother and his half-sister, and his father is also his maternal grandfather. When the truth is revealed, the wife summons her father and all three withdraw to the desert. But the devil again tempts the old father. Again he sins with his daughter. The young son finds them out, kills both parents, and goes off to the desert alone. Subsequently he becomes a saint and miracles are worked by his body. The story type is relatively rare and is found mainly in Latin manuscripts rather than in a folklore tradition. There are, however, traces of it in the *Arabian Nights*.

10. **THE BOY WHO MARRIED HIS MOTHER.** FINLAND

A father was maddened, wanted to kill his son, slashed him across the waist. The mother wanted to save the boy, put him on a piece of wood, then set him adrift. He came ashore. Someone found and raised him. Then he traveled around and came to his old home. The father had died. The boy fell in love with his mother and married her. Once, in the sauna, they learned the truth. The mother fainted.

11. **JACK AND HIS FAMILY.** UNITED STATES

O ne time the folks had went to town, and there was nobody home but Jack and his sister Jenny. Jack was fifteen years old, and Jenny must have been about seventeen. It was a terribly hot day, so the boy took off all his clothes and laid down on the floor. There was enough cracks to let a little air come through, so it was the coolest place in the house. Jenny didn't have but three things on, and two of them was hair-ribbons. Him and her got to talking about one thing and another, so pretty soon she pulled her dress off and laid down beside Jack.

They just kind of petted each other at first, but then Jenny got to playing with Jack's pecker. It swelled up surprising, and she says, "My goodness, I never seen anything so big only on a jackass, and maybe that's how they come

10. SOURCES: Primary source: Savokarjalainen Osakunta 1887; Secondary source: Edmunds 1985:142. Edmunds, Lowell. *Oedipus: The Ancient Legend and Its Later Analogues*. The Johns Hopkins University Press, Baltimore/London, 1985.

11. SOURCE: Randolph 1976:55–56. Copyright 1976 by the Board of Trustees of the University of Illinois. Used with the permission of the University of Illinois Press.

to name you Jack!" The boy didn't return no answer, and pretty soon she says, "Do you reckon you could stick that big thing in me?" Jack says there is only one way to find out, but maybe you better put a little grease on it first. So that's what she done, and everything worked out wonderful.

"My god, Jenny," says Jack, "I never had it so good in my whole life! Why, you're lots better than Maw!" The girl just wiggled her ass, and started to tickle Jack's balls some more. "Yeah," she giggled, "that's what Paw always says."

12. SOLOMON THE WISE. MEXICO

It is said that Solomon wasn't always discreet in the way he illustrated a truth.

Once he was walking along a street pondering over the weakness of human nature. One of many in a crowd that followed him asked, "Are women good or bad?"

"There are as many kinds of women as there are women," said Solomon; "but in general they are selfish, untruthful, and bad."

"In that case would it be right to point out any one of them as an example?"

"Yes," said Solomon, "we will begin with my mother." He called his mother, who was following at a distance. "*Mama*," he said, "there is a question that bothers us. We would like to know whether you are bad or good."

"Son, I am good. Do you doubt it?"

Solomon turned to the crowd and asked if anyone felt any wiser, now that his mother had made her comment.

Later that day the shrewd king called one of his servants and said, "Have no fear of consequences. Tomorrow I want you to walk with my mother into the mountains. She won't care to listen to all that you have to say; but regardless of her anger you are to tell her that she is beautiful, young, and lovely. Shower her with *piropos* [flattery]. Remember, half a word won't be enough. In short, make love to her, and tell me later what she said to you."

That afternoon the mother came to Solomon and said, "My son, I have brought you this servant. He has been provoking me. He has insulted you, his king, by saying things to me that I prefer not to mention."

"What would you have me do with him?" asked Solomon. "Let's let him go. I will take care of him later."

"Don't ask me again to associate with anyone so uncouth. This I ask as a favor," said the mother.

---

12. SOURCE: Aiken 1980:146–48.

"But I want you to go out again, with another servant. I command it."

This time she was accompanied into the fields. They came to a stream and sat on the bank. Later, when she found her son, she said to him. "Son, you are a *cornudo* [pander]. Is there no limit to you? That servant should be hanged, for he wanted to put his arms about me. He was worse than the last."

"Just one more, *mamacita*, and this will be all."

"I shall go only because you have the power to command me to do so," she said.

Solomon's mother and his servant walked along a boulevard. They came to a bench and sat for awhile to rest. This man commented on the spring flowers and particularly on the lilies of the field; he quoted poetry in which there was much mention of love. He made casual reference to this and that girl who passed by, but seemingly ignored the woman by his side.

Then she took the initiative, and before it was over she had invited him to her bedroom after night had drawn over the city. "Knock on my door three times," she said, "and I shall let you in."

The servant reported all this to Solomon. The latter changed clothes with the servant and kept his appointment for him. He knocked on the mother's door and was told to come in; but he refused, saying in a muffled voice that she should open it for him.

"My son!" she gasped when he entered.

Then she began to weep, and Solomon asked what she would have him do with the servants for their part in the trick that had been played on her.

"Nothing," she said. "Let them go in peace."

"Mother," said Solomon, "only a few days ago you told me you were good. This nature of forgiveness on your part proves that. On the other hand, it was not a good woman who invited a man to her bedroom at this hour of the night. We don't need God's help for our goodness, Mother, but we do need it to protect us from evil. Keep that in mind and we will understand each other."

13. **EUGENE THE FOUND.** GUADELOUPE

A mother had two sons, Eugene the Great and Eugene the Bohemian. Those two sons signed a marriage contract but never got married. One day Eugene the Great left Eugene the Bohemian to spend three months in a boat. There, he found a beautiful girl and fell in love with her. He went back

---

13. SOURCES: Primary source: E. Parsons 1936:205–6; Secondary source: Edmunds 1985:220–22. Edmunds, Lowell. *Oedipus: The Ancient Legend and Its Later Analogues*. The Johns Hopkins University Press, Baltimore/London, 1985.

to tell his brother about his adventure. He told him: "I found a beautiful girl who is going to marry me. The marriage contract we signed is lost." Then Eugene the Bohemian told Eugene the Great: "The first child you have, make sure you kill him, because he can be a real problem for you." Then he said: "I will!" He got married and had a baby boy. He also had a servant. He bought her a knife and asked her to take the baby with her and kill him in the forest. The maid thought that was too much for her. Instead, she bought a chicken, killed it, and left the child in the forest without killing him. She returned to the house with the bloody knife. She said, "Mr. Eugene, I killed him." Then Mr. Eugene said, "Well! I am going to give you a raise. You were making twenty-five francs, now you are going to make fifty francs."

There was an old charcoal maker who was making charcoal in the forest. He heard a baby cry. He walked straight in the direction of the voice and found a deer who was nurturing the child. He then took the child home with him. Without knowing anything about the baby's history, he called him Eugene the Found.

As the child was growing older, he started to talk. The old man was very rich and told the boy that he was so rich that he had a lot of money saved in a white silver box. This would make the child walk faster while he is on duty. He would also have the chance to meet his father, Eugene the Great, without knowing that he is his father. In fact, he saw him on a carriage that was being pulled by two horses. As he was going to pass in front of the carriage, his father barred him from passing without knowing that was his child. The boy decided to go downtown and saw a very beautiful girl. He went back and told the old man, "Any time I go downtown there is always a man who bars my way." He took a gun and went downtown with it. The man again came to bar his way. This time he pulled his gun, fired one shot, and killed Eugene the Great. Then the carriage returned to depose the dead man on the door-step of his wife's house. His wife lamented and buried him. The boy went downtown and saw a very beautiful woman and fell in love with her without knowing that she was his mother. He then decided to talk to her, and she, in turn, fell in love with him. They got married without knowing that they were mother and son. As he was taking a walk downtown, he saw Eugene the Bohemian. Then Eugene the Bohemian told him, "The man that you killed on the carriage was your father, and the woman you married and with whom you have a child is your mother. Your father's name was Eugene the Great. My name is Eugene the Bohemian, and your name is Eugene the Found." The boy left very sad. He came home at noon, dinner time, his wife said, "What's the matter with you?" And he started to cry. He said while he was crying, "My mother, my wife, and my children, all of you who are here are my brother, my sister, and my mother."

Then his mother said, "Are you joking, Eugene?" He replied, "I killed my father, Eugene the Great, on the carriage, and you are my mother. I have four children with my mother. When I was a child, my father sent his servant to kill me in the forest. By chance, the servant did not kill me, and instead she bought a chicken, killed it to let him think that she killed me, and brought the bloody knife to him. My father thanked her by giving her a raise. It was the old charcoal maker who took me and raised me. My name is Eugene the Found. By this we know that a man should not marry a widow. So I took a gun, I, Eugene the Found, killed myself, and my mother killed herself. The children are left to cry. My cousin, Eugene the Bohemian, took the children and raised them." Here, it is forbidden for a young man to marry a widow.

14. CAMOES AND HIS MOTHER. BRAZIL

I know one about Camoes, him saying that all women are unfaithful, there isn't an honest woman. Camoes went and said this to the king, that there were no faithful women, that all women were false. Then the king said, "Well, Camoes, you are going to tell me, you are going to prove this story to me, convince me of it. Because if you do not prove this story such that I can believe it, and it is untrue, I will order you beheaded right in the middle of the road. If it is true, we are the same as always, there is no problem between us."

And Camoes said, "I will prove to you My King, My Lord, how my own mother is unfaithful. My own mother! I will prove to My Lord that my mother is false. I will make a rendezvous with her, in such a way that you will see how she will fall for it. Although I cannot, since she is my own mother, at that time I will show you whether she is not on the bridge waiting for me. And when I arrive, I will prove to you that she has been waiting for me like any other unknown woman that I have arranged to tryst with."

It was said and done. He arranged with the old woman, his mother, that she should meet him where he said. Then when he arrived, he approached her, and said, "O lady my mother, how can it be you came to await this encounter with me thus, thus, thus!? I cannot." Then he asked her to bless him. The king had placed someone close by to spy on how Camoes was going to prove his case, as though it was the king himself who was watching. The king's spy saw how she was ready to yield to him. Then Camoes said, "How can woman be honest? When my own mother is like this, what are the others worth?"

Camoes was so sly, a real trickster!

14. SOURCE: Paiva, Johnson, and Soares 1991:1–2. Used by permission.

15. THE MAIDEN TSAR. RUSSIA

In a certain land, in a certain kingdom, there was a merchant whose wife died, leaving him with an only son, Ivan. He put this son in charge of a tutor, and after some time took another wife; and since Ivan, the merchant's son, was now of age and very handsome, his stepmother fell in love with him. One day Ivan went with his tutor to fish in the sea on a small raft; suddenly they saw thirty ships making toward them. On these ships sailed the Maiden Tsar with thirty other maidens, all her foster sisters. When the ships came close to the raft, all thirty of them dropped anchor. Ivan and his tutor were invited aboard the best ship, where the Maiden Tsar and her thirty foster sisters received them; she told Ivan that she loved him passionately and had come from afar to see him. So they were betrothed.

The Maiden Tsar told the merchant's son to return to the same place the following day, said farewell to him, and sailed away. Ivan returned home and went to sleep. The stepmother led the tutor into her room, made him drunk, and began to question him as to what had happened to him and Ivan at sea. The tutor told her everything. Upon hearing his story, she gave him a pin and said: "Tomorrow, when the ships begin to sail toward you, stick this pin into Ivan's tunic." The tutor promised to carry out her order.

Next morning Ivan arose and went fishing. As soon as his tutor beheld the ships sailing in the distance, he stuck the pin into Ivan's tunic. "Ah, I feel so sleepy," said the merchant's son. "Listen tutor, I will take a nap now, and when the ships come close, please rouse me." "Very well, of course I will rouse you," said the tutor. The ships sailed close to the raft and cast anchor; the Maiden Tsar sent for Ivan, asking him to hasten to her; but he was sound asleep. The servant began to shake him, pinch him, and nudge him. All in vain—they could not awaken him, so they left him.

The Maiden Tsar told the tutor to bring Ivan to the same place on the following day, then ordered her crews to lift anchor and set sail. As soon as the ships sailed away, the tutor pulled out the pin, and Ivan awoke, jumped up, and began to call to the Maiden Tsar to return. But she was far away then and could not hear him. He went home sad and aggrieved. His stepmother took the tutor into her room, made him drunk, questioned him about everything that had happened, and told him to stick the pin through Ivan's tunic again the next day. The next day Ivan again went fishing, again slept all the time, and did not see the Maiden Tsar; she left word that he should come again.

On the third day he again went fishing with his tutor. They came to the

15. SOURCE: Afanasev 1945:229–34.

old place, and beheld the ships sailing at a distance, and the tutor straightaway stuck in his pin, and Ivan fell sound asleep. The ships sailed close and dropped anchor; the Maiden Tsar sent for her betrothed to come aboard her ship. The servant tried in every possible way to rouse him, but no matter what they did, they could not awaken him. The Maiden Tsar learned of the stepmother's ruse and the tutor's treason, and wrote to Ivan telling him to cut off the tutor's head, and, if he loved his betrothed, to come and find her beyond thrice nine lands in the thrice tenth kingdom.

The ships had no sooner set sail and put out to sea than the tutor pulled the pin from Ivan's garment; he awoke and began to bemoan his loss of the Maiden Tsar; but she was far away and could not hear him. The tutor gave him her letter; Ivan read it, drew out his sharp saber, and cut off the wicked tutor's head. Then he sailed hurriedly to the shore, went home, said farewell to his father, and set out to find the thrice tenth kingdom.

He journeyed onward, straight ahead, a long time or a short time—for speedily a tale is spun, but with less speed a deed is done—and finally came to a little hut; it stood in the open field, turning on chicken legs. He entered and found Baba Yaga the Bony-legged. "Fie, fie," she said, "the Russian smell was never heard of nor caught sight of here, but now it has come by itself. Are you here of your own free will or by compulsion, my good youth?" "Largely of my own free will, and twice as much by compulsion! Do you know, Baba Yaga, where lies the thrice tenth kingdom?" "No, I do not," she said, and told him to go to her second sister; she might know.

Ivan thanked her and went on farther; he walked and walked, a long distance or a short distance, a long time or a short time, and finally came to a little hut exactly like the first and there too found a Baba Yaga. "Fie, fie," she said, "The Russian smell was never heard of nor caught sight of here, but now it has come by itself. Are you here of your own free will or by compulsion, my good youth?" "Largely of my own free will, and twice as much by compulsion! Do you know, Baba Yaga, where lies the thrice tenth kingdom?" "No, I do not," she said, and told him to stop at her youngest sister's; she might know. "If she gets angry at you," she added, "and wants to devour you, take three horns from her and ask her permission to blow them; blow the first one softly, the second louder, and the third still louder." Ivan thanked Baba Yaga and went on farther.

He walked and walked, a long distance or a short distance, a long time or a short time, and finally beheld a little hut standing in the open field and turning upon chicken legs; he entered it and found another Baba Yaga. "Fie, fie, the Russian smell was never heard of nor caught sight of here, and now it has come by itself," she said, and ran to whet her teeth, for she intended to eat her uninvited guest. Ivan begged her to give him three horns; he blew one softly, the second louder, and the third still louder. Suddenly birds of all kinds swarmed about him, among them the firebird. "Sit upon me quickly," said the firebird, "and we shall fly wherever you want; if you don't come with me, the Baba Yaga will devour you." Ivan had no sooner sat himself upon the bird's back than the Baba Yaga rushed in, seized the firebird by the tail, and plucked a large handful of feathers from it.

The firebird flew with Ivan on its back; for a long time it soared in the skies, till finally it came to the broad sea. "Now, Ivan, merchant's son, the thrice tenth land lies beyond this sea. I am not strong enough to carry you to the other shore; get there as best you can." Ivan climbed down from the firebird, thanked it, and walked along the shore.

He walked and walked till he came to a little hut; he entered it and was met by an old woman who gave him meat and drink and asked him whither he was going and why he was traveling so far. He told her that he was going to the thrice tenth kingdom to find the Maiden Tsar, his betrothed. "Ah," said the old woman, "she no longer loves you; if she gets hold of you, she will tear you to shreds; her love is stored away in a remote place." "Then how can I get it?" "Wait a bit! My daughter lives at the Maiden Tsar's palace and she is coming to visit me today; we may learn something from her." Then the old woman turned Ivan into a pin and stuck the pin into the wall; at night her daughter flew in. Her mother asked her whether she knew where the Maiden Tsar's love was stored away. "I do not know," said the daughter, and promised to find out from the Maiden Tsar herself. The next day she again visited her mother and told her: "On this side of the ocean there stands an oak: in the oak there is a coffer; in the coffer there is a hare; in the hare there is a duck; in the duck there is an egg; and in the egg lies the Maiden Tsar's love."

Ivan took some bread and set out for the place she had described. He found the oak and removed the coffer from it; then he removed the hare from the coffer; the duck from the hare, and the egg from the duck. He returned with the egg to the old woman. A few days later came the old woman's birthday; she invited the Maiden Tsar with the thirty other maidens, her foster sisters, to her house; she baked the egg, dressed Ivan the merchant's son in splendid raiment, and hid him.

At midday, the Maiden Tsar and the thirty other maidens flew into the house, sat down to table, and began to dine; after dinner the old woman served them each an egg, and to the Maiden Tsar she served the egg that Ivan had found. The Maiden Tsar ate of it and at once conceived a passionate love for Ivan the merchant's son. The old woman brought him out of his hiding place. How much joy there was, how much merriment! The Maiden Tsar left her betrothed, the merchant's son, for her own kingdom; they married and began to live happily and to prosper.

MIDDLE EAST AND AFRICA

16. **ZAHHAK.** PERSIA

It is said that Zahhak was originally called Dahhak, that is to say he had ten apparent faults and defects, and he was so ugly and bad looking that even his brothers and father hated to look at him. Zahhak's father was the master of horse for King Jasmid, and he had a very pretty wife. They say that Zahhak fell in love with his step-mother, and every day when he would take the horses to pasture, he would go sit somewhere and cry on account of his love for her. But, fearing his father, he never dared say anything—until one day the accursed Satan turned himself into an old man and appeared in front of him and said, "O Zahhak, why are you distressed?" Zahhak answered, "O old man, leave me alone, there is no remedy for my pain." Satan said, "If you will tell of your heart's pain, I will find a cure for it." And Zahhak began to talk, and the devil said, "O Zahhak, as long as your father is alive you can't do anything." Zahhak said, "Well, I knew that already." Satan said, "O Zahhak, if you want to gain your beloved, today when you go home you will find your father asleep. Pick up a stone, and hit him on the head with it hard, and after you kill your father, go to your step-mother, and marry her." Zahhak found this to be a wonderful plan. He got up, and returned home earlier than usual, and he saw that, sure enough, his father was sleeping like a log. He did not dawdle, but picked up a big stone, and hit his

---

16. SOURCES: Primary source: Anjavi-Shirazi 1975:301–2; Secondary source: Omidsalar 1980. Used by permission.

father's head very hard and killed him. Then he began to scream and moan and the people gathered and picked up the father's corpse, and buried it. After several days, Zahhak went to his step-mother, and revealed his love to her. She, knowing what a son-of-a-bitch he was, began to use delaying tactics and said, "If you go to the court of King Jasmid, and get your father's office from him, then I will consent to be your wife." She was thinking of herself all the time that as soon as Jasmid set eyes on his ugly face, he would certainly call the executioner and have him beheaded. Then she would be off the hook.

17. DIIRAWIC AND HER INCESTUOUS BROTHER. DINKA
(AFRICA)

THIS IS AN ANCIENT EVENT.

A girl called Diirawic was extremely beautiful. All the girls of the tribe listened to her words. Old women all listened to her words. Small children all listened to her words. Even old men all listened to her words. A man called Teeng wanted to marry her, but her brother, who was also called Teeng, refused. Many people each offered a hundred cows for her bridewealth, but her brother refused. One day Teeng spoke to his mother and said, "I would like to marry my sister Diirawic."

His mother said, "I have never heard of such a thing. You should go and ask your father."

He went to his father and said, "Father, I would like to marry my sister."

His father said, "My son, I have never heard of such a thing. A man marrying his sister is something I cannot even speak about. You had better go and ask your mother's brother."

He went to his mother's brother and said, "Uncle, I would like to marry my sister."

His maternal uncle exclaimed, "My goodness! Has anybody ever married his sister? Is that why you have always opposed her marriage? Was it because you had it in your heart to marry her yourself? I have never heard of such a thing! But what did your mother say about this?"

"My mother told me to ask my father. I agreed and went to my father. My father said he had never heard such a thing and told me to come to you."

"If you want my opinion," said his uncle, "I think you should ask your father's sister."

He went around to all his relatives that way. Each one expressed surprise

17. SOURCE: Deng 1974:78–90. From *Dinka Folktales: African Stories from the Sudan* by Francis Mading Deng (New York: Africana Publishing Company, 1974). Copyright © 1974 by Francis Mading Deng. Reprinted by permission of the publisher.

and suggested that he should ask another. Then he came to his mother's sister and said, "Aunt, I would like to marry my sister."

She said, "My child, if you prevented your sister from being married because you wanted her, what can I say! Marry her if that is your wish. She is your sister."

Diirawic did not know about this. One day she called all the girls and said, "Girls, let us go fishing." Her words were always listened to by everyone, and when she asked for anything, everyone obeyed. So all the girls went, including little children. They went and fished.

In the meantime, her brother Teeng took out his favorite ox, Mijok, and slaughtered it for a feast. He was very happy that he was allowed to marry his sister. All the people came to the feast.

Although Diirawic did not know her brother's plans, her little sister had overheard the conversation and knew what was happening. But she kept silent; she did not say anything.

A kite flew down and grabbed up the tail of Teeng's ox, Mijok. Then it flew to the river where Diirawic was fishing and dropped it in her lap. She looked at the tail and recognized it. "This looks like the tail of my brother's ox, Mijok," she said. "What has killed him? I left him tethered and alive!"

The girls tried to console her, saying, "Diirawic, tails are all the same. But if it is the tail of Mijok, then perhaps some important guests have arrived. It may be that they are people wanting to marry you. Teeng may have decided to honor them with his favorite ox. Nothing bad has happened."

Diirawic was still troubled. She stopped the fishing and suggested that they return to find out what had happened to her brother's ox.

They went back. As they arrived, the little sister of Diirawic came running to her and embraced her, saying, "My dear sister Diirawic, do you know what has happened?"

"I don't know," said Diirawic.

"Then I will tell you a secret," continued her sister, "but please don't mention it to any one, not even to our mother."

"Come on, Sister, tell me," said Diirawic.

"Teeng has been preventing you from being married because *he* wants to marry you," her sister said. "He has slaughtered his ox, Mijok, to celebrate his engagement to you. Mijok is dead."

Diirawic cried and said, "So that is why God made the kite fly with Mijok's tail and drop it in my lap. So be it. There is nothing I can do."

"Sister," said her little sister, "let me continue with what I have to tell you. When your brother bedevils you and forgets that you are his sister, what do you do? I found a knife for you. He will want you to sleep with him in the hut. Hide the knife near the bed. And at night when he is fast asleep, cut off his testicles. He will die. And he will not be able to do anything to you."

"Sister," said Diirawic, "you have given me good advice."

Diirawic kept the secret and did not tell the girls what had occurred. But she cried whenever she was alone.

She went and milked the cows. People drank the milk. But when Teeng was given milk, he refused. And when he was given food, he refused. His heart was on his sister. That is where his heart was. At bedtime, he said, "I would like to sleep in that hut. Diirawic, Sister, let us share the hut."

Diirawic said, "Nothing is bad, my brother. We can share the hut."

They did. Their little sister also insisted on sleeping with them in the hut. So she slept on the other side of the hut. In the middle of the night, Teeng got up and moved the way men do! At that moment, a lizard spoke and said, "Come, Teeng, have you really become an imbecile? How can you behave like that towards your sister?"

He felt ashamed and lay down. He waited for a while and then got up again. And when he tried to do what men do, the grass on the thatching spoke and said, "What an imbecile! How can you forget that she is your sister?"

He felt ashamed and cooled down. This time, he waited much longer. Then his desire rose and he got up. The rafters spoke and said, "O, the man has really become an idiot! How can your heart be on your mother's daughter's body? Have you become a hopeless imbecile?"

He cooled down. This time he remained quiet for a very long time, but then his mind returned to it again.

This went on until very close to dawn. Then he reached that point when a man's heart fails him. The walls spoke and said, "You monkey of a human being, what are you doing?" The utensils rebuked him. The rats in the hut laughed at him. Everything started shouting at him. "Teeng, imbecile, what are you doing to your sister?"

At that moment, he fell back ashamed and exhausted and fell into a deep sleep.

The little girl got up and woke her older sister, saying, "You fool, don't you see he is now sleeping? This is the time to cut off his testicles."

Diirawic got up and cut them off. Teeng died.

Then the two girls got up and beat the drums in a way that told everybody that there was an exclusive dance for girls. No men could attend that dance. Nor could married women and children. So all the girls came out running from their huts and went to the dance.

Diirawic then spoke to them and said, "Sisters, I called you to say that I am going into the wilderness." She then went on to explain to them the whole story and ended, "I did not want to leave you in secret. So I wanted a chance to bid you farewell before leaving."

All the girls decided they would not remain behind.

"If your brother did it to you," they argued, "what is the guarantee that our brothers will not do it to us? We must all leave together!"

So all the girls of the tribe decided to go. Only very small girls remained.

As they left, the little sister of Diirawic said, "I want to go with you."

But they would not let her. "You are too young," they said, "you must stay."

"In that case," she said, "I will cry out loud and tell everyone your plan!" And she started to cry out.

"Hush, hush," said the girls. Then turning to Diirawic they said, "Let her come with us. She is a girl with a heart [among the Dinka, the functions of the heart and the mind are conceptually fused; this expression therefore means wise, prudent, discreet, considerate, and the like]. She has already taken our side. If we die, we die together with her!"

Diirawic accepted and they went. They walked; they walked and walked and walked, until they came to the borders between the human territory and the lion world. They carried their axes and their spears; they had everything they might need.

They divided the work among themselves. Some cut the timber for rafters and poles. Others cut the grass for thatching. And they built for themselves an enormous house—a house for larger even than a cattle-byre. The number of girls was tremendous. They built many beds for themselves inside the hut and made a very strong door to make sure of their safety.

Their only problem was that they had no food. But they found a large anthill, full of dried meat, grain, and all the other foodstuffs that they needed. They wondered where all this could have come from. But Diirawic explained to them. "Sisters, we are women and it is the woman who bears the human race. Perhaps God has seen our plight, and not wanting us to perish, has provided us with all this. Let us take it in good grace!"

They did. Some went for firewood. Others fetched water. They cooked and ate.

Every day they would dance the women's dance in great happiness and then sleep.

One evening a lion came in search of insects and found them dancing. But seeing such a large number of girls, he became frightened and left. Their number was such as would frighten anyone.

It then occurred to the lion to turn into a dog and go into their compound. He did. He went there looking for droppings of food. Some girls hit him and chased him away. Others said, "Don't kill him. He is a dog and dogs are friends!"

But the skeptical ones said, "What kind of dog would be in this isolated world? Where do you think he came from?"

Other girls said, "Perhaps he came all the way from the cattle-camp, following us! Perhaps he thought the whole camp was moving and so he ran after us!"

Diirawic's sister was afraid of the dog. She had not seen a dog following them. And the distance was so great that the dog could not have traveled all the way alone. She worried but said nothing. Yet she could not sleep; she stayed awake while all the others slept.

One night the lion came and knocked at the door. He had overheard the names of the older girls, one of them, Diirawic. After knocking at the door he said, "Diirawic, please open the door for me." The little girl who was awake answered, chanting:

> "Achol is asleep,
> Achol is asleep,
> Nyankiir is asleep,
> Diirawic is asleep,
> The girls are asleep!"

The lion heard her and said: "Little girl, what is the matter with you, staying up so late?"

She answered him, saying, "My dear man, it is thirst. I am suffering from a dreadful thirst."

"Why?" asked the lion. "Don't the girls fetch water from the river?"

"Yes," answered the little girl, "they do. But since I was born, I do not drink water from a pot or a gourd. I drink only from a container made of reeds."

"And don't they bring you water in such a container?" asked the lion.

"No," she said. "They only bring water in pots and gourds, even though there is a container of reeds in the house."

"Where is that container?" asked the lion.

"It is outside there on the platform!" she answered.

So he took it and left to fetch water for her.

The container of reeds would not hold water. The lion spent much time trying to fix it with clay. But when he filled it, the water washed the clay away. The lion kept on trying until dawn. Then he returned with the container of reeds and put it back where it was. He then rushed back to the bush before the girls got up.

This went on for many nights. The little girl slept only during the daytime. The girls rebuked her for this, saying: "Why do you sleep in the daytime? Can't you sleep at night? Where do you go at night?"

She did not tell them anything. But she worried. She lost so much weight that she became very bony.

One day Diirawic spoke to her and said, "Nyanaguek, my mother's daughter, what is making you so lean? I told you to remain at home. This is too much for a child your age! Is it your mother you are missing? I will not allow you to make the other girls miserable. If necessary, daughter of my mother, I will kill you."

But Diirawic's sister would not reveal the truth. The girls went on rebuking her but she would not tell them what she knew.

One day, she broke down and cried, and then said, "My dear sister, Diirawic, I eat, as you see. In fact, I get plenty of food, so much that I do not finish what I receive. But even if I did not receive enough food, I have an enduring heart. Perhaps I am able to endure more than any one of you here. What I am suffering from is something none of you has seen. Every night a lion gives me great trouble. It is just that I am a person who does not speak. That animal you thought to be a dog is a lion. I remain awake all night to protect us all and then sleep in the daytime. He comes and knocks at the door. Then he asked for you by name to open the door. I sing back to him and tell him that you are all asleep. When he wonders why I am awake, I tell him it is because I am thirsty. I explain that I only drink out of a container made of reeds and that the girls bring water only in pots and gourds. Then he goes to fetch water for me. And seeing that he cannot stop the water from flowing out of the container, he returns towards dawn and disappears, only to be back the following night. So that is what is destroying me, my dear sister. You blame me in vain."

"I have one thing to tell you," said Diirawic. "Just be calm and when he comes, do not answer. I will remain awake with you."

They agreed. Diirawic took a large spear that they had inherited from their ancestors and remained awake, close to the door. The lion came at his usual hour. He came to the door, but somehow he became afraid and jumped away without knocking. He had a feeling that something was going on.

So he left and stayed away for some time. Then he returned to the door towards dawn. He said, "Diirawic, open the door for me!" There was only silence. He repeated his request. Still there was only silence. He said, "Well! The little girl who always answered me is at last dead!"

He started to break through the door, and when he succeeded in pushing his head in, Diirawic attacked him with the large spear, forcing him back into the courtyard.

"Please Diirawic," he pleaded, "do not kill me."

"Why not?" asked Diirawic. "What brought you here?"

"I only came in search of a sleeping-place!"

"Please allow me to be your brother," the lion continued to plead. "I will never attempt to hurt anyone again. I will go away if you don't want me here. Please!"

So Diirawic let him go. He went. But before he had gone a long way, he returned and said to the girls then gathered outside:

"I am going, but I will be back in two days with all my horned cattle."

Then he disappeared. After two days, he came back with all his horned cattle, as he had promised. Then he addressed the girls, saying: "Here I have come. It is true that I am a lion. I want you to kill that big bull in the herd. Use its meat for taming me. If I live with you untamed, I might become wild at night and attack you. And that would be bad. So kill the bull and tame me by teasing me with the meat."

They agreed. So they fell on him and beat him so much that his fur made a storm on his back and it fell off.

They killed the bull and roasted the meat. They would bring a fat piece of meat close to his mouth, then pull it away. A puppy dog would jump out of the saliva which dripped from the lion's mouth [although the Dinka have dogs and treat them with affection, puppies are used in folktales as symbols of wildness; presumably they recall the image of rabbid dogs]. They would give the puppy a fatal blow on the head. Then they would beat the lion again. Another piece of fat meat would be held close to his mouth, then pulled away, and another puppy would jump out of the falling saliva. They would give it a fatal blow on the head and beat the lion some more. Four puppies emerged, and all four were killed.

Yet the lion's mouth streamed with a wild saliva. So they took a large quantity of steaming hot broth and poured it down his throat, clearing it of all the remaining saliva. His mouth remained wide open and sore. He could no longer eat anything. He was fed only milk, poured down his throat.

He was then released. For four months, he was nursed as a sick person. His throat continued to hurt for all this time. Then he recovered.

The girls remained for another year. It was now five years since they had left home.

The lion asked the girls why they had left their home. The girls asked him to address his questions to Diirawic, as she was their leader. So he turned to Diirawic and asked the same question.

"My brother wanted to make me his wife," explained Diirawic. "I killed him for that. I did not want to remain in a place where I had killed my own brother. So I left. I did not care about my life. I expected such dangers as finding you. If you had eaten me, it would have been no more than I expected."

"Well, I have now become a brother to you all," said the lion. "As an older brother, I think I should take you all back home. My cattle have since multiplied. They are yours. If you find that your land has lost its herds, these will replace them. Otherwise they will increase the cattle already there, because I have become a member of your family. Since your only brother is dead, let me be in the place of Teeng, your brother. Cool your heart and return home."

He pleaded with Diirawic for about three months. Finally she agreed, but cried a great deal. When the girls saw her cry, they all cried. They cried and cried because their leader, Diirawic, had cried.

The lion slaughtered a bull to dry their tears. They ate the meat. Then he said to them, "Let us wait for three more days, and then leave!"

They slaughtered many bulls in sacrifice to bless the territory they crossed as they returned, throwing meat away everywhere they passed. As they did so, they prayed, "This is for the animals and the birds that have helped keep us healthy for all this time without death or illness in our midst. May God direct you to share in this meat."

They had put one bull into their big house and locked the house praying, "Our dear house, we give you this bull. And you bull, if you should break the rope and get out of the house, that will be a sign of grace from the hut. If you should remain outside, then we bequeath you this hut as we leave." And they left.

All this time the people at home were in mourning. Diirawic's father never shaved his head. He left the ungroomed hair of mourning on his head and did not care about his appearance. Her mother, too, was in the same condition. She covered herself with ashes so that she looked grey.

The rest of the parents mourned, but everybody mourned especially for Diirawic. They did not care as much for their own daughters as they did for Diirawic.

The many men who had wanted to marry Diirawic also neglected themselves in mourning. Young men and girls wore only two beads [for young people to be without any beads at all signifies disaster]. But older people and children wore no beads at all.

All the girls came and tethered their herds a distance from the village. They all looked beautiful. Those who had been immature had grown into maturity. The older ones had now reached the peak of youth and beauty. They had blossomed and had also become wiser and adept with words.

The little boy who was Diirawic's youngest brother had now grown up. Diirawic resembled her mother, who had been an extremely beautiful girl. Even in her old age, she still retained her beauty and her resemblance to her daughter still showed.

The little boy had never really known his sister, as he was too young when the girls left. But when he saw Diirawic in the newly arrived cattle-camp, he saw a clear resemblance to his mother. He knew that his two sisters and the other girls of the camp had disappeared. So he came and said, "Mother, I saw a girl in the cattle-camp who looks like she could be my sister, even though I do not remember my sisters."

"Child, don't you feel shame? How can you recognize people who left soon after you were born? How can you recall people long dead? This is evil magic! This is the work of an evil spirit!" She started to cry, and all the women joined her in crying.

Age-sets came running from different camps to show her sympathy. They all cried, even as they tried to console her with words.

Then came Diirawic with the girls and said, "My dear woman, permit us to shave off your mourning hair. And all of you, let us shave off your mourning hair!"

Surprised by her words, they said, "What has happened that we should shave off our mourning hair?"

Then Diirawic asked them why they were mourning. The old woman started to cry as Diirawic spoke, and said, "My dear girl, I lost a girl like you. She died five years ago, and five years is a long time. If she had died only two or even three years ago, I might have dared to say you are my daughter. As it is, I can't. But seeing you, my dear daughter, has cooled my heart."

Diirawic spoke again, saying, "Dear Mother, every child is a daughter. As I stand in front of you, I feel as though I were your daughter. So please listen to what I say as though I were your own daughter. We have all heard of you and your famed name. We have come from a very far-off place because of you. Please allow us to shave your head. I offer five cows as a token of my request" [it is customary among the Dinka for sympathizers to give cattle to an aggrieved person to end the mourning].

"Daughter," said the woman, "I shall honor your request, but not because of the cows—I have no use for cattle. Night and day, I think of nothing but my lost Diirawic. Even this child you see means nothing to me compared to my lost child, Diirawic. What grieves me is that God has refused to answer my prayers. I have called upon our clan spirits and I have called upon my ancestors, and they do not listen. This I resent. I will listen to your words, my daughter. The fact that God has brought you along and put these words into your mouth is enough to convince me."

So she was shaved. Diirawic gave the woman beautiful leather skirts made from skins of animals they killed on the way. They were not from the hides of cattle, sheep, or goats. She decorated the edges of the skirts with beautiful beads and made bead designs of cattle figures on the skirts. On the bottom of the skirts, she left the beautiful natural furs of the animals.

The woman cried and Diirawic pleaded with her to wear them. She and the girls went and brought milk from their own cattle and made a feast. Diirawic's father welcomed the end of mourning. But her mother continued to cry as she saw all the festivities.

So Diirawic came to her and said, "Mother, cool your heart. I am Diirawic."

Then she shrieked with cries of joy. Everyone began to cry—old women, small girls, everyone. Even blind women dragged themselves out of their huts, feeling their way with sticks, and cried. Some people died as they cried.

Drums were taken out and for seven days, people danced with joy. Men came from distant villages, each with seven bulls to sacrifice for Diirawic. The other girls were almost abandoned. All were concerned with Diirawic.

People danced and danced. They said, "Diirawic, if God has brought you, then nothing is bad. That is what we wanted."

Then Diirawic said, "I have come back. But I have come with this man to take the place of my brother Teeng."

"Very well," agreed the people. "Now there is nothing to worry about."

There were two other Teengs. Both were sons of chiefs. Each one came forward, asking to marry Diirawic. It was decided that they should compete. Two large kraals were to be made. Each man was to fill his kraal with cattle. The kraals were built. The men began to fill them with cattle. One Teeng failed to fill his kraal. The other Teeng succeeded so well that some cattle even remained outside.

Diirawic said, "I will not marry anyone until my new brother is given four girls to be his wives. Only then shall I accept the man my people want."

People listened to her words. Then they asked her how the man became her brother. So she told the whole story from its beginning to its end.

The people agreed with her and picked four of the finest girls for her new brother. Diirawic then accepted the man who had won the competition. She was given to her husband and she continued to treat the lion-man as her full brother. She gave birth first to a son and then to a daughter. She bore twelve children. But when the thirteenth child was born, he had the characteristics of a lion. Her lion-brother had brought his family to her village and was living there when the child was born. The fields of Diirawic and her brother were next to each other. Their children played together. As they played, the small lion-child, then still a baby, would put on leather skirts and sing. When Diirawic returned, the children told her, but she dismissed what they said. "You are liars. How can such a small child do these things?"

They would explain to her that he pinched them and dug his nails into their skins and would suck blood from the wounds. Their mother simply dismissed their complaints as lies.

But the lion-brother began to wonder about the child. He said, "Does a newly born human being behave the way this child behaves?" Diirawic tried to dispel his doubts.

But one day her brother hid and saw the child dancing and singing in a way that convinced him that the child was a lion and not a human being. So he went to his sister and said, "What you bore was a lion! What shall we do?"

The woman said, "What do you mean? He is my child and should be treated as such."

"I think we should kill him," said the lion-brother.

"That is impossible," she said. "How can I allow my child to be killed? He will get used to human ways and will cease to be aggressive."

"No," continued the lion. "Let us kill him by poison if you want to be gentle with him."

"What are you talking about?" retorted his sister. "Have you forgotten that you yourself were a lion and were then tamed into a human being? Is it true that old people lose their memory?"

The boy grew up with the children. But when he reached the age of herding, he would go and bleed the children by turn and suck blood from their bodies. He would tell them not to speak, and that if they said anything to their elders he would kill them and eat them.

The children would come home with wounds, and when asked, would say their wounds were from thorny trees.

But the lion did not believe them. He would tell them to stop lying and tell the truth, but they would not.

One day he went ahead of them and hid on top of the tree under which they usually spent the day. He saw the lion-child bleed the children and suck their blood. Right there, he speared him. The child died. He then turned to the children and asked them why they had hidden the truth for so long. The children explained how they had been threatened by the lion-child. Then he went and explained to his sister, Diirawic, what he had done.

18. UKEN. ALUR (UGANDA)

There was a youth called Uken. He was having a playful argument with his mother. "Now you are old, mother," said he. "But was I not a girl once too?" countered his mother, "surely if I dressed up the men would look at me still!" "Really, mother," answered Uken, "you who are all old now, who do you think would look at you?" Now when his mother heard what he said, his words sank deep in her heart. The next morning Uken was exchanging promises with a girl friend, and the girl promised that she would come to him that day. Then Uken's mother devised a trick. She stripped off all her old skin and there she was with complexion as clear as long ago when she had been a girl. By the time the youth came back from his walk it was night. He found his mother lying on his sleeping place.

18. SOURCES: Primary source: Southall 1958:167–69; Secondary source: Edmunds and Dundes 1983:35–38. Reproduced by permission of Garland Publishing Co.

She was beautiful from head to floor, glistening with the oil she had used to anoint her body, and wearing beads of many kinds. There she was lying relaxed on the sleeping place. So when her son came and entered the hut his eye lit up at the thought that perhaps the girl who had made him promises had really come. And so he lay with his mother that night. At first light his mother went out and left him on the bed. She returned to her hut and put on her old skin. Then when morning came Uken got up and went to his mother's hut to ask her for food. She said, "Your mother, your mother, just now you were lying with your mother there—did you know that you have a mother?" When Uken heard his mother speaking to him in this way, rage seized him and he went back to his hut without a word. Next he got out his spear and his arrows. He whetted their blades keenly. Then he set out aimlessly into the bush, with his horn to his lips blowing on it the while.

> "Mother, you have dishonoured me, Mother you have
>   dishonoured me.
> To whom will my wife fall now? Mother you have
>   dishonoured me.
> To whom will my child fall now? Mother you have
>   dishonoured me.
> To whom will my granary fall now? Mother you have
>   dishonoured me."

So he went far away. He went and found a great tree, then he planted his spear and his arrows in the ground under the tree. And after that he climbed to the top of the tree and threw himself down on to the spear and it stabbed him to death. When he had died, then his body began to decay and when it had decayed completely, mushrooms sprouted from the spot. An old woman came to uproot the mushrooms and they said to her, "Ah! uproot us gently! Don't just break us!" The old woman uprooted the mushrooms and returned to her village with them. The mushrooms said, "Don't cook us! Just store us away in a pot." So the old woman stored them in a pot. Then the mushrooms rotted and bore maggots. The maggots changed into flies. The flies changed into baby rats, and those rats into a big mother rat. Then the rat turned into a baby boy. The child began to grow bonny until slowly he began to walk. The old woman was rearing him on cow's milk. He grew up and began to herd cattle. Little by little Uken became a youth just as he had been before. When Uken saw that he was full grown he began to consider: "What shall I do to make my people recognize me?" He told the old woman to brew beer, then he held a dance. This dance gathered together many people and his own folk also came to it. Then, when the dance was in full swing, Uken began to blow his horn, singing:

"Mother you have dishonoured me, Mother you have
    dishonoured me.
To whom will my wife fall now? Mother you have
    dishonoured me.
To whom will my child fall now? Mother you have
    dishonoured me.
To whom will my granary fall now? Mother you have
    dishonoured me."

When the people of Uken's home heard the way he blew his horn they said, "But this child is like our child Uken." Then they told him that he should go back with them, but he refused and said, "If you want me to go back with you to our home, you just go and kill my mother and I will go back with you tomorrow." Then those people went back and killed Uken's mother. The next day they came back to the dance. When the sun set and the dance was over they went back with Uken to their home and the old woman who had brought him up went with him also.

19. **USIKULUMI KAHLOKOHLOKO.** ZULU (SOUTH AFRICA)

It is said there was a certain king; he begat many sons. But he did not like to have sons; for he used to say it would come to pass, when his sons grew up, that they would depose him from his royal power. There were old women appointed to kill the sons of that king; so when a male child was born, he was taken to the old women, that they might kill him; and so they killed him. They did so to all the male children the king had.

He happened on a time to beget another son; his mother took him to the old women, concealing him in her bosom. She made presents to the old women, and besought them earnestly not to kill him, but to take him to his maternal uncle, for it was a son she loved exceedingly. The mother, then, besought the old women very much, and told them to suckle the child. They suckled him, and took him to his uncle, and left him there with his uncle.

It came to pass when he had become a young man that he liked to herd the cattle at his uncle's, and followed by the boys of his uncle's kraal; they respected and honoured him. It came to pass, when they were herding, he said to the boys, "Collect large stones, and let us heat them." They collected them, and made a heap. He said, "Choose also a fine calf, and let us kill it." They selected it from the herd they were watching. He told them to skin it;

---

19. SOURCES: Primary source: Callaway 1868:41–47; Secondary source: Edmunds 1985: 214–16. Edmunds, Lowell. *Oedipus: The Ancient Legend and Its Later Analogues.* The Johns Hopkins University Press, Baltimore/London, 1985.

they skinned it, and roasted its flesh joyfully. The boys said, "What do you mean by this?" He said, "I know what I mean."

It happened one day when they were herding, the officers of his father were on a journey, being sent by him; they said, "Who are you?" He did not tell them. They took him, without doubting, saying, "This child is like our king." They went with him, and took him to his father.

When they came to his father, they said to him, "If we tell you good news, what will you give us?" His father said to the officers, "I will give you cattle of such a colour, or of such a colour, or of such a colour." The officers refused saying, "No; we do not like theirs." There was a selected herd of black oxen, at which they hinted. He said, "What do you wish?" The officers said, "The herd of black oxen." He gave them. And so they told him, saying, "It happened in our journeying that we saw a child which is like one of yours." So then the father saw that it was indeed his son, and said, "Of which wife is he the child?" They who knew that she concealed the child said, "The daughter of So-and-So, your wife, your Majesty."

He assembled the nation, being very angry, and told them to take his son to a distance. The nation assembled; his mother and sister also came. The king told them to take away his son, and to go and put him in the great forest. For it was known there was in that forest a great many-headed monster which ate men.

They set out for that place. Many did not reach it; they became tired, and turned back again. The mother and sister and the king's son went, those three. The mother said, "I cannot leave him in the open country; I will go and place him where he is ordered to go." They went to the great forest; they arrived, and entered the forest, and placed him on a great rock which was in the midst of the forest. He sat down on it. They left him, and went back. He remained alone on the top of the rock.

It came to pass one day that the many-headed monster came, it coming out of the water. That monster possessed everything. It took the young man; it did not kill him; it took him, and gave him food, until he became great. It came to pass when he had become great, and no longer wanted anything, having also a large nation subject to him, which the many-headed monster had given him (for that monster possessed all things, and food and men), he wished to visit his father. He went with a great nation, he being now a king.

He went to his uncle; but his uncle did not know him. He went into the house; but neither did his uncle's people know him. His officer went to ask a bullock of the uncle; he said, "Usikulumi, the son of Uthlokothloko, says, 'Give him a fine bullock, that he may eat.'" When the uncle heard the name of Usikulumi, the son of Uthlokothloko, he started, and said, "Who?" The officer replied, "The king." The uncle went out to see him. He saw it was Usikulumi, the son of Uthlokothloko, indeed. He rejoiced greatly, and said,

"Yi, yi, yi!!!" sounding an alarm for joy, and said, "Usikulumi, the son of Uthlokothloko, has come!" The whole tribe of his uncle was assembled. His uncle gave him a part of a herd of oxen for his great joy, and said, "There are your oxen." A great feast was made; they ate and rejoiced because they saw him, for they did not know that they would ever see him again.

He passed onward, and went to his father's. They saw that it was Usikulumi, the son of Uthlokothloko. They told his father, saying, "Behold your son, whom you cast away in the great forest." He was troubled exceedingly. He collected the whole nation, and told them to take their weapons. All his people assembled. The father said, "Let Usikulumi, the son of Uthlokothloko, be killed." Usikulumi heard it; and went outside. The whole nation assembled. His father commanded him to be stabbed with a spear. He stood in an open space, and said, "Hurl your spears at me to the utmost." He said this because he was confident he should not die; although they hurled their spears at him a long time, even till the sun set, he should not die. He merely stood, until the sun set. They hurled their spears at him without having power to kill him. For he had the power of not dying; for that monster strengthened him, for it knew that he was going to his people, and that his father did not want his son; it knew, by his own wisdom, that they would kill Usikulumi, the son of Uthlokothloko, and gave him strength.

They were unable to pierce him with their spears. He said, "Are you worsted?" They said, "We are now worsted." He took a spear, and stabbed them all, and they all died. He took possession of the cattle; and departed with his army from that country with all the cattle. His mother too went with him and his sister, he being now a king.

20. HOW THE EARTH WAS PEOPLED. NGOMBE (AFRICA)

In the beginning there were no men on earth. The people lived in the sky with Akongo and they were happy. But there was a woman named Mbokomu who bothered everybody.

One day Akongo put the woman in a basket with her son and her daughter, some cassava, maize, and sugarcane and lowered the basket down to the earth.

The family planted a garden on earth and the garden flourished through their care.

One day the mother said to her son: "When we die there will be no one left to tend the garden."

"That can't be helped," the son replied.

"You must have children," the mother said.

---

20. SOURCES: Primary source: Smith 1961:60; Secondary source: Feldman 1963:37–39.

"How?" asked the son. "We are the only people here. Where shall I find a wife?"

"Your sister is a woman," his mother replied. "Take her and have children by her." But the son recoiled from his mother's suggestion. The mother insisted, however. "That, or die childless, with nobody to continue our work. You can only get children by your sister so go and take her."

In the end the son gave in and went to his sister. The sister yielded to him quite willingly and became pregnant.

One day the sister met a creature who looked like a man except that he was completely covered by hair. She was afraid but the creature spoke so kindly to her that after a while they became friends. One day the sister took her husband's razor and went out to look for the hairy man. When she found him she made him lie down and shaved him. Now he looked like a man. His name was Ebenga, meaning the beginner.

Ebenga bewitched the woman, so that when her child was born it brought witchcraft into the world. The child grew up under the spell of Ebenga. He practiced witchcraft and brought evil and sorrow to men.

In the course of time the brother and sister had other children. So the earth was peopled. But evil and witchcraft continued to the present.

21. **KAUHA.** !KUNG (AFRICA)

The wives lived in discontent for some time. Kauha was satisfied and fed them well, but they were discontented just the same. One day one of the wives said, "I think I'll go visit my family." Kauha refused, and said, "No, you're not: we're staying here. Why should we go visit them—they never visit us." So they stayed. But the wife grew restless. "How can I get away?" she wondered. One day when Kauha and his son went hunting, she simply ran off alone. The other wife sat in the camp alone and waited for her husband to return.

The wife who had left did not return. The other wife stayed at the camp alone, waiting for her husband. He was off hunting but he did not bring home anything for her to eat. Hunger began to work upon her, and she grew very thin. Soon she had no fat on her buttocks—they were nothing but skin.

One day Kauha killed a fat eland far from his camp, and came home at last to bring the news. "Hai? Where's my other wife?" he asked. "Oh, she's left," sniffed the wife who had stayed. "And you?" asked Kauha, "why do you look so terrible?" "Hunger, obviously," she replied. "Well, if you're go-

21. SOURCES: Primary source: Biesele 1975:266–70; Secondary source: Edmunds and Dundes 1983:39–42. Reproduced by permission of Garland Publishing Co.

ing to look like this I'm leaving," said Kauha. "You're probably just starving yourself so you'll have an excuse to leave me and run after other men. I'm leaving, and you'll just have to sit here. I'm not interested in a woman who's so thin. You're awfully thin and ugly and you don't interest me at all." With that, Kauha took his son and began packing up their belongings. The wife just sat there. Kauha packed all his things into a string carrying bag. As they were leaving, his son put out his hand and drew his mother to her feet. "Please, mother, follow us, I beg you," he said. So she walked secretly behind them when they left.

After they had walked a long while, father and son sat down to rest. The son sneaked to where his mother was and found her a comfortable place to sit. Kauha rested and ate something and then they traveled further. After a while the son asked his father, "Are we almost there?" "Don't worry—the meat is there. We'll come to it," answered Kauha.

When they came to the dead eland, Kauha and his son began cutting it up right away. Kauha skinned it and broke his body open. Then he took out its intestines. He dipped out the chyme with his cupped hands and dumped it on the ground. He was still dipping out the chyme when his son said to him, "Father, let me take the chyme and throw it away for you. I want to watch the dung beetles eat it." (The son wanted the chyme to smooth on the ground for his mother, so she would have a nice place to sit.) So the father gave it to him and the child sat his mother upon it. Then he came back. "Father!" he said, "Won't you give me that bit of fat so I can watch the dung beetles eat it?" Kauha cut out the piece of fat for him and he went and gave it to his mother to eat. The son went back and forth between his father and his mother. He spent the whole day taking bits of food to his mother one by one. He and his father would eat a little and then he would take something like the bladder and go to his mother. "I'm going to go play with the dung beetles and eat my meat over there," the son would say. Then he would go give whatever it was to his mother.

At last the sun hung low in the sky. Kauha said, "Since it's so late already, I think we'll just go to sleep and wait until morning to fetch water." "All right," said the son. He went and told his mother. Then they all went to sleep. The wife slept in one place and her husband and son slept together not far away. In the night the son went to check on his mother several times. In the morning Kauha went off to fetch water, leaving his son in their new camp. When he was gone, the son told his mother to come sit with him in the camp. Today she was fat, and *very* beautiful! She sat with her son in the camp as if she were a lovely python girl.

When a little time had passed, Kauha returned and saw her. "Hai? Is this my son who's sitting with such a beautiful woman? Who can it be?" he asked his son, "Has your mother returned?" "Yes, mother has come," he answered. "What has she been eating that makes her look so good?" "I don't know: she looked like this when she got here," he said.

Kauha dropped his water containers and ran to his wife. He climbed on top of her and right away he began screwing her very hard. Her son cried, "Hey! Didn't you nearly kill my mother with hunger, and then abandon her so that I had to feed her myself? Who do you think made her beautiful again? If you think you're going to screw her now, I'll fix you!" Kauha was still lying on top of his wife and refused to get off. "Father, give me your axe so I can sharpen it and eat the eland bones," said his son. "Hand me the whetstone too." All the while Kauha lay on top of his wife and continued to screw her. Suddenly . . . (snap!). The boy had chopped his father in two with the axe! He did it to get him off his mother. (He no longer wanted his mother to be his mother; he wanted to marry her.) Then he lifted up his father's body. He took the top half and threw it one way and threw the bottom half the other way. "When did you suddenly grow up?" asked his mother, as she sat up.

"Will you make a fire so we can warm ourselves, mother?" he asked. "Certainly, my son." "I'm not 'your son' any more." "Well, what am I going to call you now? How about 'my little brother'?" But he refused that name too. "My nephew?" But he refused again. "What am I going to call this child?" she wondered out loud. "My husband?" (Snap!) That was all he wanted. He jumped and ran to the fire. He was looking for *tutus*, these little black insects that smell bad and crawl around near the fire. When he saw some he lay down in their midst. He wanted them to bite his penis so it would swell up and he would be able to do what he wanted. Well, the *tutus* bit him nearly to death. His penis swelled up until it was enormous. It was so big he couldn't take his mother with it. He had spoiled his own chances! The things that went on long ago . . . ! This is what the old people tell, and this is what I have heard.

22. THE CHIEFTAIN'S SONS. TOGO-BASSARI (AFRICA)

T here was once a very rich and important chieftain who had six wives each of whom had borne him a son. He also had a young and very beautiful wife. The chieftain's six sons were already grown up. Every day they went to look after the chieftain's cows and oxen. One day they were tending the cows out in the fields. They had eaten yams. They were talking together.

The eldest son said: "For six days I would like to own all of my father's cows. Then, every day, I would have them led past me. Every day I would have one slaughtered, I would share out the meat, and use everything up.

---

22. SOURCE: Frobenius 1971:221–26.

Then, for all I care, I could die on the seventh day. But during the first six days I would like to do exactly as I please."

The second son said: "For six days I would like to own all of my father's corn and yams. Then every day I would summon all of the women from all the villages and every day I would order them to make food and brew beer and so use everything up in six days. Then, for all I care, I could die on the seventh day. But during the first six days I would like to do exactly as I please."

The third son said: "For six days I'd like to occupy my father's leather seat. I would summon all of the people. I would distribute gifts, I would have all disputes brought up before me, I would kill people and deal with everything in a manner such as in my opinion befits an important chieftain. I would ride, make war, and take prisoners. Then, for all I care, I could die on the seventh day. But during the first six days I would like to do exactly as I please."

The fourth son said: "For six days I would like to have all of the meat that my father's village could provide. During these six days, I would have everything slaughtered, cooked, and shared out. I would eat what I liked and make free with everything. Then, for all I care, I could die on the seventh day. But during the first six days, I would like to do exactly as I please."

The fifth son said: "For six days I would like to be in command of all of my father's young men. I would send for some of them and order them to dance. Some of them I would send hunting. Some of them I would send to work in the fields. Some of them I would send to war. Some of them I would sell, and anyone I did not fancy I would have put to death. Then, for all I care, I could die on the seventh day. But during the first six days I would like to do exactly as I please."

The sixth man said: "For six days I would like to live in a hut with my father's young wife. I would sleep with her in the morning, I would sleep with her in the afternoon, I would sleep with her at night. I would never let her out of my arms, even if it killed her. Then, for all I care, I could die on the seventh day. But during the first six days I would like to make love to this wife so often that I would not have any strength left."

A man had overheard all that the six brothers had been saying. He went and told the chieftain what he had learned. The chieftain sent for his sons and said to the eldest: "Take all my cows." To the second he said: "Take all my corn and my yams." To the third he said: "Take my place on the leather seat." To the fourth he said: "Take all the meat there is." To the fifth he said: "Take all the young men." To the sixth he said: "Take my young wife."

The six sons took everything that their father had given them in response to their wishes. For six days each son lived in accordance with his heart's desire. All of the chieftain's cows and oxen were slaughtered, all of his corn and yams were used up, all of his meat was boiled or roasted, all of his beer was drunk, all of his men were sent fighting, hunting, and dancing. Many of them were killed, sold, or driven away. Everything was turned upside down. The sixth son, however, shut himself up with the chieftain's young wife whom he held constantly embraced, while the young wife kept repeating: "Your penis is sweet! Your penis is sweet! Your penis is sweet!"

At the end of the six days all of the chieftain's possessions had been destroyed, all of his forces dispersed, and his peaceful relations with his neighbors disrupted. But meanwhile the chieftain had obtained six lions. He placed one lion outside each son's dwelling. The six lions were put there so that they might devour the six sons when they came out on the seventh day. When the six days were over, the eldest son came out and was devoured. When the six days were over, the second son came out and was devoured. When the six days were over, the third son came out and was devoured. When the six days were over, the fourth son came out and was devoured. When the six days were over, the fifth son came out and was devoured.

On the seventh day the sixth son, too, said: "Today is the seventh day. Today I shall die." The young wife said: "No, you must not die. We will escape. I will show the way." The young wife went to the far end of the hut where she lifted the straw thatch off the top of the wall. She said: "Come out with me this way." The young man climbed out with the young woman. The young man and the young woman walked for some distance. The young woman said: "Now we must kill a cow and cut off its four legs. They may well be of use to us." The young man killed a cow. They cut off the legs and went off with them.

When the fugitives had gone some way further the lion came up behind them. The lion had almost caught up with them. Then the fugitives threw it a cow's leg. The lion flung itself on the cow's leg and began to crunch it up. Meanwhile the fugitives hastened on their way. But as soon as the lion had finished eating the cow's leg, it set off in pursuit until it had almost caught up with them. Then the fugitives threw it the second cow's leg. The lion flung itself on the cow's leg and began to crunch it up. Meanwhile the fugitives hastened on their way. But as soon as the lion had finished eating the second cow's leg, it set off in hot pursuit until it had almost caught up with them. Then the fugitives threw it the third cow's leg. The lion flung itself on the cow's leg and began to crunch it up. Meanwhile the fugitives hastened on their way. But as soon as the lion had finished eating the third cow's leg, it set off in hot pursuit until it had almost caught up with them. The fugitives threw it the fourth cow's leg. The lion flung itself on the fourth cow's leg and began to crunch it up.

Meanwhile the fugitives had come to a river that could not be crossed, for it was wide and deep and there were no boats. But a young girl was walking on the far bank. She was Unji-bugara's daughter. The girl shouted across the river to the young man: "You cannot get across this river. But if you will marry me I will help you." The young man said: "Yes, I will marry you." The girl hurried away. She came back with her uncle whose beard was huge and long. The man threw the end of his beard across. The young man caught the end of the beard. The young man and the young wife that he abducted from his father's house got to the other side. Hardly had they got across than the young man's father arrived with his men. He had gone forth himself on hearing that his son and his young wife had succeeded in escaping the lion. But now the young man and the young woman had got across to the other side, and his father and the men he had with them could do nothing.

When the young man had reached the other side with the help of the old man's beard, the young girl said to him: "You promised that you would marry me." The young man said: "I shall gladly do so." The girl said: "Then I will take you to my father's farm. My father is a very important chieftain. He often kills people. Therefore you must remember what I tell you. My father's name is Unji-bugara. He has ten wives, nine of whom are good. Unjankann, however, is bad. My father always asks people which of his wives is the bad one. If you can point her out and say her name you will no longer be in danger." The young man arrived at the farm. The young girl pointed to a woman saying: "Look, that is Unjankann, my father's bad wife."

They appeared before Unji-bugara. Unji-bugara ordered food and drink to be brought and a hut to be prepared for them. Later he sent a message to the young man, saying "We will play *jworra* [a game played on a board] together." The young man came and played with Unji-bugara. Unji-bugara said: "I have ten wives one of whom is bad. If you cannot single her out I will have you beheaded. But if you succeed, you may slit my throat." The young man said: "I agree." Unji-bugara said: "Let all of my wives assemble." The ten wives came. Unji-bugara said: "Tell me which of them she is." After looking at each wife in turn, the young man pointed to the tenth and said: "This is the bad one amongst your wives and her name is Unjankann." Unji-bugara said: "You are right. Slit my throat." The young man slit Unji-bugara's throat.

The young man fulfilled his promise and married Unji-bugara's daughter. In addition he inherited all ten of Unji-bugara's wives and Unji-bugara's thousand cows. He was now a rich man and a very important chieftain. His cows were very large and white. Amongst them was one cow that was large as a hill and completely white all over.

Unji-bugara's daughter became pregnant and bore her husband a son. The young man's first wife also became pregnant and gave birth to a child. Both the children grew and learned to walk. They played together. Unji-bugara's daughter's child said: "The white cow's tail belongs to me!" The other child said: "Why do you say that? I want the tail." The first child said: "No, the tail is mine!"

The children's father heard this exchange. He gave orders that the big white cow should be slaughtered. He had its tail cut off. He had the severed end bound with brightly colored leather, in the style of the Dagomba leather workers. Then he took it and called the two children to him. He said to them: "You were quarreling about the white cow's tail. You must not quarrel. Now I am going to throw the tail into the air and whoever catches it when it comes down can keep it." The two children stood there ready to jump or run after it. The father threw the tail of the large cow that was completely white all over high up into the air. Up and up went the tail. The tail turned into the moon and its hairs turned into stars.

And since that time cows have never been as big as they once used to be.

23. **THE MOTHER'S BOY.** MUNTSHI (AFRICA)

A man married. His wife became pregnant. His wife bore a child and the child was a boy. The wife took the child out to the farm with her. The child grew up on the farm. He always worked alongside his mother. The child grew into a strapping youth. The youth's mother always cooked his meals for him and the youth himself always worked on the farm. The youth grew big and strong and his mother went on cooking for him and he went on working on his mother's farm.

Some people came to the farm. The people saw the youth. The people said: "That is a fine, strapping youth!" The people asked the youth: "Do you not want to take a wife?" The youth said: "No. All I want is my food, and what my mother gives me is both good and ample."

One day the father came to the farm where the youth was living with his mother. The father said to the youth: "Do you not want to take a wife so that you can beget a son? Come back with me now to the village!" The father took the youth back with him to his village. The father shaved his son's head. When he finished, he gave him many beautiful beads. He put strings of beads around his neck. He wound strings of beads around his toes and ankles. He put fine bracelets on his arms. He rubbed his body with red dye. He gave him a new loin-cloth. Then his father said: "Now go and look for a wife with whom you can beget a child."

The youth went. The youth walked about the place and looked at the girls. He took a girl and brought her home to his father. He said to his father: "I want to marry this girl." His father said: "That is good." The father led his son and the girl to a hut. The father said: "Go in there with the girl and lie

23. SOURCE: Frobenius 1971: 230–31.

with her so that she becomes pregnant." The youth went into the hut with the girl. But when he had laid the girl down on the bed, he came out again and hurried back to his mother's farm. He said to his mother: "Mother, I am hungry. Cook me a good meal." The mother cooked a meal for the youth. Then he stayed with her.

The newly married girl ran out of the hut. The girl went hurrying to the youth's father and said: "Your son did not lie with me. He took me into the hut and then he hurried out again." The father got up and went. He went to his wife's farm. He said to his wife: "Is my son here?" The mother said: "Yes, your son is here. Last night he came and said: 'Mother, I am hungry. Cook me a good meal!' Then I cooked him a good meal. He ate it and stayed here."

The father said: "My son got married yesterday. But he did not lie with his wife last night. He came running to you and asked for food. Something must be done. I think that the next time he asks for food you must give him terrible food or none at all. Then he will go hurrying back to his wife." The mother said: "I will do as you say." The father went back to town.

Presently the youth came to his mother and said: "Mother, I am hungry. Cook me a good meal!" The mother said: "Did you not marry a wife yesterday?" The youth said: "Yes, I did marry a wife yesterday." The mother said: "If you married a wife yesterday, then go to her and ask her to prepare you a meal." The youth went. The youth went to his father and said: "My mother will not give me food any more." The father said: "Did you not get married yesterday? Did you lie with your wife?" The youth said: "No, I did not lie with my wife." The father said: "Then go to your wife and lie with her. Then tell her to cook a good meal for you. Then your wife, too, will be able to satisfy your appetite."

The youth went. He lay with his wife. Afterwards his wife washed herself and cooked him a good meal. The youth watched her at her work. The young wife brought him food. The youth ate it. When he had eaten enough he said to his wife: "Come indoors. I want to lie with you again!" Not long afterwards the young wife became pregnant. She gave birth to a son.

A father should bring his son up to be a man and a husband, for if he stays with his mother he will only learn to eat.

24. **A BOY WHOM THE GIRLS LOVED.** MUNTSHI (AFRICA)

A man married a woman. The woman bore two children. One was a girl and the other a boy. The children grew and throve. When the girl was fully grown, the father lay with his own daughter. When the boy was fully grown he gave him a wife.

---

24. SOURCE: Frobenius 1971:226–30.

The man had a big farm. His son and his slave worked on the farm. A small boy hiding nearby overheard what the two were saying. The youth and the slave did not know it. The youth had nothing to eat. He said to the slave: "I am hungry. I would like a dish of beans today." The slave, too, had had nothing to eat. He said to the youth: "I am hungry. I would like a dish of chicken today." The boy had heard what they said. He ran to the house of the youth's father and said: "Your son has said that he would like a dish of beans. Your slave has said that he would like a dish of chicken." The father said: "Very well." The father ordered a dish of beans and a dish of chicken to be prepared.

When the youth and the slave had finished working on the farm they set off for home. They found the man at home. In front of the man were two covered gourds. The man asked his son: "What would you like to eat today?" The son said: "Today I would like a dish of beans." The father gave his son a gourd. The son took off the cover. There were beans inside. The man asked the slave: "What would you like to eat today?" The slave said: "Today I would like a dish of chicken." The man gave the slave the other gourd. The slave took off the cover. There was chicken inside.

The youth said to the man: "O father, as you are granting every wish today, there is something else that I want." The father asked: "What is it?" The youth said: "I want to lie with my sister!" The father said: "But that is not done! You cannot lie with your own sister!" The youth said: "There are other things that are not usually done. You lie with your own daughter." The father said: "I will not permit you to lie with your sister!" The son said: "But I want to lie with my sister!"

The father said: "That you will not do!" Taking hold of the youth, his father led him into a house. The father locked the door behind him. On his way back to his own house, the father met his daughter. The daughter said: "Father, I would like to sleep with my brother!" The father said: "I will not permit my son to sleep with my daughter!" The daughter said: "But I want to sleep with my brother!"

The father said: "In that case I shall shut you both up in the same house." Then the father took hold of his daughter and led her to the house where his son was already confined. He locked both of his children in together.

Now the son had a friend called Hingaga. Hingaga came to visit his friend. Hingaga searched the whole farmstead but could not find his friend. Hingaga went to the youth's father and asked him: "Where is my friend? I have been looking for him and cannot find him." The father said: "I have locked up your friend together with his sister in that house." Hingaga said: "Can I perhaps visit my friend?" The father said: "You may visit him just once more." The father ordered the door to be unlocked for Hingaga. Hingaga went inside.

Hingaga asked his friend: "What is wrong?" The youth said: "I wanted to lie with my sister. My sister wanted to sleep with me. I told my father. My father locked us up in here. Tomorrow my father will put us to death." Hingaga said: "I do not think that you will have to die. I will show you how you can get away with your sister." Hingaga began digging inside the hut. First Hingaga dug a shaft. Then Hingaga dug an underground passage that led right under the village, only coming to the surface on the far side of it.

When Hingaga had finished the tunnel he hurried back along it to the hut where the youth and his sister were confined. Hingaga said to the youth: "Come with me. Now we can all leave together. I will go ahead. You and your sister can follow me." Hingaga went down the shaft and then along the underground passage. The youth and his sister followed after him. Beyond the village Hingaga emerged from the tunnel. Beyond the village the youth and his sister emerged from the tunnel.

The youth and his sister hurried away as fast as they were able. When they had been walking through the bush for some time the youth was bitten by a snake. He fell down dead. The girl screamed and wept. Presently a Jukum girl came through the bush. She asked the sister: "Why are you crying? Why are you screaming?" The sister said: "My husband and I were walking through the bush. My husband was bitten by a snake and now he is dead!" The Jukum girl said: "I have medicine with me. I can restore the young man to life and health. But when I have done so he will have to take me with him as his wife." The first wife said: "Bring him back to life and health and then he will do as you wish." The Jukum brought out her medicine. She put the medicine under the young man's nose.

The young man woke up. He looked about him. The young man said: "What is happening?" His first wife said: "You were bitten by a snake. You were dead. I was sitting here and crying. Then this Jukum girl came along. The Jukum girl had medicine with her. The Jukum girl said: 'I can restore the young man to life and health. But when I have done so he will have to take me with him as his wife.' Then she brought you back to life and health." The young man said: "Very well. I will continue on my way with two wives."

The youth set out with his two wives. With the two of them he went further and further into the bush. They walked a great distance. They came to a river. They could not find any place where they could cross the river. They went up and down the river bank. At last the Jukum woman caught sight of a fishing boat. There was a girl in it. The Jukum woman said: "Take us across to the other side." The fisher girl brought her boat closer to them and said: "Who am I to take across?" The Jukum woman said: "There are three of us; the young man here and we, his wives." The fisher girl looked at the young man. The fisher girl said: "I will ferry you across, but when I have done so, this young man here must take me with him as his wife." The young man said: "Very well. Then I shall continue on my way with three wives!"

The fisher girl ferried the young man and his two wives across the river.

When she had done so, the young man went on his way with his three wives. When they had covered a very great distance they came to a big city. The *toro* [king] of the city saw the young man and his three wives. The *toro* said to his servants: "This young man has three beautiful young wives. I will take them all away from him." The *toro* said: "Take a big crock of beer for the young man's wives and a small one for the young man. You must poison the beer in the small crock." The servants did as he had told them. The servants brought the big crock containing good beer to the young man's wives. They brought the small crock with the poisoned beer to the young man himself. When the beer arrived, the Jukum woman tasted the beer in the big crock. The Jukum woman said: "This beer is good." The Jukum woman tasted the beer in the small crock. She spat it out, saying: "This beer is poisoned. The *toro* of this city is trying to poison our husband. Let us drink the beer from the big crock." Thereupon she emptied the beer out of the small crock and they all four drank out of the big one. When the servants returned to the king, they said: "The wives have thrown the poisoned beer away. They and their husband are drinking the good beer."

The next day the *toro* sent for the young man and said to him: "If you can tell me which is my first wife, I will not kill you. But if you fail to do so, then I shall kill you." When all of the people were assembled, the *toro* sent for his wives. The *toro*'s wives were all lined up in a long row. When all of the people and all of the wives were there, the *toro* said: "Now, which is my first wife? Can you tell me or can you not?" The young man looked along the row of women. He did not know which of them was the first wife. The king's first wife, however, was thinking to herself: "The *toro* must be wanting to kill this young man. I would rather be his wife than the *toro*'s wife. I will give the young man a sign." The *toro*'s first wife signalled with her hand. The young man saw it. The young man went up to the first wife and said: "This is the *toro*'s first wife."

Everybody began to shout: "The young man is right! The young man is right! Do not kill the young man! Kill the *toro*, for he is wicked!" Everybody ran towards the *toro*. They caught hold of him. They took him into the bush. They killed the *toro*.

Then they made the young man their king.

25. **THE LOVE BETWEEN BLOOD.** NUPE (AFRICA)

A young woman became pregnant. She gave birth to a son. At his birth he was already a grown man. The son said to his mother: "Take these three thousand cowries. Go out and fetch me a wife so that I can sleep with

25. SOURCE: Frobenius 1971:239–46.

her." The mother took the three thousand cowries. She went out to fetch a wife. She met a man. She owed the man three thousand cowries. The man saw the money in her hand. The man took the three thousand cowries away from her, saying: "You owe me these three thousand cowries. I will take the money." The woman said: "Do not take the money. Leave me the money. The money does not belong to me. It belongs to my son. My son sent me out to fetch a wife for him to sleep with." The man said: "That is nothing to me!" The man kept the money. The man went off with the money.

The mother went home. The son asked her: "Have you brought me a wife?" The mother said: "In five days' time a wife will be here to sleep with you." When five days had gone by the son asked: "Where is the wife that is going to sleep with me?" The mother said: "The wife will come to you to-night." Now the mother had just been having her period. That evening the mother washed herself thoroughly. She put on freshly laundered clothes. In the evening the son lay down on his bed. When it was dark the mother went in to him. The man asked: "Who is there?" The mother did not answer. The son wanted to blow on the embers of his fire. Seizing the water pot, the mother poured water on the fire. Then the mother lay down on a mat near the door.

When it was past midnight the son rose and went over to the woman who was lying near the door of his house. He lay with the woman. He lay with his mother. Then he went back and lay down again on his bed. Towards the morning the woman got up. She left the house. She went out. The son followed her. The woman did not know it. The woman went towards her hut. The son saw that it was his mother's hut. The son called out: "Mother! Mother!" The woman screamed. The son saw that it was his mother. The son said: "I have lain with my own mother!"

When day came the son went to see his friend. He said to his friend: "I gave my mother three thousand cowries. My mother was to find me a wife to sleep with. My mother did not bring me a wife. I grew impatient. Yesterday I asked my mother what had happened to the wife I wanted to sleep with. My mother said I should have her that night. During the night a woman came to me. The woman did not speak. She poured water on the embers of my fire. She slept in my house. Towards morning I lay with her. When it was almost dawn the woman went out. I followed her. The woman went towards my mother's hut. I called after the woman. She ran away. I saw that it was mother. I have lain with my own mother. Do not tell anyone. You are my friend. I had to tell you about it. Do not tell anyone. Nobody must know." The friend said: "I will not tell anyone."

The son had lain with his mother just after her period was over. The mother became pregnant and at the end of three months her belly grew big. People said: "The woman is pregnant. Who did she sleep with?" People asked the man's friend. They said: "The woman is pregnant. Who did she sleep with?" The friend said: "The son lay with his mother. You must not tell anyone." A few days later the son was walking through the town. He met a man. The man said: "Go away from here! You have lain with your own mother!" The son went on his way. He passed another man. The man said: "Go away from here! You have lain with your own mother!" The son hurried back to his house. He packed up his things. He ran out of the house. He ran out of the town. The son ran through the Nupe country. The son ran through the Hausa country. The son came to Kano. In Kano the son went to a *mallem*. The son said to the *mallem*: "Be my father and my mother, I beseech you! Let me stay with you!" The *mallem* said: "Very well!" The *mallem* said to his first wife: "This youth has asked me to be father and mother to him. Look after him!" The wife said: "Very well." The son remained with the *mallem*.

Nine months after the son had lain with his mother, the mother gave birth to a child. The child was a girl. The child grew and throve. The girl played with other children. When the girl was grown up, the other girls said to her: "Go away! Before you were born, your brother lay with your mother!" The girl was ashamed. The next day the other girls said to her: "Go away! Before you were born your brother lay with your mother!" The girl was ashamed. The girl packed up her things. The girl left home.

The girl wandered through the Hausa country. The girl came to Kano. The girl came to Kano marketplace. In the marketplace was the wife of the *mallem* who had taken the mother's son into his house. The girl said to the *mallem*'s wife: "Will you be my mother?" The woman said to the girl: "What has happened to you?" The girl said: "When my mother gave birth to my brother he was already full-grown. My mother had no wife for him. My mother's son gave her three thousand cowries with which to get him a wife. He wanted to sleep with a woman. The mother went off with the money. She met a man to whom she owed three thousand cowries. The man took the money away from her. My brother grew impatient. My mother went to my brother in the night. The son lay down with his mother. The mother had just had her period. The mother became pregnant. I was born. All the other girls shouted after me: 'Go away! Before you were born your brother lay with your mother!' I was ashamed. I packed up my things. I ran away. I came here. I beseech you to be my mother!" The *mallem*'s wife took the girl home with her. She said to the *mallem*: "Today a young girl came to me. The girl asked me to be her mother. I took the girl with me." The *mallem* said: "Very well."

After a time the *mallem* said to his wife: "Now, I have this young man who once upon a time asked me to be both a father and mother to him. And you have the girl who asked you to be a mother to her. I have no wife for this man. You have no husband for the girl. Should we not marry them to each other?" The wife said: "As you wish." Thereupon the *mallem* and his wife married the mother's son to the girl.

Two months after the mother's son and the girl had gotten married, the mother's son said to the girl: "When my mother bore me I was already full-grown. My mother had no wife for me. I gave my mother three thousand cowries with which to get a wife. I wanted to sleep with a woman. My mother went out with the money. She met a man to whom she owed three thousand cowries. The man took the money away from her. I grew impatient. My mother came to me during the night. I lay with my mother. My mother had just had her period. My mother became pregnant. Everyone called out after me: 'Go away! You have lain with your own mother!' Then I was ashamed and ran away. Then I came here. I asked the *mallem* to be both father and mother to me. The *mallem* took me in. The *mallem* gave you to me as my wife. That is how it was."

The young wife said: "When my mother gave birth to my brother he was already full-grown. My mother had no wife for him. My mother's son gave her three thousand cowries with which to get him a wife. He wanted to sleep with a woman. The mother went out with the money. She met a man to whom she owed three thousand cowries. The man took the money away from her. My brother grew impatient. My mother went to my brother in the night. The son lay with his mother. The mother had just had her period. The mother became pregnant. I was born. All the other girls shouted after me: 'Go away! Before you were born your brother lay with your mother!' I was ashamed. I packed up my things. I ran away. I came here. I met the *mallem*'s wife. I asked the *mallem*'s wife to be a mother to me. The *mallem*'s wife took me in. The *mallem* gave me to you as your wife. That is how it was."

The mother's son asked his wife: "What town did you come from?" The wife told him the name of the town. It was the town from which he himself had come. Then the mother's son knew that he had married his mother's daughter. The mother's son knew that he had married his own daughter. His wife fell asleep. The mother's son packed up all his things. The mother's son quietly opened the door. The mother's son hastened away.

The mother's son went a long way away. He went further and further. The mother's son arrived in Mecca. The mother's son hurried to the imam. The mother's son said to the chief imam: "I was a grown man when my mother bore me. I gave my mother money to fetch me a wife. A man took the money away from my mother. My mother came into my house in the night. I lay with my mother. I saw that I had lain with my mother. I told my friend. The people heard that I had lain with my mother. The people hurled insults at me. I was ashamed. I ran away. I fled to Kano and took refuge with a *mallem*.

I had lain with my mother just after her period. My mother became pregnant. She gave birth to a daughter. The girl grew up. The people hurled insults at the girl. The girl was ashamed. The girl ran away. The girl fled to Kano and took refuge with the *mallem*'s wife. The *mallem* gave me the girl as my wife. I married the girl. I have lain with my mother. I have lain with my mother's daughter. What will become of me?"

The chief imam said: "Nothing can be done to help you. When you come to die the great fire awaits you." The mother's son said: "Can nothing at all be done to help me?" The chief imam said: "No, nothing at all can be done to help you." The mother's son said: "Is there no chance that it might be otherwise?" The chief imam said: "Should an old, dead branch which has not borne a single leaf for three whole years once again bring forth leaves and twigs, then it will be otherwise." The mother's son heard what he said. The mother's son went away.

The mother's son said to himself: "When I die the great fire awaits me. It cannot be otherwise. A branch that has borne no leaves for three whole years cannot bring forth twigs and leaves. It will never be otherwise." The mother's son went into the bush. The mother's son cut himself a staff. Its wood was hard and dry. The mother's son went along the road that leads from Kano to Mecca. The mother's son lay in wait beside the road. A merchant came along it, carrying goods from Kano to Mecca. The mother's son leapt out and killed the man with his staff. The mother's son took the murdered man's load and carried it to his house. The mother's son went back to the road. He lay in wait beside the road. He killed many people who were travelling with their loads from Kano to Mecca. The mother's son took all their goods to his house. For three years the mother's son lived beside the road from Kano to Mecca. For three years he murdered the merchants who travelled along it by striking them dead with his staff.

In Kano there was a rich *Madugu*. He had a beautiful young wife. The *Madugu* wanted to go to Mecca with his wares. A young man in Kano saw his wife. He wanted to possess the wife. He went to the *Madugu* and said: "Have you any need of a porter to carry your load to Mecca?" The *Madugu* said: "Certainly I would have use for a porter to carry my load to Mecca." The young man said: "I will go with you as porter. The *Madugu* said: "Very well."

The *Madugu*, his beautiful wife, and the porter set off for Mecca. They reached the spot at which the mother's son was lying in wait with his staff. At this spot the *Madugu*'s beautiful young wife fell to the ground. She was dead. The *Madugu* said to the porter: "Carry my load as far as the next village. Then come back here and help me bury my young wife. I will stay with her in the meantime." The young man said: "I only became your porter so that I could be with your beautiful young wife. Now you can carry your load yourself. I will go no further with you. I shall stay with the corpse." The *Madugu* said: "I beseech you to carry my load to the nearest village and then come back and help me." The porter said: "No, I will not! I do not want to have anything more to do with you!" The *Madugu* said: "Many have already been robbed of their loads in this part of the bush. Help me to carry my load away!" The young man said: "Help yourself!" The *Madugu* put the load on his head. He hurried with his load to the nearest village.

When the *Madugu* had gone away with his load, the young man threw himself down beside the corpse of the beautiful woman. He flung himself on top of the beautiful young woman. He made love to her. The young man made love to the corpse of the beautiful woman. The mother's son was lying in the bush with his staff. The mother's son leapt out of the bush. The mother's son leapt out upon the young man. The mother's son cried: "How can you make love to the corpse of a dead woman?" Seizing his staff, the mother's son killed the young man. Then the mother's son buried the corpse of the beautiful young wife. He did not bury the corpse of the young man.

The mother's son went back to his house. He lay down in his house. He went to sleep. While he was asleep the people from all around came to the spot. They entered the house. They went up to the mother's son. They said: "This is the man who murders people on their way from Kano to Mecca. Let us take him prisoner." They took him to Mecca. They brought him before the chief imam.

The chief imam saw the mother's son. The chief imam said: "This man lay with his own mother. This man married his mother's daughter. This man married his own daughter. This man has murdered and robbed many people seeking to travel from Kano and Mecca. Put him to death!" The chief imam had spoken. Men came to put the mother's son to death. Then a leaf fluttered down out of the sky. The leaf came to rest at the imam's feet. The imam picked up the leaf. There was writing on the leaf. The imam read what was written on the leaf. The writing on the leaf said: "The mother's son lay with his mother. The mother's son did not know that it was his mother. The mother's son fled. The mother's son married his mother's daughter. The mother's son did not know that it was his mother's daughter. The mother's son married his own daughter. He lay with his own daughter. He did not know that it was his own daughter. The mother's son fled. The mother's son came to Mecca. The mother's son came to the chief imam. The chief imam said to him: 'Nothing can be done to help you. When you come to die the great fire awaits you.' The mother's son said: 'Is there no chance that it might be otherwise?' The chief imam said: 'Should an old, dead branch which has not borne a single leaf for three whole years once again bring forth leaves and twigs, then it will be otherwise.' The mother's son went into the bush. He cut himself a staff. Its wood was hard and dry. The mother's son went along the road that leads from Kano to Mecca. He killed many people with his staff. He buried them. A young man came along and made love to the corpse of a young woman lying in the road. The mother's son killed him. The mother's son buried the young woman's corpse. Go and look at his staff which for three years has borne no leaves."

The people hastened to the place. On the staff there were leaves and twigs. The chief imam said: "Help has come for the mother's son." The mother's son was set free. Everyone congratulated the mother's son. The mother's son remained in Mecca. Three months later the chief imam died. Then the people made the mother's son chief imam.

26. CHILD OF THE VALLEY. HAYA (AFRICA)

Now then, I go and I see.
    I see a woman
bears children of her own,
    a boy and a girl . . .
    two children . . .
Now those two children take goats to pasture . . .
While pasturing the goats . . .
    they lie with one another.
When you come to see the girl, look, a belly.
You children, what have you done? They had a big rock there.
    They had looked it over and said, "When the child is born,
    we'll put him in there."
The child was carried
    and when it was born, it was born
    in the fields, and they kept it there.
Now the rock
    rose up, and below there was a hole.
They cut grass for the infant, and whatever else [it needed]
    they did for it.
They put it in there.

Now they come home.
They find their mother has already cooked. The food was ready,
    they ate, and they finished.
When they had finished eating,
    when they had finished eating,

---

26. SOURCE: Seitel 1980:91–94, as told by Ms. Kokubelwa Ishabakaki. Reproduced by permission of Dr. Peter Seitel.

they wrap up some food in a package and take it along—
the food of their parents—to eat in the fields.
They say, "Now the goats don't return at lunchtime. They stay
the whole day."
"Yes, they stay the whole day."
The girl stands by the rock.
(sings)   "Little mountain, little mountain, child of the valley,
Of anthills that are spotted,
Of termite hills that are red,
Come and see, little milk-fed one, little father.
Come and see, little one of the valley."
"E-e-eh [child's cry]
E-e-eh"
She picks up the things she covered the infant with, takes it out, and gives it
her breast. It nurses.
She goes.
One day. In the morning she returns.
And whenever she comes, she stands by the rock and calls the same way. In
the morning they come and call. In the morning they nurse it.
                                                                    Now
one day an old woman comes cutting grass [for the floor
of a house] . . .
Now, they . . .
come . . .
to take goats to pasture.
The old woman stoops in the grass. Now they stand there.
The old woman's back is bent as she ties up
her bundles of grass.
Now the girl stands by the rock.
"Little mountain, little mountain, child of the valley,
Of anthills that are spotted,
Of termite hills that are red,
Come and see, little milk-fed one, little father.
Come and see, little one of the valley."
"E-e-eh
E-e-eh"
The old woman cocks her ear like this.
She keeps quiet.
The girl takes out the rock
and picks up what she used to
cover the infant. She goes inside and nurses her child.
She finishes.

They round up the goats and they take them here and there.
They judge the hour
     to go to nurse.
The old woman says, "I'd better spread my grass to dry
     and look more closely at what I saw."

They return and stand at their rock. They call.
They nurse and finish nursing. The old woman ties up her grass
     and goes home.
When she comes to their mother, she says, "Bojo,"
     she says, "what I saw . . ."

She says, "Tomorrow we'll go to cut grass."

The mother says, "Mh?" Then she says, "E-e-h" [first she
     questions, then she agrees]. She says, "But what
     will I wear?" [so as not to be recognized]. She says,
     "I'll give you my leather skirt."
She gives her the leather skirt. [The next day] she leaves while everyone is
     still at home.
Before they had gotten up, and while the children are going
     to untie the goats,
     the woman is the first one out there.
Among the rocks she cuts and cuts grass. The old woman
     also cuts and cuts.
Now when they came and stood by the rock,
       "Little mountain, little mountain, child of the valley,
       Of anthills that are spotted,
       Of termite hills that are red,
       Come and see, little milk-fed one, little father.
       Come and see, little one of the valley."
       "E-e-h
       E-e-h"
"IY"
    THE WOMAN SAYS, "WHAT'S THIS?
WHILE IN THIS PLACE, HAVE THEY BORNE A CHILD
    AND HIDDEN IT AWAY?
SO THAT'S WHY I SEE HER BREASTS BECOME HEAVY.
    SHE HAS A CHILD HERE!"
She goes home . . .
She hits her husband with the news . . .
The husband comes and stands at the rocks. They come
     and call . . .

The child cries . . .
When they open it, look, a child.

The parents stay there and wait. The children round up
    the goats and take them.
The father asks, "Whose child is that?"
"The girl
    and her brother."
They go and find a watery place among the papyrus stalks.
In a reedy swamp like the one at Kyabagenzi.

It was the final act. [Literally, "You did not see the danger." The girl, her
    brother, and their child were drowned in the swamp.]
When I had seen these things . . .
I said, "Let me go and report to them." It's finished. What is it you say,
    "The news of long ago"?

27. MUHAMMED OTHMAN, THE SULTAN'S SON.

KAMALAB ABBASIYA (AFRICA)

They say that there was a boy whose father loved him dearly. He was born
to him after a long period of sterility and the father made a big roofed
courtyard for him, and put him in it. He had a female servant to look after him.
She even took his morsels of bread for him and rolled them for eating. She also
picked off pieces of meat and gave them to him. In a short time, the boy grew
to be a big man, and the horse grew with him. One day, the slave brought to
her master the meat with its bones, and milk with froth, and bread not ready
for eating. "This is food as it is seen outside," she said. The boy said to his slave:
"Bring me the horse to go out with the boys." Then there came a gazelle which
was owned by a nomad girl. The boy pursued the gazelle until he reached the
place of its owner. The girl came out, and when the boy saw her, he was struck
dumb. "Should I give you water?" she said. But he did not reply. "Should I give
you bread?" she said. But he did not reply. Then he returned to his father, still
dumbstruck. His father could not find out anything from him, until he wrote
down where the girl's people were for his father. His father, who was Sultan, at
once said to him: "Let us go to her."

The Sultan and his son went to the girl's family and asked for her hand.
The reply was: "We warn you that we are very busy; it would be better for

27. SOURCE: Al-Shahi and Moore 1978:151–55. © Ahmed Al-Shahi and F. C. T. Moore
1978. Reprinted from *Wisdom from the Nile* translated by Ahmed Al-Shahi and F. C. T.
Moore (1978) by permission of Oxford University Press.

you to leave us." But the boy's heart was set on the girl. Well, to cut a long story short, they married the girl to him, and then the man said: "I have many sheep and goats, and your land would not be sufficient for them." "Not at all," came the reply, "there is enough land, and no one will enter it, either slave or free." So the contract was completed, and they came in from outside, and were given the island.

Then there came an old woman, a bastard, carrying a pot containing beer. Now the boy was throwing stones, and one of them fell into the pot. The old woman said to him: "Muhammed Othman, I shall turn the tables on you." She went to the nomads and said to them: "Do you realize that the Sultan's son whom you are getting is an idiot?" The nomads took their daughter and went away. Now when the girl was playing *sija*, she wrote a note to him, saying that if he didn't catch up with her family within seven days, they would marry her to someone else.

The boy found this note, took money from his father, and set off after them. On the way, he found some people holding on to a coffin to prevent it being buried until they should recover the money owed to them by the dead man. Muhammed Othman paid the money and was about to leave when the people prevented him. They married the dead man's daughter to him.

They said that there were two roads, one difficult and one easy. The boy took the difficult road. They say there was a woman blocking the road. People were afraid of her, and she had cut off the heads of ninety-nine men. This time, when the woman came, she found Muhammed Othman lying in her court-yard; now Muhammed Othman had put some grease on his sword. "Who is this cavalier," she said, "resting in the house of a cavalier who has killed ninety-nine men?" "Don't be proud," said the boy, "come in and meet me." "Come and wrestle," said the woman, "and the one who throws the other shall dis-embowel him." Muhammed Othman made no obstacle. First, they wrestled, and he said: "This is for your shade." The second time, he said: "This is for your water," and the third time: "This is for your food." On the fourth round, he was on the point of killing her, when she cried out: "I'm a woman!" At this, he cried: "May God fail me if I do not leave you be." "Now that I am known to be a woman," she said, "I shall not leave you unless you marry me." So he married her, and afterwards she went with her slave, and after two days they reached a settlement of nomads. There they were met by a female slave. "Did some nomads come here a week ago?" they asked. "They did," she replied, "and tomorrow is their daughter's wedding." He took a jar, put his ring in it, and said to her: "Take this water to her and say: 'Muhammed Othman, your master, says that you must drink this holy water.'" The girl did drink the water, and she found the ring. She said to the slave: "Take me to him." The slave took her, and went to him. During the night, he took her, and left with their slaves. They walked all night, and in the morning they rested.

The nomads followed them, but the wife and her slave repelled the nomads and sent them away while the husband was asleep. When he awoke, he found his wife in tears, and asked what was the matter. She said: "My brother told me that he was going to kill me." After this, they went to the wife who was a highway robber, and spent two days with her. "Everything that lives I take and sustain, but what is dead I leave where it is." They packed up, and travelled until they reached the daughter of the blacksmith—of the man who died. The woman who was a robber said to him: "Come and beat me, so that we may take your wife. Say to them that you want to kill me because I kill people." When they met him they intervened between the two, and the three wives left together. When they reached home, they settled outside the village.

The Sultan and his minister came to visit the boy and his wives. Well now, the Sultan was taken by the beauty of the girls, and he declared that he was looking for a ruse by which he could kill the boy and take his wives. An old lady in the village, a real she-devil and clever as well, told them to put poisoned nails in his path, and make sure that when the boy came to his father's house he would not go in wearing his slippers.

But early in the morning the nomad girl was reading her husband's palm, and she said to him: "When you go to your father, do not enter barefooted to see him." The next day, the old woman said to them: "Poison his chair." Again, when the next day came, the nomad girl was reading her husband's palm, and she said to her husband: "When you go to your father's house do not sit in the chair which you are offered, but sit in your father's chair." On the third day, they poisoned his cup. But the nomad girl said to him: "On the third day, do not drink the cup which you are offered, when you take coffee, but take your father's cup."

The father declared that this solution was useless. They must look for another. One day, the nomad girl forgot to read her husband's palm. They were joking and wrestling with him and said: "Why can't you be thrown?" He replied: "To get the better of me, a man must take me by my tuft of hair." At once, they took hold of his tuft of hair, and he found their hands all over him. They pierced his eyes, and threw him under a tree. There, small birds came and settled on him, and one said: "This is the Sultan's son. It was his father's wish that his wives should pierce his eyes." Another replied: "His medicine is in my liver and in your lung." With his dying breath, the boy caught one, slaughtered it, and rubbed his eyes with its liver. By the grace of God, his eyes opened.

Then he went and stayed with a blacksmith, who gave him food and drink for a month, and then filled a saddle-bag with earth and said to him: "Throw this on your back. If you can do it, you are well. If you can't, stay longer." The boy threw the saddle-bag, and his hands did not bleed.

When he left, only the procession of the bridegroom was left. His father wanted to marry his wives. So the boy took a lame horse from the black-smith, and left. By palmistry the robber woman found out that he was coming. She sent him his horse and his sword, and asked her slave to take them to him on the edge of the crowd where he was to be found. She herself attacked the Sultan wearing men's clothes, and cut off his head. The boy said to her, "Stop! Do not cut off the head of the minister." He brought two she-camels, of which one was thirsty and the other hungry, put down water for the thirsty one, and fodder for the other, tying the minister between the two she-camels. The thirsty camel pulled towards the water, and the hungry one towards the fodder, and so they tore the minister in half between them. He took his father and buried him. Then he found his mother on the ground, and took her with him. He brought the blacksmith, and made him his minister. He remained himself as Sultan, and lived with his wives in prosperity and happiness.

28. FATMA THE BEAUTIFUL. SHAIQIYA ABBASIYA (AFRICA)

Fatma was a comely girl; her face was white as the moon, and her hair was long, reaching down to her legs. She lived in a village on the Nile. The villagers were always talking about her beauty, and all the young men hoped for her hand. The strength of their admiration lured her brother, Muhammed, into the resolve to marry her himself.

One day, when Fatma had left to fetch water in a bowl, her brother asked his parents for her hand. Now Fatma and Muhammed were their parents' only children. His parents did not want to anger Muhammed, so when Fatma returned from the river and asked her mother to help her take the bowl from her head, her mother promised to help Fatma if she would say: "My mother is my mother-in-law," trying to persuade Fatma to marry her brother Muhammed. But Fatma refused. She asked her father to take the bowl, but he made the same demand as his wife. Fatma refused it. Then she asked her brother to take the bowl, but he said: "First, you must say—Muhammed is my bridegroom."

Fatma grasped the situation, and was dumbfounded. She threw down the bowl, and ran away from the house. She collected together all the girls from the settlement, and she told them that the men of the village had decided to marry each one of them to her brother, and asked them to run away with her. They fled with her, and ran a considerable distance from the village. In the evening, they saw a big fire, and they walked towards it. As they drew

28. SOURCE: Al-Shahi and Moore 1978:110–14. © Ahmed Al-Shahi and F. C. T. Moore 1978. Reprinted from *Wisdom from the Nile* translated by Ahmed Al-Shahi and F. C. T. Moore (1978) by permission of Oxford University Press.

near, they saw a woman with a gigantic body. This woman had large teeth, and red eyes. They greeted her: "Peace be upon you!" And she replied: "Welcome! Whoever brought you here, may he bring those who will come after you." The girls said: "We want to spend the night with you." "You are welcome," said the woman. Then she took them into her house, sat them on a bedstead, and told them that she would prepare dinner for them.

But when she went out, Fatma warned the girls: "This woman is an ogress and she eats people. So do not eat any of her food, because it is made from human bones, and if you eat it, you will never walk on your feet again, and the ogress wants to eat us." Fatma told each of them to dig a hole underneath herself to hide the ogress's food while appearing to eat it. The woman prepared the food, and the girls did what Fatma had told them, with the exception of the youngest, who ate it, in spite of Fatma's advice.

After dinner, Fatma thought of a means of escape. She asked the ogress to bring her water in a gourd without a hole in it, or in a net made of string. Further, the water should be brought from the seventh sea. The ogress set off, thinking that the girls would never leave. But after her departure, Fatma and the other girls escaped, except the youngest, who was unable to, because she had eaten the flesh of human beings. When the ogress reached the seventh sea, she tried to put water into the net or into the gourd, but she failed. So she pierced the gourd, put water into it, and returned home, to find that all the girls had vanished, except the youngest, who said: "Fatma told me to run away with them, but I said I could not leave my mother alone."

So the ogress ran off on the track of the girls, and when she failed to reach them, she said: "Please to God, Fatma and your friends, may you find heaps and heaps of gold which will keep you busy, and then I will reach you." The heaps and heaps of gold appeared in front of Fatma. "Girls," she said, "take only one or two pieces, and then run away from the ogress." Then the ogress said: "Please to God, may you find silk *thawbs* which will keep you busy, and then I shall reach you." Again Fatma warned the girls when they came upon the silk *thawbs*: "Girls, take one or two *thawbs* and then run away from the ogress."

When all these tricks had failed, the ogress said: "Please to God, may you girls come upon a big river which you cannot cross." And a wide river appeared in front of Fatma and her friends. They did not know what to do, and they were frightened by the approaching danger. Fatma thought for a while, and suddenly a huge crocodile appeared. Fatma called to him, and asked him to take them to the other side of the river, where she would give him one of the girls to eat. The crocodile told the girls to put weeds on his back to sit on. When they had done this, he took them to the other side, and as soon as they had arrived the ogress appeared on the opposite side. Fatma said to the crocodile: "Go back and bring our mother from the other side," but their "mother" was really the ogress. The crocodile went back, and the ogress mounted his back. When he had got half-way across, Fatma shouted: "Mr. Crocodile, your prey is on your back, your prey is on your back." The crocodile dived with the ogress, and took her with him, and she became his food.

On the other side, the girls saw six young boys grazing their camels, and near them was an old man. The girls searched for a place in which to hide. They found a big cave, and went inside. Fatma went up to the old man, and started talking to him; during the conversation, she said:

"We shall stay, old man,
By what you say, old man.
What will remove the skin of an old man?"

And he told her to find a thorn from an acacia, and put it in the old man's head. Fatma went and searched for the thorn until she found one. Then she came back to the old man, and, without being noticed, stuck the thorn in his head. His skin fell off in one piece, and Fatma put it on. Disguised as an old man, she went back to the cave.

Now a little bush hid the entrance to the cave, and one of the camels came over to eat the leaves of the bush, but one of the girls shooed it away. The camel kept coming, and kept being shooed away by the girls. One of the boys noticed this, and told his friends. They all went up to see what was behind the little bush. They found the cave, which they had not noticed before. One of them went into the cave to see what was inside; he saw one of the girls, and took her away with him. Then the second boy went in, saw the second girl, and took her away with him. So it went until the turn of the sixth boy, whose name was Wad al-Amin, a quiet, respectable and at the same time simple youth. When he went in, he saw Fatma the Beautiful in the shape of an old man. So he carried him out. When his friends saw him, they laughed at him, pointing out what beautiful girls they had. The news spread in the village how Wad al-Amin's bad luck had brought him the old man.

But Wad al-Amin accepted his bad luck, and was content. He asked the old man to graze his camels, but the old man said: "I am old, and I cannot!" So Wad al-Amin asked the old man to graze his sheep, but he refused because he could not run after them. But the old man said that he could graze pigeons, and could take them to the river for watering. Wad al-Amin agreed to this, and gave him the task of grazing pigeons, and assigned a dumb slave to accompany the old man. Fatma, clad in the old man's skin, took the pigeons and went to the river. There she took off the old man's skin and appeared. She was a beautiful sight, bewitching the eyes and the heart. She went down to the river to swim, and after bathing came out dancing with her long hair on the bank. Being dumb, the slave could not express his surprise and admiration, astonished as he was at her beauty and her rich clothes. Eventually, Fatma put the skin on again and went back home with the pigeons. There, the slave wanted to tell what he had seen, but he could not. He stood in front of Wad al-Amin, and started jumping up and down, a gesture that he had seen something beautiful, but his master could not understand. He asked the old man what had happened to the slave, and the reply was that the slave was ill. To cure him, his chest should be burnt with fire. The master did this.

The next day, the old man and the slave went to graze the pigeons, and at the river the slave saw exactly what he had seen the day before. When he went back, the slave again started beating his chest in front of his master, and his master beat him once more. This happened many times, until Wad al-Amin decided to hide himself to see what was happening. When he reached the river, he saw the old man take off his skin and appear as a girl among the most beautiful in the world. Wad al-Amin fainted. When he came to, the old man and the slave had gone home. He returned home, and asked the old man to play chess with him: the winner would skin the loser. The old man agreed, and the game started. The old man won, but he refused to skin Wad al-Amin. Again, they played, and Wad al-Amin won; he did not hesitate to skin the old man, and there appeared Fatma under the skin in her real form. He was taken with her beauty, and hid her from everyone. But the news spread; Wad al-Amin refused to show her to the villagers, and asked them to prepare for his wedding. The preparations took place for this great wedding in order to see Wad al-Amin's wife on the day of the wedding—or, as some of them who saw her said: "To see the moon!" On the day of the wedding, all the people of the village gathered, and dancing and festivities took place in expectation of the arrival of Fatma the Beautiful. Before sunset, Fatma appeared with her husband, Wad al-Amin, coming to the place of the festivities. She lighted the open space, as though she the beautiful were a new sun, destined to replace the sun now sinking in the sky.

29. **THE WIFE OF THE PRINCE'S SON.** FARADIYIN JUHAINA
(AFRICA)

The wife of the prince's son was barren, and had no children. So she went to a holy man in the village so that he might pray for her to have children. The holy man told her to go and slaughter a sheep, to roast it, and

29. SOURCE: Al-Shahi and Moore 1978:79–81. © Ahmed Al-Shahi and F. C. T. Moore 1978. Reprinted from *Wisdom from the Nile* translated by Ahmed Al-Shahi and F. C. T. Moore (1978) by permission of Oxford University Press.

to bring it to him on a tray. The woman did as she was told, and brought the roast sheep to the holy man, who then read some verses from the Koran over the sheep, and gave it back to the woman, warning her not to eat the meat until midnight. She went home, and left the roast sheep hanging up in her house while she visited the neighbours. While she was out, her husband came and found the roast sheep in the house and ate the meat. So the wife on her return found the meat gone, and told her husband that a holy man had read verses from the Koran over it.

After some days, the man felt his belly getting larger, and in the end he realized that he was pregnant and that this was because of the meat over which the holy man had read his incantations.

So the prince's son went to a place far away from the village in the desert, where he prayed: "O God, what Thou has created in my belly, be pleased to lower to my leg." And indeed, God fulfilled his desire, and lowered the foetus from his belly to his leg.

The prince's son then opened up his leg with a razor, and out came a small girl, whom he covered with straw and left in the desert. Now a bird came and found the baby under the straw. He carried her off to his nest in a tree, where she grew up to be a lovely and charming girl.

Now one day Wad al-Nimair came by with some merchants, and they all sat under the tree for a rest. While they were there, Wad al-Nimair noticed the beautiful girl in the tree, but he kept quiet. Later, when they had left and gone a considerable distance from the tree, Wad al-Nimair said to his companions: "I have left my ring under the tree." So he went back and brought the girl down from the nest. He carried her back to his village, and gave her to his mother to look after.

In due course the girl grew up. When she reached marriageable age Wad al-Nimair married her, and she became pregnant. Now Wad al-Nimair's mother became irritated with her daughter-in-law because of the way her son coddled her and gave her all she asked for. And in her son's absence, she told one of the slaves to take her daughter-in-law to the forest, to kill the girl, and bring back her blood. The slave took the woman to the forest but could not bring himself to kill her. Instead he killed a gazelle and brought its blood to Wad al-Nimair's mother, leaving his wife in the desert unharmed. The girl wandered until she found an island where she settled.

A long time later, Wad al-Nimair came home from his journey. He was met by his mother, who said: "Your mother has died, and I am your wife." Wad al-Nimair suspected nothing. But one day, she said to Wad al-Nimair that she wanted *mulukhiya*; and in fact the only place to find this *mulukhiya* was on the island where the girl was. So Wad al-Nimair sent one of his slaves to bring the *mulukhiya*, and the slave when he arrived called out:

"O mistress of the green isle,
Your lion and your crocodile
Will not let me cross the Nile.
But the pregnant wife of Wad al-Nimair needs saving—
A little *mulukhiya* is her craving."

And the girl replied:

"My mother prayed for me,
My father was pregnant with me,
And the green bird took and nested me.
Wad al-Nimair who made his mother pregnant—
Why does he come for me?
Scissors fly for me!
Cut out the slave's tongue and bring it to me."

And the scissors flew and cut out the slave's tongue, and the slave returned without the *mulukhiya*. He went back to the village, but what he said was unintelligible. Wad al-Nimair sent another slave in his place, but the same thing happened to him. In fact all his slaves were sent and came back with their tongues cut out. Finally, Wad al-Nimair went himself, and when he reached the island he said:

"O mistress of the green isle,
Your lion and your crocodile
Will not let me cross the Nile.
But the pregnant wife of Wad al-Nimair needs saving—
A little *mulukhiya* is her craving."

And the girl replied:

"My mother prayed for me,
My father was pregnant with me,
And the green bird took and nested me.
Wad al-Nimair who made his mother pregnant—
Why does he come for me?
Scissors fly for me!
Cut out the slave's tongue and bring it to me."

But when the scissors flew, Wad al-Nimair deftly caught them. And when he came to the girl, he found out the full story. He brought her back to his palace, and when he arrived, he installed her in his palace and dismissed his mother.

30. THE NEW OR THE OLD?   EGYPT

When Goha was young, he lived with his father and his mother. His mother was getting old and his father wanted to marry a younger woman. People said to him, "Why do you have to do this?" 'Um Goha [Goha's mother] is a good woman."

His father answered, "I need a young wife to patch up my bones."

People said, "May God lead your path. May God satisfy you [i.e., please change your mind]!"

He said, "Never!"

His father married a young girl and brought her home to live with his old wife and Goha. Because she was the new wife, the old man became like a piece of dough in her hand. She drove Goha and his mother out of their minds and "made them see the stars at mid-day."

Finally, Goha said to himself, "By God, I must show this woman whose house this is!"

He waited until his father bought a new pair of slippers. And on a Friday, his father ordered him, "Goha, go get me my new *bulgha* [soft, slipper-like shoes], for I want to go to the mosque."

Goha ran inside to his stepmother and said to her, "My father ordered me to sleep with you."

The woman was startled and said, "What did you say? Your day is black!"

Goha put his head out of the door and shouted, "Hey father, the new or the old?"

The father replied in anger, "I told you a hundred times, the new, stupid!"

And the woman had to let him do what he said he would do.

31. THE ELDER BROTHER AND HIS YOUNGER SISTER.

FULFULDE (AFRICA)

There were an elder brother and his younger sister.

Now, the brother said he would marry no one but his sister. The sister said: "My elder brother, you will not marry me. How could you marry me? You are my elder brother, and you want to marry me?"

Well, that elder brother said he would marry only her, and as for her, she said: "My elder brother, you will not marry me." He said: "Then if I cannot

---

30. SOURCE: El Shamy 1980:222–23. From El Shamy, *Folktales of Egypt*, published by the University of Chicago Press, 1980. Reproduced by permission of the publisher.

31. SOURCE: Eguchi 1984:921–27. Reproduced by permission of Paul K. Eguchi.

marry you, I am going to kill myself. If you say that I should not marry you, I will go and kill myself." She said: "My elder brother, whether you kill yourself or not, you will not marry me."

Well, the older brother went to a deep river.

Well, away he went. When her elder brother went, the girl came out.

Well, she followed him. She followed him. They kept going till they arrived at the river. He took off his shirt and put it down. Then he went into the river. The girl was standing by the river. She said:

> "My elder brother, do not drown.
> Elder brother born from my mother, do not drown.
> Handful of money, do not drown.
> *Garbi* stick, do not drown."

Well, he said to her:

> "Indeed leave me to drown,
> my true sister."

Now the water came up to his knees.
Now, again, she said:

> "My elder brother, do not drown.
> Elder brother born from my mother, do not drown.
> Handful of money, do not drown.
> *Garbi* stick, do not drown."

Now, he said:

> "Indeed leave me to drown,
> my true sister."

The water came up to his waist.
Now, she said:

> "Elder brother, do not drown.
> My brother born from my mother, do not drown.
> Handful of money, do not drown.
> *Garbi* stick, do not drown."

Now, he said:

> "Indeed leave me to drown,
> my true sister."

The water came up to his breast.
Now, she said:

"Elder brother, do not drown.
My brother born from my mother, do not drown.
Handful of money, do not drown.
Garbi stick, do not drown."

He said:

"Indeed leave me to drown,
my true sister."

Now his whole head sank into the water.

Now, she was standing there. She saw his head disappear into the water.
Now, she said:

"Elder brother, do not drown.
Elder brother born from my mother, do not drown.
Handful of money, do not drown.
Garbi stick, do not drown."

He came out up to his breast. His breast came out of the water.
Now, she said:

"Elder brother, do not drown.
Elder brother born from my mother, do not drown.
Handful of money, do not drown.
Garbi stick, do not drown.
Heey, do not drown.
Heey heey, do not drown."

Now, he said:

"Indeed leave me to drown,
my true sister."

He said:

"Wait. Let me drown,
my true sister."

Now, again, she said:

"Elder brother, do not drown.
Elder brother born from my mother, do not drown.
Heey, do not drown.
Heey heey, do not drown.
Handful of money, do not drown.
Garbi stick, do not drown."

He said:

> "Indeed leave me to drown,
> my true sister."

Now he came out of the water. He then took his trousers and put them on. He took his shirt and put it on. His younger sister kept following him. They came back to the *saare*.

> Now, they became engaged.
> Now, they were married. They were living together.
> That's the end of the story.

32. SHANGO THE USURPER. YORUBA (WEST AFRICA)

["Shango was a warrior king who led his armies in all directions and exacted tribute from all the neighbors of the Oyo kingdom. But his people became tired of fighting and they pleaded with him to cease the endless raids."]

One day Shango turned himself into a small child and he went to confront the king on his throne. He told him to leave the throne; that he, Shango, was the real king. The king called everybody and asked who was the father of this child that wanted to disturb him on his throne. No one knew him. The king ordered his servants to kill the child and throw him in the river. They took him away. The servants returned from the river. But before their arrival, the child had already reappeared before the throne. The king was amazed. He said: "How is this possible? He was killed by these men, and now he has returned. Perhaps if I have him killed by women, he will not return."

But when the child heard him, he began to jump and play around and perform miracles; the women pursued him. He saw a big hole; he jumped over it; he jumped up a tall tree, he climbed down again; he ran to the forest and found a mighty tree; he jumped and appeared to hang from the tree with a rope; he was dead. The women returned to the palace and said: "The little child has hanged himself."

The king ordered a big sacrifice to be made. He bought a cow, a ram, a cock, a chicken, oil, snail, shea butter, tortoise, wild duck, guinea fowl, and pigeon. He ordered his servants to dig a ditch underneath the tree where the child hanged himself. He asked them to throw all the sacrifices into the ditch and to cut the rope.

---

32. SOURCE: Beier 1980:25–26. From Ulli Beier, *Yoruba Myths*. Reprinted with the permission of Cambridge University Press. NOTE: This story was collected in Brazil by Pierre Verger.

But as the corpse fell from the tree the child came back to life and everybody was amazed. The child said: "I did not hang myself." They went to see the king. He was surprised and went to the forest to see if it was really true.

When he returned to the palace the child was sitting on his throne. The king commanded him to surrender it. But the child refused. He said that his name was Oba Koso and that he had now become the sacred vehicle of the king.

Thus Oba Koso seized the throne.

33. SHAKA. ZULU (SOUTH AFRICA)

Shaka is born an unwanted child, the failure of his father, Senzasakuna, to observe the limits of customary intercrural intercourse—*ukuhlobonga*—with his mother Nandi. Nandi's mother was a Quabe whose clan intermarriage with the Zulus was taboo. Shaka thus springs from a union with incestuous implications. Marriage takes place but soon the father rejects the mother and child and they go to live at Nandi's people's kraal. When Nandi was pregnant, because of the incest involved, it was given out that she was simply harboring an intestinal beetle, *I-Shaka*. Hence his name. It can also mean—as *chaka*—a poor fellow, a menial, a servant. Shaka is bullied and mocked by the elder herd boys. Shaka vows to repay them. At fifteen he is brought to his father's kraal for puberty ceremonies (*thomba*) but he is recalcitrant and refuses to fully participate. He is said to have refused the loingirdle—*umutsha*—because he wants to demonstrate he has grown to become a man. (Shaka is commonly credited with having abolished circumcision among the Zulu though it is practiced among other members of the Nguni family.) The hostility in his father's kraal causes Shaka and Nandi once again to leave. They live with Gendeyana to whom Nandi had borne a son Ngwadi, Shaka's maternal half-brother, with whom his relations were always friendly.

But Shaka has no rightful place in this kraal. Escaping his father's emissaries who bargain for his death he finally settles with Ngomane, headman of the Dletsheni clan of the Mtetwas. This is the kraal of his mother's father's sister. The Mtetwas are ruled by King Jobe. At the time Jobe's two sons had conspired against him. One had been put to death and the other, Dingiswayo, fled. When Jobe dies, Dingiswayo returns and Shaka, because of his energy and bravery, is made an important member of his army. Here he invents the short stabbing *assagai* so crucial to his military successes. Its use made Nguni warfare much more bloody and devastating than the previous skirmishes carried on at a distance with throwing spears. Shaka adopts the draconian custom of accepting no prisoners. He kills all the enemy wounded and those of his own wounded incapacitated by their wounds.

33. SOURCE: Fernandez 1971:340–42. Used by permission.

Dingiswayo, whose reputation in Zulu history is one of moderation and conciliation, attempts to restrain the zeal of his chief lieutenant. Shaka is partially reconciled with his father who, however, dies shortly. Shaka sends his maternal half-brother to waylay and kill his paternal half-brothers and prevent them from taking the chieftainship. Installed as chief he has all those who mocked him and Nandi put to death. "Now the Zulu knew what kind of a chief they had!" He does the same for those elder cousins in his mother's family.

He enforces exasperatingly long celibacy upon his warriors. He himself forms a large seraglio of women sent him in homage or from capture but visits them rarely. He is no sensualist and he vows he will never marry and cast "little bulls" to challenge the big bull of the kraal. His preferred form of dalliance seems to be "Zulu love play"—intercrural intercourse. Pregnant women of the harem are killed usually on the pretext of adultery. He refers to his wives as his "sisters"! He adopts the custom of a daily bath entirely nude before any of his people present.

Shaka's personality and draconian methods so impose their will on his councilors and advisors that they are virtually reduced to compliant adulation and obsequiousness. He is followed everywhere by his slayers who crush skulls and break necks at the slightest nod of his head. Albeit he as frequently demonstrates a spontaneous and generous sentiment as this merciless and arbitrary discipline. He is a curious and unpredictable combination. Only Nandi is completely influential with him.

Shaka's conquests have reverberations on all of southern Africa as various of the Nguni flee north, south, and east to escape him. He dominates Natal. The English traders visit him. He boasts of the orderly, moral, and lawabiding condition of his kingdom, but inquires with great interest after European custom.

Now Nandi dies. Shaka is thrown into a profound and malevolent grief. "I have conquered the world but lost my mother." At times uncontrollably homicidal, there is great danger in his presence. In mourning, he decrees no crops should be planted for a year. In that time couples which allow pregnancy to occur will be slain. Minor reverses in his campaigns are answered by the annihilation of the truant regiments involved. To test the state of mourning among some of his long celibate troops he strips them naked and has maidens dance before them. Those who show sexual excitement are killed for their disrespect to his poor mother.

His people grow restive of his rule. His paternal half-brothers, Dingane and Mhlangane, respond to the malaise and plot his assassination. They spear him to death. Dying he turns to them and asks, "Ye children of my Father, what is the Wrong?"

SOUTH AND
EAST ASIA

34. THE BODHISATTVA AT TAKKASITA. ANCIENT INDIA

Women are always given to lechery." Thus spoke the master when he was staying in Jatavana and reproving a monk who had been led astray by a woman. "They are lecherous, evil, vulgar and low." To illustrate this doctrine, he told the following story. Once upon a time the Bodhisattva had been reborn in a Brahman family in Takkasita and grew up to be a very learned man. At the same time, another Brahman boy was born at Benares, and when he was old enough, his parents sent him to Takkasita to learn wisdom. Having returned home without having learned something his mother considered essential, to wit, the vicious character of women, he was sent to Takkasita a second time, with the request that the Bodhisattva teach him that doctrine also. Now the teacher had an old mother who had reached the venerable age of 120 years and whom he took care of as a dutiful son should. When he heard the pupil's request, he immediately hit upon a plan. He asked the boy to take care of the old woman, flattering her and praising her beauty. The result of his obsequiousness he was to report to his teacher.

The young Brahman does as he is bidden and is so successful in his enterprise that the poor old woman takes him seriously and is willing to

---

34. SOURCES: Primary source: Dutoit 1906:251ff.; Secondary source: Krappe 1927: 185–86.

let herself be seduced by him. When he expresses fear of his master's severity, she urges him to kill her son. When he declares himself unable to do so, on account of moral considerations, she is ready to accomplish the deed. The pupil informs his teacher of what is going on. The Bodhisattva carves a wooden statue (for his mother was blind with age) and bids the boy hand her an axe while giving her an appropriate hint. After making him promise not to desert her, she resolutely deals a blow to the statue which she believes to be her son. From the cracking of the wood she concludes that a prank has been played upon her, and when she hears her son's voice calling her and asking her what she is doing, she is so overcome with shame that she dies on the spot. The Bodhisattva drives home the lesson while offering to the deceased the last rites. The pupil is so deeply impressed with this experience that he decides to renounce the world and to become a hermit.

35. **KUTSA SEDUCES INDRA'S WIFE.**   ANCIENT INDIA

Kutsa Aurava ["Thigh-born"] was made out of the two thighs of Indra. Just as Indra was, so was he, precisely as one would be who is made out of his own self. Indra made him his charioteer. He caught him with his wife, Saci the daughter of Puloman, and when he asked her, "How could you do this?" she replied, "I could not tell the two of you apart." Indra said, "I will make him bald, and then you will be able to tell the two of us apart." He made him bald, but Kutsa bound a turban around his head and went to her. This is the turban that charioteers wear. Indra caught him again [with his wife] and said to her, "How could you do this?" She said, "I still couldn't tell the difference, because he bound a turban around his head and then came to me." "I will smear dirt between his shoulders, and then you will be able to tell the difference between us." He did smear dirt between his shoulders—and so charioteers have dirt between their shoulders—but Kutsa covered it up and went to her. Indra caught them again and said, "How could you do this?" and again she said, "I still could not tell the two of you apart, for he covered up his upper torso and came to me." Then Indra bound Kutsa and said, "Now you are a wrestler [Malla]." Kutsa said, "Generous one, do not ruin us. Give us something that we can live on, for truly we were born from you." Indra said, "Shake the dirt off from between your shoulders." Kutsa shook it off, and it became the Rajas and Rajiyas, a great people.

---

35. SOURCE: O'Flaherty 1985:75–76.

36. THE UNCLE WHO TRIED TO MURDER THE NEWBORN CHILD. ANCIENT INDIA

When Vyasva, the son of Sakamasva, was still in the womb, his paternal uncle, Gaya, realized that he would be a great sage as soon as he was born. When he was born, Gaya ordered them to throw him out and to say that he was born dead. But the child's shadow did not leave him, and his own two thumbs gave him milk. Then they told Gaya, "The little boy that you ordered us to throw out is still alive." Gaya took his club and went out to kill the child. But Vyasva prayed, "Let me get out of this; let me find help and a way out." He saw this chant and sang it over Gaya, and so Gaya's club fell backwards and split open his own head.

37. DEVI. ANCIENT INDIA

The Goddess in her full primeval form became lustful and created a male to impregnate her. She became a bird and laid an egg, out of which Brahma, Visnu, and Siva hatched. When she lusted after them and asked them to satisfy her desire, they protested that she was their mother, that they came from her womb; but she insisted that the egg was their mother, that she was only their grandmother, and that it was therefore all right for them to do as she asked. They fled from her, and ultimately Siva and Visnu tricked her into giving her third eye to Siva, thereby causing her to lose both her strength and her desire.

38. PURUSA. ANCIENT INDIA

In the beginning this world was Soul [atman] alone, in the form of Purusa. He had no joy, and desired a second. Now he was as large as a woman and a man in a close embrace, and so he caused his self to fall into two pieces, which became a husband and a wife. Therefore it is said, "Oneself is like a half-fragment." He copulated with her and produced human beings. But then she thought, "How can he copulate with me when he has just produced me from himself? I will hide." She became a cow; he became a

36. SOURCE: O'Flaherty 1985:79.

37. SOURCES: Primary source: Oppert 1893:465–66, 472–74; Secondary source: O'Flaherty 1980:99. From O'Flaherty, *Women, Androgynes, and Other Mythical Beasts*, published by the University of Chicago Press, 1980. Reproduced by permission of the publisher.

38. SOURCE: O'Flaherty 1980:311. From O'Flaherty, *Women, Androgynes, and Other Mythical Beasts*, published by the University of Chicago Press, 1980. Reproduced by permission of the publisher.

bull, copulated with her, and produced cattle. She became a mare; he a stallion. . . . Thus were born all pairs there are, even down to the ants.

39. PRAJAPATI. ANCIENT INDIA

Prajapati became pregnant and created progeny from his right thumb, nipple, and other organs, without the benefit of mothers. But he became dissatisfied with this creation, and so he divided his body in half and made one-half a woman. He tried to make love to her, and although she and her brothers were shocked at this incestuous act, he eventually married her and created progeny with her.

40. ARJUNA AND THE BABHRUVAHANA. ANCIENT INDIA

The great Pandava hero Arjuna is roaming about India in the train of Yudhisthira's sacrificial horse. According to the custom, the kings into whose territory such a horse wanders must either submit and become tributaries of the sovereign in whose name the sacrifice is to be conducted or capture the beast and offer battle to its armed escort. Arjuna, following the horse, defeats a number of kings in the name of his elder brother. Ultimately the horse wanders into the kingdom of Manipur ruled by Arjuna's own son Babhruvahana. Babhruvahana is confronted with a real dilemma: he is torn between his duty on the one hand as a self-respecting *ksatriya* to fight the intruder and on the other his duty of filial submissiveness. Yet the prince gives no immediate sign of the ambivalence which the situation must engender in him with respect to his father. Hearing that his father has arrived in Manipur, Babhruvahana goes forth humbly to greet him with brahmans and welcoming offerings. Arjuna, rather than his son, must point out the conflict inherent in the situation. Far from showing pleasure at his son's meek devotion, the hero is enraged. He rejects the welcome prepared for him and unleashes a torrent of verbal abuse upon his son, reviling him as an unmanly coward and betrayer of the knightly tradition.

> Then the wise Phalguna [Arjuna], his mind fixed on what is proper, recalling what is proper for a warrior, did not approve and, angered, he said to him, "This conduct is not appropriate for you. You are beyond the limits of what is proper for a warrior. My son, why have you not attacked me who have crossed the border of

---

39. SOURCES: Primary source: Maity 1966:199–200; Secondary source: O'Flaherty 1980:312. From O'Flaherty, *Women, Androgynes, and Other Mythical Beasts*, published by the University of Chicago Press, 1980. Reproduced by permission of the publisher.

40. SOURCES: Primary source: *The Mahabharata* (Buck 1973); Secondary source: Goldman 1978:330–32. Reproduced by permission of Kluwer Academic Publishers.

your kingdom guarding Yudhisthira's sacrificial horse? Damn you! You fool. You know the rules for warriors yet you greet me peacefully when I have come to fight! Living here you accomplish none of the goals of a man greeting me gently, like a woman, when I have come to fight. Idiot! Lowest of men! If I had come to you unarmed only then would this conduct have been proper."

In the face of this startling reaction on the part of his father, Babhruvahana is confused. Hesitant, he stands with his face downcast, unable to act. It is only when his father's wife, the serpent princess Ulupi, who stands in the relation of a mother to the prince, appears and urges him to fight, assuring him that this will please Arjuna, that Babhruvahana agrees to comply with his father's wishes. Abandoning his earlier hesitation, the prince prepares for battle and has his men seize the sacrificial horse. As predicted by Ulupi, this pleases Arjuna and an unequalled battle begins between the father and his son, both of whom are described as being delighted. The son scores the first hit. Laughing, he shoots his father through the collarbone. Arjuna is seriously injured and appears to be dead but soon regains consciousness and praises his son: "Well done. Well done, my boy, great-armed son of Citrangada. When I see a deed that so befits you, my son, I am delighted."

The battle begins anew and when Babhruvahana, his chariot rendered useless by his father's arrows, descends in fury to fight him on foot, Arjuna is still more pleased with his son's courage and increases his own efforts. Babhruvahana, however, since he is but a child, finally shoots his father in the heart and kills him.

When Arjuna falls the young prince himself succumbs to the wounds he has already received at his father's hand and falls unconscious. At this point, Arjuna's second wife, Citrangada, Babhruvahana's actual mother, appears and laments her husband's death, rebuking Ulupi for her part in inciting Babhruvahana. She remarks, interestingly enough, that she does not grieve for her son but only for her husband for whom such a welcome was prepared. At this point Babhruvahana, who had only been stunned, recovers consciousness and, his boyish ardor for battle now cooled, succumbs to massive guilt for his act of parricide. He calls upon the assembled brahmans to witness his foul crime and to prescribe some expiation. He then proposes a grisly expiation for himself, saying that as a parricide he should live for twelve years clothed in his father's skin begging with pieces of Arjuna's skull. Finally he concludes that there is no expiation for a sin so great and he resolves to fast to death on the battlefield unless Ulupi can restore his father to life.

Then, as the grieving king and his mother begin their fast unto death, Ulupi calls to mind the magical life-restorative jewel that is used to revive the slain *nagas*, her own people. She urges Babhruvahana to abandon his grief and conveys to him some astonishing information:

"Arise my son. Do not grieve. You have not killed Jisnu [Arjuna]. He is not to be conquered by men or even by the gods including Indra. Rather this is a kind of magical illusion known as 'Delusive' that I have employed today for the sake of pleasing this foremost of men, your glorious father. For, my son, O king, this Kaurava, this slayer of opposing heroes, came here wishing to ascertain your strength when you fight in battle. Therefore, I urged you on to battle. My son, my lord, do not imagine that you have incurred even the most minute sin. He is a seer of great power, the eternal and unchanging Purusa. My son, not even Indra is able to defeat him in battle."

She then describes the magic jewel and the method of its use. Babhruvahana places it on Arjuna's chest and to the delight of his son he arises as though from sleep. The restored Arjuna embraces his son and, in the typical gesture of paternal affection, sniffs his head. Then, seeing his two wives on the battlefield, he inquires as to the reason for this unusual situation. Ulupi explains to him the reason for the whole bizarre sequence of events.

Her explanation is of considerable interest to our understanding of the epic approach to the oedipal encounter. Asking her husband not to be angry with her, she announces that she has staged the whole affair to please him. This time, however, she is not referring to his desire to test his son's martial prowess but something much more serious. She tells Arjuna that his "death" at the hands of his son is in fact his penance or expiation for his immoral killing of Bhisma during the great Bharata war. She reminds him that since he wrongfully killed the great Kuarava patriarch while he was engaged with Sikhandin, he would, by virtue of this crime, have gone to hell forever had he died without having expiated it. The expiation fixed is death at his own son's hands. The rationale given for this sequence is that the Vasus, divine figures reckoned to be the older brother of Bhisma, learning of the unchivalrous murder of that hero, resolved—with the concurrence of their mother, the sacred river Ganges—to curse Arjuna. Their resolution is overheard by Ulupi's father, who becomes alarmed at the fate of his son-in-law and manages to propitiate them to the extent of their allowing for Arjuna to be freed from the curse but only through death at the hands of his own son.

Thus we see that Ulupi, a devoted and clever wife, has acted chiefly in order to free her husband from being cursed to eternal damnation. Finally, with a piece of sophistical argumentation of a sort found frequently in the epic texts, Ulupi reassures Arjuna that no one has conquered him at all, that he has in fact killed himself! "For not even the king of the gods could defeat you in battle. It is said that 'The son is the self.' Therefore you have been defeated here by him."

In this Ulupi manages to clear herself of any trace of wrongdoing and any taint of sin. She concludes her speech to her husband: "I don't think that there is any fault of mine in this. What do you think, my lord?"

Arjuna, in keeping with his extraordinary good humor that he maintains throughout this tale of his own death, is perfectly delighted with Ulupi's cleverness and after exchanging a few more affectionate words with his son, departs in the train of the sacrificial horse.

41. **GARPAKE BABA.** LEPCHA (NEPAL)

The tutelary divinity of the Magars is called Garpake Baba. His wife Raimala gave birth to nine sons and then died. Garpake Baba remarried. His second wife, Philmala, was quite beautiful and the nine sons, being envious of their father, decided to kill him in order to marry Phimala. "How can we get rid of the old man?" They thought about it for a long time. "We will go hunting with our father and when we arrive at the hunting ground, the tiger will eat him." They suggested the hunt to their father but Garpake Baba took the tiger by surprise and killed him with one arrow.

The sons met once again to decide on another way of eliminating their father. "We will go for honey by the cliff. Father will go down to gather it and once he has descended, we will cut the rope ladder." The sons and their father left for the jungle, and arrived at the top of the cliff. Halfway down the cliff were the beehives. The father asked his sons to go down for the honey, but each of them found a pretext to refuse. The father descended alone.

Once he had arrived near the beehive, he threw aside the empty containers and kept those that were full of honey. "Have you finished?" his sons asked. "No, not yet." The third time his sons asked this question, the father became suspicious and said to his sons: "I've finished gathering the honey." The sons cut the ropes of the ladder and returned home.

Garpake Baba stayed on the cliff for twelve years, eating nothing but honey.

One day, two black-feathered vultures [*garud-garudni*] finally came by the cliff. "What are you doing here?" they asked the old man. "I came here to gather honey with my nine sons, but once I had gone down the cliff, they cut the rope and left me for dead." "We will stretch our wings out together and carry you back home." Garpake Baba hesitated: "My sons will kill me, and can I trust these birds?" He said to them, "First, in order to prove your strength to me, bring a large boulder here on your wings." They carried a large boulder on their spread wings. The father thought: "Yes, these birds wish to help me." "Drop me off near the spring, right next to the house." *Garud-garudni* carried Garpake Baba, who weighed next to nothing, since he was so dehydrated.

---

41. SOURCE: Jest 1976:299–300. Reproduced by permission of John T. Hitchcock.

His despondent wife, who wore her clothes inside out and hair hanging down, went to the spring of water. She was about to drink some water when Garpake Baba stirred the water with a leaf from a *ruru* tree. The woman wondered: "Who could be stirring this water?" She looked up and saw a *palcaura* bird fly away crying *chak*. She said to him, "I'm unhappy and you're stirring up my water. I hope you get trapped in a slip-knot made of an ox hair . . ."; and she cast this spell on him. A second time, a *dhabini* bird troubled the water. The third time, the woman saw her husband and cried when she saw how thin he was. "You must quickly return home."

During this time, the nine sons were practicing archery. The winner was to marry his stepmother, but none of the brothers could hit the target. "I don't want to go home, my sons will kill me. But if you insist, you must bring me a large grain basket [*thun*], a bamboo stick, and a white cotton veil nine cubits long." The woman put her husband in the basket, covered it with the cloth, picked up the stick, and carried it all back to the house. After climbing the nine-notched ladder, she set her husband down on the upper floor.

The nine sons continued their archery. The father saw them and thought, "I am alive after twelve years of suffering. My sons covet my wife, but none of them can hit the target. I myself will shoot the arrow." Garpake Baba took his bow, aimed carefully, and hit the target with the first arrow. Each claimed that the arrow was his own, and a quarrel broke out. But the youngest son thought, "Only my father with his strength and skill is capable of hitting the target. He's alive!"

Garpake Baba cast a spell and transformed six of his sons into jungle animals. The three sons who had taken pity on their father were spared; the eldest *jetho*, the second *mailo*, and the youngest *kancho*. The eldest son must sacrifice a rooster, the second must sacrifice *kodo* [Eleusine?] on the threshing-floor near the house, the third must offer a white ram whose meat is to be distributed among the members of the lineage.

42. **TIBETAN INCEST MYTH.** TIBETANS IN NEPAL

A brother and sister go hunting. They kill a deer, but as night closes in they must stay together in a hut in the forest. To avoid incest they make a vow to sleep back to back and not turn over in the night. The boy breaks the vow, however, when he turns over to grab some meat from the fire. At that moment a tiger enters the hut and eats the boy.

His sister heard the sound of jaws chomping meat, but refused to break

42. SOURCE: Mumford 1989:143. Reproduced by permission of the University of Wisconsin Press.

her vow and turn over, thinking "my brother is eating the meat." In the morning she awoke and saw what had happened. She pledged to get revenge and crossed nine passes and nine valleys to find the killer. She saw a tiger and aimed her arrow, saying, "If this tiger is indeed the one that killed my brother, may my arrow hit its heart. If not, may the arrow hit a rock or a tree." She let loose the arrow. It struck the tiger and it fell dead.

43. GARA. SINHALESE (SRI LANKA)

Gara was the son of a king. At his birth royal astrologers predicted that he would desire his own sister. To avoid this calamity the king sent his son to live away from home with the king's brother. As the prince grew up he was called Dala Kumara, or Tusk Prince, because of his tusklike canines.

The prince's mother gave birth to a beautiful girl named Giri Devi, but Dala Kumara was never told about this. The girl grew up and it was decided to give her in marriage. The king's brother was invited, but not Dala Kumara. However, the prince heard about the wedding and went home to attend the nuptials. He demanded to see his sister, and in his rage he smashed everything around him and ate all the food. Ultimately he was shown the princess. Dala Kumara was seized by a deep passion; he carried his sister away to the forest and lived with her there, subsisting on wild foods. One day, when her brother-husband was away, Giri Devi ran away and hanged herself from some forest vines.

Dala Kumara was in a rage; he caused great havoc. Even the gods were afraid of him since he shook the wish-fulfilling tree [*parasatugaha*] under which the gods assembled. [It is this event that is represented in the shaking of the swing (*ayile*) in the ritual.] Ultimately he was shown his sister's corpse; but his rage, fever, and thirst grew worse. Finally the gods pleaded with him to desist from killing and destruction. He was given twelve attendants by the king of demons, Vessamuni.

44. SATWAI'S DAUGHTER. MARATHI (INDIA)

Everyone knows the Goddess Satwai. She has to write the future of every child on the night of the fifth day after its birth; and what she writes must happen. Now, Satwai had a daughter. Every night she was left alone

43. SOURCE: Obeyesekere 1984:183–84. From Obeyesekere, *The Cult of the Goddess Pattini*, published by the University of Chicago Press, 1984. Reproduced by permission of the publisher.

44. SOURCE: Karve 1950:71. Reproduced by permission of *Man*.

when her mother went to write out some baby's fate. She asked her mother one day, "Mother, why do you go out every night and leave me alone?" Satwai answered, "Daughter, I have to perform the task for which I am appointed by God. I must therefore go and write the fate of newborn babies." "Can one read what you write?" "No, not even gods know what I have written out for them." "But, mother dear, you must tell me what you have written for me." Satwai refused this request and went out as usual. But her daughter allowed her no peace and threatened to leave her house if her request was not complied with. At last Satwai told her, "My daughter, it is your fate to marry your own son." Shocked at this revelation, the daughter begged to know whether her fate could not be changed. Satwai answered, "No, my daughter, as I have told you, my writing cannot be reversed. It must happen as I have told you." The daughter, however, was determined to cheat her fate. She resolved not to marry, not even to see a man, and so went into a deep forest, built a hut there and lived all alone for some years until she grew up to be a young woman. Now it happened that a king, while hunting, passed through the forest. He came to a lovely lake filled with clear sweet water. As his mouth was parched he took some water in his cupped hand, gargled with it and threw it back into the lake, and then rode away. The maiden arrived soon afterwards at the same lake. She had been gathering fruit and roots since morning and was tired and thirsty. She stopped, took some water in her cupped hands and drank it. Now that water contained the mouthful ejected by the king. As soon as the water reached her belly she became pregnant. At first she did not know that anything had happened to her, but after a few months she became frightened and did not know what to do. In due course a handsome male child was born to her. As she knew the prophecy she determined to destroy the baby, so she tore her sari in half, wrapped it round the child, and threw it from a steep mountain side. Below the cliff lived a gardener and his wife, who had a beautiful grove of closely planted bananas. The bundle in which the child was wrapped alighted on top of some thick and stout banana leaves and remained there until it was found by the gardener, who took it home and handed it over to his wife. As the couple were childless they were thankful for this gift of the gods, and the baby grew and thrived until it became a very handsome man.

Satwai's daughter lived on in the forest for years until she grew tired of the lonely life. She thought that as she had killed her son she might go back to the world, and started to find a path through the forest. She rounded the great cliff and came on the homestead of the old couple. She was received with hospitality and as she had nowhere to go she lived and worked in their house. She was liked by all as she was both comely and industrious. In a few months the old couple thought that God, who had sent them the boy, had also sent them this girl as a daughter-in-law, and so performed the marriage with the boy. The young bride became the mistress of the house and in her household duties could go anywhere she liked. One day she was seeking some old pots in the loft and came across the torn piece of a sari which she recognized as her own. To make sure, she went down and asked her mother-in-law about the old piece of sari, and was told the whole story. She realized that what Satwai had written was fulfilled, did not tell anybody about her knowledge, and lived happily with her husband, blessed by her aged parents-in-law to whom she was always kind and dutiful.

45. **VASANTATILAKA.** ANCIENT INDIA

In the city of Ujjayini in the kingdom of Avanti lived a rich merchant called Suhasta. Vasantatilaka was his beautiful mistress. She conceived twins and was greatly troubled by morning sickness. Suhasta left his mistress in disgust when he saw her in this condition. In due time a boy and a girl were born. When Vasantatilaka saw them she thought "these wretched creatures deprived me of my patron, the rich Suhasta; I had better abandon them," so she wrapped the girl in a beautiful blanket set with precious stones and left her at the southern outskirts of the city. There she was found by the merchant Suketu, travelling from Prayaga, who being childless adopted her as his daughter and named her Kamala. The male twin was similarly left at the end of the northern end of the city, and was found and adopted by a merchant from Saketa, who named him Dhanadeva. After some years Dhanadeva married Kamala and lived happily with her in the city of Saketa. One day Dhanadeva, together with other merchants, came to Ujjayini to sell some merchandise. There he saw the beautiful Vasantatilaka and lived with her, forgetting his wife Kamala. Vasantatilaka bore him a son. Kamala awaited the return of her husband for a long time, until she was told his whereabouts by a pious sage. Disgusted with the world, she renounced it, became a religious mendicant, and wandered about begging from town to town. She thus happened to come to Ujjayini and saw Vasantatilaka's son crying in front of her house. By her sacredness she was gifted to see everything and she knew instantly who the child was. [Here follows a long narrative about the previous birth of all the characters in the story.] She took up the child in her arms and addressed him thus: "Child, you are my son, you are my uncle, my brother, my brother-in-law. Your father is my husband. Child, be still, don't cry." Vasantatilaka heard

---

45. SOURCE: Karve 1950:72. Reproduced by permission of *Man*.

the address and came out with her husband, and when they were told the story of their past and present life, repented of their sin and renounced the earth.

46. **THE INDIAN OEDIPUS.** INDIA

A girl is born with a curse on her head that she would marry her own son and beget a son by him. As soon as she hears of the curse, she willfully vows she'd try and escape it: she secludes herself in a dense forest, eating only fruit, forswearing all male company. But when she attains puberty, as fate would have it, she eats a mango from a tree under which a passing king has urinated. The mango impregnates her; bewildered, she gives birth to a male child; she wraps him in a piece of her sari and throws him in a nearby stream. The child is picked up by the king of the next kingdom, and he grows up to be a handsome, young, adventurous prince. He comes hunting in the self-same jungle, and the cursed woman falls in love with the stranger, telling herself she is not in danger any more as she has no son alive. She marries him and bears him a child. According to custom, the father's swaddling clothes are preserved and brought out for the newborn son. The woman recognizes at once the piece of sari with which she had swaddled her first son, now her husband, and understands that her fate had really caught up with her. She waits till everyone is asleep, and sings a lullaby to her newborn baby:

> Sleep
> O son
> O grandson   O brother to my husband
> sleep O sleep
> sleep well

and hangs herself by the rafter with her sari twisted to a rope.

47. **TAMIL TALE.** INDIA

A king has no children. He prays to Siva, who appears to him and tells him, "You have a choice. You can either choose one ordinary son or four beautiful talented daughters." The king chooses the daughters [note the preference!]. They do grow up to be four talented, divinely beautiful young

---

46. SOURCE: Ramanujan 1983:237. Reproduced by permission of Alan Dundes.

47. SOURCES: Primary source: Sastri 1884–88; Secondary source: Ramanujan 1983:249–50. Reproduced by permission of Alan Dundes.

women. One day the daughters are watching from the balcony while a clumsy tone-deaf masseur is patting oil into the king's body with all the wrong rhythms. The daughters are disgusted with the unmusical performance, come down from the balcony, dismiss the lout, and proceed to give the delighted father an oil-bath, all four of them massaging and patting oil into his limbs in pleasing rhythms, conducting a very orchestra of touch. After the bath, which sends the king into an ecstasy of pleasure, he is filled with desire for them and goes into the dark room specially reserved in ancient Indian palaces for doldrums, tantrums, and sulks. When the family and the counsellors gather to ask him why he is sullen and unhappy, he asks a question similar to the one in the Kannada Jaina legend: "If I have something precious, should I enjoy it myself or give it away?" The unsuspecting ministers tell him, "Go ahead. Enjoy what you have." Delighted, he answers, "I'm in love with my daughters. I want to marry them right away. Make the necessary arrangements." The ministers think he is mad, but humor him by saying that they would take care of it. Then they rush to the daughters with the bad news; the resourceful daughters pray to the goddess Parvati who transports them into a sealed lacquer palace in the heart of a jungle—a seven-storied palace, with living quarters on the first, and food and clothing of every kind stored up in the six upper stories to last several years. The palace has no doors or windows; a good image for virginity, indeed. Several years later, a prince strays into the jungle and hears strange vina [lute] music which lures him to the sealed palace, and it opens miraculously to let him in. He falls in love with all four of them and marries them. The young women's virginity was offered only to the rightful young man, after being denied to the incestuous father.

48. **DAITEN.** MEDIEVAL JAPAN

A version that can be traced to a Buddhist source appears in *Konjaku*, ca. 1050, v.4:23. "Daiten, a man in India, some four hundred years after the nirvana of Sakya, married his own mother while his father was away on business overseas. When his father's boat returned, Daiten met the boat and slew his father. He then killed his mother out of blind jealousy. He fled and lived in a remote country. One day a Buddhist priest of his native country came by, and Daiten murdered him also, lest the latter should reveal Daiten's sins." The rest of the story has been lost. The tale is again listed in *Sangoku Denki*, 1394 A.D., v.3:28.

---

48. SOURCE: Daiten (931 "Oedipus . . . *Tenjiku no Daiten*"), Ikeda 1971:210. Reproduced by permission of FF Communications.

AJASE. JAPAN

any years ago, in the time of Buddha, there lived a king named Binbas-
hara. His wife, Idaike, fearing the loss of her husband's love as her
beauty faded, longed to have a son with which to secure the king's love for as
long as she lived. Hearing of her intense wish, a prophet told her that, within
three years, a hermit living on a mountain would die a natural death and
start his life afresh to become her son. However, the queen, who so deeply
feared the loss of her husband's love, chose to kill the hermit before the three
years had passed. She wanted to have her son, who was to be reborn from
the dead hermit, as soon as possible. As soon as the prophet had said, she
conceived and gave birth to a boy [Ajase]. However, during her pregnancy,
she had been beset with fears of being cursed by the hermit she had killed
and at one time had even tried to induce a miscarriage.

Although Ajase's birth had sprung out of such a fatality [called in
Buddhism: *mishoon*, in-born resentment], he spent a happy youth, with his
parents' love centered upon him, knowing nothing of the secret of his conception. However, one day, after he had reached manhood, during a bout of
melancholy, he was approached by Daibadatta, one of Buddha's enemies
[Buddha's Iago], who revealed to Ajase the secret of his birth, saying: "The
cause of your melancholy is your mother's evil deed." At first, Ajase reacted
against his father, feeling sympathy for his mother's agony over his father's
love and anger against his father who had so distressed his mother. He
helped unseat his father and then had him imprisoned. [Up to this point, the
son's reaction was probably no different from what might be expected in
the Western psyche. But, at this point, the story departs sharply from the
Western pattern.]

Ajase soon learned that his mother was feeding his imprisoned father
honey which she had first rubbed onto her body. This honey saved his father
from starvation. Ajase then became so angry with his mother that he tried to
kill her with his sword, blaming her for the attempt to save his father, who
was his enemy. However, he was dissuaded from slaying her by a minister
who counseled that, while there were some sons who tried to kill their fathers, there were none who attempted to kill their mothers. At that moment,
Ajase was attacked by severe guilt feelings and became afflicted by a terrible
illness called "Ruchu"—a severe skin disease characterized by a so offensive
odor that no one dared approach him. Only his mother stood by and cared
for him.

---

49. SOURCES: Primary source: Kosawa 1950; Secondary source: Okonogi 1979:353–54.
Reproduced by permission of S. Karger AG, Basel.

Thanks to his mother's compassionate nursing, Ajase recovered from the illness and was forgiven by the mother he had intended to murder. As a result, he was awakened to a real love for his mother, discarding his grudge against her. His mother, for her part, was able to develop a natural maternal affection for her son beyond her original self-centered attachment to him.

50. ADVICE TO SON WHO HAS INJURED OWN FATHER (MOTHER). CHINA

The son of a rich man has had a fight with his father and (a) knocked off his father's molar(s) or (b) injured his face, etc. As such an offense is considered a very serious crime in Old China, the son has to seek advice from a clever man. It is a sultry summer day. The clever man bites his arm or his ear, and makes it bleed (c) while sitting by the fire with heavy clothes on. Then he teaches the youth to plead at court that his father (d) made love to his own wife, and (e) bit his arm or ear. While struggling to get free, he injured his own father unawares. The youth is acquitted. (f) Later, the son has a compunction of conscience and joins his father in suing the clever man. When made to describe the circumstances in which he received the advice, the son appears to have given absurd testimony.

51. THE BUDDHIST CONCEPTION OF THE INTERMEDIATE STATE (AFTER DEATH). TIBET

He [the deceased] sees all sorts of things such as are seen in dreams, because his mind is confused. He sees his [future] father and mother making love, and seeing them a thought crosses his mind, a perversity rises in him. If he is going to be reborn a man he sees himself making love with his mother and being hindered by his father; or if he is going to be reborn as a woman, he sees himself making love with his father and being hindered by his mother.

It is at that moment that the Intermediate Existence is destroyed and life and consciousness arise and causality begins once more to work. It is like the imprint made by a die; the die is destroyed, but the pattern has been imprinted.

---

50. SOURCE: Ting 1978:191. Reproduced by permission of Academia Scientiarum Fennica.

51. SOURCES: Primary source: Conze 1964:283; Secondary source: Ramanujan 1983:258. Reproduced by permission of Alan Dundes.

52. PAUK TYAING. BURMA

There came from the land of Thingatha six brothers of royal birth, and founded the city of Tonnge and afterwards that of Tagaung. One of the brothers, Thado Saw, became king of Tagaung, and his queen was Kin Saw U. Now the foundation-post of the palace was brought from Momeik, and from a knot in it sprang a dragon, which took the form of a man; and he was loved by the queen, and slew her husband with a prick from his poisoned fang, and the king's brother Thado Pya reigned in his stead, and took Kin Saw U to wife. But he also was slain by the dragon, and likewise all the rest of the brothers in turn. Then Tagaung was a kingdom without a king, and the ministers sought for a king, and sent out a magic car to bring him. Now Kin Saw U had a son Pauk Tyaing, who was lost in the forest when a boy, and was brought up by Po Byu and Me I. His foster-parents would have taught him his letters, but he was too dull to learn anything but these sayings from them:

> Thwa: ba mya: 'kayi: yauk
> Me: ba mya: zaga: ya
> Ma eik ma ne athet she.

> Keep going, if you want to get anywhere.
> Ask questions, if you want to learn.
> Wake, if you want to live long.

With this learning Pauk Tyaing set out in obedience to the first precept, and he was met by the magic car and taken to the palace and offered the kingdom. But he bethought him of the second, and asked what had become of the former kings and husbands of Kin Saw U; and he learnt that the reason of their death was unknown, but each one had the mark of a single tooth upon him. And he waited seven days, and accepted the kingdom and Kin Saw U as his queen. Then the dragon came to him in the night to kill him like the others, but he was awake and ready for him in accordance with the third precept, and slew him with his sword. So the dragon became a nat, and is worshipped under the name of Bodawdyi, "the Great Father."

Then the queen made hairpins of the beast's backbone, and a pillow of his skin. And she paid a thousand pieces for stripping off the skin, and a hundred for making the pillow; and she asked her husband this riddle, and they made covenant that she was to die if he guessed it, and he if he could not:

---

52. SOURCE: R. Brown 1917:742–48.

'Taung pe: lo 'sok.
Ya pe: lo chok.
Chit-te. lu ayo: sado: lok.

Give a thousand for flaying:
Give a hundred for binding:
Hairpins of the loved one's bones.

Seven days were given to Pauk Tyaing to guess the meaning of this riddle. Now his foster-parents had come in search of him, and rested beneath a banyan-tree near the palace. And they heard a crow say to her mate (for they understood the language of birds), "For to-day we have enough, but to-morrow where shall we get our food?" to which he replied, "Be not anxious. To-morrow Paul Tyaing will die, being unable to guess the queen's riddle, and there will be a great feast." And he told her the riddle and its answer. Then fear filled the hearts of Po Byu and Me I, and they hastened to the palace, where they found their foster-son and told him what they had over-heard from the crows. So he gave the true answer to the riddle, and lived: yet he spared the queen, and she bare him sons, called Maha Thanbawa and Sula Thanbawa, whom the emanation of the dragon within her womb caused to be born blind. They, when they became youths, were set adrift on a raft down a river; and upon it they caught an ogress stealing their food, and she gave them their sight because they spared her life. At last they reached the place where is now the city of Prome. Here lived as a hermit Maung Dwe, brother of the queen Kin Saw U, and his daughter Ma Be Da by a *thamin* doe, which had conceived by lapping that which ran from the hermit's body. And be-cause it was not right that a woman should be seen at a hermit's dwelling he sent her every day to the river to fill with water a gourd having a hole no bigger than could be made by a needle. Here the young men met her, and enlarged the hole, so that Ma Be Da returned early to her father. And he questioned her, and heard the reason, and he went for the youths, and knew that they were his kin, and gave the elder his daughter in marriage. Thereafter Maha Thambawa founded the city of Tharekittara, and his brother was king after him when he died, and he also took Ma Be Da to be his queen.

53. **MAUNG BA CEIN.** BURMA

The tale concerns one Maung Ba Cein, a traveler, who came to a cer-tain kingdom and was told that a *naga*, a mythical dragon, had killed the king, taken the queen as his wife, and satisfied his hunger by eating

---

53. SOURCE: Spiro 1973:392. Copyright 1973 by Williams & Wilkins. Reproduced by per-mission of Waverly Publishers, Baltimore, Md.

people. After hearing this tale, Maung Ba Cein decided that he would become king. One night he entered the queen's chamber, and placed a banana stalk in the queen's bed, so that, when both were covered with a blanket, it would appear as if the queen were sleeping with a man. Hiding behind the curtain, Maung Ba Cein then waited for the arrival of the *naga*. When he entered the chamber, the *naga*, seeing what he took to be the body of a sleeping man, pierced it with his sword. Just as Maung Ba Cein had planned, the sword stuck in the banana stalk, and, as the *naga* attempted to extricate it, Maung Ba Cein stepped from behind the curtain and slew him. He then took the queen as his wife and he himself became the king.

[Spiro (1973:392) prefaces this account with the following: "When I then asked if they knew any Oedipal legends or myths, they knew only the Thihabahu myth [54]. However, the above-mentioned woman said she knew yet another, but after thinking a few moments she expressed surprise that she had characterized it as Oedipal. When she recounted the tale, it became apparent that on the manifest level it indeed was not an Oedipal tale, for although the theme was Oedipal, the *dramatis personae* were not. That, however, she had originally offered it as one, suggested that this was what it signified to her at a latent level."]

54. THIHABAHU. BURMA

As told in Yeigyi, the tale begins with a young princess who was a nymphomaniac. As a young woman, her sex drive was so insatiable that once she was abducted by 500 robbers in the forest, and although each of them had sexual intercourse with her, she was still not satisfied. Her father, ashamed of his daughter's nymphomania, banished her from the court. While wandering in the jungle, she met a lion, with whom she had intercourse, and since he alone could satisfy her sexually, she married him. Eventually they had two children, a son (who was eventually be become the Buddha) and a daughter. The son, Thihabahu, was ashamed that his father was a lion, and he persuaded his mother and sister to abandon him. They left the jungle while the lion was away, and eventually returned to the court where the princess's father, the king, warmly welcomed them.

In the meantime, the lion, who was filled with grief, set out to find his family. As he wandered through the villages, the people were frightened and asked the king for protection. When the king asked his court whether any would volunteer to hunt down the lion, Thihabahu, realizing that the lion must be his father, volunteered to kill him. So he set out for the jungle, and

54. SOURCE: Spiro 1973:391–92. Copyright 1973 by Williams & Wilkins. Reproduced by permission of Waverly Publishers, Baltimore, Md.

eventually found his father. Although the latter was overjoyed to see him, the son slew his father with a bow and arrow.

As a reward for slaying the lion, Thihabahu was made king of a new kingdom. However, shortly after ascending his throne he was struck blind and the court physicians were unable to cure him. One day, however, a hermit came to the court and informed Thihabahu that his blindness was retribution for his patricide, and that his sight could only be restored if he would repent of this sin. He told him to construct an image of a lion in honor of his father, and to pay homage to it. Ashamed to be seen doing homage to a lion image, Thihabahu ordered the image to be placed in front of a pagoda where, if he did obeisance to it, people would think that he was really worshipping the pagoda. This done, Thihabahu prostrated himself before the image, and his sight was restored.

55. **THE FLOOD.** HMONG (LAOS)

A very long time ago, the whole universe turned upside down. The earth tipped up, the sky rolled over, the whole world was flooded with water. All living things were killed, except one brother and his sister, who had run and taken refuge in an unusually large wooden funeral drum.

The water rose higher and higher until it reached the sky. Then this drum bumped against the land of the sky and made a sound like NDOO NDONG! NDOO NDONG!

Heaven heard the sound made by the drum and said, "Go and visit the earthly world, to see why it's making this noise. What could be happening?"

Heaven sent people to go down and observe, and they saw that water had already covered the earth and had reached even up to the sky. Then the sky people said, "Let us use copper lances and iron spears to puncture holes in the earth, so that the water can flow away."

So the sky hurled copper lances and iron spears to pierce holes in the land of the earth. Then the water flowed down and away, and the big drum finally descended back down to the surface of the earth.

When the brother and sister heard the noise, they knew their drum had landed on earth, so they broke open the drum and got out of it. Now by this time, all living beings: all people, all animals, whether squirrels, rats, or birds, even all worms, insects, and ants, had been killed, every single one. There was nothing left alive. The brother and sister looked all around, and there was no one.

---

55. SOURCE: C. Johnson 1985:115–17. From "Dej Nyab Ntiaj Teb: Hmoob Lub Xeem" ("The Flood and Hmong Clan Names") as told by May Yang, written and translated by Se Yang, Tou Doua Yang, and Charles Johnson.

They were alone, just the two of them, in all this vast world. There was no one to give life to other beings and to repopulate the world.

So the brother said that he wanted to marry his sister and have her for his wife. But the sister was not willing, and refused him. However, she said, "If you really want to marry me, we must do this: you and I will each bring a stone and we will climb up on that mountain. When we get there, we will roll your stone down one slope of the mountain, and roll mine down the other side. The next morning, if both stones have gone back up the mountain and we find them lying together on the mountain top, then I will agree to marry you."

But since the brother wanted very much to marry his sister, he got up during the night and carried his own stone and his sister's stone back up the mountain and put them together on the summit.

The next morning, when they went to look, they wanted to take someone along to be a witness, but unfortunately, there was no one to take. So the two of them, brother and sister, went back again alone, up to the top of the mountain. Lo and behold! They saw that the two stones which they had rolled down the two opposite slopes had come to rest together, in the same place, on the mountain top! When the sister saw this, she said, "We are really brother and sister, but these stones have come back and are lying together. Therefore we can be married, if you wish it to be so."

OCEANIA

56. **TANE AND HINE-HAU-ONE.** MAORI (NEW ZEALAND)

SONG OF THE MYTHOLOGY OF TANE

Tane took Hine-ti-tama to wife.
Then night and day first began;
Then was asked, "Who is father by whom I am?"
The post of the house was asked,
    but its mouth did not speak;
The side of the house was asked,
    but its mouth did not speak.
Smitten with shame, she departs, and is hidden
In the house called Pou-tu-te-raki . . .

    The host of heaven called to Tane, and said, "O Tane! fashion the outer part of the earth: it is bubbling up." Tane repeated his incantation, and went and formed the head, then the hands, arms, legs, and feet, and the body of a woman. There was no life in the form, and she adhered to the earth. Her name was Hine-hau-one [daughter of earth-aroma]. Tane used his procreating power, and a child was born, which he called Hine-i-tauira [the model daughter]. She was reared by the people to become a wife for Tane, and to him she was given. When Tane had been absent for some time she asked the people, "Where is my father?" They replied, "That is your father with whom

---

56. SOURCE: White 1887−90:131−32.

you live." She was overwhelmed with shame, and left the settlement. She killed herself. She went down to the world of spirits by the road called Tupu-ranga-o-te-po [the expansion of darkness]. Her name was altered and she was then called Hine-ti-tama [daughter of defiance]. She was allowed to enter the world of darkness, where she remained, and her name was again changed, and she was there called Hine-nui-te-po [great daughter of darkness]. Tane followed his wife, and on his arrival at the door of the world of darkness he found it had been shut by her. He was in the outer portion of the world of spirits when he heard the song of his wife, which she sang to him thus:

Are you Tane, my father,
The collector at Hawa-iki, the priest of the
    sacred ceremony of the kumara crop?
My sin to Raki made you leave me
In the house Rangi-pohutu [Heaven uplifted].
I will disappear, and weep at
The door of the house Pou-tere-raki
    [Heaven floated away].
O me!

When she had ended her song she said to Tane, "Go you to the world and foster our offspring. Let me stay in the world of darkness to drag our offspring down."

She was lost in darkness, but Tane lived in the light—that is, the world where death was not like the death in the world of darkness.

Tupu-ranga-te-po [growth of darkness] led Tane to see his wife, and opened the door of the world of darkness to allow Tane to follow her; but when he had seen the blackness he was afraid, and was not brave enough to follow her, and drew back.

57. TIKI. MANGAREVA

Tiki took Hina-one as his wife, and a female child was born who was named Tiaki-te-keukeu. One day Hina-one asked Tiki to go to the Underworld to obtain fire for them. Tiki refused and his wife said, "Then I indeed will go to the Underworld to get fire for us." Tiki replied, "No! Let us stay quietly here." His wife said, "You have your daughter. I will go to the Underworld and become a goddess." In the myth, the full moon is a symbol

---

57. SOURCE: Hiroa 1938:307. From Sir Peter Buck, *Ethnology of Mangareva*. Reproduced by permission of the Bishop Museum. NOTE: The tale is reported by the author, whose glosses are interspersed.

of the pregnant abdomen of Hina-one, for she was pregnant when she left. In the Po she was delivered of twin sons, Kuri and Kuro.

Tiki remained in the upper world with his daughter but did not dare to possess her openly. He affected to live on the other side of the mountain but told her that she might be visited at night by one of her brothers from the Underworld. He visited his daughter at night but left before daylight, lest he be recognized. After some time, Tiaki-te-keukeu became disgusted with her father and left to join her mother in the Underworld. The mother and daughter planned to kill Tiki and they lit an oven in which to cook him. Kuri and Kuro, however, objected and prevented the killing of their father. A man named Katiga, who had been brought from the upper world by the god Tuako, was consigned to the oven in Tiki's place.

58. MAUI KISIKISI AND HINA. TONGA

The husband of the goddess Heimoana, whose incarnation was the sea snake, was Malekulaulua. Heimoana's first son was Maui Motua, her second son was Maui Atalanga, her third son Maui Kisikisi, and her fourth child was Hina, a girl.

After attaining maturity the sons went to their work, leaving Hina and their parents at home. One day, while Hina was thus remaining at home, Maui Kisikisi hung chestnut leaves about his neck and stole back to his parents' house. He touched Hina's chest just above her breasts and she became pregnant. She was delivered of a male child, who was called Tangaloa. Again she became pregnant and gave birth to Io. Once more she gave birth to a girl, who was called Kohai, and lastly to a male child, who was named Afulunga. The offspring of Hina intermarried and from their progeny sprang the dynasty of Tui Tonga.

59. TUI TUITATUI. TONGA

The following account concerns the Tui Tonga Tuitatui and what he did on the raised platform house. His sister went to him. Her name was Latutama and she was female Tui Tonga. Her attendant followed her to Tuitatui's house. After his sister arrived Tuitatui ascended to his platform and then he began his lies, for, behold, he had desire for his sister to go up to the platform, so that they might have sexual intercourse. From above he said to

---

58. SOURCE: Gifford 1924:19–20. From E. W. Gifford, *Tongan Myths and Tales*. Reproduced by permission of the Bishop Museum.

59. SOURCE: Gifford 1924:29. From E. W. Gifford, *Tongan Myths and Tales*. Reproduced by permission of the Bishop Museum.

his sister below: "Here is a vessel coming, a vessel from Haapai very likely; a very large vessel."

And Latutama answered: "Oh, it is your lies." "It is not my lies," retorted Tuitatui. "Come up and see the vessel yourself." Then his sister climbed up and sat with him on the platform, while her attendant remained below, and Tuitatui and his sister had sexual intercourse. That was the way of that Tui Tonga, and it was known to the attendant.

60. **TIKOPIAN TALE.** TIKOPIA

In Raropuka, a brother and sister determined to live together. They married and the woman became pregnant. Then they left Raropuka and came to live in Rarovi. The man then went to the realm of the gods while the woman dwelt on and gave birth in the world of men, in Rarovi. Then she dwelt with her children among men. When Tafaki and Karisi came, the children had grown big—they were twins. Then they began to build their house, and went to various lands getting things to prepare it properly. Then they went off to the realm of the gods, hanging up their objects in the grove of Rarovi. Then the house of mother and children was built, standing in Rarovi. They came again, and commanded that a shelf should be made for them. There it stands in the house, with a name of its own. There are two of them, like adze handles—the embodiments of Pu Ma, of Tafaki and Karisi.

61. **TEBAGUGU.** RENNEL AND BELLONA ISLANDS

Tebagugu just lived at Tehakagaba, and Kagobai killed him because he spread vicious stories about him and his parent. Tebagugu said that Kagobai had abducted his own mother, Temota. That was the reason Kagobai killed Tebagugu, because he was ashamed about this evil report.

[Samuel Elbert's note: This came when I asked what the vicious stories were. SE: "Do you think the stories were true?" Informants: "We think so, Kagobai would not have killed him." SE: "Could Tebagugu have lied about the snake and also about Kagobai?" Informants: "We don't think so. We think both are true." SE: "Was incest common?" Informants: "It was sometimes done." (The informants seemed surprised that I could doubt either story.)]

---

60. SOURCE: Firth 1961:75. From Raymond Firth, *History and Traditions of Tikopia*, published by the University of Hawaii Press, 1961. Reproduced by permission of the publisher.

61. SOURCE: Elbert and Monberg 1965:241–42. From Samuel H. Elbert and T. Monberg, *From the Two Canoes*, published by the University of Hawaii Press, 1965. Reproduced by permission of the publisher.

62. THE TALE OF THE IMMORAL NGARARA. MAORI

(NEW ZEALAND)

U ruhape was a chief who possessed such powers over the unseen world that everybody thought he would have respected such personal property as he had made *tapu*, or sacred, to himself. But Tonga was a woman who lacked foresight, a creature of impulse and carelessness, who could not realize the awful responsibility of living in close contact with a wizard, the hair of whose head she was not worthy to comb. And, strangely enough, it was a comb which caused all her trouble.

Uruhape went on a journey to the Urewera Country, where lived relations of his whom he had not seen since he was a child. He left all his belongings in his hut, knowing full well that nobody in Hauraki would be so foolhardy as to rob him in his absence. His mats of ceremony and his weapons he took with him; but such things as his fish-hooks, his *mata-tuhua*, used for tonsorial purposes, and the combs with which he was wont to deal with the *kutu* which took refuge in his locks, he left in a carved *kumete* in his wife's keeping. Everything in the box was sacred to himself, and of that fact Tonga was fully cognizant. However, in the mind of a foolish woman familiarity breeds contempt. Uruhape had treated his wife with such consideration and affection that she had forgotten the gulf fixed eternally between her mediocrity and his sanctity. So that he had been gone hardly a week when, being much troubled with the *kutu* in her own hair, Tonga lightly seized one of her husband's combs to rid herself of the pest.

She finished the operation without realizing the enormity of her offence against her spouse's *tapu*; she returned the sacred comb to its box; and full of satisfaction she went down to the sea-shore to eat mussels. There retribution overtook her. While she bent over the succulent bivalves and drank the juice out of their nacreous shells, there hovered on the horizon a dark and ominous object, which flying swiftly over the surface of the sea, rapidly swept down on the misguided woman. Too late she heard the flapping of the great membranous wings, too late she saw the black abhorrent form. She had barely time to cry, "The Ngarara! The Ngarara!" when she was seized, and borne captive over the desolate sea.

That, you will think, was the end of the unhappy Tonga, that was the last ever heard of the woman who failed to respect her husband's *tapu*. But it was not so. All day the Ngarara flew over the sea with his prey, and as night fell he reached a solitary island, where he had made his home in a dark, unwholesome cave; and there he deposited his living burden.

---

62. SOURCE: Grace 1907:209–11.

Of course the terrified woman imagined that she was to be eaten alive; but the Ngarara had preserved her for a fate even more terrible. "You are to be my wife," said the monster in a language which Tonga could not as yet understand, but which she was to speak with fluency ere she had lived out half her days. "I have not the least intention of hurting you; I have brought you here simply to love you," said the Ngarara, and he took her on his knee, and wrapped her in his dreadful pinions.

Now, it so happened that Tonga had been married to the Ngarara only a couple of months—and such was her womanly ability of adapting herself to circumstances that she had become almost resigned to her new manner of living—when she gave birth to a dear little brown girl.

"This," said the Ngarara, "is no daughter of mine—she has no wings, no webbed feet."

"No," replied Tonga; "she is the daughter of Uruhape, my former husband."

"Then I will eat her," said the Ngarara.

"Don't do that," exclaimed his wife. "She will grow up to be more beautiful than I am, and then you will be able to have two wives."

"I never thought of that," said the Ngarara. "That is a very good idea." And such was his immoral nature that he determined to carry out the plan.

There was one advantage, however, in being married to the Ngarara—he caught plenty of fish, and these Tonga cooked for herself and her child, to whom she had given the name of Kura. And this little girl throve and grew, but without knowing the fate that was in store for her; for when Kura had grown up, the Ngarara turned the faded mother out of his cave and took her daughter to be his wife.

The aged Tonga wandered over the island till she came to a sheltered cove at the end furthest from the den of the horrible monster, and there she made herself a hut out of flax leaves and *manuka* boughs, in which she lived a comparatively happy, if lonely, existence.

63. TIKI TAKES HIS DAUGHTER HINA TO WIFE. TUAMOTUA

Hina grew up in the care of her maternal grandparents, Mati and One-ura. When she reached young womanhood she resolved to go to the land of her father. When she announced her intentions, Mati willingly consented but One-ura would not acquiesce. She said to her, "If you go to the land of your father you will become his mistress—for Tiki has no wife. Your

63. SOURCE: Stimpson 1937:6–9. From J. F. Stimpson, *Tuamotuan Legends*. Reproduced by permission of the Bishop Museum.

mother is dead, you have reached the age of puberty, and indeed you are a winsome girl."

Then they argued together—Hina and Mati on one side, and One-ura on the other. Finally against her better judgment, One-ura consented.

So Hina went to Havaiki-nui-a-na-ea, the land of Tiki. As soon as she arrived, her father's parents, Ahu-roa and One-rua, welcomed her to their home. Tiki was not there at the moment—he had gone inland to seek for food. Finally Tiki returned and saw them sitting together. He realized that this young girl must be his own daughter. Tiki advanced to meet her and looked at her long and intently—Hina was indeed a very beautiful girl.

Soon Tiki's parents went away to prepare the evening meal. In a little while the food was ready and they took their repast together. Afterwards Ahu-roa and One-rua went to their house to prepare a sleeping place for Hina. This was soon ready, and then they came back for Hina and Tiki.

"Hina is going to sleep in my house," Tiki told his parents.

"It is unseemly that you should both sleep in the same house since you have no wife—for Hina has reached the age of womanhood," they replied.

Then they argued over the matter, but Tiki was so obstinate that his parents at last consented against their will, and allowed Hina to sleep beside him in his own house.

Tiki and Hina had been living in Tiki's house for quite a long time when an evil thought arose in his mind. This was that thought—he would sleep with his own daughter, with Hina.

During the nights that followed, they slept in the same house. At dawn, Tiki marked the position in which his daughter lay. If she lay on her back, he would lie upon her, face down, pressing his nose against hers and uttering words of fatherly affection. Hina, on awakening, thought that Tiki's conduct was an expression of the natural affection of a father and so did not resent it.

Tiki one day told Hina he was going out fishing. He instructed her to follow some time after with a basket for the fish. She was to follow the southern shore and go to a place on the beach where she would see birds flocking and hovering about. When she saw something sticking up from the sand, she was to pull it up as it was their pointed stick for stringing fish.

Later Hina followed with her fish basket. On seeing a flock of birds hovering around some object on the shore, she approached it. Thinking that the object protruding from the sand was the stick for stringing fish, she grasped it and pulled. At once Tiki who had covered himself with sand, leaped up crying, "Who is this person pulling on my phallus?"

Tiki began laughing and when Hina saw it was her father, she reproached him saying, "O Tiki! This is an unworthy performance—a most despicable act. Therefore, indeed, you are called 'Tiki-the-trickster,' 'Tiki-the-tumid,' 'Tiki-the-slimy!'"

[Tiki seized Hina and after ravishing her, he chanted a passion-song (Tiritiri na Tiki) in which the copulative act is described. In the chant Tiki applied the following epithets to himself, his name being symbolic of the phallus: Tiki-te-peu (Tiki-the-trickster), Tiki-te-maineine (Tiki-the-tingling), Tiki-te-goru (Tiki-the-distended), Tiki-te-hakupekupe (Tiki-the-smeared), Tiki-te-hagaregare (Tiki-the-slimy), Tiki-mara-uta (Tiki-the-tumescent-upon-land), Tiki-mara-tai (Tiki-the-tumescent-upon-the-ocean).]

Tiki and Hina then lived together as lover and mistress in Tiki's house.

64. SIKHALOL AND HIS MOTHER. ULITHI ATOLL

A very beautiful young woman by the name of Lisor was married to a chief by the name of Sokhsurum. She became pregnant, and the child was born prematurely at seven months. The infant was still covered by the amniotic membrane, and the mother did not know there was a baby inside. She put the membrane in a coconut spathe and set it adrift on the ocean.

On the east end of the island, separated from the main village, there lived about ten people. One of them was Rasim, a man who had a large stone trap for catching fish. The spathe with the baby drifted against the sides of the trap and one day when Rasim went out to see if he had caught any fish he saw the infant lying on the coconut bract. He lifted it up and took it home. He then performed some magic so that it would grow up. Everyday he would repeat the magic, at the same time giving the infant nourishment. This went on for many days and in a month the baby had grown to be a young man. Rasim had guessed the identity of the child from the beginning, for he knew that a girl from the village had been pregnant and had had a premature baby at the same time he had found the infant on the spathe.

Rasim made a small canoe for the youth, whose name was Sikhalol. One day, Sikhalol went sailing on the reef with some youths from another village. Their canoe passed by the menstrual house where his mother happened to be confined because she was menstruating. Lisor saw her son and said to herself, "Who is this handsome youth?" She waded out into the water and caught hold of the canoe, which was being pushed near shore by the wind while the boys swam playfully after it. Sikhalol told her to give him back his canoe. She told him to come over to her as she wanted to tell him something. He replied, "I cannot come ashore as I do not have on a loincloth." Lisor walked over near to him, still holding the canoe, and said, "Come and see me tonight and we shall spoon." The youth told her he did not know where

64. SOURCE: Lessa 1961:49–50. From William Lessa, *Tales from Ulithi Atoll: A Comparative Study in Oceanic Folklore*, published by the University of California Press, 1961. Reproduced by permission of the publisher.

she slept and Lisor told him she was staying in the menstrual house. Sikhalol said he would come. Then he sailed away with the other boys who were with him.

Sikhalol waited for darkness to fall. When nighttime arrived he went to see the beautiful young woman in the menstrual house. They made love. About four in the morning he returned to his house. These visits were repeated for several days in succession. After the tenth day, the chief, Sokhsurum, went to see his wife at the menstrual house to find out why she was staying there so long. She did not want to return with him so she lied and said her period had not yet ended. The truth was that she wanted to continue making love with the handsome youth.

Sikhalol's foster father, Rasim, suspected that the youth was visiting a girl each night so he asked him if he had a sweetheart in the village. Sikhalol replied that he had. Rasim asked him where the woman lived and he answered that she lived in the menstrual house and was the wife of the chief. Rasim told him he was making a great mistake, for the woman was his own mother. Then he related the story of how he had removed him from the sea and raised him.

When Sikhalol went the next night to see Lisor he revealed to her that he was her son—the child she had set adrift on the sea. He said they had better stop their love-making. But his mother did not care and said they should continue, and so they did. When Sikhalol returned home in the morning he had a talk with his foster father, telling him he had spoken to his mother but that she did not care and wanted to go on making love. Rasim replied, "All right. I don't care, either." Sikhalol returned to his mother the next night and many nights thereafter, making love to her for three months. On one of these occasions he happened to scratch her with his fingers on the side of her face.

The chief had meanwhile become very impatient with Lisor and one day he went to see her and demanded that she leave the menstrual house, saying she was lying to him since she had been there for four months. She refused to leave, whereupon Sokhsurum became angry, so she returned with him.

Lisor's face still bore the scratches that she had got from Sikhalol. She was afraid her husband might see them and guess their origin, so in order to conceal them she kept her hair, which was long, close to the sides of her face. But Sokhsurum knew she had the scratches and had made up his mind how she had got them; therefore one day he suddenly pulled back her hair away from her face and exposed them. He demanded, "Have you been making love to someone else?" Lisor replied, "No"—but he did not believe her. He took a conch shell and blew it. All the men of the village assembled to see what was the matter. The chief told them to step up one by one and put their fingers near his wife's face so that he could see which ones fitted the marks.

As each man did so Sokhsurum held an ax poised to strike him down if he were the guilty one. When they had all submitted to the test he realized that none of them was responsible for the scratches.

The next day he sent word for the handful of men in the nearby village where Rasim and Sikhalol lived to come to see him. Rasim told the men to go one at a time and return. While they were doing so, he told his foster son that he was going to teach him to wrestle, and Sikhalol learned how to protect himself. When all the other men had completed their tests Rasim himself went and then returned. Now only his foster son was left and all the people in the little village surmised that he was the guilty one. Thinking he was about to be killed they decorated him with turmeric, arm bands and anklets of young coconut palm leaves, and a sweet basil wreath, and dressed him in a new hibiscus-banana fiber loincloth. Then they accompanied him to see the chief.

As the group approached the chief's house, Lisor looked at Sikhalol and began to cry. The other people sat down near the house. Sokhsurum called over to the youth to come and put his fingers alongside his wife's face. He told him as he held up the ax that he would kill him if he were guilty. When the youth put his fingers near the scratches Sokhsurum saw that he was the guilty one. He began to swing the ax on Sikhalol but the youth knew how to defend himself, for his foster father had taught him. He seized the ax and with it cut off the head of the chief—his real father.

Sikhalol then took Lisor back to his village, and they lived together from then on.

65. MANDAYA TALE. PHILIPPINES

The Mandaya of Cateel believe that many generations ago a great flood occurred which caused the death of all the inhabitants of the world except one pregnant woman. She prayed that her child might be a boy. Her prayer was answered and she gave birth to a son whose name was Vacatan. He, when he had grown up, took his mother for his wife and from this union have sprung all the Mandaya.

66. THE ORIGIN OF LOVE AND MAGIC. TROBRIANDS

The source [of love and magic] is Kumilabwaga. A woman there brought forth two children, a girl and a boy. The mother came [and settled down] to cut her fibre skirt; the boy cooked magical herbs [for the

---

65. SOURCE: Cooper-Cole 1913:173–74.
66. SOURCE: Malinowski 1929:456–59.

magic of love]. He cooked aromatic leaves in coco-nut oil. He hung the vessel with the fluid [on a batten of the roof near the door] and went away to bathe. The sister arrived from her firewood-breaking expedition; she put down the firewood; she asked the mother: "Fetch me some water, which my brother has put in the house." The mother answered: "You go and fetch it yourself, my legs are burdened with the board on which I cut the skirt."

The girl entered the hut, she saw the water-bottles lying there; with her head she brushed against the vessel with the magic fluid; the coco-nut dripped; it trickled into her hair; she passed her hands over it, wiped it off, and smelt it. Then the power of magic struck her, it entered her inside, it turned her mind. She went and fetched the water, she brought it back and put it down. She asked her mother: "And what about my brother? [Where has the man gone?]"—The mother gave voice: "O my children, they have become mad! He has gone to the open seashore."

The girl ran out, she sped towards the eastern shore, to the open sea. She came to where the road abuts on the sea beach. There she untied her fibre skirt and flung it down. She ran along the beach naked; she ran to the Bokaraywata beach [the place where the Kumilabwaga people usually bathe, and where they beach their canoes]. She came upon her brother there—he bathed in the Kadi'usawasa passage in the fringing reef. She saw him bathing, she entered the water and went towards him, she gave him chase. She chased him towards the rock of Kadilawolu. There he turned and ran back. She chased him back and he went to the Olakawo rock. There he turned round and came back running. He came back and went again to the Kadi-'usawasa passage [i.e., where he was bathing first]. There she caught him, there they lay down in the shallow water.

They lay together [and copulated], then they went ashore and they copulated again. They climbed the slope, they went to the grotto of Bokaraywata, there they lay down again and copulated. They remained there together and slept. They did not eat, they did not drink—this is the reason why they died [because of shame, because of remorse].

That night a man of Iwa had a dream. He dreamt the dream of their *sulumwoya* [the mint plant which they used in their love magic]. "O my dream! Two people, brother and sister are together; I see in my mind; they lie by each other in the grotto of Bokaraywata." He paddled over the sea arm of Galeya; he paddled to Kitava and moored his canoe—he searched all over—but nothing was to be found. He paddled over the sea arm of Da'uya, he came to Kumilabwaga, he paddled towards the shore, he landed. He saw a bird, a frigate-bird with its companions—they soared.

He went and climbed the slope; he went and saw them dead. And lo! a mint flower had sprouted through their breasts. He sat by their prostrate bodies, then he went along the shore. He looked for the road, he searched and found it, he went to the village. He entered the village—there was the mother sitting and cutting her fibre skirt. He spoke: "Do you know what has happened by the sea?" "My children went there and copulated and shame overcame them." He spoke and said: "Come, recite the magic, so that I may hear it." She recited, she went on reciting, he listened, he heard till he had learnt it completely. He learnt it right through to the end. He came again, and asked: "What is the magical song of the coco-nut oil?" He inquired, that man from Iwa. "Come now, tell me the song of the coco-nut oil."

She recited it to the end. Then he said: "Remain here, I shall go. Part of the magic, the opening part, let it remain here. The eye of the magic, the finishing part, I shall take, and let it be called Kayro'iwa. He went off, he came to the grotto, to the *sulumwoya* plant which sprouted and grew out of their breasts. He broke off a sprig of the herb, he put it into his canoe, he sailed, he brought it to Kitava. He went ashore in Kitava and rested there. He then sailed and landed in Iwa.

These are his words [which he spoke in Iwa]: "I have brought here the point of the magic, its eye [the sharpest, that is the most efficient part of the magic]. Let us call it the Kayro'iwa. The foundation, or the lower part [the less important part], the Kaylakawa remains in Kumilabwaga." [Henceforth the words of the speaker refer not to Iwa, but to Kumilabwaga. This is obviously an inconsistency, because in the myth he is speaking in Iwa. This probably was due to the faulty recital of the myth.] The water of this magic is Bokaraywata; its sea passage Kadi'usawasa. There [on the beach] stands its *silasila* bush, there stands its *givagavela* bush. If people from the lagoon villages would come to bathe (in the waterhole or in the sea passage), then the bushes would bleed. This water is taboo to them—the youth of our village only should come and bathe in it. But a fish caught in these waters is taboo to them [the young people of our village]. When such a fish is caught in the nets, they should cut off its tail, then the old people might eat it. Of a bunch of coco-nuts washed on the beach, they [the young people] must not eat a single one—it is a taboo. Only old men and old women may eat them.

When they come and bathe in the Bokaraywata and then return to the beach, they make a hole in the sand and say some magic. Later on in their sleep they dream of the fish. They dream that the fish spring [out of the sea] and come into that pool. Nose to nose the fish swim. If there is only one fish they would throw it out into the sea. When there are two, one female, one male, the youth would wash in this water. Going to the village, he would get hold of a woman and sleep with her. He would go on sleeping with her and make arrangements with her family so that they might marry. This is the happy end, they would live together and make their gardens.

If an outsider would come here for the sake of the magic, he would bring a magical payment in the form of a valuable. He would bring it and give it to you, you might give him the charm: the spells of the *isika'i* leaves, of the betel pod, of the washing charm, of the smoking charm, of the stroking charm; you might give him also the charm of the obsidian blade, of the coco-nut, of the *silasila*, of the *buresi* leaves, of the coco-nut husk fibre, of the *gimgwam* leaves, of the *yototu* leaves, of the comb—and for all this, they ought to pay the substantial payment of *laga*.

For this is the erotic payment of your magic. Then let them return home, and eat pigs, yams, ripe betel-nut, yellow betel-nut, red bananas, sugar cane. For they have brought you valuables, food, betel-nut as a present. For you are masters of this magic, and you may distribute it. You remain here, they may carry it away; and you, the owners, remain here, for you are the foundation of this magic.

67. DOKONIKAN AND TUDAVA. TROBRIANDS

Humanity led a happy existence in the Trobriand Archipelago. Suddenly a dreadful ogre called Dokonikan made his appearance in the eastern part of the islands. He fed on human flesh and gradually consumed one community after another. At the north-western end of the island in the village of Laba'i there lived at that time a family consisting of a sister and her brothers. When Dokonikan ranged nearer and nearer to Laba'i the family decided to fly. The sister, however, at that moment wounded her foot and was unable to move. She was therefore abandoned by her brothers, who left her with her little son in a grotto on the beach of Laba'i, and sailed away in a canoe to the south-west. The boy was brought up by his mother, who taught him first the choice of proper wood for a strong spear, then instructed him in the *Kwoygapani* magic which steals away a man's understanding. The hero sailed forth, and after having bewitched Dokonikan with the *Kwoygapani* magic, killed him and cut off his head. After that he and his mother prepared a taro pudding, in which they hid and baked the head of the ogre. With this gruesome dish Tudava sailed away in search of his mother's brother. When he found him he gave him the pudding, in which the uncle with horror and dismay found the head of Dokonikan. Seized with fear and remorse, the mother's brother offered his nephew all sorts of gifts in atonement for having abandoned him and his mother to the ogre. The hero refused everything, and was only appeased after he had received his uncle's daughter in marriage. After that he set out again and performed a number of cultural deeds, which do not interest us further in this context.

---

67. SOURCE: Malinowski 1927:111–12. Published by Routledge and Kegan Paul, 1927. Reproduced by permission of ITPS.

68. **MOMOVALA.** TROBRIANDS

Momovala goes with his daughter to the garden and sends her up a tree. He looks up and sees her genitals, and emits the long-drawn *katugogova*. This is produced by giving voice on a high-pitched note, while the sound is interrupted by the rapid beating of the mouth with the hand. It is used to express intense emotional excitement of a pleasant kind. She asks him why he screamed. "I saw a green lory," he answers. The same sequence is repeated, and he mentions another bird, and so on for several times over. When she comes down from the tree, the father has already discarded his pubic leaf and is in a state of erection. She is very confused, and weeps. He, however, seizes her, and copulates and copulates. After all is over, she sings a ditty which may be rendered: "O *Momovala, Momovala*! Gut of my gut, father of my father. Father by name, he seized me, he brought me, he wronged me." The mother hears her and guesses what has happened. "Already he has got hold of the girl and copulated. I shall go and see."

The mother meets them, the girl complains, and the father denies. The girl goes to the seashore with all her belongings, and sings to a shark to come and eat up, first her wooden board for the making of grass skirts, then her basket, then one arm, then the other arm, and so on, interminably singing the same ditty for each object. Finally she sings: "Eat me up altogether," and the shark does so.

At home Momovala asks the mother where the girl has gone, and learns of her tragic death. His answer is to ask the mother to take off her grass skirt and copulate with him. The story describes his horizontal motions, which are so strong that his wife complains: *Yakay*, *Yakay*, an expression of pain. But he only pushes deeper and deeper. She complains again to no purpose. She dies after the act.

Next day people ask him in the garden what has happened. He says that his wife has been speared. "Where?" "In her vagina." Momovala then cuts off his penis and dies.

69. **THE REVENGE OF AIO.** EASTER ISLAND

Once upon a time there was a jealous man called Aio, who used to strike his wife all the time. One day when Aio had gone to a *koro* feast, his wife went fishing and caught *patuki* and *tuamingo* fish. She made an earth oven and cooked the fish.

---

68. SOURCE: Malinowski 1929:346–47.

69. SOURCE: Metraux 1971:385–86. Used by permission.

When Aio came back from the *koro*, she opened the oven and brought the *tuamingo* fish to her husband. He ate until he was satisfied and then fell into a deep sleep. The woman stabbed his stomach with an obsidian spear. The blood flowed, the intestines fell out from the stomach. The woman took her belongings and went to Vaiatare, but she forgot to take her youngest child.

The child stayed in the house, hungry and crying. He crawled toward his dead father and licked the blood. Four days later an old woman saw the rotten body of the man and this child, whose intestines were filled with the corrupted blood of his father, crying and licking the corpse. The old woman took the child and went down to the beach to wash him. She threw him into the sea and forced him to swallow salt water so that he would vomit the rotten stuff he had in his stomach. His intestines finally subsided because there was no more filth within him. The old woman took him to her house. There he remained and was fed with good food. He lived with the old woman ten years.

Years passed and he became an adult. The old woman had given him the name of Aio. The child asked, "Old woman, who is my father?" The old woman answered, "I am your father." "No, tell me who is my father." The old woman said, "Don't you want me to be your father?" "No, I want my own father." The old woman said, "Your father was killed by your own mother. She lives in the direction of the black clouds."

Aio planted bananas, sugar cane, and potatoes, and made heaps of soil for yams. When these plants were ripe, he prepared a big feast above the little mountain called the "Mountain of Aio." He plucked sugar cane and bananas and buried them in a big pit to hasten their ripening. He dug out yams and sweet potatoes and caught tuna, *pei* fish, and eels.

He sent a messenger to his mother in the mountain to invite her with his brothers to eat at the *koro* feast. She came with his aunts, uncles, and cousins. Not a single relative, even far apart, was forgotten. When they arrived the earth oven was opened. Aio said, "My mother and I are going to stay outside. You enter the *koro* house and eat." The uncles, aunts, the brothers, the cousins, the distant relatives entered the *koro* hut and ate. Aio cried to his people, "Put in bananas, put in sweet potatoes, put in sugar cane." "The sugar cane in the house is not finished," said the people in the house, "Stop sending more, be moderate, the house is already full." But Aio said to his men, "Press it, make it tight." They pressed the food in the house very tightly. The people in it could hardly breathe. Then Aio said to his men, "Burn the house."

After this, Aio said to his mother, "I am going to take care of you. I made a pile of sugar cane and shall put the load on your back." The mother said, "Aio, put a smaller load." He piled up more and more sugar cane until the woman succumbed under the weight and died. This was Aio's revenge.

70. **LUMIMU-UT.** CELEBES

In the beginning there were only the sea and a great rock which was washed by the waves, and which, after first giving birth to a crane, sweated, from the sweat being produced a female deity called Lumimu-ut. Advised by the crane of the existence of the "original land," she got from thence two handfuls of earth which she spread upon the rock, and so she created the world, on which she planted the seeds of all the plants and trees, obtaining them from the same "original land." Having thus made the earth, Lumimu-ut ascended a mountain, where the west wind blew upon her and made her fruitful. In due time she bore a son, and when he had grown to manhood his mother advised him to seek a wife, but though he sought far and wide, he could find none. So Lumimu-ut gave him a staff, whose length was equal to her own stature, bidding him to seek for a woman who should be less tall than the staff, and telling him that when he should find such a person he would know that she was the one he was destined to marry. Mother and son then separated, one going to the right and one to the left, and travelled around the whole world until at last they met again, without recognizing each other, and lo! when he set the staff beside her, its length was greater than her stature, for without his knowledge the rod had increased in height. Believing, therefore, that the woman, who was indeed his own mother, was she of whom he had been told, he married her, and she bore him many children who became gods.

71. **THE LEGEND OF TANGKUBAN PARAHU.** WEST JAVA

[Prayatni's note: There is a mountain in West Java called Mt. Tangkuban Parahu, which is, according to the following legend, considered to be an overturned boat, with the Bandung Plateau being a vast lake.]

The legend of Tangkuban Parahu tells the story of Sangkuriang, a prince who unknowingly comes across his long exiled mother, Dayang Sumbi, who has retained her youth and beauty, and falls in love with her. They plan to marry and one day caressing Sangkuriang's head she finds the scar of the wound that she had inflicted on him when he was a child and realizes who he is. Not wanting to tell him the truth, she sets some impossible tasks for him. A day before the wedding feast she demands that he build a boat in one night and also a lake so he can enjoy a cruise. Unaware that he has supernatural powers, she is aghast to find that before the end of the night,

70. SOURCE: Dixon 1916:157–58.
71. SOURCE: Prayatni 1989.

the boat is almost finished so she makes a last effort to stop him. She takes her *lesung* [wooden pounder for rice] and starts pounding it. The sound awakens the cocks and their crowing indicates an early dawn. Finding that he has failed, Sangkuriang kicks the boat, overturning it to become the legendary Mt. Tangkuban Parahu.

One version says that he then pursued the beautiful princess and her lightning in the area indicates that he has almost caught her. The lake later dried up to become the Bandung Plateau. Another version has it that he drowned and the princess jumped into the lake too in despair.

72. SEUFA AND HIS NEPHEW.   TRUK

Seufa used to live on Fefan [an island in Truk] and had five wives. He decreed that if any of the women of Fefan were to give birth to boys they should kill them, but if they bore girls they should take care of them. Seufa made this rule because he did not want anyone to speak to his wives.

The people of Fefan were in great distress, for they pitied their sons. By and by, one of Seufa's sisters gave birth to a son. She loved him greatly. She sent him to Eater-of-the-Wind [a moth or a bird] to take care of him. Eater-of-the-Wind took him and she raised him until he was big.

One day, the boy heard the people doing much clapping down by the sea and he asked his mother [Eater-of-the-Wind] what it was. She told him the people of Fefan were holding a model canoe race. He told her he wanted her to carve out a canoe for him so that he could join them. So Eater-of-the-Wind carved a model canoe for her child. He took his toy canoe and went off and set it on the sea. His canoe sailed off among all the other toy canoes. As the canoe traveled along it sped with the outrigger float out of the water. In his happiness the boy clapped the hollow of his bent elbow, for his toy canoe had left all the others behind. The boy chased after his canoe and directed it toward land.

Seufa's wife caught sight of the canoe, and of the boy, too. She greatly liked that fellow. She kept running to wherever the boat was headed. She seized the canoe, but the boy ran up and wrenched it away from her. His fingernails indented the hands of Seufa's wife. The people kept on sailing their toy canoes until the canoe game was finished; then each returned to his house.

---

72. SOURCES: Primary source: Fischer n.d.:1011–23; Secondary source: Lessa 1961:174–76. From William Lessa, *Tales from Ulithi Atoll: A Comparative Study in Oceanic Folklore*, published by the University of California Press, 1961. Reproduced by permission of the publisher. NOTE: The tale is being presented by Lessa, who summarizes a portion of it in his own voice.

Evening came, and Seufa said to his wives, "Come, let us eat." So they ate. And that woman would dig into her breadfruit poi and keep her hand turned to one side. Seufa ordered her to straighten out her hand. So the woman straightened out her hand, and Seufa saw the mark of that fellow's fingernails. He asked her, "Who scratched your hand?" The woman did not reveal him. So Seufa dashed out by his feast house and blew his shell trumpet.

All of the people of Fefan assembled. They asked what the trumpet was for, and Seufa said, "A trumpet for you to come and impress your fingernails on my wife's hand." So they each measured their fingernails in the marks of that certain person's fingernails, but none of them fit. Seufa said to them all, "All right, let us think whose these fingernail marks may be." Someone called out for them to try and see if they were the marks of a certain youth who had joined in the canoe racing that day, for he was very handsome. Seufa asked where he came from, and the fellow spoke and said, "It seems as if he came down from up on that mountain."

Seufa sent someone to go up and see if there was a youth in the house of Eater-of-the-Wind. The fellow arrived and the youth was there. He told the youth that he was to go to see Seufa. The youth went along with that fellow. They entered Seufa's feast house. Seufa said to the youth, "Come here and try fitting your fingernails [to see] if these are the marks of your fingernails on my wife's hand." The youth tested his fingernails, and they fitted perfectly.

[At this point there follows a long series of attempts on the part of Seufa to have the boy killed. These accounts form the greater part of the story but are irrelevant for our present purposes. Briefly, Seufa tries to kill the boy by having a post rammed down on him while he is digging a posthole; by having him burned to death; by having him showered with spears; by having him lowered into the sea in a wicker fish trap; and by having him abandoned on a small uninhabited island. The boy escapes each time by means of various tricks, except in the last instance when he is aided by the God of the Rainbow, who, delighted at coming upon the boy as he is making offerings to him, helps him return home. He does this by drawing a canoe for the youth in the sand. He then kicks it into the water. It is a fine ocean-going sailing canoe. The boy gets on the canoe and sails for Fefan. From here on the story again becomes relevant.]

When the youth arrived near Fefan the people of the land watched him. They said, "What canoe is that, that is so fast? For there has never been a vessel of this land as fast as that." Seufa told the people to watch the canoe, and they peered and peered at it. They told him there was only one person on it, and that he was "that fellow." Seufa gave orders that the youth was to moor his canoe and leave it for Seufa to sail the next day. The youth came ashore with a cargo of one thousand and five fish. He took one for his mother to eat, and all the rest he set down before Seufa. He said to Seufa,

"Your expedition didn't catch anything, because I was all by myself." Seufa said to him, "Why look, here is your catch." Then the youth went to see his mother, and he told her that Seufa had said he was going to use his canoe. His mother said, "Well, that's fine."

Night fell and day rose. Then Seufa and his brothers—his group—set forth on that canoe. The youth climbed up a tall coconut tree and watched them. His mother told him not to play with Seufa's canoe, and he said to his mother, "No, I'm going to sorcerize it." Then the youth said a sorcery spell over the canoe: "Run along, my canoe; run, run, flee, run, run." And the canoe started to fly over the sea. He repeated the spell a second time. The canoe went much farther than before. Then a third time. And then he said a spell for the canoe to disintegrate: "Ball of sand, scatter; scatter into sand." And Seufa's group swam about in the sea. Sharks appeared and bit them all, and they died.

73. TWO BROTHERS WHO COVETED THEIR SISTER.

ULITHI ATOLL

There lived all alone·on an island a man, his wife, and their three children—two boys and a girl. The mother and father often cautioned their children against having incestuous relations with one another. The two sons and the daughter promised to do as they were told.

In time, the father became very sick and approached death. He told his wife and children that after he had died he should be buried near the house. Then he passed away and they buried him in accordance with his instructions.

Soon the mother too became sick. She told her children that after she died they were to put her in the same grave as the father. She died, and the children buried her where she had said they should. Thus, only the three children were left on the island, living together in one house.

The two brothers were desirous of lying with a girl, but there were no women on the island except their sister. One day, the two boys came together and discussed how they could have intercourse with her. The older brother said to the younger one that he had a plan, and related it to him. He said that he would go fishing and when he returned he would pretend to be a spirit and command their sister to lie with the younger brother.

That night, as arranged, the older brother went fishing. He caught a lot of

73. SOURCE: Lessa 1961:51–53. From William Lessa, *Tales from Ulithi Atoll: A Comparative Study in Oceanic Folklore*, published by the University of California Press, 1961. Reproduced by permission of the publisher.

fish and started to take them home. As he was walking toward the house his sister saw the fish gleaming in the darkness and cried out to her brother, "What is that!" She thought she was seeing a spirit. But her younger brother, who was reclining in another corner of the house, knew it was not a spirit and he said nothing. The sister then called out, "Who are you!" The brother with the fish replied, "I am a spirit." The girl did not hear him clearly, so she asked the brother in the house what it was that the voice had said. He replied, "The spirit says we should lie with one another." But the sister replied, "We must not do that, for our father and mother told us we must never have intercourse." Her brother said, "If we do not lie with one another, perhaps the spirit will kill us." The girl said she did not think that would happen, whereupon the younger brother said he would ask the "spirit" what it was he had told them. He asked the "spirit" to repeat what he had said. The "spirit" replied, "Get on top of your sister and have intercourse with her. If you do not, I will kill you both!" The brother turned to his sister, saying, "See! That is what I told you before, but you would not believe me." The sister did not know how to reply effectively to her brother, so she consented to do what the "spirit" had ordered. Her brother got on top of her and they had intercourse.

The older brother, who was outside the house, gave them enough time to finish. Then he entered the house, which was dark. His sister called out "Who are you!" and he replied that he was her brother, returning from fishing. He said he had hung the catch of fish outside the house. Then he and the other two, who had already separated from each other before the brother came in, went to sleep.

The next morning the brother who had acted as the spirit had a talk with the younger brother. He asked him if he had lain with his sister as they had schemed, and the latter said he had. The older brother then said, "You have lain with her, but how am I going to do so?" The younger brother said he would go inside their parents' grave and remain there during the day, and that if their sister were to ask where he had gone he should tell her he was out fishing. Then he should tell her to go with him and collect breadfruit from the trees. He then gave him the other details of his scheme. The older brother agreed to the plan.

That day, the younger brother went and hid in the grave and the other one called his sister to come and collect breadfruit with him. They went off into the woods. The youth climbed a breadfruit tree, while his sister stood below waiting for the fruit to fall. Suddenly the brother pretended to slip. He seized a branch as he fell, hanging from it with one arm and crying, "I am going to fall!" His sister was panic-stricken and shouted, "What can I do to help you!" He told her to go to the grave of their parents and ask their ghost for advice.

The sister ran quickly to the grave, calling, "Mother! Father! How can I help my brother, who is hanging with one arm from a breadfruit tree!" The brother inside the grave answered, "Go and have intercourse with your brother." She ran back to the breadfruit tree saying, "They said, 'Go and have ———.'" But she stopped, unable to utter the wicked word. Her brother, hanging from the tree, told her to go back again and ask once more what to do. She left for the grave, and when she returned she started all over again: "They said, 'Go and have ———,'" but again she was unable to bring herself to speak the horrible word. Her brother then told her to go once again to the grave.

This time, when she returned, she sputtered out the rest of the sentence: "——— intercourse with your brother." Immediately, her brother seized the branch with both hands and then made his way down to the ground. He and his sister then lay with each other under the breadfruit tree.

The younger brother, who had been hiding in the grave, waited until they had had time to finish and then he went to where they were. He said, "I have returned from fishing, but I did not catch anything." Then all three returned to the house.

74. JAVA TALE.

The ruler of Daha [in Java] urinated in a hollow stone. A pig drank the urine and became pregnant, giving birth to a girl. The girl was raised by some *widiadari*, or heavenly maidens. She had intercourse with a black dog who had brought her the bobbin that she had dropped from her house to the ground. In shame the girl took a knife and cut the dog and herself [note: this is said to be the origin of the "circumcision" of all Moslem men and women]. The dog went away. The girl gave birth to a son, and when the son grew up the dog returned to see his child. The son went into the forest with the dog on a leash, and they hunted. The boy there met his grandmother, the pig. The dog was very malicious and killed the pig. The boy went back to tell his mother to come and see the pig he had killed. The woman recognized the pig as her mother and told the boy. The boy also learned that the dog was his father, and in shame he killed him. The woman sent the boy to find a wife, giving him a ring into which his intended spouse must fit her forefinger. He was unsuccessful in finding a girl whose finger fitted the ring.

---

74. SOURCES: Primary source: Eerde 1902:36–39; Secondary source: Lessa 1961:180. From William Lessa, *Tales from Ulithi Atoll: A Comparative Study in Oceanic Folklore*, published by the University of California Press, 1961. Reproduced by permission of the publisher. NOTE: The bracketed additions are Lessa's comments.

In fact he complained that he had nowhere met a human being and did not know where to look further. He asked his mother why she did not try the ring. She did, and it fitted exactly. They then married. The boy went to the mountains to seclude himself in devotion, but salvation did not come to him. He sailed to Macassar and there became the ancestor of the Kampung people, that is, all the foreign elements living on the island of Lombok—in this instance the Macassars and Bugis from Celebes.

Meanwhile his mother [his wife] waited a long time, sorrowing. One night she had a dream, and someone said she should go to Sumbawa, where salvation awaited her. She went there on a piece of driftwood. The people there asked her where she had come from—whether she was an Islamite or a Balinese. She answered that she came from Lombok and had come to Sumbawa because of her sorrow. She married the ruler of Sumbawa and became the ancestress of all the rulers of Sumbawa.

75. PUTRI. JAVA

A Sunda Strait version tells how Putri [Princess] Dajang Sumbi did not want to marry because her only passion was for the hunt. One day, she disappeared while hunting with her faithful dog. After six years the princess reappeared, together with her dog and a beautiful boy. She brought up the boy as her own son, without mentioning his father, and he became a great hunter like his mother. Once, when he asked his mother about his father, she whispered some words into his ear which made him run off into the woods full of horror, after first calling the dog. The boy disappeared in the woods, but the dog was found with a kris in his heart. Putri recognized her son's weapon, but did not tell anybody. Many years passed. Putri's beauty remained—a gift of the god Siva. She withdrew to a mountain, spending her days in solitude at her loom. A strange knight of great courage and beauty appeared in the country and fell in love with her. She recognized him as her son and withstood his advances. But again she went hunting with him every day. When she could no longer hold out against her son's passion for her she promised to marry him if he fulfilled a seemingly impossible task. But the task was not impossible for her son, and only his mother's prayers to the gods prevented him from fulfilling it on time. Putri showed him the kris with which he had killed the dog, his father, and told him who it was that he demanded in marriage. Thereupon he disappeared forever.

75. SOURCES: Primary source: Juynboll 1912:54; Secondary source: Lessa 1961:181–82. From William Lessa, *Tales from Ulithi Atoll: A Comparative Study in Oceanic Folklore*, published by the University of California Press, 1961. Reproduced by permission of the publisher.

76. MASINGBAL AND HIS SON METINGLAUG. ALOR

A man named Masingbal had six sons. His wife became pregnant once again, and when he left he told her that if the child were born a male it must be killed, but if it were a female she should keep it until he returned. The woman bore a son. Instead of killing the child she hid him on top of a mountain with a large supply of food and male adornments. When the husband returned he thrust a spear into the supposed grave of the boy, and some coconut milk seeped out, for his wife had buried a coconut. He thought she had killed the boy, but a rooster betrayed the secret to him. He then set out with his six sons and his adopted male slave to kill his son, whose name was Metinglaug. He sent each of his sons in turn up the slope to kill the boy, but each was offered food and accepted it, whereupon each felt unable to kill his young brother. When each returned to his father and confessed he could not kill the boy, he gave as an excuse that the son's face resembled that of his father. At last the father himself went up. He refused the food his son offered him. Instead, with the son offering no resistance, he first blinded him, slashed his mouth, cut off his hand, and cut open his abdomen. After three days two women found him and replaced his organs with those of a dog. They brought him back to life with a fire fan and a fire tube. When he was revived, they fed him and told him what he must say when he met their father. In the course of time he returned to his native village, where his father again tried to kill him. He was once more revived and later ascended to live in a village in the sky.

77. ABORIGINAL TALE. ARANDA (AUSTRALIA)

The man of the Rat totem made his camp at Tara [Rock] near Henbury on the Finke River. Two women camped there, a mother and her daughter. The man made his camp near theirs. All day long he decorated himself with his pubic tassel and his head band. All day long he "sang" the women. One of the women was old and fat. She stood in the relationship of wife to him. The other woman was his classificatory daughter. He "sang" and decorated himself for many days. When the mother and the daughter went to gather seeds, he followed them. When they returned to their camp, he danced for the whole night. The next day, they went to gather seeds once

---

76. SOURCE: Du Bois 1944:168. Copyright © 1944 by the University of Minnesota. Reprinted from *The People of Alor*, by Du Bois, by permission of the University of Minnesota Press.

77. SOURCE: Roheim 1974:190–91. Pages 190–91 from *Children of the Desert* by Geza Roheim & W. Muensterberger. © 1974 by Werner Muensterberger. Reprinted by permission of HarperCollins Publishers, Inc.

more. This time he caught his classificatory daughter. She cried out, "You are my father! Leave me alone!" But he would not release her. He said only, "Come along. I am going to take you."

He dragged her a little way and then made her lie down. He tried to have intercourse with her, but he failed. He dragged her further away from there and tried again to cohabit with her. Again he failed, for the girl was ashamed. "You are my father," she said. "Leave me alone." But he would not release her. She cried as he dragged her away from the camp.

"Where are you going?" she asked. "North!" The man dragged her on and on against her will. As they went along, he danced, for he was very happy. He had captured a young girl and he was well decorated with bandicoot tails. They went through Nyeingu-kona and finally came to Karilkara [Buck-bush-plain]. There they rested. While they were resting, he became so excited that he bit his beard. He rushed at her and they cohabited.

Again he danced as they hurried along. They went through Jay to Iltira-puta [White-stone]. As they walked to the north, the girl cried. They climbed a big hill to a place called Ankalla [Cousin] or Itirka or Tjirke-wara [Incestuous]. There they camped. The girl cried all the harder as she looked back toward her own country. "We do not have much further to go," said the man. When they came to Worra-tara [Two-boys] he cohabited with her. Then they walked past Tjoritja [Stony-country] to Burt Plain.

Together they made a camp there, although she first tried to run away. Again he forced her to have intercourse with him. A rock hole called Nura arose on the spot where he put his knee. They then went past Arkaianama [Legs-sit-down, i.e., taboo] and on to Paraltja [Dry-bush]. There they sat on the top of a hill and the man showed the girl his own country. "There are many people. Do you see the pine trees? That is where we are going."

They walked a little further and rested at a place called Alakala [Father-and-child]. There was another man of the Rat totem at that place. He was performing the last part of the initiation ceremony. One of the initiates saw the man and the girl coming and ran to tell the old man that a man was coming from the south with a captured woman. The old man of the Rat totem decorated himself. He even donned the *wallupanpa* [the long strings of hair].

When the man of the Rat totem who had come from the south with the girl saw the old man and the initiates coming toward them, he knelt down and told the girl to stand on his belt and to hold on to his shoulders. The old man threw his *wallupanpa* around them and dragged them toward him. He placed them in a hole and got in after them. All the initiates followed their mentor, the man, and the girl into the hole. They were all covered with the decorations used in the initiation ceremony. They carried their bull-roarers. They wore their head bands, arm strings, and were covered with birds' down. They all went right into this hole in the earth and became *tjurunga*.

78. MYTH OF NATA (LAP). RATAPA (AUSTRALIA)

A woman came from Maurungu and gave birth to a child at Nata (Lap). The boy became big and walked on all fours, looking for his mother. He had a little *papa* [stick] and he always tried to get up with it. Then he walked on all fours again and found his mother's track. One day he went to Maurungu and his mother saw him coming. This must be my child, she thought. She sat down, squatting with her legs open, and put a *tjurunga* on her head. She called him with open arms and she squatted on the ground with her vagina wide open. He went right in with the papa and he *borkeraka* [became tired] and became a *tjurunga* in the mother. The baby inside was too big, so she too *borkeraka* and *tjurungeraka* (became a *tjurunga*) there.

79. MURNGIN TALE. AUSTRALIA

T he Murngin relate the following story: In the mythical times a boy was groaning in the camp. His mother asked him what was the matter, but he kept on groaning.

"Shall I give you honey?" she asked. "No," he groaned.

"Do you want some kangaroo?"

"No," he groaned.

And so on through a series of questions, until at last she says, "Would you like my vagina?" "Yes!" he cries, "that is what I want."

80. THE WITCH OF NORMANBY ISLAND.

T here was an old witch who lived with her granddaughter. They went to the garden to drive the birds away. She took her vulva and put it on the top of her head so that it gave light. All the others were astonished. They went to sleep [the witch and her granddaughter] and then they came again before daybreak with their light. The other people took the light away. She was delivered of a child and they performed the smoking ritual for her. As soon as her son was born he had intercourse with his mother while her blood

---

78. SOURCE: Roheim 1945:208. From Geza Roheim, *Eternal Ones of the Dream*. Reproduced by permission of International Universities Press, Inc.

79. SOURCE: Roheim 1945:208–9. From Geza Roheim, *Eternal Ones of the Dream*. Reproduced by permission of International Universities Press, Inc.

80. SOURCE: Roheim 1952:483; cf. Roheim 1948:280. From Geza Roheim, *The Gates of the Dream*. Reproduced by permission of International Universities Press, Inc.

was still flowing. The child went up and became the moon. When women are menstruating they are having intercourse with the moon and men stay away from them. The moon is also regarded as light itself, as the *kaya* kept by witches in their vulva.

81. GANUMI I. KIWAI (NEW GUINEA)

Ganumi was an infant when his mother became pregnant again. This turned her milk so he did not like it. She gave Ganumi the blood that had been stained by her second delivery to lie upon. The blood changed into a red parrot.

The red parrot flew away and landed on a sago tree over a water-hole where it saw its reflection in the water.

Girls came to draw water and one of them called Gebae saw the reflection of the parrot. She dove, but she caught nothing. Then they saw the real bird, caught it, and put it in a basket. At night he became a man, had connection with Gebae, and in the morning he became a bird again. Gebae became pregnant and the parrot [Ganumi] flew away.

The girl's parents and other people wanted to kill him. He called for his mother and she tried to get hold of him in order to hide him in her basket. She unfastened the string with which her grass petticoat was tied on and threw one end up to Ganumi but it was too short. Then she did the same thing with the navel cord which she had preserved since his birth. Ganumi now told his mother that he was the moon. Then he said, "You throw that to me." She flung one end of the navel cord up to him, holding the other tightly in her hand. She meant to draw him down from the tree and to put him in her basket. But he gave a pull to the cord, the tree bent toward his mother, and the next moment he hurled his mother up to the sky and hoisted himself up after her. She caught hold of him and put him in her basket and there she is still carrying him in the sky.

[Roheim 1952:484: "When Ganumi's face peeps out a little from his mother's basket he appears as the new moon and gradually more and more of his face will appear. Sometimes the mother hides the basket behind her and then the moon cannot be seen at all. The mother herself is invisible except her fingers which are sometimes outlined against Ganumi's face and they are the spots on the moon. *Ganumi married his own mother.*"]

81. SOURCES: Primary source: Landtman 1917:484–86; Secondary source: Roheim 1952: 483–84. From Geza Roheim, *The Gates of the Dream*. Reproduced by permission of International Universities Press, Inc.

82. GANUMI II. KIWAI (NEW GUINEA)

An old married couple have a child and people make them ashamed. The child Ganumi was put in a bowl and the bowl floated on the water. A girl named Gebae had borne a child with bad sores. When the basin came floating in she picked Ganumi up and let her own child drown.

Once after seeing two girls with their petticoats in disorder, Ganumi, who was still a little boy, cried, "Mother, I want that red thing."

Red flowers, fruit, etc., he rejects. Finally he was put to sleep between the two girls but he was too small for intercourse. Therefore they were dissatisfied with him and put him on top of a sago palm. A red-feathered bird named *wiowio* [cf. his mother's name in another version] alighted above him and her droppings made him grow feathers so that he became a *wiowio* bird.

Now all the girls wanted him but he only yielded to Gebae, his foster mother. Then because he was ashamed at the idea of having slept with his mother he jumped into the water and hid for a month among the water spirits. When he came home all the women rejected him, they all told him to go to his mother. One night he and his mother ran away into the bush and then climbed up into the sky by means of Ganumi's navel cord [the foster mother idea is here forgotten].

83. NUMBOOLYU AND CHENCHI. SAMBIA (NEW GUINEA)

PART 1.

Numboolyu and Chenchi emerged from the trunk of the *dowutu* [softwood] tree. Numboolyu came outside first, and he was followed by that other "man," Chenchi, a Nokwai [tribesman], his age-mate. This occurred at Kokona.

Numboolyu was the first man. He had a very small penis. He did not know what his penis was. It was so small. He kept it hidden with rubbishlike things. One day Numboolyu pulled his penis out from his pubic area. It became a bit longer. He continued to hide his penis several days more. But he did not sleep well at night for his penis was intensely erect.

Then Numboolyu had his first ejaculation by masturbating himself. When he ejaculated, his semen fell on the ground. Later he urinated nearby. He compared the two substances. The urine, he noticed, was only water. But the semen looked just like snot. He thought it looked just like the juice of pan-

---

82. SOURCES: Primary source: Landtman 1917:486–87; Secondary source: Roheim 1952: 484–85. From Geza Roheim, *The Gates of the Dream*. Reproduced by permission of International Universities Press, Inc.

83. SOURCE: Herdt 1981:256–60.

danus nuts. So he knew it was something good. Then he decided to copulate with his partner.

Numboolyu showed his age-mate "woman" [who is verbally transformed at this point from male to female gender] his penis, asking, "What is this? I don't know why it [penis] won't rest." Then Numboolyu began copulating with the [age-mate] woman in her mouth. But soon she complained to him, objecting that the intercourse was not enjoyable. She said this was because Numboolyu's penis was too short. Whereupon she fetched a bamboo knife and slit open his foreskin, exposing the glans penis. The penis grew bigger and nicer. The "woman" declared: "Now it is good; I will eat it [suck the penis, ingest the semen]."

At this time both Numboolyu and his partner had enlarged breasts [like a normal woman's]. As Numboolyu began copulating with the woman in her mouth, however, his own breasts fell "flat" [like a normal male]. Yet the "woman's" breasts grew larger and swollen. She had no genitals at all; she possessed only a mouth and an anus.

The woman's stomach then began to swell. The couple wondered what could be the cause: "What has produced this great belly? Has she eaten too many sweet potatoes, or what?" The woman started having abdominal pains, and from the pain she began screaming. She screamed and screamed. She retired to a small, shabby house—the *pulungatnyi-angu* [menstrual hut]—that the couple had built away from their house. The woman continued to scream from her stomach pains; then Numboolyu thought to himself: "What can I do to relieve her pain?" So Numboolyu entered the menstrual hut. With his bamboo knife he made a vertical slit in the woman's pubic area. When he made the cut a child fell outside. Some of the birth blood splashed onto Numboolyu's face. A female child was born, and when he saw it, Numboolyu proclaimed: "Another kind [a female person] has come out!" Then he covered the child with banana leaves. He then used his hand to remove the birth fluids from his brow.

The birth blood flowed into the river Tekutaalyu ["taro place"] at far away Menyamya. Now the Green people [a Sambia hamlet in the Lower Green River Valley] are forbidden to drink this river water when their wives have menstrual periods.

Our women, at their menarche, go to the menstrual hut. Their menstrual blood flows and they have the fashion of sleeping in that house. When women kill the moon [menstruate], they go to the menstrual house. This means they are ready for marriage since their menstrual blood is flowing.

When women give birth, they do not let us [males] see the birth. This is because at the first birth [of Numboolyu's wife], when the "man" had a child, Numboolyu didn't reveal the child, he hid it. Likewise, women today do the same: they hide during childbirth.

Since a girl child was the firstborn, girls always grow faster than boys now. The firstborn girl child "grew" first; now girls grow faster than boys. Boys would grow faster than girls, but the firstborn child of Numboolyu was a girl.

The woman [the new mother] continued to live in the menstrual hut. Numboolyu went to the forest. He felt it was wrong to have cut open the woman and he wanted to be in the forest. There, Numboolyu trapped possum and birds. He brought his catch back to his mate. The fur of the *wakoogu* possum Numboolyu and his "wife" used to cleanse their hands [of the birth-blood pollution]. Now our wives use this possum fur to cleanse themselves following birth.

Numboolyu speared birds for his wife and child to eat. Because of this, now we men have the bow and arrows [for hunting]. Numboolyu also cut a digging stick for his wife. Now our women use them for planting sweet potatoes.

After the birth, Numboolyu's wife had a vagina [where he had made a vertical slit at the pubic area] so he could copulate with her down below. He proceeded to copulate with her—sometimes in fellatio intercourse and sometimes in vaginal intercourse. In time his wife became pregnant again. This time she produced a male child.

After he had created the vulva, Numboolyu said he then had two pathways [orifices] for sexual intercourse: the mouth and the vagina. First he had copulated with his wife's mouth for two years. Then he made her vulva. But now we know that a woman must be copulated with in her vagina to produce a child; fellatio alone will not produce a child. Before there was no vulva; now women have the vagina. The semen of Numboolyu alone created the pathway into the vagina.

PART 2.

One day Numboolyu's eldest son came to him. He said, "Father, my penis is erect. What can I do about it?" Numboolyu thought to himself: "My wife is here, but she is my scale [sexual partner]. I can't send my boy to my wife." The son reiterated to his father: "Father, I have no woman, but my penis is erect; what can I do?"

Numboolyu instructed his eldest son to go and copulate with his younger brother [in homosexual fellatio]. [In telling the myth, Tali interrupted at this point and said: "If Numboolyu had sent his oldest son to copulate with the boy's mother we (men) would also give our wives to our sons when the boys reach puberty! But he didn't, so we don't share our wives! Had Numboolyu sent his son to his wife, she wouldn't have refused him; she wouldn't have said no. She would have copulated with the boy."] Later, Numboolyu thought to himself: "It would be bad if the boy became pregnant from sucking his older brother's penis." But their father decided to wait and see what would happen. He thought that if the younger boy did become pregnant, he could then tell the older son to cut open the boy's stomach to make birth possible [as Numboolyu had previously done]. But Numboolyu did not tell his wife about this. He thought that if the younger boy became pregnant then he would tell her.

So Numboolyu waited, but the younger boy did not become pregnant. ["Now we can copulate with boys without worrying that they will become pregnant," Tali said. "We do not tell women that we do this. For Numboolyu first hid it (his sons' homosexual fellatio) from his wife."] If the younger boy had become pregnant then Numboolyu would have told his wife: "Oh, wife, before we had intercourse [fellatio]: this boy, he did the same to his younger brother, who has become pregnant." But the younger boy did not become pregnant and Numboolyu hid the boys' homosexual practices from his wife.

The elder son did not go to his mother and ask her what he could do about his erect penis. He went to his father instead. And his father sent him to his younger brother. Numboolyu thought: "Why should I send my boy to my wife? She is my scale. I have two roads for my penis [vagina and mouth]!" Numboolyu thought: "It wouldn't be good if the boy copulated with my wife and then the two of us [father and son] fought." [Tali: "If he (Numboolyu) had not done this, now we would copulate with our mothers and sisters."]

84. **THE DEATH OF THE FATHER.** MURINBATA (AUSTRALIA)

[Allen's note: In the northwestern region of Port Keats, the Murinbata people tell of the Rainbow Snake who appeared in the form of the man Kunmanggur. Kunmanggur created the people and taught them how to live in peace. In this myth, Kunmanggur sends his two daughters on a trip. On the way their brother, Jinamin, forces one of them to commit incest with him. The sisters use magic to punish Jinamin, but he returns to camp and spears his father, Kunmanggur. Jinamin turns into a bat and Kunmanggur once again becomes the Great Rainbow Snake, who can be seen as one of the bands of color in the rainbow (p. 81).]

In the Dreamtime when the earth was young and people had not yet come to be, lived Kunmanggur, the first ancestor of the Murinbata people. Kunmanggur had the form of a python. His home was in a deep pool on top of the mountain, Wagura. By day he rose from the depths of the water hole and lay coiled in the sunshine, his scales glowing with all the colors of the rainbow.

Kunmanggur looked down from the mountaintop to the land that undu-

---

84. SOURCE: Allen 1975:81–88. Selection from pages 81–88 from *Time Before Morning: Art and Myth of the Australian Aborigines* by Louis A. Allen. Copyright © 1975 by Louis A. Allen. Reprinted by permission of HarperCollins Publishers, Inc.

lated green and brown to the sea. He saw there were no people. "I shall create men and women," he decided.

So Kunmanggur fashioned a *didjeridu*, which he called *maluk*, from a bamboo stalk and sang a song of power. Then he blew on the *didjeridu*. As the first resonant notes sounded, several flying foxes popped out of the *didjeridu* and flew off in a chorus of squeaks.

"I want to make people," said Kunmanggur. Again he blew, long and hard. This time a boy and girl emerged from the end of the *didjeridu*.

Now Kunmanggur was pleased. "I shall keep the *didjeridu*. It will bring much good," he said. He changed himself into a man and sat with the children on a rock that rose above the surface of the water hole. Swallows dipped and swooped in the sharp, clear air; a hawk poised on bent wing and hurled itself at a mouse; dragonflies darted back and forth in the sedge by the waterside.

And while these small events occurred, the two children grew to man and woman. Kunmanggur told them how to live in peace, then he sent them away to populate the land.

"I shall go live among the camps of my people," said Kunmanggur soon after, and he went to a place called Kimmul where the river brawls from the hills, levels through a plain, and flows quietly to the sea. Kunmanggur made camp near a grove of baobab trees, took a wife, and fathered two daughters and a son. The children were close in age, and they grew happily together until the boy passed the initiation ceremony and the swelling breasts of the girls marked their first blood.

The older girl, Biligmun, and the younger one, Ngolpi, were pleasant, attractive, and obedient. But their brother, Jinamin, had a headstrong nature that sometimes offended his father. So it was that Kunmanggur taught his daughters certain power songs with which they could work small magic— foretell the rain and summon small creatures like flies and wasps to do their bidding. But because his son displeased him, Kunmanggur taught Jinamin nothing.

The pubic hair had come to Biligmun and Ngolpi and their breasts were large and full. The girls were ready for husbands. However, no suitable matches had been found, although from the time of their birth, as was the custom, Kunmanggur had urged their maternal uncles to betroth them. But a great plague had killed many men, and no young men in a marriageable relationship were available.

Jinamin, a year younger than his admiring sisters, was quick and alert. When he strode into camp with a wallaby over his shoulder, even the older women looked at him with desire. The pubic shield he wore indicated he had been circumcised. Still, he had not yet passed through the rites that qualified him to marry.

Jinamin and his two sisters were fond of each other. But now, when talking to them, he ceremoniously averted his face and eyes, for so he had been taught when he had entered the boys' camp to prepare for initiation. At times he still affectionately embraced his sisters, and they in turn often let their fingers linger softly on his arms when they talked to his averted face.

One day Jinamin came upon Biligmun picking figs among the mangrove trees. As she stretched down a branch beyond her reach, Jinamin leaned over to help. Her body moved against his as she stepped back. In quick response, Jinamin put his arms around his sister and pressed her close.

"Come to the pool at the river and lie with me," he invited.

But Biligmun shook her head. "We are brother and sister; it is forbidden," she replied. "Our father will kill us if we disobey."

Jinamin walked away disconsolately. From the shade of the fig tree, *karrak*, the kookaburra or laughing jackass bird, cocked its head, eyed the youth, and uttered a harsh, mocking cry. Jinamin winced, but his thoughts soon turned to Ngolpi, her swelling breasts and long, slender legs. He had seen her leave camp, and now he set off to find her.

"Your work is good," he said when he came upon her stripping sheets of bark from a paperbark tree. She placed more bark on the pile. "The bark is deep," Jinamin continued, sitting on a pile to test it. Ngolpi cut more bark and pushed Jinamin aside.

"I work and you rest. You could help me," said Ngolpi with irritation.

Jinamin caught her arm. "The bark is soft. Sit with me and try it," he replied and pulled her down beside him.

When his hand sought her breast, Ngolpi sprang up. "It is forbidden; you are my brother," she said.

"You have no husband and I no wife. Lie with me," urged Jinamin. But Ngolpi did not yield and drove Jinamin away.

At this time, the men were assembling spears, woven rope, and net baskets to carry for ceremonial exchange to the Fitzmaurice River, Djamanjung, which was several days distant. Frustrated and unhappy, Jinamin set off with the trading party. After some time, the sisters began to miss him, and they went to Kunmanggur for counsel.

"Father, we are sad," they explained. "We desire men but do not yet have husbands. What shall we do?"

"I have talked with the men of your mother's tribe," replied Kunmanggur, "and they seek husbands for you. But men in the proper relationship are few. It will take much time. To pass the days, journey to the land of your mother's people and take my greetings to them."

The sisters set out as their father advised. They followed the winding river, found groups of their kin, and visited the women. For many days they traveled from camp to camp. Everywhere the suitable men were married, and their possessive wives hurried the comely sisters on their way.

Meanwhile, Jinamin had returned to the camp of his father and had learned of his sisters' departure. Again he grew restless. He thought of Biligmun and Ngolpi and the soft hair that grew to shield their places of pleasure.

"I go to visit our clanspeople," he told Kunmanggur. He tied an opossum band on his forehead and set out down the river, in the opposite direction from that which his sisters had taken. As soon as he was out of sight, he turned and swiftly followed the tracks of his sisters. As the blazing torch of the Sun Woman dropped toward the horizon, Jinamin killed a wallaby and began to look for a place to pass the night.

Nearby the two sisters had also stopped to make camp. Each stripped sheets of paperbark from the trees and placed them in a pile. Then they gathered firewood for the night.

"We will sleep here, sister," said Biligmun. "But now let us go find food."

While the girls were gone, Jinamin came upon their camping place. He saw the two piles of paperbark and the firewood stacked close by. Quickly, he put all the bark sheets in one pile, then removed his pubic covering and carefully pulled the bark over him until he was concealed. He poked a hole through the layers to breathe, then he waited.

When the sisters returned with fish for their supper, they immediately saw that the two piles of bark were now one. "The wind has blown our bark sheets together. We must sort them out," Biligmun said. They began to separate the sheets, but when they reached the last one, something began to move.

"Oh! There is something here," cried Ngolpi, backing away.

Jinamin leaped up and threw off the bark. "The trading party returned and our father sent me to find you," he said. "I will travel with you. Now let us share the wallaby I speared." The sisters silently watched Jinamin clean the wallaby. "We will catch more fish while you make the fire," Biligmun finally announced and went with her sister to the river nearby.

"Jinamin intends to lie with us. What shall we do?" asked Ngolpi.

But Biligmun frowned and did not respond. They caught several fish and carried them back to the fire. Jinamin offered them the wallaby, but they refused the meat. "We will eat the fish," they said.

As the Sun Woman dropped below the horizon, Jinamin helped the sisters arrange their bark beds once again. "We will sleep here together," he said and went into the bush to relieve himself.

"It is not good for our brother to sleep here, for he means to lie with us," Biligmun whispered. But when Jinamin returned to camp he lay down between the sisters and prepared for sleep.

The night was filled with the laughing clamor of the kookaburras that congregated in the nearby bushes. When Biligmun stirred restlessly on her bark bed, Jinamin edged close to her and said, "Lie with me."

"I cannot, I am your sister," Biligmun replied.

Jinamin moved to the bark of the younger sister. "Lie with me," he again invited.

"I am too young; I cannot," came Ngolpi's reply.

Now Jinamin seized her roughly. "I will not hurt you," he said and forced himself upon her. Though she cried out in pain, Jinamin had his way.

The two sisters awoke to the racket of the kookaburras as soon as the morning star touched the treetops and in a few moments they were ready to leave. As Biligmun lifted her dilly bag over her shoulder, Jinamin sat up and yawned.

"There is no need to hurry. Tarry with me," he said.

The girls ignored him and quickly set off down the trail. "I will catch up with you," Jinamin called after them. He lit a fire and warmed the last of the wallaby meat for breakfast.

As they hurried away, Ngolpi said, "Sister, we must do something to stop him from following us."

Together they sang a magic song to call up a great cloud of wasps, which they sent to Jinamin, who had just left camp. The wasps settled upon his head, his neck, his shoulders, and began to bite. His face became puffy. His arms and legs reddened and swelled. But still Jinamin followed, the slits of his eyes bright with anger and desire.

"Hurry, sister! We must cross the river," cried Biligmun. When the girls reached the far bank, they waited for Jinamin to wade to mid-stream. "Come across quick," Biligmun called.

Then Biligmun sang a magic song to bring up the tide. The water rushed in, as Jinamin hurried forward, knocking him off his feet and carrying him away in its raging current.

Relieved, the sisters climbed a cliff that rose beside the river and stopped to rest. But when they looked down, they saw that Jinamin had been washed ashore and was now pulling himself onto the rocks.

"Sisters, help me!" he called.

They made a long rope of vines and lowered it over the cliff. "Climb up," they shouted.

Jinamin began to pull himself up with the rope. As he labored up the face of the cliff, he saw Ngolpi's pleasure place as she spread her legs to brace the rope. Jinamin became excited.

"Sister, tarry with me; we need not return yet," he shouted.

But Ngolpi, still in pain from the previous night, became angry. She reached for a sharp stone that lay at her feet, severed the rope Jinamin was clutching, and watched in satisfaction as he crashed to the rocks below.

The sisters lost no time in returning to their father's camp and telling him all that had happened. "Jinamin did wrong," Kunmanggur said. "Now he is dead. He was your brother and we will forgive him."

But Jinamin had not died. Bruised and broken, he crawled to a hunter's camp at a place called Punyitti and after a time was healed. "I will return to my father," Jinamin decided. He took a sharp stone from the end of a spear and cut his face and chest so the blood flowed freely.

Jinamin returned to the camp of his father at Kimmul. His face was bloody and his body gashed and bruised. His spirit was filled with anger, for he had suffered much. Kunmanggur welcomed him, but gave him a stern warning to stay away from Biligmun and Ngolpi. At this, the son's anger grew, for he was determined to continue relations with his sisters.

To celebrate Jinamin's safe return, Kunmanggur arranged a great corroboree. Everyone danced and sang, while Kunmanggur played the *didjeridu*, *maluk*, and his daughters kept time with tapping sticks. Jinamin danced with the men. He danced the story of the water spirit and the man who fell in love with her. He danced close to his sisters and swung his hips provocatively. Kunmanggur observed Jinamin and blew hard on his drone pipe in warning.

"I'm going to kill him," Jinamin muttered, but he spoke in the language of his mother's people, the Jangman, which nobody else could understand.

"What did you say?" a woman asked.

"I'm thirsty, get me some water," Jinamin replied.

The woman brought a bark container of water to the edge of the crowd. When he went to drink, Jinamin took his spear and laid it on the ground.

The people danced and stamped. The dust rose. The shouting and singing grew to a din. Darkness fell. The people grew hungry. "Let us eat," they said.

Jinamin had not yet been able to approach Kunmanggur. "Let us dance the flying fox dance, the snake dance, and the fire dance; then we will eat," he called to his father over the heads of the dancers. To humor him, Kunmanggur agreed and began to blow the song of the flying fox on the *didjeridu*.

Now Jinamin danced toward his spear and began to push it over the ground with his toes. Gradually, he moved toward Kunmanggur.

"How many more dances?" asked Ngolpi.

"Two more," replied Kunmanggur.

"How many more dances?" inquired Biligmun.

"One," said the father.

Now Kunmanggur blew the melody for the last dance, the dance of fire. The singers' voices rose. The dancers' feet pounded the earth. The dust thickened in the firelight. Night fell.

Jinamin clutched the spear with his toes and lifted it to his hand as the dance reached its height. No one observed when Jinamin leaped from the shadows and thrust the spear with all his might into Kunmanggur's side. Blood spurted from the old man's wound and splashed down his legs. Kunmanggur uttered a great cry. He staggered. He lifted the *didjeridu, maluk,* that had brought good to the people; with his last strength he smashed it to the ground so it broke in two. Then Kunmanggur fell to the ground. Several men rushed forward. Quickly they broke off the point, removed the spear, and placed hot stones on the wound to stop the bleeding.

"Get the killer! Take revenge!" rose the cry as the men ran for their spears.

Now Jinamin feared for his life. With a thin, high shriek, he leaped into the night sky and was instantly transformed into a bat. To this day he has so remained, squeaking his fear and dismay through the night.

Though sorely wounded, Kunmanggur did not die. "I shall go among the people I have created, and once more I shall teach them to live in happiness and peace," he said. So Kunmanggur traveled among them. But his wound did not heal, though at each camp the people heated stones to stop the bleeding. Day by day the old man weakened. As his strength ebbed, he began to leave signs for the people. At a place called Miwa, he painted his marks upon the walls of a cave; at another place, he embedded the imprint of his foot in a large, flat stone. He taught his people many sacred songs but steadily he lost his strength, so that the strongest men had to give support to Kunmanggur's frail body as he walked.

At last, one day he wearily reached a place called Toitbur where the river forms a deep pool as it joins the sea. "Here I shall leave you," he said. "But with me I shall take the fire so that the people will know they have done wrong."

He lifted the fire stick from its embers and fixed it in his thick hair with the glowing end upright. Then he walked into the pool. The water rose to his waist, to his chest, to his chin. The water lapped at the fire stick.

"We shall lose the fire forever," cried a man called Kartpur in alarm. He jumped into the pool, snatched at the fire stick, and carried it to shore. There he set the grass ablaze so that fire would stay with them.

Kunmanggur disappeared beneath the surface of the water. Down he went, far down to the bottom. As he sank, the water welled up in great bubbles that expanded to the banks of the pool and broke. In the depths Kunmanggur transformed himself once again into the Rainbow Snake. Beside the deep pool where fresh and salt water meet, he fashioned stones in the shape of children and placed them upright in the shallow water near the banks. Thus he created all the spirit children, *ngaritj-ngaritj,* who became the ancestors of the people who live in that country.

Today, when the women hunger for children, they come to the pool of Kunmanggur. There they heat bushy twigs in a fire and strike them against the stone figures so that Kunmanggur will know their wombs ache with emptiness and will send them children.

85. THE MILKY WAY. YUMU (AUSTRALIA)

The boy belongs to the ant totem and the story is localized at Linga-kura [ant]. The Milky Way itself [*tukalpa*] consists of two big *kuntanka* [kangaroo ancestors] standing crosswise. At Lingakura a boy of the ant totem had been circumcised. The women were *untingu* [ceremonial dancing = Aranda] for the boy, but a *kunka mamu* [devil woman] had been hiding behind a windbreak. When the men had left the boy alone the *mamu* woman came up and pulled his penis into her vagina and there she held it fast with the labia. In this position they ascended to the sky hanging to each other, the boy being above. Some other men were looking for the boy and then they said: "There they are above." Then they threw *mapanu* [invisible magical stones] at them but could not hit them because they were too high. The Milky Way or the woman and the boy they call also *ngantanuta*—that is, stuck together in coitus. There is another earth up there and the woman and the boy live there alone.

The third piece of the tradition is contained in the exoteric name given by the Pitchentara to the Milky Way. When speaking to the women they call it Ngaltarara, that is "with the mother," and say it is a kangaroo mother with her son. They also call it Warapulena-pulena (O hurts, hurts), because the boy had a sore after the circumcision and he exclaims "hurts, hurts" when she sits on his penis. She played the active or male part in cohabitation.

86. LORO SAMA LILAKA. TETUM (TIMOR, INDONESIA)

A long time ago a king married a queen, and the two of them had a son, Loro Sama Lilaka; only one. He was almost grown up when his mother died, and the king's two sisters brought up the boy while his father went looking for another queen. [Hicks' note: In the original text the story is confused at this point.] The new queen, Larakak, wanted to kill the lad, and eat his liver. So her two sisters cut out a buffalo's liver and brought it to her. She said that it was not Loro Sama Lilaka's liver, but that of a buffalo. They tried the same with the liver of a pig, and a horse, but each time the answer was "No!!" This time the two sisters (who were called Nai Bui and Nai Lalu) killed the king's son, cut out his liver, and brought it to his father and mother. They said that this time it really was the boy's liver.

With difficulty, the king unwillingly had a coffin made, which was then

85. SOURCE: Roheim 1934:90. Reproduced by permission of *Psychoanalytic Quarterly*.
86. SOURCE: Hicks 1984:102–5. Reproduced by permission of Michael Aung-Thwin, CSEAS, Northern Illinois University.

taken to a big *hali* tree, and lifted up into its branches. Seven strong women, some time later, from over the sea, came to collect some dye. They sniffed a nasty smell, and divined that the aristocrats in that area were being evil to a virtuous relative. They found him, lifted down the coffin, and opened it. Inside, they saw the king's virtuous son. Of the seven women, one, who was the eldest sister, ordered the youngest, Ali-iku, to return over the sea to get her mother's winnowing fan, and bring it back to make the lad come alive again. Ali-iku brought back the fan, and her eldest sister fanned the dead boy's head. Her fan was then given to a younger sister, but one still older than Ali-iku, who continued fanning. But the body rotted more and more. It was then given to another sister, who was between the ages of the eldest sister and the youngest sister, and she fanned, but again the body continued decaying. The six sisters all failed to bring life to the decaying body, but when Ali-iku fanned the body the lad came to life. The seven women then took the king's son over the other side of the sea. The eldest sister asked her five sisters if Ali-iku could marry the king's son. They were married.

Five years later, the prince's son was out hunting when his dog chased a deer for a long way—over the sea! The dog killed the deer in a patch of *lontar* palms owned by the prince's mother's brother. During the night the mother's brother came to tap the wine from the palms, and there found the king's son. "Old man, my friend, my dog chased a deer and killed it in your patch of wine trees. Tap your wine, then, and let us two cook the deer in *tuquir* fashion, and drink your wine." They both ate. Having eaten and drunk, the king's son pushed the meat away, and looked at his old friend. The king's son knew the old man but did not recognize him as a true friend. He knew him as his mother's brother, but the mother's brother didn't know his sister's son. Then the king's son returned over the sea.

Five days later the king's son went out hunting again and his dog chased a pig a long way over the sea. Arriving at his mother's brother's patch of wine trees, it killed the pig, and in the evening the mother's brother came to tap the tree. The king's son saw his mother's brother, but called him "my friend, the old man" instead of by the term "mother's brother." "You came to tap the wine tree. My dog has killed a pig in your grove. Tap the trees after you have cut them, and then let us cook the pig, old man." Having tapped the wine, and eaten, the mother's brother recognized his friend, the young man. "Let us go to my house, friend. Eating here alone in the wine grove is not much good. At home we can cook meat, eat it, and drink."

The two of them took the wine to the house, which was the house of the young man's father's sisters, Nai Bui and Nai Lalu. It was their house. Nai Bui and Nai Lalu looked at the two men cooking the meat, and the old man went over to talk with Nai Bui and Nai Lalu. "The king's son is very like your son, Loro Sama Lilaka." When they had cooked meat and the rice, Nai Bui and Nai Lalu said, "The rice is cooked, and the salt is mixed with meat. So let's start eating."

Nai Bui and Nai Lalu put the rice onto a plate and brought it to the table. They pounded the meat and brought it onto the table. When the four were together, Nai Bui and Nai Lalu looked closely at the king's son and began crying. The king's son did not eat, for he was thinking hard. The old man said to him, "Lad, you're not eating, and the two old women are crying so much." "It's all right now," said the boy, "you mustn't cry. I died, you see, and my two father's sisters, Nai Bui and Nai Lalu, really killed me. They put me in a coffin and lifted me to the top of a small *hali* tree. Seven ladies came and fanned me to life again, and then took me back over the sea. That's how it was. Really. Today I'm just recalling what happened. I've come back. My father's sisters, Nai Bui and Nai Lalu, can't talk to each other. I'm Sama Lilaka. I'm going tomorrow and I can't talk. Tomorrow I shall return over the sea. Seven days and seven nights later I would like to come and live in Nai Bui and Nai Lalu's house. I'll invite the king to celebrate, have a cock fight, and invite nocturnal singers. We shall tell them that the king's son, recently arrived from across the sea, has come just for the cock fight."

The king's son brought only one cockerel in his sailboat when he came to the fight. The king wanted to see how well the cockerel belonging to the visitor from over the sea could fight. "I can come," he said, "I have lots of cockerels." The event started with a feast, and everyone could see the king's son had brought only one cockerel to compete with those of the king. In the first fight the young man's cockerel killed that of the king. Then the king ordered all his people to put up their cockerels against that of the visitor. Although they all did so, not one could kill that of the king's son. The king's son had only one cockerel, but it killed all the cockerels in the land. Then the king and his subjects had no more money left to bet, but they had one more fight. This time it was without any money. The old king said, "You, my lad! I have no money for betting, so the best thing for me is to wager myself against your money." The two cockerels fought, and that of the king's son killed its rival. Later, everyone danced to the nocturnal songs. Then the king's son attacked the old king and his sisters, killing them. "Oh!" said the king's subjects, "This is really our lord." The king's son returned over the sea to fetch his belongings. He brought them back, and then ruled the old king's people. Everyone in the kingdom was happy with this arrangement.

NATIVE NORTH AMERICA

87. TRICKSTER MARRIES HIS DAUGHTER. SOUTHERN UTE

Sunawavi had two daughters and a son. One day he was lying down in a little brush lodge. It was raining and the roof leaked so he asked his daughters to fix it. While they were doing this he caught sight of his elder daughter's genitalia, which were large, and began to lust for her. He thought of possessing both his daughters and considered how he might do so. He went out to hunt rabbits. He found an old rabbit bone, and stuck it up in front of his tipi. There was snow on the ground, and in cleaning it from his feet he purposely stepped on the bone. He cried out and his family came out. His wife pulled out the bone, but he pretended to be sick. He continued ailing for a long time, at last he said he was about to die. He told his family that after his death they should move far away to a big village. When they were there, some visitors were going to come from another part of the country. One was going to ride a gray horse, and he was the one his elder daughter should marry. There would be a lot of gambling there. This visitor would stand there. He would be good-looking, have his hair wrapped with otterskin and carry an otterskin quiver. "He is a good fellow, and if my daughter marries him she will never starve." He pretended to get worse. "When I die, I want you to burn me up. Roll me up in blankets on a pile of wood and burn me. Don't look back. If anyone looks back, someone else will die, it will bring

87. SOURCE: Schmerler 1931:196–98. Reproduced by permission of the American Folklore Society from *Journal of American Folklore*, 44:196–98, 1931. Not for further reproduction.

bad luck." So they tried to burn him and went off without turning back. However, the little boy turned back and said, "My father rolled off." The old woman said, "Your father told you not to look back."—"My father rolled off."—"Well, then he is dead."

They went to the next village and told the people about the death; they were very sad. After several days visitors came from different parts of the country and they looked out for a man riding a gray horse, but he did not come, until one day they espied him. "That is the young man your father told us about. When he gets to those lodges, we'll tell him we want him." He stopped in the camp and stood behind the gamblers. He was carrying an otterskin quiver and his hair was decorated with otterskin. The little boy went up to him and ran back telling his mother it was the man his father had spoken of. Then he was sent again to invite him to become the old woman's son-in-law. The boy called him, but the man replied, "Wait till sundown." The boy returned with the message. Sunawavi spoke to the sun and made him set soon. He went to the family, who were seated, and sat between his daughters, who did not recognize him. The little boy, however nudged his mother, saying, "He looks like father." His mother pushed him. "Don't say that,he is dead." But the boy repeated, "His face resembles father's." The old woman was ashamed to look at him and went to bed. "Take whichever girl you want." He chose the elder daughter. They went to bed. In the night he had his will and the girl screamed. The old woman said, "What's the matter? When I was young, it was the same way. At first it hurts, but later it does not."

The next morning the old woman asked the man to go where her husband had been in the habit of catching rats. He went off with the little boy. When they got to the big rat's house, the boy teased them out of the holes with a stick, while the man turned small, entered the holes, ate up the big ones inside, and threw out the little ones. The boy said, "I think it is my father, this is the way he used to do." So he looked sharply and caught sight of four marks on Sunawavi's teeth. Thus he recognized his father. He pushed his stick into the hole and rushed home. Sunawavi said, "Go on teasing the rats. What is the matter?" There was no answer; he saw the boy running off.

When near home the boy shouted, "That husband of yours is your father!" The people were scared. The old woman asked her daughter what her husband had done while cohabiting. She said, "He sucked my breast." "That's what he does with me, it is your father." She was furious and cut up his quiver, bow and arrows, threw them into the fire, and said, "Let us run away." They went up toward heaven. Sunawavi got home and said, "Wait for me." His wife answered, "You are no good, you did a dirty thing with your daughters. We will not live with you any more, but are going to the sky."

"Wait for me."

"No, it is too late. You are going to be turned into a wolf. At sundown you will go round the country and cry biting your tail." Sunawavi said, "You shall be stars."

"It is well." Thus they became the four stars to be seen in the evening and named Soneyan.

88. COMANCHE TALE.

Once a young man had a separate lodge and a woman came to him in the night for several nights. He found her very attractive and was curious as to who she was, so he rubbed his hand in red paint and in the course of the embrace rubbed the paint on the back of her buckskin robe. The next day when the girls were out playing, he recognized his mark and knew that the girl was his sister. He was much horrified and got a dogwood stick, sharpening it at both ends, and waited until the next night. He placed the stick upright between them, and when the girl came they were both pierced and killed. The boy's body was honored, but her body was mutilated and thrown out.

89. HASTIIN GAAGII ("MR. CROW"). NAVAJO

Crow had many children and they all lived together. His oldest daughter was the prettiest of them all. So Crow decided to make his oldest daughter to become his wife. So he played that he was very ill. He said to his wife, "I am very sick. I want you to make a nest for me yonder in that cottonwood tree. Then take me over there and put me to bed." Then his wife made the nest in the cottonwood tree as she was told.

After the nest was made Crow crawled up into it and went to bed. From somewhere he got hold of an old rotten liver of some kind. He put it under him. Then he again said to his wife, "You must sweep the ground under me every day. If the worms should start falling from the nest then you'll know that I am dead. When I die you all move away some place. After that the first individual [crow] you see carrying four big fat prairie dogs you must let him have my oldest daughter," he said to her.

Crow did all these things just to have a chance to have intercourse with his daughter. But there is one thing wrong with this Hastiin Crow's looks. There is a big scar on the side of his head. Every day his wife sweeps the ground under his nest. Then one day the liver he had up there got real

---

88. SOURCE: Kardiner 1945:70–71. Reproduced by permission of Columbia University Press.

89. SOURCE: Landar 1972:118–33. Reproduced by permission of Mouton de Gruyter, a division of Walter de Gruyter & Co., Berlin.

wormy. Then some of the worms began to fall to the ground below. His wife saw the worms on the ground when she came to sweep the next day. Then she ran back to her children wailing.

Then she said to her children, "The worms are falling from the nest. So now it's time for us to move away. He told us to move away when we notice some worms on the ground," she said to her children. Then they started to move. Before they went out of sight the last child looked back and saw his father jump out of the cottonwood tree over yonder. Then he said to his mother, "Mother, I saw my father jump out of that cottonwood tree." Then his mother said, "Don't say that, my baby, father died long ago. So don't speak any more about him," she said.

Even then the little boy spoke again to his mother. "No, it's true, I know it's father. I know it's so because I saw him," the little boy says. Then his mother told him to keep quiet and they kept moving farther and farther away.

As they moved farther away Crow met his own family, with four prairie dogs in his hands. Crow's wife did not recognize him. When Crow met his family he spoke to them. "Why do you look so sad and where are you going?" he said to them. Then the woman replied to him. "When the worms fall yonder, go away from the body, he told us, and now the worms have fallen. That is why we are moving away. Now that man is dead," she said. The woman says this.

So then that Crow, just talking about himself continued to speak to his wife. "That old man was really smart. He must have given you some kind of instructions to follow. Did he?" He spoke thus to her. Then the woman replied to him. "Yes, he told me to give our oldest daughter to the first individual I saw carrying four prairie dogs." She says this. So then Crow replied to his wife. "That's just what I thought. I knew I was right. That man was smart," he said.

He just made a crude hogan for his oldest daughter and she was given to him. So his own daughter became his wife. They sat down on the sunny side of the hogan. Then he spoke thus to his daughter who has just become his wife. "My wife, clean my head of lice." He said that to her. He put his head in front of his wife and she began to hunt for lice on his head. He knew that his daughter could recognize him if she saw the scar on one side of his head so he kept it away from her. Occasionally she would run her hands close to the scar and he would turn his head.

Then Crow spoke to his daughter. "The lice are only on this side, on this side," he said to her. He did not want her to get her hands on the scar. Then Crow suddenly went to sleep. Then the girl thought to herself: "I wonder why he does not want me to touch the other side of his head," she thought. Then she took a look at the other side while the man was asleep. Then she saw a big scar. "This is my father," she thought. Then she sneaked away while the man slept. Then she ran to her mother. "Mother, that man is my father. He still has a big scar on his head. I know him by that scar." She said this to her mother.

She came back with her mother while he was still asleep. They both examined the scar. They were sure it was him all right. Then her mother picked up a big rock. She raised it high while she stood over the man. Then she threw the rock down on top of the man's head. That's how Hastiin Crow was killed.

90. THE WOMAN AND HER HUSBAND. ESKIMO

There were people just beyond Kotzebue. This man was a real good hunter. There was always plenty to eat. Finally he drifted out on the ice. He tried to get back, but the ice drifted farther and farther away. After two winters and two springs his wife decided he must be dead, so she got married.

All this time her husband was thinking about his wife from out on the ice. He couldn't get home, even though he kept trying. Finally he decided he would never get home, so he sent his soul home. The wife was busy with her new husband's catch. The soul said, "*Arunga*" [I came home]. The wife lifted her head to hear better. The husband repeated, "*Arunga!*" The wife said, "My ears are ringing." The husband repeated as loud as he could, "*Arunga!*" This time the wife said happily, "*Euii!* [Oh, boy!] My ears are ringing" [a sign of good luck]. This time the husband got so mad he kicked his wife in the ribs as hard as he could, so she had a sharp pain in her side.

The moment he kicked his wife, the soul became unconscious. When he became conscious again he found he was inside the womb of his wife. The woman had never had children, but soon she noticed she was pregnant. Whenever she ate, her husband ate also, inside the womb. Finally she gave birth.

When she gave birth, the baby looked a bit like her former husband, so they named him after the former husband. When the baby became old enough to sit up by himself, but not yet old enough to crawl, he looked more than ever like the former husband.

One night the second husband and the wife were having sexual intercourse. When they looked at the child he seemed to be envying them. That night the woman woke up and felt that it was crowded in bed. She looked back to where the baby was supposed to be sleeping and he was a full grown

90. SOURCE: Hennigh 1966:357–58. Reproduced by permission of the American Folklore Society from *Journal of American Folklore* 79:312, April–June 1966. Not for further reproduction.

man. He hadn't been able to sleep for envying; that was why he was like that. She recognized him as her former husband.

When she recognized him as her husband, she nudged her second husband and told him, "This, our child, is my husband. He is fully grown now." The second husband got up immediately, got dressed, took his things and went out as quickly as he could, without saying anything.

While the second husband was dressing, his *apak* [term referring to the male member of a wife exchange] told him not to rush, that he was thankful to him for taking care of his wife and that he was not trying to scare him. But this man rushed out anyway. He took his kit of tools and went out.

This first husband was still a good hunter. He got lots of animals. Whenever he got animals he gave some to his *apak* because he was grateful to the man for having taken care of his wife, but the *apak* never said very much. That is all.

91. THE WOMAN AND HER BROTHER. ESKIMO

There was a people by a beach, a big village, and they had a *kazzigi* [community house], a big *kazzigi*, and there were two orphans living together, a sister and a brother. This sister didn't want to get married. Lots and lots of young men tried to go after her, but she didn't want to get married.

When they weren't hunting, the young people stayed in the *kazzigi*. They slept there every day, and each night, after the old folks went home, they started to play games. On most nights some young man or other would go to her house and ask her to marry him, but she always told him she didn't want to get married. They must have gone on for years like that. The girl was always alone because her brother never came home from the *kazzigi* to sleep.

Sometimes her brother told her to get married so that he might have a helper in providing for her, but she told him she wouldn't get married because she didn't want to have intercourse. Besides, she had lots of things to eat in her home.

One night she went to bed, trimmed the lamp, and started to go to sleep; then after a while some apparition started to come into the room. It was not like any of the young men who had come before. She was scared, so she let it do whatever it wanted. She let it go to bed with her. Before day broke it went out of the room, so she didn't find out who it was.

Some evenings after that, he came back, and slowly she became less afraid of him but she still let him do whatever he wanted. Finally she decided to

91. SOURCE: Hennigh 1966:365–66. Cf. Boas 1888:597; Levi-Strauss 1969:296–97. Reproduced by permission of the American Folklore Society from *Journal of American Folklore* 79:312, April–June 1966. Not for further reproduction.

find out who he was. One evening she prepared the light on her lamp, moved her bedding close to the lamp, then trimmed it, and waited for that man. When he came in she let him get into bed with her; but carefully, so he wouldn't know what she was doing, she sooted one hand in the lamp and marked the man on the cheek.

Toward morning, when the old folks finally got home from the *kazzigi*, she started out to find which man had a mark on his cheek. When she reached the *kazzigi*, she took covers off the skylight, opened it a little and peeked in. She saw lots of young men playing games. She looked from face to face, trying to see who would have a mark on his cheek. She didn't expect her brother to have one, so she looked at him last. Finally she saw him, and he had a soot mark on his cheek. She was so surprised she almost fainted.

She got down from the *kazzigi* and started to go home. When she got inside her sod house, she got her *ulu* [woman's knife], a big *ulu*, and a wooden bowl. Then she took off her parka. She cut off both her breasts and put them in a bowl. Then she started back toward the *kazzigi* without putting her parka back on. Much blood marked her tracks.

When she got to the *kazzigi* she went right in. She put the bowl with her breasts in front of her brother, and said: "Here is your meat, brother! So you want to eat these! I have nothing else to give you; you have to eat these!" Then she turned and ran out, with her brother right after her, trying to catch her.

She started running around that *kazzigi*, staying ahead of her brother. He almost caught her but not quite. On the third time around she started to go up in the air. When her brother reached the spot where she left the ground, he started to go up in the air also. They kept going around and around, following each other in wider and wider circles. The people were out of the *kazzigi* watching by that time. They saw the two of them go higher and higher until they disappeared in the air.

The girl kept on to become the sun and her brother the moon. When that girl's breasts bleed too much, the clouds get red. When that boy gets tired, his face gets pale. When it is too pale, the moon is bright. That is all.

92. MONO TALE. WESTERN MONO

A girl, Kaneo, was importuned by her brother-in-law. She built a fire under a cliff where he was; suffocated, he fell and died. Kaneo took his roasted flesh home; people ate it. She sang, disclosing the truth. The outraged people chased her into a creek, trying to shoot her. She traveled upstream

---

92. SOURCES: Primary source: Gayton and Newman 1940:58; Secondary source: Levi-Strauss 1969:297. From Anna Gayton and Stanley Newman, *Yokuts and Western Mono Myths*, copyright © 1940. Reproduced by permission of the University of California Press.

under water. She was pursued far up into the mountains to a lake where she disappeared, at the same time causing a snowstorm. She stayed under the waters of the lake; she had children; she sometimes peers at people on the trans–Sierra Nevada trail.

93. THE GIRL WHO MARRIED HER BROTHER. SHASTA

A mother and her ten children were living together. The oldest was a girl. She was mean; and her mother had to hide from her the youngest child, a boy. The girl was wont to ask her mother, "Where is that child you bore some time ago?" to which her mother would reply, "Oh, I lost him long ago." Every morning the daughter saw her mother go down to the spring. She followed her, and noticed that the water was disturbed, as if some one had been swimming there.

One day she found a long hair in the water. She measured it with the hair of her other brothers, and found it to be too long. So she decided to learn whose hair it was. Every night she camped at the spring, until one morning she saw a strange man come down to bathe. Then she knew who had been disturbing the water, and to whom the hair belonged. It was her youngest brother. She fell in love with him, and decided to marry him. She went home and asked her mother to prepare some food for her, as she was going away. Her mother gave her food, and the girl asked, "Who wants to accompany me?" The oldest brother said, "I."

"No," replied the girl, "not you." In a similar manner she refused to go with any of her other brothers. Finally she ran to the side of the house, put her hand there, and said, "This is the one I want to take along." Then the younger brother came out from where he had been hidden all these years, and said, "All right! I'll go with you."

They travelled all day. When night came, she said, "Let us stop here!" So they stopped there, and the girl began to prepare the bed. The boy suspected what she wanted of him, but he said nothing. He only wished she might fall sound asleep, so as to be able to run away from her. When she was sound asleep, he put a log in his place and left her, returning to the house. He ran home, and shouted, "Let all get ready to come with me!" They did so, and before departing cautioned everything in the house not to tell his sister where they had gone. But they omitted to tell Ashes.

Early in the morning she woke up and began to speak to the log, thinking it to be her husband; but soon she found out the deception, jumped up in anger, and cried, "I'll kill you!"

---

93. SOURCES: Primary source: Farrand and Frachtenberg 1915:212; Secondary source: S. Thompson 1929:196–98.

In the meantime the brother and his family had entered a basket and were drawn up to the sky. The sister came home, and inquired of everything in the house as to the whereabouts of her mother and brothers. No one would tell. Finally she asked Ashes, and was told that they had gone up to the sky. She looked up, and saw her family half-way up the sky. She began to weep, and called for them repeatedly to come down. But the boy had told them not to look back, no matter how often she might call. Soon, however, the mother looked back, and the basket began to fall. The daughter was glad when she saw the basket coming down. She made a big fire, intending to kill her family as soon as the basket should fall into it. The basket came down; but, when the youth hit the ground, he flew right up and floated away. The girl thought she had killed them all, and was very glad.

After a while the brother came down on the ocean beach, where two Sea-Gull girls found him. At first the girls were afraid of him; but he assured them, saying, "Don't be afraid of me! Touch me, wash me, and you will find that I am all right!" The girls did as directed, and he married them. After a while his wives became pregnant and gave birth to a boy and girl. As soon as the children grew up, the father gave them a bow and arrow, and taught them how to shoot, saying, "When you grow up, I want you to go to my sister over yonder, and watch her secretly." The children grew up and went to their aunt's house, who scared them so, that they ran back in a hurry. Then he said to his children, "Let us all go and kill my sister! She is mean. She killed my family." The children promised to help him.

So they all went, and the young man began to fight with his sister; but he could not kill her, because the only vulnerable spot, her heart, was in the sole of her foot. In vain he shot arrow after arrow at her. He could not kill her. His arrows were all gone, and he was almost exhausted, when Meadow-Lark came to his help. She told him to look at her heel. He did so, and saw something bright and shining. On Meadow-Lark's advice he directed an arrow at that spot, and thus succeeded in killing the terrible sister.

94. **THE JEALOUS FATHER.** CREE

O nce there was an old man named Aioswe who had two wives. When his son by one of these women began to grow up, Aioswe became jealous of him. One day, he went off to hunt and when he came back, found marks on one of the women [the co-wife with his son's mother] which proved to him that his son had been on terms of intimacy with her.

One day the old man and the boy went to a rocky island to hunt for eggs. Wishing to get rid of his son, the old man persuaded him to gather eggs

94. SOURCE: Skinner 1911:92.

farther and farther away from the shore. The young man did not suspect anything until he looked up and saw his father paddling off in the canoe. "Why are you deserting me, father?" he cried.

"Because you have played tricks on your stepmother," answered the old man.

When the boy found that he was really left behind, he sat there crying hour after hour. At last, Walrus appeared. He came near the island and stuck his head above the water. "What are you crying for, my son?" said Walrus. "My father has deserted me on this island and I want to get home to the mainland. Will you not help me to get ashore?" the boy replied. Walrus said that he would do so willingly. "Get on my back," said Walrus, "and I will take you to the mainland." Then Walrus asked Aioswe's son if the sky was clear. The boy replied that it was, but this was a lie, for he saw many clouds. Aioswe's son said this because he was afraid that Walrus would desert him if he knew it was cloudy. Walrus said, "If you think I am not going fast enough, strike on my horns [tusks] and let me know when you think it is shallow enough for you to get ashore, then you can jump off my back and walk to the land."

As they went along, Walrus said to the boy, "Now my son, you must let me know if you hear it thunder, because as soon as it thunders, I must go right under the water." The boy promised to let Walrus know. They had not gone far, when there came a peal of thunder. Walrus said, "My son, I hear thunder." "Oh, no you are mistaken," said the boy who feared to be drowned, "what you think is thunder is only the noise your body makes going so quickly through the water." Walrus believed the boy and thought he must have been wrong. Some time later, there came another peal of thunder and this time, Walrus knew he was not mistaken, he was sure it was thunder. He was very angry and said he would drop Aioswe's son there, whether the water was shallow or not. He did so but the lad had duped Walrus with his lies so that he came where the water was very shallow and the boy escaped, but Walrus was killed by lightning before he could reach water deep enough to dive in. This thunderstorm was sent to destroy Walrus by [the boy's] father, who conjured for it. Walrus, on the other hand, was the result of conjuring by his mother, who wished to save her son's life.

When Aoiswe's son reached the shore, he started for home, but he had not gone far before he met an old woman, who had been sent as the result of a wish for his safety by his mother [or was a wish for his safety on his mother's part, personified]. The old woman instructed the lad how to conduct himself if he ever expected to reach his home and his mother again. "Now you have come ashore there is still a lot of trouble for you to go through before you reach home," said she, and she gave him the stuffed skin of an ermine [weasel in white winter coat]. "This will be one of your weapons to use to protect yourself," were her words as she tendered him this gift, and she told him what dangers he would encounter and what to do in each case.

Then the son of Aioswe started for his home once more. As he journeyed through the forest he came upon a solitary wigwam inhabited by two old blind hags, who were the result of an adverse conjuration of his father. Both of these old women had sharp bones like daggers protruding from the lower arm at the elbow. They were very savage and used to kill everybody they met. When Aioswe's son approached the tent, although the witches could not see him, they knew from their magic powers that he was near. They asked him to come in and sit down, but he was suspicious, for he did not like the looks of their elbows.

He thought of a plan by which he might dupe the old women into killing each other. Instead of going himself and sitting between them he got a large parchment and fixing it to the end of a pole, he poked it in between them. The old women heard it rattle and thought it was the boy himself coming to sit between them. Then they both turned their backs to the skin and began to hit away at it with their elbows. Every time they stabbed the skin, they cried out, "I am hitting the son of Aioswe! I've hit him! I've hit him!" At last, they got so near each other that they began to hit one another, calling out all the time, "I am hitting the son of Aioswe!" They finally stabbed each other to death and the son of Aioswe escaped this danger also.

When the young man had vanquished the two old women he proceeded on his journey. He had not gone very far when he came to a row of dried human bones hung across the path so that no one could pass by without making them rattle. Not far away, there was a tent full of people and big dogs. Whenever they heard anyone disturb the bones, they would set upon him and kill him. The old woman who had advised Aioswe's son told him that when he came to this place he could escape by digging a tunnel in the path under the bones. When he arrived at the spot he began to follow her advice and burrow under. He was careless and when he was very nearly done and completely out of sight, he managed to rattle the bones. At once, the dogs heard and they cried out, "That must be Aioswe's son." All the people ran out at once, but since Aioswe's son was under ground in the tunnel they could not see him, so after they had searched for a while they returned. The dogs said, "We are sure this is the son of Aioswe," and they continued to search.

At length, they found the mouth of the hole Aioswe's son had dug. The dogs came to the edge and began to bark till all the people ran out again with their weapons. Then Aioswe's son took the stuffed ermine skin and poked its head up. All the people saw it and thought it was really ermine. Then they were angry and killed the dogs for lying.

Aioswe's son escaped again and this time he got home. When he drew near his father's wigwam, he could hear his mother crying, and as he approached still closer he saw her. She looked up and saw him coming. She cried out to her husband and co-wife, "My son has come home again." The old man did not believe it. "It is not possible," he cried. But his wife insisted on it. Then the old man came out and when he saw it was really his son, he was very much frightened for his own safety. He called out to his other wife, "Bring some caribou skins and spread them out for my son to walk on." But the boy kicked them away. "I have come a long way," said he, "with only my bare feet to walk on."

That night, the boy sang a song about the burning of the world and the old man sang against him but he was not strong enough. "I am going to set the world on fire," said the boy to his father, "I shall make all the lakes and rivers boil." He took up an arrow and said, "I am going to shoot this arrow into the woods; see if I don't set them on fire." He shot his arrow into the bush and a great blaze sprang up and all the woods began to burn.

"The forest is now on fire," said the old man, "but the water is not yet burning." "I'll show you how I can make the water boil also," said his son. He shot another arrow into the water, and it immediately began to boil. Then the old man who wished to escape said to his son, "How shall we escape?" The old man had been a great bear hunter and had a large quantity of bear's grease preserved in a bark basket. "Go into your fat basket," said his son, "you will be perfectly safe there." Then he drew a circle on the ground and placed his mother there. The ground enclosed by the circle was not even scorched, but the wicked old man who had believed he would be safe in the grease baskets was burned to death.

Aioswe's son said to his mother, "Let us become birds. What will you be?" "I'll be a robin," said she. "I'll be a whisky jack [Canada jay]," he replied. They flew off together.

95. IT HAPPENED AT "COARSE-TEXTURED ROCKS LIE ABOVE IN A COMPACT CLUSTER." APACHE

It happened at "coarse-textured rocks lie above in a compact cluster."
Long ago, a man became sexually attracted to his stepdaughter. He was living below "coarse-textured rocks lie above in a compact cluster" with

95. SOURCE: Basso 1984:37–38. Reproduced by permission of the American Anthropological Association from *Text, Play, and Story*, 1984. Not for further reproduction.

his stepdaughter and her mother. Waiting until no one else was present, and sitting alone with her, he started to molest her. The girl's maternal uncle happened to come by and he killed the man with a rock. The man's skull was cracked open. It was raining. The girl's maternal uncle dragged the man's body up above to "coarse-textured rocks lie above in a compact cluster" and placed it there in a storage pit. The girl's mother came home and was told by her daughter of all that had happened. The people who owned the storage pit removed the man's body and put it somewhere else. The people never had a wake for the dead man's body.

It happened at "coarse-textured rocks lie above in a compact cluster."

96. **RAVEN AND THE GIRL.** TSIMSHIAN

Raven lives with his wife, who has a daughter by another husband. He covets the girl. He tells her to bathe. Raven goes to the trees and asks them whether they emit sparks when burning. The hemlock sends him inland to the spruce, the spruce to the fir, the fir to the red cedar, the red cedar to the yellow cedar, which says that it sends its sparks beyond the people who sit near the fire. Before it is taken the yellow cedar asks to be wedged into small pieces, so that it can fly far. Raven tells it to fly into the lap of the girl. The girl comes back from bathing, and is told to warm herself by the fire [first the back, then the front, of her body, then to sit in front of the fire with legs spread]. The sparks fly into her lap and burn her, so that she is very ill. Then he advises the girl who has been burnt to go into the woods and to call for medicine. She is told that when she is far it will shout loud, when nearby in a low voice. [When it was said that the plant had sprouted a straight stalk without foliage, she went to investigate it. When she came up to it, she put it in her just as the stalk "enters" the husk. When the girl quit investigating the plant, Raven ran stealthily to the moss around it and hid under it so that his penis stuck out of it. And thus he awaited the girl.]

[Volume editor's note: The last part, in brackets, was rendered in Latin by Boas: Eam herbam quandam esse dixit quae musco innasceretur, recto culmo, sine foliis. Hanc investigaret; in hac, cum invenisset, considerat, ita ut culmus in vaginam iniret; quo facto; vollus sanatum ivi. Itaque, postquam puella ad herbam illam investigandam abiit, Corvus clam furtim ad muscum cucurrit, sub quo se celvait, ita tamen ut penis tantum exstaret et sic puellam expectavit.]

[The present translation is by Arthur Gribben, Ph.D.]

---

96. SOURCE: Boas 1909–10:707–8.

97. **THE HERO TWINS.** NAVAJO

Changing Woman [or Turquoise Woman] gives birth to twins, the Sun being their father. The older boy was Nayenesgani the Slayer and the younger was called Child of the Water. The Sun warned his wife Changing Woman to hide her sons from the giant Yeitso. She dug a hole in the floor, and every time she heard Yeitso coming she put them in it and covered the hole with a flat stone. The great giant came often *for he was in love with her* and jealous of the Sun, but she kept the little ones hidden. The children grow up quickly and go to seek their father, the Sun. He had a wonderful palace in the east where White Shell Woman was his wife. When they arrive *he cruelly attempts to kill his own offspring.* Finally, when he fails to kill them, the Sun gives them the straight lightning and the crooked lightning. Then they kill Yeitso, the Giant, who was the Sun's eldest child. The gigantic stature of Yeitso and the diminutive size of his antagonists are emphasized. But it is really the Sun who kills the giant and when the elder brother rushes in, he does so with his father's stone sword.

[Roheim (1950:322) comments: "We note that (a) the Sun tries to kill his own children, (b) the children kill the giant who had made amorous advances to their mother, i.e., that the giant is a father substitute, and (c) it is really the Sun (or Monster Slayer with the Sun's sword) who kills his own child."]

98. **THE YOUNG MAN LIVED WITH HIS GRANDMOTHER.**

COOS

The young man was making an elk fur blanket. And now this is what the young man said, "Uh. I wish I could sleep with the sister of yip-yibu'la'i!"

"He'i! what did you say, grandson?"

"Why I did not say anything!"

"Uh I heard you say something!"

"But I did not say anything!" She just kept on asking him.

"Why do you want to know? Well I did say it. I wish I could sleep there with the sister of yipyibu'la'i."

"Uh. I know it. When she comes you must not be bashful. You should go to bed with her."

---

97. SOURCE: Roheim 1950:321. From Geza Roheim, *Psychoanalysis and Anthropology.* Reproduced by permission of International Universities Press, Inc.

98. SOURCE: Jacobs 1940:172–73. Reproduced by permission of the University of Washington.

And then indeed the girl came. He did go and lie down with her. Now they lay down, and then the young man got on top of her. "Oh I almost have to urinate."

"Oh just keep pushing it further in, grandson!" Now the young man was angry, [discovering that] she was only his grandmother. The young man got up, and he went down below to the water.

He was not there long, and then a person came downstream [in a canoe]. "What is the news?"

"The next person along will tell you."

It was no long time before another [person] was coming downstream, and then he asked again. "Oh. The next person along will tell you." In just the same manner they told him, five canoes passed by [in that manner. And then the fifth canoe told him,] "Why must you ask that? [The news] is only that yipyibu'la'i copulated with his grandmother." Now then they came to war upon him and his grandmother, and then they killed his grandmother. The young man was ashamed, because his grandmother had lied to him.

The people can still see her blanket, and also the old woman lying on her back on the rock there. There the people still see her [turned into rock at a place near the mouth of the Coquille River].

99. NIH'ANÇAN AND HIS MOTHER-IN-LAW.

SOUTHERN ARAPAHO

Nih'ançan, his wife, and his mother-in-law, camped alone. He had his own tipi and did a great deal of work and errands for the mother-in-law (such as is the custom of the Indians). He became quite fond of her, at a distance, because of her pretty looks, but he could not get to talk with her.

One day Nih'ançan went out for game and returned with some beef for the family. His wife brought some beef or meat, which the mother-in-law had prepared. He was not in good spirits, and didn't feel like eating. "What is the matter with you? Are you sick?" said the wife. For some time, he didn't eat his meat, but looked very sad. Finally he told his wife that he was anxious to go out on the war-path, but he could not go alone. "I would be too glad if I could have a companion, like the others," said he, taking a few bites of food. "What do you want to do? Tell us!" said the wife. "Well, I saw a party of young men passing through with their mothers-in-law, all fixed up in warlike appearance. There were several parties, going in all directions," said Nih'ançan. "I would like to take my mother-in-law along, if it is possible," said he. "Well, eat your food, I will ask her, and let you know if she can do it or not," said his wife.

---

99. SOURCE: Dorsey and Kroeber 1903:75–77.

So this wife went out and told her mother that her husband had seen a war-party of young men with their mothers-in-law; that he wanted to know if she would consent to go with him. "Well, if that is the case, it is not a hard thing to do, simply to go along as company to wait on him. Tell him that I can go along any time," said the mother-in-law. "She said she is willing to go," said his wife to him. "You may then tell her to get ready, for I want to catch up with the rest of the crowd, before they get too far off," said Nih'ançan. So they started off, leaving the daughter behind. They traveled for miles, and it was late in the afternoon that Nih'ançan stopped and said to his mother-in-law, walking behind her, "Let us climb this high hill, and see if there is any sign of them ahead of us. You may take the lead, fix yourself up lightly, and tie your dress higher so that you can ascend more easily, and I will follow you and shall watch for any danger behind," said Nih'ançan. So the mother-in-law climbed the high hill, using a stick for a cane. "Hold your dress higher and walk faster! I think that the enemy is following us," said Nih'ançan. He was looking at her fat legs and in the course of time, while she was climbing fast, he saw her privates, which made him laugh secretly. After they had reached the top of the hill he told her that the pursuing party, the enemy, had disappeared and that they were safe for the night. The mother-in-law believed whatever he said, and she was more handsome than ever to him. While they were resting he sang a song, beating his bow with an arrow, saying, "There was a dark spot, I saw," meaning her privates. "My mother-in-law, don't feel hurt by the words, for I am singing about those people. I saw them behind us. It is the way that the war-party of young men do and they have all kinds of songs to stir their feelings and rouse their ambitions. Say, mother-in-law, I think that we have to turn around and go back, for we cannot see them. We might get lost. I see that we cannot overtake them. So it is best for us to go back now, and we will go as far as we can to-day," said Nih'ançan. So they went down the hill and reached a creek, which had much timber and grass. "Say, mother-in-law, we shall have to camp out for the night, and we shall take time to-morrow to reach home," said Nih'ançan.

Both of them together erected a shelter and made separate beds. Late in the night, Nih'ançan complained of being too cold. The mother-in-law gave him more cover, but he was knocking his teeth together, and rolled about. "Are you still cold, son-in-law?" said the woman. "Oh, yes! I can't lie still," said Nih'ançan. [The woman said, "Come, you can lie with me." And so he lay down and although he soon warmed up, he still shivered. "What are you doing?" said the woman. "Why mother," said he, "a part of me is frozen and unless you assist me I will be annoyed," said Nih'ançan. "Which part is that? Come," said the woman, "get on me and it will be warmed." When Nih'ançan mounted her, he began to work. His penis was so big that the woman tried to flee. She begged him to withdraw and get off her. He replied,

"Mother dear, be still. Father. Let you and me be joined in union." So all night long he lay with her. Then they set out for home. The woman was not able to walk very well because all night long they had sex and she was quite stretched out.] Finally they reached their home feeling very tired. "Well, what made you return so soon?" said the daughter. "My dear wife, when we climbed the hill, I saw the enemy below, after us, and we just barely escaped from them. Besides, the other parties had gone so far that we could not begin to catch up with them, and the journey was dangerous, too, so we returned. I am glad to see you, wife. I might have been killed if I had been in the fight," said Nih'ançan.

[Volume editor's note: The part in brackets above was rendered in Latin by Dorsey and Kroeber: "Age dum," inquit mulier, "potes mecum reclinari." Itaque reclinatus est et quamquam mox calefiabat tame horrebat. "Quid nunc agis," inquit mulier. "Quid mater," inquite ille, "una pars corporis mei gelata est et nisi tu me juvabis, molestiam hebelo," inquit Nih'ançan. "Quae est pars illa?" inquite Nih'ançan. "Age," inquit mulier, "ascende in me id calidum faciam." Nih'ançan cum in eam ascendisset, laborari coepit. Membrum eius tam magnum erat ut mulier effugere conaretur. Hare flens ex eo petivit ut descenderet. Ille respondit: "Mater cara, tace; pater; ego et tu in flumine coitus coimus." Sic per totam noctem cum ea coibat. Mane domum profecti sunt. Mulier non bene ambulari poterat quod per totem noctem coierant et multum patebatur.]

[The present translation is by Arthur Gribben, Ph.D.]

100. THE GRANDMOTHER DISGUISED AS A MAN.

THOMPSON INDIANS

An old woman called Skaiya'm lived all alone. She created two granddaughters for herself out of fish roe. When they became adult they desired to have husbands. Their grandmother feigned death and fixed herself up to resemble a man; she tied the loose skin of her breasts under each armpit so that she acquired a man's flat chest; for penis and testicles she hung between her legs a chisel made from deer-horn and a stone hammer with a handle in the middle. She passed herself off as a young stranger and, at nightfall, slept with the young girls. Bruised by the hard, artificial member, they suspected some ruse and tickled their lover, forcing him to laugh. As soon as the stranger opened his toothless mouth, they recognized their grandmother. They were angry with her for deceiving them, and threw her into the river.

---

100. SOURCES: Primary sources: Gunther 1925:166; Teit 1912:283–85; Secondary source: Levi-Strauss 1981:474–75. Excerpt from pages 474–75 from *The Naked Man* by Claude Levi-Strauss. English translation copyright © 1981 by Jonathan Cape Limited and Harper & Row, Publishers, Inc. Reprinted by permission of HarperCollins Publishers, Inc.

The old woman drowned; she laughed as she sank and made the kind of bubbles which can often be seen rising to the surface of a river or lake (Gunther 1925:166).

The young women travelled down river, and stole a baby which was being nursed by its blind grandmother. They put a piece of rotten wood into the cradle in place of the child. When the old woman realized what had happened, she called her husband who was away fishing, and their son. All three set off in pursuit of the kidnappers. From time to time the old woman drew up the loose skin of her breasts into a bunch and at once the distance between pursuer and pursued became shorter. The distance increased every time the tired old woman let go of her skin. The kidnappers were not overtaken.

The old woman made another child with the rotten wood in the cradle. He grew up, learned to hunt, and one day met his elder brother who had married the roe-women who had abducted him. After a farewell visit to their grandparents, the brothers returned together to the mountains; the elder gave one of his wives to his younger brother. Thus the women each had a husband (Teit 1912:283–85).

101. **WREN AND HIS FATHER'S MOTHER.** CLACKAMAS CHINOOK

Wren and his father's mother lived at their house there. Now they were starving. She told him, "Son's son! You might go [hunting and] find something, kill something [for us to eat]."

Then the next day he made ready, and he went to somewhere in the mountains. He sat down and he started to halloo. He said, "Come out [from the woods and] play push-one-another!" Rabbit emerged. He said to him [to Rabbit], "[So it is] you! With your Rabbit eyes! It is you I am calling!" So then he [Rabbit] went into the woods. Now he hallooed again, and then again little Chipmunk emerged [from the woods]. Now he said to her, "So it is you I have been calling! You Chipmunk eyes!" So away she went. Then again he hallooed. Then again little Grey Squirrel came out of the woods. He said to him, "It is you I am calling! You Squirrel eyes!" [whereupon Grey Squirrel dashed back into the woods]. Now he hallooed again, and soon Doe got to him. He said to her, "So I am calling you! Doe eyes!" So then away she went. Now he hallooed again, and shortly a Deer came out of the woods. He said to him, "I am calling you [humph]! You Deer eyes!" Again away he went [back into the forest].

101. SOURCE: Jacobs 1958:199–207.

Now he hallooed again, and soon then a big Horned Elk came out of the woods. He [Elk] said to him, "Whom are you calling? You what-do-you-call-it!" Right after that then Wren said, "Where shall I enter you? In your eyes? Where shall I enter you? In your nose? Shall I enter you by way of your ears? Shall I enter you? Where shall I enter you? Shall I enter you at your mouth? Where shall I enter you? Shall I enter you at your anus?"

He [Wren] disappeared. Now he went inside him. Elk thought, "Where has he gone?" Shortly now his nose itched. He sneezed. He [Wren] jumped out, chewing on something. He [Elk] asked him, "What are you eating?" "Your heart fat." "Oh yes I suppose you are! [You liar!] But it might be so anyway." He [Wren] swallowed [whatever it was that he had been chewing].

Now again he did the very same thing. "Where shall I enter you? Shall I enter you at your ears? Where shall I enter you? Shall I go into you at your mouth? Where shall I enter you? Shall I go into you at your anus?" Now again he disappeared, he went inside him [entering in an eye of Elk]. Elk continued right there, he thought, "Where did he go?" Soon then again his eye itched and itched. He moved [blinked] it, there he [Wren] jumped out from his eye. He was chewing and chewing something. He [Elk] said to him, "What are you eating, Wren?" He replied to him, "Your heart fat." "Oh yes indeed [You liar]!" He [Wren] ran about, he swallowed it [the thing he had been chewing] again.

Now he again did like that. He went inside [Elk by way of the ear of Elk], and he cut and cut at his heart fat. Done. Soon then as Elk was remaining there, now again his ear itched and itched. He emerged right there, chewing and chewing. Now it seemed that Elk was becoming sleepy. He [Elk] said to him, "What are you eating, Wren?" "Your [heart] fat." "Oh yes you are (you liar)!"

He [Wren] ran here and there, and then again, "Where shall I enter you? Shall I go into you at your anus? Where shall I enter you? Shall I go into you at your eyes? Where shall I enter you? Shall I go inside you at your mouth?" He went inside at his mouth. Elk just sat there, and he was nodding off to sleep. Soon now his mouth itched and itched, and there out he came, chewing and chewing. He [Elk] said to him, "What are you eating, Wren?" "Your [heart] fat." "That is what you say [you liar]!" Now it was a long time before he said something, for Elk was now [seemingly] falling off to sleep [and actually he was moribund].

Then again, "Where shall I enter you? Shall I go inside you at your mouth? Where shall I enter you? Shall I go inside you at your eyes? Where shall I enter you? Shall I go inside you at your ears?" He went inside at his anus [this fifth and last time]. Now he had vanished again, and he remained inside there. Then he pulled out his heart fat. Presently while he was inside there, then he [Elk] fell. Now he had killed him, and so he emerged, and he butchered him.

When completed, then he went back home, he packed him [some of Elk]. He got to his father's mother. He said to her, "Help me now. We shall go bring him [all] back." "All right," she said, "grandson!" She made ready, and then they went. They went on and on [until] they got to the [cache of] meat.

He said to her, "What will you pack, father's mother? Pack this [part of Elk's carcass]!" "No." "Then what [part] will you take along? This [part] is light in weight." "No. Not it." "What then will you take along?" This [other part] is light." "No." He became angry. He said to her, "What then will you take along? This [part]? The hips [hind quarter including the genitals]?" "Yes, yes! Son's son! Long, long ago when I was still an unmarried girl, that is the only thing that I ever carried back." "Where is your packstrap?" "Oh no." "What then will you pack it with? Long twisted hazel sprouts?" "No." "[With] what then? Here is a rope." "No." Now he again became angry. He said to her, "With these intestines [of Elk] then?" "Yes, yes! Son's son! Long, long ago when I was still an unmarried girl, those were the only things that I used for packing things." So accordingly he himself made a pack [of parts of elk], he packed it on himself, and he went along.

And as for her, she tied up her pack [of Elk's hind quarter and genitals], and then presently she packed it along herself. Now the [packstrap of] guts broke. So then again she fixed them. Wren got back to her, his father's mother was there yet. Now he made up another pack, he put it on his back, he went homeward, he got to their house. He piled it neatly. Then he turned back again, he went along, and far yonder he encountered his father's mother [who was still at that place]. Then he again made up his [third] pack, he put it on his back, he went on, he got to there [to their house]. Now no father's mother [had arrived yet]. Again he returned [to the cache]. Now he did not see his father's mother. And there was only the hide [left]. He took it along, he went homeward, he went along. No father's mother at all. He thought, "Possibly she got lost somewhere." So then he butchered [the meat], and again he roasted it on spits, some of it he boiled. All done, so then he looked for his father's mother. No [sight of her anywhere].

He merely went to the sweathouse, he found her at that place. She was sitting on the hindquarter [masturbating with Elk's organ]. He seized her, he threw her off it, he took the hindquarter, he threw it aside.

Presently then she went inside, and they ate. They finished eating. Now he lay down. And she lay down in the same way too on the other side of the fire. As he was lying there then he soon remarked, "Oh how I wish that a Klamath woman would come from somewhere and copulate here with me." She said to him, "What did you say, son's son? What did you say?" He paid no attention to her. Again she asked him, "What did you say, son's son?" He said to her, "What I was saying, I was merely saying that I wished some Klamath would copulate here with me." She arose, she said to him, "Son's son! My body is half Klamath." She went, she sat on him to copulate with him. Now they [two] did it right there.

Shortly afterwards then they heard *quow quow* [noise of paddling of canoers]. She said to him, "Son's son! Noise! Noise! Son's son! Noise! Son's son!" It was quite some time before he arose, he went outside, he noticed that a canoe was passing by them. He called out, he said to them, "What is the news?" "Oh yes they are telling one another that Wren [and] his father's mother are doing it to [copulating with] each other." "Hm" [expressing humiliation and anger], he thought. He went inside. She asked him, "What did they tell you?" He said to her, "What they said to me [is as follows], they told me that Wren [and] his father's mother are doing it to each other." He took Elk's hide, he wrapped her in it, he took her away, he threw her into the river. She floated downstream. Now he lived all alone.

Blue Jay [and] his older brother [Jay Bird] were canoeing along. Jay Bird saw something [the Elk hide floating]. He said, "This is my elk hide!" Blue Jay said, "I saw it first." He [Jay Bird] said to him, "Where is it?" "Why here it is, right here" [said Blue Jay who actually had not seen it]. Jay Bird said, "You did not see it anywhere." Presently as they [two] were going along [in their canoe], now he [Blue Jay] seized hold of something, he hauled it out of the water there. They took it along [Wren's grandmother in the Elk hide], they took her back with them. They unwrapped her, indeed it was Wren's father's mother.

So then they got [three] shamans, and now they doctored her.

> "Drum drum drum drum
> they use me for sewing canoes."

> "I flow thickly
> I flow very, very thickly.
> I flow thinly-like-water."

Now one of them made her come to, and [in fact it was] . . . Bird made her come to.

> "I wish my younger sister would move.
> I wish my younger sister would turn over on her side.
> I wish my younger sister would sit up."

They said, "Take off her wrinkles." So they sat down [beside her] her wrinkles [which were actually her elk hide cover which they now removed from her]. They said, "This thing [the elk hide cover of wrinkles] is her mother's mother." Only her teeth they were unable to fix well. Now then she stayed there [and seemed to be a pretty young woman]. They said, "Tomorrow they will tell Wren, we will sell the girl to him [to become his wife]." "All right," they said. The following day then one of them went, he reached there [at Wren's place], he said to him, "They want to offer an unmarried girl to you [to purchase]." "All right," he said to them.

And then indeed he went, he got to there, he saw a nice unmarried girl sitting there. "All right," he said to them. "I will take her." Now he became married [to his grandmother who lacked her hide of wrinkles and had no teeth]. The next day then he took her with him. They had told him, "Do not leave her mother's mother [that is, her hide]." They went away [Wren, his bride, and her hide].

They had said to the girl, "If you play, do not laugh big [loudly with your mouth open lest you reveal your toothless gums]. Just [laugh] m m m [with your mouth shut tightly]."

Now they went along, they got to there. They lived there. Then they would play. He would tickle her, she would laugh m m m m. Sometimes he would think, "Why does she laugh like that?" Then he would tickle her, he would tickle her, until she just began to laugh, [whereupon] she opened her mouth. Behold her [elk hide of] wrinkles came back onto her. He turned and looked, he saw [that she actually was] his father's mother. "Oh," he thought, "they just deceived me with my father's mother."

So then he again wrapped her up, he again hurled her into the water. She floated downstream, and again Blue Jay [and] his older brother noticed her [and once more took her out of the water and brought her to their home]. And again they doctored her. But no, they could not make her come to. Now they lived there [without her because she could not be resuscitated.]

Now all of the story.

102. ORIGIN LEGEND OF THE MOTH WAY CEREMONY.

NAVAJO

Begochidi lives with the butterfly [moth] people. He raises and takes care of them, never letting them out of his sight. As a *berdache*, he is in the habit of putting his hand to the crotches of the butterfly boys and girls, but he will not let them marry. Begochidi leaves for country where there is game. The butterfly people hold a discussion and appoint chiefs who check

---

102. SOURCE: Spencer 1957:149–50. Reproduced by permission of the American Folklore Society from *Memoirs of the American Folklore Society*, vol. 48, 1957. Not for further reproduction.

each night to see if all have returned, thus maintaining his rules in his absence. When the butterfly boys and girls are asked in marriage by aliens, the chiefs refer these requests to the parents, who are reluctant to give their children in marriage. "As for me when I think of this, is it for a man who has been raised in some other place that a person is nursing his baby here? And after having raised it what an awful thing it would be should one give her to a man elsewhere." They move camp several times for pollen gathering, and each time there are more fruitless marriage proposals from aliens.

A council of all the people is called. The method of recognizing someone who wants to speak to council is specified, that the speaker must stand rather than sit while talking. A chief presents the problem for consideration—what is to be done about marriage. He reviews their relationships with Begochidi, that he had great love for both the men and women and they in turn for him, that he had forbidden them to marry, and that now in his absence they are still guided by his wishes in refusing marriage. On the other hand, the butterfly parents have not wanted their children to marry aliens and thus be taken from them. The possessiveness of parental love and responsibility is emphasized again: "at the time you became pregnant with those children, no help came to you in any way" from the people who are now asking for these children in marriage. If their offers are accepted, "your daughter would be one place somewhere and your son would be another place, but you would be crying for them." To solve the difficulty and keep the families together the chief proposes that brothers and sisters shall marry each other. "So this coming evening you children, some of whom are boys, some girls, those that love each other shall prepare their bedding for one another, they shall lie together, everyone of them you must place under one another's cover. That alone will be a good thing in my opinion, because you love your children and they themselves love one another." The other chiefs agree to this proposal and it is carried out.

"On the following morning everybody [seemed] happy as moving again began, and brothers and sisters had their arms around each other." They start traveling again and at one stopping place four fires are built some distance apart. "Then it seems they rushed into those fires one on top of the other, burning themselves up. They simply tramped over each other from all sides in a mad rush to get into the fire." Finally the chiefs extinguish the fires, but the people are wild as though they have drunk whiskey. A rock ledge is made to separate them so that they cannot see one another [presumably the men and the women], and both sides quiet down. Since no cure is known for such a condition, "Therefore there is absolutely a mutual fear of their lower parts between brothers and sisters, the mere thought of such a thing is to be feared."

103. **THE BIRD NESTER.** KLAMATH

There is a story that at the beginning of time, Kmukamch, the demiurge, who lived with his son Aishish, began to create things and beings, and in particular, all kinds of fish. He made a dam so that the Indians could scoop up the fish every time the south wind blew and left the bottom of the rivers dry.

But Kmukamch fell in love with one of his son's wives and tried to get rid of him. He claimed that the young birds nesting on a Kenawat stalk were eagles. He commanded his son to capture them, after taking off his shirt, his belt and his hair-ribbon. Aishish, now naked, climbed up but found only little birds of a very common species. Meanwhile the stalk grew as he climbed and Aishish was unable to get down; he went back to the nest and waited.

Kmukamch took all Aishish's clothes away, dressed himself in them, and took on his son's physical appearance. Only the daughter-in-law whom he coveted did not suspect his duplicity; the others refused to consort with him, since they were convinced he was not their husband.

Aishish, marooned at the top of the tree and with no food to eat, became nothing but skin and bones. Then two butterfly-females saw him in the nest. They brought him water and food, combed his hair, poured oil on his emaciated body, and carried him down in their basket.

Aishish set off to look for his wives. He found Tchika [chaffinch] and Kletish [sandhill crane] busy digging roots. Tchika's child recognized him first. The two wives, then a third called Tuhush [mud hen, *Fulica americana*], rejoiced to see their husband whom they had believed dead. To all three he gave neck-wear made from quills of porcupines he had killed.

On hearing that his son was still alive, Kmukamch prepared to greet him. Aishish enjoined his young son to jerk his grandfather's pipe off into the fire. When the pipe was completely burnt, Kmukamch died. He came to life again later and tried to make his revenge on his son, by daubing pitch all over the sky and setting it on fire. The pitch turned into a lake which covered the whole world: only Aishish's home remained untouched. His third wife, Tuhush, tried to put her head out and a drop of pitch landed on her forehead. Ever since, this mark has remained on the mud hen.

---

103. SOURCES: Primary source: Gatschet 1890:94–97; Secondary source: Levi-Strauss 1981:31–32. Excerpt from pages 31–32 from *The Naked Man* by Claude Levi-Strauss. English translation copyright © 1981 by Jonathan Cape Limited and Harper & Row, Publishers, Inc. Reprinted by permission of HarperCollins Publishers, Inc.

THE STORY OF AISHISH. KLAMATH

O nce, they say, there lived a woman who had many children: one only was a girl with long red hair who got married to someone from the Gowasdi area. However, she kept coming back home for she was in love with her youngest brother and she always insisted that he should take her home.

Once they had to camp for the night and the girl crawled into bed beside her brother. Then he woke up and was shocked to find her next to him. "What a fool she is! Whatever will she do to me being a wife to her own brother!" He crawled slowly out and found a big tree-limb and pillowed his sister's head on it. Then he returned home. When he told his mother what had happened she feared that something very bad would come upon them.

The sun had long been up when the woman awoke. In her fury at being abandoned, she started a huge fire, burning up everything, her brothers and their wives. But she spared her mother. While searching around in the ashes, the old woman found the corpse of Meadow Lark, one of her daughters-in-law, who, being pregnant, had buried her stomach under a mortar. From her burned-through back the mother picked up two children, a boy and a girl. She was very much afraid that the girl would be just like her aunt, so she stuck the children together with pitch, making a single male creature with two heads. Then she advised the little boy never to bend down to look at his shadow and never to shoot an arrow into the sky.

The child grew up and began to suspect something mysterious was going on. A shrill-voiced bird, the killdeer plover . . . persuaded him to shoot his arrow into the air. The arrow came straight down and split the children in two. The boy, who had never seen the other head, was surprised to find a little girl beside him. Then she told him she was his sister. When they went home the grandmother realized she knew all the time what would happen.

The little girl always went hunting with her brother and kept asking him questions. "Who are we? Why are we without a father and a mother? Why does our grandmother always cry? Why do we live this way? Let us go over there and ask the sun and we will shoot him if he does not tell us."

When the sun rose, they questioned him, but as he paid no attention to them, the little girl shot an arrow into the sun's cheek, leaving a black mark which is still there. The wounded sun begged them to pull the arrow out quickly and agreed to tell them. He explained that the woman who had orphaned them lived in the water and he showed them exactly at which spot.

---

104. SOURCES: Primary source: Barker 1963:158; Secondary source: Levi-Strauss 1981: 49–51. Excerpt from pages 49–51 from *The Naked Man* by Claude Levi-Strauss. English translation copyright © 1981 by Jonathan Cape Limited and Harper & Row, Publishers, Inc. Reprinted by permission of HarperCollins Publishers, Inc.

When winter came, the sister planned to go to this spot, on the pretext that she was going torch hunting. Night after night, they brought back many, many fish and water fowl. At last they heard the murderess's cry "gochgoch-gochgodjip!" The grandmother too heard it and she was afraid she would find her daughter's head in with the fish. This in fact was what happened, but she was very sad and frightened because she loved her daughter, even though the latter had killed her own kin.

Fearing the old woman's anger, the young people decided to escape through the hearth ashes, advising all the domestic utensils not to say where they had gone, and shut the hole behind them with a piece of coal. But they forgot Awl, who showed the old woman how they had escaped. She at once followed them.

But the children had had several days' start. . . . On one occasion the boy shot an arrow up into a tree and was unable to get it back down. He asked his sister to get it for him. She refused to do so unless he told her how he was related to her. "You are my sister?" "No." "Aunt?" "No." "How is it— mother?" "No." Then he named every relation one after another, but the little girl rejected them all until the brother said, "Then you're my wife!" So, at the little girl's suggestion, they lived together as husband and wife, although they were brother and sister.

Knowing they would do this, the grandmother was still pursuing them. While inspecting the ashes of their sleeping-places, the grandmother saw the impression of the little girl's stomach and realized the latter was pregnant. She also found the skin of a bear which her grandson, having now become a man, had killed. She crawled into the fur.

Meanwhile, the young couple had a child and, in accordance with custom, the young man went off into the brush in order to pray, fast, and obtain the protection of the spirits. The old woman changed into a bear, caught up with him, killed, and ate him.

Then she returned to her grand-daughter's house and asked for water. While she was drinking, the little girl threw red-hot stones into her anus. Then, on the pretext of making her vomit up the excess water she had drunk, she stepped on the old bear's stomach so that the hot stones would bring the water to the boil and cook her. Then that bear [ogress] died.

NATIVE SOUTH AMERICA

105. **KARUETAOUIBO AND WAKURUMPO.** MUNDURUCU

Once upon a time there lived two men, named Karuetaouibo and Wakurumpo, who were married to each other's sisters. The latter was a man of normal appearance, but Karuetaouibo was very ugly. He was so ugly that his wife no longer wanted him and not only refused to accept his kill of fish and game, but had relations with another man.

One day the men of the village went to a stream far in the forest to fish with *timbo*. When the others returned, Karuetaouibo remained in the shelter that they had built and contemplated his unhappy situation. He was disgusted with life and reluctant to return to a wife who did not want him. As he was sitting there, the Sun came with his wife and asked him what he was doing. "Nothing," replied Karuetaouibo, "I am only sitting here because my wife has relations with another man and no longer wants me because of my ugliness."

The Sun wished to verify the truth of this and told his own wife to have coitus with Karuetaouibo in order to see if he was capable of pleasing a woman. The wife tried him out, but his penis was soft and would not enter. She went back and reported this to the Sun. To see if his wife was telling the truth, he passed his hand down the front of her body and then down her back to see if he could bring out semen. Nothing could be discovered, and he knew his wife told the truth.

The Sun then said, "Let us see what we can do for him," and he passed his

---

105. SOURCE: Murphy and Murphy 1985:122–25. Reproduced by permission of Columbia University Press.

hands over the body of Karuetaouibo, making him very small. He placed him inside his wife's womb, and after three days he was reborn. The Sun worked on him and fashioned him into a beautiful man of normal size. He then went to the stream and caught a basketful of fish, which he gave to Karuetaouibo, saying, "Return to your village, but do not go back to your wife. Go instead to a woman named Painun who weeps constantly for her husband, who was killed by the enemy." The Sun then brought him to the edge of the village and left him to enter by himself.

As Karuetaouibo approached the village, he signaled that he was coming. He first went to the men's house and there hung a hammock so small that there was no room for another man to climb in and bother him. Everybody gathered around him and admired his new beauty. The men said, "Ah, I wish that I were a woman so that I could have him for myself." Karuetaouibo's wife heard this, but she did not bother to look up, thinking that he had merely painted himself. Finally, she went outside the house and saw that her husband had indeed become very beautiful. The wife was under the impression that her husband still wanted her, and she made haste to make herself appear industrious. She went to her mother-in-law, who was grating manioc, and said, "Let me grate the manioc, mother-in-law." The old lady replied, "No, he does not want you to do it." In the meantime, Karuetaouibo ignored his wife and said, "Mother, go to the edge of the forest and pick up my basketful of fish." The wife offered to go, but Karuetaouibo refused.

When the mother returned with the fish, Karuetaouibo instructed her, "Go to the house there and give the woman who is weeping some fish and tell her to be consoled and cry no more." The old woman did this, and the woman in mourning said to her, "How can it be that your son wants me. I am ugly and dirty now." The mother replied, "It was he himself who sent me. He wants you." At this moment, Karuetaouibo entered the house and said to the woman, "Go to the stream and wash yourself and return to be my wife." She made herself clean and beautiful, and when she returned they started their life together.

When Karuetaouibo returned to the men's house, he got into his tiny hammock. Wakurumpo approached him and said, "Let me get into your hammock so that you can tell me how you became so beautiful." Karuetaouibo replied, "No, the hammock is too small." But Wakurumpo was extremely persistent, and after a number of days Karuetaouibo surrendered and told him the story. "But," he added, "this can mean nothing to you for you are not ugly, and your wife wants you."

The envious Wakurumpo wanted, however, to get rid of his wife and be as handsome as Karuetaouibo. He accordingly pretended that he was ugly and that his wife had rejected him for another man. Like Karuetaouibo, he went on a *timbo*-fishing expedition and stayed behind when the others returned to the village. Soon the Sun arrived and, pretending at first that he did not recognize Wakurumpo, eventually asked him what he was doing. Wakurumpo repeated the same story that Karuetaouibo had told, and the Sun proceeded to take the same measures. He instructed his wife to see whether Wakurumpo was capable of satisfying a woman, and the Sun's wife proceeded to have coitus with him. However, Karuetaouibo had neglected to tell this part of the story to Wakurumpo, and the latter completed satisfactory relations with the Sun's wife. The wife told the Sun what had happened, and he verified it as he did in the case of Karuetaouibo.

The Sun then made Wakurumpo very small and inserted him into his wife's womb, whence he was reborn three days later. He proceeded to make him big again and to remodel him. But this time, he made him ugly and hunchbacked and told him, "Now go home. But go home to your wife." The Sun and his wife did not fish for him or carry his basket back to the village, and Wakurumpo had to do all this himself. When he neared the village he signaled his arrival, and all the people who came to greet him stood about and stared at his ugliness. He had to go back to his wife, who accepted him.

When Wakurumpo went to the men's house to hang up his hammock, Karuetaouibo was lying there in his hammock, playing the following song on a flute:

> It was your fault, Wakurumpo
> It was your fault, Wakurumpo
> You were curious for your mother's vagina
> You were, you were.

Wakurumpo and Karuetaouibo were killed by enemies, who cut off their heads and placed them on top of posts. A small fat boy was posted to guard the heads. This boy had inherited shamanistic powers, but neither he nor the other people knew this. One day the heads began moving and talking, but only the boy could hear them, because of his special power. He shouted to the older men. "The two heads are moving and saying to each other, 'When will we rise to the sky?'" The elders scoffed and said, "How can heads without bodies or eyes move, and how can a dry mouth talk?" This happened many times, and the men still thought that the fat boy was lying to them.

A few days later the men adorned the heads with *urucu* paint and feathers, and after some days the heads said to each other, "Today we ascend." The boy spread the alarm, but none of the men heeded this warning. At noon the heads were seen to start rising to the sky, accompanied by their wives. Karuetaouibo and his wife rose rapidly, but Wakurumpo ascended slowly because his wife was pregnant. The men of the village shot arrows at the heads, and all missed except one shaft sent by the fat boy, which put out the eyes of Wakurumpo.

Wakurumpo and Karuetaouibo, both children of the Sun owing to their magical rebirth from the womb of the Sun's wife, are now in the sky and appear as the visible sun. The wife of Wakurumpo is Parawabia, the moon. When it is sunny and bright, this is because Karuetaouibo is in the sky; he is beautiful and his eyes shine a bright red. However, when it is dark and cloudy, it is because Wakurumpo is in the sky. Wakurumpo is ashamed to show his ugliness, and his eyes are dull and lifeless. For this reason he hides, and we do not see the sun.

106. SHAKANARI. MATSIGENKA

There was a young man who lived with his father and mother. One day he went to his uncle's house to ask to marry his daughter. He stayed for a month, working for his uncle, then asked for his daughter. His uncle said it was good, that he should come to live with him. The young man went home to get his things. When he got home he was angry and he beat his mother. His father said, "Why did you beat your mother? I will beat you."

And the son said, "Who are you?" His father went and got a club and beat him.

The son said, "Why are you beating me? You are like the head of the *makosomakosoimatake* bird."

His father said, "I am going to correct you."

"I am going to live with uncle's daughter," Shakanari said.

"You are a bad person," replied his father. "You will not live well with them. Her brothers will be angry with you. Your life there will not be peaceful."

But the son said, "No, I am going," and packed his net bag.

His father took his net bag away from him and made him stay home. The next day they went out and placed bird traps in the forest. The young man's uncle waited several days for his nephew to return. When he did not return, he went with his sons to the young man's house. When he arrived, he asked Shakanari's mother where he was. She replied, "In the forest."

So the uncle waited until the son and father returned. When they did, Shakanari was so angry he did not see the guests. His father greeted them, then Shakanari noticed them and said, "Greetings, Uncle." They sat down and ate and drank manioc beer. When they had finished, the uncle asked his nephew, "Why haven't you come to marry my daughter?"

"No, I am staying here with Father."

"I have prohibited him from going," said his father, "because he beat his mother. I have beaten him. If he goes to live with you he will treat his wife badly."

"I did not ask him to take my daughter," said the uncle. "He came and

---

106. SOURCE: Johnson and Johnson 1991a. Used by permission.

asked me for her. I said yes. Now his aunt is waiting for him to return to my house. If he does not want to come and live in my house, he can bring my daughter here."

They spent the whole night in discussion, and in the morning Shakanari went with his uncle. When they arrived at his uncle's house, his aunt said, "I have been waiting for you because you said you wanted my daughter." His uncle then told her the story, repeating what the father had told him. He said, "His mother says our daughter can go live in their house."

So Shakanari took the girl to live in his house. He built a new house and lived in it with his wife. After a time, his father died and his mother got angry at her son's wife. When her son went hunting and brought home meat to give to his mother, she never gave any to her daughter-in-law. Shakanari began to live in his mother's house, and left his uncle's daughter alone and without meat. Shakanari treated his mother in all respects as a wife.

One day his uncle said, "I will go visit my nephew. He is a good hunter and he will give me meat." He went with his wife and many sons and daughters. When they arrived, they saw his daughter all alone in her house.

"Where is my nephew?" asked the uncle.

"I don't know," said his daughter. "He left me here alone and went to live somewhere else."

"Why did he come and ask for you, if he did not want to live with you?"

She served them manioc and manioc beer, but no meat. When they had finished eating, she told them the story of what had happened.

"I am here alone, hungry, without meat, and he is living with his mother."

"Why is he living with his mother instead of you?"

"I don't know."

There followed a long silence in the house until Shakanari returned from the forest with his mother. He greeted everyone, then his mother greeted everyone. She ran to her house, carrying a guan her son had killed. As she ran, the bird cried, "*Hak! Hak!*"

The mother said to the girl, "Niece, come help me pluck the feathers of this bird."

"No. When my father was not here you never gave me meat. Now I won't eat any."

When the food was ready, Shakanari said, "Come and eat guan, Uncle."

But his uncle said he had drunk too much beer and was not hungry. The daughter refused to eat also, but the other members of the family went to eat. When they were finished eating, the uncle said, "Nephew, I came to visit you and my daughter. Because you took my daughter and because you are a hunter, I came to be invited to eat meat." His nephew said nothing.

"Why have you left my daughter alone and taken your mother? It is bad that you live with your mother. You should live with your wife."

Shakanari said nothing. He went to his mother's house. He blamed his mother: "You were angry at my wife, and never gave her any of the meat I gave you. Now what can we do?"

The next day his uncle said, "I am going. I came to visit you and see my daughter."

"Maybe you will take her with you," said Shakanari, but when he went to his house, she was already gone with her mother.

After that, Shakanari lived in his mother's house and hunted in the forest. One day, when he sat in the patio delousing his mother, his uncle's sons arrived and shot him behind the ear with an arrow. Shakanari lay like a dead man out in the sun, and the sun burned him. Then his mother heated water and bathed his body. Then it began to rain and Shakanari began to live again. He sat up in the patio and said, "Mama, they have shot me with an arrow." His mother brought him water to drink and he took it inside to drink. He suffered much. Worms grew in his wound. But slowly he got better.

When he was well, he and his mother lived together. Shakanari ate so many plantains that he finished theirs off, and began to eat the plantains of his neighbors. They said, "Who is eating all the plantains?"

"Maybe coati," he replied. "You should cut your plantains and keep them in your house."

The neighbors cut their plantains and kept them in their houses to ripen. When they were ripe, Shakanari went in to steal them. In the morning, the neighbors said, "Who is eating our plantains?"

"Wait for him at night with a club and kill him," Shakanari advised.

The neighbor said he would and late at night, around midnight, Shakanari stole in on hands and knees to get the plantains. The neighbor hit the thief with his club and broke his head open. The neighbor ran out of the house calling, "Shakanari! Shakanari! Shakanari! I have killed him!"

But Shakanari did not answer. In the morning, the neighbor went back to his house and saw that it was Shakanari he had killed. He took him and buried him in the forest.

Now, that's all.

107. TULUMA, THE WOODPECKER.   MEHINAKU

Tuluma was sick in his hammock, very, very sick. Or so he pretended. He saw his daughter, the line of her labia, her black pubic hair. He wanted to have sex with her.

---

107. SOURCE: Gregor 1985:63–64. From Gregor, *Anxious Pleasures*, published by the University of Chicago Press, 1985. Reproduced by permission of the publisher.

Tuluma called his daughter to him: "Come here, my daughter. In the future, I will send your cross-cousin to you. He calls me 'mother's brother,' he is your real cross-cousin, your father's sister's son. He looks just like me. He has my nose, my eyes, my body, my feet. Just like me. You'll see in the future, my nephew will come to you. When he does come, I want you to marry him; I want you to have sex with him."

Ah, then the daughter began to cry, out of sorrow for her dying father: "*Papai yu, papai yu*. Oh, my father," she wailed.

"Come to me, my daughter, I will soon die. When I am dead, I want you to have me buried under a ceramic cauldron, in the ground. But don't bury me too deep—just a shallow grave, not too deep."

"Yes, I will do it," said the daughter.

Then Tuluma completely relaxed his body and played dead. They decorated his body and put him in his hammock, painting his head with a red design, like that of a real woodpecker. They carried him out in his hammock, and he was buried under the ceramic cauldron, in a shallow grave.

Later that night, when it was very dark, Tuluma began to peck at the cauldron: "*Tak, tak, tak* . . ." It broke. The cauldron broke! Tuluma came up from the grave, in the middle of the night. All that night, Tuluma hid in the forest. The next day, he went to his daughter and said, "My uncle, Tuluma, has he died?"

"Yes he has."

Tuluma pretended to cry for his "uncle": "*Ua ku, ua ku, ua ku, ua ku.* Oh, my uncle . . ." Then he said, "Let me tell you what my uncle told me: "When I die in the future, my nephew, I want you to marry your cousin, my daughter."

"Yes, so my father told me."

Tuluma tied his hammock above his daughter's, and he had sex with her.

But then, a few days later, Tuluma called to his daughter: "Come over here to groom me for head lice." She sat down beside him and began to look through his hair for lice: "Ah, here is one. And here is one . . . here is one—What's this!?" All over Tuluma's scalp she found earth, earth from the grave.

"Mama! This one—my husband—he is my father!"

They struck him with clubs. Up, up, up, he flew away over the village to the forest and landed on a tree limb.

"*Tsiik, tsiik, tsiik hururu* . . . I had sex with you . . . I had sex with you . . . I had sex with you," he said to his daughter.

108. EWEJE AND HIS DAUGHTER KWALU. MEHINAKU

Eweje left the Mehinaku. He took refuge in another tribe because he feared he would be killed. He was a big witch, and everyone knew it. His daughter, Kwalu, was a little girl when he left, but she entered adolescent seclusion and grew into a beautiful woman.

When Eweje returned to the Mehinaku, his wife had died and his daughter was living with kin. He took his daughter off to the woods and said, "Let's have sex."

"Oh, no," she cried, "you are my father."

But Eweje threw her on the ground and raped her. When he returned to the village, he hung his hammock over his daughter's. Everyone was very much afraid of him. None of Kwalu's lovers continued to see her because they were afraid of Eweje's anger. Only one man dared criticize Eweje openly, and that was an old man, one of Eweje's close kin who did not fear his sorcery. All the others taunted him in falsetto voices from behind the houses at night so that he could never be sure who it was: "Woodpecker, woodpecker, you have sex with your daughter," they shouted. But none of that stopped Eweje. He lived with Kwalu as her husband until he himself died from witchcraft.

109. TAPIR WOMAN. MEHINAKU

A child was alone in the house. His mother had left him there alone. He cried and cried for his mother, but no one came. But then Tapir Woman heard his crying, and she came to comfort him. "Don't you know me?" she asked. "I am just like your mother. Don't cry."

Bending over, Tapir Woman said, "Put your arm into my rectum." "No!" replied the child. "I won't do that."

But Tapir Woman urged and begged and urged and begged, and at last the child slid his entire arm inside her, up to his shoulder. Tapir Woman tightened herself around the arm and raced off, dragging the little boy behind her. The little boy tried to pull himself free, but he could not; his arm was squeezed and crushed, tight inside. Tapir Woman dragged him through the forest, through the swamp, day after day. He was cut with thorns and bloodied. He was covered with the tapir's ticks and biting insects. But then Tapir

---

108. SOURCE: Gregor 1985:65. From Gregor, *Anxious Pleasures*, published by the University of Chicago Press, 1985. Reproduced by permission of the publisher.

109. SOURCE: Gregor 1985:178–79. From Gregor, *Anxious Pleasures*, published by the University of Chicago Press, 1985. Reproduced by permission of the publisher.

Woman come [*sic*] to a grove of fruit trees and ate and ate and ate. She filled herself with fruit. She ate more and more fruit. Later that day, she defecated the fruit. Out came all the fruit. Out came the arm of the little boy. But the arm came out shriveled and tiny. Too tiny, too shrunken for the boy to use it at all.

110. ARAUKUNI. MEHINAKU

Araukuni was in seclusion with his sister, a beautiful girl. Her thighs and calves were big and firm, and for that reason he wanted to have sex with her. Finally he did. He had sex with her, he had sex with her, he had sex with her. No one knew. But then Araukuni's sister became pregnant. "Who has been having sex with you?" said her mother. "I have seen no one coming to visit you."

"My brother has given me a child," she replied.

Oh, the mother was angry. She struck Araukuni and beat him with a club. She cut down his hammock and burned it. She burned his bow, his arm bands, and his belt. All of these she burned. She would not make bread for him. She would not give him manioc porridge or fish stew. All she would do was beat him, beat him, beat him. All the time she beat him.

Araukuni grew sad. He went off into the forest and wove a great canoe of bark fiber, bigger than a house. It could fly through the air like a plane, and it made frightening sounds like a shaman's rattle as it moved through the sky. In his village, Araukuni's family and friends said it was so much better that he had gone. "Good riddance," said the father. "He had sex with his sister."

But they came to miss him. They went to find him in a place where the waters were so deep that the sun could not be seen on the bottom. Araukuni lived deep in these waters. He ate birds that came near the water.

His sister came to him. "I want to be your wife," she said.

"No," replied Araukuni. "I don't want you. I don't want my mother or my father. They have missed me."

Then some of Araukuni's friends came to him. They saw that fur was beginning to grow all over his body, on his arms and legs. A long beard came down to his lap. His hair grew to his waist. He was changing into a spirit.

"If you come here again I will kill you and eat you," he said.

All of Araukuni's friends left and warned everyone else to stay far off. None came back. And Araukuni went off to a distant place, far away in the north.

---

110. SOURCE: Gregor 1985:180–81. From Gregor, *Anxious Pleasures*, published by the University of Chicago Press, 1985. Reproduced by permission of the publisher.

111. BAT ('ALUA'). MEHINAKU

In the village of the vultures, the birds were holding the ear-piercing festival for their sons. They were sad, since they had no headdress with which the boys could dance on the plaza. But then Vulture looked at Bat's mother-in-law, and he saw that her labia were enormous. "There," he said, "are the headdresses we need."

Bat decided that he would get the headdresses for the birds and lured his mother-in-law to a distant village where there was only one house. "You will not be alone," Bat told her. "Look at all the footprints on the trail. Everyone is already there." But the mother-in-law did not know that Bat had previously covered the trail with his own footprints.

When they arrived in the village, Bat pretended to be surprised: "Where is everyone?" he asked. "There is no one here!" Bat and his mother-in-law went into the one shabby house in the village and tied their hammocks at opposite ends. Suddenly, a bird screeched in the night, and the mother-in-law called to Bat: "What is it saying?" "It is saying you should move closer to me," Bat replied.

And so the mother-in-law moved closer each time an animal called in the night. Finally, after the jaguar growled, the mother-in-law got into Bat's hammock. There they had sexual relations. Bat then cut away his mother-in-law's labia with a clam-shell manioc spear and filled many, many baskets with her genitals.

All the baskets he carried to the village of the vultures. There the ear-piercing ceremony was still underway. Bat gave the labia as headdresses to the ducks and the turkeys and all the other birds. And that is how the birds first got their headdresses, their crowns, their crests, their throat folds.

112. ORIGIN OF THE STARS AND OF CERTAIN ANIMALS.

BORORO

Every time the women went to the corn plantation they came back to the village empty-handed, without so much as an ear of corn for their husbands and children. To insistent demands they replied: "Be patient a little longer; the corn is not yet ripe."

111. SOURCE: Gregor 1985:191–92. From Gregor, *Anxious Pleasures*, published by the University of Chicago Press, 1985. Reproduced by permission of the publisher.

112. SOURCES: Primary source: Albisetti and Venturelli 1969:473–75; Secondary source: Wilbert and Simoneau 1983:48–51. Reprinted, with permission, from Johannes Wilbert and Karin Simoneau, eds., *Folk Literature of the Bororo Indians* (Los Angeles: UCLA Latin American Center Publications, 1983), pp. 48–51.

One day an intelligent little boy began to doubt the sincerity of his mother and the other women. Waiting until they left for the field one day, he armed himself with his little bow and arrows and followed them. Near the plantation he clearly heard the rhythmic pounding of the pestle and the women's merry laughter. When he went closer the women discovered him and exclaimed to his mother: "Look who's here! It's your little boy!" Then, amiably inviting him to help himself to roast corn, cakes, and a corn drink, they generously gave him some of everything. But the boy thought to himself: "What liars you are! You have so much, and you say there's no corn!"

After eating his fill the boy began to play, hunting lizards and running after them into the cornfield, where he was hidden from prying eyes. There he gathered a lot of ripe corn and hid the grains inside his hollow bamboo arrows. Returning to the women, he found them getting ready to go home, empty-handed as usual. They made the boy promise not to say anything to the other Bororo. In return for his silence he would be allowed to accompany them freely to the field and enjoy the food they prepared. But since he was not at all interested in spending his time with the women, he decided never to go back to the field. His mother, fearing that he might talk, tried to force him to go, but when her son kept resisting her efforts she lost her calm and began to beat him mercilessly. The boy pretended to be bleeding copiously from the mouth. In fact, foreseeing that his mother might punish him, he had earlier filled his mouth with red clay; when he spat out the clay mixed with saliva he gave the impression that he was vomiting blood. Alarmed by the spectacle, the other women persuaded the boy's mother to refrain from further violence. All the women then returned to the field.

Free from his mother, the boy happily joined his playmates, to whom he said: "Friends, come over here, all of you! See how much ripe corn there is in the field!" He took the kernels from his arrows, and with the corn the boys made gruel and broth.

After considering how best to take revenge on their mothers, the boys finally decided to hide in the sky. They immediately made a very long rope to climb up on, and then they asked all the birds that were good fliers to tie one end of the rope to a secure place in the sky. When none of the birds was able to carry out the task, the boys appealed to the little hummingbird. Needing no persuasion, he quickly flew up until he reached the sky. He returned exhausted, fainting at the boys' feet. They revived him by fanning him and asked: "Did you manage to reach the sky and tie the rope firmly?" "Yes," he replied jokingly. "I tied it lightly to an old *sucupira* tree stump."

Satisfied with their first success, the boys noticed that only an old woman and a parrot remained in the village as sole witnesses to their actions, for the other women were all in the field and the men had gone hunting. To prevent the woman and the bird from telling what they had seen, the boys tied them up and cut out their tongues. Then, carrying the youngest boys on their backs, the older boys began to climb up the rope.

By the time they were halfway up, the women had begun to return to the village. Finding it silent and deserted, without the merry noise of children's voices, they went at once to the old woman and bombarded her with questions. Unable to answer, she simply raised her eyes to the sky. At this indication the women looked up and saw their sons, climbing rapidly. They called lovingly to the boys, offering them their breasts, but in vain, for the boys continued to flee toward the sky. The women started after their sons and had come up right behind them when the last boy, jumping into the sky, quickly turned and cut the rope. It fell and all the women came tumbling down with it.

Then an extraordinary thing happened: the women who remained in a sitting position while falling were transformed into tapirs, wild boars, peccaries, pacas, agoutis, and capybaras. The rest, falling into trees, turned into monkeys, howler monkeys, coatis, coendous, small and large anteaters, white monkeys, and tayras. Also, those who kept their waist bands well in place during their fall turned into animals without tails. Those whose bands came loose in front and were hanging down in the back were transformed into animals with tails.

The rope on which the boys climbed up is the present-day "ladder liana." It is still marked by their footprints, and the stars that glitter at night are the handsome faces of the sons of the Bororo.

113. THE STORY OF THE WOMAN ARARUGA PARU. BORORO

The Indian Butore Kurireu gave his daughter Araruga Paru in marriage to Araru Kurireu, who loved her very much. The father-in-law, however, did not want the couple to have sexual relations, so every night, whenever the boy wanted to initiate something, he revived the fire, brightly lighting up the inside of the hut. As an extra preventive Butore Kurireu made the girl wear a belt with pendants of wild-boar claws. Thus every time the husband wanted to caress the girl the rattle of the claws awakened her father, who then warned his son-in-law not to exercise his marital rights.

But one night Araru Kurireu found his wife without her belt and was easily able to sleep with her. Then he realized that her father had had relations with her before him. Furious at the discovery, he at once plotted re-

113. SOURCES: Primary source: Albisetti and Venturelli 1969:865–68; Secondary source: Wilbert and Simoneau, eds. 1983:187–91. Reprinted, with permission, from Johannes Wilbert and Karin Simoneau, eds., Folk Literature of the Bororo Indians (Los Angeles: UCLA Latin American Center Publications, 1983), pp. 187–91.

venge. He went hunting and killed a fat heron, which he cleaned and filled with the fat of the entrails, mixed with the pith of a gourd. Then he went away. His father-in-law, seeing a bird so nice and fat, could not resist temptation: he cooked it and ate it greedily. He had not quite finished eating the fowl when sharp abdominal pains made him cry out that he had been poisoned by his son-in-law. That night he died.

Losing no time, the murderer took his wife and left the village. But Araruga Paru sensed that the journey was bound to end badly, for the dead man was a spirit shaman and would take revenge on his assassin wherever the latter was. So she warned her husband: "Don't be careless; be on your guard, for my father was evil and very powerful." Concerned for her husband's life, she walked ahead of him in dangerous places, and when he lost his arrows in dense thickets or inaccessible places, she picked them up.

One day, when the couple came to a riverbank, Araru Kurireu decided to shoot at a shoal of silvery *piraputanga* fish, despite his wife's apprehension. He missed his shot and the arrow fell into the middle of the river. Immediately he ran to retrieve it, deaf to his wife's pleas not to expose himself to danger. As he ran into the water he stepped on a bank of quicksand, which rapidly swallowed him up to his neck.

In despair Araruga Paru cried: "I told you so! Before you die at least give me something to remember you by—your belt, or your bracelets, or your armband, or your lip pin!" "No," replied Araru Kurireu, "I won't leave you anything, for I don't want you to marry these ornaments." But the woman was insistent, making one last plea: that he give her his earrings. Tired of her begging, Araru Kurireu acquiesced, and before drowning he instructed her: "Continue your journey. Visit the clans of my friends Cibaiwu, Otokoe, and Kuje, but remember that the path leading to their village goes past the house of Rie. Be careful not to make a mistake. You'll see that the first one has his face painted red and has straight hair and white skin; the second also has straight hair and white skin, but the lower part of his face is light yellow; Kuje likewise has a light complexion but his hair is wavy."

Placing her husband's earrings in her basket, Araruga Paru abandoned him and resumed her journey. After walking a long time she heard merry conversation and laughter behind her. She tried to find out where it came from, and she discovered two beautiful children in the basket on her back. She understood at once what had happened: her husband's earrings had impregnated her and she was the mother of a pair of healthy twins.

After the little boys had grown up a bit, they would walk ahead of their mother and eat everything they found in order to satisfy their appetites. When they reached the foot of a huge *jatoba* tree they took a tasty fruit and split its strong shell to get at the sweet pulp inside. Suddenly there appeared an old man who was the spirit of the *jatoba*. He went over to the woman and said: "Why do you eat what belongs to me? I like this fruit very much. Go away! And may your children be attacked by wasps!" This was the first plague that he called forth, but it was in vain; the woman replied: "What you say is useless, for the wasps are my totem."

Becoming more and more furious, Ciriwore, as the spirit was called, continued to threaten Araruga Paru: "May your boys be stung by the hairy caterpillar and bitten by the snakes, by the pit viper, and by the *jararaca* viper; may they be devoured by the jaguar, the puma, and the leopard cat; may they be attacked by the whites, by the enemies!" Attentive despite the noise of the children, the mother answered readily: "Your curses are no good; none of these creatures will do us any harm, for they are my totems." The spirit, however, refused to give up. He redoubled his imprecations amid the shouting of the twins and the replies of the woman. Eventually there were curses that she was unable to answer, for she could not hear them because of the noise made by the boys.

Finally the old man stopped talking, and Araruga Paru, filled with forebodings of danger, took the children and continued her search for her husband's friends. The three walked a long distance through an arid region, and the children began to feel thirsty. When they least expected it they found a small pool of water, and against the advice of their mother they dipped into the pool to refresh themselves. No sooner had they entered the water than an eel caught and devoured them, leaving only their little lungs, which at once floated to the surface.

The woman cried and cried, and alone she continued her search for the friends of her husband. She reached a village, and immediately a man emerged from his hut, went toward her, and asked: "Where are you going?" She replied: "I'm looking for Cibaiwu, Otokoe, and Kuje, who are friends of my husband." Then Rie—for it was none other than he—told her a lie: "I am the very person you are looking for." Although she realized that the man was not telling the truth, she slept with him.

At daybreak her host said to her: "I'm going hunting to get us some food. Stay here, and don't go into the forest." Closing the door tightly he asked his mother not to look into the hut, but as soon as he had left the old woman, unable to restrain her curiosity, looked in and saw Araruga Paru, all decorated and painted like a bride. She understood everything, went to the woman, and said: "My daughter-in-law, let's go out and watch the dance of the boys while I begin to delouse you." They went out and sat down on the ground, leaning against the wall of the hut. As the boys passed before them, the old woman said to Araruga Paru: "There's Cibaiwu; look at Otokoe and Kuje." Imagine the joy of the woman at finding her husband's friends! She was so happy that she joined the boys in their dance and, as soon as it was over, went with them to the central hut.

Meanwhile Rie had returned from his hunting expedition. Seeing the house completely empty, he realized that his orders had not been obeyed. He did not believe his mother when she claimed that she had not even looked into the hut. At once he began to consider how to take revenge on his rivals. He filled his stomach with *coroata* fruit and immediately began to belch. Then he went over to Cibaiwu, Otokoe, and Kuje, who were asleep, and vomited the sticky fruit that he had eaten into their faces. They were disfigured at once, and their hair turned white. In the morning Araruga Paru saw the damage that Rie had done. She led her merry companions to the river, washed them, and massaged their stomachs with her feet. In this way she managed to remove all the ugliness from their faces and to restore the color of their hair. Then she happily returned to the village with them.

114. THE LEGEND OF THE HERO TORIBUGU. BORORO

A boy named Toribugu was the son of Kiare Ware. When his mother died another wife of his father's began to look after him, and his maternal grandmother raised his younger brother.

One day Toribugu's stepmother, carried away by an unnatural affection, decorated the boy beautifully with paint and little feathers, and then she let him sleep with her. When Kiare Ware returned to his wife's hut he noticed some white down on her belt. Unable to explain this ornamentation, he guessed that something irregular or illicit might have taken place. He called his son and ordered him to organize a dance for all the Bororo. To his surprise Kiare Ware saw that only Toribugu was wearing a feather ornament at the dance. He asked that the dance be repeated, and then his suspicions were confirmed: his son had broken one of the strictest clan laws relating to marriage by committing incest with a woman of the same clan as his mother.

Kiare Ware immediately plotted to kill his rival without letting the victim know what his intentions were. First he asked the boy to go hunting for the most ferocious animals, saying that he wanted to eat their meat. He thought that the boy would probably fall prey to a jaguar. But Toribugu, following the advice of his maternal grandmother, had an unusually good hunt and brought his father lots of meat.

Impatient to get rid of his son, Kiare Ware thought up another test. He said to the boy: "Go to the land of the spirits and get me one of the rattles they use to accompany their songs." The father knew very well that the own-

114. SOURCES: Primary source: Albisetti and Venturelli 1969:303–7; Secondary source: Wilbert and Simoneau, eds. 1983:198–204. Reprinted, with permission, from Johannes Wilbert and Karin Simoneau, eds., *Folk Literature of the Bororo Indians* (Los Angeles: UCLA Latin American Center Publications, 1983), pp. 198–204.

ers, in protecting their instruments, would kill the intruder. The boy ran at once to his grandmother who instructed him: "Try to find Mamori, the big locust, and tell him to go and get for you what your father wants." Toribugu called Mamori who flew to the land of the spirits, saw a rattle, and snatched it, holding it by the string by which it was hanging in a hut. The spirits were lying down, but when they heard the sound of the rattle they sat up immediately, moaning "Um, um, um." Then they let fly a rain of arrows at Mamori which, though not knocking him down, did inflict many scars which he still has on his wings to this day. The locust flew back quickly to Toribugu and gave him the rattle, which the boy handed over to his father.

Kiare Ware was still not discouraged in his plans for revenge. Again he called his son and said: "I want to eat the nuts of the babassu palm that grows right in the middle of the swamp and is guarded by the *buiogoe* spirits." Again consulted on the best way to fulfill the order, Toribugu's grandmother did not deny the difficulties it involved. But she had an idea: "The spider Ieragadu is used to walking on water; ask him to carry on his back Kodokodo, the squirrel, who can thus get to the palm tree and climb up to pick the fruit." The boy obeyed, and Kodokodo found a good cluster of fruit. But the unforeseen happened: while the squirrel was gnawing on the stem a piece of it fell from his mouth into the swampy water. Alerted to the presence of an intruder, the spirits made the water rise until it reached the crown of the palm tree. But Kodokodo, by climbing to the top of the tree, was able to escape the flood, which subsided after a while. He finished gnawing and when he saw that the spirits were quiet he climbed down. Again riding on Ieragadu's back he went back and gave the fruit to Toribugu, who took it to his father.

Kiare Ware had one last test to try. He suggested to his son: "Let's go to a high rock wall where there are many macaws. I want to take some of the young birds so I can raise them for myself." Before leaving Toribugu once more consulted his grandmother. She did not conceal the risky nature of the expedition, but she gave the boy a magic stick of hers which might help him in the most difficult situations. When father and son had reached their destination Kiare Ware cut a long sturdy stick and leaned it against the rock wall so that Toribugu could climb up to the birds' nest, which was dug into the rock, and grab the young ones. When he was quite high up his father kicked the lower part of the stick so that the boy was in danger of falling into the deep precipice below. In a flash Toribugu drove the magic stick into the stone wall. He clung to it but soon realized that he had no way of descending from such a height. Then he had some good luck: he saw lianalike roots hanging from a bush on the plateau at the top of the rock wall. The boy tested the strength of the roots, and finding it sufficient he climbed up to the top of the rock.

Unfortunately Toribugu found there only bushes and grass; there was neither water nor food. His main concern then was to climb down from the rock. From a twig he made a small bow, used thread pulled from his cotton ornaments as a string for it, and fashioned little arrows from the woody stalks of the grass. Using these improvised weapons he caught a large number of *batarereu* and *kukaga-doge* lizards and tied them to the threads and tassels hanging from his ornaments. When he was practically covered with the little animals, which he realized were rotting because of the bad odor, he lay down and pretended to be dead.

Attracted by the smell of the decaying meat, Ciwaje, the vulture, flew down and bit hard into Toribugu's buttocks. The boy, who of course was not dead, stirred because of the pain. Ciwaje thought to himself: "This animal is still not dead. I'll call on other vultures like the *bae*, *pia-doge*, and *pobureu*, and on the caracara hawk to help me." When they got there they too furiously dug into the boy's buttocks. Their horrible feast made them thirsty, and so they decided to move their victim to a place where there was water. It was agreed that Ciwaje would carry the boy on his back to the foot of the rock. As soon as Ciwaje landed on the soft grass near the water the boy jumped from his back and fled. While they were descending, however, Toribugu had been leaning on the vulture's wings, bending them. To this day this defect disfigures Ciwaje's wings.

When he examined his buttocks Toribugu discovered that his entire anal region had been destroyed. Undaunted, he immediately went in search of his friends but found the village completely abandoned. Going to his grandmother's hut, he saw inside it some food that the old woman had purposely left for him. He was so hungry that he quickly gulped down the food, but he noticed that it did not remain in his stomach because of the damage done to his anal tract by the vultures.

Continuing on this journey, Toribugu found another abandoned village. In his grandmother's house he retrieved a well-cooked *pobodori* tuber that was buried under the still-glowing ashes. He applied the tuber to his wounded anus; not only did it fit perfectly, but it remained in place. Happy to have his buttocks restored, the boy ate what his grandmother had left behind and found that the operation had been completely successful; the food remained in his intestines in the normal manner.

Thus recovered, he continued to follow after his companions, again and again finding abandoned villages and welcome food in his grandmother's huts. After walking a long time he heard cries of sadness. They came from his grandmother, who thus showed her grief while accompanying the Bororo whenever they moved. Immediately Toribugu transformed himself into a little bird and flew into the old woman's face. She found this very strange but calmed down when Toribugu's brother said that it was nothing very extraordinary. The boy then turned himself into a lizard and hit the end of the stick that she was holding. "Boy," she said to her grandson, "what's this?" "Nothing," he replied. "It's just a little insignificant lizard bumping against your stick." Reassured, she continued her journey, but the lizard touched her cane once more. Again she spoke to her grandson: "Take a look behind us to see what's going on." "My brother has come!" exclaimed the boy when he saw the lizard transformed into a man. Happily the old woman picked up Toribugu and made him sit on her lap, crying with joy over his return.

After this display of emotion Toribugu said to the old woman: "My grandmother, my grandmother, don't tell anybody that I have come back. When we get to the site of the new village, build your hut well away from the others so that I can come and go without being seen. Then send the children to hunt for lizards; thus I'll be able to enter your house easily in the form of a lizard, with the ones caught by the boys. If anybody runs after me you must pretend to catch me with a mat and tell him to leave the house." The old woman obeyed, and everything happened as planned.

At sunset a violent storm broke with rain, thunder, and lightning. It put out all the fires of the Indians, except that of Toribugu's grandmother, which was as large as an enormous lagoon. At dawn Kiare Ware asked one of his wives to to his mother-in-law's hut and fetch a firebrand so that he could light his fire again. The wife reached the hut quickly, entered, and to her great surprise she saw Toribugu. She took the firebrand and told her husband that she had seen his son. Kiare Ware, though highly displeased at the reappearance of his son, who he had thought was dead, pretended to be happy and ordered a beautiful song to be sung and a hunting expedition to be undertaken in the boy's honor.

After some time had passed Toribugu, who was waiting for a suitable moment to get rid of his rival, sent his youngest brother to ask the father to have another song sung and to organize a deer hunt. Kiare Ware agreed at once. Toribugu then instructed his brother to tell his companions that if a stag should appear they were to spare it so that he could kill it and make a handsome rug from its hide for his father. With his plans made, Toribugu found a beautiful *paratudo* branch which he fitted to his head to look like horns, but it was not strong enough. Next he tried a *sucupira* branch, which did have the desired strength, so the boy could transform himself into a handsome deer when the right moment came. Once more he called his brother and told him to run among the Bororo in the form of an agouti to find out exactly where their father was waiting to hunt. When he saw an agouti between his legs Kiare Ware tried to put an arrow through it but he missed. As the rodent happily sped away it was cursed by Kiare Ware: "Vile animal, with your huge rump!" The agouti, panting for air, reached his elder brother and pointed out exactly where their father was waiting for a stag to appear.

Toribugu arranged the *sucupira* branch on his head and magically turned himself into a majestic stag. Swiftly he ran to the center of the circle formed by the Bororo, all of whom were eager to catch him. They attacked once, but he disappeared in the direction of the place where he knew his father was waiting. Kiare Ware wanted to frighten the stag so that it would turn its side and thus present a better target. But he tried in vain: the animal advanced swiftly and drove its horns into the father's stomach, lifted him about its head, and threw him into a lagoon infested with piranhas. Thus did Toribugu kill his father. All the Bororo were saddened by what had occurred, for a deer killing a man is an ill omen. Feeling downcast, they returned to the village, with Toribugu and his brother walking behind them.

Still not satisfied with his revenge, the murderer once more instructed his brother: "When we get to the village I'll carry my father's weapons, and I'll even imitate his walk and wear his ornaments. Then I'll go into his wives' hut, and they will certainly be deceived and will give me a nice bath and delouse me. In so doing they may discover the scars made by the horns I used as a stag. If they suspect anything, give me a quick wink so that I can defend myself." Toribugu had guessed correctly. The women, seeing the traces of the horns, looked at each other and understood everything, but they had no time to react. Toribugu's brother gave the sign agreed upon, and in a flash Toribugu stood up, seized his club, and shattered the heads of Kiare Ware's two wives.

These events are briefly referred to by the members of the clan of the Paiwoe in one of their songs.

115. TRANSFORMATION OF A BROTHER- AND SISTER-IN-LAW INTO BOAS. NIVAKLÉ

There was a very beautiful girl whom her brother-in-law loved very much. Her sister was the wife of this man.

Having found out about the relationship, the father of the girl planned to kill his son-in-law by shooting him with an arrow. As the old man, accompanying himself on his drum, sang to Tsintsex, the pink heron [which is a benevolent thunderbird], the latter spoke to him to dissuade him. The bird told him that he should only throw a cord down in front of his son-in-law.

The old man spent all night making the rope. At midnight he finished it, and early in the morning he knelt down to toss the cord before his son-in-

---

115. SOURCE: Wilbert and Simoneau, eds. 1987b:296–97. Reprinted, with permission, from Johannes Wilbert and Karin Simoneau, eds., *Folk Literature of the Nivaklé Indians* (Los Angeles: UCLA Latin American Center Publications, 1987), pp. 296–97.

law, asking him to pick it up. The father-in-law tossed it, and the very moment that the son-in-law picked it up, he turned into a boa constrictor.

All who witnessed what happened were surprised, wondering about the reason for the transformation, since they knew nothing about it. The fact was that the old man had become angry with his son-in-law because he wanted his own sister-in-law for his wife. The older man had not liked this, and for this reason had cast the cord at the young man's feet.

Once the man who had been changed into a boa had gone into the forest his wife did not cry for him, as must be done when someone disappears or dies. The only one who cried for the disappearance of the man was his sister-in-law, the younger sister of his wife.

Before his transformation the man had realized what his father-in-law's plans were. Convinced that he could not have his sister-in-law, one day in the forest in search of honey he had mixed water boa eggs with the honey in his leather pouch. Returning to the village, he had given the bag to his sister-in-law so that she might eat. She had consumed the honey mixed with the eggs. This mixture, which we new men never make, is dangerous, but the first men had this custom.

When the girl mourned the disappearance of her brother-in-law, she finally said: "I will go with him and will transform myself into a water boa." Then she went to a thicket of *caraguata* and in it found a burrow. She went into it and there became a water boa.

Those who saw what had happened to the son-in-law and his sister-in-law said: "The same thing could not happen to us; it could have happened only to them."

Ever since then, whenever the father-in-law sang to Pink Heron he was sad and he cried, because he remembered his son-in-law who had become a boa, and whom he had loved.

116. THE INCESTUOUS YOUNG MAN WHO WAS TRANSFORMED INTO A JAGUAR. CHAMACOCO

There was a heavy rainfall, and the mother of a young man placed a shelter made of mats over him. From below he saw her vagina, and since that time he would not eat any kind of food. The rain ended, days went by, and still he refused to eat. Then he told his mother that he wanted to eat

116. SOURCES: Primary source: Cordeu 1980; Secondary source: Wilbert and Simoneau, eds. 1987a:194–99. Reprinted, with permission, from Johannes Wilbert and Karin Simoneau, eds., *Folk Literature of the Chamacoco Indians* (Los Angeles: UCLA Latin American Center Publications, 1987), pp. 194–99.

algarrobo flour, and she told his father to bring the bread which they kept in the forest. After the man had left she asked her son why he did not want to eat. He replied: "I saw your vagina, and now I want to have relations with you." "All right, then do it; it's all right." So the son copulated with his mother, and afterward he ate everything there was. When the husband returned she told him that their son was fine again, and that his journey had been for nothing. The father realized that what had been happening was not because of the food, and he guessed that the boy had had relations with his mother. "That's why he likes to eat again and doesn't cry anymore," he thought.

A long time passed. Then the father announced that he was going fishing. He took his younger son along, leaving the elder at home. When they got to the place where there were eels he gave his son the digging stick and told him to dig a hole, because there was an eel there which he wanted to catch but had been unable to. When the hole was waist-deep he told his son to run back and get his brother so he could enter it. The boy went and saw his mother, who said: "Don't let your brother stay there, for he has just finished his initiation. As a new initiate he must not get dirty." Then she let him go, and the two boys went off and found their father. He said, "There's an eel here which I can't get out." They used to insert their fingers into the gills to catch them. "My hand is too big; why don't you try?" The boy stuck his hand in, but there was no eel there, only an empty hole. Suddenly the man seized his legs and pushed him head first into the hole, and then he covered it. Although he had ordered the younger boy to go away for a while the latter saw what happened. Afterward the father went away, leaving his sons there, the dead one and the younger boy.

The latter did not want to leave his brother, and cried until it grew dark. The next day he had lost his voice and could not cry anymore. Some storks wanted to descend to eat the fish there, but they were kept away by the presence of the boy. Finally one bird flew down and asked him what he was doing. The boy wanted to answer, but his voice was choked from all his weeping. Instead he signaled that they had dug a hole there and that someone was inside it. The stork did not understand and sent for all the herons to find out what the boy needed. They were all there, but could not understand what he was saying. "Call the *carau*!" said someone, and the *carau* came. "There's a boy here who can't tell us what's wrong. Maybe you can cure him!" The *carau* took a large, round snail shell with a cover underneath, took out what was inside, and made the boy swallow it. But still he could not talk. The *carau* took another snail and again made him eat, and this time he recovered his speech: "My brother is here. My father killed him and buried him there." He explained to them what had happened to his brother. The birds told him that they were going to save him, and began to remove the mud with their feet. The dead boy was already swollen and decomposing, but they began to resuscitate him, trying to give him power. Finally the young man sat up and spoke to his brother: "Why are we here?" "Father killed you; he brought you here and killed you. You were resuscitated by these storks and herons!" Thus he found out what had happened.

The storks asked: "Would you like to become birds like us?" They wanted the boys to turn into birds so that they, too, would be able to fly. "No," replied the older boy, "because if you turn me into an animal I'll be killed and eaten." "But there are jaguars around here, and those aren't eaten!" "Yes, all right; nobody eats them, and as jaguars we'll be left alone!" Then the herons gave the two boys shamanic power, and they were transformed into jaguars.

The two jaguars left, and one said to the other: "Let's go to father's house, since he killed me. When they go to defecate we'll kill them." Although the boy who had been killed had become a jaguar, his younger brother saw that his body was no good anymore; he had lost his strength while he was in the hole. "You have no more strength left, but I still have plenty. Let's go, and since you have grown weak you will bite mother, and I'll bite father." They traveled until they reached the house. After taking up separate positions they began calling their father and mother with their magic power, until finally their parents came. They went apart and defecated, and when the father came back the jaguars bit them and killed them. Morning found them dead there, and the other people saw the two jaguars eating them. Then they grew afraid of the jaguars. The older boy ate his mother.

Later, when the two boys were in the forest, they wanted to have intercourse with a woman. Although they were jaguars they were also young men, and they thought as we do. They wanted a wife, and thought of having a woman with them. One day a hunter came with his wife. They were both gathering food, but proceeding separately, the woman from the Rio Paraguay and the man in the direction of the center of the Chaco. The two jaguars gathered the other jaguars, and took ten or fifteen of them along like dogs. They heard that there was a woman there. When the husband called to his wife to find out where she was, one jaguar likewise called out in a man's voice. She was surprised when she heard it, for her husband's voice was less coarse. Seeing all the jaguars the man thought: "I don't stand a chance against them!" He started to run, leaving his wife behind. She had a very small son, and the man, who was now in a way a widower, took care of him.

When the woman saw the jaguars she climbed up in a tree, and they stood below, pleading: "Come down; we won't hurt you! We want you to come and live with us, for we need a wife!" Then she climbed down and joined the jaguars, and they had intercourse with her.

After hunting, jaguars eat their prey raw, but when they brought the woman raw meat she did not want it. She made a separate fire, roasted the meat, and ate it. She did not want to eat raw meat.

She lived in the forest for many years. Her son was already big. Once he went out to hunt birds, and as he was shooting at them a bird addressed him. It did not really speak, but it sounded as though it did. There was a bird which calls *etuxa*, *etuxa*, a word meaning "fatherless" or "motherless" [orphan]. The boy left the bird, went to his father, and said: "When I shot at a bird just now, it called me '*etuxa*.' I don't know why. I want you to tell me what happened to my mother." Then his father had to explain to him that the jaguars had probably eaten her. The boy asked whether they had eaten her or taken her away, but the father did not know, for he had fled. "Where is the place? I'm going to look for my mother and kill those jaguars." His father showed him the place.

In the morning the boy prepared his club and left. He saw the tracks of the jaguars and of his mother, but they were old, and the mud was dry. He went on. After a few days he found a spot where the jaguars had eaten. He touched the ashes, and finding them still warm he said: "This is my mother's fire; the jaguars didn't eat her after all, and she's living with them. I'm certain my mother made this fire." He was only guessing, for he still did not know. Farther on he found another fire, and he touched the ashes and found them warm: "I'm sure my mother is with the jaguars. Now I'm going to sleep." In the morning he saw the smoke from a fire rising from his mother's house. When the woman looked toward the edge of the forest she knew at once that the one who was coming was her son. She ran toward him and embraced and kissed him, saying: "Poor boy who has come here! There are many fierce jaguars here, and they will bite you! But it is still early; they won't come until the afternoon." Then she made a small hut for him: in among some strands of weeds she made a funnel-like clearing and placed a mat over it, and there she hid her son. "Hold on to your club, for you have many jaguars as your stepfathers." All used to copulate with her. "If they see you by yourself they will eat you, so stay in this little hut which I've made for you, and they won't know. After they arrive and put down what they have killed, they lie down to rest. When the first one comes I'm going to delouse him. Let him fall fast asleep, and then kill him!"

In the afternoon the boy was waiting inside the hut. He killed the first jaguar that came, and cut off his tail, and then he carried off the body and threw it to the side so that the others would not see it. Thus he went on killing many of them until there was only a single jaguar left. She happened to be very fond of that jaguar, the one with the white head, whose back was white all the way down to his tail. She did not tell the boy that he was her husband. His name was Kumarxuo and he was the Lord of the Jaguars, the biggest jaguar of all.

When he came, the last of the jaguars, his wife examined his head, picking off the lice and the thorns. Then she made a sign, and her son came out. He dealt the jaguar a blow, but not a serious one; he was in a hurry, for that was the last victim. His mother stopped him: "Enough! Leave your stepfather alone! Don't bother him; let him go away." She loved that jaguar. Her son, though, had no interest in any jaguar and wanted to kill them all, but she prevented him. The jaguar left.

The young man set off toward home, bringing his mother. It was their custom when traveling to orient themselves by the sun and the direction of the wind. But the woman did not really want to leave, for she was now at home with the jaguars. At night when they lay down to rest the boy fell asleep, and his mother returned from where they had come. When he woke up he took his club and started to follow her. Finding her on the path he took her with him once more. The same thing happened: she wanted to go back, and would not let her son rest. "All right," he finally said, "if you don't want to come with me I can't force you. Go, then." And his mother went away forever.

Morning came, and his mother was no longer there; he had let her go. He himself returned home, bringing only the tails of the jaguars he had killed, as proof of what he had done. After showing them off he told everyone that his mother had not wanted to go home, and that he was now very tired.

The people thought afterward that he should have killed that jaguar. Because of that woman there are many jaguars today.

117. THE INCEST AND THE BIG BULL. GUAJIRO

A woman was living in seclusion in her house. She had two children, a boy and a girl. She stayed confined so that no one would see her. Her children looked after their animals, the boy tending the horses and the girl the goats and the cows. She never went out but lived like a young girl, a *majayura*. [Volume editors' note: Although she was married and a mother, this woman was living in seclusion, i.e., like a young girl. This is an abnormal situation for a Guajiro woman].

When the boy had grown into a young man he said to his sister: "It's not our mother who's shut up in the house." He did not believe that she was his mother. "Yes, it's our mother!" replied the girl. "No, it's not; she looks like a

---

117. SOURCES: Primary source: Perrin 1973:3–22; Secondary source: Wilbert and Simoneau, eds. 1986: vol. 2, 780–92. Reprinted, with permission, from Johannes Wilbert and Karin Simoneau, eds., *Folk Literature of the Guajiro Indians, Vol. 2* (Los Angeles: UCLA Latin American Center Publications, 1986), pp. 790–92.

young girl. You're lying, it's not our mother!" And in fact the woman was behaving like a young girl.

One day the boy returned early after tending the horses. When he arrived his sister was not yet there. He went to the woman and asked her to copulate with him. "No! I'm your mother," she said. But the boy forced her to have relations with him. "No, you're not my mother; you're lying!"

Immediately afterward the woman left. It was said that up in the mountains there lived a big bull that ate people and was as ferocious as a jaguar. The woman decided to go there to disappear.

Just after she had gone her daughter came home. She put on a red scarf and ran off after her mother, crying. Her brother was left all alone.

The mother reached the place where the bull lived. She stopped in the shade of some big calabash trees where the bull used to come every day at noon. When the daughter was nearly there she saw the big bull coming. Very quickly she climbed up into one of the calabash trees. "Climb up, mother!" she called but her mother did not listen; she stayed at the foot of the trees. "No, I don't want to climb up. I won't do it!" The bull came and swallowed her.

After he had eaten her he began to dig at the foot of the trees. He wanted to devour the girl who was in the top of a tree. When the tree was about to fall she jumped over into another tree. Immediately the bull attacked it. When the tree was about to fall she changed again.

Soon there was only a single calabash tree left. The young girl took the red scarf that she had with her and began to wave it about like a flag. From far away the owner of the bull saw the piece of red cloth. He knew that the animal ate people. "Someone has probably climbed up into the trees to get away from him. Poor man! I'll go and take a look," he said. After saddling his mount he went off toward the flag.

He arrived as the bull was about to bring down the last tree. He scared the animal, which went running off. The young girl was calling to the man from the top of the tree. The bull wanted to eat her. He had already eaten her mother, who was inside his stomach. The girl climbed down.

She asked the man to get her mother out from the bull's stomach. He asked her to go with him. "How could I kill my bull?" he said. But she insisted so strongly that he felt sorry for her and killed the animal with his revolver. He opened the stomach and took out the girl's mother, who was whole. The bull had swallowed her.

The man took the girl to his house, and also the body of her mother. "We'll give her a big funeral and invite a lot of people," he said. He arranged a big ceremony.

Afterward he asked the girl to be his wife. She wanted to, but he had to wait for several years.

Many years went by. The girl married him. He became her husband.

118. THE ORIGIN OF A HILL. GUAJIRO

A long time ago there was a *majayura* [virgin] who had sexual relations with her father. When she knew she had become pregnant she was so ashamed that she wanted to hang herself to atone for her offense, and she did so. Mareiwa, the god of the Guajiro, then said that as punishment for what she had done he would turn her into a hill. The Indians say that that is why the hill of Katetamana has the form of a hanged woman. Since then the Indians frequently hang themselves whenever fortune goes against them.

119. INCEST. GUAJIRO

A *majayura* was in her period of seclusion. She had a brother. When she emerged from her seclusion she was pregnant, having been impregnated by her brother. When she realized her condition she was beside herself, and her first thought was to throw herself into a sea. She did so, but she fell into the water instead of on the rocks. Mareiwa said to her: "You shall turn into a rock; you have committed a bad deed, and other people will follow your example." That is why today brothers sometimes have relations with their sisters.

120. THE BIRTH OF KWANYIP. SELKNAM

T he parents of Kwanyip were good people. His father [Hais] was an accomplished *xon*. Hais had a strong adversary in powerful Nakenk, who had a daughter named Hosne. She was very beautiful. Hais fell in love with the daughter of Nakenk and wished to make her his wife.

These two had met in secret, tasting much of love. One day they were again playing with each other, Hais lying on top of Hosne. Unbeknownst to the two Nakenk saw this. He became very angry. Hais had a long penis and therefore Nakenk did not want to give him his daughter.

Nakenk thought it over; he wanted to play a devastating trick on Hais, and

118. SOURCES: Primary source: Pineda Giraldo 1950:76; Secondary source: Wilbert and Simoneau, eds. 1986:45–46. Reprinted, with permission, from Johannes Wilbert and Karin Simoneau, eds., *Folk Literature of the Guajiro Indians*, Vol. 1 (Los Angeles: UCLA Latin American Center Publications, 1986), pp. 45–46.

119. SOURCES: Primary source: Chaves 1946; Secondary source: Wilbert and Simoneau, eds., 1986: vol. 1, 46–47. Reprinted, with permission, from Johannes Wilbert and Karin Simoneau, eds., *Folk Literature of the Guajiro Indians*, Vol. 1 (Los Angeles: UCLA Latin American Center Publications, 1986), pp. 46–47.

120. SOURCES: Primary source: Gusinde 1931:584; Secondary source: Wilbert 1975:30–31. Reprinted, with permission, from Johannes Wilbert, *Folk Literature of the Selknam Indians* (Los Angeles: UCLA Latin American Center Publications, 1975), pp. 30–31.

in this he succeeded. Hais's own daughter Akelkwoin lay down in the place where Hais had always met Hosne. When Hais came full of desire he threw himself immediately on the girl, on his own daughter! He did not know it! Akelkwoin became with child. She gave birth to Kwanyip. Evil Nakenk had brought that about!

Later Hais discovered that he himself had begotten this child with his own daughter. Terribly enraged, he sought at once to revenge himself on Nakenk. But the latter kept himself well hidden.

The family of Hais originated in the north. There Kwanyip fetched tame guanacos for himself. Many ancestors also left the north and came to our country.

121. **THE GUANACO-MAN AND HIS DAUGHTERS.** SELKNAM

Once there was an old guanaco-man who lived during the time of the ancestors. When he had become a widower he fell in love with his two daughters. He particularly liked his older daughter, with whom he wanted to sleep. He did not know how he might accomplish this, however; after all, he was her father! But after thinking it over for a long time he said to his two daughters: "I am going to die soon. Just see how old I am already! So let me lie here, and cover up my body; but let my head stick out!" His daughters wept bitterly. Their father comforted them and said: "Nearby here lives another man who desires you. He wishes to marry you and that is fine with me. That way you won't be alone. Don't be afraid!"

Then their father died. But he was only pretending to be dead. His daughters cried much and let him lie there. They covered his body with his robe but left his head free. Then those two girls immediately painted themselves. Even today one still sees the black line that they carry on their chests. They also made motions with their arms, crying loudly at the same time.

Then they left that place. After some time a guanaco came toward them. It was their father, but the girls did not recognize him. The guanaco made a sound: "Rsr, rsr, rsr." The two girls answered at once: "Srr, srr, srr." They came closer to one another and caressed each other. It pleased the guanaco-man very much to have relations with each of the two girls. All of them were now guanacos. Since that time fathers have relations with their own daughters, for they stay together for a long time in the same herd.

121. SOURCES: Primary source: Gusinde 1931:650; Secondary source: Wilbert 1975:107–9. Reprinted, with permission, from Johannes Wilbert, *Folk Literature of the Selknam Indians* (Los Angeles: UCLA Latin American Center Publications, 1975), pp. 107–9.

THE WILD GOOSE COUPLE. YAMANA

In the old days, to cover their bodies women wore only their *masakana* [loincloth] and a short cover hanging down the back. They always took off the back cover when inside the hut. There once lived a woman who had a little son. One day her husband went out to hunt for several days. As usual, the woman devoted herself to her work in the hut. She did not pay too much attention to herself whenever she bent down, but her little son was watching her attentively and could see her private parts from behind. He took great pleasure in this and thought about it constantly. From then on he cried over and over: "I like that thing there! I like that thing there!" Since he was constantly crying the same words his mother wanted to let him have his wish. She brought edible mussels and snails, sea urchins and crabs, fish and berries, showed him one after the other, and offered it to him kindly. But discontentedly he rejected every single thing, turned away his head, and only repeated: "I like that thing there!" At the same time he pointed to his mother's private parts, but she did not understand what he wanted. She brought little baskets and necklaces, feather ornaments and beautiful stones, weapons and tools, even small birds and a small dog. But the boy angrily rejected all this and turned away from it, saying again and again: "I like that thing there!" Finally the mother was completely at a loss and embarrassed; she no longer knew what to do. She was unable to discover what her small son really wanted and could not understand why he was always screaming: "I like that thing there!" She had shown and offered him everything within her reach, but nothing had calmed him down.

Finally the mother pretended to be very tired. She lay down and acted as if she were going to sleep, for she expected her little son soon to fall asleep, too. He did indeed remain still, likewise pretending that he was going to sleep. The mother got up after some time and looked for her baskets, talking quietly to herself as she went: "I'll go to the beach now to collect mussels." She took her basket and left the hut. Just a few steps from the hut she came across some big mussels. She bent down and gathered them in her basket. Meanwhile her little son had half sat up on his bed and turned his eyes on his mother. When she was thus gathering mussels in a bent-over position he again saw her private parts from behind and was delighted. He quickly got up and painted his head, his face, and the upper part of his body all black with charcoal dust, but his legs he covered with *imi* [red soil for painting].

---

122. SOURCES: Primary source: Gusinde 1937:1195–97; Secondary source: Wilbert 1977: 73–75. From Johannes Wilbert, *Folk Literature of the Yamana Indians: Martin Gusinde's Collection of Yamana Narratives*, published by the University of California Press, 1977. Reproduced by permission of the publisher.

He left the hut and hurried down to the beach where his mother was. He went by some women who were also gathering mussels. Unobtrusively he looked at their private parts from behind but did not touch any of these women. When he was standing close by his mother he put his hand on her genitals and began to play with them. He liked this play very much and it increased his pleasure. His mother liked it, too, and she gave in to him. But so that the other women would not notice what the two were doing to each other they hurried to their canoe, got in, and went over to an island nearby. Here they were all alone. They lay down and had intercourse. They stayed together for a long time in this way. During this they were eventually transformed into birds.

The following day both left the desert island and flew back to the shore where the huts of the people were. Here they sat on a stone exactly in front of the hut where they had lived until the day before. In the meantime the man had come back from the hunt, and when he could not find his wife and his son in the hut, he anxiously inquired among the other people: "Where are my wife and my little son? I see them neither in the hut nor elsewhere." The people answered him: "Just look at that stone: two birds are sitting there that were not there before. Those two *sekus* [the powerful, heavy wild goose] are your wife and little son. They fell head over heels in love and were turned into birds." Since that time the two accompany each other constantly and, to this day, live together exclusively by themselves.

123. **THE LITTLE WOODPECKER.** YAMANA

Although little *detehurux* [small woodpecker] was still very young, he had already fallen in love, and with his own mother, at that. She was always carrying her little son around with her. For that purpose she had made a bag from pieces of hide; she put the little *detehurux* into it and constantly carried him around on her back. She never took the little boy out of the bag, and whenever she left her hut she slung the bag on her back. That way the small boy was never without his mother.

This woman went frequently into the forest. She told the people: "I find the *esef* [mushroom] so delicious that I always have to go out into the forest to collect a lot of these mushrooms." But she always went alone, taking only her son along in the bag. As soon as she found a hidden place in the forest she stopped. Her little son became a full-grown man and quickly left the sack

---

123. SOURCES: Primary source: Gusinde 1937:1197–99; Secondary source: Wilbert 1977: 75–78. From Johannes Wilbert, *Folk Literature of the Yamana Indians: Martin Gusinde's Collection of Yamana Narratives*, published by the University of California Press, 1977. Reproduced by permission of the publisher.

in which he had been sitting. Without delay he climbed up into the trees and picked *esef*. Then he threw many of them down to the woman below who gathered them up. After some time he called to his mother from up there: "Lie down on the ground and part your legs as far as you can; I want to throw *esef* into your vagina!" The woman immediately lay down on the ground with great pleasure, and with her legs stretched far apart she opened her vagina very wide. The son hit his mother's vagina with the *esef* thrown from the tree, which was a very great pleasure for both of them. After playing like this for a rather long time the son climbed down from the tree. Then he lay down on his mother and she received him with great pleasure, for his penis was extremely large.

After they had spent a long time doing this they finally got up. The son got into the bag, became smaller and smaller, until he had become an infant again. The mother hurried back to the hut with him. Again they had returned with a large amount of *esef*. These they distributed among the other women; all ate a lot and appeared very content. The mother and her son went often to the forest, but always alone, and every time they played around in this wicked manner.

The other women were mystified and asked the woman: "How do you manage to gather that many *esef* in so short a time? You always bring a large amount to the camp." Calmly the woman replied: "I always go out alone into the forest and climb into the trees to quickly pick a lot of *esef*." From then on the other women did exactly as that mother had told them; but still they were unable to gather that many *esef* in so short a time.

Finally one day several women followed the mother unnoticed as she again disappeared alone into the forest. As usual, she was carrying only her son in the bag. When the two had gone far into the forest the astonished women saw how the little son quickly left the bag and became a full-grown man. He promptly climbed up into the trees and rapidly broke off a large number of *esef*. Then after a while the son again called to her from above: "Lie down on the ground and part your legs as far as you can, I want to throw *esef* into your vagina!" The woman immediately lay down on the ground with great pleasure, and with her legs stretched far apart she opened her vagina very wide. The son hit his mother's vagina with the *esef* thrown from the tree, which was a great pleasure for both of them. After playing like this for a rather long time the son climbed down from the tree. Then he lay down on his mother and she received him with great pleasure, for his penis was extremely large.

The women saw and heard all this from their hiding place and were horrified. Unnoticed, they rushed back to their huts and soon revealed to the husband of the woman that the two of them, the mother and the son, would go off together and yield to incestuous pleasure. He seemed very surprised, for until then he had believed his son to be very small still. Indeed his mother always carried him in the bag on her back without ever letting him out; the father had so far only seen his face. In fact, the mother had never allowed the little boy to leave the bag if another person was in the hut. She carried the bag firmly strapped to her back. For she said to herself: "If I let my son out of the bag his father will notice at once that his penis is very long. In view of this he will start to suspect that he has intercourse with a woman!" Thus she kept the son always tied up in the bag and carried him constantly around with her. She did not let him out at night either, because he had nothing with which to cover his body.

The husband now considered what those women had revealed to him. He took a knife and made it sharp enough to cut leather. The following day his wife hurried again into the forest and did not return until evening. As usual she was carrying her little son in the bag on her back. She brought very many *esef*. Then he spoke to her in a friendly tone: "Why do you never put down the bag with the little boy? After all, that load must be very heavy if you carry it around with you all day." She replied curtly, fending him off: "Our little son is still very small, so that I have to protect him extra carefully! Actually I don't notice any burden at all; our boy is still very small, you know." But the husband quickly replied: "Do rest a little now and trust me with the bag!" In saying this he took his sharp knife and severed the leather straps by which the bag hung from his wife's back. At once the bag dropped down and tore apart. The little boy fell to the ground and on his back with his legs far apart. Then the father could see his son's large penis, as he was not dressed. Now he knew enough! Beside himself with horror he seized the knife he had sharpened, and cut off his son's large penis. Although much blood flowed, the furious man let him lie there. Finally the little boy became a bird. Since then he has stayed in the forest and never again returned to his parents' hut. That is the little *detehurux* who even today has a powerful beak with a long, red tongue inside.

124. **THE WOODPECKER BROTHER AND SISTER.** YAMANA

The two *lana* [large woodpecker] were brother and sister. From their earliest youth they lived with their parents and grew up together. When they had grown a bit older they began to meet in a hiding place. Here they caressed each other and yielded to their desire. For a long time they secretly carried on their evil pleasure in this way.

124. SOURCES: Primary source: Gusinde 1937:1199–1200; Secondary source: Wilbert 1977:79–80. From Johannes Wilbert, *Folk Literature of the Yamana Indians: Martin Gusinde's Collection of Yamana Narratives*, published by the University of California Press, 1977. Reproduced by permission of the publisher.

The other people finally noticed that the two were meeting secretly. They became very upset over this, loudly criticized the evil doings of the brother and sister, and threatened them with severe punishment because of their disgusting behavior. But neither the boy nor the girl listened to people's scoldings; they met secretly and carried on with each other as before. After a long time all the people were extremely angry and would no longer stand for the improper behavior of the brother and sister. They explained everything in detail to their parents. When the father heard this he became furious; he was beside himself with anger over what his degenerate children were doing. He summoned both of them, took some *imi*, and painted his daughter's head with it. At the same time he said furiously: "Since you are doing such bad things you shall henceforth remain together always! Now get out of my hut!"

Then the two left their parent's hut and fled into the forest where they had been meeting for their evil doings. Since then those two, brother and sister, have stayed together and to this day live all by themselves as husband and wife.

125. THE WOODPECKER COUPLE. YAMANA

A brother had fallen in love with his own sister. He therefore tried in every way possible to meet and sleep with her. His sister had long noticed his intention. She avoided him every time for she did not want to have forbidden intercourse with him. Yet she was of two minds, half willing, half unwilling. The brother considered what pretext to use to lure her out of the hut.

One day he discovered big berries in a clearing in the forest. A sly thought occurred to him. He said to himself: "I shall tell my sister now that I have found big berries here. After that I'm sure she'll come here." He promptly ran back to the hut and told his sister: "I have found big berries in a certain place in the forest; you should go there and get them!" The girl took her basket and hurried into the woods.

Without anybody noticing it the brother quickly sneaked after her. He hid in a place where his sister had to pass. Once she had gotten close enough he embraced her. Then both lay down and yielded to their desire. But when they wanted to get up after the wicked thing they had done, they found themselves turned into birds. Both were all black. In addition, the brother has since had a bright red head; it was those big, red berries that he pointed out to his sister in order to do bad things with her.

125. SOURCES: Primary source: Gusinde 1937:1201; Secondary source: Wilbert 1977:80–81. From Johannes Wilbert, *Folk Literature of the Yamana Indians: Martin Gusinde's Collection of Yamana Narratives*, published by the University of California Press, 1977. Reproduced by permission of the publisher.

126. THE SEVEN STARS (THE PLEIADES). GE

An Indian who had seven sons lived alone with them and his wife. The boys were already men, and they were all handsome. They all decided to isolate themselves from their village and after moving away, they built a house for themselves. The mother fixed dinner, and the father went out to hunt. The boys were men and wanted women. The eldest thought about it; all the brothers thought about it.

"Have you eaten?" asked the eldest son. "Let's go. I'm thinking about something. Is it possible that we could take our mother?"

"You ought to know," said the others. "But there's our youngest brother. Let's see what he says. Is it possible that you could also bring yourself to take our mother?" The youngest thought deeply about it and then they fought about it. The younger brother became afraid of his brothers and said: "I will do it."

Their mother was bringing in potatoes in a large container. The father was out hunting. Then she said: "Boys, come and get some potatoes to eat." The eldest said: "Oh, I don't like potatoes, but perhaps you will give me something else." "What?" asked the mother. The eldest replied: "This thing is in your possession, and we want it more than potatoes." The mother lowered her head, thinking, and said: "I don't know, but you do. Have you already talked to your brothers?" "Yes," he said. "The youngest, too?" she asked. "He wants it too," he replied. "All right," she said.

They all had intercourse with their mother. At first the youngest didn't want to do it, because he was ashamed. But after a lot of urging he did it too. Then he was ashamed and went to cry in the woods where his father was. He stayed away from the house and didn't eat anything. He just cried until his father arrived, carrying a deer. The father said: "Why are you crying?" "I'm going to tell you something," replied the youngest son. "Your sons had sexual relations with their mother and talked me into doing it, too. I'm overwhelmed with shame. I've been crying here for an hour."

The father didn't say anything. He was just thinking it over. The he said: "All right. It's all right. Never mind. Let's go home." They went home. The father said: "Well I'm home. Make my dinner. Hurry up; I'm hungry. Later on I want to talk to all of you." His wife made dinner and served him. He ate and slept.

Early in the morning he got up and went to cut switches to whip the boys.

---

126. SOURCES: Primary source: Chiara 1961–62:333–39; Secondary source: Wilbert and Simoneau, eds. 1978:81–87. Reprinted, with permission, from Johannes Wilbert and Karin Simoneau, eds., *Folk Literature of the Gê Indians, Vol. 1* (Los Angeles: UCLA Latin American Center Publications, 1978), pp. 81–87.

He made a bunch this size. He called the eldest and asked him: "Why did you do that with your mother?" The boy explained. The father said: "Now you are going to see something pretty." He grabbed the whip and beat his son. A man does not cry, so the son bore it until his father stopped. He called another son and then another until he finished with all seven of them, from the eldest to the youngest.

It is said that in earlier times there wasn't a hawk that liked lizards. The father thought: "What am I going to do? I'm going to go away."

His wife was outside the house. The man closed the door and locked it. He set the house on fire with the door locked. He turned into a *curica* hawk, one that doesn't attack little chickens or anything else. Then he left the house and went away shrieking like a hawk, "Que e, que e, que e." The woman lowered her head crying. "I'm going with him."

She also turned into a *curica* hawk. She flew away through the smoke, also shrieking. Then the youngest brother cried with pity for his father and mother. The eldest brother said: "Don't cry because our father is going far away from the village. We needed it, so we did it. Now we are going away too." They made bundles of their clothes and traveled a long distance. They all slept alone in the woods. The youngest was thirsty and spoke up: "I'm thirsty."

There was a pretty creek but it was dry. "Let's see if we can dig and get water," said the eldest son. They dug near the upper end of the bed. They dug and dug. I don't know how far down, until the water finally appeared.

"Drink then. Drink until you quench your thirst," said the eldest. The water was bubbling and coming up fast. The eldest boy jumped into the bed. The water filled up the bed and made a big river. They were all swimming. The eldest and the others jumped up on the other side of the river. Only the youngest was left.

"Jump!" called his brothers.

"I'm afraid."

"We'll grab you. The water is high. Jump!"

"No, I'm afraid."

They called him, but he didn't come.

"Then stay there," they said.

He stayed. As the others left, he was shouting to them: "How can I cross?" [*Nhum, nhum ketore*: "Who is going to carry me across?"]

An alligator was listening.

"Who is crying?"

The alligator lifted his head slowly up out of the big river and said again: "Who is it?"

"I want to cross but my brothers left me here."

"Do you want me to take you across?"

"No you'll eat me."

"No I won't eat you!"

Meanwhile, the middle brother began to miss the youngest brother and said: "The rest of you go on. I will wait here."

Back at the river the alligator understood the situation and thought it over.

Then the youngest boy dived into the water carrying his bow, and came up swimming. When he reached the middle of the stream the alligator grabbed him and they went down together. They remained at the bottom. Then the alligator let go of the boy's bow, and it floated to the top. The middle brother pulled it out and wondered what had happened. He slept there by the river. Nothing happened. He slept there again, and again nothing happened. The others were waiting, but I'm not sure where; perhaps it was in Atore's house. He is a little bird that likes to walk on the ground.

The brothers were waiting and thinking. One of them said: "What is our brother doing? If the youngest has drowned, perhaps he may still show up."

On the bottom of the river the youngest boy was saying to the alligator: "Oh, Uncle."

"What?"

"I want to lie down on your back."

The alligator said: "No, my back is too thin. It tires quickly."

"Oh, Uncle. Then I want to lie on your arm."

"No, my arm is too thin."

"Then I want to lie on your shoulders."

"No, that won't do either. I get tired too easily."

"Uncle, I'm cold. Carry me to the bank of the river."

"All right. You're cold?"

"I am. When I get warm, we'll come back."

"All right."

The boy got on the alligator's back and they started up through the water.

"Where is the bank?"

"Over there."

Then the river became shallow.

"Here?"

"No."

The alligator pointed his head in another direction and asked: "Here?"

"No, go further."

They had almost crossed to the other side of the river.

"Closer to the bank," the boy said.

"All right?"

"No, go further. You can get closer."

The alligator got closer. The boy caught hold of a branch hanging above his head.

"Is this all right?"

"A little more."

"Like this?"

"Yes. You can go out of the water a little more."

The boy was thinking: "What am I going to do? I'll jump off and perhaps I'll find my brothers."

"Ready?"

"No, let me warm up a little more."

The boy rose slowly from the alligator's back, took hold of the branch, got off, and ran and ran. The alligator was at the bank looking for the boy but he saw nothing. The boy had gotten away. Still, the alligator picked up his trail. The boy ran until he got to Atore's house, with the alligator not far behind him.

"Hide me so the alligator won't eat me!"

Atore hid him. The bird told the boy he had been harvesting his fields, and that a lot of cut bushes were piled up in mounds. The boy went to the fields and hid among the bushes. The alligator reached Atore's house.

"Where is that shameless boy? I know he came here. His trail leads here."

The bird said: "I didn't see him. If I had seen him, I'd tell you."

The alligator looked all around but couldn't see the boy, and so he decided to leave. He left by way of the fields and was about to enter the area where the mounds were when the bird said to the boy: "He will pass by here, and then you can come out. Now he is leaving. Go and tease him a little."

The boy taunted the alligator: "*Miyti tokohyti kryryti!*" [Alligator with a face full of scales and with a turned-up nose!"]

The alligator heard the boy talking.

"Wait there, you disgraceful boy!"

He started back after the boy. The boy ran and ran and got to the house of the emu bird who was at home making string.

"Hide me! Hide me! The alligator wants to eat me."

He hid in the emu's armpit. The emu stayed there with her arm bent close to her body. The alligator arrived and began to look around for the boy.

"Where is the boy?"

"I don't know. I got up with a fever because of a growth in my armpit."

"Is it possible that he is in your armpit?"

"No. It isn't possible. My armpit hurts. The growth just appeared."

"Lift your arm up!"

"No, I won't!"

She kept her arm close to her body. The boy was afraid, but finally the alligator went away. Then the boy came out and asked: "Did my brothers come by here?"

"They came, slept here, and went away."

"Now I want to taunt that alligator."

The alligator heard, turned around, and ran for the boy. The boy ran too and got to the house of the *macaco* monkey. The monkey was cracking *jatoba* shells and a lot of them were lying about. The boy said: "Hide me! Hide me! The alligator is after me. He wants to eat me! Where can I hide?"

"Here. Over here."

He hid the boy under a pile of shells. The alligator came running up and said: "Where is the boy? His trail ends here."

"I don't know. I was just about to set these shells on fire."

When the alligator went away, the boy asked: "Did the alligator go away?"

"He did."

"Did my brothers come by here? There are six of them."

"Yes, they did. They slept here, and they left yesterday. Perhaps you can still reach them."

The alligator was going away. The boy crept out from under the shells and began to scold him again. The alligator heard the boy and ran until he came close to him.

There is an animal called opossum whose urine has a terrible odor. The brothers were all in the opossum's house.

"Hide me! Hide me!"

"No. Stay there. Wait right there," the opossum said.

He raised his tail and urinated on the alligator. The alligator went mad, rolled around, and then died because of the awful smell of the opossum's urine. The boy came up to his brothers.

"The alligator wanted to eat me. I slipped away from it and finally got here."

The opossum called the bird Atore, and they rolled the alligator along to the bank of the river and threw him in. That was the end of that.

Then the brothers discussed their plans.

"What are we going to do? Let's go away."

They traveled and traveled.

"Now what are we going to do?"

"Let's live here by the bank of the river all our lives because it is good to dive only into very big rivers. Now you, the eldest, stay right here; you stay here, you here, you here. Now then, the youngest, stay back the farthest."

Thus they became the seven stars.

And now we know that they are not ghosts but are real people.

Afterward they arranged themselves along the bank until they got to the place where they could dive in. When they dive we can hear the noise they make. When they hit the water in the month of June they make a very loud noise: "Brrao." I don't know how long it takes them to come out on the other side. It seems to me they come out in July. The name of this group of seven stars is Krodre.

127. THE ADVENTURES OF PEDWO AND HIS DAUGHTERS.

GE

Pedwo went to the garden. His son had something wrong with one eye. Pedwo's wife looked at the eye, put some medicine on it, and said: "You're having sexual relations with someone else, and I'm angry with you!" She added: "Do it with me!" The son did as she asked and had intercourse with his mother. Afterward the two of them slept together, and his penis was in her vagina.

Then Pedwo returned. He noticed them, and was silent. He took some feathers in order to put them on his arrows, and remained outside, silent. When his daughter arrived with potatoes he said to her: "I'm ashamed of your mother who is lying with your brother; I'm ashamed and I don't want to enter the house." His wife got up to urinate and saw Pedwo who was in the shadows. She said to him: "What are you looking at outside?" He replied: "I don't want to come in. I'm not speaking to you, I'm really ashamed."

In the afternoon Pedwo went out quietly without saying anything to his daughter. He arrived at the garden, thinking: "What am I going to turn into? I'll turn into manioc." And he transformed himself into manioc. Then he thought: "No, I don't want this, for if I turn into manioc they'll pull me up, grate me, put me in a pan, and heat me. No!" He thought, and turned into yams. But later he thought: "No, this way they'll heat me." After thinking it over he turned into a *croata* [*pertxo*]. There was a lot!

But then he thought: "No, I don't want to become a *croata*, for this way they'll grate me. I'll turn into a horse." And he turned into a horse. He was on the footpath eating grass. Then his three daughters came and asked: "Well, where's father?" "I don't know, let's look for his tracks." The oldest girl said: "There he is. Let's turn into horses!" Two of them turned into horses, but the youngest was wearing a small decorated gourd [*kradre*] and did not turn into anything. The youngest kept walking with her father, who had turned into a horse, and with her sisters, who had turned into mares. They walked.

---

127. SOURCES: Primary source: Melatti 1978:318–20; Secondary source: Wilbert and Simoneau, eds. 1984a:432–35. Reprinted, with permission, from Johannes Wilbert and Karin Simoneau, eds., *Folk Literature of the Gê Indians, Vol. 2* (Los Angeles: UCLA Latin American Center Publications, 1984), pp. 432–35.

Autxetpirure, who was a real Indian, was catching fish with *timbo*. Then the father and the daughters turned into Indians again. They hid in a thicket, and only Pedwo turned into a kingfisher and caught fish. Autxetpirure noted: "Ah, Tepkriti, you're catching my fish!" The daughters also wanted fish and turned into kingfishers, except the youngest, who was wearing the decoration [decorated gourd] and who did not turn into anything. The oldest became a kingfisher and caught fish. The other also became a kingfisher and caught fish. The youngest did not become anything, and she went to catch fish herself. But Autxetpirure saw her and came out: "Ah, you're taking my fish!" He asked her: "What are you doing here?" "I'm not doing anything." Autxetpirure asked Pedwo: "What did you do to be painted that way?" The other lied: "We made stone ovens. Then we lay down on them, and that's how we became painted like this." "All right, make an oven so I can be painted, too." Pedwo ordered his daughters to make an oven. They made one and put Autxetpirure inside, and put fish inside, too. They covered it with straw and put soil on top of it, and then they ran off. But the youngest forgot her decorated gourd and returned to look for it. She thought: "Let me take some fish [from the oven] to eat." As she began to uncover the oven Autxetpirure asked: "How am I? Am I painted yet?" "No, you're only partially painted," she said. "There's a lot left." Autxetpirure lowered his head back into the oven and waited.

Pedwo and his daughters ran along the footpath. Then he asked the *buriti* palm to shrink so that he and his daughters could sit in it and hide from Autxetpirure.

Autxetpirure remained lying there for a long time, and then got up, looked for the others, followed their tracks, and came cursing. He came up to the foot of the palm tree and looked around it, but could not find any more tracks. The youngest daughter spat from up above and the spit fell into the water. Autxetpirure saw it. He then asked Pedwo: "How did you get up there?" "I took some *embira* from the palm and tied our arms, and we climbed up to the top." "All right, do the same so that I can climb up." Pedwo mended a strip of the palm top and threw it down, and Autxetpirure took it and tied it. Then Pedwo pulled him up close. But the oldest girl said: "No, let's cut it so he'll fall down and die." They cut the cord and Autxetpirure fell, but as he fell he thought: "No, I'll turn into something else." He turned in to a crab. Pedwo said to the palm: "Shrink! Shrink!" The *buriti* obeyed. Pedwo jumped down and turned into a stag, and his daughters turned into deer.

The youngest remained alone on the ground. She went walking alone on the savanna until she arrived at the bathing place of the *seriemas* [kind of bird]. It was a *seriema* village. A *seriema* father asked his son to go and get water. The youngest girl was hidden in a thicket. She spat—*pfu, pfu, pfu*—and the boy's gourd vessel broke. He returned to his father, crying, fearing that he would get spanked. The *seriema* put some green banana on the embers and then ground it in the mortar. *Seriema's* son said to his father: "Give me of the bananas and I'll tell you a good story." The other *seriemas* said: "Give him of the bananas so that he'll tell us the story!" The father gave him one, and the boy said: "You already gave me the banana and I'll eat it, and I do not have anything to tell you." Then the father took the banana from him. The son cried and said: "No, give it to me! I saw a girl there; she's behind the thicket!" Then all the *seriemas* went to the spring to look. The girl was behind the thicket. They saw her and grabbed her. The *seriemas* wanted to have sexual relations with her, and they copulated until they killed her. They introduced their penises everywhere: in her armpits, her eyes, her nose, her mouth, her ears. The girl died from the loud noise of her attackers. She grew so tired that she died. Afterward the *seriemas* decided to remove her vulva, and each of them received a small part of it. They tied the little pieces with *embira*, and each piece became an Indian woman.

128. THE "ME-BE-NGO-DJU-TI KAMRI". GE

In those days the *me-be-ngo-dju-ti* [boys aged from eight to twelve, before entering the men's house] were very big, with a lot of pubic hair. A group of them went to copulate with some *me-printi* girls and some *me-kra-poyn* women. They went into the forest with their own sisters.

The *me-be-ngo-dju* were completely covered with feathers, as though they were birds.

As this was happening near a plantation and the women were laughing a lot, some other women asked them, from afar, what was going on.

"There are enemy Indians here, but they aren't killing us, they only want to copulate. We enjoy it, and they aren't going to take us away."

They are making the rounds [*me-a-ngiei*; when a group of men meet a woman outside the village and have sexual intercourse with her].

Afterward the *ngo-dju-ti* went to bathe to remove all the feathers, and then they gathered in the place where they used to sit together.

A little *ngo-dju-ti* was hungry and went home to get some food.

His sister called him to delouse him.

128. SOURCES: Primary source: Vidal 1977:214–15; Secondary source: Wilbert and Simoneau, eds. 1984a:468–70. Reprinted, with permission, from Johannes Wilbert and Karin Simoneau, eds., *Folk Literature of the Gê Indians*, Vol. 2 (Los Angeles: UCLA Latin American Center Publications, 1984), pp. 468–70.

Parting his hair she found feathers which she put away under her thigh.

Then she told the other women: "It wasn't enemy Indians who were copulating but the *me-be-ngo-dju.*"

The boy heard, and went to tell his companions. All became quiet and downcast.

In the afternoon the boys went to gather palm fronds. Leaving some of them in the forest they carried the rest to the men's house. In the evening they fetched them and made feathers of dry palm leaves.

At night the *ngo-dju-ti* put on the feathers, transforming themselves into jabiru storks.

They were angry.

Then they went to take their nephews, pulling them from the arms of their sisters, who were asleep.

An old man who was sleeping in the men's house in the middle of the plaza looked out and saw the *ngo-dju-ti* flying hither and thither like birds.

He informed the others.

A sister woke up and realized that she no longer had her son in her arms.

She got up and saw her brother in the distance, with her son in his arms and covered with feathers.

When she was close to them her brother pierced her eye and went away with his small nephew.

They turned into white jabirus [*kamri-aka*] and bald-headed jabiru [*kamri kra-kei*].

They left with their nephews and never returned again.

129. **THE SHAMELESS MOTHER AND SON.** GE

Long ago a young boy [*ayrepudu*] used to accompany his mother when she went to gather *buriti* fruit. It was at the beginning of creation. They went out to lie down together in the forest.

"*Whose mother?*"

His mother. She would take her son with her to look for *buriti* fruit. For they did something that one should not do. The mother corrupted her son. For that reason the father sent his toddler son [*watebremi*] to follow them.

"*How did he go?*"

He went on foot from the village.

129. SOURCES: Primary source: Giaccaria and Heide 1975:115–20; Secondary source: Wilbert and Simoneau, eds. 1984a:470–73. Reprinted, with permission, from Johannes Wilbert and Karin Simoneau, eds., *Folk Literature of the Gê Indians, Vol. 2* (Los Angeles: UCLA Latin American Center Publications, 1984), pp. 470–73.

Only when their tracks turned off in another direction did the boy who was following them turn into a hummingbird.

In the form of a hummingbird he entered the forest and saw the tracks where they had passed. Then he thought about what to do in order to find them.

"How can I follow them?" he was saying to himself. "I don't know. I'll enter the forest as a hummingbird."

He flew off, making his humming sound, and went into the forest. He looked for *buritis* in order to find the two, but did not see anything. He flew deep into the forest and then turned back, emerged, and went into the forest once more to search, until at last he found them. They were lying down, one on top of the other. The hummingbird flew over them, and then settled in a tree to watch.

"The bird is flying over us."

The boy turned to throw a piece of wood, but missed his aim. Once more the hummingbird returned to fly around them. After a thorough investigation he went home, leaving the forest. He went to where he had left his bow and went home with it. (*Perhaps that bow was an object for turning oneself into a hummingbird.*)

"*I'm not going to say anything!*"

That is how the story goes. This story does not end; it is always told in this way.

He reached home, they say. When he got home he lay down on his bed, overcome by shame.

"Did you see the two of them?"

"No," he replied to his father. "I came up behind them. It's ugly."

"Why? How did you see them?"

"My mother is not taking her son along to gather nuts. I do not like mother; she does not know how to respect her son. And I do not like my brother, either; I do not like him. I saw the two of them, one lying on top of the other."

"What did they say to you?"

"I did not get there as myself, in my own body; I was up in the air. My body became very small to go there."

"What were you?"

"What I had decided; I followed them in the form of a hummingbird. That's how I flew. They did not know it was I. I am telling you so you will know. I do not like it. They put new *buriti* leaves on the ground to lie down on. That is what my mother takes him along for; that is why she always takes her son with her, saying that she is going to look for *buriti* fruit."

"That is the reason why I sent you after them to discover what is going on."

"Yes."

"Well, now I know. Just let her come home."

He prepared the *buriti* switches [*wayhi*] to have them ready.

"First I'm going to beat the boy, and then his mother, if she says anything. After beating them I am going to throw them out of the house, leaving them abandoned behind the house."

All this because the son had told his father what he had seen. The man waited. In the afternoon the two returned. He asked his wife: "Where are the *buriti* fruit so I can suck them?"

"The *buriti* fruit have not fallen yet."

"Then how come you two are always going out to look for them, if they are not falling yet?"

"The *buriti* fruit have not fallen yet. We were looking for some, but we did not find even one."

"The two of you don't go out to look for *buriti* fruit but to do something bad."

"To do what?"

"To deceive me."

He stood up to give his son a beating. After thrashing him he threw him out. His mother said to her husband, "Why did you beat him?"

"Aha!"

He had kept another bundle of switches with this in mind, and he got up to beat his wife. He gave her back and shoulders a sound thrashing, and the woman was screaming in pain: "Oh, oh . . ."

"Stop beating her now," said the youngest girl to her father.

After beating her he threw her out. The two were crying behind the house. They cried a lot: it grew dark while their tears were falling. They had not arrived home early but had been late.

Night fell. The two stopped crying, and sat there. They wanted to flee.

"Shall we return [to the buriti place]?"

The father had abandoned them. They left and kept walking all night. Then the two of them turned into tapirs. (They were the ones that died and whose meat all the people ate.) The women saw the tapir tracks and told the men.

"Where are they?"

"Over there at the headwaters in the middle of the forest. Maybe they were crossing over to the other side."

"We must go there and take a look," said the husband.

"Let them go. No one is going to hunt!"

"I shall go myself. First I am going to make the arrows."

After attaching the feathers he made the arrowheads. "Now I am going. Perhaps their bodies are already complete. It must be those two; there are no other tapirs."

He went off and saw the old tracks. He crossed another part of the forest and saw the tracks.

"Ah, they are going this way!"

He followed, and they entered the forest. Keeping a close look-out he found the two tapirs lying on the ground. The mother was already covered with hair, but the boy was not yet complete; only his face was hairy. First he shot the female tapir with his arrow, and then the male. Thus we call the male tapir *idzu*. He shot the *idzu*, which was screaming. After killing the male he went back to look at the female. She was dead. He went home, having killed the two tapirs.

"I came back to tell you to go and look for the two tapirs."

Everybody went. Enjoying the way it smelled they ate the meat of the ones who had turned into tapirs for doing something a mother and son should not do. The two who were dead were tapirs. Its name is *uhodo* [tapir]. We, the Shavante, call the name of the tapir correctly.

130. PICO-KAMCWU, BOYS WHO TURNED INTO BIRDS.

APINAYE GE

[Wilbert's note: *Pico*, banana plant; *kamcwu*, to pierce. The story accounts for the Apinaye ceremony of this name.]

While their parents were engaged in farming, the boys and girls, led by an older boy, gathered together and marched into the steppe near the village. The girls brought a quantity of manioc paste along and built a hut while the boys hunted birds and rats in order to make meat-pies. Then the older boy called his companions aside and proposed that each boy was to deflower his own sister. He himself went into the bush first, the others sent his sister to him. She cried and would not go, but the other boys forced her to do so. They acted similarly with the other girls. Then they ate meat-pies, decorated themselves with the feathers of the birds killed, made themselves wings of the grass-like foliage of the *bacaba* palm, and returned to the village.

There the oldest of the boys went to an adviser and asked him to induce the parents to make ornaments for them. In the meantime he had a banana plant put up, into which the boys discharged their arrows. Then they danced round the house circle and thence to the place, flapped their wings, and flew up like birds. The youngest at first had difficulty flying, but the rest helped

130. SOURCES: Primary source: Nimuendaju 1939:182; Secondary source: Wilbert and Simoneau, eds., 1978:268–69. Reprinted, with permission, from Johannes Wilbert and Karin Simoneau, eds., *Folk Literature of the Gê Indians, Vol. 1* (Los Angeles: UCLA Latin American Center Publications, 1978) pp. 268–69.

him rise. They flew to a lake, put the little one on a tree-stump in the middle of the water, crushed *tinguy* roots, and poisoned the water with them to drug the fish. They caught plenty and fed the raw little fish to the little one.

The little boy's mother wept bitterly for him and went after the fugitives. Seeing her child from afar sitting on the stump in the lake, she made herself a mask of *buriti* palm leaves and dived into the lake. But when she had already got close to the lad and was emerging panting, the rest caught sight of her. They at once flew up, taking the little one along. They transformed themselves into *maguary* and other swamp birds and flew off in the direction across the Tocantins.

131. THE DAUGHTER OF THE SUN. TUKANO

The Daughter of the Sun had not yet reached puberty when her father made love to her. The Sun committed incest with her at Wainambi Rapids, and her blood flowed forth; since then, women must lose blood every month in remembrance of the incest of the Sun and so that this great wickedness will not be forgotten. But his daughter liked it and so she lived with her father as if she were his wife. She thought about sex so much that she became thin and ugly and lifeless. Newly married couples become pale and thin because they only think of the sexual act, and this is called *gamuri*. But when the Daughter of the Sun had her second menstruation, the sex act did harm to her and she did not want to eat anymore. She lay down on a rock, dying; her imprint there can still be seen on a large boulder at Wainambi Rapids. When the Sun saw this, he decided to make *gamu bayari*, the invocation that is made when the girls reach puberty. The Sun smoked tobacco and revived her. Thus, the Sun established customs and invocations that are still performed when young girls have their first menstruation.

132. THE STAR IBESNUI. AYOREO

Those who marry their relatives act like Ibesnui. Now he is a star. When he was human he said that he had no desire for women and would rather live alone. His brothers, the Utigamisnami, however, always travel together.

One day as Ibesnui was out walking he came across Oroho, a bee that lives

---

131. SOURCE: Reichel-Dolmatoff 1971:28–29. From Reichel-Dolmatoff, *Amazonian Cosmos*, published by the University of Chicago Press, 1971. Reproduced by permission of the publisher.

132. SOURCE: Wilbert and Simoneau 1989:35–36. Reprinted, with permission, from Johannes Wilbert and Karin Simoneau, eds., *Folk Literature of the Ayoreo Indians* (Los Angeles: UCLA Latin American Center Publications, 1989), pp. 35–36.

in the ground. He said: "I'm going to dig up the honeycomb I found." Several of his brothers went along with him. Ibesnui began digging and soon earth started to pile up where he dug. His sisters said to one another: "Let's test our brother since he says he has no desire for women." So they lay down on their backs. Their brother saw their genitals exposed and threw himself on them. They asked him: "How can you say that you do not desire women?" He covered his sisters with a blanket.

One day the brother forgot to cover his sisters. When he was in the forest, he said: "I forgot to cover them." The women went up into the sky. Ibesnui wanted to be with them, but his sisters, the Dayade, did not want him. They did not like what he did nor did they want him marrying his own sisters. That is why they threw him out. He left and ever since he has been alone. The song that goes with this story is *tabu*. When it is sung it causes miscarriage.

133. ETABI, THE INCESTUOUS WIDOW, AND HOW FIGHTING ORIGINATED. AYOREO

Among the ancient Ayoreo, fighting originated with a man called Etabi who went around cutting people's throats. Etabi means throat, which is why they gave him that name; when he killed anyone he would always cut his throat. His name was Dachagaide but they called him Etabi.

One day his brothers-in-law went out hunting in the forest, and they were away several days. Etabi had remained in the camp, but when he saw that his wife's brothers did not return, he said: "When will my brothers-in-law come back? If they stay away much longer they will bring back illness." That is the way it is among us. If someone stays away a long time we say: "Oh! When he returns he will bring back a grave illness."

Etabi's wife asked her husband not to harm her brothers who were calmly returning to camp. The husband paid no heed to what she said, but went to wait on the road for his brothers-in-law in order to kill them. Before leaving he told his wife: "I'm going to kill my brothers-in-law. Once I have killed them you will know it because I am going to be very happy. When I come back to camp I will whistle giving praise. However, if they vanquish me you will not hear my voice again."

So Etabi waited on the road and when two brothers-in-law passed by, he threw his spear at the one who was out in front and wounded him in the leg. The man who was wounded called to his brothers, asking them to come and

133. SOURCE: Wilbert and Simoneau 1989:151–52. Reprinted, with permission, from Johannes Wilbert and Karin Simoneau, eds., *Folk Literature of the Ayoreo Indians* (Los Angeles: UCLA Latin American Center Publications, 1989), pp. 151–52.

help him. Etabi was unaware that the others were so near. They caught him by surprise and hit him on the neck, whereupon he died.

When they returned to camp they ran to tell Etabi's wife the news. She said: "I begged him over and over not to harm my brothers but he would not pay attention to my advice," and she lamented her lot and cried a great deal.

Ebati's wife's brothers threatened to kill her. They thought that she was sad because they had killed her husband, and so they decided to kill their sister. A woman who had no bad feelings toward her warned her to leave. So Etabi's wife fled with all her children. When her brothers arrived at her house she was no longer there; the house was empty.

Etabi's wife was very fearful, though. She was frightened of the rain, and so she wanted to return to her brothers. She approached them, crying out: "I want to come back, my brothers." They replied: "Why did you not give your husband Etabi good advice? He harmed us first." They chased the woman away, but could not catch her to kill her.

The day came when she went to her brothers' fields to steal from them. She stole their beans, but she told her children not to touch any of her brothers' things. They were only to take things from the part of the field where the crops had begun to be harvested. That way they would not notice it.

Her children asked their mother to speak to her brothers and ask to be allowed to return to their camp. The woman saw one of her brothers and asked him to take her as his wife. So at night she would sleep with him and during the day she would go back to the forest. She slept with him to overcome his enmity. Finally that brother asked his other brothers to put aside their hostility toward their sister and allow her to return to their camp. However, she was already pregnant.

134. **YAKOVIRI.** MATSIGENKA

Yakoviri lived in a house with his wife and daughter. His nephew came to ask him for his daughter. Yakoviri asked his daughter and she said she wanted him. His nephew was a hard worker and a good hunter. He would work all morning in the garden and spend the afternoons hunting. Yakoviri's daughter went with him to the forest. Yakoviri worked in the garden and his nephew brought in plenty of meat. But his wife objected and Yakoviri told his daughter, "You should not go into the forest every day. You should help your mother grind corn." She was a hard worker, so she was able to finish the work her mother gave her and still spend the afternoons out hunting with her husband-to-be. The next day her mother did not want

---

134. SOURCE: O. Johnson 1978:308–10. Used by permission.

her to leave at noon, and Yakoviri told her sternly not to go; her mother brought her an enormous amount of maize to grind.

Yakoviri's nephew came at noon and asked his daughter to go with him to the forest.

"How can I go?" she said. "I have so much maize to grind."

"Leave it for your mother," said the nephew.

"I cannot."

"Then I will go alone to the forest," he said. He went into the forest and began to clear underbrush in order to be able to hunt [get a clear shot at] Katsari [bird]. He thought the girl might come later, so he waited for her along the beach. She did not come and it began to rain. He built a shelter of *caña brava* and waited. After dark he went home. Yakoviri had taken ayahuasca and was up on the stairs singing *nenenenenene*. His spiritual nephew came into his body just as his own spirit travelled to the land of the good spirits. Yakoviri's spiritual nephew spoke to his wife, saying, "I will cut the edge of the sky so it will fall on you and destroy you."

"Daughter," Yakoviri's wife said, "ask my 'nephew' to come make love to you."

"Yes, come here," his daughter said, and he made love to her. Afterward, he said, "Now that I have been with you, I will not destroy you."

This spirit left Yakoviri's body and another, Yakoviri's spiritual brother, came to take his place. He said he would destroy them unless Yakoviri's wife made love to him. She refused, and his daughter became so frightened she asked her mother, "Call Father back to be with you." She did and Yakoviri came back. He said, "Build up the fire so we can go outside to sit where the spirits may more easily reach us."

As he went outside he saw the figure of a man. At first he thought it was a demon, Sevatasirira. Then he saw that it was his human nephew. He said, "Nephew, you are here."

"Yes, I am here."

"I should not take ayahuasca again," said Yakoviri.

His nephew was angry with him, saying, "I am going to live with another uncle."

"Come inside and sleep," said Yakoviri.

"No, it will be better if I sleep out here."

He slept outside, and Yakoviri's daughter went outside to sleep with him. He said, "No, you go inside. I will come in later."

In the early morning Yakoviri's nephew went away. He caught many *etari* fish, started a fire, and ate breakfast. On the way he shot many small *tsimeri* birds and then came to his other uncle's house. He exchanged greetings with his uncle, who said, "Why have you come? You never came to visit us before."

"I am grown now and I wanted to visit you," he replied. He took out a small bird and gave it to his uncle, and then said, "Uncle?"

"Yes?"

But the nephew said nothing. After a pause, he repeated, "Uncle?"

"Yes?"

But again he said nothing. From this the uncle concluded he was hungry and went inside to tell his wife that he had arrived. Then he served him manioc, meat, and manioc beer. After the meal, he went to work in his garden, and his nephew went with him.

"Uncle?"

"Yes?"

Again no reply. He worked alongside his uncle but was afraid to ask his question. Finally, he said, "Can the good spirits come and make love to our women?"

"I don't know," replied the uncle. "Why do you ask?"

"I have been to visit your brother." And the nephew told the story of what had happened that evening. "I have come here to ask you for your daughter."

"I will have to think about it," said the uncle. He went home and discussed it with his wife.

"It depends on whether he wants to live here or not," she said.

"I will always stay here," replied the nephew, so they gave him two daughters as wives. "Come with me, Uncle, to get my arrows at Yakoviri's house."

They went and arrived in the afternoon at Yakoviri's house. Yakoviri said "Greetings" and sent his daughter to get manioc beer. She brought some but the nephew said, "Give it to your father. I'm not thirsty." His other uncle said the same thing. In the late afternoon this other uncle had ayahuasca brought out. Both Yakoviri and his brother drank and began to sing. Yakoviri climbed up to his platform to sing. His brother, to distract him [to test his authenticity as one capable of communicating with the spirit world], began to pester his wife, who told him to stop—but when she said it, Yakoviri stopped singing and descended the stairs saying "Yakovikovikovikovi . . ." [at which the storyteller laughed, explaining its meaning as "I am not angry." This proved that Yakoviri was not really in the spirit world and had intentionally had incest with his daughter.]

In the morning Yakoviri's wife prepared food but the nephew refused to eat it; Yakoviri's brother did eat. Afterwards, Yakoviri's brother got ready to leave. The nephew (pretending that he was not going to abandon Yakoviri's daughter) said, "I'll go with you part way." As they left Yakoviri told his daughter to go with them, but the nephew said, "No, don't bother—I'm not going far." But he went to his uncle's house and never returned.

The girl was very sad and cried, but said, "It's not my fault—it's my father's fault."

lal was the son of the daughter of the field mouse. Field mouse raised him from very small because his mother had died. Elal grew up in the place where his grandmother had her *toldo*, a place up north which became known as Agua Linda, close to the Senguer River.

The grandmother's name was Terrguer, which means field mouse. Elal had changed her into a mouse because she misbehaved toward him. After bringing him up, she wanted to live with him, with her grandson! But Elal said: "I am ashamed of my grandmother! What resentment I feel for this grandmother of mine! And this after you have raised me! Do you know what I am thinking about your folly, little grandmother?" And he grabbed her head and twisted it until she ended up with the elongated head of a field mouse. Said Elal: "Now you are good for nothing, and I am leaving you in the earth below. I am turning you into a mouse for what you have done to me. Kill you I cannot do, but you will have to live underground; and I shall fly away."

Elal flew away on a swan, which to him is like an airplane. He went to where the sun rises because of what he had done to his grandmother.

When Elal was a small boy of about four or five years of age, he was already playing his pranks around there, killing birds. So his grandmother said to him: "Don't do such evil things; they are small." But Elal answered: "I killed a little bird with this very thing here, with a small arrow. That's what I did it with: the bird was perched, I let fly an arrow, and killed it." Said the grandmother: "Don't say such dumb things." When Elal had grown a little bigger he did more such things. Originally all the animals in the open country were wild. But Elal arranged it so that they stopped causing harm; he tamed them all. [The informant said that the guanaco, the rhea, and others used to killed people.]

They say that the condor (which one could see very small in the sky) used to come to carry off the small children of the ancient ones. But they did not know who took them. Instead, they went to the mountains, thinking it was the puma who carried off the little ones. But one day the condor got caught. It was the four-year-old Elal who caught it. Lying on his back, he shot an arrow high into the sky upon seeing the bird up there very small. Imagine the strength he had! And he brought the condor down. It came down screeching; it was able to speak. Elal asked the condor for a feather. But it replied, saying: "I won't give it to you. I won't give you a feather!" And then the condor arrived. When it had come close to Elal, the youngster got up

135. SOURCE: Wilbert and Simoneau, eds. 1984b:50–51. Reprinted, with permission, from Johannes Wilbert and Karin Simoneau, eds., *Folk Literature of the Tehuelche Indians* (Los Angeles: UCLA Latin American Center Publications, 1984), pp. 50–51.

and grabbed the bird. He made it drowsy with his power, held it, and plucked the feathers from its head. That is why the condor is now bald-headed. Elal said: "I am not going to kill you. Instead, I will let you go free." He just pulled out the feathers and then let it fly away.

136. TAWKXWAX AND THE BIRDS. MATACO

The birds, who had changed into men, gathered to make a feast. Many women had come to join them and also to become their wives. They drank and they sang. Their songs were very beautiful and the women chose their men and married them. Tawkxwax was the only one who sang a dirty song and the two girls who were going to marry him ran away. Tawkxwax noticed he was alone; the girls had hidden themselves and his friends were with their women. It was because of his dirty song that he was alone. He went back to his village where the only woman left was his mother. He slept with her and she became pregnant. When her child was delivered she said: "Lift your child." Tawkxwax was ashamed and he said: "Oh, Mother, do not say that; tell me to lift my little brother."

The men who sang then are now the singing birds in our forests.

137. OSHETO (SPIDER MONKEY). MATSIGENKA

Long ago there was a man, Osheto, in human form. Then his sister was born. His mother said, "Keep her with you, take care of her." He took care of her. When she grew up, he did not want to leave her. He married her. His mother was furious and beat him.

"I told you to take care of your sister, not to marry her. You are a demon." She put pepper on his penis, on his sister's vagina. When his father was in the house she did nothing, but when he went away she would hit Osheto with a stick, bathe him in scalding water, hit him with nettles, put pepper on his genitals. He really suffered.

His father said to his mother, "Now don't be angry with him. There are no other women for him. You are at fault. You should have taken her to sleep next to you. If he doesn't marry her, he will have no wife."

When Osheto grew up, he ran away with his sister. He planted a garden. He climbed high in a tree and built a house, with a palmwood floor that he kept extending out into a path among the trees. His father went to look for him, in the direction away from where he usually hunted. He found the tree

136. SOURCES: Primary source: Metraux 1939:34; Secondary source: Wilbert and Simoneau 1982:232. Reproduced by permission of Etnografiska Museet.

137. SOURCE: Johnson and Johnson 1991b. Used by permission.

and climbed to the house where he found his daughter, who took him along the palmwood path to her brother, who by now had become a demon who could kill by stabbing with his penis.

"Hello, Father. Mother hated me. She peppered me. I suffered. I took my sister, yes. Mother said, 'Take care of her, keep her close to you, look after your sister.' Otherwise I wouldn't have seen her, I wouldn't have taken her. There were no others, I wanted her, I took her. You weren't angry with me. If you were, you wouldn't be alive."

The father held his newborn grandson in his arms, then invited his son and daughter to come home. But Osheto refused, saying his mother was too angry with him. The father made repeated trips to invite his children home, but they refused. Then the mother said she was no longer angry and she would visit to see her grandson. When she got there her daughter said, "Mother, where are you going?"

"I came to see you. Your father told me I have a grandson. I came to hold him and kiss him."

"You won't kiss him. I married my brother. You said, 'You married incestuously your brother.' If I hadn't, you could kiss him. If I had taken your nephew, you could kiss him. Now go back home. You got too angry, you never forgave him. He will attack you with his penis. He will attack you now."

But the mother remained unafraid. She reached for her grandson, but heard Osheto running along his path and fled down the tree. Osheto caused a sudden rainshower to fall on her, drenching her. He climbed down after her but then came back up. If he had gone all the way down, he would have remembered her anger and had intercourse with her. He said to his sister, "Why didn't you hold her? I would have screwed her in exchange for the pepper she put on me that caused me so much suffering."

The mother went home soaking wet. She was pale, shivering, nearly dead from the cold.

"He almost killed me!" But the father just reminded her that it was all her fault.

After a while, the father visited his children again. Their son was now bigger, and they had him leashed to a post. He jumped at his grandfather like a vicious dog. If he hadn't been tied down, he would have raped his grandfather. The daughter said, "Don't come any closer. Your grandson is growing up." Osheto, Spider Monkey, was there and warned his father to keep his distance in the future. Next time his father visited, he saw more children. The oldest had now become huge and fat.

During his next visit, Spider Monkey told his father, "Father, don't come back. You are very close to the place I am going to."

His father could see it, the large soft shale outcrop where the Spider Monkey Spirit lives. He went home.

Many days later, he went to the forest. So many spider monkeys. They said, *"Koren! Koren!"* Lots of black animals, spider monkeys, there. Plenty of them. They lived there.

Now, that's all.

138. **BACHUE.** MUISCA

In the vicinity of the city of Tunja, four leagues from a native village called Iguaque [*gua* = ridge of mountains; *que* = strong, vigorous], lies a lake set among rugged mountains. The climate in these mountains is very cold and most of the year a dense fog covers everything, hiding the mountains, which are only visible on certain days in the month of January. From this lake arose the human race. Once light and other things had been created, there emerged from the water a woman called Bachue.

The word "Bachue" signifies "worthy mother," also known by the name of Furachogua, meaning "good woman." Bachue brought out with her, by the hand, a boy of three years and, descending with him from the lake, arrived at the village of Iguaque, where they built a house. There they lived until the youth reached an age appropriate for marriage with her. After the marriage, Bachue gave birth to four to six children at a time and in this way populated the entire earth. After many years the married couple grew old and, accompanied by many people, returned to the lake from which they had emerged. Bachue spoke to the people, exhorting them to comply faithfully with her precepts, especially to honor the cult of the gods; taking their leave amidst great outcry and weeping, man and wife transformed themselves into two great snakes and disappeared into the depths of the water.

139. **LA CACICA (THE CHIEF'S WIFE).** MUISCA

According to the description we have from Triana, the wife of Guatavita [a Muisca chief] was accused of the terrible sin of adultery with a gentleman of the court, and the offended chief condemned the seducer to death, according to the law of the time; and he forced the adulteress to eat at a public banquet, amidst the merry-making of the guests, that which according to Triana could be called the "corpus delecti." Unable to tolerate such an affront, the Cacica slipped away with her young daughter and fled through a ravine to the lake. She swam across it a few minutes and then disappeared forever into the water.

---

138. SOURCES: Primary source: Simon 1891; Secondary source: de Zubiria 1968:168–69. Reproduced by permission of Roberto de Zubiria.

139. SOURCE: de Zubiria 1968:164. Reproduced by permission of Roberto de Zubiria.

Frightened, the sorcerers ran to notify their master who, deeply repentant of what he had done, ordered the most powerful of them to search the lake and return his wife and child to him. The sorcerer returned to Guatavita with the news that the Cacica had married the dragon of the lake and was happy with her new life. Unsatisfied with this news, the chief ordered the sorcerer to dive once again in search of his daughter, who turned up dead with her eyes eaten by the dragon.

[Comments by de Zubiria (p. 165):
    La Cacica is a symbol of the mother and therefore, like mother Bachue, returns to the lake. The chief is a symbol of the father, who kills the offending prince. A very important aspect of the myth is the punishment of the offender; the punishment is death and the loss of the "corpus delecti," as Triana says; castration or fear of it, which according to Freud is the most important element in the development of neurosis, appears with total clarity in the Muisca myth. The punishment of loss of virility is comparable in the story to the loss of life. The noble offender is dead and castrated.]

REFERENCE MATTER

REFERENCES CITED

✓ = Ill July 27, 2002
Y = I have

Aarne, Antti, and Stith Thompson. 1961. *The Types of the Folktale*. Helsinki: Suomalainen Tiedeakatemia.

✓ Abend, Sander M. 1988. Intrapsychic Versus Interpersonal: Different Theories, Different Domains or Historical Artifacts. *Psychoanalytic Inquiry* 8:497–504. *Ill came.*
Is w/ Freud
Afanasev, A. N. 1945. *Russian Fairy Tales*. New York: Pantheon.
8 notes,

Aiken, Riley. 1980. Solomon the Wise. In *Mexican Tales from The Borderland*. Dallas: *not*
Southern Methodist University Press, pp. 146–48. *w/*

Albisetti, Cesar, and Angelo Jayme Venturelli. 1969. *Enciclopedia Bororo*. Campo *Oedipus*
Grande, Brazil: Museu Regional Dom Bosco.

Allen, Louis A. 1975. *Time Before Morning: Art and Myth of the Australian Aborigines*. *notes*
New York: Crowell.

Al-Shahi, Ahmed, and F. C. T. Moore. 1978. *Wisdom from the Nile: A Collection of Folk-Stories from Northern and Central Sudan*. Oxford: Clarendon Press.

Anjavi-Shirazi, Sayyid abu al-Qasim. 1975. *Mardum va Firdawsi*. Tehran: Markaz-i Farhang-i Mardum.

Barker, M. A. R. 1963. Klamath Texts. *Publications in American Archaeology and Ethnology* 30. Berkeley: University of California Press.

Basile, G. B. 1932. *The Pentamerone of Gioambattista Basile*. Trans. from the Italian of Benedetto Croce by N. M. Penzer. New York: Dutton.

Basso, Keith H. 1984. "Stalking With Stories": Names, Places, and Moral Narratives among the Western Apache. In Edward M. Bruner, ed., *Text, Play and Story: The Construction and Reconstruction of Self and Society*. 1983 Proceedings of the American Ethnological Society.

Bauman, Richard. 1975. Verbal Art as Performance. *American Anthropologist* 77: 290–311.

Beier, Ulli. 1980. *Yoruba Myths*. Cambridge: Cambridge University Press.

Benedict, Ruth. 1933. Myth. *The Encyclopaedia of the Social Sciences* 11:179.

Bettelheim, Bruno. 1976. *The Uses of Enchantment: The Meaning and Importance of Fairy Tales*. New York: Knopf.

Biesele, Marguerite Anne. 1975. Folklore and Ritual of !Kung Hunter-Gatherers. Vol. 1. Ph.D. diss., Harvard University.

Bixler, Ray H. 1982. Sibling Incest in the Royal Families of Egypt, Peru, and Hawaii. *Journal of Sex Research* 18:264–81.

Blanck, Gertrude, and Rubin Blanck. 1979. *Ego Psychology II: Psychoanalytic Developmental Psychology*. New York: Columbia University Press.

Bly, Robert. 1990a. *A Gathering of Men*. New York: Mystic Fire Video. (With Bill Moyers.)

———. 1990b. *Iron John: A Book About Men*. Reading, Mass.: Addison-Wesley.

Boas, Franz. 1888. The Central Eskimo. *Report* 6. Washington, D.C.: Bureau of American Ethnology.

———. 1909–10. Comparative Study of Tsimshian Mythology. *Annual Report* 31. Washington, D.C.: Bureau of American Ethnology.

Breal, Michel. 1877. *Melanges de Mythologie et de Linguistique*. Paris: Hachette.

Briggs, Jean. 1970. *Never in Anger*. Cambridge, Mass.: Harvard University Press.

Brooks, Cleanth, J. T. Purser, and R. P. Warren. 1938. *An Approach to Literature*. New York: Crofts.

Brown, Donald E. 1991. *Human Universals*. New York: McGraw-Hill.

Brown, R. Grant. 1917. The Dragon of Tagaung. *Journal of the Royal Asiatic Society of Great Britain and Ireland 1917*, pp. 741–51.

Buck, William. 1973. *The Mahabharata*. Berkeley: University of California Press.

Callaway, Henry. 1868. *Nursery Tales, Traditions, and Histories of the Zulus*. Westport, Conn.: Negro Universities Press.

Campbell, Joseph. 1959. *The Masks of God: Primitive Mythology*. New York: Viking.

Carroll, Michael P. 1979. A New Look at Freud on Myth: Reanalyzing the Star-Husband Tale. *Ethos* 7:189–205.

———. 1986. The Trickster-Father Feigns Death and Commits Incest: Some Methodological Contributions to the Study of Myth. *Behavior Science Research* 19: 24–57.

———. 1992. Folklore and Psychoanalysis: The Swallowing Monster and Open-Brains Allomotifs in Plains Indian Mythology. *Ethos* 20:289–303.

Chaves, Milciades. 1946. Mitos, Leyendas y cuentos de La Guajira. *Boletin de Arqueologia* (Bogota) 2:305–31.

Chiara, Vilma. 1961/62. Folclore Kraho. *Revista do Museu Paulista* (Sao Paulo), n.s., 13:333–75.

Chodorow, Nancy. 1974. Family Structure and Feminine Personality. In Michelle Rosaldo and Louise Lamphere, eds., *Woman, Culture, and Society*. Stanford: Stanford University Press, pp. 43–66.

———. 1978. *The Reproduction of Mothering*. Berkeley: University of California Press.

Cleeve, Lucas. 1984. *Tales of the Sun, or, Folklore of Southern India*. Collected by Mrs. Howard Kingscote and Natesa Sastri. New Delhi: Asian Educational Services.

Comparetti, M. 1867. *Edipo e la Mitologia Comparata*. Pisa: Nistri.

Conze, E., ed. 1964. *Buddhist Texts Through the Ages*. New York: Harper and Row.

Cooper-Cole, Fay. 1913. The Wild Tribes of Davao District, Mindanao. *Field Museum of Natural History Anthropology Series* 12(2).

Cordeu, Eduardo Jorge. 1980. Aishtuwente: Las Ideas de Deidad en la Religiosidad Chamacoco. Ph.D. diss., University of Buenos Aires.

Cosmides, Leda, and John Tooby. 1989. Evolutionary Psychology and the Generation of Culture. Pt. 2, Case Study: A Computational Theory of Social Exchange. *Ethology and Sociobiology* 10:51–97.

Cox, George W. 1870. *The Mythology of the Aryan Nations*. London: Longmans.

de Navarre, Marguerite. 1960. A Tale of Incest. In Maurice Valency and Harry Levtow, eds., *The Palace of Pleasure: An Anthology of the Novella*. New York: Capricorn.

Deng, Francis Mading. 1974. *Dinka Folktales: African Stories from the Sudan*. New York: African Publishing Co.

Devereaux, George. 1953. Why Oedipus Killed Laius. *International Journal of Psychoanalysis* 34:132–41. *Iu come. Is w/ Oedipus notes.*

de Zubiria, Roberto. 1968. *Origenes del Complejo de Edipo: De la Mitologia Griega a la Mitologia Chibcha*. Bogota: Tercer Mundo.

Dixon, Roland B. 1916. *Oceanic Mythology*. Boston: Marshall Jones.

Dorsey, G. A., and A. L. Kroeber. 1903. Traditions of the Arapaho. *Anthropology* 5. Publication 81. Chicago: Field Columbian Museum.

Du Bois, Cora. 1944. *The People of Alor*. Minneapolis: University of Minnesota Press.

Dundes, Alan. 1980. *Interpreting Folklore*. Bloomington: Indiana University Press.

———. 1985. The Psychoanalytic Study of Folklore. *Annals of Scholarship* 3:1–42.

———. 1987. *Parsing Through Customs: Essays by a Freudian Folklorist*. Madison: University of Wisconsin Press.

Dutoit, J., trans. 1906. *Jatakam*. Vol. 1. Leipzig: Lotus-Verlag.

Edmunds, Lowell. 1985. *Oedipus: The Ancient Legend and Its Later Analogues*. Baltimore: Johns Hopkins University Press.

Edmunds, Lowell, and Alan Dundes, eds. 1983. *Oedipus: A Folklore Casebook*. New York: Garland.

Eerde, J. C. van. 1902. De Kalanglegende op Lombok. *Tindschrift voor indische Taal-, Land- en Volkenkunde* 45:36–39.

Eguchi, Paul Kasuhisa. 1984. *Fulfulde Tales of North Cameroon*. Vol. 4. Tokyo: Institute for the Study of Languages and Cultures of Asia and Africa.

Elbert, Samuel H., and Torben Monberg. 1965. *From the Two Canoes: Oral Traditions of the Rennell and Bellona Islands*. Honolulu: University of Hawaii Press.

Eliade, Mircea. 1967. *From Primitives to Zen*. London: Collins.

El Shamy, Hasan M. 1980. *Folktales of Egypt*. Chicago: University of Chicago Press.

Erikson, Erik. 1963. *Childhood and Society*. New York: Norton.

Farrand, L., and L. J. Frachtenberg. 1915. Shasta and Athapascan Myths from Oregon. *Journal of American Folklore* 28:212.

Feldman, Susan, ed. 1963. *African Myths and Tales*. New York: Dell.

Fernandez, James. 1971. Bantu Brotherhood: Symmetry, Socialization, and Ultimate

Choice in Two Bantu Cultures. In F. Hsu, ed., *Kinship and Culture*. Chicago: Aldine.

Fields, Suzanne. 1983. *Like Father, Like Daughter*. Boston: Little, Brown.

Fingarette, Herbert. 1969. *Self-Deception*. London: Routledge.

Firth, Raymond. 1961. *History and Traditions of Tikopia*. Wellington, N.Z.: Polynesian Society.

Fischer, John. n.d. *Fieldnotes*. Honolulu: Bernice Pauahi Bishop Museum.

Frazer, Sir James George. 1919. *Folk-Lore in the Old Testament: Studies in Comparative Religion*. Vol. 2, *Legend and Law*. London: Macmillan.

Freeman, Derek. 1967. Totem and Taboo: A Reappraisal. *Psychoanalytic Study of the Child* 4:9–33.

Freud, Sigmund. 1900. The Interpretation of Dreams. *Standard Edition* 4.

———. 1905. Three Essays on the Theory of Sexuality. *Standard Edition* 7:123–243.

———. 1913. Totem and Taboo. *Standard Edition* 13:1–161.

———. 1915. Repression. *Standard Edition* 14:141–58.

———. 1916. Introductory Lectures on Psychoanalysis. Pts. 1 and 2. *Standard Edition* 15.

———. 1917. Introductory Lectures on Psychoanalysis. Pt. 3. *Standard Edition* 16.

———. 1920. The Psychogenesis of a Case of Homosexuality in a Woman. *Standard Edition* 18:145–72.

———. 1923. The Ego and the Id. *Standard Edition* 19:12–66.

———. 1925. An Autobiographical Study. *Standard Edition* 20:7–74.

———. 1930. Civilization and Its Discontents. *Standard Edition* 21:59–145.

———. 1931. Female Sexuality. *Standard Edition* 21:221–43.

———. 1940. Splitting of the Ego in the Process of Defence. *Standard Edition* 23:275–78.

Freud, Sigmund, and Ernst Oppenheim. 1911. Dreams in Folklore. *Standard Edition* 12:180–203.

Friedman, Lawrence. 1988. *The Anatomy of Psychotherapy*. Hillsdale, N.J.: Analytic Press.

Frobenius, Leo, ed. 1971. *African Nights: Black Erotic Folk Tales*. New York: Herder and Herder.

Fromm, Erich. 1947. *Man for Himself: An Inquiry into the Psychology of Ethics*. New York: Rinehart.

———. 1948. The Oedipus Complex and the Oedipus Myth. In Ruth Nanda Anshen, ed., *The Family: Its Function and Destiny*. New York: Harper.

Funke, Friedrich. 1969. Religioses Leben der Sherpa. *Kumbu Himal* 9. Innsbruck: Universitatsverlag Wagner.

Galenson, Eleanor. 1978. The Psychology of Women. *Journal of the American Psychoanalytic Association* 26:163–77.

Gatschet, A. S. 1890. The Klamath Indians of South-Western Oregon. *Contributions to North American Ethnology* 2. Washington, D.C.: Government Printing Office.

Gayton, A. H., and S. S. Newman. 1940. Yokuts and Western Mono Myths. *Anthropological Records* 5 (1). Berkeley: University of California Press.

Gedo, John E. 1979. *Beyond Interpretation*. New York: International Universities Press.

Giaccaria, Bartolomeu, and Adalberto Heide. 1975. *Jeronimo Xavante Conta*. Publicacao No. 1, 2 da "Casa da Cultura." Campo Grande, Mato Grosso, Brazil.

Gifford, Edward W. 1924. Tongan Myths and Tales. *Bernice P. Bishop Museum Bulletin* 8. Honolulu: The Museum.

Gill, Merton M. 1983. The Point of View of Psychoanalysis: Energy Discharge or Person? *Psychoanalysis and Contemporary Thought* 6:523–51.

Girard, Rene. 1979. *Violence and the Sacred*. Baltimore: Johns Hopkins University Press. ~~Loncash has?~~

Goldman, R. P. 1978. Fathers, Sons and Gurus: Oedipal Conflict in the Sanskrit Epics. *Journal of Indian Philosophy* 6:325–92.

Goodall, Jane. 1986. *The Chimpanzees of Gombe: Patterns of Behavior*. Cambridge, Mass.: Belknap.

Grace, A. A. 1907. *Folk-Tales of the Maori*. Wellington, N.Z.: Gordon and Gotch.

Graves, Robert. 1955. *The Greek Myths*. Vol. 2. Mt. Kisco, N.Y.: Moyer Bell.

Gregor, Thomas. 1985. *Anxious Pleasures: Sexual Lives of an Amazonian People*. Chicago: University of Chicago Press.

Gricourt, Jean. 1954. Epona-Rhiannon-Macha. *Ogam* 6:75–79.

Gunther, E. 1925. Klallam Folktales. *Publications in Anthropology* 1. Seattle: University of Washington.

Gusinde, Martin. 1931. *Die Feuerland-Indianer*. Vol. 1, *Die Selknam*. Vienna: Moedling.

———. 1937. *Die Feuerland-Indianer*. Vol. 2, *Die Yamana*. Vienna: Moedling.

Hagglund, Tor-Bjorn, and Vilja Hagglund. 1981. The Boy Who Killed his Father and Wed his Mother. The Oedipus Theme in Finnish Folklore. *International Review of Psychoanalysis* 8:53–62. ~~ILL come. Is w/ Oedipus notes.~~

Harris, Marvin. 1977. *Cannibals and Kings: The Origins of Cultures*. New York: Random House.

Hartmann, Heinz. 1958. *Ego Psychology and the Problem of Adaptation*. Trans. David Rapaport. New York: International Universities Press.

Hennigh, Lawrence. 1966. Control of Incest in Eskimo Folktales. *Journal of American Folklore* 79:~~357–58~~. ~~356–69. ILL come. Is w/ Oedipus notes.~~

Herdt, G. 1981. *Guardians of the Flutes: Idioms of Masculinity*. New York: McGraw-Hill.

Herman, Judith. 1981. *Father-Daughter Incest*. Cambridge, Mass.: Harvard University Press.

Hesiod. 1993. *Works and Days and Theogony*. Trans. Stanley Lombardo. Cambridge, Mass.: Hackett.

Hicks, David. 1984. A Maternal Religion: The Role of Women in Tetum Myth and Ritual. Special Report 22, Monograph Series on Southeast Asia. Center for Southeast Asian Studies. Dekalb: Northern Illinois University.

Hiroa, Te Rangi. 1938. Ethnology of Mangareva. *Bernice P. Bishop Museum Bulletin* 157. Honolulu: The Museum.

Hopkins, Keith. 1980. Brother-Sister Marriage in Roman Egypt. *Comparative Studies in Society and History* 22:303–54.

Horney, Karen. 1937. *The Neurotic Personality of Our Time*. New York: Norton.

———. 1939. *New Ways in Psychoanalysis*. New York: Norton.

Ikeda, Hiroko. 1971. A Type and Motif Index of Japanese Folk-Literature. *Folklore Fellows Communications* 209. Helsinki: Suomalainen Tiedeakatemia, Academia Scientiarium Fennica.

Ingham, John. 1963. Malinowski: Epistemology and Oedipus. *Kroeber Anthropological Society Papers* 29:1–14.

Jacobs, Melville. 1940. Coos Myth Texts. *Publications in Anthropology* 8 (2). Seattle: University of Washington.

———. 1958. Clackamas Chinook Texts. Pt. 1. *International Journal of American Linguistics* 24 (2).

Jest, Corneille. 1976. Encounters with Intercessors in Nepal. In John T. Hitchcock and R. L. Jones, eds., *Spirit Possession in the Nepal Himalayas*. Warminster, Eng.: Aris and Phillips, pp. 299–300.

Johnson, Allen W., and Timothy K. Earle. 1987. *The Evolution of Human Societies*. Stanford: Stanford University Press.

Johnson, Allen, and Orna Johnson. 1991a. Shakanari. Translation from Field Notes. Manuscript, 6 pp.

———. 1991b. Osheto (Spider Monkey). Translation from Field Notes. Manuscript, 3 pp.

Johnson, Charles. 1981. *The Flood: How Hmong Names Began*. St. Paul, Minn.: Linguistics Department, Macalester College.

———. 1985. The Flood and Hmong Clan Names (Dej Nyab Ntiaj Teb: Hmoob Lub Xeem). *Dab Neeg Hmoob: Myths, Legends, and Folk Tales from the Hmong of Laos*. St. Paul, Minn.: Linguistics Department, Macalester College.

Johnson, Orna. 1978. Interpersonal Relations and Domestic Authority Among the Machiguenga of the Peruvian Amazon. Ph.D. diss., Columbia University.

Jones, Ernest. 1925. Mother-Right and the Sexual Ignorance of Savages. *The International Journal of Psycho-Analysis* 6:109–30.

Jung, C. G. 1956. *Two Essays on Analytical Psychology*. New York: Meridian Books.

———. 1964. *Man and His Symbols*. New York: Doubleday.

Juynboll, Hendrik H. 1912. *Supplement op den catalogus van de Sundaneesche handscrhiften en catalogus van de Balineesche en Sasaksche handschriften der Leidsche Universiteits-Bibliotheek*. Leiden: E. J. Brill.

Kardiner, Abram. 1939. *The Individual and His Society*. New York: Columbia University Press.

———. 1945. *The Psychological Frontiers of Society*. New York: Columbia University Press.

Karve, Irawati. 1950. A Marathi Version of the Oedipus Story. *Man* 99:71–72.

Kern, O. 1963. *Orphicorum Fragmenta*. Berolini: Apud Weidmannos.

Kestenbaum, Clarice J. 1983. Fathers and Daughters: The Father's Contribution to Feminine Identification in Girls as Depicted in Fairy Tales and Myths. *American Journal of Psychoanalysis* 43:119–27.

Kirk, G. S. 1970. *Myth: Its Meaning and Function in Ancient and Other Cultures*. Cambridge: The University Press.

Klein, George S. 1976. *Psychoanalytic Theory: An Exploration of Essentials*. New York: International Universities Press.

Kluckhohn, Clyde. 1959. Recurrent Themes in Myths and Mythology. *Daedelus* 88: 268–79.

Kohut, Heinz. 1977. *The Restoration of the Self*. New York: International Universities Press.

Kosawa, H. 1950. Two Kinds of Guilt Feelings (Ajase Complex). *Japanese Journal of Psychoanalysis* 1.

Krappe, Alexander H. 1927. *Balor with the Evil Eye: Studies in Culture and French Literature*. New York: Institut des Etudes Françaises.

———. 1983. Is the Legend of Oedipus a Folktale? In Lowell Edmunds and Alan Dundes, eds., *Oedipus: A Folklore Casebook*. New York: Garland.

Krauss, Friedrich S. 1935. The Oedipus Legend in South Slavic Folk Tradition. *Imago* 22:358–67.

Kroeber, A. L. 1920. Totem and Taboo: An Ethnologic Psychoanalysis. *American Anthropologist* 22:48–55.

———. 1939. Totem and Taboo in Retrospect. *American Journal of Sociology* 45: 446–51.

Kurtz, Stanley N. 1991. Polysexualization: A New Approach to Oedipus in the Trobriands. *Ethos* 19:68–101.

La Barre, Weston. 1957. Freud and Anthropology. *Archives of Criminal Psychodynamics* 2:450–51.

———. 1984. *Muelos: A Stone-Age Superstition About Sexuality*. New York: Columbia University Press.

Landar, Herbert. 1972. Themes of Incest in Navajo Folklore. In S. Ghosh, ed., *Man, Language and Society: Contributions to the Sociology of Language*. The Hague: Mouton.

Landtman, G. 1917. The Folk-tales of the Kiwai Papuans. *Acta Societatis Scientiarum Fennicae Tomus* 47. Helsingfors: Printing Office of the Finnish Society of Literature.

Langness, L. L. 1990. Oedipus in the New Guinea Highlands? *Ethos* 18:387–406.

Lefkowitz, Mary. 1986. *Women in Greek Myth*. London: Duckworth.

Lessa, William A. 1956. Oedipus-Type Tales in Oceania. *Journal of American Folklore* 69:63–73.

———. 1961. Tales from Ulithi Atoll. *Folklore Studies* 13:172–214.

Levi-Strauss, C. 1967. *Structural Anthropology*. New York: Anchor Books.

———. 1969. *The Raw and the Cooked*. New York: Harper.

———. 1981. *The Naked Man*. New York: Harper.

Lichtenberg, J. 1989. *Psychoanalysis and Motivation*. Hillsdale, N.J.: Analytic Press.

Loewald, Hans. 1979. The Waning of the Oedipus Complex. *Journal of the American Psychoanalytic Association* 27:751–75.

Maity, Pradyot K. 1966. *Historical Studies in the Cult of the Goddess Manasa*. Calcutta: Punthi Pustak.

Malinowski, Bronislaw. 1922. *Argonauts of the Western Pacific*. New York: Dutton.

———. 1923. The Psychology of Sex and the Foundations of Kinship in Primitive Societies. *Psyche* 4:98–128.

———. 1924. Psycho-Analysis and Anthropology. *Psyche* 4:293–332.

———. 1927. *Sex and Repression in Savage Society*. London: Routledge.

———. 1929. *The Sexual Life of Savages in North-Western Melanesia*. London: Routledge.

Mardrus, J. C. 1972. The Tale of Ala al-Din and the Wonderful Lamp. *The Book of the Thousand Nights and One Night*. Vol. 3. New York: St. Martin's Press.

Matisse, O. Vernon. 1990. *Father-Daughter Incest in the American Middle-Class Family: An Ethnographic Study*. Ph.D. diss., University of California, Los Angeles.

Mead, Margaret. 1930. An Ethnologist's Footnote to "Totem and Taboo." *Psychoanalytic Review* 17:297–304.

Melatti, Julio Cezar. 1978. *Ritos de una Tribo Timbira*. Sao Paulo: Editora Atica.

Metraux, Alfred. 1939. Myths and Tales of the Matako Indians. *Etnologiska Studier* (Goteborg) 9:1–127.

———. 1971. Ethnology of Easter Island. *Bernice P. Bishop Museum Publications* 160. Honolulu: The Museum.

Money-Kyrle, R. 1929. *The Meaning of Sacrifice*. London: Hogarth.

———. 1951. *Psychoanalysis and Politics*. London: Duckworth.

Moore, Sally Falk. 1964. Descent and Symbolic Filiation. *American Anthropologist* 66: 1308–20.

Mosko, Mark S. 1991. The Canonic Formula of Myth and Nonmyth. *American Ethnologist* 18:126–51.

Mozart, Wolfgang Amadeus. 1959 [1786]. *Le Nozze di Figaro (The Marriage of Figaro)*; opera in four acts. Music by W. A. Mozart, libretto by Lorenzo Da Ponte. English version by Ruth and Thomas Martin. New York: G. Schirmer.

Müller, F. Max. 1983. *Theosophy; or Psychological Religion*. The Gifford Lectures 1982. Glasgow: University of Glasgow.

Mumford, Stan. 1985. *Transmutation and Dialogue: Tibetan Lamaism and Gurung Shamanism in Nepal*. Princeton: Princeton University Press.

———. 1989. *Himalayan Dialogue: Tibetan Lamas and Gurung Shamans in Nepal*. Madison: University of Wisconsin Press.

Murphy, Yolanda, and Robert F. Murphy. 1985. *Women of the Forest*. New York: Columbia University Press.

Nimuendaju, Curt. 1939. *The Apinaye*. Trans. Robert H. Lowie and John M. Cooper. *Anthropological Series* 8. Washington: Catholic University of America Press.

Obeyesekere, Gananath. 1984. *The Cult of the Goddess Pattini*. Chicago: University of Chicago Press.

O'Flaherty, Wendy Doniger. 1980. *Women, Androgynes, and Other Mythical Beasts: Tales of Sex and Violence*. Chicago: University of Chicago Press.

———. 1985. *Tales of Sex and Violence: Folklore, Sacrifice, and Danger in the "Jaiminiya Brahmana."* Chicago: University of Chicago Press.

Okonogi, Keigo. 1979. Japanese Psychoanalysis and the Ajase Complex. *Psychotherapy and Psychosomatics* 31:350–56.

Omidsalar, Mahmoud. 1980. Oedipus Complex in the Shahnameh: Textual, Folkloristic, and Psychoanalytical Studies on the National Persian Epic. Ph.D. diss., University of California, Berkeley.

Oppert, Gustav. 1893. *On the Original Inhabitants of Bharatavarsa or India*. New Delhi: Unity Book Service.

Ovid. 1955. *Metamorphoses*. Trans. Mary Innes. London: Penguin.

Paiva, Zeca, Allen Johnson, and Carlos Soares. 1991. Camoes and His Mother. Manuscript, University of California, Los Angeles.

Parsons, Anne. 1964. Is the Oedipus Complex Universal? The Jones-Malinowski Debate Revisited. *Psychoanalytic Study of Society* 3:278–328. *Is w/ Oedipus notes*

Parsons, Elsie Clews. 1936. Folk-lore of the Antilles, French and English. Pt. 2. *Memoirs* 24 (111):205–6. Washington, D.C.: American Folklore Society.

Paul, Robert. 1976. Did the Primal Crime Take Place? *Ethos* 4:311–52.

———. 1979. Dumje: Paradox and Resolution in Sherpa Ritual Symbolism. *American Ethnologist* 6:274–304.

———. 1982. *The Tibetan Symbolic World*. Chicago: University of Chicago Press.

Perrin, Michel. 1973. Contribution a L'etude de la Litterature Goajiro. These de troisieme cycle. Coll. No. 1 (1969) 03.22. Paris: University of Paris.

Piers, Gerhart, and Milton B. Singer. 1953. *Shame and Guilt: A Psychoanalytic and a Cultural Study*. Springfield, Ill.: Thomas.

Pineda Giraldo, Roberto. 1950. Aspectos de la Magia en la Guajira. *Revista del Instituto Etnologico Nacional* 3:76. Bogota.

Pinker, Steven. 1991. The Rules of Language. *Science* 253:530–35.

Pollock, George H., and John Munder Ross, eds. 1988. *The Oedipus Papers*. Madison: International Universities Press.

Prayatni. 1989. The Legend of Tangkuban Parahu. *Inflight Magazine*, July. West Java: Garuda Indonesia Airlines.

Propp, Vladimir. 1983. Oedipus in the Light of Folklore. In Lowell Edmunds and Alan Dundes, eds., *Oedipus: A Folklore Casebook*. New York: Garland.

Proskauer, Stephen. 1980. Oedipal Equivalents in a Clan Culture: Reflections on Navajo Ways. *Psychiatry* 43:43–50. *Lancaster has. Is w/ Oedipus notes*

Radin, Paul. 1956. *The Trickster: A Study in American Indian Mythology*. New York: Shocken.

Raglan, Lord. 1936. *The Hero: A Study in Tradition, Myth, and Drama*. Westport, Conn.: Greenwood Press.

Ramanujan, A. K. 1983. The Indian Oedipus: In Lowell Edmunds and Alan Dundes, eds., *Oedipus: A Folklore Casebook*. New York: Garland, pp. 234–61.

Randolph, Vance. 1976. *Pissing in the Snow*. Urbana: University of Illinois Press.

Rank, Otto. 1992. *The Incest Theme in Literature and Legend: Fundamentals of a Psychology of Literary Creation*. Baltimore: Johns Hopkins University Press. (Originally published in German in 1912.)

Reichel-Dolmatoff, Gerardo. 1971. *Amazonian Cosmos: The Sexual and Religious Symbolism of the Tukano Indians*. Chicago: University of Chicago Press.

———. 1975. *The Shaman and the Jaguar*. Philadelphia: Temple University Press.

Riklin, F. 1908. *Wunscherfullung und Symbolik im Marchen. Schriften zur Angewandten Seelenkunde*. Vol. 2. Leipzig: Deuticke.

Robert, Carl. 1915. *Oedipus*. Berlin: Weidmann.

Roheim, Geza. 1932. Psychoanalysis of Primitive Cultural Types. *International Journal of Psychoanalysis* 13:2–224.

———. 1934. Primitive High Gods. *Psychoanalytic Quarterly* 3 (Supplement).

———. 1941. Play Analysis With Normanby Island Children. *American Journal of Orthopsychiatry* 11:524–59.

———. 1945. *Eternal Ones of the Dream*. New York: International Universities Press.

———. 1948. Witches of Normanby Island. *Oceania* 18:280.

———. 1950. *Psychoanalysis and Anthropology: Culture, Personality and the Unconscious*. New York: International Universities Press.

———. 1952. *The Gates of the Dream*. New York: International Universities Press.

———. 1974. *Children of the Desert*. New York: Basic Books.

Saperstein, Jerome L., and Jack Gaines. 1973. Metapsychological Considerations on the Self. *International Journal of Psycho-Analysis* 54:415–24.

Sastri, S. M. Natesa. 1884–88. *Folklore in Southern India*. Bombay: no pub. given.

Savokarjalainen Osakunta. 1887. The Boy Who Married his Mother. Trans. Marja Henonen. Helsinki: Suomalainen Kirjallisuuden Seura.

Schmerler, Henrietta. 1931. Trickster Marries his Daughter. *Journal of American Folklore* 44:196–98.

Seitel, Peter. 1980. *See So that We May See: Performances and Interpretations of Traditional Tales from Tanzania*. Bloomington: Indiana University Press.

Shaheen, Jack G. 1992. Arab Caricatures Deface Disney's "Aladdin." *Los Angeles Times*, Calendar Section, p. F3, Dec. 21.

Shostak, Marjorie. 1981. *Nisa: The Life and Words of a !Kung Woman*. Cambridge, Mass.: Harvard University Press.

Simon, Bennett. 1991. Is the Oedipus Complex Still the Cornerstone of Psychoanalysis? Three Obstacles to Answering the Question. *Journal of the American Psychoanalytic Association* 39:641–68.

Simon, Fray Pedro. 1891. *Noticias Historiales*. Bogota.

Skinner, A. 1911. Notes on the Eastern Cree and Northern Saulteaux. *Anthropological Papers* 9. New York: American Museum of Natural History.

Slater, Philip. 1968. *The Glory of Hera: Greek Mythology and the Greek Family*. Boston: Beacon Press.

Smith, E. W., ed. 1961. *African Ideas of God*. London: Edinburgh House Press.

Southall, A. W. 1958. Oedipus in Alur Folklore. *Uganda Journal* 22:167–69.

Spencer, K. 1957. *Mythology and Values: An Analysis of Navajo Chantaway Myths*. Philadelphia: American Folklore Society.

Spiro, Melford. 1973. The Oedipus Complex in Burma. *Journal of Nervous and Mental Disease* 157:389–95.

———. 1979. Whatever Happened to the Id? *American Anthropologist* 81:5–13.

———. 1982. *Oedipus in the Trobriands*. Chicago: University of Chicago Press.

———. 1992. Oedipus Redux. *Ethos* 20:358–76.

Steinmetz, Devora. 1985. Oedipus Again! Kinship and Continuity in Ancient Literature. *Annals of Scholarship* 3:43–64.

Stephens, William N. 1962. *The Oedipus Complex: Cross-Cultural Evidence*. New York: Free Press.

Stimpson, Frank J. 1937. Tuamotuan Legends (Islands of Anaa). *Bernice P. Bishop Museum Bulletin* 148. Honolulu: The Museum.

Stoller, Robert. 1973. The Sense of Femaleness. In Jean Baker Miller, ed., *Psychoanalysis and Women*. Baltimore: Penguin Books.

Stritmatter, Roger. 1987. Oedipus, Akhnaton and the Greek State: An Archeology of the Oedipus Complex. *Dialectical Anthropology* 12:45–63.

Teit, J. A. 1912. *Mythology of the Thompson Indians*. Memoirs 12. New York: American Museum of Natural History, 12.

Thompson, Stith. 1929. *Tales of North American Indians*. Cambridge, Mass.: Peabody Museum, Harvard University.

———. 1949. Folktale. In Maria Leach, ed., *Dictionary of Folklore, Mythology and Myth*. Vol. 1. New York: Funk and Wagnalls.

———. 1952. Letter to William A. Lessa. In William A. Lessa. 1956. Oedipus-Type Tales in Oceania. *Journal of American Folklore* 69:73.

Thomson, George. 1977. *Studies in Ancient Greek Societies: The First Philosophers*. London: Lawrence and Wisehart.

Ting, Nai-tung. 1978. *A Type Index of Chinese Folktales*. Helsinki: Suomalainen Tiedeakatemia Academia Scientiarum Fennica.

Tooby, John, and Leda Cosmides. 1989. Evolutionary Psychology and the Generation of Culture. Part 1, Theoretical Considerations. *Ethology and Sociobiology* 10: 29–49.

Trivers, Robert. 1985. *Social Evolution*. Menlo Park, Calif.: Benjamin/Cummings.

Trosman, H., A. Rechtschaffen, W. Offenkrantz, and E. Wolpert. 1960. Studies in Psychophysiology of Dreams: Relations among Dreams in Sequence. *Archives of General Psychiatry* 3:602–7.

Turner, Terence. 1969. Oedipus: Time and Structure in Narrative Form. In Robert F. Spencer, ed., *Forms of Symbolic Action*. Seattle: American Ethnological Society.

Vernant, J. P. 1972. Oedipe sans Complex. In J. P. Vernant and Pierre Vidal-Naquet, *Myth et Tragedie en Grece Ancienne*. Paris: Francois Maspero.

Vidal, Lux. 1977. *Morte e Vida de uma Sociedade Indigena Brasileira: Os Kayapo-Xikrin do Rio Catete*. Sao Paulo: Editora Hucitec, Editora da Universidade de Sao Paulo.

Voegelin, E. W. 1950. Myth. In Maria Leach, ed., *Dictionary of Folklore, Mythology, and Myth*. Vol. 2. New York: Funk and Wagnalls.

Waal, F. B. M. de. 1982. *Chimpanzee Politics: Power and Politics Among Apes*. New York: Harper and Row.

Westermarck, Edward. 1922. *The History of Human Marriage*. New York: Allerton.

White, John. 1887–90. *The Ancient History of the Maori, His Mythology and Traditions*. Wellington, N.Z.: G. Didsbury.

Whiting, John, and Beatrice Whiting. 1975. *Children of Six Cultures: A Psychocultural Analysis*. Cambridge, Mass.: Harvard University Press.

Wilbert, Johannes. 1975. *Folk Literature of the Selknam Indians*. Los Angeles: UCLA Latin American Center Publications.

———. 1977. *Folk Literature of the Yamana Indians: Martin Gusinde's Collection of Yamana Narratives*. Berkeley: University of California Press.

Wilbert, Johannes, and Karin Simoneau, eds. 1978. *Folk Literature of the Gê Indians, Vol. 1*. Los Angeles: UCLA Latin American Center Publications.

———. 1982. *Folk Literature of the Mataco Indians*. Los Angeles: UCLA Latin American Center Publications.

———. 1983. *Folk Literature of the Bororo Indians*. Los Angeles: UCLA Latin American Center Publications.

———. 1984a. *Folk Literature of the Gê Indians, Vol. 2*. Los Angeles: UCLA Latin American Center Publications.

———. 1984b. *Folk Literature of the Tehuelche Indians*. Los Angeles: UCLA Latin American Center Publications.

———. 1986. *Folk Literature of the Guajiro Indians.* With Michel Perrin. 2 vols. Los Angeles: UCLA Latin American Center Publications.

———. 1987a. *Folk Literature of the Chamacoco Indians*. Los Angeles: UCLA Latin American Center Publications.

———. 1987b. *Folk Literature of the Nivaklé Indians*. Los Angeles: UCLA Latin American Center Publications.

———. 1989. *Folk Literature of the Ayoreo Indians*. Los Angeles: UCLA Latin American Center Publications.

Williams, F. E. 1936. *Papuans of the Trans-Fly*. Oxford: Oxford University Press.

Willner, Dorothy. 1984. Definition and Violation: Incest and the Incest Taboos. *Man*, n.s. 18:134–59.

Winnicott, D. W. 1965. Ego Distortion in Terms of True and False Self. *The Maturational Processes and the Facilitating Environment: Studies in the Theory of Emotional Development*. New York: International Universities Press, pp. 140–52.

Wolf, A. P. 1966. Childhood Association, Sexual Attraction, and the Incest Taboo: a Chinese Case. *American Anthropologist* 68:883–98.

PERMISSIONS TO
REPRODUCE THE FOLKTALES

1. Hesiod, *Works and Days*, translated by Stanley Lombardo, 1993, Hackett Publishing Co., Inc. Reproduced by permission.

2. Same as 1.

3. From *The Greek Myths*, vol. 2, by Robert Graves, published by Moyer Bell, Kymbolde Way, Wakefield, RI, 02879. Reproduced by permission.

4. From Joseph Campbell, *The Masks of God: Primitive Mythology*. New York: Viking, 1959. Copyright © 1959, 1969, renewed 1987 by Joseph Campbell. Used by permission of Viking Penguin.

5. From Wendy Doniger O'Flaherty, *Women, Androgynes, and Other Mystical Beasts*, published by the University of Chicago Press, 1980. © 1980 by The University of Chicago. All rights reserved. Reproduced by permission of the publisher.

6. From Alexander H. Krappe, *Balor with the Evil Eye: Studies in Culture and French Literature*. New York: Institut des Etudes Françaises, 1927.

7. From Marguerite de Navarre, "A Tale of Incest," in Maurice Valency and Harry Levtow, eds., *The Palace of Pleasure: An Anthology of the Novella*. New York: Capricorn, 1960.

8. From Lowell Edmunds and Alan Dundes, eds., *Oedipus: A Folklore Casebook*, published by Garland Publishing Company, 1983. Reproduced by permission of the publisher.

9. Same as 8.

10. Edmunds, Lowell. *Oedipus: The Ancient Legend and Its Later Analogues*. The Johns Hopkins University Press, Baltimore/London, 1985.

11. Copyright 1976 by the Board of Trustees of the University of Illinois. Used with permission of the University of Illinois Press.

12. Reproduced by permission of Beulah Aiken.

13. Same as 10.

14. Reproduced by permission.

15. From *Russian Fairy Tales* by Aleksander Afansev, translated by Norbert Guterman

Copyright © 1945 by Pantheon Books, Inc. Copyright renewed 1975 by Random House, Inc. Reprinted by permission of Pantheon Books, a division of Random House, Inc.

16. Reproduced by permission of Mahmoud Omidsalar.

17. From *Dinka Folktales: African Stories from the Sudan* by Francis Mading Deng (New York: Africana Publishing Company, 1974). Copyright © 1974 by Francis Mading Deng. Reprinted by permission of the publisher.

18. Same as 8.

19. Same as 10.

20. From Susan Taubes Feldman, ed., *African Myths and Tales*, published by Dell, a division of Bantam, Doubleday, Dell Publishing Group, Inc., 1963. Reproduced by permission of the publisher.

21. Same as 8.

22. From Leo Frobenius, ed., *African Nights: Black Erotic Folk Tales*, published by Herder and Herder, 1971.

23. Same as 22.

24. Same as 22.

25. Same as 22.

26. From Peter Seitel, *See So that We May See: Performances and Interpretations of Traditional Tales from Tanzania* as told by Ms. Kokubelwa Ishabakaki. Reproduced by permission of Peter Seitel.

27. © Ahmed Al-Shahi and F. C. T. Moore 1978. Reprinted from *Wisdom from the Nile* translated by Ahmed Al-Shahi and F.C.T. Moore (1978) by permission of Oxford University Press.

28. Same as 27.

29. Same as 27.

30. From Hasan M. El-Shamy, *Folktales of Egypt*, published by the University of Chicago Press, 1980. © 1980 by The University of Chicago. All rights reserved. Reproduced by permission of the publisher.

31. Reproduced by permission of Paul K. Eguchi.

32. From Ulli Beier, *Yoruba Myths*, published by Cambridge University Press, 1980. © Cambidge University Press 1980. Reprinted by permission of Cambridge University Press.

33. Reproduced by permission of James Fernandez.

34. Same as 6.

35. From Wendy Doniger O'Flaherty, *Tales of Sex and Violence*, published by the University of Chicago Press, 1985. © 1985 by The University of Chicago. All rights reserved. Reproduced by permission of the publisher.

36. Same as 35.

37. Same as 5.

38. Same as 5.

39. Same as 5.

40. Reproduced by permission of Kluwer Academic Publishers.

41. Reproduced by permission of John T. Hitchcock.

42. From Stan Mumford, *Himalayan Dialogue: Tibetan Lamas and Gurung Shaman in Nepal*, published by the University of Wisconsin Press, 1989. © 1989 The Board of Regents of the University of Wisconsin System. All rights reserved. Reproduced by permission of the publisher.

43. From Gananath Obeyesekere, *The Cult Goddess of the Pattini*, published by the University of Chicago Press, 1984. © 1984 by The University of Chicago. All rights reserved. Reproduced by permission of the publisher.

44. From Irawati Karve, "A Marathi Version of the Oedipus Story," *Man*, 1950. Reproduced by permission.

45. Same as 44.

46. Same as 8.

47. Same as 8.

48. Reproduced by permission of FF Communications.

49. From Keigo Okonogi, "Japanese Psychoanalysis and the Ajase Complex," *Psychotherapy and Psychosomatics*, 1979. Reproduced by permission of S. Karger AG, Basel.

50. Reproduced by permission of Academia Scientiarum Fennica.

51. Same as 8.

52. From R. Grant Brown, "The Dragon of Tataung," *Journal of the Royal Asiatic Society of Great Britain and Ireland*, 1917. Reproduced by permission of Cambridge University Press.

53. From Melford Spiro, "The Oedipus Complex in Burma," *Journal of Nervous and Mental Disease*, 1973, 157, pp. 391–92. Reproduced by permission of Waverly.

54. Same as 53.

55. From "Dej Nyab Ntiaj Teb: Hmoob Lub Xeem" ("The Flood and Hmong Clan Names") as told by May Yang, written and translated by Se Yang, Tou Doua Yang & Charles Johnson. In *Dab Neeg Ymoob: Myths, Legends & Folk Tales from the Hmong of Laos*. St. Paul, Malacaster College. 1985.

56. From John White, *The Ancient History of the Maori, His Mythology and Traditions*. Wellington, New Zealand: G. Didsbury, 1887–90.

57. From Sir Peter Buck, *Ethnology of Manganera*. Reproduced by permission of the Bishop Museum.

58. From Edward W. Gifford, "Tongan Myths and Tales," *Bernice P. Bishop Museum Bulletin*, 1924. Reprinted by permission of the Bishop Museum.

59. Same as 58.

60. From Raymond Firth, *History and Traditions of Tikopia*, published by the Polynesian Society (incorporated), Wellington, New Zealand, 1961. Reproduced by permission.

61. From Samuel H. Elbert and Torben Monberg, *From the Two Canoes: Oral Traditions of the Rennell and Bellona Islands*, published by the University of Hawaii Press, 1965. Reproduced by permission of the publisher.

62. From A. A. Grace, *Folk-Tales of the Maori*. Wellington New Zealand: Gordon and Gotch, 1907.

63. From Frank J. Stimson, "Tuamotuan Legends," *Bernice P. Bishop Museum Bulletin*, 1937. Reproduced by permission of the Bishop Museum.

64. From William Lessa, *Tales from Ulithi Atoll: A Comparative Study in Oceanic Folklore,* published by the University of California Press, 1961. Copyright © 1961 by The Regents of the University of California. Reproduced by permission of the publisher.

65. From Fay Cooper-Cole, "The Wild Tribes of Davao District, Mindanao," *Field Museum of Natural History Anthropology Series* 12 (2): 173–74.

66. From Bronislaw Malinowski, *The Sexual Life of Savages in North-Western Melanesia*, published by Routledge, 1929. Reproduced by permission of the publisher.

67. From Bronislaw Malinowski, *Sex and Repression in Savage Society*, published by Routledge and Kegan Paul. Reproduced by permission of ITPS.

68. Same as 66.

69. Courtesy of Bishop Museum Press, Bishop Museum, Honolulu, Hawaii.

70. From Roland B. Dixon, *Oceanic Mythology*. Boston: Marshall Jones, 1916.

71. From Prayatni, "The Legend of Tangkuban Parahu," *Garuda Airlines Inflight Magazine,* July 1989.

72. Same as 64.

73. Same as 64.

74. Same as 64.

75. Same as 64.

76. From Cora Du Bois, *The People of Alor*, published by University of Minnesota Press, 1944.

77. Pages 190–191 from *Children of the Desert* by Geza Roheim & W. Muensterberger. © 1974 by Werner Muensterberger. Reprinted by permission of HarperCollins Publishers, Inc., and Frances Collin Literary Agent.

78. From Geza Roheim, *Eternal Ones of the Dream*, published by International Universities Press, 1945. Reproduced by permission of the publisher.

79. Same as 78.

80. From Geza Roheim, *The Gates of the Dream*, published by International Universities Press, 1952. Reproduced by permission of the publisher.

81. Same as 80.

82. Same as 80.

83. Reproduced by permission of Gilbert Herdt.

84. Selections from pages 81–88 from *Time Before Morning: Art and Myth of the Australian Aborigine* by Louis A. Allen. Copyright © 1975 by Louis A. Allen. Reprinted by permission of HarperCollins Publishers, Inc.

85. Reproduced by permission of *The Psychoanalytic Quarterly*.

86. Reproduced by permission of Northern Illinois University.

87. Reproduced by permission of the American Folklore Society from *Journal of American Folklore* 45: 176, 1932. Not for further reproduction.

88. Reproduced by permission of Columbia University Press.

89. From Herbert Landar, Themes of Incest in Navajo Folklore, 1972. In S. Ghosh, ed., *Man, Language and Society: Contributions to the Sociology of Language*. The Hague: Mouton. Reproduced by permission of Mouton de Gruyter, a division of Walter de Gruyter & Co., Berlin.

90. Reproduced by permission of the American Folklore Society from *Journal of American Folklore* 79: 312, April–June 1966. Not for further reproduction.

91. Same as 90.

92. From Anna Gayton and Stanley Newton, *Yokuts and Western Mono Myths*, published by University of California Press, copyright © 1940. Reproduced by permission of the University of California Press.

93. From Stith Thompson, *Tales of North American Indians*, published by Harvard University Press, 1929.

94. From A. Skinner, "Notes on the Eastern Cree and Northern Saulteaux," *Anthropological Papers,* 9. New York: American Museum of Natural History, 1911.

95. Reproduced by permission of the American Anthropological Association from *Text, Play, and Story*, 1984. Not for further reproduction.

96. From Franz Boas, "Comparative Study of Tsimshian Mythology," *Bureau of American Ethnology Annual Report 31*. Washington, D.C.: Bureau of American Ethnology, 1909–10.

97. From Geza Roheim, *Psychoanalysis and Anthropology*, published by International Universities Press, Inc., 1950. Reproduced by permission of International Universities Press, Inc.

98. Reproduced by permission of the University of Washington.

99. From G. A. Dorsey and A. L. Kroeber, "Traditions of the Arapaho," *Anthropology* 5. Publication 81. Chicago: Field Columbian Museum, 1903.

100. Excerpts from pages 31–32, 49–51 and 474–75 from *The Naked Man* by Claude

Levi-Strauss. English translation copyright © 1981 by Jonathan Cape Limited and Harper & Row, Publishers Inc. Reprinted by permission of HarperCollins Publishers, Inc.

101. From Melville Jacobs, Clackamas Chinook Texts, *International Journal of American Linguistics* 24 (2), published by the University of Chicago Press. Reproduced by permission of the publisher.

102. Reproduced by permission of the American Folklore Society from *Memoirs of The American Folklore Society*, Volume 48, 1957. Not for further reproduction.

103. Same as 100.

104. Same as 100.

105. Reproduced by permission of Columbia University Press.

106. Reproduced by permission.

107. From Thomas Gregor, *Anxious Pleasures: Sexual Lives of an Amazonian People*, published by the University of Chicago Press, 1985. © 1985 by the University of Chicago. Reproduced by permission of the publisher.

108. Same as 107.

109. Same as 107.

110. Same as 107.

111. Same as 107.

112. "The Origin of the Stars and of Certain Animals." Reprinted with permission, from Johannes Wilbert and Karin Simoneau, eds., *Folk Literature of the Bororo Indians* (Los Angeles: UCLA Latin American Center Publications, 1983), pp. 48–51.

113. "The Story of the Woman Ararúga Páru." Reprinted with permission, from Johannes Wilbert and Karin Simoneau, eds., *Folk Literature of the Bororo Indians* (Los Angeles: UCLA Latin American Center Publications, 1983), pp. 187–91.

114. "The Legend of the Hero Toribúgu." Reprinted with permission, from Johannes Wilbert and Karin Simoneau, eds., *Folk Literature of the Bororo Indians* (Los Angeles: UCLA Latin American Center Publications, 1983), pp. 198–204.

115. "Transformation of a Brother- and Sister-in-law into Boas." Reprinted with permission, from Johannes Wilbert and Karin Simoneau, eds., *Folk Literature of the Nivaklé Indians* (Los Angeles: UCLA Latin American Center Publications, 1987), pp. 296–97.

116. "The Incestuous Young Man Who Was Transformed into a Jaguar." Reprinted with permission, from Johannes Wilbert and Karin Simoneau, eds., *Folk Literature of the Chamacoco Indians* (Los Angeles: UCLA Latin American Center Publications, 1987), pp. 194–99.

117. "The Incest and the Big Bull." Reprinted with permission, from Johannes Wilbert and Karin Simoneau, eds., *Folk Literature of the Guajiro Indians*, vol. 2 (Los Angeles: UCLA Latin American Center Publications, 1986), pp. 790–92.

118. "The Origin of a Hill." Reprinted with permission, from Johannes Wilbert and Karin Simoneau, eds., *Folk Literature of the Guajiro Indians*, vol. 1 (Los Angeles: UCLA Latin American Center Publications, 1986), pp.45–46.

119. "Incest." Reprinted with permission, from Johannes Wilbert and Karin Simoneau, eds., *Folk Literature of the Guajiro Indians*, Vol. 1 (Los Angeles: UCLA Latin American Center Publications, 1986), pp. 46–47.

120. "The Birth of Kwányip" Reprinted with permission, from Johannes Wilbert and Karin Simoneau, eds., *Folk Literature of the Selknam Indians* (Los Angeles: UCLA Latin American Center Publications, 1975), pp. 30–31.

121. "The Guanaco-man and His Daughters." Reprinted with permission, from Johannes Wilbert and Karin Simoneau, eds., *Folk Literature of the Selknam Indians* (Los Angeles: UCLA Latin American Center Publications, 1975), pp. 107–9.

122. From Johannes Wilbert, *Folk Literature of the Yamana Indians: Martin Gusinde's Collection of Yamana Narratives*, published by the University of California Press, 1977. Copyright © 1977 by The Regents of the University of California. Reproduced by permission of the publisher.

123. Same as 122.

124. Same as 122.

125. Same as 122.

126. "The Seven Stars (The Pleiades)." Reprinted with permission from Johannes Wilbert and Karin Simoneau, eds., *Folk Literature of the Gé Indians*, Vol. 1 (Los Angeles: UCLA Latin American Center Publications, 1978), pp. 81–87.

127. "The Adventures of Pëdwö and His Daughters." Reprinted with permission from Johannes Wilbert and Karin Simoneau, eds., *Folk Literature of the Gé Indians*, Vol. 2 (Los Angeles: UCLA Latin American Center Publications, 1984), pp. 432–35.

128. "The Mē -be-ngo -dj u-ti Kamri." Reprinted with permission, from Johannes Wilbert and Karin Simoneau, eds., *Folk Literature of the Gé Indians*, Vol. 2 (Los Angeles: UCLA Latin American Center Publications, 1984), pp. 468–70.

129. "The Shameless Mother and Son." Reprinted with permission, from Johannes Wilbert and Karin Simoneau, eds., *Folk Literature of the Gé Indians*, Vol. 2 (Los Angeles: UCLA Latin American Center Publications, 1984), pp. 470–73.

130. Same as 126.

131. From Gerardo Reichel-Dolmatoff, *Amazonian Cosmos: The Sexual and Religious Symbolism of the Tukano Indians*, published by the University of Chicago Press, 1971. © 1971 by The University of Chicago. All rights reserved. Reproduced by permission of the publisher.

132. "The Star Ibesúi." Reprinted with permission, from Johannes Wilbert and Karin Simoneau, eds., *Folk Literature of the Ayoreo Indians* (Los Angeles: UCLA Latin American Center Publications, 1989), pp. 35–36.

133. "Etabi, The Incestuous Widow, and How Fighting Originated." Reprinted with permission, from Johannes Wilbert and Karin Simoneau, eds., *Folk Literature of the Ayoreo Indians* (Los Angeles: UCLA Latin American Center Publications, 1989), pp. 151–53.

134. Reproduced by permission.

135. "Birth and Infancy of Elal." Reprinted with permission, from Johannes Wilbert and Karin Simoneau, eds., *Folk Literature of the Tehuelche Indians* (Los Angeles: UCLA Latin American Center Publications, 1984), pp. 50–51.

136. From Alfred Metraux, Myths and Tales of the Matako Indians, *Etnologiska Studier*, 1939. Reproduced by permission of Etnografiska Museet.

137. Reproduced by permission.

138. Reproduced by permission of Roberto de Zubiria.

139. Same as 138.

INDEX

Because of the very different nature of the two parts of this book, and the difficulty in knowing how to index the folktales in a meaningful way, this index covers only the analysis in Part I. An "f" after a number indicates a separate reference on the next page, and an "ff" indicates separate references on the next two pages. A continuous discussion over two or more pages is indicated by a span of page numbers, e.g. "57–59." *Passim* is used for a cluster of references in close but not consecutive sequence.

Library of Congress Cataloging-in-Publication Data

Johnson, Allen W.
    Oedipus ubiquitous : the family complex in world folk literature /
Allen Johnson and Douglass Price-Williams.
        p.   cm.
    Includes bibliographical references and index.
    ISBN 0-8047-2576-4 (cloth : alk. paper). —ISBN 0-8047-2577-2
(pbk. : alk. paper)
    1. Tales—History and criticism.   2. Oedipus complex in
literature.   3. Family violence—Folklore.   4. Incest—Folklore.
I.   Price-Williams, Douglass Richard.   II. Title.
GR75.03J65   1996
398.27—dc20
95-41368   CIP

⊗ This book is printed on acid-free paper.

Last figure below indicates year of this printing:

05 04 03 02 01 00 99 98 97 96